Parody Paradise

Parody Paradise

By
Jay Dubya

www.bookstandpublishing.com

Published by
Bookstand Publishing
Pasadena, CA 91101
4959_3

Cover art and design by Al Margolis

ISBN 978-1-956785-59-3

For Anne, Steve and Skip

Other Books by Jay Dubya

Adult Fiction

Black Leather and Blue Denim, A '50s Novel
The Great Teen Fruit War, A 1960' Novel
Ron Coyote, Man of La Mangia
Frat' Brats, A '60s Novel
Pieces of Eight
Pieces of Eight, Part II
Pieces of Eight, Part III
Pieces of Eight, Part IV
The Wholly Book of Genesis
The Wholly Book of Exodus
The Wholly Book of Doo-Doo-Rot-on-Me
Thirteen Sick Tasteless Classics
Thirteen Sick Tasteless Classics, Part II
Thirteen Sick Tasteless Classics, Part III
Thirteen Sick Tasteless Classics, Part IV
Thirteen Sick Tasteless Classics, Part V
So Ya' Wanna' Be A Teacher!
Mauled Maimed Mangled Mutilated Mythology
Fractured Frazzled Folk Fables & Fairy Farces
FFFF & FF, Part II
Nine New Novellas
Nine New Novellas, Part II
Nine New Novellas, Part III
Nine New Novellas, Part IV
One Baker's Dozen
Two Baker's Dozen
RAM: Random Articles and Manuscripts
Time Travel Tales
Modern Mythology
UFO: Utterly Fantastic Occurrences
Prime-Time Crime Time
Snake Eyes and Boxcars
Snake Eyes and Boxcars, Part II
The Psychic Dimension
The Psychic Dimension, Part II
Shakespeare: Slammed, Smeared, Savaged and Slaughtered
Shakespeare: S, S, S & S, Part II
First Person Stories
The Arcane Arcade

vi

Thirteen Tantalizing Tales
PLOTS
PLOTS, Part II
THEMES
Hawthorne: Hacked, Shakespeare: Sacked, & Thurber: Thwacked
Hawthorne: Hazed, Hooked, Hammered and Hijacked
Suite 16
The FBI Inspector
Poe: Pelted, Pounded, Pummeled and Pulverized
Twain: Tattered, Trounced, Tortured and Traumatized
London: Lashed, Lacerated, Lampooned and Lambasted
O. Henry: Obscenely and Outrageously Obliterated
Homer's Odd Sea Odyssey
HOMER'S ILL Iliad
The Timeless Time Machine
War of the Worlds
The Invisible Man

Young Adult Fantasy Novels and Stories

Pot of Gold
Enchanta
Space Bugs, Earth Invasion
The Eighteen Story Gingerbread House

Introduction

Parody Paradise is a compilation of twenty-nine rewritten satirical short stories and plays from famous authors, featuring adult language and situations. Author Jay Dubya *equally* sideswipes *(parity/parody)* and lampoons popular and classic stories authored by Edgar Allan Poe, Jack London, O. Henry, Mark Twain, and Nathaniel Hawthorne. Other authors' works that are lambasted and thoroughly corrupted are James Thurber, Washington Irving, Sir Arthur Conan Doyle, Miguel Cervantes, and also several William Shakespeare plays are also savagely brutalized.

Parody Paradise is Jay Dubya's 63rd published book. Besides Adult Satire, the prolific author writes in seven other separate genres: Action/Adventure Novels, Non-Fiction Books, Mythology, Science-Fiction, Detective Stories, Paranormal Short Stories, and Young Adult Fantasy Novels.

Contents

"A Descent into the Maelstrom"
Edgar Allan Poe

My very elderly Norwegian guide and I had finally reached the summit of the ridge's loftiest crag, which majestically lorded over a beautiful-deep fiord situated within the valley below to our right. The climb to the pinnacle had been quite arduous, and I suspected that the old wrinkled-faced, gray-haired fellow was exhausted from his three-hour-long labor. Finally, the old codger inhaled a quantity of oxygen and began speaking.

"You know, Mr. Poe. Not too long ago there happened to me an event of terror, that to my knowledge, no mortal man other than myself has ever survived," Hans Jorgensen claimed before having a three-minute allergic sneezing fit. "Just look at my goddamned hair! It's fuckin' white as snow! But let me explain to you, Mr. Poe; the color had changed from pure black to snow white in just six hours of extremely horrifying danger!"

"Ha, ha, ha," I lustily laughed, believing that I was being lured into listening to an obscure Norwegian tall tale. "Your hair fuckin' sounds like Snow White without the dick-head Seven Dwarfs, and your dandruff must've been the goddamned snow; you old flakey Asshole! And probably you had had your hair dyed, but you forgot to die yourself, ha, ha, ha! Hans; it's a good thing I'm not made out of glass, because your story's already cracking me up, and you haven't even gotten past the friggin' preface!"

"Laugh if you must, Mr. Poe. But I can scarcely look-out over this cliff without feeling sick in my stomach and giddy in my head," Hans Jorgensen continued his tale's lengthy and monotonous introduction. "If you think our vantage point on top of this wind-blown crag is precarious, it is nothing when compared to the perilous adventure, or should I say *misadventure,* that I had once experienced in that treacherous strait of water down there," my guide elaborated. "It was so horrendous that I had shit my pants five times a day for a full year, until I finally decided not to wear any goddamned underwear or pants at all. And as sure as sin, that's the honest-to-God naked truth I'm telling you, Mr. Poe."

"Sounds like you had been suffering from a rare combination of diarrhea, colitis, and dysentery to me," I ridiculously jested. "Your good heredity should've given you a more efficient colon, and a more durable asshole. And how the hell do I really know Hans that you still aren't farting around using your hyperactive mouth instead of your irritated asshole?"

"Stop acting like my asshole *used* to behave after I had endured and survived my crisis misadventure," Hans angrily chastised. "As you can perceptively fathom from our present mutual high-in-the-sky observation point, we're overlooking the Norwegian coast in the great Nordland Province."

"I never overlook overlooking," I foolishly joked. "Just as long as the coast is clear, ha, ha, ha!"

"Keep fuckin' making asinine remarks like that one, and I'll tell you the whole fuckin' story in medieval Norwegian Viking words," my thoroughly aggravated guide threatened. "Now then, Mr. Poe. We're precisely in the sixty-eighth degree of latitude in the always dreary district of Lofoden. We're currently sitting on top of Mt. Helseggen the Cloudy," Hans academically related as I yawned. "Now, I strongly recommend, Mr. Poe, that you look-out beyond the vapor belt below us, and focus your eyes upon the sea."

Feeling dizzy from my high altitude (and from my guide's attitude), I gazed-out, grabbing and holding onto thick grass clumps so that I would not be suddenly sent airborne by the gusty winds. In the distance, a certain group of small islands randomly dotted the dark blue water, and to my left and right were impressive-looking promontories, with the total panorama suggesting to my vivid imagination a deplorably desolate-yet-pristine landscape.

"That island in the far distance is called Vurrgh," Hans knowledgeably informed me. "And the larger island in the middle is Moscoe, which incidentally is not in Russia, you American dumb-ass! I thought I would say *that* dumb-shit remark before *you* ever fuckin' thought of uttering the idiotic comment," Jorgensen sternly lectured. "Then, a mile to the north is Ambaaren; and yonder are Islesen, Hotholm, Keildhelm, Suarven, and Buckholm. And further off between Moscoe and Vurrgh are Otterholm, Flimen, and finally, Sandflesen," my ancient-looking, encyclopedic mentor lectured in what sounded like a rather boring Homeric catalog. "Do you now hear anything inordinate or see any dramatic change in the water's behavior, Mr. Poe?"

"No, I don't hear a toot; I don't smell a fart, and I don't see shit!" I sarcastically answered. "Wait a minute, Hans! I'm noticing that the sea is becoming disturbed over there in the distance near Moscoe, and the rough waves are rapidly moving towards Vurrgh. Now look!" I pointed in an animated fashion. "It's bubbling and rapidly whirling, and the sea appears to be almost-boiling as it approaches. It looks like a fuckin' tsunami coming our way! It's a good thing we're way up here upon this cliff; otherwise, we could be wiped into oblivion by a mammoth tidal wave!"

A minute later, the distant sea's surface ceased its awesome swelling, and eventually again became rather smooth. The separate swirling whirlpools gradually dissipated one by one; all-the-while prodigious streams of white foam became abundant almost everywhere, forming an

2

enormous circle, surrounded by a gleaming girdle of spray, approximately a mile in diameter.

And then, a fantastically huge and powerful sea-funnel appeared, dizzily swirling around; its erratic motion and size easily capable of sucking-up the entire cataract discharge of the great Niagara Falls. This mind-boggling phenomenon that my disbelieving eyes and brain were interpreting immediately gave legitimate credence to Hans Jorgensen's recent fantastic narrative. I then felt the mountain's base trembling, as the recently generated terrible waves smashed against its rock foundation several thousand feet below.

"I almost pissed my pants!" I screamed at Hans above the roar of the pounding surf surges. "That giant whirlpool out-there would easily suck Zeus's dick off, if the Olympian ever got caught stranded here on this mountain! Does it have a name?"

"Yes; it's the Maelstrom of Moscoe, but we native Norwegians simply call it 'the Maelstrom'! Just like you Mr. Poe, that colossal mother-fucker out there really sucks!"

"What's the depth of the water out near Moscoe?" I curiously asked, suddenly turning serious in defiance of my normal stupid-shit obnoxious personality.

"About forty fathoms deep; can you fathom that Mr. Poe?" Hans challenged my academic acumen by cleverly employing the use of a poly-semantic English word.

"Yes, Hans. About two-hundred-and-forty-feet-deep, one fathom being equivalent to six-feet," I replied as I remembered how Mark Twain had acquired the first and last parts of his pen name. "I'll tell you Hans; that must fuckin' be Jupiter's brother King Neptune down there having a goddamned orgasm!"

"I've seen several large fishing vessels get vacuumed-down inside the hungry Maelstrom, and I also witnessed a bear on one occasion and a whale on another disappear into its voracious throat," Hans recollected and disclosed. "And once, Mr. Poe; I even saw an immense oak tree and a huge pine get ripped to splinters, and then violently deposited onto the shore."

I could not resist the opportunity to again clown around and aggravate Hans. "Once my girlfriend back in Baltimore wanted me to buy her a mink coat for Christmas, but I bought her a Douglas fir instead," I inanely quipped. "You should've opened a toothpick factory, Hans. It looks like that friggin' Maelstrom had done most of the goddamned hard work for you!"

"Mr. Poe; it's been chronicled in various historical accounts that in the year 1645, on the morning of Sexagesima Sunday, the Maelstrom had raged with such impetuosity that the stone buildings and homes of the village residents all simultaneously collapsed to the ground. The only

3

survivors were those devout souls that had remained inside the safety of the church."

"Hans, those stupid assholes that stayed home and were having sex on Sexagesima Sunday had to have the greatest, most-sensational climaxes of their lives, dying while achieving tremendous orgasms. What a fuckin' way to go!"

"Mr. Poe, are you for real? Aren't you ever serious or earnest?" Hans austerely asked.

"Mr. Jorgensen; first of all, *Sirius* is a bright star in the constellation Canis Major; and furthermore, if I were Earnest, then quite obviously, my fuckin' name couldn't possibly be Edgar Allan!" I crazily answered.

* * * * * * * * * * * *

"Okay, Mr. Poe," Hans Jorgensen said with palpable conviction. "I'll now tell you all about my more-than-decent descent into the Moscoe Maelstrom, even though talking to you is like trying to communicate with a deaf, dumb, and blind mute on opium. And if you had half a brain," my illustrious guide added, "you'd be only one-fourth as sagacious as I am!"

My impatient storyteller then related to me that he and his two brothers were famous area fishermen that owned a schooner-rigged smack that got caught in the turbulent eddies, smack-dab between the familiar islands of Moscoe and Vurrgh. "We three dumb-ass sailors were the only assholes around that had the balls to venture-out there in those wicked straits and soon thereafter, we really found our dumb asses in real dire straits," Hans obtusely explained. "For you see, Mr. Poe; the fishing was really excellent between those two islands, but if you're there throwing nets over the gunwales at the wrong time, then there's a really heavy penalty the ambitious fool has to pay; namely, risking the loss of your life."

"Come on Hans, get on with your glorious story," I begged. "Surely you must've survived your major problem; otherwise, you wouldn't be here reliving it at my auditory expense!"

"Well, Sir, on July 18th of that epic year, a really nasty hurricane invaded the Norwegian coast that afternoon while the three of us were out sailing between Moscoe and Vurrgh, casting our dependable nets," the decrepit old man shared. "But let me now emphasize something important. That freaky storm was enough to scare the living semen out of any seaman."

"Stop trying to be so melodramatically funny and resume orating your damned exaggerated story," I entreated, feigning heightened anger. "And please stop attempting to imitate my propensity for telling irrelevant jokes. Now Hans, I'm beginning to understand exactly how annoying I must seem to others. I'm finally learning to detest hyperbole, falsehoods, and the like."

"Well, Mr. Poe, the wind was for once calm, and then it began blowing our smack all over the fuckin' place, and my brothers and I were suddenly caught-up in *current* events, so to speak," Hans preposterously told me. "In less than ten minutes, the devastating storm was upon us, and literally kicking the shit out of our schooner. Then, my happy-go-lucky youngest sibling Thor said, 'Let's get the fuck out of here; the *schooner* the better,' the pathetic jokester yelled as the asshole adroitly tied himself to the main mast. Well, Mr. Poe," Hans proceeded with his oddball recollection. "No sooner had that dumb-fuck Thor hollered those stupid-assed words that a titanic gust of wind broke the fuckin' mast off, and the whole beam and Thor, who was already lashed to the object, went flying-off the deck and were hastily deposited into the choppy, white-capped sea."

Before I could even fart or curse, Hans then orally recounted to me that after what he had witnessed happening to Thor, Jorgensen fearfully slid his body over to a ring bolt that had been fastened to the deck near the second mast, and then the desperate man securely grasped the metal loop and held on for dear life, fearing that the boat would certainly capsize. Next, Jorgensen's other brother Ingemar came sliding-over to the ring bolt, and frantically struggled to also hold on in a genuine effort to save *his* own life.

"Ingemar could've measured your head and taken your cap size during the capsize," I moronically jested. "Did you let Ingemar have a piece of the iron ring after he rolled to your location?" I ignorantly asked. "Surely, you must've exhibited brotherly love, despite the fact that you're definitely not from Philadelphia."

"Well, Mr. Poe," my accommodating guide elucidated with a mild sneer evident upon his austere-looking visage. "Brotherly love only goes so far. Even though I loved Ingemar, when self-preservation is involved as the chief factor in the equation, I soon learned that I loved myself more than I did him. I wildly kicked, pushed and shoved Ingemar away from the iron ring, which in fact was only big enough to allow one man to grip properly. And then, before I could succinctly yell 'Fuck you Ingemar!', the ship canted, and then tilted, and my middle brother joined Thor exploring down in Davy Jones's locker. But at that moment, Mr. Poe," Hans stressed and reiterated, "I felt that I was just as doomed to die on that half-demolished schooner the same as if I had been cowardly hiding in the hull of a hundred-gun warship."

"So, Hans. You were courageously battling two very formidable enemies; the savage hurricane on the one hand and the omnipotent Maelstrom on the other," I perceptively comprehended and interrupted.

"I'll bet you didn't even have time to wipe your ass or scratch your balls!"

"Mr. Poe; if I dared to do either of those two dumb-fuck things, I'd be sailing right off the deck and would've wound-up joining my kin Thor and Ingemar in the drink," Hans insisted. "Surely, I didn't have an icicle's chance in hell of living through my traumatic dilemma, but somehow, basic instinct gave me the wherewithal to persevere. But then, Mr. Poe," Hans pontificated before coughing-up and spitting out a green lunger that splattered against my chest. "I heard a loud sucking sound that made my wet, jet-black hair stand-up on end. I thought that some prehistoric dinosaur or prehistoric sea creature was either going to devour my ass, or take a healthy shit on top of me, and sink the goddamned boat right-down to the sea bottom. But truthfully, Mr. Poe," Jorgensen continued before again clearing his lungs with me instantly ducking-down. "My terror had all been used-up, and I was no longer petrified to either act or die. In my heart, I didn't give a goddamned shit about dying, and in reality, I was actually resigned to the fact that it should fuckin' happen pretty damned soon. Yes, Mr. Poe; the prospect of me dying just didn't matter one iota to me! I remember thinking, 'Dying isn't so fuckin' bad. Look how easily Thor and Ingemar managed to do it'!"

I again felt compelled to open my big mouth and articulate something truly fucked-up. "Yes, Hans. Plunging-down into the bowels of the abyss would certainly be pretty abysmal," I chuckled, and then involuntarily farted three loud times. "What the hell happened next Hans? Did a gorgeous mermaid with big succulent breasts rescue your grungy ass when you heard her alluring siren's call? Did you finally wake-up from your mind-boggling, heinous nightmare? Did Thor and Ingemar wake you up from your slumber and cook breakfast for you?"

"Well, Mr. Poe. The devastating Maelstrom then sucked-up the entire schooner as if it was a chicken feather, and I was being whirled-around like a spinning top, as I still desperately clung to the metal ring bolt," Hans sternly articulated. "Despite the fact that the ship was whirling-around in an orbit all along the circumference of the Maelstrom, in sheer desperation, I managed to use my right hand to grab a rope, and luckily tie my torso to an empty cask that had rolled over to my vicinity upon the deck."

"Was it the Cask of Amontillado?" I idiotically jested. "Excuse me Hans, but *that* reference was a private joke that only I could understand and appreciate."

"As I glanced-out at the churning sea," Hans said, pausing a moment to recapture his faltering breath. "I noticed all sorts of junk drifting by: bones, fish skeletons, wine racks, barrels, hogsheads, bottles, chests, liquor cabinets, dildos; well, you name it; the debris was all rapidly swirling-around in concentric orbits, that amazingly, paralleled the

6

schooner's orbit. It was far worse than the most peculiar, bizarre, fucked-up nightmare a man could ever have! If I was insanely drunk and on marijuana and cocaine addiction," Hans hypothesized and unconvincingly communicated, "then Mr. Poe; I couldn't have hallucinated anything more outlandish!"

"I'm getting pretty damned dizzy just listening to your fanciful, nautical bullshit," I disgustingly opined. "I mean, who in the world could jerk-off let alone get laid under such non-propitious conditions? If a half decent whorehouse had flown by your accursed schooner," I insisted, feigning seriousness, "you could've hopped from the swirling schooner directly inside the front door, and maybe gotten laid or blown during the climax of your abominable ordeal. Don't you agree, Hans?"

Jorgensen was not especially humored or impressed by my fertile imagination. "Well, now, dubious Mr. Poe. More freakin' fragments went zooming and zipping by the spinning schooner; weird things like furniture, desks, chairs, lamps, cartons, drawers, the kind of drawers in desks, and not the kind that's men's or women's underwear; and also, timbers and snuff boxes were twirling and swirling all over the goddamned place," Hans narrated with a poker face. "I hadn't been that fuckin' dizzy since I was a kid in kindergarten getting sick and nauseous playing 'Pin the Tail or the horned helmeted Fat Lady singing at the end of the opera, or 'Spin the Bottle, with *me* being assigned being the goddamned bottle!"

"A spendthrift sort of woman might describe your Maelstrom misadventure as a whirlwind shopping trip," I giggled and then indulgently laughed. "I can't believe it, but I actually find your terrifying story quite amusing. It's so damned hilarious, Hans, that I think I'm becoming delirious, ha, ha, ha! This fucked-up fisherman's tale could make a fairly enjoyable comic short story, if not the essential premise for a cornball novel."

"Well, in conclusion; my hands, legs, wrists, fingers, shoulders, elbows, along with my knees and testicles, were all chafed-up and badly lacerated," Hans Jorgensen regretfully testified and then spit a huge lunger into the wind, the green glob instantly being deflected right onto my face. "Now, Mr. Poe. I thought I was going to fuckin' bleed to death before I ever had a chance to drown, or commit suicide. It was the biggest friggin' bummer of my life, and I futilely wished that I was dead and playing strip-poker with Thor and Ingemar down there in Hell, or Hades, or Purgatory, or wherever the fuck my immortal soul was heading."

"Well, Hans. It certainly wouldn't be Heaven," I cynically commented. "Paradise would certainly reject your wrinkled-up ass," I facetiously *anal*yzed. "That St. Peter who guards the Pearly Gates is a pretty damned fussy son-of-a-bitch, or so I hear. But please Hans," I diplomatically urged. "Finish-up your goofy story because I think I'm going to have an intense bowel movement within the next five minutes. My erratic intestines won't allow me to sit here and listen to your absurd jargon too much longer. Did you finish your nautical dilemma at the Finnish Line?"

Hans lucidly communicated to me that the Old Salt had calculated that lighter objects like the pine tree parts that had drifted to the beach from previous Maelstrom activity would tend to rise and not sink during the culmination/termination phase of *his* whirlpool's "spin cycle". And the hoary tour-guide continued his spectacular story by saying, "So, I intrepidly let go of the iron ring, lifted-up the empty cask with my girth still lashed to it, and then without hesitation, jumped my ass off of the schooner directly into the Maelstrom's swirling mass."

"Did you collide with either Thor or Ingemar after your valiant plunge?" I asked with an expressionless face, enunciating each word tongue-in-cheek. "You three knuckleheaded fuck-heads sound to me like you were already way *out there* revolving around and rotating in some distant solar orbit, long before your doomed schooner ever began swirling and orbiting around inside the Maelstrom. Are you a fucked-up space alien or what? Did you get to meet Scylla and Charybdis having tea time down there?"

"Stop being so nasty, or I'll refuse telling you the unbelievable ending of my Maelstrom misadventure," Hans aggressively reprimanded me. "Show me more courtesy and respect."

I figured that I had to be a bit more contrite and considerate. "Well; who the heck rescued you from the formidable waves? Was it John Paul Jones or was it Eric the Red?" I laughed, ripping a large hole along the crotch seam of my pants. "How about that dumb-fuck barbarian Viking rascal, Leif Erickson?"

"Some very surprised fishermen from my village salvaged my ass from the great waves, and then lugged me aboard their rescue boat," Hans recalled and maintained. "But unfortunately, Mr. Poe. The avid tuna hunters hadn't detected any vestiges of either Thor or Ingemar. My brothers must've really enjoyed Death, because they never returned after experiencing it!"

My felicitous mood was about to sober-up in a hurry. Much to my consternation, Hans patiently and persuasively divulged to me a statement that sent my skeptical mind shifting into a sudden grim reality check. I was absolutely unprepared to hear his startling revelation, which quite candidly, scared the living feces out of my rear-end, and also, frightened the yellow piss out of my kidneys.

"After my fishermen colleagues pulled me on board, the sailors were shocked to see that my hair had turned from raven jet-black to snow white in less than a day. Furthermore," Hans Jorgensen stated with a powerful countenance that thoroughly-expressed his sincerity, "I had aged over fifty years in less than twenty-four hours. More specifically, Mr. Poe. I had aged over half a century during the six-hour crisis I had experienced swirling around and around in my drastic descent into the Maelstrom."

"Dr. Tarr and Professor Fether"
Edgar Allan Poe

Someone might think my tale is humorous, but to me, it was all quite disconcerting. During the mild autumn of 1840, I was touring France's southern provinces, trying to locate a certain *Maison de Sante*, or a notorious local nuthouse that specialized in advanced psychology methods and techniques. Since I had never had the pleasure of visiting an eminent "experimental asylum" of that kind, I proposed to my French traveling companion that we should set aside an afternoon, so that I could avail myself of the opportunity to gather some pertinent research for a short story on mental health I had wished to author.

"This place to which you allude is a lunatic magnet, and I wish not to visit it," my Parisian friend replied. "If I were you, I'd fuckin' seek asylum from that wacky asylum, and avoid the goddamned place as quickly as you can. But if you insist, I'll tell you how to get there, but I intend to ride on to Marseilles and rest my weary bones. I'll meet you at the designated waterfront inn that is expecting us later tonight. Then, we could enjoy an excellent supper together."

"Do you know the superintendent of *Maison de Sante*, a distinguished fellow named Monsieur Maillard?" I asked my French friend Gaston. "I had heard his renowned name mentioned while I had been speaking with some notable published men in the medical profession, back in Paris."

"Unless you have some meritorious letter of recommendation or an official state certificate of admission from the national government," Gaston revealed in a regretful tone of voice, "then I doubt whether this Monsieur Maillard will ever allow you to enter and tour his avant-garde facility. Quite frankly, I've heard that Maillard is a trifle fucked-up in his organizational skills, and that the weird personage is quite suspicious about unexpected or uninvited visitors," Gaston confided. "But Edgar, since I'm a medical doctor and had known this Maillard five years ago back in Lyons, I'll accompany you to his clinic and introduce you to him. The rest will be entirely up to you."

"I see," I answered Gaston, with my ordinarily rational mind being somewhat confused. "You *are* a doctor of the body, and just like your Parisian colleagues, you condescend those that study the activities of the human mind, thinking that they're all a monstrous gaggle of fucked-up incompetent quacks involved in perpetuating an ongoing fiasco!"

We rode our fatigued horses upon a dirt trail that meandered through a dank and dismal forest, and at the base of a mediocre-sized mountain we finally arrived at *my* destination, the *Maison de Sante*. At first glance, the edifice was a fantastic-looking chateau, but upon closer scrutiny, its appearance was a bit dilapidated from neglect and from lack of maintenance. My initial inclination was to turn around and head towards Marseilles with Gaston, but then my heart gathered the courage to stay and satisfy my original curiosity about the rather intriguing facility.

Monsieur Maillard was quite a vigilant administrator, who immediately detected our presence while peering-out of an iron-barred window. The short, portly superintendent anxiously exited his clinic, and upon recognizing Gaston, courteously invited him and me inside. Maillard, at first impression, struck me as a man of genteel and polished manners, whose general demeanor reflected dignity and authority. 'Always trust your first perception,' I thought as I keenly evaluated the strange-looking fellow from head-to-toe.

"My friend, Mr. Poe, would like to stay the afternoon and tour your nationally-famous *Maison de Sante,*" Gaston blandly disclosed. "Unfortunately, Monsieur Maillard, I have important business to attend to in Marseilles, and will have to take a rain-check on your gracious offer to stay. Would you mind accommodating my dear friend, Mr. Poe, in my absence?"

"No, not at all," Superintendent Maillard benignly indicated. "Why don't you dismount from your horse, Mr. Poe, and I'll gladly give you a guided tour of the premises."

After I thanked Gaston for his invaluable assistance, and after my friend rode-off in a fury towards Marseilles, Monsieur Maillard politely ushered me into his modern "experimental facility". A cheerful fire blazed upon the hearth, and a very beautiful and talented young woman was preoccupied playing an aria from Bellini on the piano keys. The young lady paused upon realizing my intrusion into the room, casually greeted me with a graceful smile, and then continued with her rehearsal of the complicated composition.

I had instantly detected an element of sorrow and melancholy in the young woman's disposition, but being a refined gentleman of good breeding, I never explored pursuing *that* possibly embarrassing aspect of conversation. I had heard at the recent academic conference in Paris that the acclaimed *Maison de Sante* (under the direction of Monsieur Maillard) had been managed (by the vulgarly used term) "system of permissive soothing", so I asked the now-garrulous superintendent about his innovative method of mental care.

"Well, you see Mr. Poe, according to my revolutionary creative method, all types of punishments have been disposed with, and the novel concept of 'rewards' is implemented at this innovative institution, whenever possible," the superintendent enthusiastically explained. "Although the patients are secretly watched, the subjects do have liberty of the house; that is to say, they have and enjoy complete freedom of mobility. And instead of wearing uniforms like inmates in prisons do, my pampered patients are allowed to cavort around at will in civilian apparel, and mingle and bond with their peers whenever each individual so desires," the esteemed executive of the asylum informed. "Such a tolerant and lenient atmosphere could only engender the development of independence and self-sufficiency among my 'guests', as I like to call them."

"I see, Sir. You run your remarkable institution, as if it were a high society hotel," I perceptively commented. "Very interesting indeed, Mr. Maillard. Very fascinating, too, if I may add."

At that time, I had resolved in my always-skeptical mind to confine my remarks to general topics, so as not to offend either Monsieur Maillard or his sensitive-minded mental-patients. A footman then brought a tray of fresh fruit into the room, along with wine and other suitable refreshments, and I made myself comfortable, taking a glass of merlot along with a red ripe apple.

"Was that young lady in the other room playing the piano one of your patients?" I diplomatically asked my host. "She seemed very normal to me."

"No, Mr. Poe. That pretty young lady is pretty young, and she happens to be my beloved niece Florence, just visiting here for the week," Monsieur Maillard laughed, and then loudly burped, nearly regurgitating a large chuck of cheese he had just swallowed. "Flossie, as I affectionately call her, is a most accomplished musician, and plans to do some major Parisian theater concerts in the near future. All she really needs right now is a trifle more experience, along with a skilled booking-agent, and a scrupulous business manager!"

"Are you feeling all right?" I asked Maillard as the director began burping and farting loudly. "I do have adequate knowledge about gastro-intestinal remedies, you know!"

"You must excuse my chronic belching," Maillard replied, while exhibiting a minor degree of mortification. "For you see, Mr. Poe, under the previous system that was in place here; a harsh system that enforced martinet discipline and punishment; the inhibited patients were often savagely abused. So, that's why with the utilization that my new 'permissive soothing method' employs, I had to exclude visitors from the outside interfering with my new program's initial administration. My patients must learn to trust the friendly staff in the building, and not be subject to the prejudices and discriminations of those encroaching outsiders, most of whom can't relate to *their* own often-complex mental health issues."

"How long has your 'permissive soothing system' been in operation?" I innocently asked as I began to think that Maillard was an idealistic, impractical, quixotic, dumb-fuck university academic, doing irrelevant quack research on his own. "I would like to analyze and document the entire intricate process, if I may?"

"Why that would be impossible, Mr. Poe!" Monsieur Maillard surprisingly exclaimed. "Just last week, I found it necessary to return to the formerly obsolete martinet discipline approach. I'm sorry, Mr. Poe, that you had not visited us last month when the controversial 'permissive soothing method' was being fully employed."

'This dumb-fuck is really a fickle, doltish asshole,' I instinctively concluded. 'No doubt he farts and shits out of his mouth, and probably eats and drinks out of his asshole. What a fucked-up, hypocritical, omnivore this pathetic jerk-off Maillard is!'

"You see, Mr. Poe, while I was utilizing the highly controversial 'permissive soothing method' of mental treatment," Maillard defensively stated and equivocated, "some of the men actually thought that they were chickens; more specifically roosters, and the fellows would run around the house trying to screw any female whether the ladies said or screamed cock-a-doodle-doo, or not! And then we had several gay roosters in the pack, who were trying to have sexual intercourse with other male patients! And then, a few of the more serious hens spent their entire day attempting to lay actual chicken eggs! The entire psychological experiment proved to be an abominable, abysmal failure, where all semblances of civility had been abandoned with the ineffective ultra-liberal 'permissive soothing philosophy' going completely amok!"

"Did you still have dancing, music, sports, card playing, and reading books as alternative amusement activities?" I inquired.

"Well, Mr. Poe. For a while, we did try those standard therapeutic activities, and we also relied upon the patients admonishing each other for alleged misbehaviors and indiscretions," Millard lectured without a lectern. "But the really bad maniacs in our care had to be discharged to a local regular hospital for rehabilitation. We wanted to find a perfect medium; somewhere between those punitive methodologies of the ruthless Marquis de Sade, and those Christian charity-oriented methods of Jesus Christ. But specifically, Mr. Poe," Maillard warned. "I strongly advise you to believe nothing that you hear, and only half of what you see, in regard to you assessing the avant-garde *Maison de Sante*. Whatever you do," the rather strange superintendent cautioned me, "don't be misled by the false teachings of those medical ignoramuses over in Paris! Now then; I'll show you the gardens and the conservatories, and next we'll have a delicious dinner after six."

"Mr. Maillard, where the hell are your patients?" I inquired. "I haven't seen one of them since I've been here."

"Oh, they're meandering around here, somewhere," the chief administrator obtusely answered. "I'm sure they're hiding from us somewhere in the dense outside foliage, or perhaps playing Hide and Seek behind sofas and chairs, just to break our balls!"

14

And before I could explore the next uncultivated garden and weed area, I heard around twenty zany voices all zestfully yelling-out in unison, "Cock-a-doodle-doo!" in a queer dissonant cacophony, sounding much like some sort of out-of-control, lunatic community chicken coop.

* * * * * * * * * * * * *

At six o'clock, dinner was announced, and the oddball French superintendent, and his twenty-four-inch-tall footman, conducted me from the chateau's comfortable-but-sterile living room, through in-need-of-repair French doors, into a large dining area containing a huge eighteen-leaf solid oak table, with what I assumed to be thirty dignified people seated around it. Twenty-five of the chatty diners were well-dressed women, all of whom were wearing expensive-looking evening gowns, necklaces, wrist and arm bracelets, gold medallions, and finally, jeweled diamond rings. Upon first impression, the ostentatious women all seemed gregarious, charming, and also appeared to be dominating the myriad trivial conversations that were occurring at the huge oval table.

I next noticed that the warped floor was rug-less; that the dirty windows were indeed barred (both horizontally and vertically), and that the oak table had been set with an abundance of food with veal and ham as the principal meats, and with rice, salad, potatoes, yellow squash, and corn being the main vegetables. A great many trite anecdotes were being exchanged among the guests, and my mind tried to absorb all that was being discussed around the gigantic table.

"We had a gentleman here about a year ago," prefaced a man seated two chairs down from my right, "and the old geezer fancied himself being a goddamned teapot, always whistling, not like a human would, mind you, but like a goddamned common, ordinary kitchen stove teapot. And do you know what?" the self-serving speaker continued his unsolicited monologue. "The dumb-shit jerk, I think he was from Cannes, would polish himself every night to stay shiny and silvery."

"It's a good thing he didn't think there was a hurricane inside of him, or else I believe that the gentleman would've been a wicked 'tempest in a teapot'!" I mused and then foolishly declared.

Next, a tall gentleman seated three down from Monsieur Maillard piped-up, "About eight months ago, we had a stubborn asshole staying here, who thought he was a hungry donkey, and the mule-headed asshole would eat pine cones, hay, and thistle all day long," the fellow possessing the good memory stated. "Well then, when I kindly asked to see his animal pecker, I saw that the lying son-of-a-bitch didn't have any goddamned donkey-dick after all, ha, ha, ha!"

Immediately, Superintendent Maillard felt obligated to reprimand and chastise the loose-tongued resident. "Mr. DeKock," the flustered administrator austerely chastised. "Stop acting so naughtily. You're beginning to make an ass out of yourself, just as our former guest Mr. Muleskin had done when he was hee-hawing his damned tonsils out every single morning, noon and night."

Everyone at the table was merrily drinking delicious wine, as if it was fresh cold water. Bottles of chardonnay, of cabernet-sauvignon, of merlot, and of white zinfandel were randomly scattered (or distributed) all over the immense table. I was busily feasting on ham and veal, and was so engrossed in my consumption of tasty food that I paid little heed to the nonsensical hubbub happening all around me. But in retrospect, the scenario was even worse in magnitude than any chaotic, nonsensical episode out of *Dante's Inferno*.

And then, a cadaverous-looking lady sitting six chairs down to my right testified, "We had a screwed-up patient living here at the chateau a while back, who thought she was a slice of Cordova cheese, and every time she picked up a knife at breakfast," the raunchy old bag emphasized, "at lunch, or at dinner, the naked Lady Cordova would attempt to slice-off a sliver of herself, honestly thinking that she was the goddamned Big Cheese around here!"

"I'm Mr. Chardonnay, and I'm a chilled bottle of red wine," the transsexual cross-dressing woman four chairs down to my left announced, as the crazed female put her finger inside her mouth and made the popping sound of a cork flying off a champagne bottle. "Now, which of you asshole men wants to corkscrew me into a mattress, so that I can pop your weasel, too!"

"These weird stories are not only amusing, but they're quite visceral and graphic, too," I leaned-over and confidentially related to Monsieur Maillard. "Are these people fucked-up, or are *we* fucked-up just sitting here and listening to their incredible bullshit?"

Before Maillard could reply to my keen observation, the asshole woman sitting thirty-feet down at the far end of the table boisterously yelled-out to Maillard and me, "Hey you two shit-heads down there! Don't you know I'm a frog? Yesterday, I was a horned toad, but now I've changed into a horny frog that doesn't want to croak until I get laid at least twenty times tonight." And then the dumb-shit, toothless woman noticed a huge disgusting insect crawling on the wood-planked floor; got down on her hands and knees, and then extending her long tongue, captured the very large black bug in her mouth, and began chomping away."

My mind was in a dizzy quandary, but I was again subjected to listening to additional bizarre bullshit. "And what about that fuck-head Petit Gaillard, who thought himself to be a box of snuff, and wanted everyone in the house to sniff his smelly asshole that he thought was his box's opening?" a chatty woman in the center right of the expansive oak

16

table hollered-out for all to hear. "And don't forget that dumb-shit Jules Descartes, who believed he was a pumpkin, and who would beat-up and injure the cook before every meal, because Jules suspected that the always bruised-up chef was going to change him into a pumpkin pie to be eaten by all at dinner."

"What the hell is this stupid shit all about?" I demanded to know from Maillard. "Either these pea-brained fuck-heads at the table are all raving imbeciles, or they're an insolent pack of retarded morons? Which is it Monsieur?"

Before the beleaguered superintendent could ever garner and utter a respond to my imperative/interrogative statement, a really ugly lady, who was now half-naked shouted-out, "What about good old Bouffon Le Grand, who thought he had two heads; the first one being Cicero, and the second one being Demosthenes. And then, good old debonair Bouffon would leap-up upon this same dinner table, and render to us in an extemporaneous speech saying, "That asshole Greek Demosthenes might have pebbles in his mouth, but that fuckin' roamin' Roman Cicero always had rocks in his head! Ha, ha, ha!" the female zoo candidate shrieked. "And then good old bonny Bouffon finally graduated into being a toy top, and would spin-around all-night-long, until the dumb-fuck finally shit and pissed his pants!"

'My riding companion Gaston was indubitably right,' I finally realized and concluded. 'I too need asylum from this fucked-up asylum! These son-of-a-bitches sitting here have to be the fucked-up mental patients, and I now think that the deranged retards certainly aren't goddamned sophisticated aristocratic guests at all!' I determined.

But before I could grab Maillard by the collars and start strangling my host, and also before any feasible explanation could exit out of his chubby throat, an elderly, gray-haired, promiscuous bitch (with her hideous, flabby tits hanging out of her dress) stood-up and began redundantly bellowing, "Cock-a-doodle-doo; any cock'll do! Cock-a-doodle-doo! Any cock'll do!"

"Monsieur, she's trying to start a sex orgy at the dinner table! Do something, Maillard! I say fuckin' do something before I violently squeeze your neck until your goddamned windpipe disintegrates!" I boomed as I took-out my frustration by pounding my right hand against the asshole superintendent's chest, but regrettably, to no avail or personal satisfaction.

"Mr. Poe, I must tell you that Madame Honeywell is in heat," Maillard explained to me with a very pallid facial expression. "She thinks she's a female poodle in estrous. There's little I can do to salvage Madame Honeywell, or 'the Bitch' as she wants to be called! And incidentally, Mr. Poe. Madame Honeywell sometimes thinks she's a modest young lady, who, when she meticulously dresses herself, she always gets outside rather than inside her clothes."

"Just like the goofy Cicero/Demosthenes jerk-off that was just discussed, your Madame Honeywell is what the modern psychologists call a person suffering from a split personality. Yes, I believe that the mental condition is now referred to as schizophrenia! But truthfully Monsieur Maillard," I screamed above the ever-ascending dining room din. "I now truly feel like I'm the goddamned chief cashew speaking inside this nuthouse!"

And before basic order could be intelligently restored, Madame Honeywell again stood-up, and once more cockily yelled out, "Cock-a-doodle-do! Any cock'll do! Cock-a-doodle-do! Any cock'll do!" while ripping-off her ornate dress and accompanying undergarments, and then the crazy old bag "Bitch" began wildly masturbating her vulva and her clitoris in public.

"Milliard," I asked. "Who has devised this retroactive treatment of a compromised medium existing between your former liberal 'permissive soothing method' and the more Draconian Marquis de Sade martinet punishment method?" I hoarsely gasped.

"Why it was none other than that famous dynamic duo, Dr. Tarr and Professor Fether," Maillard recollected and loudly replied. "Don't tell me you've never heard of those two very prominent contributors to the psychology field?"

"I must admit that I'm presently forced to acknowledge my uneducated ignorance," I confessed in a raspy, hardly audible voice. "If I recall, those two gentlemen were not in attendance at the recent Paris medical conference."

Suddenly, a massive food fight originated at the other end of the colossal oval table with apples, oranges, bananas, ham, veal, and hot potatoes flying all over the damned place. And soon, the airborne objects were accompanied by torrents of wine from recently opened bottles of chardonnay, cabernet-sauvignon, merlot, and white zinfandel. I stood-up and weakly screamed, "You're all going berserk! Stop this bullshit buffoonery right this second!" at the top of my faltering lungs and vocal cords, but unfortunately, the voice of a minnow swimming under faraway Niagara Falls could have been heard much better at that crazy fiasco scene located not far from the Riviera in Southern France. "Maillard, if you can't immediately put these thirty insane lunatics in straight-jackets, then I suggest that you get out the fuckin' crooked jackets instead!"

"Certainly, Mr. Poe," the short, obese, baldheaded superintendent loudly articulated into my ear. "These thirty patients need one-on-one individual attention, which because of economic reasons, cannot be adequately supplied. I have only two reliable employees assisting me, and we're pretty damned overwhelmed, wouldn't you agree?"

18

"Well then," I yelled in a puzzled frame of mind. "Where the hell are Dr. Tarr and Professor Fether? Can't they help you re-tool and reorganize this fucked-up place?"

"I'll tell you a little secret, Mr. Poe. They're both locked-up in the chateau's cellar," Maillard confessed without remorse. "Dr. Tarr and Professor Fether had taken over this institution from me, but then I became an activist patient here myself, and shrewdly coordinated a counter-revolution just like Napoleon Bonaparte had done. And I coyly got together these thirty uncouth rebels, and convinced the nutcases to recapture the asylum from the control of those two quack shrinks, Tarr and Fether."

"Holy shit!" I exclaimed amidst the tumult of the ever-escalating dining room food fight. "Then, really and truly, Maillard. The insane patients have, in reality, taken-over the goddamned asylum! That's fuckin' even worse than the goddamned chicken hawks and foxes being given the keys to the chicken coop!"

Three nude men then clumsily hopped onto the table, and started kicking plates, serving bowls, and eating utensils off the already-abused oak surface, while the deranged triumvirate simultaneously and in-harmoniously were singing "Yankee Doodle".

And while all of the unbearable noise and frenzy was in progress, and reaching a crescendo, a formidable army of experimental baboons and chimpanzees (that had been caged-up in the asylum's cellar) savagely invaded the dining room, and the vicious animals were led by the demented Dr. Tarr and the equally-demented Professor Fether, who both had broken free of their shackles and had gotten the Simian troops to support *their* current battle assault.

Needless to say, during the hectic and ferocious combat that ensued, I had received a tremendous brutal thrashing, and was maliciously scratched all over my face, hands, chest, testicles and arms, just for sitting next to Monsieur Maillard. I instinctively feigned mortal injury by falling to my hands and knees, and then accelerating my ass by swiftly crawling to the front exit door, and miraculously escaping out of the terrible madhouse *Maison de Sante*. I staggered and hobbled across the lawn to the chateau's outbuildings, and I next struggled to saddle and then mount my refreshed horse, which had been moved to the nearby stone barn. Five minutes later, my rested steed was ambitiously galloping in the direction of Marseilles.

After my hasty departure from the crazy asylum, I traveled extensively throughout France, and researched inside each and every Paris, Marseilles, and Lyons' library for the collective thesis works of Dr. Tarr and Professor Fether. But alas, in the end, my well-intentioned efforts all proved to be abject failures.

"The Story of Keesh"
Jack London

When I first heard the name Jack London (1876-1916) as an eighth-grade student attending a Levittown, Pennsylvania parochial school, I naively believed that the famous author was from England. London was born and raised in abject poverty in San Francisco. Although he resented formal education, Jack London was an avid reader and a frequent visitor to the local public library. As a roving teenager, Jack lived a rather unorthodox lifestyle where the adventurer was an oyster pirate, a sailor, a tramp, and the itinerant youth eventually wound-up in jail on vagrancy charges.

Jack London ought to be admired as a role model for young people, because he turned his life around full circle. He took night courses at the *University of California*, studied literature, and developed a respectable vocabulary. The reformed young man soon got caught-up in the Alaska gold rush fever. The avid reader didn't find gold nuggets up in the Klondike and in the Yukon, but he found something as good as gold if not better than the precious ore: Jack London discovered a wealth of material, settings, themes, and characters to construct and support imaginative plots for wonderful novels and novellas.

The versatile author refined the writing technique known today as "Realism", and that very evident quality is reflected in his major novels like *The Call of the Wild* and *White Fang*. Most of Jack London's tales are about strong men, or animals, and their instinct to survive in very harsh environments. Realism is also definitely apparent in London's classic short fiction works such as "Love of Life," "To Build a Fire" and "The Story of Keesh".

Keesh was an Eskimo boy, who never in his life made or sold an Eskimo Pie or a Klondike Bar to anyone. Through courage and wisdom, the audacious youth ascended to the position of village chief, despite opposition from senile village elders, and from jealous village rivals and hunters. By demonstrating steadfast virtue and an indomitable will, the lad was able to advance from the most-humble igloo in the village to becoming the most prosperous clansman. Here's how this incredible bullshit all happened.

Keesh was a bright boy, who sometimes glowed in the dark. At age thirteen, the healthy, strong lad had seen "thirteen suns", but not all at the same time during the same year. That's the terminology his Eskimo clan used in their native village to describe thirteen years, so naturally, the inhabitants probably also must have called the sun "a year", if they called a year "a sun".

Keesh's Eskimo elders were totally fucked-up. That's why he had to straighten all of the stupid assholes out, so that the proper things could be called the proper words and names; some of which might also have been proper nouns that were *commonly* used, and common nouns that were *improperly* used.

Keesh's father Bok had been a valiant fellow that had died during a *grave famine* when all the burial plots in the icy cemetery had also become frozen. Bok sought to save the weaker members of the village by setting-out to hunt and kill a great polar bear, but unfortunately, the great dark beer drinker never came *bok*.

Keesh was Bok's only son, and over the years, the people forgot about Bok's bravery, so the proud boy and his poor indigent mother were demoted in rank to live in the village's smallest and most shabby, dirty-iced, small-assed, ghetto igloo. The igloo was made out of ice cubes from an ancient icebox, rather than constructed out of traditional large, carved, rectangular ice blocks as was the norm according to Eskimo construction codes. Keesh was pretty pissed-off about his relegation to the lowest social and economic echelon in the Eskimo community, which incidentally, also included the fucked-up Eskimo gay and lesbian community.

A council meeting in the big igloo of Chief Klosh-Kwan was rudely interrupted by a complaint from an angry upstart sitting in the rear. Keesh rose to his feet, showing the strong dignity of an elder, and demanded to be heard amidst the babble of a chorus of critical condescending voices.

"Oh, great Klosh-Kwan," the acne-faced juvenile began his oratory. "The meat my mother and I have been apportioned has entirely too much fat, too much gristle, and too many bones. Hell, I demand better quality meat, and make 'no bones' about it. Know what the frig' I'm bitchin' about!"

The grizzled, elder, veteran hunters were appalled and aghast at Keesh's confident attitude, which the senile idiots interpreted as brash brazenness. The council lawmakers were perturbed that an audacious punk pretending to be a man was attempting to arbitrarily break their balls in front of the entire Eskimo community, which included the fucked-up Eskimo gay and lesbian sub-community.

"Who is this impudent child that talks like a man?" one councilman asked. "He has absolutely no reputation as a skilled hunter, nor any track record as a proven scout. Sit-down Macho Boy, before we throw your ass out of the big igloo, and ostracize you from the entire Eskimo village, including banishment from the influential gay and lesbian village people, along with other less powerful heterosexual village idiots!"

Keesh was undaunted by the sudden outburst of criticism directed against him, so the lad stubbornly continued with his grievance. "I've heard from many of you demented charlatans that my father Bok was a fantastic hunter. It's said that Bok brought back to the village twice as much meat to share than any two other hunters combined. And it's also reputed that my father also knew how to beat his meat better than anyone else in this clan," Keesh reminded his disinterested listeners. "And Bok would then generously give his meat to the old toothless women of the village to suck on!"

"Nay, nay!" the old prune-faced men on the council *neighed* like discontented horses. "Put the disrespectful delinquent out of our company!" and "Send the infant wanna'-be back to his crib!" is what the incensed crowd boisterously yelled. "No man would ever insult the long graybeards as this lazy, juvenile punk delinquent is attempting to do!"

Keesh patiently waited for the assembly's clamor and the elders' protests to calm-down. Then, the determined lad incisively continued his critique, much to the chagrin of his already-peeved adult audience. "Ugh-Gluk," the Eskimo adolescent said to one of the humiliated hunters smugly sitting on the council. "Thou hast a wife, and for her do you speak."

"That's right!" The old man sitting in the assembly hollered-out. "Ugh-Gluk has some *ugly luck* with both married and unmarried squaws. Ha, ha, ha!"

"The old coot's insulted wife punched him squarely in the face as Klosh-Kwan banged his two hunting spears together to reestablish order above the hoots and jeers of the assembled crowd inside *his* huge igloo. Then, the wise old chief motioned for Keesh to continue his brazen oratory.

"And thou, Massuk, you have a mother, and for her do you speak. My mother has no one to speak on her behalf, except me, so that's why the hell I'm here," Keesh boldly declared. "Bok is dead because he hunted too fanatically for the benefit of others, who have now regrettably forgotten his glory," Keesh emphasized for everyone's consideration. "So based on my father's great contributions to this community, including the fucked-up gay and lesbian sub-community," the teenager cautiously proceeded, "I insist that my mom Ikeega and I be given better meat as long as this tribe has a plentiful supply. I, Keesh, the son of Bok and of Ikeega, have spoken. I say this just in case some of you deaf sons of bitches seated on the other side of the igloo, and some of you deaf and dumb sons of bitches whose smelly asses sit on the council, were wondering what the hell I was doing when I was moving my mouth and jaws!"

The brash kid sat-down in a huff with his ears perceiving the abundant dissension and commotion that his stinging words had generated. Keesh then alertly absorbed the intense, malignant harangue being channeled in his direction.

"That ungrateful boy talks disease out of his ass and shits out of his unwise mouth!" Ugh-Gluk mumbled to Massuk. "Let's face the music Massuk. Keesh is a sick, young, walrus pup trying to *seal* an easy life for his big fat cow mommy, and also for Keesh'! Ha, ha, ha!" Ugh-Gluk robustly laughed. "Massuk; tell that ambitious roughneck to fuck-off and quickly leave the council's igloo, so that we can conduct our important business!"

"Fellow Eskimos, shall the babes in arms tell us veteran experienced men how we must distribute meat?" Massuk implored those parents still grumbling in the general attendance. "If Keesh was to have more meat, tell him to live in a 'porterhouse' instead of in the smallest igloo in Alaska! Ha, ha, ha!"

The entire assemblage. with the exception of saddened Ikeega, mocked and jeered Keesh's brashness. After order had again been restored, Klosh-Kwan commanded Keesh to bed to have 'white dreams' of delicious polar bear carcasses. "You shall have scheduled beatings administered to you by the council's administrators!" the livid Chief thundered at Keesh. "You're a most rambunctious, presumptuous, little tyrant, whose all-too-thin hide needs to be tanned! Have *you* no modesty or humility?"

Keesh's eyes flashed with heightened anger, and the blood within his veins, arteries, and capillaries promptly boiled. The defiant young prodigy/progeny jumped to his feet to challenge the council's supreme adult authority, all happening before the entire appalled village population. "Hear me speak elderly retards and pedophiles!" the youth hostilely replied. "These are my last words to you. Bok was a great hunter. I, his son, shall prove to be a great hunter, also. I shall go and hunt the meat I shall eat without your goddamned, unjust welfare system, and I shall divide my meat and apportion it fairly," the agitated lad boldly stated. "First, I shall share my meat with widows whose husbands have been killed. Secondly, I shall share my meat with the mothers whose sons are dead; and thirdly, I shall give my meat to the impotent old men that sit on council and can go longer get erections or shoot an ounce of sperm juice. And I predict," Ikeega's son loudly communicated, "that in the days to come, the gluttonous, fat old men that arrogantly sit on this sham council shall know the meaning of the word 'shame' without the aid or use of a dictionary! I, Keesh, have spoken."

"You ain't gonna' screw me up the ass, you arrogant, piss-ant mother-fucker!" Massuk yelled at the audacious upstart like a raving maniac. "Just come over here and suck my dick to see exactly how *impotent* I am in this damned village!"

Keesh did not answer Massuk's degrading insult, because the youth had told everyone at the meeting that he had spoken all he had wished to say. Jeers and abundant scorn filled his ears as the mocked lad abruptly left the meeting with his head raised high. Keesh's jaw was set tight, for the teen Eskimo looked neither left nor right as he silently battled his sudden lockjaw attack.

The next morning, the determined boy trekked along the coastline where the sea's ice met the hard frozen land. Several elders had witnessed him leaving the village with his bow, a handful of bone-barbed arrows, his father's enormous hunting spear, and a bulging hard-on sticking out from his thigh-length fur coat, which was made from the skin of Bok's last polar bear kill.

Never before had a thirteen-year-old fledgling gone-out to hunt, let alone gone out to hunt all by his lonesome. Many horny women stared with pity in their hearts at Ikeega, whose facial expression reflected both grimness and melancholy. "He'll be back before long, Ikeega," the considerate women encouraged their disconsolate, grieving friend. "He'll become tired, and return to the village, and eventually learn to curb his rash tongue. Your obstinate son is rebelling against a gross injustice, and blaming it all on adult authority."

"Let the junior jerk-off go; let him learn the meaning of 'disgrace' *without* the aid of an elementary school dictionary," the hunters laughed while mimicking Keesh's council meeting presentation. "And the callow wise-ass will come back soft of tongue and meek in speech, and he'll finally respect the wisdom of his sage elders; that young punk double-fuck!"

And three days passed with strong gales and ten inches of snow, but there was no sign of Keesh. Ikeega pulled-out her hair and smeared soot all over her face as tokens of sorrow, symbolically telling everyone it was better to do that than to smear soot onto her scalp, and to pull her face off. The village women all openly criticized their husbands for mistreating the haughty, naughty boy at the council meeting, and the clever wives had cut-off their spouses' sex lives, and no longer sucked their partners' dicks, telling their husbands that those practices would only be resumed when the women could eat and enjoy Keesh's meat. The men of the village felt guilty, and were totally pissed-off by the stubborn women's statements, so the adult males reluctantly organized search parties to track-down and find the adamant, opinionated "lost boy".

On the fourth morning, Keesh entered the village, but the boy was wearing a cheerful, confident face. A bountiful supply of freshly-killed meat was carried across his scrawny shoulders. Ikeega's son had triumphantly returned, and his success gave his militant personality a new-found cockiness.

"Go ye' men with your dog sledges, and travel my trail for a full day," the "Macho Boy" commanded the astonished residents, which included the gay and bisexual village people. "I've left much meat on the ice. A she-bear and two cubs."

Ikeega was filled with happiness at her son's apparent good fortune, and at his safe completion of his daring one-boy expedition. "Come Ikeega; let us eat meat inside our tiny little igloo. After that, I shall sleep, for I'm quite exhausted from beating my meat out there on the cold ice!" Keesh suggested and confessed. "In the future, I'll have that ugly bastard Massuk pound my meat so that I can conserve my energy for future hunting expeditions!"

'Oh boy,' Ikeega proudly thought. 'Now Keesh will become rich and will give me enough money to open a village furniture store!'

Much discussion and debate abounded throughout the small tribal village concerning Keesh and his "lucky hunting foray". The killing of a she-bear attending to her cubs was very dangerous, considering *her* inbred maternal instinct to protect her young. The men could not believe that Keesh was a better hunter than *they* were, but the knuckleheads were glad that the youngster had come back, because now the jerk-offs could again receive decent sex and stimulating blowjobs from their sometimes-faithful wives, who actually preferred lesbian homosexuality to heterosexual activity with their marital partners. So, the grumbling men departed the village to retrieve the polar bear kills, remembering their wives' memorable, familiar refrains, "No sex or blowjobs until you retrieve and finally return with Keesh's fabulous meat!"

In northern Alaska, it was imperative that the polar bear carcasses be located as soon as possible. Wild animals in search of scarce food might discover the remains, or the exposed meat could freeze so solidly that it could break even the sharpest cutting knife. A three-hundred-pound polar bear is not easy to lift and deposit onto a sled when it is frozen-solid *dead weight*. But when the recovery team eventually reached the dead animals' location, the searchers observed that Keesh had already neatly and impressively quartered the prey in true hunter practice.

Keesh's mysterious hunting prowess became more and more evident with the passing weeks. On his second mission, the wonder boy killed a nearly adult-sized male bear, and on his third expedition into the Alaskan wilderness, a male and its female companion were slain. Both of those remarkable exploits had been condensed into rather short three-or-four-day journeys that Keesh had conducted into the snow-covered, frontier barrens.

"How does he do it?" the very concerned Massuk asked Ugh-Gluk. "He never takes dogs with him, and certainly, dogs can be of great assistance. I believe that Keesh is possessed."

"Daaa, I don't know!" the over-challenged Ugh-Gluk replied. "Daa, I don't know!" the old senile fool reiterated.

"Let's ask the lucky punk about this good-luck skein he's been on!" Klosh-Kwan chimed-in. "And let me do all the talking, you two old stupid jerk offs!"

The three decrepit council members ate humble pie (which is not as tasty as hair pie), and approached the valiant Keesh standing outside his humble igloo. "Why do you hunt only polar bear, Keesh?" Klosh-Kwan curiously asked. "Why not also go after Christmas and Easter Seals, and also sea lions?"

Keesh contemplated Klosh-Kwan's motivation for wanting to ask such a silly, damned, asinine question, and then the lad illustriously responded, "Are you three, ancient, cretin, stupid assholes, or what?" the teen scolded his elders. "Every Eskimo from here to the North Pole knows that there's more meat on a polar bear than on a seal, or on the kind of sea lions that frequent this God-forsaken part of the known world!"

"I think you practice witchcraft!" Massuk openly accused Keesh. "You hunt with evil spirits that gladly help you in exchange for selling your soul! You are an evil sorcerer!"

"Maybe the spirits that help me are good ones and not evil ones," Keesh alertly challenged. "Maybe my noble father's spirit is expertly guiding me, and allowing me to attain excellence and tribal reward through *his* fine example and wisdom."

"I think you beat and have pounded your meat too much!" Massuk criticized his young adversary. "That's exactly your fuckin' problem! You beat your meat too much! Ha, ha, ha!"

"At least I have meat that can be pounded!" Keesh smartly answered his narrow-minded opponent, whose last valid erection was on his eightieth birthday three decades before.

Keesh's accumulative kill production was quite prolific by Eskimo standards. The lesser skilled hunters were kept busy going-out and hauling in sleds full of polar bear carcasses. Just as Bok had done before him, Keesh's distribution of the meat was fair, and the village elders became extremely pissed-off when the popular boy became the first official Eskimo meat distributor getting advanced orders from neighboring villages.

The teenager was both just and democratic in his allocations, providing the least of the women and the weakest of the grandfathers (not on the council) with abundant portions. The lad was achieving great prestige and honor from his peers, along with recognition from the women, and many knowledgeable gossipers predicted that Keesh would replace ancient Klosh-Kwan as the village chief. But the obstinate boy remembered his promise, and never returned to the village council until Keesh would be invited by the bullshitting ruling elders to share *his* unique experiences, his expertise, and his precocious philosophy about village affairs. The sanctimonious, bureaucratic, senile elders were too proud and too ashamed to publicly compromise, relent, and invite the impetuous boy to address them in council.

One morning, in the center of the icy village, Keesh confronted Klosh-Kwan, Ugh-Gluk, and Massuk, who were eagerly looking for a fourth member to sing bass to form a sort of un-harmonious Eskimo barbershop quartet.

"I'm considering constructing an igloo," Keesh began his oral statement. "And it shall be a very tremendous igloo to accommodate my mother Ikeega, and also my super-big ego. In fact, you wrinkled old farts, it will definitely be the largest and most spectacular igloo in the whole damned village."

"Ay!" the three nodded in amazement. "Ay!" they hypnotically repeated and nodded.

"Ay! Ay! Ay!" Klosh-Kwan exclaimed. "Ay, Ay, *I* wish I was in *Dixie,* hooray, hooray, In Dixieland I'll take my stand, to live and die in *Dixie!*"

"Away, away, away down south in *Dixie!*" Massuk and Ugh-Gluk idiotically joined-in with Klosh-Kwan, to further aggravate their principal nemesis.

"Stop this crazy nonsense right now!" Keesh indignantly yelled. After silence reigned supreme, the boy continued his braggadocio-type monologue. "But I have no time to build my igloo because of my scheduled commitment set aside for hunting polar bear meat for the entire village," Keesh boastfully maintained. "I recommend that the old men and widows that eat my meat should construct my huge igloo during my absence."

And much to the council elders' humiliation, a week later the giant iced edifice was almost completed and being constructed to Keesh's strict specifications, and the huge structure was especially designed to be three times as massive as Klosh-Kwan's meeting hall. The spacious home was the first material comfort Ikeega would experience since the death of Bok, who according to village scuttlebutt, only came *bok* as a benign spirit, assisting Keesh in *his* celebrated hunting exploits.

Keesh's mother also earned admiration and recognition from the other village women, and Ikeega became the First Lady of the settlement, despite the fact that the place had no President, and that her husband was deceased. Many squaws asked the matriarch's sage advice on sensitive female matters like dealing with menstruation, and having multiple sex partners, and Ikeega competently showed the other women how to masturbate like crazy using both hands, and how to use a whalebone dildo to achieve multiple orgasms when not engaged in formerly forbidden lesbian sex.

One day, Klosh-Kwan, Massuk, and Ugh-Gluk accosted Keesh in front of the youngster's work-in-progress, almost completed igloo. The three elders appeared rather annoyed and in prosecutorial moods, despite the fact that the trio had recently found a talented bass singer to complement the correct rhythm for their inharmonious Eskimo barbershop quartet.

"What's this shit about a new culinary sensation being attributed to you?" Klosh-Kwan jealously asked the Eskimo boy prodigy. "Stop stealin' our fuckin' thunder!"

"My new eating delight is when a person puts seven slabs of polar bear meat on a skinny stick, and flame broils the flesh over a fire," the now-famous young hunter gloated. "Ikeega calls the new fabulous dish Eskimo *Keesh-ka-bob!*"

"It is charged," Ugh-Gluk yelled, deliberately changing the topic of conversation, "that thou Keesh dealest with an evil spirit; wherefore thou hunting expeditions are rewarded by dead demon shamans with plentiful polar bear meat."

"There is 'spirit' involved," Keesh readily acknowledged, "but it's not an evil spirit. When I see a polar bear about to attack me, I simply *spear-it!* Ha, ha, ha! Get it! Spear-it, ha, ha, ha!"

"Don't give us any of your polar bear comedy shit, or we'll excommunicate you from the village!" Massuk sternly warned his young formidable enemy. "Your new ice house is probably held together by E-glue because types A, B, C and D glue were ineffective."

"Is not the meat good that I give you?" Keesh objected while getting back on subject. "Has anyone in our village taken sick from eating it? Is your accusation of witchcraft being involved in my skill a slick cover-up for the envy and jealousy that consumes your black, selfish souls?"

"That's enough out of you; you disrespectful, insolent, walrus pup!" Klosh-Kwan admonished the proud youth. "Keep your nasty fucked-up thoughts to yourself!"

"You three senile, deranged, stupid shits can *Keesh* my smooth, white Eskimo ass!" the boy-prodigy/genius contemptuously answered his mortified superiors.

And the three elder councilmen fearfully withdrew from Keesh's illustrious company with their hands trembling, and the gossipy eavesdropping village women intensively snickered at the "three charlatans" failure to effectively intimidate the emboldened lad. At a council caucus meeting, the trio of embarrassed elders asked for "suggestions from the ice" on how to deal with Keesh's blatant defiance of their authority.

After much discussion, it was finally decided to send four scouts out on patrol to spy on Keesh, and to see if witchcraft was indeed associated with his sinister hunting activities, or if skill was the dominant factor responsible for the boy's uncanny success. Four crafty hunters, Bim, Brim, Baum and Bum were assigned to trail the boy wonder into the icy wilderness, and then report back to the pissed-off council elders precisely what they had witnessed.

Five days later, the four fatigued spies re-entered the shabby village and addressed a closed-session of the council. Their eyes were bulging out of their sockets, and the neurotic men's hands were shaking as if each spy had contracted Parkinson's disease during the five-day absence. Klosh-Kwan requested that one of the four hunters step forward to the front table, and then orally review exactly what the spy had personally observed.

Bim reluctantly approached the elders seated behind a rudely fabricated table made from timber imported to the northern tundra from the Alaskan taiga forests. "Aged Brothers; the four of us had done as commanded by the council. We cunningly trailed Keesh, and we did it so secretly that he never suspected our furtive presence; our eyes scrutinizing his every move," Bim prefaced.

"Get to the point, or we'll have Bum tell us what the fuck happened!" Klosh-Kwan characteristically chastised the all-too-vociferous, gossiping villager. "You have a shit-mouthed tendency to prevaricate and equivocate!"

"Well, midway in the first day, Keesh encountered a ferocious large bear with teeth longer than Bum's dick!" Bim cockily asserted.

"I've never seen such a gargantuan bear in my entire life!" Baum verified. "But the amazing thing was that although provoked by Keesh's spear, the monster refused to fight him. It all was quite fuckin' extraordinary to witness, to say the least."

"And what transpired next?" Massuk demanded to know. "Make it short and sweet, just like Bum's abbreviated dick. I gotta' leave the meeting soon, Bim. It's almost time for my ugly wife to give me my nightly enema."

"The strange-acting bear turned and moped slowly over the ice," Bim elaborated with mild excitement. "And Keesh chased after the beast, which became very much unafraid. And the obnoxious boy shouted insults at the great brute, which just ignored the dumb kid's nasty comments. Some jerks get all the friggin' luck!"

"And then," Brim enthusiastically interrupted Bim. "The bear became so antagonized that it stood-up on its hind legs and growled fiercely. But Keesh stepped right up to the giant polar bear as if it were a baby seal pup."

"Next," interrupted a very nervous and stuttering Baum, "Keesh ran-up to the enraged ferocious bear, and prodded him with his father's magical spear. I thought that the asshole must be insane to be acting so aggressively!"

"Ah, witchcraft!" Ugh-Gluk surmised and exclaimed. "The little bastard was using witchcraft! The spear is bewitched! I knew all along that *he* was fuckin' communing with evil spirits!"

"Perhaps!" Baum continued and acknowledged. "Keesh then ran away, and the aggravated mammoth bear took-off in pursuit of his ass. But Keesh then dropped a little red round ball upon the slippery ice, and the mammoth bear amazingly stopped, smelled it, and finally chewed and swallowed the circular sphere!" Baum exclaimed. "And then Keesh dashed-away some more, and dropped his balls all over the ground, and the irate bear continued to devour them."

"What are you four fucked-up simpletons expecting us to believe?" Massuk incredulously asked. "Are you four assholes fuckin' delusional or what? I think the four of you neurotic, imbecilic cunt-lappers are infected with evil spirits, too!"

"We all saw it with our own eyes!" Bim confirmed.

"With our own eyes!" Bum corroborated.

"With our own eyes!" Brim affirmed.

"With our own eyes!" Baum verified.

"Fuck your own eyes!" Klosh-Kwan boisterously derided. "Your eyes can only behold evil witchcraft, and nothing else!"

"But eminent elders," Baum facetiously answered. "This red-ball activity continued until the immense polar bear stood erect, cried-out in agony, and then thrashed its forepaws wildly about as if it was going absolutely crazy. The lunatic bear paid no attention to Keesh as it growled and groaned in excruciating pain," Baum added. "The goddamned polar bear became very weak and exhausted, rolled over on its back, and then seemed to beg Keesh to kill it, which he soon accomplished with his father's bewitched, supernatural spear."

"The spear was a charm! It was an evil object not intended for Eskimo use in this accursed world!" Ugh-Gluk exclaimed. "The spear definitely belongs to an evil sorcerer! A fuckin' shaman of the forbidden black arts!"

"Exactly what happened after Keesh killed the bear with Bok's haunted spear?" Klosh-Kwan insisted on learning.

"When we left the incredible scene," Bim summarized almost out of breath, "Keesh was preoccupied skinning the bear, so we came sprinting back to the village in record time to accurately reveal the unearthly truths that we had witnessed."

"All four of you shit-head clowns, get the fuck outa' here right this instant!" incensed Klosh-Kwan nastily screamed. "Besides sucking Keesh's dick, you four assholes must also eat his little red balls, too!"

That afternoon, the humble women of the village all earnestly pounded Keesh's meat, while their aggravated husbands attended an emergency council session in Klosh-Kwan's igloo, now the second largest ice building in the whole damned village. A courier was dispatched to Keesh, ordering the vernal hunter to attend the important meeting, and of course the young man considered and then declined to go, even though he believed "the order" was "an invitation" by the elders to formally address the council. "I'm too tired and hungry this time," the polar bear killer told the shocked and disappointed messenger. "But my new igloo is the largest in the village and can easily accommodate all of the councilmen, along with the gay and lesbian sub-community," the kid just entering puberty shrewdly answered, effectively breaking everybody else's testicles and tits.

Klosh-Kwan and the others were so curious about inspecting Keesh's new igloo that the ignoramuses all got their asses up and paced over to the recently-constructed "Ice Palace". Keesh was busy eating his one-man banquet, but he took the time to welcome the elders and the rest of the 'rank' and file clan, and next seated them according to their positions of importance. Ikeega was proud of her son's evident haughtiness, and the loyal mother became the hostess, going around the tremendous-sized igloo and cordially serving everyone delicious Eskimo pies without any pubic hairs in them.

During the formal council meeting, Klosh-Kwan presented the testimonies of Bim, Brim, Baum and Bum. "So young Keesh," the tribal chief concluded and articulated, "I believe that an explanation of your fantastic activities is indeed warranted. Describe to our village people, Macho Boy, your secret method of hunting polar bears. Is there any witchcraft or evil spirits involved?"

Everyone listened intently for Keesh's explicit accountability. "Nay, old Klosh-Kwan," the lad nonchalantly answered. "A boy, such as I, knows little about witches or about the forbidden black arts. I have but cleverly developed a means to successfully kill ice bears. I assure you, Mighty Assholes perched on the council, my genuine hunting methods involve good head-craft, and not evil witchcraft as you presume."

"And may any hunter perform the same method?" Massuk inquired. "Could I be able to kill a polar bear?"

"Yes, even you Massuk!" Keesh amusingly responded as the other men in the audience loudly heckled and jeered the village's old codger. "If you can still pop a load into a hairy pussy, you could kill a polar bear with my proven strategy."

"And will thou share with us this wonderful hunting secret?" the aged Ugh-Gluk pleaded. "I'd love to kill more polar bears if the process could be made easier, and if it didn't involve any fucked-up satanic witchcraft!"

"Yes, I'll tell thee now that the council has had the courtesy to assemble in *my* igloo!" Keesh lectured and stated. After sucking on a rich marrowbone, the lad stood on a crate and again spoke to the astonished Eskimo community, including the influential gay and lesbian Eskimo sub-community. "It is all quite easy and simple to comprehend, you asinine simpletons!"

The lad picked-up a thick strip of whalebone cartilage and showed it to his captivated audience. The ends were honed like sharp needle-points. Keesh then meticulously coiled the cartilage strip until it released and sprang open in the palm of his hand. He next picked-up a piece of red blubber, and made the mass hollow on the inside.

"Then, I place the coiled whalebone cartilage inside the blubber, add another layer of red meat, and next form the mass into a rounded red ball," the young hunter orally described and demonstrated for all to see. "Next, I take the Eskimo 'meatballs' and allow them to freeze outside. The bear swallows the red ball, thinking that it is delicious food, which in a way it is," Keesh convincingly explained. "But it happens to also be deadly food. When the blubber melts, the whalebone cartilage either uncoils in the bear's throat, or in its stomach. The polar bear becomes ill, chokes incessantly, suffers from internal bleeding, and when it's too weak to fight, I kill it with my father's trusty spear that is not haunted, as *you* especially fucked-up idiots on the council falsely presume."

And Ugh-Gluk exclaimed "Oh!" and Klosh-Kwan yelled out "Ay!" and old Massuk boomed-out, "You conniving smart-assed little bastard!"

Soon, Keesh became the eminent chief of the remote village, located on the rim of the great polar sea. His loyal hunters practiced good head-craft instead of evil witchcraft, and the Eskimo village was soon the most prosperous on the entire Alaskan coast. Neither widow nor weak grandfather clamored for fresh food, even during the fiercest winter blizzards.

Keesh instituted a tradition in the village that is still practiced today. The new teen Chief declared the warm month of July "Polar Bear Month", and every resident was required by law to crawl around stark naked on all fours inside his or her igloo in imitation of the great white animals whose flesh and meat sustained the village's population. The horny men would sniff their wives' hairy asses and crotches all day long for that whole warm summer month, and every calendar period between March and April of the following year, the village was blessed with many new baby Eskimos.

The promulgation of surplus Eskimos trained in the art and skill of "head-craft" led to the tribe's great prosperity, and vastly expanded the clan's already-renowned reputation. Even some of the avowed village lesbians surprisingly became pregnant, and reproduced their own kind, thanks to wonderful Keesh's incomparable genius and indispensable wisdom.

"Love of Life"
Jack London

The two very fatigued men hobbled-down a steep embankment, and staggered across rough jagged rocks. Each was heavily encumbered with blanket packs strapped to his shoulders. while having head-straps across the forehead, used for stabilizing and supporting cumbersome camping paraphernalia. The very tired men both wished they were situated in a more pleasant and less hostile natural environment.

"I wish we had a couple of those cartridges in that cache of ours," the second man disgustedly stated to his traveling colleague. "Then, we could either shoot an animal and live, or pop a few slugs into our brains and get the fuck outa' this goddamned cruel world."

The man's disgruntled tone of voice was very mechanically spoken without evident emotion or motivation, and his utterance was completely ignored by the second man, who was thinking about getting laid on a tropical island, and not about trekking across the worst, desolate part of Alaska.

Soon, the two gold prospectors splashed and staggered through a stream of icy cold water, making their feet and ankles even more numb than they already were. The trailing man slipped on a smooth, underwater rock and uttered a sharp expletive.

"Fuck!" the follower exclaimed and objected. The trailing trekker reeled around and attempted to balance himself from falling over into the icy water. "Thank God the ice will make the goddamned swelling go down!" the staggering gent yelled as the man thought about his throbbing ankle, and not about his throbbing dick penetrating the lead man's gorgeous native princess on the ideal tropical island. But the lead man was still thinking about getting laid on the tropical island paradise, and ignored the following man's loud cry for assistance.

"I say Bill; I've fuckin' double sprained my right ankle!" the second injured victim hollered. But the man in front again ignored his companion's entreaty, as the leader awkwardly stumbled onward through the icy-cold, shallow river. The first fellow's eyes were like those of a dazed, wounded deer, as his distracted mind pleasurably imagined experiencing a wonderful sperm ejaculation. Then Bill ascended up the stream's embankment without ever looking back and acknowledging his faltering companion. 'I'll now think about my next fuckin' sexual fantasy!' the lead hiker selfishly considered. 'Yes, fantasy! That's really the only fuckin' thing that's keepin' me alive,' Bill concluded, trudging ahead.

The man left stranded in the stream still had sufficient energy to give his abandoner a stiff middle finger. His lips were trembling from his pain and from his general exhaustion. A rough mustache and a thatch of brown hair encircled his quivering lips. The beleaguered man's tongue moistened his mouth, and the fellow was pretending that he was licking the imaginary native princess's hairy beaver on that wonderful, fanciful tropical island.

"Bill!" the left-behind man yelled with all of his strength. "Don't leave me out here all alone, you fuckin' degenerate!"

But Bill never turned his head to recognize his friend's desperate plea. William kept on lurching forward up the embankment toward the dull gray skyline, where his sex-starved mind now imagined that a dozen horny babes on another tropical island were wildly masturbating and waiting for him to arrive. 'I hear the bastard callin' me, but I don't give a shit about Jack!' Bill thought. 'I don't care Jack about Jack. I'm gonna' keep all my gold, and sail from Tahiti out to Samoa, so that I won't have to dream about *some moa'* goddamned pretend sex! I want the real fuckin' thing!'

The deserted man stared ahead in the direction of Bill, and Jack observed his friend's form passing through the mists and vapors as if he had entered an atmospheric portal into another weird dimension. While placing his weight on his good ankle, the abandoned man standing in the frigid stream still possessed the wherewithal to pull-out his watch, which faithfully indicated four o'clock.

'It's just about the First of August, and the damned sun is in the northeast,' Jack perceptively reckoned. 'The Great Bear Lake is to the south, and then after that lies the Canadian Barrens. I wanta' fuckin' stay away from that desolate place. And this stream I'm in feeds into the Coppermine River, which flows into Coronation Gulf near the Arctic Ocean. God, I'm sure glad I won that shitin' Geography Bee in elementary school!'

The man again surveyed his bleak environment of low-lying hills that were devoid of vegetation. 'No damned trees, shrubs, grass or ladies' bushes,' Jack regretted. 'And Bill still has two good legs, and the determined bastard is liable to eventually make it back to civilization and to the nearest whorehouse, way before I do. Fuck you Bill, even if ya' gotta' be sodomized! Fuck you I say!' Jack mentally repeated in what constituted an introspective rage.

The abandoned man stood shivering in the icy water, cowered- down, and then examined the empty gun in his hand. His shaking allowed the gun to fall from his grasp into the cold stream, and the almost-delirious fellow groped in the water until his searching hands finally located the weapon. Then, Jack weakly trudged-out of the stream onto the solid, hard, frozen land. 'Why the fuck did I ever leave San Diego?' the prospector wondered and regretted. 'Now I remember. I wanted to find gold up here in Alaska. I'd rather die of venereal disease recalling fond prostitute memories than drown is this lousy, scumbag creek, and wind-up being polar bear food,' the wincing man mused.

Next, the determined stream escapee struggled-up the rise and gradually reached the hill's crest. Jack noticed no trace of Bill limping forward, anywhere. Instead, the fellow's weary eyes perceived a shallow valley showing no signs of life, so Jack stubbornly lurched forward thinking about how Bill had left him in *his* moment of dire need, even though his fiendish friend was hallucinating and didn't know what the hell he was actually doing.

'Jack and Bill went up the hill, to fetch two sacks of gold,' the man from sunny California recollected and laughed. 'Jack fell-down and sprained his leg, and Bill never heard his partner beg! Fine partner I've been fuckin' associated with!'

The valley's basin was extremely soggy, and moss-covered rocks were prevalent in that God-forsaken sector of the Alaskan Tundra. Each time the man struggled a step forward, the muddy water squirted out from under his boots, causing a sucking sound, which immediately made the survivor fantasize about getting the best Samoan blowjob of his life. Jack slowly meandered through the muskeg *marsh,* looking for delicious marshmallows to eat, and then sampled the disgusting mint-green moss, only to spit the foul-tasting slime out of his mouth. But Jack was as doomed as Biblical Abel.

'I'm not lost, even though I'm all alone,' Jack pensively and hopefully pondered. 'Pretty soon, I'll be south enough to reach the dead, stunted trees on the shores of the little lake the Eskimos call the *titchin-nichille*. That means 'little sticks', and logically, they're the only kind of erections the damned Eskimos could achieve in this fuckin' frigid temperature. I'll locate the stream and follow it to the Dease River, where *our* cache of supplies is hidden under the overturned canoe. I'll be able to find my gun bullets, fishhooks, lines, a small net, flour, bacon, beans, and my treasured porno' magazines,' Jack remembered, enjoying a brief moment of felicity. 'Yes; the memory of those fuckin' porno' magazines; *that* is really the only goddamned thing keepin' me alive. There aren't any boondocks out here to be out in the boondocks, and there are no sticks around here to be even out in the goddamned *titchin-nichille!'*

'When I regain my full strength,' Jack reckoned, 'I'll locate the hidden canoe and paddle-down the Dease to the Mackenzie River, and successfully race south ahead of the encroaching winter. Next, I'll finally reach the Taiga, where the frontier Hudson Bay Company post had been constructed in the northernmost coniferous tree line. Food will be aplenty, and after being rejuvenated, I could then use my precious gold to hire the myriad services of several enterprising, itinerant Eskimo prostitutes.'

And meanwhile, Jack still possessed some semblance of distorted reality. 'Bill will probably be waiting at the cache with Tippycanoe and Tyler, too,' Jack's inventive mind fabricated. 'I haven't eaten for two days, and for the first time in my life, I actually desire chomping on food more than eating juicy, succulent pussy!'

So, the man stooped-down and picked-up a handful of bitter-tasting muskeg berries and carefully chucked them into his mouth. And as Jack chewed on the sour-flavored vegetation, he imagined that even dingleberries would taste better than a handful of friggin' mushy muskeg berries.

The distracted trekker seriously stubbed his big right toe on a protruding rock at nine o'clock. Jack faltered and then toppled over in response to the pulsing excruciation inside his big right toe, which augmented the pulsating pain in his double sprained right ankle. He knelt-down on the permafrost and roughly slipped off his backpack straps, wishing that he could convert to being a Muslim, die, and then shack-up in heaven with a minimum of seven virgins eager to lose their virginity. As twilight settled in the eastern sky, the man built a fire out of dried moss, and then heated a tin pot of water to drink in the absence of good hard whiskey.

Jack next unwrapped his pack, and with his mind in a bewildered, fuzzy state, meticulously counted his remaining matches, and twelve consecutive times the counter reached the sum of sixty-seven, wishing he had two more so that he could contemplate 'sixty-nine'. Bill's paranoid, left-behind companion divided the matches into three piles, and then placed one pile into his empty tobacco pouch, the second handful in his pants' pocket, and the third batch inside his battered and tattered hat's headband.

'I can't remember how many matches I have,' Jack thought while doubting his own judgment. So, the perplexed survivor counted his three sums an additional time to verify the validity of his former mathematical determination.

Jack placed his wet boots next to the smoldering fire, and then he briefly removed his socks and examined his abused feet, which were pallid, lacerated, and bleeding. 'I'm glad my dick and my ass aren't in the same condition,' his twisted mind considered. 'Then, I would need four socks. Two socks would cover my tender feet, and another pair for my dick and my ass to wear. And my ankle's' now the size of my knee, and my knee looks like a baby watermelon. Christ! I must have *water*melon on the knee!' his warped, exhausted, deteriorating mind deducted. 'And this fuckin' swollen big toe is really aggravatin' my excruciating gout condition.'

The gold prospector tore the seam strips from one of his two blue blankets and recklessly bound them around his severely injured right ankle. The rest of the strips Jack ingeniously used to wrap around his feet to serve as suitable protection until his saturated socks would dry near the gentle fire. Next, Jack poured the hot water into a tin cup and greedily drank, pretending that the bland liquid was powerful rye whiskey. He next wound-up his watch, momentarily studied the heavens, crawled between his blue blankets, and finally dozed-off.

The Land of the Setting Sun had only brief darkness around midnight, and soon, the Earth's nearest star rose in the northeast, and the flickering object was discernible amidst ominous gray clouds. Jack woke-up hungry, and realized that he required nutrition to continue his arduous journey to the hidden cache stashed under the hidden, inverted canoe. He turned over and then shrieked to the barren wilderness, "Holy shit! I need a delicious fuckin' sizzlin' steak!"

A nearby bull caribou had been inspecting with curiosity Jack sleeping, tossing and turning on the cold ground. The nervous man heard snorting and then fully awoke. 'That bastard animal probably wishes he was a wolf rather than a weak grass eater,' the man suspected. 'I sorta' wish that he was a goddamned wolf, too!' "Eat me, you son-of-a-bitch!" Jack futilely screamed, scaring the bull caribou into thinking about flight and about sex with its mate, rather than wasting time studying a stupid, silly, sleeping human stranded many miles from civilization.

Jack instinctively reached for his gun, pulled the trigger, but no bullet was released from the chamber. The bull caribou soon had escaped the desperate man's range of vision. At that moment, the lonely human wished that he did have a bullet in his pistol's chamber to blow his own brains out, and escape to Muslim heaven and start pumping the poop out of those seven gorgeous, horny virgins.

In sheer contempt of his hostile environment, the miserable fellow groaned and finally managed to stand and assume an erect posture. The commonplace task of standing required a full minute to complete, because Jack's joints felt like rusty door hinges needing lubrication, and his tender ass felt like it weighed the equivalency of a ton of bricks. Next, the aggrieved prospector attempted taking a leak, but that simple process required a full half hour to perform, mostly because of faulty internal plumbing, along with a bad case of bladderwort infecting his aching bladder.

The weary survivor stumbled and crawled up a small knoll, and still had the presence of mind to survey the distant scenario. Everything appeared gray, including the prospect of *his* returning to the overturned canoe. The lakelets, sky, moss, rocks, streams and distant caribou all were gray, symbolizing stark uncertainty, old age, and the encroachment of death. 'I've lost my fuckin' sense of direction!' Jack eventually realized. 'But now, I remember! I'll just proceed in the opposite direction from which I came! I say, how many fuckin' matches do I have left! I'd better count the suckers again just to make sure I'm in control of my sanity!'

After carefully tabulating and double-checking his matches, Jack seriously considered having 'sixty-nine' instead of '67' with the bull caribou, but then immediately exited his peculiar delusion when the beast (in his mental manifestation) started kicking the man's face with its hooves as it started to orgasm. 'Christ! My mind is really fucked-up now!' Jack concluded. 'I gotta' use-up another match, burn and singe my numb finger, and get this friggin' sixty-nine bullshit fixation out of my goddamned head!'

Then, the delusional prospector assessed his moose-hide sack containing fifteen-pounds of gold nuggets. 'Should I discard this precious ore?' Jack wondered and evaluated. 'It's fuckin' weighin' me down, and it means nothin' at all to the goddamned caribou and wolves in this most secluded part of Alaska. Oh well, I'll take it with me in hopes that I can reach the Hudson Bay outpost and buy some sixty-nine with a decent hooker rather than dream a nightmare of doin' it with a fuckin' male caribou! Damn it! I gotta' use up one more of my freakin' matches, or else I'll fuckin' go insane!'

Hunger pangs gnawed-away inside Jack's stomach as he fancifully craved all sorts of food, and would even kill and cannibalize a weak vegetarian caribou if one were within choking range. He haphazardly descended into the ugly-empty valley, where rock ptarmigan rose with flapping wings, pecking away at the scattered muskeg berries. "Ker, ker, ker" the birds squawked as their beaks picked at the tart berries randomly growing between rocks and ledges. Jack pathetically stalked the bad-tempered birds on his knees, just as a hungry cat might hunt a family of yard birds (outside a prison). His abused legs left a blood trail as the hapless man squirmed and wriggled over wet moss and rocks, futilely attempting to clutch and strangle an unwary mother ptarmigan nesting its young.

"Ker, ker, ker," the disturbed birds mocked as they communicated danger to one another.

"Fuck! Fuck! Fuck!" Jack answered in frustration, repeating in his language what he had interpreted "Ker, ker, ker!" had meant to the apprehensive wary ptarmigans.

Almost in tears, the thwarted man crawled-upon what must have been a sleeping deaf bird. Jack impetuously grasped at the suddenly surprised creature, which quickly regained its consciousness, and frantically flew-off. Only three gray tail feathers were present in the man's dirt-smeared palm. "Come back and retrieve your ass-end steering feathers!" Jack yelled to the escaped ptarmigan flying overhead in a circle. "Come back you fuckin' birdbrain, and I'll surely kill your ass the second time around!"

40

The dazed man rose and clumsily tripped his way forward. In the afternoon, the disoriented fellow entered a valley of marshes where animal life was more abundant. Twenty caribou played peek-a-boo with him, and aimlessly ambled and grazed a hundred yards away. 'If only I had a loaded rifle,' Jack thought. 'I would easily take-down the biggest of the herd. And if I could sprint, I could surely catch the swiftest of the pack. Holy Christ! Are my totally angled thoughts fucked-up, or what?'

A black fox accidentally came ambling toward the incoherent man, and it was carrying a squealing ptarmigan in its mouth. "Drop that fuckin' bird!" Jack shouted at the sly fox, which quickly and skillfully leaped-away onto higher rock ledges, and then hastily disappeared over a hill's crest. 'Even sloppy seconds from a wily fox seems tantalizing,' the desperate man supposed in self-sympathy.

Jack then glanced-down at his dungaree zipper. 'The next thing I gotta' prevent from happenin' is to keep that freakin' fox away from *my* damned bird, especially since *he* carries his cherished food away to eat and enjoy in secrecy!'

The overwhelmed man came upon a milky, lime-colored stream that flowed through multi-shaped patches of green grass. Jack pulled the grass rushes up from their roots, which to his jumbled mind, reminded him of onion sprouts, hardly the size of a pinky fingernail. The fibers were tough and stringy, and the small bulbs were hardly as palatable as the famished man had wished.

And next, the tenacious struggler got-down on his hands and knees and wildly foraged and munched the grass like a distraught bovine would, even though Jack hated everything about cows, including their sweet milk. 'I'd much rather have a nice juicy *Porterhouse* and chew the fat with a homosexual friend, rather than to suffer the indignity of lying here in this isolated marsh imitating a lowly cow chewing its cud!' the weary wanderer decided. Then, another basic consideration surfaced in the all-too-frustrated prospector's troubled cerebrum.

'Damn it; I wanna' find some nourishing food,' Jack lamented. 'I need meat! I'd even eat live frogs, or squiggly worms, if I could only find them!' the pathetic wanderer thought as he aggressively dug away into the muddy marsh grass with his fingernails. 'I'd even eat a horny toad! God, how I really love frog legs! Shit! No frogs, toads, or worms live in this far-northern wasteland, but I'm gonna' keep on diggin' for reptiles and amphibians, anyway!'

Jack searched every shallow water pool hoping, to see a small fish. And then, almost miraculously, the fanatic spotted a tiny old *minnow* that, to his warped mind, looked like it was a carryover from the ancient Greek *Minoan* civilization. The starving fellow plunged his arm up to his shoulder into the cold pool, but the daylight had been refracted, going from the medium of air to the medium of water, and the slippery minnow eluded his frantic lunge. The incensed man then used both hands exploring the depths of the pool, trying to use tactile sensation to locate the tiny old fish, which nearly had died from fright during its most recent misadventure. The unfortunate human fell and splashed into the murky marsh, getting wet up to his chest.

'I have to wait until the sediments settle so that the water is clear again,' he concluded. 'I must stay on task and not lose sight of my *mission!*' the food searcher thought as his destitute mind conjured-up an image of the *Alamo.*

After the muddy water became somewhat clear again, Jack attempted capturing the evasive minnow, which again wildly avoided his frenetic effort. The encumbered man anxiously began bailing water out of the pool with his tin cup, while boisterously screaming, "Everybody out of the pool! Everybody out of the fuckin' pool!" the asshole shrieked as if he was a maniacal lifeguard. His freezing hands were shaking, and his heart was rhythmically pounding inside his chest cavity. In a half hour, the pool was nearly empty. The tiny fish had managed to squeeze itself though a tiny crevice between two stones, and had escaped to a larger adjoining pool that was big enough for a small whale to swim in.

'Damn it!' Jack mentally cursed. 'If I had known of that fuckin' crevice, I could've plugged it up.' Then, the famished fellow's attention was directed toward his rusty zipper. 'Shit!' he realized. 'My limp pecker will never again plug-up any damned female crevice, diminutive or otherwise, unless I fuckin' find some food fast!'

The virtually-defeated, lost rambler slowly climbed out of the freezing-cold pool and rolled over upon the wet ground. Jack cried loudly to the apathetic and heartless marshes, mountains, hills, and dull gray sky. His soul felt as desolate as his insensitive surroundings seemed to be.

In a moment of sheer inspiration, the stubborn survivor managed to build a campfire and warmed several quarts of hot water, which he indulgently gulped-down to keep his fragile body warm. Jack next conscientiously checked his supply of matches, and ascertained that they were still dry. 'Now I think I only have sixty-five.' he sulked. 'How the hell do you do sixty-five with a naked woman?'

Jack's blue blankets were moist and clammy, and his right ankle, knee, and big toe ached with incredibly intense pain. He again wound his watch and eventually fell asleep, dreaming of Viking feasts, of huge wedding banquets, of exotic Hawaiian luaus, of cheap Eskimo smorgasbords, and of fast-food brothels. The dozer awoke from his disturbing slumber feeling physically cold and emotionally irritated.

'What the fuck's goin' on?' the lost gent thought in disgust. 'Snow flurries are ornamentin' the hills, makin' them pure white; and a heavy wind is blowin'. The dampness from the larger flakes has put out my fire! Why the fuck was I ever born!'

The poor soul carelessly packed his wet gear, awkwardly strapped the blankets to his back, and proceeded onward. 'Fuck the land of the little sticks, and the cache under the canoe on the bank of the Dease. All I wanna' do is eat some grub. I can't believe I'd rather eat broccoli or celery than savory wet pink pussy! I must be turnin' into either a goddamned lame wimp, or a fuckin' gay son-of-a-bitch! One thing's for damned sure!' Jack irrationally decided. 'I'll never follow Bill into the goddamned wilderness again, gold or no goddamned gold nuggets!'

The pessimistic adventurer again stared at his heavy moose-hide sack of gold. 'This sucker's weighin' me down,' the trekker assessed. 'It's worth a fortune anywhere in the Klondike or the Yukon, but it ain't worth shit out here with the various hungry animals. No creature would accept a fuckin' ransom for me, that's for damned sure! But I'll try and preserve my strength to carry the sack to the damned Dease. Then, the gold will be worth something again!'

Jack re-cinched his ankle with his blanket strips, and blood oozed through the fabric. The hilltop snow had partially melted, and after identifying the position of the morning sun, the man valiantly set-out on his quest to reach the secret cache. 'I gotta' go about five degrees to the right,' the left-behind man roughly estimated. 'I believe I've gone slightly off course. I don't want to wind-up somewhere in shitin' Siberia or fuckin' Antarctica.'

The man's tongue felt dry and enlarged as he trudged along. He frequently paused to rest, and his heart was irregularly palpitating, going "thump, thump thump" as if it was a big brass drum lodged deep in his thorax. 'My goddamned parched tongue feels like it's growin' hair!' Jack thought. 'Could it be that it's turnin' into a woman's fuzzy beaver?'

The woebegone trekker came upon a fairly large marsh pool with two minnows darting about in it. 'This damned basin is too large to bail-out!' the observer accurately determined. Showing less excitement at finding a marsh pool than he had exhibited before, Jack slowly pushed his tin prospecting bucket through the water's surface and (through noteworthy perseverance) managed to isolate and catch several of the small creatures. And then after taking a deep breath, he thrust the wiggling fish into his mouth, and avariciously chewed them raw, all-the-while imagining that he was enjoying a wonderfully delectable baked flounder dinner.

That evening, Jack successfully caught three more minnows and saved them for breakfast. 'I gotta' cover at least ten miles a day,' the prospector reckoned. 'I gotta' stay strong. The goddamned wolves are huntin' the old and weak caribou. I can hear the carnivorous critters howlin' in the distance. Fuck breakfast! I better *wolf* down these three squiggly fish before those friggin' wolves wolf both me and my arrogance down.'

The perplexed man had a tough decision to make, and finally rationality triumphed over greed. Jack divided his gold nuggets into two piles. He stashed half into a crack in a prominent ledge inside some blanket material, and the remaining half he returned to his *moose-hide* sack, which entirely was too small for even a baby moose to hide inside of. 'I'll keep my gun for as long as I can,' the grim-faced struggler convinced himself. 'I can get ammo' when I finally reach the overturned canoe. I might even need bullets to kill Bill, that fuckin' dirty, faggot prick!'

Jack was overwhelmed from giddiness that had been caused by a lack of nutrition and plenty of weariness. His bewildered and befuddled brain was as befogged as the strange-looking atmosphere. He stumbled and fell five times, got-up, and continued his weird one-man procession. His bedraggled body stumbled a sixth time, falling squarely into a well-concealed ptarmigan nest. Jack's blurred vision detected four squealing, newly hatched chicks, little day-old specks of life. The man honored his impulse to act quickly.

The desperate human eagerly hi*jacked* the tiny birds, flung them into his mouth, and chewed them ravenously (ptarmiganly), his teeth crunching them as if they were shelled peanuts. 'These little critters taste much better than those tart minnows did,' the starving trekker reasoned and appreciated. 'I can't wait to find and catch a warty frog, or a couple of earthworms, and see if I like the taste of them better!'

The alarmed mother ptarmigan returned from scavenging food, tried protecting her nest, and chirped and squawked all about, just managing to elude Jack's wild lunges. The prospector endeavored using his gun as a suitable club, but the annoyed bird dodged his erratic thrusts. He then hurled stones at the protesting bird, one of which injured her right wing. The distressed mother ptarmigan forgot all about her maternal instinct, entered a survival mode, and subsequently always maneuvered to stay several steps away from Jack's incessant clutching and smashing.

'Those chicks have whetted my appetite,' Jack realized. 'A bird in the hand is worth two in the bush!' the crazed Californian concluded as he lustily rubbed his limp *Johnson* while pursuing the thoroughly agitated 'lady-bird'.

The chase brought Jack across several swampy swales in the bottom of the valley where his fertile mind conjured-up a half-dozen valley girls masturbating like crazy. Then, amazingly, the dazed pursuer discovered recently formed footprints. 'Those suckers look like Bill's,' Jack theorized. 'They must be Bill's. That snot-nosed bastard must not be far ahead. I know the six valley girls are safe from molestation, because my buddy Bill's a goddamned, impotent, one-balled, homosexual.'

44

The mother ptarmigan lay exhausted ten feet in front of Jack's grasp, but the exhausted predator lacked the stamina or the will to leap and land upon her. But the man and the bird required rest, and both existed only ten-feet apart from one another. 'No more smorgasbords!' Jack mused in despair. 'And when the guy mustered-up sufficient power to lurch forward, the petulant-but-frightened mother bird also had reserve energy to elude his exaggerated effort by nervously fluttering and hopping forward. Jack tripped and fell flush on his face, cutting his pallid cheeks and chin between two sharp-edged stones. The courageous man did not move a muscle for an hour. Then, he diligently wound his watch, shit his pants, and went to sleep.

The following foggy morning, a nasty wind and a light drizzle had completely obscured Bill's footprints. By midday, the weight of the backpack became too oppressive, so Jack discarded the balance of his gold nuggets, and blatantly cursed man's proclivity toward valuing avarice. Starvation was setting in, so the temporarily lost soul also threw-away several items of necessity, and carried only his blanket, the tin sifting bucket, his knife, and his gun.

'I'm so goddamned hungry I'd even eat a smelly Eskimo hair pie,' Jack whimsically reflected for a moment. 'I believe I have one bullet remaining in my gun.' He industriously checked the weapon and was dismayed that his hope turned-out to be a mere fantasy. Jack next plodded and tramped ahead in disappointment, trying to ascertain how reality and his imagination had merged into one entity.

During the next two hours, the plodder fancifully inspected his gun six times, searching for the indispensable bullet that his undependable mind had created. The serious hunger pangs were increasing in severity and in frequency. The man robotically advanced southward, acting like a strange automaton devoid of compassion, self-sympathy, or other common human feelings. Suddenly, a fierce sight caught the trekker's immediate attention.

'Holy horseshit!' Jack's mind thought. 'It's a giant bear lookin' for its next meal!'

The ferocious carnivore was studying the pathetic hiker with bellicose scrutiny. 'I must do something before the animal goes into an irreversible attack mode!' Jack decided. 'If I run, I'm dead meat; and if I fight; I'm dead meat! I'm about to get my ass kicked and eaten! This is all ironically fuckin' un*bear*able!'

Jack remembered that he had not thrown away his trusty hunting knife that remained fastened to a leather sheath strapped to his belt. He touched its pointed blade, making certain that it was sharp. The worried gold rush participant's strained heart again began beating irregularly, and he felt as if his knees were wobbling and about to buckle. 'I'm going to pass out!' he frightfully thought.

In a gesture of total desperation, the dumb-ass man rushed forward with his raised knife and screamed as loud as he could, 'I'm gonna' kill you, you fuckin' ugly brown bastard!' The bear reared-up in a defensive, combative posture, considered its circumstances, and then retreated back three steps. Jack's grisly eyes met those of the big grizzly, and the man menacingly growled as the shouter crazily gestured with the raised knife. His startling animation had effectively intimidated the fierce predator, which was momentarily stunned by the mysterious human's uncharacteristic antics. Jack stood still as a statue, and then commenced roaring in imitation of a vicious circus lion he once saw as a boy. The gigantic, brown bear scampered-away on all fours, figuring that it would judiciously select a less insane and more predictable prey for its next meal.

The man wept and sobbed for a full half-hour; his psyche had been completely overwhelmed by his latest bizarre ordeal. 'I don't give a flyin' shit about dying like a man!' Jack contemplated and wept. 'I don't want to be violently ripped to shreds and then devoured by a fuckin' wild, ferocious Alaskan bear, or consumed by a pack of savage wolves. Oh, dear God; isn't my troubled soul deserving of a more favorable fate?'

Over the next several hours, full-bellied wolves crossed his path in packs of three and four, but the wily predators steered clear of the vertical creature weeping and screaming like a mental patient escaped from an insane asylum. The carnivores were hunting and feasting off of old, weak and young caribou, which did not stab, or scratch, or bite like the weird human standing and shouting crazy expletives in a threatening, erect, defensive stance.

An hour later, Jack discovered scattered caribou *calf'* bones. The backpacker felt the rear of his knees and thought, 'I'm fuckin' lucky to still have my two *calves* attached to my legs. Look what the fuck those carnivorous wolves have done to this poor, innocent, grass-eating animal!'

And then, the unstable man did something grotesque and unthinkably primitive. He solemnly touched the bones and thought, 'Is this what the fuck I'm gonna' look like tomorrow? These remains can't be Bill's dismantled skeleton!' And then an additional thought brought some consolation to *his* chaotic mind. 'There is no pain or suffering in death! Only the desire to live brings about misery, hurt, and anguish! Heaven, please help me! I'm not ready to fuckin' die!'

Jack was soon squatting in the damp moss, and sucking on a pink bone, biting off every savory shred of flesh and available sustenance left behind by the already-satisfied wolves. The sweet meaty taste sent Jack's mind into a mild ecstasy. He chomped-down on the bone with his weak jaws. Sometimes the caribou's bone broke exposing its rich marrow. Sometimes the intense crush broke several of Jack's molars.

Then, the almost-vanquished man had an inspiration. He smashed the bones against the nearby rocks, pounding them into small fragments, and then Jack swallowed the almost-pulverized remains. His fingers were bleeding from the times his descending rock missed the bone, or when the white femur or clavicle broke, scraping the skin off of his exposed knuckles and wrists. 'I'm livin' like a freakin' caveman!' the man sobbed and anguished in languish. 'Neanderthals had more dignity than I have right now. At least those primitive assholes had the security of bein' with their moronic family upon leaving *this* life!'

The next two days featured a mixture of snow, sleet, and rain, and Jack behaved like a machine that was not synchronized with its environment. His sleeping patterns were irregular, with him traveling both during the day and at night. Sometimes, the despondent man gingerly walked, and other times, he irresponsibly crawled and groveled. Jack was unwilling to surrender his soul to death's beckoning. He repeatedly made, and then quickly broke camp at whim, and did not honor any standard practice or regular habit.

The desperate survivor carried in his pack remnants of the caribou calf's bones, and he actively sucked and crunched them whenever he felt a need to react to his biological compulsions to eat and live. Jack now loyally followed a wide, fast-flowing stream, and his hazy mind was filled with exotic visions and mirages, none of which were entirely comprehensible.

The following morning, the tormented nomad awoke; his body lying on a rocky ledge. The wanderer felt the sun's rays shining upon his countenance, and heard the sounds of curious caribou calves to his left. 'I want to live, and I also want to die!' he ambivalently thought as his disoriented mind grappled with fathoming the significance of the two extreme alternatives. 'But if pain, anguish, and suffering are all that fuckin' life has to offer,' the lost fellow regrettably pondered, 'in the final analysis, I would prefer dying.'

But the warm sun reflected off his bearded face, and provided the obstinate man with encouragement to continue his intrepid travail. He rolled onto his side and perceived the wide fast-flowing stream, the identity of which challenged and puzzled his memory. Jack observed the dismal, bare, distant hills devoid of vegetation. Only the river valley had grass and caribou feeding off the vegetation supply, and eager wolves feasting off the healthy, captured caribou. The worried man's emotional state was very melancholy, and quite apparently, now lacked interest, motivation and enthusiasm.

As the pitiful human gawked into the distance, he believed his mind was playing cruel tricks on him. 'There's a ship out there on the shining sea,' Jack interpreted and comprehended. He closed his eyelids, opened them, and then rubbed his face to confirm his recognition of the familiar object outlined on the horizon. 'It is a ship anchored in a bay, and several small islands are surrounding it. I wonder if they're the friggin' *Illusion Islands* between Alaska and Siberia!' his giddy mind mused. 'I gotta' get my bearings straight!'

The hopeful vision persisted, and did not fade into oblivion, and *that* particular realization (mirage) energized Jack's spirit and afforded his weakened heart the far-fetched prospect of being rescued.

But then, the obstinate trekker's soul plunged into despair. 'There's no bullet in my friggin' gun,' he sadly remembered. 'And also, no ship on the shining sea. What a fuckin' living nightmare those goddamned lousy illusions are!'

The vanquished explorer soon heard a snuffle behind him, that was actually a combination cough and pant. He shifted his body weight and witnessed a most despicable companion. Jack noticed the gray head of a wolf, and its primitive-looking jade eyes were greedily peering at him through several jagged rocks, twenty or so feet away. The predator's green eyes were glassy and bloodshot, and its head was drooping, and almost crestfallen. The animal blinked as if it too was witnessing a terrible mirage.

'What the fuck's this shit?' Jack thought in total consternation. 'A fuckin' sick wolf! And the goddamned bastard is waitin' for me to expire so that it could enjoy its last meal. What a travesty of justice if a dumb abstraction such as justice exists in this survival-of-the-fittest animal world!' the giddy man neurotically considered. 'If there's justice anywhere in this fucked-up misadventure of mine, it must indeed be a freakin' miscarriage of justice!'

Jack turned his bloodied head left toward the nebulous ship upon the shining sea, and then rotated it right toward the very real diseased wolf, and the befuddled observer attempted to plausibly distinguish between the 'dual mirages'. Then, the suffering man chuckled. 'A weak dying wolf! What utter irony! What a fuckin' appropriate fateful conclusion to a goddamned, meaningless human life!'

The whimpering sufferer closed his eyes and reviewed the dramatic events of the past few days. His difficult journey had been heading south by southwest, moving away from the Dease Divide in the direction of the fabled Coppermine River. His unexpected destination was well-defined on the wall map at the Hudson Bay Company outpost. 'That damned shining sea is the majestic Arctic Ocean!' Jack hypothesized. 'And there's a damned whaling ship anchored in Coronation Gulf! God save both the Queen of England and my lily-white ass!'

The hope of deliverance gave the temporarily defeated man additional emotional energy. He carefully felt his aching feet, which were now deformed lumps of raw meat. 'My fuckin' gun and knife are now several miles behind me,' Jack reasoned. 'I still have matches in my pocket. It's eleven o'clock,' his brain realized and stared blankly at his still-ticking watch. 'I've been through too much to simply give-up and sacrifice my life and my body to a goddamned, sick, gangrened, lustful wolf!'

The beleaguered man attempted remaining calm and prudent. All awareness of pain had now disappeared, and even his lips and fingertips had little sensation. Jack thought of swallowing food, but that ignorant idea made him feel nauseous, and his stomach felt like vomiting. The unfortunate gold prospector re-cinched his swollen ankle, causing blood to drip upon the surrounding rocks. 'I still have my tin cup and my matches,' he doggedly considered. 'I'll be able to drink boilin' water and kill off the bacteria. I wonder if I could set the wolf on fire? That's one fuckin' advantage I still have. The wonder of fire is my staunchest ally over that repulsive, sick animal.'

Jack's hands now shook as if he was afflicted with a palsy. He gathered dry moss into a heap to ignite into an improvised blaze. Man's mastery of fire could be used against the filthy offensive wolf. 'He's probably been abandoned by his pack, just like Bill had abandoned me,' Jack accurately concluded. 'How terribly merciless and inhumane could nature be?'

The brave man inched forward toward the diseased wolf and peered directly into the creature's glassy, bloodshot eyes. The animal was still fearful of Jack's unorthodox behavior, and the wolf reluctantly yielded territory to the crazed, strange-behaving human. The wolf greedily licked the sides of its mouth, contemplating food (once Jack would die), but the man noticed that the revolting beast had hardly the strength to curl its flaccid tongue.

'Jesus H. Christ!' the dejected man thought. 'The goddamned enlarged tongue isn't even red! It's yellowish-brown, and coated with a layer of thick, germ-infested mucus! I'm not goin' to be this hideous, diseased animal's next son-of-a-bitchin' meal. No way!'

After Jack drank nearly a liter of hot water, the injured prospector found that he still possessed adequate strength to rise-up on his abused feet and stand almost erect. 'If I die, it'll be with a man's dignity, and not with a sheep's cowardice!' Jack proudly thought. 'I can walk at least four-miles toward the ship anchored on the bay, even in this debilitated condition. I hope the ship's not an illusion created by my horribly stressed-out psyche!'

All night long, Jack habitually blinked his eyelids and could not fall asleep. The sick wolf's coughing and wheezing, along with the squawking of distant ptarmigan and caribou, kept him awake. 'I am this sick wolf's only hope of living,' Jack pragmatically evaluated. 'If I live, it fuckin' dies! If I die, it fuckin' lives! Fuck philosophy! The basic formula is so amazingly simple, yet at the same time, so terribly brutal!'

The repulsive creature stood on its four legs, assessing Jack's every movement, including his most recent bowel movement. Its mangy tail was tucked between its legs in a subordinate, defensive position, and the sickly animal lacked the strength to even snarl or moan. It very deliberately and slowly skulked in a circle around the frightened human, who now regarded the dying beast as a mutual companion in suffering. The infected wolf even seemed to broadly grin at Jack's rueful face, when the shocked human orally addressed the disgusting, sick animal, using sarcastic and obscene language.

That afternoon, the weak man's legs dragged his vulnerable frame three-miles forward, but fatigue rapidly set-in, and soon Jack was slowly advancing on all fours, just like the sick wolf that was avariciously trailing him. 'Thank God it's an Indian summer day. If it were three weeks from now, my Caucasian butt couldn't be distinguished from an icicle's asshole in broad daylight!'

As Jack slowly progressed on all fours toward the glittering ship on the shining sea, his form came across a small pond where he triumphantly captured four minnows in his tin cup. "Here," he declared to the diseased wolf while tossing the smallest of the fish before the creature's maw. "Eat to your goddamned heart's content. You've been officially reduced to a lousy, goddamned scavenger, just like me, but I see that you don't give a shit!"

Jack crawled along for several-hundred-yards, following the trail of another man that had also crawled that doomed path. A heap of fresh-chewed bones was surrounded by wolf footpad marks that had been imprinted in the soggy moss. The recent arrival observed a moose-hide sack, similar to the one he had been carrying, and Jack automatically theorized that the skeletal remains were those of Bill. "These pinky, white bones are yours, Bill," Jack acknowledged and sobbed with tears forming in his eyes. "But don't worry, good buddy! I will not suck your bones. I'm not a fuckin' cannibal, or any goddamned fuckin' civilized queer, either. I'll never suck another man's bone! Never I say!"

An hour later, the distraught, paranoid man arrived at a deep pond of water where the deflected sunlight reflected his wretched-looking face. He spotted three minnows swimming inside the pool, and thrust his arm inside the cold water in an unsuccessful attempt to acquire his next snack. 'I'm afraid that if I accidentally tumble into the pond, I'll certainly drown,' Jack regretted. 'And I know that I could easily friggin' drown in only six inches of water if I was lyin' on my face. Tell me, bitter destiny; explain to me, fate; how the hell did I get to be so totally fucked-up in this totally fucked-up world?'

The next morning and afternoon, Jack was able to exhaustively stumble and crawl three-additional-miles towards the tantalizing gleaming ship upon the shining sea, and the following day, his labor gained him two-more-miles. 'This is how Bill expired,' Jack remorsefully thought. 'He was crawling, and fainting, and sleeping, and inching his way, but his labor was all in vain. Who needs this raunchy crap? Who needs this fuckin' Alaska Tundra shit?' the man's addled and cluttered mind questioned.

And then, as Jack turned his head, his pupils observed the lugubrious-looking, infected wolf diligently licking *his* trail of crimson with its gruesome, enlarged, yellowish-brown tongue. But the defiant man was adamant about persevering and enduring, so he pulled and dragged his abused carcass across the desolate ground with the wolf scavenging and licking-up his recently shed blood.

'If the wolf were a healthy one, I would gladly surrender to death,' Jack contemplated. 'But since the ugly bastard is diseased, the thought of him eating my flesh is absolutely repugnant. I'd prefer sucking Bill's raunchy dick when *he* was alive rather than have this son-of-a-bitchin' loathsome disgrace of its breed biting my tender ass and sensitive balls off!'

Jack's intervals of lucid mental activity now alternately appeared into, and then quickly faded from his addled mind, in more rapid succession. Hallucinations perplexed his perception and cognizance, and doubt plagued his sensibilities, especially his misgivings about the 'artificial glistening ship on the shining sea'. Late that afternoon, the man was awakened from a deep slumber by a faint sniffle at his ear. When Jack reflexively moved his head, the rancid-furred wolf leaped back and stumbled, exhibiting an almost ludicrous, awkward demonstration of its current pathetic plight.

'I guess that the glowing ship's only about four-miles away now,' Jack estimated. 'That is to say, it's four-miles away if it's really a ship anchored in the bay.' The survivor rubbed his eyes so that his peepers could focus with more clarity. 'It has white sails; but fuck! I can't even crawl a half-mile, let alone four wicked miles! Why the fuck didn't I join the navy like my parents wanted me to do!' his wild madness sarcastically concluded. 'Then, I'd be a safe, contented sailor, standing at attention aboard that gleaming ship on the shining sea!'

The grief-stricken man closed his eyes and visualized his existence speeding toward a tunnel's entrance with a small intense bright light glowing at the other end. 'I'm dying!' he happily thought. 'Thank God I'm fuckin' finally dying!'

As Jack lay on his back gasping for his next breath, his left hand felt the sick wolf's putrid-smelling breath wheezing against his left cheek. Next, the petrified fellow felt the sick wolf's huge, discolored tongue pressing against his mud-smeared face. It's persistent lapping had the horrible feel of sandpaper grating against his almost-numb skin. 'I'll not move until the exact right moment!' Jack promised his in-flux conscience.

The wolf showed tremendous cunning and patience, but Jack's stubborn attitude was equal to his adversary's resolve. The man lay still for a whole half-day, allowing the wolf to gain confidence and to begin initiating its disrespectful feast. Jack dreamed of a spectacular beautiful blonde whispering in his ear, only to awaken to the despicable wolf's harsh, coarse tongue caressing his face and lips. 'This must be a gay fuckin' wolf that only wants to eventually lick my dick!' Jack conjectured during that very traumatic moment. 'I'm still vulnerable in the neck, and this scumbag scavenger is liable to accidentally puncture my throat and sever my goddamned jugular!'

Soon, the infected dying wolf's tongue began lapping at Jack's bleeding right hand. The animal's fangs pressed against the man's palm, and the diseased creature attempted to penetrate the already-lacerated skin. Jack wrapped his left arm around the wolf's neck, and the prey's mouth was soon full of flea-ridden, stench-smelling, dark, gray fur. 'I can't choke him to death, but I think I can sever the gross creature's throat with my teeth!' he hoped. 'Maybe I can smother the damned carnivorous wolf. Take that; you mangy, ugly, foul mother-fucker!'

Five-minutes later, the pathetic man's entire weight had pinned-down his immobilized adversary, and thirty-minutes thereafter, Jack felt a very unpleasant warm trickle rolling down his throat. 'He's dead!' the man realized and concluded. 'The mother-fucker's dead! My will has prevailed!' Then, the victor slowly rolled over, closed his bleary eyes, and dozed-off.

* * * * * * * * * * * *

A whaling ship, *The Bedford,* had brought a contingent of scientists to northern Alaska to expertly conduct pertinent experiments, and to assiduously record observations of polar flora and fauna. The alert sailors on the ship's main deck had binoculars, and noticed a large, strange creature moving like a crippled crustacean along a riverbank. The mariners instantly climbed into 'a whaling harpoon boat', and set-out to discover exactly what they had seen. Jack was squirming forward like a mammoth worm. He then was writhing and twisting about, wrangling and wrestling with an imaginary sick wolf in his volatile, semi-conscious mania.

Three weeks later, Jack sat-up in his bunk bed on *The Bedford* to disclose to his fascinated audience the elements of his incredible tale, which the listeners regarded as mostly bunk being told from a *bunk* bed. Tears cascaded down the man's cheeks as he recalled and vividly described each episode of his extraordinary adventure. Intermixed with

52

his revelations about caribou, a bear, the gold, the ptarmigans, the sick wolf, and Bill's morbid fate, were recollections about his mother, his family, and sunny California. Somehow, orange groves got blended in with muskeg berries, and semi-tropical flowers were intermingled with lichens upon hard Arctic rocks, which added a certain dimension of implausibility to Jack's disheveled presentation.

The following morning, the rescued man sat in the ship's galley, and he gobbled-down his hardy breakfast as if he had just survived a horrendous famine. 'They're goin' to steal my fuckin' food!' the distrustful eater imagined and believed. 'These fuckin' surreptitious sailors and scientists are no different than that black fox and that bastard dying wolf! The scumbag bastards think my story's a gaudy lie!'

After breakfast, the rescued man briefly toured the ship, and paid particular attention to where all of the food had been stored. And he voraciously ate like a hog in heat, stuffing every available morsel into his mouth, making each bite swiftly disappear into his esophagus before any crumb could be stolen by his 'jealous and envious ship mates'. In three weeks, Jack had added four inches to his waist, and began exhibiting a most prodigious girth.

All the way from Alaska to San Francisco, Jack hoarded hardtack biscuits, filled his pockets with the crunchy crackers, and ate with suspicious eyes. He clandestinely hid and stuffed biscuits inside his mattress and also inside his bunk bed. Jack steadfastly guarded his 'highly coveted food supply' from the *Bedford's* 'less intelligent crewmembers'.

'I must take precautions so that no one pilfers my goddamned food,' Jack greedily imagined. 'All of these treacherous son-of-a-bitches are ruthless! I must and will survive for the sake of my love of life!'

"The Ransom of Red Chief"
O. Henry

As most everyone who is literate knows by now, O. Henry was the 'penname' used by William Sydney Porter (1862-1910), because the famous author couldn't think of an appropriate pencil name. After Porter moved from Greensboro, North Carolina to Austin, Texas, the future writer worked as a bank clerk, and got into a big heap of trouble. William Sydney was accused of embezzling money while transferring account funds. Porter became a fugitive from justice, and then swiftly fled to South America to avoid trial and certain imprisonment.

After being notified that his wife was seriously ill, Porter returned to the United States, was jailed, and then sentenced to a federal penitentiary. While incarcerated (with plenty of time on his hands), O. Henry wrote many of his classic short stories. It is believed that the author derived his famous pseudonym from the name Orrin Henry, a prison guard at the Ohio Penitentiary where William Sydney Porter had been sentenced by a judge that believed in short paragraphs in addition to long sentences.

O. Henry never produced or vended any candy bars of the same name, and spent a good deal of time in turn-of-the-century New York. The writer really loved that grand city, especially the Greenwich Village area. The author would often sit on a park bench and converse with derelicts, or with prominent citizens, getting fresh material for new stories from other people's lives. Porter's tales are notorious for their surprise or "twist endings", where an unexpected coincidence (or parallel coincidences) usually occurs. The author produced over two-hundred-and-fifty imaginative stories during his short forty-eight-year-life. Some of O. Henry's more notable tales are "The Last Leaf," "The Gift of the Magi," "Twenty Years Later," "The Cop and the Anthem", and "The Ransom of Red Chief".

The felony looked like a decent scam, but just let Old Sam the Narrator tell ya' everything that my forgetful mind remembers about it. Old Bill Driscoll and I were down South in Alabama, the armpit of *Dixie,* when this asshole kidnappin' brainstorm hit us like the midnight freight train out of Mobile. As Bill appropriately described our outlandish little scheme, "It was a temporary *apparition* that had more than a friggin' ghost of a chance at succeeding." Of course, my distinguished accomplice meant to say *aberration,* because at the time, both Bill and I were experiencing dual escapes from sanity, while also badly suffering from a lack of adventure.

Summit was a town down there in Alabama that was as flat as a Coney Island pancake. Its small hick population was comprised mostly of harmless, dull inhabitants, whose prime source of recreation was not doing anything except engaging-in perpetual gossip. Bill and I decided that the country bumpkins of Summit, Alabama needed some essential amusement as a diversion from their mediocre, brain-dead, level of existence.

Bill and I had a joint wallet asset of about *six hundred bucks,* an awful lot of male deer, but not nearly as much cash as we needed to get to a more prosperous city, and start pulling-off some big swindles that we were surreptitiously planning. We required just two-thousand-dollars more in capital to initiate our fraudulent town building lot scheme up in western Illinois, where (believe it or not) the citizens were actually dumber than we were. Bill and I talked it over in our informal sartorial splendor in front of the lackluster Summit Hotel, which looked on the outside like a cheap New York City Bowery bordello catering to drunken sailors and resident homosexual degenerates.

"Philoprogenitiveness," I academically said to Bill, "happens to be strong in these backwoods' quaint, semi-rural hamlets. Summit, Alabama isn't any damned different from the rest of the God-forsaken boondocks."

"Speak fuckin' plain English," Bill insisted and reprimanded. "I ain't got no shit-eatin' idea what the hell a goddamned hamlet is! Isn't that some kind of play by Shakespeare? Oh, I'm sorry Sam. I was thinking of omelet instead of hamlet!" Bill characteristically joked. "I got confused because both fuckin' plays have somethin' to do with breakfast foods!"

"I meant to say," I interrupted my expert-bullshitting colleague, "people around these parts love their children so much, that the strange local yokels are willin' to pay a handsome ransom fee for the safe return of their precious little piglets."

"What about police pursuit after we manage to kidnap some lucky little tyke?" Bill inquired.

"Well, the best they can muster-up around these parts are a few droopy, constipated constables, and several underfed bloodhounds with rotten teeth," I attested, employing a degree of hyperbole. "And the local gazette might feature a back page article about our great achievement, after we've cunningly skipped town with the ransom loot. The moon, along with all its moonshine, has more competent policemen on its surface than the lazy village of Summit does."

"Well, in that case," Bill amiably agreed, "let's give your prospective crime a serious go. Our illicit act will be a lot easier to accomplish if we could only catch some stupid-assed *kid napping* somewhere under a tree near a deserted fishin' hole!"

So, the fucked-up idea looked and sounded good to Bill Driscoll and me, right from the get-go. We did some diligent research on the matter, and selected for our targeted victim the only son of the town's prominent banker that answered to the weird Biblical-sounding name, Ebenezer Dorset. The financial wizard was a respected mortgage fore-closer that attended church every Sunday, and then the following Monday morning, repossessed the house of the parishioner that had been sitting next to him in the same damned church pew. Dorset's type was a patriotic citizen that had money to burn, or to throw away on an imaginative kidnapping of his only son, which, of course, would be skillfully executed by clever professional renegades on the lam like Bill Driscoll and me.

The ornery kid we had selected for bagging was ten-years-old, and had elevated freckles dotting his entire body, or at least the parts of his anatomy we could see from a distance. The kid's hair was flaming red, the color of certain alluring girly magazines you see exhibited for sale at a New York City newsstand. Bill suggested that Ebenezer Dorset would gladly fork-over a fair ransom of two thousand bananas to a cent, but wait until I tell ya' the entire damned hairy story.

A little mountain was situated about two miles outside Summit, so why the town (with the name it sported) wasn't built on top of that enormous molehill, defies human logic. Anyway, a dense forest of cedar trees covered most of the whole shittin' mountain. A cave without any prehistoric Neanderthal men living in its cavity was conveniently located on the ass side of the mountainous incline. Bill and I clandestinely stored our supplies in that dark, dank cave, as if we were preparing to commit the ultimate crime of the century, and then live like reclusive homosexual hermits.

Bill and I vigilantly went-out on surveillance patrols to scout the prospects of pulling-off our grand kidnapping heist. We drove our rented horse and buggy past Ebenezer Dorset's small brick mansion, and spotted the young rascal we had targeted throwing rocks at a meowing kitten, and its hissing mother, conveniently trapped between Ebenezer's and the neighbor's fences.

"Hey little boy!" Bill yelled in the startled kid's direction. "Would ya' like to have a bag of candy, and then go for a nice buggy ride in the country?"

"Don't you clowns have any whiskey or chewin' tobacco to offer?" the tiny tot criticized. "You two jerks ain't child molesters, are ya'?"

"Why no!" Bill answered with surprise and regret. "We're just two nice men lookin' for juvenile companionship."

"Then, fuck-off, assholes!" the little squirt yelled as the brat threw several rocks at our buggy, one of which clipped Bill above his right eyebrow.

"That act of defiance will cost old Ebenezer an extra five hundred buckeroos," Bill promised me as my accomplice wiped-away some scarlet from his forehead with his right hand. "That little punk got an accurate throwin' arm, and could be a startin' pitcher with the *Yankees.*"

My loyal companion leaped-out of the buggy, and old William required my deft and daft assistance to effectively subdue the ornery young Turk. We finally got the screaming and cursing urchin on the ground, where the little critter clawed, scratched, and bit us like he was a cross between a welterweight cinnamon bear and a vicious bobcat. Bill and I tossed the still-struggling and bitching kid into the back of the buggy. I expertly applied a half-nelson around the boy's left shoulder and neck, and then Bill adroitly took command of the wagon and hightailed it out of Summit to our cozy mountain retreat.

I hitched the horse to a cedar tree located in the hill's posterior, and we tugged, dragged and wrestled the little scamp up to the dingy cave. After dark, I dutifully returned the horse and buggy back to the small livery rental business on the other side of Summit, where Bill and I had hired them, and then I swiftly paced the three arduous miles back to the isolated cave.

I spotted Bill pasting court plaster over a series of cuts, scratches, and bruises that decorated most of his facial features. My eyes looked to the right, and noticed the little smart-assed imp guarding a pot of coffee burning on a fire, all situated behind a small boulder at the cave's entrance. I observed with fascination that the freckle-faced brat was wearing two buzzard tail feathers sticking-out like respectable erections from his flame-red hair.

The kid instantly detected my presence, and then menacingly pointed a stick at my throat and said in a feigned accented voice, "Ha cursed paleface! Do ya' have the balls to enter the camp of the brave Red Chief, the no bullshit Indian terror of the plains?"

"Er, yes," I replied with a weak grin. "Why do ya' ask me that illogical question, Red Chief?"

"Because if ya' give me any crap," the kid tyrannically warned, "I'll cut off your vitals and hide them in the wilderness while you're too busy countin' stupid sheep in your sleep to do anything about it!"

I glanced over at Bill in a bewildered manner, looking for some rhyme or reason to what my eyes had been observing and my ears had been hearing. My usually dependable associate seemed rather perturbed and upset about his own singular predicament.

"Sam, the kid's all right now, ever since the lad finally calmed- down from his French hemorrhage," my partner nervously began. Driscoll then rolled-up his trousers to show me some rather nasty battle scars, which my distinguished colleague had already-received from his new-found junior nemesis.

"We were attemptin' to rehearse a few scenes from Buffalo Bill's Travelin' Show, Sam, but then the obnoxious kid wanted to change the venue from Buffalo Bill to a prolonged Indian hostage situation," Bill explained as my comrade applied some salve to a laceration above his right wrist. "I was appointed Old Hank the Trapper by that miserable little cutthroat coyote with the blazing-red hair," my super-sensitive friend angrily pointed-out. "And the little nefarious jasper then changes his illegitimate Indian name from Red Chief to Geronimo. I've been assigned to be his personal captive, and when I resisted him punching and clawing-away at my sensitive skin, the little jerk-off kicked me at least two dozen times in the shins, and then smashed me really hard in my already-sufferin' swollen testicles. Now Sam, the little terror has threatened to scalp me at daybreak," Bill lamented and reported. "Can't this little *scalper* do his thing outside some local *Minor League* baseball park?"

"Relax Bill," I calmly recommended in a disgusted tone of voice. "If ya' don't learn to relax, you're gonna' cardiac-out on me, and leave me all alone in this pathetic situation with this fifty-pound human alligator!"

Yes sir, that little rogue was having the time of his life at our expense. Immediately, the temperamental little Napoleon announced that he was changing his name from Geronimo back to Red Chief, because the twerp had heard somewhere that Geronimo was an "Indian-giver", and that Red Chief had no *reservations* about killing annoying trespassing palefaces like Bill and me.

Red Chief immediately labeled me Snake Eye the Spy. and claimed that I had been officially captured along with Old Hank the Trapper. Old Bill was still being sentenced to be scalped before daybreak, and *my* singular punishment for being apprehended was that I had been scheduled to be broiled at the steak at the morning sun's rising. I humorously told Red Chief I'd rather be broiled "at the *steak*" than "at the hamburger", and the dysfunctional lad didn't take too kindly to my Vaudeville sense of amusement. The little wise guy poured a cup of hot steaming coffee down my pants, and quite effectively scalded my sensitive rooster, along with my vulnerable sperm ducts.

After I recovered from the demented tyke's violent assault, *our* little abductee ate supper with Bill and me, and stuffed his mouth full with bread, bacon, gravy, and sausage, and spoke incessantly with his jaws full. The punk kid's thought patterns were erratic, and his words slurred by all the damned food in his mouth, but this is exactly what his speech sounded like:

"I like this here arrangement just fine. I ain't never camped-out before. I have a pet possum, and a pet skunk, and I was ten my last birthday. I ain't never had no sex with girls, or even felt their tits. I hate to go to school. Rats ate all twenty-four of Jimmy Taylor's hen's speckled eggs, and then Jimmy and I killed all of the raunchy rodents with baseball bats and clubs. That was really fun! Are there any real savage Indians in these here woods? I want some more gravy and bacon. Sam, can ya' still piss after I burned your thingy and your balls good with the hot coffee? Do the trees movin' make the damned wind blow? My dog has five puppies. Hank, how come your nose is so red? Are ya' an alcoholic? Are the planets and stars hot? My dumb-ass old man has lots of money, and thinks everyone else in the world is an asshole."

The tiny tyrant paused for a moment to gulp-down and devour the excess food in his mouth and throat. Then, Red Chief continued his incredible monologue. "I really kicked Ed Winters' ass good twice last Saturday for throwin' cat turds inside my bedroom window! I don't like girls, but only want to see and smell their pussies, and maybe feel their tits! Ya' can't catch toads right unless ya' use a string. How come some farts don't make noise? Why are oranges round and apples and bananas not? Have we got beds to sleep on in this shitty-lookin' cave? Amos Murphy has got six toes on both feet! I especially like to fart in the bathtub! A parrot can repeat some of the shit it hears, but a fish or a raccoon can't. Snake-Eye, why ya' holdin' your balls like that with both hands?"

Every few minutes, the pesky mop-head would remember he was supposed to be Red Chief, and pick-up a stick he pretended was a rifle, and point it threateningly at Bill and me. Then, the end of the stick the kid had been brandishing as a gun penetrated Bill's right nostril, and a stream of blood came trickling-out. And before Driscoll could latch on to the irritating pest, Red Chief ran to the front of the cave to feign being a sentinel waiting for more interloping palefaces to arrive and raid "the fort". I looked over at Bill, and my chum had his bloody handkerchief held-up to his nose. My poor buddy was erratically shivering as if a sudden fever was invading his entire body.

"Red Chief," I yelled at the young whippersnapper. "Would ya' like to go home and be reunited with your parents?"

"Aw, what for Snake-Eye?" the pesky scamp rhetorically objected. "I don't have any fun at home. My old man is just as corny as you two nutcases are when pop clowns-around. In fact, his jokes are even worse than the bullshit I hear from you two bozos, if ya' can believe that horse manure! And if I'm home," the little hot-shot persuasively continued, "I'll have to go to school. I'd rather camp-out with you two ugly, fat, funny-lookin' palefaces. Ya' won't take me back to my goofy old man now, would ya' Snake-Eye?"

"Not right away," I amenably replied. "Your father's safer if ya' stay put right here in the cave with us. I'm surprised your old man hasn't appeared in the obituaries yet, as a suicide case havin' an undisciplined little cannibal like you around to pester the hell out of his sanity."

"That's all right," the ornery kid answered rather nonchalantly. "My uncle's the town undertaker, and will know what to do with my old man's body. I really like stayin' here in this fort," the weird boy admitted with a smile. "I never had such great fun playin' torture with any of my asshole friends."

At eleven p.m., I extinguished the fire, and we went to sleep on tattered blankets and goose-feathered pillows that Bill and I had confiscated from the last fleabag hotel we had stayed at somewhere in Missouri. We made sure Red Chief was safely stationed on a quilt, situated between Bill and me. The diminutive scoundrel kept us both awake, until three in the morning, with the miniature rascal yelling-out "Ready braves!" and "Let's scalp the damned intrudin' palefaces!" At last, I fell into a restless sleep, dreaming that a ruthless freckle-faced diabolical pirate had hostilely kidnapped me. The sadistic junior swashbuckler in my extensive nightmare had inhumanely chained me to a sassafras tree, and was making me eat and swallow fire from a blazing torch.

When daybreak finally came, I was awakened by a series of ear-shattering screams originating from Bill's vibrant vocal cords. The shrieks weren't masculine shouts or howls. Instead, the shouts were analogous to the sissy-type screams you hear when women see ghosts, mice, or slimy wall slugs. Naturally, I promptly leaped-up to determine the cause of Bill's sudden fright.

Red Chief was doggedly sitting upon Bill's exposed hairy chest. One of the runt's hands was inside Bill's curly black hair, and the other fist held the sharp knife we had been assiduously using to slice the bacon. The young ruffian was endeavoring to realistically remove Bill's scalp to satisfy the harsh frontier Indian justice sentence that *he* had unilaterally pronounced and was officially imposing and enforcing on my discomfited and totally-insecure traveling acquaintance.

I deftly gained control of the knife by smacking the kid on both sides of the head with a large metal spoon I had used to stir stew inside the black kettle. Luckily, the industrious little punk instinctively dropped the sharp knife, when the diminutive pretend Indian raised his hands to massage the outer covering of his thick skull. I instinctively picked-up the knife, and tossed it toward the cave's mouth. Then, I had to grapple on the ground with the little dynamo until I finally and decisively subdued him with a hammerlock, four exhaustive minutes later.

Bill's pipsqueak but un-daunting adversary had amazingly broken my partner's adventurous spirit. Driscoll just stayed on his side while lying on his blanket, whimpering like a petrified puppy dog about to be assaulted by a big ferocious tomcat. I didn't bother Bill, figuring that his mindset was not conducive to intelligent conversation, because of *his* extended emotional trauma. I then scrutinized Red Chief closing his eyes and succumbing to sleep a half-hour later, but I could not satisfactorily visit the Sandman, since I had remembered the adolescent Indian's personal pledge that I was to be burned and barbecued at the stake at sunrise.

Bill sat-up and noticed that I was still wide-awake, and seriously worrying about current circumstances. "How come you're up so early Sam?" William Driscoll curiously asked. "Ya' sufferin' from a bad case of insomnia?"

"Oh me," I said creatively faking emotional security. "I have a sharp pain in the shoulder, and I thought sittin' up would alleviate the intense throbbin'."

"Pain in the shoulder, my left nut!" Bill yelled so loudly that Ebenezer Dorset down in Summit might have heard him. "I think you're up all night, not because of any damned pain in the neck. Ya' can't catch forty regular winks because of that little pain-in-the-ass savage lyin' over there!"

"What do ya' mean?" I weakly and lamely challenged my paranoid and now-neurotic colleague.

"I mean that Red Chief sleepin' over there promised to burn your ass at the stake at sunrise, and you were afraid that the junior rogue would enact his mean-spirited prediction. Make sure we search his pockets for matches. Sam, do ya' really think any parent in their right mind would pay-out good American money to get that miniature demolition machine back home? I personally doubt that prospect very much."

"Sure, I do," I boldly lied. "That kid is so damned rambunctious, just because his parents placate him and dote on him all the freakin' time. That's why the little scoundrel is so damned fuckin' rowdy and insubordinate. He's an egotistical, spoiled, undisciplined brat. Now Bill," I continued my evaluation. "You and Red Chief get some wholesome breakfast prepared while I climb-up to the mountaintop to see if there's any activity goin' on searchin' for the missin' bundle-of-joy we got stashed here with us!"

On top of the mini-mountain, I expected to see all kinds of search and rescue teams combing the hinterlands for the missing little snot-nosed, third-grade pugilist. Instead, I saw during my reconnoitering a very peaceful landscape, devoid of human activity or minimal parental concern. One country farmer was tilling the soil with a dun mule. No couriers or constables were scurrying about, and no one was desperately dragging the nearby creek for a discarded body. It was as if no one in or around Summit gave a flying shit about the missing little ball-breaker. I decided to descend to the secluded cave, and have some nourishment and commiserate and prevaricate with Bill.

I found Old Driscoll standing-up against the cave's left-side-wall, breathing heavily like a person that was about to die from severe tuberculosis. The obnoxious boy was threatening to clobber some part of Bill's already-tortured body with a rock the size of a head of cabbage.

"Sam, that young lunatic put a red-hot potato along with one of *his* soft human turds down my back when I was dozin' off," Bill gasped.

"And then the insufferable aggressor mashed them-down with his foot, and performed a brief war-dance all over my whole damned spine. I got-up off the ground and boxed his ears really hard, and I think I gave him the beatin' that his old man must've always been afraid to deliver. Sam, can I use your gun for protection?"

I gently removed the huge rock from the kid's sweaty hands, and attempted to patch-up the existing disagreement between kidnapper and kidnappee. In truth, I was not a very effective arbitrator.

"I'll fix you," young Johnny Dorset warned my exasperated and defeated colleague. "No white man ever violently struck the Red Chief before. My honor and name must be avenged in a wicked fight to the death!"

"See what I mean," Bill maintained with real dread showing in his eyes. "This toxic kid is very vindictive, and if I may add, extremely vengeful. He won't rest until I've been successfully castrated and assassinated."

"Don't worry Bill," I assured my disheveled friend. "I don't think anyone in Summit has yet realized that this blasted, peppery hooligan is missin'. His folks must think he spent the night at a friend's house, or at a relative's place. That's the way things are in these lazy rural mountain communities," I philosophically added. "Tonight, I plan to get the ransom note to Ebenezer Dorset, so that we can eagerly grab the two-thousand-clams and hastily skip town to pursue greener pastures."

"I wish ya' wouldn't make us sound like a couple of dumb mooing cows with all this 'green pastures' jargon," Bill answered and protested. "That Red Chief little varmint might be fixin' to slaughter us right now, so that the juvenile terrorist could sell our meat and testicles to the neighborhood grocery store."

"Hey!" Red Chief yelled in our faces, after awakening from his phony slumber. "Sally Norton once promised she'd show me her pussy, but then the little bitch pulled-down her pants, turned around, and showed me her asshole instead. The damned smelly red hole looked the same as mine does in a hand mirror!" our fake Indian captive vociferously complained. "Was I totally pissed-off!" the small villain continued his monologue. "Hey; either of you two guys ever had sex with a young girl?"

"Well," I replied. "Old Hank the Trapper and I try to keep our personal lives out of our professional relationships," I diplomatically returned to the despicable young wise-ass. "But we do prefer grown women to girls."

Just then a healthy war whoop was emitted from Red Chief's powerful lungs. The lethal kid had assembled a rudimentary slingshot during my absence from the cave, while Bill had been getting some much-needed shuteye. The repulsive twerp was whirling the ancient-looking weapon around his head, possibly pretending he was David about to slay the giant Goliath. 'Who knows what kind of crap is lodged in that kid's fucked-up mind?' I wondered as I ducked an errant stone heading in my direction.

I heard a heavy thud, and next a bone-chilling moan was emanating from abused Bill's larynx. A rock the size of a tennis ball had caught Driscoll just behind the left ear, making a good-sized gash. William felt the pain behind his earlobe, and then gaped in disbelief at a handful of wet crimson in his palm. The man became nearly comatose, staggered backwards, fell across the morning fire's flames, and nearly incinerated himself before my associate awkwardly tumbled to the rock-solid ground.

I altruistically dragged Bill outside the cave, poured cold water over his scalp and injured ear, and then cleaned the exposed cut as best as I could until the bleeding finally stopped. Then, I role-played being a psychologist and consoled my friend, who really desperately needed the advanced services of a skilled psychiatrist.

"Simmer-down Bill, before you're ready for either the funny farm or the county morgue," I sagely suggested. "Relax. Your heart is beating two-hundred-times a minute and is about to explode out of your chest! Take it easy, or you'll go into a wild seizure!"

"Ya' gotta' appreciate, Sam," Bill told me. "Do ya' know who my favorite Biblical character is?" my best pal erratically asked in almost a delirious state of mind.

I was going to answer 'David', but then realized that the recent stone incident might have been based on the slaying of Goliath of Gath by the Israelite boy hero, and Johnny Dorset might have been coincidentally impersonating the legendary David. "No, Bill. Please tell me if it'll make ya' come to your senses and not go deep into schizophrenia, or some other nasty and distasteful form of insane asylum psychosis."

"King Herod is my favorite Biblical character with what the monster did to the kiddies in Bethlehem, while his army was searchin' for the Christ child," Bill stressed under stress. "And I only wish that his royal highness was here right now to take care of that little banshee that's got my mind seriously reconsiderin' this entire lousy kidnappin' caper."

I stepped inside the cave, caught the young antagonist by the arm, and shook his frame until his red freckles rattled against each other. "If ya' don't behave Johnny," I shouted like a maniac, "I'll take ya' straight to your daddy, and then ya' could listen all day and all night to *his* asshole sick puns! Now are ya' gonna' honor my simple fair rules, or not?"

"I was only funnin' with Old Hank," the boy explained a little sullenly with a trace of guilt added-in. "I didn't mean to upset or injure Old Hank the Trapper. But I had to get even after he hit me hard behind my ears!"

"Then, you're hereby promisin' me that you're gonna' settle- down and quit clownin' around?" I demanded.

"I'll behave Snake-Eye! I promise!" the boy answered, crossing his heart with the pinky finger on his right hand. "I pledge I'll not cause any more ruckus if ya' let me play the Black Scout. I'm sick and tired of bein' the Red Chief, and sick and tired of bein' dumb-ass Geronimo, too."

"I don't know the Black Scout game," I honestly confessed. "So, that's up to you and Mr. Bill to invent the rules. Now come and sincerely apologize to the man ya' almost sent speeding to the nearest insane asylum!"

I made the insolent Black Scout and the shell-shocked Bill Driscoll shake hands, but was worried that the new truce wouldn't last too long. I told my co-conspirator I was heading over to Poplar Cove, a village three miles from the cave, the hamlet existing just north of Summit. First, I intended to glean some relevant scuttlebutt that might be circulating around the area concerning a "high profile kidnapping". Then, I also planned to mail a decent and reasonable ransom letter to Mr. Ebenezer Dorset.

"Sam, ya' won't leave me long with this small package of dynamite, will ya'?" Bill pleaded. "I oughta' curse that Nobel guy a thousand times over for inventin' the stuff."

"Just keep the boy amused and occupied with you playin' the popular Black Scout game with him," I strongly emphasized, without me having any knowledge of *that* particular form of recreation. "I'll be back sometime this afternoon, but first we gotta' organize the right language for the all-important ransom note."

Red Chief (or Geronimo or the Black Scout, take your pick) had wrapped a blanket around his shoulders, and was strutting back and forth "guarding the fort" from an imaginary posse of paleface fugitives. Bill had an urgent request to make before I prodigiously applied the fountain pen to the blank sheet of paper.

"Sam, it ain't human for any God-fearin' parent to surrender two-thousand-dollars for that chunk of freckled wildcat," Bill candidly pleaded. "I hate to sound redundant, Sam, but please lower the demand to fifteen-hundred. Ya' can charge the difference to my burgeonin' ongoin' expense account."

I tried to dicker with Bill, but then I reluctantly conceded and wholeheartedly endorsed his fairly legitimate request. We then collaborated on the following missive:

Ebenezer Dorset, Esquire

We got your nice shy boy hidden in a remote place far away from Summit. Not even the most highly-skilled detectives given good directions would be able to find him. You can have little Johnny back if you comply with the following plain and simple conditions.

We demand fifteen-hundred-dollars for your boy's safe return. Leave the money tomorrow night in a box we will have set aside at a designated spot. Send a messenger tomorrow night at 8:30 p.m. to Poplar Cove Road. Have him stop just beyond Owl Creek. Three oak trees are clumped together there. Your cooperative messenger will find a cardboard box behind the first and second oak trees. Have him put the money in the box. We guarantee your precious, well-mannered son will then be safely returned to your splendid residence within four short hours.

If you dare attempt any treachery or deviation from this well-designed plan, you'll never see your boy again.

Two Desperate Desperados

I addressed the envelope to the very discreet ransom letter to Dorset, and placed it inside my coat pocket. When I was about to exit the cold and damp cave, the crazy kid came-up to me and said, "Aw, Snake-Eye. Ya' said I could play bein' the Black Scout while you was away on important business."

"Sure, play it with Mr. Bill," I defensively and suavely answered. "He said he'd give ya' his full adult cooperation. What are the rules to this special game?"

"Well, ya' see. I'm the Black Scout," the former Red Chief and Geronimo explained. "And I have to ride my horse to the damned stockade to warn the stupid deaf, dumb, and blind settlers that the Indians are comin'. I'm tired of being a dumb-ass Indian, so now I'm the Black Scout workin' on the side of the damned deaf, dumb, and blind palefaces."

"Mr. Bill will help ya' tame those wild hostile savages, won't ya' Bill?" I chuckled and asked my dismayed traveling-business partner.

"You're the hoss," Black Scout identified to Bill. "So, get-down on your hands and knees and start whinnyin' and neighin' like one. How the hell can I ride all the way to the stockade without a damned horse?" the bratty kid questioned.

"Ya' better keep him interested until I return," I mentioned to Driscoll with a cute wink. "I think we're truly dealin' with a dedicated juvenile delinquent with a complicated mercurial and mercenary conscience."

"When ya' return, ya' might discover both a homicide and a suicide here!" Bill yelled on his hands and knees before the terrified fellow was commanded again to whinny and then to neigh. "I just hope I'm alive to go to prison."

"Be a good *neigh*bor to the Black Scout!" I joked and advised Bill as I turned and rapidly exited the cave before the Black Scout could initiate any further disruptive interaction.

I briskly ambled-over to Poplar Cove, and parked my corpulent butt onto a wooden stool inside the combination post-office-general-store. I discussed some generic politics and religion with a couple of old chaw-bacons that came-in to trade money for food and merchandise. Both amiable hicks claimed that they had been lieutenants for the *Confederacy* during the *Civil War.* so obviously their overall credibility was suspect from the outset.

Then, one of the two bullshitting whiskerandos seated at a cracker-barrel, playing cards, and sitting next to a rusty black potbelly stove, disclosed that the population of Summit all had their bowels-in-an-uproar on account of elder Ebenezer Dorset's only heir being either lost or pilfered. I nonchalantly bought a pouch of smoking tobacco, checked-out the exorbitant retail price of a can of *black-eyed* peas, and had to chuckle thinking that Bill Driscoll was probably already "black-eyed" from the Black Scout's persistent abuse right that very minute. I furtively posted my ransom letter as unobtrusively as possible, and I overheard the postmaster remind a clerk that the mail carrier was scheduled to transport the daily post and a few parcels over to Summit in an hour.

When I arrived back at the dismal, dank cave, Bill was wobbling all around as if my confederate had been riding upside-down on a Ferris Wheel for forty-eight hours straight. My loyal associate removed his hat and appeared overjoyed to see me. Driscoll then also removed his bloodstained handkerchief from his soiled pants' pocket. I noticed that the irascible kid was stationed three-feet behind my then neurotic amigo.

"Sam, I gotta' confess that all the damned semen in my testicles has evaporated," Bill angrily began his testimony. "I'm a grown man with masculine proclivities and propensities," Sir William went-on, trying to impress me with his brilliant nomenclature. "But there comes a time when a man's proud ego disintegrates into plain vanity and basic survival. The boy has disappeared, run-away from the damned cave. I don't think any Biblical martyr had to endure the crazy crap that that young tiger has administered to me. I tried bein' faithful to our sacred criminal code," Bill summarized and sobbed, "but I guess ya' can label me a total failure!"

"That was some dramatic speech," I reckoned and commended. "Bill, what's the goddamned trouble?" I asked while keeping one eye on my suffering and apologetic accomplice, and the other on the predictably unpredictable child gorilla standing in the background.

"I was ridden the full ninety-miles to the stockade by the hyperactive Black Scout, not excluding an inch of dusty trail," Bill un-sentimentally disclosed. "Then, after four hours of heavy difficult ridin', Black Scout's horse was given oats to swallow without any damned milk to wash them down. I believe I would've preferred eatin' a pound of sand, instead. Sam, I tell ya'; I nearly choked to death on them stale dry oats!"

"Is that all?" I asked while fully aware that Bill was *unaware* of the terrible terror lurking behind him.

"Then Sam, I was forced to explain to the miniature cyclone why holes were empty; what makes the grass green, and why girls his age show him their assholes but won't show him their hairless pussies," Bill regretfully reported. "Then, the irascible scalawag asked me if I got hair on my balls, and if it looked like a goddamned toupee. I tell ya' Sam; a human can only stand so much freakin' physical and mental punishment, before the recipient distinctly rebels and outright murders someone."

"What happened next?" I inquired as I continued to survey the Black Scout, whose face was grimacing behind poor old Bill.

"Well, Sam. I dragged the little discipline problem outa' the cave, and then the little package of destruction kicks both my legs black-and-blue, and I ain't got no skin left between my ankle and my knee on my lower right appendage. I also need my left thumb and my right hand cauterized with a brandin' iron because of a vicious series of teeth bites applied by that junior juvenile delinquent."

"Bill," I slowly replied, so that my assistant could be somewhat rational for a minute. "Is there any history of heart disease or strokes in your family tree?"

"No," Bill softly answered in a seemingly vanquished tone of voice. "Nothin' chronic except maybe diabetes, malaria, alcoholism, consumption, migraine headaches, diarrhea, and numerous accidents. Why do ya' ask?"

"Just turn around and take a peek behind ya'," I suggested. "I don't think any Summit hospital ambulance wagons come-out this damned far from town!"

Bill turned around and all the blood from his head rushed somewhere else in his body, as my partner-in-crime clumsily fainted to the ground. I slapped his face silly and revived my colleague back to consciousness by pouring a cold bucket of water over his head and face. I then told Driscoll that the kidnapping scheme was all set to come to fruition, and that only a mere day remained for us to finally cash-in on the fat ransom.

68

"Let's reduce the ransom to a thousand-dollars just to be sure," Bill argued to me like someone under heavy sedation. "I think I'd rather be tortured by the Marquis de Sade than spend another hour with this freckled-faced midget barbarian."

"Okay, but until we get the money," I reminded my nervous companion, "ya' also promised the Black Scout you'd play the Russian in a Japanese war with him when our uncooperative hostage got tired of ridin' his well-trained hoss to the settler's stockade."

The next evening, Bill stayed in the cave playing a game of "pin the tail on the donkey's asshole" with the irrepressible young Johnny Dorset being the pinner, and beleaguered Bill Driscoll being the recipient pinned participant. In the meantime, I set-out to stealthily witness the ransom money being carefully placed by Ebenezer Dorset's courier inside the appointed cardboard box I had conveniently left behind the first and second oak trees in a clump of three next to Owl Creek. I climbed-up and hid inside the foliage of the third oak tree waiting for the messenger to deliver *our* hard-earned cold cash.

After the contemporary Hermes arrived on a bicycle, placed something inside the designated box, and then departed, I hastily slid down the tree's bark, nearly spraining my ankles with the last ten-foot leap, since I had been precariously hanging from a weak branch. I was extremely frustrated to find a written 'note' inside the box, rather than fifteen crisp, hundred-dollar government *notes*.

I anxiously read the correspondence, which contained the following disappointing words:

Two Desperate Desperados:

Gentlemen; I received your wonderful letter by post. In regard to the specific ransom that you're asking in return for my defiant and recalcitrant son, I consider you to be a little unreasonably high in your excessive demands. I hereby offer you a genuine counter-proposal.

You bring Johnny home and pay me two-hundred-and fifty-dollars, and I agree to take the little terror out of your custody. Please do it while my neighbors are asleep, because they might dynamite my house knowing that the kid's safely back home terrorizing the immediate environment.

Very truly yours,
Ebenezer Dorset

I took the creative letter back to the cave and showed Bill its entire unsavory narrative. "Great Pirates of Penzance!" my theater-going colleague lividly exclaimed. "The despicable kid's despicable old man's a much bigger and much more-clever, detestable thief than either you or I will ever be!"

"Don't be ludicrous!" I intelligently admonished. "The stubborn father's just stallin' to see how we're gonna' react to his wily subterfuge! Let's ignore his preposterous counterproposal."

"Hank," the rascally kid hollered over to Bill. "I'm tired of killin' ya' all sorts of ways in this stupid Japanese war. You're no longer gonna' be a dumb Russian hostage. Now I'm gonna' be Jack the Ripper, specializin' in removin' assholes, and you're gonna' be my first victim!"

"Sam," Bill solemnly cried and whimpered. "I ain't never had this much shit-stains in my underwear before! I'll gladly contribute the two-hundred-fifty-dollars to that rich son-of-a-bitch. No wonder why old Ebenezer Dorset can put on the *Ritz,* and enjoy the high-fallutin' lifestyle the shrewd bastard maintains!" Bill enviously regretted. "I've already reserved a stay in Bedlam when we finally get out of Alabama, return to modern civilization, and take the first scheduled steamer across the *Atlantic* to London."

We convinced young Johnny to accompany us home by telling him that his penitent "Old Man" had bought his cuddly pampered son a mounted silver rifle, a pair of Indian moccasins, a knight's metal uniform, with accompanying combat armor, and an authentic *Civil War* cannon.

Bill and I had little time to procrastinate. It was midnight when we knocked on Ebenezer's expensive, imported-wood front door. Bill counted out the designated cash into the shrewd banker's hands, and then at that very moment, young Johnny let-out a shriek that sounded something like a circus calliope gone amok with its shrill music. The violent, impudent runt kicked Bill four additional times in the man's already skinless right leg and shouted, "I didn't want to come back to this crappy shit hole so damned soon, and now I have to put-up with my old man's ridiculous happy horse crap!"

Before Bill and I ran down the street and headed for the railroad tracks leading out of Summit, I diplomatically said to the understanding Mr. Dorset, Esquire, "Here's your perverted kid back. Heaven help ya' after the potential nationally infamous criminal goes through puberty, and grows red hair on his enlarged brass balls!"

Bill and I sprinted as fast as our chubby legs could carry us, and although my good buddy was suffering from multiple leg injuries, I still had trouble keeping-up with *his* incredible speed for the first mile and a half away from Ebenezer Dorset's tranquil, fancy-looking Summit, Alabama palace.

70

"A Retrieved Reformation"
O. Henry

On February 13th, a blue-uniformed guard entered the prison shoe-shop where notorious inmate Jimmy Valentine had been diligently preoccupied stitching leather.

"This shoe is a lot like a policeman," Jimmy complained to a fellow prisoner. "It's a big heel with no friggin' *soul!*"

"Okay Valentine," the guard began his announcement. "I gotta' escort ya' over to the front office. The warden wants to see your wise-ass right now!"

"Is the Warden a certified proctologist?" Jimmy humorously yelled to the martinet guard. "I want him to check my prostate while he's probing away in *that* sensitive area."

Five minutes later, the Warden transferred to Jimmy Valentine *his* official pardon, which had been signed by the accommodating state governor *that* very morning.

"Ya' only served ten months on a four-year sentence," the Warden griped. "That's only just enough time for a woman to get pregnant and have a crying baby."

"Warden, ten-month-sentences take a long time to write, and the grammar also must have a lot of commas and colons," Jimmy joked. "Actually Warden; I had expected to be outta' here in only three months, or just about as much time as a woman takes to have a goddamned abortion."

"I guess your powerful high-society friends on the outside are dying-off and losing their influence with the state's corrupt politicians," the Warden sarcastically concluded and opined. "Look at it this way, Valentine. You've gotten ten-good-haircuts that cost ya' absolutely nothing; not to fully mention a good bunk bed, along with three-square-meals to round-out your day. You're luckier than most damned lottery and sweepstakes' winners are after taxes!"

"Everybody on earth would be luckier if the dumb-shits were never born in the first place," Valentine weirdly objected. "And stop talkin' to me like I was born yesterday."

"Now Valentine; I have a word of sound advice," the all-too-conscientious Warden preached. "You'll be officially outa' the pen in the morning. Correct your errant ways, and lead an honest life. You're not an evil person at heart, and you've got a good personality goin' for yourself," the prison director commended and praised. "Stop cracking safes, and start pumping safe cracks of the feminine variety, if ya' know what the hell I mean!"

"Me?" Jimmy Valentine questioned while feigning surprise. "Why Warden; I've never cracked a blessed safe in all my life!"

"Oh no!" the Warden laughed. "Let's establish a little time line now, Valentine. How was it that you happened to get convicted on that widely publicized Springfield heist? Was it because your alibi might have compromised an important Congressman, or an unethical Senator?" the warden candidly accused. "Or maybe it was because a mean old jury finally decided to render an honest verdict based on the damned evidence? It's always some lame-brain excuse with you innocent victims that have somehow been deprived, depraved, and exploited by our unparalleled American free enterprise society!"

"Not me!" Jimmy answered with a broad smirk exhibited upon his face. "Why Warden; I've never been inside Springfield in all my life? I'm not too proficient at geography. What damned state is Springfield in, anyway?" Valentine virtuously replied.

"Okay Cronin, I've listened to enough of *this* wise-ass prisoner's arrogant malarkey," the Warden indicated. "Take Mr. Valentine to the prison tailor-shop, and have him fitted with some decent street-worthy haberdashery. Then, unlock Jimmy Boy at seven sharp tomorrow morning, *Valentine's Day*. What a fuckin' holiday misnomer in addition to being a bizarre fuckin' coincidence!"

"What should I do after that?" Cronin asked. "Sacrifice him to Zeus or Neptune?"

"Then take Mr. Valentine to the bullpen to warm-up. Keep him in the bullpen until it's time for us to release him after the tenth inning," the Warden jested and specified. "The barred room will help Jimmy V. meditate about reforming to an honest future. You'd better carefully weigh my advice, Valentine!"

At seven-thirty, on February 14th Jimmy Valentine impatiently stood in the Warden's outer office, studying and admiring the prison official's secretary's solid rock-hard breasts. 'Maybe I should imitate my throbbing dick and go straight!' Jimmy thought as the sex-starved jailbird squirmed-around in his chair, attempting to diminish his huge erection. 'Going straight with the right woman sounds like a pretty sound suggestion. But straight women nowadays are as hard to find as men with Z-shaped erections!'

Jimmy was villainously wearing a black pinstriped suit; a felt hat, and a pair of rigid squeaky shoes that he himself had personally stitched for his recently announced prison departure. 'These are standard items of apparel that the state provides for all its compulsory detainees,' Valentine deducted. 'God; I gotta' get me an inflatable rubberized woman to sleep with; one who has got solid firm tits like the Warden's knockout personal secretary has!'

The prison clerk presented Jimmy with a complimentary railroad ticket and a crisp five-dollar bill, which the naïve law establishment provided its former residents to hopefully rehabilitate into good prosperous, contributing American citizens.

"Here Valentine, take this cigar with my best wishes," the Warden requested. "I hope ya' don't choke on it before it explodes in your goddamned criminal face."

Jimmy thanked the prison operator for *his* exceptional wisdom and for his mediocre gifts, and soon "Inmate Valentine, 9763" was recorded on the books as being "Officially Pardoned by the Governor". At eight a.m., James Valentine stepped out of the front gates and into the dull February sunshine. The area winter songbirds chirping away in the barren deciduous trees seemed to be singing: "Go back to a life of crime, Jailbird! You have no fuckin' alternative! Go back to engage in crime!"

'I'll head for a restaurant and have a delectable meal,' Jimmy thought. 'I'll have some barbecued chicken, and a cheap bottle of white wine. Then, I'll puff on a new fancy Cuban cigar!' Valentine decided, as the released former convict chucked the lousy nickel cigar that the Warden had given him into a convenient street corner waste receptacle.

Having enjoyed his tasty meal, Jimmy leisurely exited the ordinary restaurant and headed toward the local train depot. After casually tossing a coin into a blind beggar's hat, the notorious safecracker purchased his railway ticket, and casually boarded a westbound train. Three hours later, the liberated man stepped off the *Pullman* and into a little hamlet located near the Illinois/Iowa state line. The paroled gentleman entered a popular local watering-hole and shook hands with the proprietor, a certain old acquaintance named Mike Donaldson.

"I'm sorry Jimmy my boy that we couldn't arrange this little conference seven months sooner," Mike whispered and confided. "But the big boys had that legal complaint from Springfield to iron-out, and the wimpy politician Governor had to be negotiated with. Now tell me, Doctor V. How the hell are ya' feelin' after your unfortunate tenure in the pen?"

"Just as fine as could be under the circumstances," Jimmy admitted. "Some shit-faced inmates tried to sodomize me on two separate occasions in the middle of the night, but I punctured one of the prick's balls with an ice pick, and I flipped the second fucked-up asshole into the other homo's bunk, and listened all friggin' night to them getting it on. Say Mike; doesn't anybody just jerk-off any more? The whole fuckin' world is getting into this perverted and gay sex bullshit!"

Mike Donaldson smiled and handed Jimmy the key to *his* old upstairs room, which had remained unoccupied since *his* ten-month incarceration. Valentine climbed the rickety steps, and then soon found that everything in the modest quarters was exactly as it had been situated the previous

April Fools' Day. The detective Ben Price's collar button (that had been torn in an intense scuffle) even still remained on the floor. 'That police raid was rather rough and disrespectful,' the gentleman criminal remembered. 'Why the hell don't they go after blue-collar criminals like pimps, prostitutes, and transvestite bank robbers! This white-collar professional, namely me, felt friggin' humiliated when the rambunctious cops had the unbridled audacity to put the goddamned cuffs on my wrists! And that totally fucked-up extended two-month criminal court trial was nerve-racking, too!'

Jimmy slowly pulled-out the folding bed from the wall, and behind a well-concealed sliding panel was stashed his dust-layered suitcase containing his indispensable safecracking tools. Valentine gingerly opened the piece of luggage and admired the finest set of vault neutralizers in the entire Central United States. 'I feel like popping two loads just lookin' at these magnificent babies!' Jimmy laughed as the owner respectfully touched the fabulous assortment of drills, augers, clamps, special screwdrivers, "Jimmy's jimmies," braces, and drill bits. 'I've even meticulously designed and manufactured several of these tools all by myself'.'

A half-hour later, Jimmy Valentine was standing downstairs inside the small café, reminiscing shared history with his old loyal colleague, Mike Donaldson. The suave white-collar criminal was now dressed in more dapper apparel, which was reflective of his high society lifestyle. Jimmy's recently-cleaned black suitcase remained on the café's floor at *his* side.

"Got any jobs goin'?" Mike personally asked. "I really like harboring a person of your high caliber upstairs, and I treasure our memorable gigs done in area banks. Jimmy, ya' really taught me plenty about the profession."

"Are you referring to me?" Jimmy answered in a feigned bewildered tone of voice. "Mike, I'm now a top salesman for the California Amalgamated Short Crispy Biscuit, Cracker and Scumbag Frazzled Wheat Company, Incorporated!" Valentine imaginatively replied. "We specialize in distributing hookers and madams, all having shaved beavers of course, all over the country. Next year, my fledgling company plans to go international."

The safecracker's witty comment delighted Mike Donaldson, who had gone through three separate divorces, and had envied Jimmy Valentine's class and style with the ladies; those dolls having either shaved crotches, or those horny whores having wonderfully hairy bushes of all pubic colors.

The following week in late February, the Midwest newspapers accurately reported a well-performed bank-safe burglary in a Richmond, Indiana institution, with "no apparent significant clues left behind'. Two

74

weeks later, a highly touted burglar-proof safe in Logansport had been opened; its contents heisted, and a large sum of stock securities, currency, gold and silver had been purloined. Detective Ben Price and his acclaimed team of rogue-catchers took immediate notice, and the federal authorities catalogued the pattern that was rapidly developing.

"It sounds like Valentine's on the march again," Ben Price informed his incompetent investigative partners. 'I'm targeting Valentine for a cardiac arrest! Ha, ha, ha!"

"How the hell can Jimmy V. be on the *march* when it's still only friggin' February?" Price's fellow detective answered and chuckled.

"Stop talkin' like a stupid shit-head and get serious about the art and science of detective investigating," Inspector Price chastised his wisecracking novice colleague. "You would make more fuckin' sense to me if you had been born in the China hinterland, and never learned a damned word of English!"

"Okay, the recent job's gotta' be Dandy Jimmy Valentine's signature," Detective Price's numbskull associate deduced and offered. "The tumblers were punched-out clean, and there was only one hole that had been neatly and skillfully drilled. That reminds me, Ben. My wife also has one hole including her ass, and I drill it all the goddamned time! In fact, sometimes three times a day! Every once in a while, my deep drilling hits oil!"

"When I capture the evasive bastard this time," Ben Price predicted as the renowned federal inspector gritted his teeth, "he'll serve his full sentence. The next time, I'll get my hanging judge brother-in-law to show Valentine no clemency for his incessant insolence to my regional authority!"

Ben Price was an expert on the proclivities of the criminals whom the detective adroitly followed, and the investigator kept a keen eye on every reported Midwest bank robbery. "Valentine's established pattern is long distances established between larcenies; rapid getaways; no accomplices, and a definite flair for high society vogues and habits. Yes Harry, Jimmy's a quick dodger of law apprehension," Ben told his pathetic apathetic assistant. "And the slippery felon is as elusive as a frightened cheetah fartin' its ass off in the open field. If I were a vile criminal, I would indeed model myself after stealthy Jimmy Valentine."

One morning in June, the accomplished safecracker and his heavy suitcase climbed out of a horse-drawn carriage that incidentally was used to send mail from one rural Arkansas village to another. Jimmy had landed in Elmore, a town of three thousand hicks, located five miles off the nearest railroad in the Arkansas blackjack territory. Valentine looked like a handsome *Yale* senior in search of his first authentic piece of ass. The visitor ambled down the board sidewalk in the direction of the

Planter's Hotel, where all guests mysteriously always wound-up with gigantic in-grown warts on their feet.

A comely young lady wearing a semi-formal floral-designed dress and carrying a matching colorful parasol above her sophisticated bonnet, entered the Elmore Bank. Jimmy took one glance at the attractive vixen and immediately fell in love. 'Women like that make instant male erections and premature ejaculations possible,' Valentine mused. 'Even when those kind of gorgeous, cock-teasing, vivacious women have all their goddamned clothes on, the dolls still heighten a male viewer's sex urge into overdrive. Who the hell needs pornography with lovely, sophisticated bitches like her struttin' all around?'

Jimmy accosted a young boy, who was loitering in front of the livery station across the gravel street from the Elmore Bank. Valentine asked the acne-faced kid a catalog of questions about the special sights of the town. Jimmy kept transferring dimes to the receptive lad with every positive answer provided, as if *he* was an accomplished animal trainer rewarding a seal or a tiger with food after the creature had successfully performed each successive circus trick. Then the beautiful well-endowed lady exited the bank and acted unaware of Jimmy's or anyone else's presence. The gorgeous female then nonchalantly sauntered down Elmore's Main Street.

"Isn't that knockout bitch, er, I mean that proud young lady Miss Jennifer Sampson, the horniest and kinkiest woman in the whole southeastern United States?" Valentine very deliberately asked the callow lad.

"Naw," the ornery adolescent honestly returned. "Her name's Annabel Abrams, and her rich pa' owns the darn bank. Hey Mister; that particular information will cost ya' a quarter instead of a mere dime. Say, Mister. Why in tar-nation did ya' come to a freaky, country-bumpkin town like Elmore for? Did ya' fall off the stage coach or something?"

"No son," Jimmy laughed. "I'm lookin' for a decent little community in which to settle-down in. I'm tired of travelin' all over creation searchin' for my seven-year-niche, ha, ha, ha!"

"Say Mister, is that a gold watch chain ya' got there?" the all-too-curious kid asked. "I'm savin' up money to buy a pedigree bulldog to scare the crap outa' senior citizens in wheelchairs that live in my neighborhood. Say Mister, ya' got any more dimes or quarters?"

Jimmy left the youthful informant's fantastic company, and ambled over to the *Planter's Hotel* that originally accommodated only vegetable and cotton farmers who habitually did only a *sow-sow* job. The Elmore visitor imaginatively signed the register as *Mr. Ralph D. Spencer*, pretending to be a prominent national salesman of primitive, prototype vending machines.

"What brings you to Elmore Mr. Spencer?" the amiable (but nosy) hotel clerk inquired. "Are ya' a Yankee trying to flee the Civil War fifty years too late?

"I wanta' get out of the machine dispenser business and find something more profitable and lucrative," Jimmy Valentine, alias Ralph D. Spencer, fibbed. "I've noticed you hicks around here ain't got no exclusive shoe store in this primitive-lookin' village, so I'm plannin' to open a fine shoe business right here on Main Street."

"The General Store down the block sells shoes," the slightly-offended clerk corrected in defense of Elmore. "But quite truthfully, its limited selection is rather shitty, er, I mean 'meager'. Most Elmore folks go into Little Rock to buy their foot-gear."

"Yes, but those obsolete-lookin' shoes in the General Store's window look like they're used leftovers from the time of the Massachusetts Pilgrims and the early western pioneers," Ralph (Jimmy) humorously maintained. "And if I ever need a diamond wedding ring, I'll surely go into Little Rock to purchase one."

"Well, Mr. Spencer, I'm really quite impressed with your city slicker clothes and shoes," the envious desk clerk confessed. "Show me how you achieve that exquisite tie-knot, and I'll introduce you to every damned whore in town that frequents the *Planter's,* and the *hot* bitches expertly giving their customers fantastic venereal warts rather than common ordinary planter's warts."

"This remote burg looks like a very pleasant community, and the people seem to be obnoxiously sociable," Jimmy congenially responded. "Say, could I pay my bill in rare porno' magazines?"

"Sure can," the young hick clerk concurred with a smile. "I'll buy 'em from you, and then you can pay me back so that I could put the money in the cash register. But I warn ya'; I wanna' see lots of wet pink hairy beaver slits, or it's no damned deal!"

"Now then, I'll stay here for three nights and check-out all aspects of beautiful metropolitan downtown Elmore," Jimmy politely returned. "And you needn't call a bellboy to carry my suitcase. It's rather heavy and loaded with the latest porn' mags' from around the globe. Those Danish and French model bitches are really super-hot? I'd give ya' one of my mags' right now as a deposit, but then you'd be squirtin' sperm juice all over the damned lobby, and that obviously would be detrimental to conductin' civil business."

Ralph D. Spencer felt like the proverbial *Phoenix.* He had risen out of his own criminal ashes, and now the free man had designs on leading a moral, straight life, especially with his new hard-on for Miss Annabel Abrams. 'I'm gonna' remain here in Elmore, run a legitimate shoe business, marry and screw Annabel Abrams, and then get promoted to vice-president of the bank.'

True to his promise, a month later, Ralph D. Spencer opened a modern shoe store with the latest available styles, and the handsome entrepreneur attracted a respectable trade, knocking the shoe department of the Elmore General Store into economic extinction. Socially, the new arrival instantly made many friends, and in a matter of three months, became Master Sergeant-at-Arms of the eminent "Elmore Perverted Sex and Dildo Society".

Ralph finally managed to meet Annabel Abrams, selling her a pair of black leather army combat boots, and then smelling and licking her rancid putrid bare feet. Spencer soon became fascinated with Miss Abrams's many appealing 'charms', and the reformed safecracker asked Annabel where she had purchased her glittering bracelet, along with all its dangling cheap, tawdry trinkets.

By the following April Fools' Day, Ralph D. Spencer had been elected President of the Elmore Perverted Sex and Dildo Society, rising to that high privileged office in the shortest time of any newly sponsored member. His popular shoe store was prospering, and his kinky sex reputation was rapidly proliferating. Even Annabel's stringent father, a demented pedophile child molester, found favor with the new Elmore businessman. Mr. Abrams already liked Ralph better than his other daughter's irrelevant husband, Waldo, who was leading a unique double-life as an area Catholic priest in another backward Arkansas community. Martha and Waldo had two children, Agatha and *May*, who were both born in September of different years.

Jimmy Valentine was now happily reformed as the socially reincarnated Ralph D. Spencer. The satisfied gentleman sat-down at his apartment desk and authored a letter of regret and happiness. Then, the shoe entrepreneur mailed the informative missive to a former criminal confederate in St. Louis:

Dear Louie the Lip in St. Louie:

I want to meet you at Riley's place in Little Rock next Wednesday night at nine p.m. I intend to consummate some final details with you professionally representing me as my personal fence. My kit of precious tools is now available for instant black-market resale. You couldn't duplicate the special set for many thousands of bucks. Perhaps you can negotiate a sale to one of those new upstart male/female Little Rock amateur felony teams, either Bonnie and Clyde or Bill and Hillary.

Now, I shall regretfully review the personal sentimental crap. Louie, please don't give me any lousy lip about my expressed intention that I'm confidentially sharing with you. I've retired from the unpredictable safecracking banking business, and have purchased a fine shoe store down here in rural Arkansas. I'm making an honest living, and I'm going to wed the most gorgeous bombshell this side of the Hudson, or is it the Mississippi? Anyway, the straight life is the only life for me, Louie; and my throbbing dick also intends to go straight, along with my budding professional shoe store occupation.

After I get married, I plan to sell my upstart business, and take my new wife to California where Ben Price will probably never track me down, since his law enforcement office has a very scarce budget for traveling expenses.

I tell you Louie, my new girlfriend is an absolute angel, who believes in me as if I'm a true religion. I wouldn't perform another crooked thing in my life, especially with my erect straight pecker. Be sure to be at Riley's place in Little Rock to negotiate the final specifics of the anticipated transaction. From now on, I'll just be using the tool between my legs.

Your old buddy,
Jimmy V.

On the following Monday, after Jimmy's posting of the letter, Ben Price unobtrusively arrived in Elmore, searching for the whereabouts of an infamous, itinerant safecracker. The nationally celebrated detective casually strolled around the town, telling every inquisitive native who asked that he was a tourist in quest of founding a "Pet Shop" business in a vacant storefront situated off of Main Street. The clever detective carefully scrutinized Ralph D. Spencer's shoe store from a rented room's window above the Elmore Drug and Marijuana Shoppe, centrally located directly across Main Street from Ralph's flourishing commercial enterprise.

'Well Jimmy, I understand you have designs of marrying the banker's unsuspecting daughter,' the eminent detective imagined. 'Now that's what I really call an inside job! What a fuckin' impractical dreamer and schemer you are, Mr. Ralph D. Spencer!'

The next morning, Jimmy was enjoying a country breakfast at the Abrams' spacious kitchen. The conversation was both genial and genteel. But Annabel's always-suspicious banking father was quite inquisitive with his interrogatives.

"Why are you going to Little Rock?" Mr. Abrams asked his ambitious, future, favorite son-in-law.

"I'm going to *Little Rock* to buy a *big rock* for your daughter's hand," the gleeful soon-to-be fiancé ludicrously replied. "And I gotta' purchase my fancy wedding togs, too. This will be the first time I'll be leaving

Elmore in over a month, Mr. Abrams, so I sorta' have island temperature living isolated here in Elmore, or cabin fever, or some other crazy mental condition like that!"

Two hours after consuming the very spectacular breakfast meal, Mr. Abrams, Mrs. Abrams, Annabel, Martha, along with her two daughters, visited Jimmy at his apartment to say "farewell" and to wish him "Godspeed" on his prospective shopping expedition to Little Rock, Arkansas.

"What's in the suitcase?" Annabel Abrams innocently asked Ralph. Then she tried lifting it. "It feels like it's got gold bricks inside. Are you a slippery, side-winding goldbricker!"

"Oh, it's just a few blacksmith anvils and plenty of nickel-plated shoehorns," the shoe store owner defensively laughed. "I'm gonna' sell them in Little Rock to cover the expense of your soon-to-be-coveted big rock, and also use the excess money to pay for my extravagant wedding costume."

"Okay," Mr. Abrams lustily laughed. "Carry your heavy luggage downstairs. I've hired Adolph Jensen to take you in his buckboard to the railroad station. But Ralph, first I want to show you a surprise. Let's all go over to the bank and inspect my most recent prized acquisition! It's a real dandy!"

Everyone else hopped into two carriages, while Ralph D. Spencer (alias Jimmy Valentine) almost got a double hernia lifting the heavy suitcase onto Adolph Jensen's classic taxi-buggy.

Five-minutes later, the merry entourage excitedly entered Mr. Abrams' landmark Elmore Bank. The town's financial kingpin (and the principal pillar of the community) had recently installed a new vault that had been especially obtained for holding safety deposit boxes and major cash storage. The new steel enclosure featured a modern-designed, patented door, configured with three solid bolts that latched simultaneously, and the massive safe also had an accurate clock timer, which constituted a novel, avant-garde technological addition. Naturally, the new vault represented an alluring temptation to one Jimmy Valentine.

"This vault is the most advanced one in this section of Arkansas," Mr. Abrams proudly articulated. "And not even Bonnie and Clyde or Bill and Hillary could break into it."

Martha's children, May and Agatha, took an instant interest in the new contraption, but Ralph D. Spencer prudently showed a courteous-but-remote fascination with the new-fangled enclosure. While the family was marveling at the bank's latest advancement, Ben Price strolled inside and observed the occupants chatting and complimenting Mr. Abrams on his impeccable judgment to safeguard his cherished customers' accounts.

"I don't want to make a deposit or withdrawal," the master detective informed the listless teller, who was preoccupied reading the latest gay and lesbian county LBTQAKRFP pamphlet. "I'm just waiting to speak with someone I know who's intendin' to open a sizable savings account here."

Suddenly, a loud, shrill, scream permeated the air, and the shriek immediately threatened to ruin the momentous occasion. The alarmed elders all turned their heads to learn the cause of the great commotion. Five-year-old May had been playing an impromptu game of "Hide and Seek" with nine-year-old Agatha, who had accidentally locked her younger sister in her grandfather's shiny, new steel bank vault. The emergency presented itself as a tremendous mental dilemma to Ralph D. Spencer.

The elderly bank executive hastened to the vault and vainly tugged at its immovable handle. "I can't budge the damned door!" Mr. Abrams bellowed and hollered. "The clock hasn't been synchronized, and the combination hasn't been set yet! Woe is me'! Woe is me'!"

Martha was screaming hysterically, as if a porcupine and a saguaro cactus had been shoved-up her sensitive love canal.

"Hush Martha!" Mr. Abrams admonished his older daughter as the rattled bank executive raised his right hand to fend the emotionally distraught mother off. "Your maternal instinct can only complicate matters right now! Shut the hell up, so that I can think rationally for a goddamned minute! Panic will not solve this friggin' crisis!"

"My precious May!" "My precious May!" Martha hysterically and repeatedly yelled. "She'll die of fright! Break open the damned door! Can't anyone here do something!" the distraught mother wailed.

"The closest expert that can open this door is a hundred-miles away in Little Rock!" Mr. Abrams answered in a defeated tone of voice. "Spencer, what the hell can we do? May is an epileptic, and will surely go into convulsions, and soon have a wicked seizure! She'll most certainly use-up all of the goddamned oxygen in that confounded airtight safe," the melancholy bank director informed. "And in a matter of minutes, when May wildly rolls around the vault's floor, swallowing her tongue, she'll eventually be dead!"

Martha was frantic and began having her own epileptic fit, deliriously rolling around on the bank's floor, and being awkwardly attended to by Annabel and by Mrs. Abrams.

"Ralph, can't you do anything?" Annabel cried and pleaded from her kneeling position. "Why are you looking so dazed and puzzled?"

"Dynamite is not a dynamite idea!" Mr. Abrams boomed. "It might blast poor May and my expensive, uninsured vault all the way to Kingdom Come!"

Ralph D. Spencer momentarily studied Annabel's large, bloodshot, blue eyes that profoundly reflected both anguish and fear. The former safecracker felt compelled to intervene in the dire situation to rescue

May, knowing full well that his past clandestine activities, and his widespread disreputable safecracking identity, would be discovered.

'Oh well; my inglorious past is gonna' jeopardize my secure future,' Jimmy Valentine realistically thought. 'And I must do what is right and save May's life, even though I despise with a passion the raunchy, little spoiled bitch!' Then Ralph D. Spencer gazed again into his woman's despairing eyes. A smile from his lips brought hope to her soul.

"Annabel," Ralph said. "Please give me that rose that's pinned on your dress. It will give me emotional strength."

Annabel stared at Ralph incredulously as if he was mystically speaking to her from another dimension. The future Mrs. Ralph D. Spencer did exactly as the safecracker had strangely requested, and gently handed him the flower, which Spencer immediately stuffed into his exposed vest pocket. With the transfer of the symbolic red rose, shoe-man Ralph D. Spencer instantly transformed back into the notorious high society rogue, Jimmy Valentine.

"Get away from the door, all of you!" Jimmy commanded the still-shocked, helpless family members. Valentine then dashed outside, obtained his heavy suitcase from Adolph Jensen's buggy, carried the necessary tools into the Elmore Bank, and then assiduously went to work practicing his ignoble craft. Jimmy laid-out his wonderful equipment upon the bank's white marble floor, and strangely (to the consternation of the Abrams' family members), whistled a cheerful tune. Everyone watched spellbound as the former convict confidently demonstrated his very remarkable (formerly secret) skills.

A minute later, Jimmy's favorite drill was smoothly biting a small cavity into the vault's solid steel door. Breaking his fastest entry record, Valentine adroitly moved back the three bolts and then easily opened the sturdy portal.

May was gasping and panting, wildly rolling around on the vault's metal base. Annabel dragged her niece out of the compartment, and used Jimmy's augers as convenient tongue depressors for both the almost-paralyzed girl, and next, *her* hysterical, epileptic mother, still rolling around on the white marble floor while frantically clutching *her* aching throat.

Jimmy Valentine put on his suit jacket, stepped outside the vault area, and paced toward the front doors as if in a mesmerized trance. The safecracker hesitated as he felt a hand on his shoulder, and a bass voice saying, "Hello Ralph!"

"Oh, hello Ben!" Jimmy greeted his old nemesis. "I figured you might catch-up with me sooner or later! Well, let's go and get my arraignment started over at the courthouse. Take me into custody, so that I can be spared the embarrassment of having to explain my arrest to my beautiful fiancée and her rather prudish, very wealthy, WASP family!"

"What the hell' are you talkin' about Mr. Spencer?" Ben Price surprisingly answered. "I don't believe I've ever met anyone by the name of Ralph D. Spencer before today. But I gotta' admit; that rescue was a damned wonderful humanitarian thing I had just witnessed, perhaps the greatest act of self-sacrifice and courage my eyes have ever seen."

"Do you mean I'm not goin' back to the slammer?" Jimmy Valentine asked in amazement, as the reformed criminal realized his possible retrieved reformation. "I mean, I've feared all throughout the Elmore bank caper that *that* was my ultimate fate!"

Ben Price simply winked at the new straight contributor to Elmore, Arkansas high society. The famed police investigator knew quite well when the exercise of moral justice should be warranted and justified, and now the acclaimed detective's keen eyes and mind had ultimately recognized it. A brief announcement ensued.

"Well, Ralph," Ben Price declared. "Strange and peculiar things often happen on April Fools' Day," the famous inspector coyly commented. The master detective courteously doffed his felt derby in respect to Ralph D. Spencer, and then slowly ambled out of the Elmore Bank onto gravel-topped Main Street. The flabbergasted, notorious safecracker now had permission to start a new life with a clean slate; thanks to the wise and sage discretion of the very judicious Detective Ben Price.

"Tom and Huck's Gang"
Mark Twain

Samuel Langhorne Clemens (1835-1910) was undoubtedly one of the most influential American authors, and was also a prolific contributor to United States literature. Sam Clemens was born in the year 1835 when *Haley's Comet* (Halley's Comet) made an appearance, and the literary master died seventy-five years later, predictably when the celestial object made another solar system pass past the earth, and then began another journey around the sun.

Sam Clemens acquired the writing pseudonym "Mark Twain" from Mississippi River steamboat jargon. A worker on the riverboat would toss a lead weight attached to a rope overboard and "mark the twain". If the water was two-fathoms-deep (twelve feet), then a riverboat could safely navigate past a shoal, or over a hidden underwater reef.

Growing-up in the quiet town of Hannibal Missouri, young Sam Clemens knew more about the Mississippi River's 'muddy waters' than the celebrated blues/jazz musician Muddy Waters ever conceived or imagined. As an impressionable boy, Twain's prime ambition was to become a Mississippi riverboat pilot. When the *Civil War* broke-out, the mighty Mississippi was shut-down to commercial boat traffic, so the unemployed riverboat pilot went west to first try his hand at gold prospecting, and later Clemens chose to become a newspaper reporter.

Mark Twain was a trendsetter, because the writer was one of the first authors to present characters speaking dialogue using poor grammar (the way ordinary people would converse), rather than the stilted, formal, academic author's style practiced by his literary predecessors, and also by his envious New England contemporaries. "Tom and Huck's Gang" is a thoroughly corrupted version of the beginning of Mark Twain's classic novel, *Huckleberry Finn*.

You probably don't know about Huckleberry Finn unless you've read a slanderous bullshit book by the name of *The Adventures of Tom Sawyer*. But I honestly believe all that particular bull-crap doesn't really friggin' matter an inch up a pig's ass. In that singular *Tom Sawyer* classic novel, some truths were exaggerated, but nevertheless, the essential facts were all goddamned bona-fide fucked-up truths from stem to stern.

I mean, just about any shit-head on this totally weird planet fibs and lies at one time or another, unless of course, their names happen to be the Widow, or Mary (not the Blessed Virgin), or *Aunt Polly*, who never wanted any goddamned cracker to eat. Tom Sawyer's Aunt Polly and the Widow Douglas are both told about in that first spectacular book, which (as I've already mentioned) is mostly true and contains a few deliberate *stretchers,* but no damned ambulances anywhere in it.

Now, here's the way that exciting *Tom Sawyer* manuscript concluded: Tom and me skillfully found the money that the ferocious robbers had hidden in the cave, and instantly, we both became rich as all hell. We got six-thousand-dollars each, all in gold. It was a lot of friggin' money when all accumulated on one table to look at and appreciate. Tom wanted to buy a national whorehouse franchise with his end, and I planned to hire a famous engineer and then construct a new type of portable outhouse suitable for utilization during circus and carnival events. But the all-too-sagacious Judge Thatcher had other designs.

"Boys," the wise Judge announced. "I believe you two lads got more *bucks* that amount to more doe (dough) than any hunters' club could ever wish for. Now I strongly suggest you two wet-behind-the- ears lucky dumb-ass kids invest your money scrupulously, rather than speculate puttin' it into a bordello franchise; into an illegal gambling casino, or into a national chain of newfangled metal outhouses for people with asses of all sizes."

"Well, Your Honor, what does ya' have in mind?" Tom crankily asked. "Huck and I are as darin' and stubborn as all hell!"

"Well boys," the Judge pontificated. "You two ain't got no say in the matter because, you're both under-aged, obnoxious turd-heads. I'm gonna' rule that the money be put into the bank, and you two lucky stiffs are gonna' each earn a dollar a day interest on your *principal*, even though your little two room schoolhouse ain't got no damned principal."

Then, the Widow Douglas took me (Huckleberry Finn) into her personal custody and predicted that she would civilize my ass, so that I didn't grow up to be a Vandal, a Visigoth or a *Hun,* even though she believed I had no observable homosexual tendencies, perverted or otherwise. The damned spinster was too decent, and too honest, and too kind in all of her ways, so it was sure rough living under her oppressive Spartan dominion. So, when I couldn't stand her demanding rules and her stern regulations, I hastily ran-away to gain freedom and independence from what I intelligently considered "fucked-up adult morals".

I got into my old rags (that I preferred wearing rather than formal school and church togs), and I happily lived out of an old abandoned hogshead down by the town livery stable. I was satisfied jerkin' off in a big old barrel, rather than pulling my meat in some fancy bed with four curtained posts erected around its frame. But then, Tom Sawyer hunted me down and said that he was "hankerin' to start a *band* of robbers" that would attack innocent civilians without using any friggin' musical instruments.

"Want to join my robber gang?" Tom persuasively asked. "You'd make a damned fine outlaw!"

"Maybe," I answered while coyly playing hard-to-get. "But why don't ya' form a gang of rapers, or a gang of hostile gay and lesbian bashers? I mean Tom; I ain't never licked a girl's beaver before, straight or lesbian, and I really never beat the shit out of a faggot minister tryin' to abduct me in the church choir loft!"

"We might do those things in addition to robbin' rich people like Robin Hood did in *Sherman Forest*," Tom authoritatively replied. "But instead, I think we'll rob from the rich, and keep all the damned easy money for ourselves. To hell with the damned poor, and with their damned stupid problems, and with their dumb livin' habits."

"What do I havta' do to join your thoroughly-neat gang?" I inquired.
"Screw a woodchuck?"

"Ya' gotta' get out of this stupid barrel you're livin' in, and go back to the Widow Douglas's place," Tom assertively and firmly reprimanded. "Once you're respectable again, you'll qualify to be in my gang of fearful robbers. We're only gonna' do white collar crime to gullible white collared people, ya' understand?"

The Widow Douglas cried and slobbered all over me, and called me a poor lost lamb when I returned to her undesirable custody. The old bag also called me a "son-of-a-bitch", and a "no-good dirty little pecker-head" under her breath on Sundays, before goin' to church and receivin' communion. The demandin' widow made me dress in new clothes all over again, and I hated sweatin' in general; and I resented sweatin' my balls and ass off in that silly tight formal uniform. Truthfully, I was all *cramped-up* without even havin' my first monthly period.

Anyway, the old, damned-ugly practices of honoring customs and rituals commenced again. The Widow rang the dinner bell, and I had to report for supper on time, or else have to wash and dry the goddamned dishes and clean-off the really big supper table. And I couldn't begin eatin' my food until the old witch would tuck my head-down where I would have to listen to her say some incomprehensible holy words over the victuals. I mean to say that in the barrel filled with my personal belongings, items got all mixed-up, but in the Widow Douglas's rigid universe of ten thousand dumb-ass habits, things like laws and traditions got all muddled-up, and I had to honor each one of the strict prudish woman's goddamned Puritan WASP values.

After supper, the overprotective, overbearing widow got-out her *Bible,* and busted my balls good, reading all about Moses and the ancient Pharaoh. And I had to sit there sweatin' in my formal clothes, even when I had to take a long piss or a healthy crap. But then, I found-out that Moses and the Pharaoh had both been dead for many centuries, so I didn't take no more stock in her bullshittin' articulations, because I don't like hearin' about dead people that posed no particular, immediate, imminent threat to either Tom Sawyer or me.

I asked the self-righteous widow if I could smoke, so she set my old hogshead clothes on fire with me in them and laughed, "Smoke all ya' want Huckleberry! Next time wear your cute little blazer!" And I had to listen to her loquacious lectures about how smokin' was a vulgar habit that wasn't clean, or sanitary or healthy. I did have a maximum tolerance for her nauseous dia*tribe*, often wonderin' what Indian council she belonged to."

"But ya' don't know anything about smokin', or about sex?" I futilely criticized. "How come ya' could tell me what the hell to do about things you ain't no damned expert at!"

"Huckleberry; now don't you get overly sassy with me!" the austere widow threatened. "Next time I set you on fire, I'll let the blaze burn right to the end until you've been reduced to charred bones and ashes, just like the unfortunate residents of Sodom and Gomorrah had perished!"

"But ya' always read and talk about Moses killin' Egyptians in that *Red Sea*, and ya' don't say anything nasty about the jerk, because he had all those pyramid people slaughtered with God's help!" I ranted without achievin' any favorable results. "But ya' always find fault with me smokin' when all I'm really actually hurtin' is me, and not me drownin' an entire army in chariots chasin' my ass all over the desert! And besides, I see ya' takin' snuff and getting high, which in my honest opinion, Widow, is twice as damned deadly as puffin' masculine tobacco!"

Well, in order to reform my vulnerable soul, the determined Widow Douglas began talkin' about the "Good Place" in the afterlife. The old maid explained that all a person would have to do all day long was go around heaven on a cloud playin' a silly harp, and singin' praise forever all the way into infinity.

"Do ya' think Tom Sawyer will also be in heaven?" I asked the inflexible old Bible-totin' lady.

"No, Huckleberry. I don't think that Tom will amass the grace credentials to ever be qualified to live in heaven," the widow lamented and maintained. "Thomas Sawyer is too rebellious, insolent, defiant and insubordinate."

'That's good!' I mentally concluded. 'I wanna' be with Tom in the afterlife in a thrillin' place where we both could screw around, get drunk, get laid, rape women, and rob angels and saints on surprise raids from hell.'

The widow's sister, Miss Watson, was a slim, frigid, old maid, but certainly more tolerable than the Widow Douglas ever was. Miss Watson came to town to live with her martinet sister; wore glasses that looked like swimming goggles, and besieged my ass every night with the contents of a stupid spellin' textbook. Every evening after prayer readin', Miss Watson would break my stones about how to spell stupid-ass words like "dynamic" and "revolutionary". I instinctively went from nervous, to fidgety, to rebellious in imitation of my personal hero, Tom Sawyer. Miss Watson's imperial, condescending rhetoric was deadly dull, and her ridiculous nomenclature reminded me of the preacher's damned deadly and dull fire and brimstone sermons articulated during wholly monotonous Sunday church services.

"Don't put your feet up on the furniture," Miss Watson commanded like A Prussian officer.

"Don't slouch-down like that, Huckleberry Finn," the Widow automatically would chime-in.

"Sit up straight!" Miss Watson would imperatively add.

"Don't stretch your arms over your head in public," the Widow impolitely insisted.

"Try to always behave," Miss Watson snootily lectured. "Conformity breeds good manners."

Then, the two old bitches described in detail the "Bad Place," and after I told them "I want to go there and meet the really interestin' people that have lived on the earth," I got dual simultaneous uppercuts to the jaw, that the combination sending my ass reeling over the impeccable parlor's very ancient couch.

The two old hags didn't realize that all I desired was a change of scenery from formal rules and from their perpetual dictatorial tyranny, but the weird disciplinarian old bags would defensively go into their hyper-aggressive behavioral mode, and then effectively and systematically beat the shit out of me.

"That's very wicked Huckleberry!" the Widow boisterously chastised. "What you're sayin' is very wicked and sinful!"

"Christ, m'am!" I yelled in defense of my often-abused ego. "Beatin' the shit out of me is what is sinful and wicked. Words ain't never killed no one all by themselves!"

"The Widow and I are both preparin' to go to the glorious Good Place!" Miss Watson shrieked like a virgin maniac. "That's why we're tryin' our best to reform you to conform to good Christian teachings!" the female nutcase bellowed, before tossin' me up against the wall like I was some sort of very dangerous criminal.

"I ain't never goin' to go to heaven and be with you two Amazons," I yelled-back. "I don't need the crap and piss beatin' out of me for all eternity, if you two ugly bitches are there!"

Miss Watson and the Widow Douglas both kept verbally badgerin' and browbeatin' my stellar personality and my pristine character, and when matters didn't go their way, the old hags resorted to clobberin' and maimin' my entire body. I got tired of their sanctimonious and irrelevant bullshit, which they alternately falsely called "Christian morality" and "Western Civilization". Sometimes, the two insane hoary women would fetch the niggers into the house, and the group would pray together to escape goin' to hell, and then everybody would go to their respective beds dreamin' of heaven, and forgettin' all about the evils of child abuse, exploitation, human misery, and slavery.

I climbed the steps up to my room and intensively stared at a clean sheet of paper on my desk. 'I gotta' think of somethin' cheerful to write, tellin' the two witches of my intentions. I'm scootin' away from home once and for all!' I pondered and decided. I sat restlessly in the chair over near the window, and seriously contemplated what the hell I wanted to tell the two psychotic churchgoin' bitches.

I wished I were dead and in hell with my pal Tom Sawyer. I glanced-out the window and noticed the stars shining up in the night sky, and listened to the leaves and branches rustling against the house and shutters. I heard an owl hootin', and accordin' to local superstition, somebody in town had just died; and then my ears perceived a whippoorwill and a dog makin' oddball sounds, tellin' me that somebody else was about to croak other than a sick frog. 'I wish they're makin' noise about Tom and me both kickin' the bucket,' I imagined. 'That would be the greatest joy, if *we* could get the hell outa' this life and swiftly go to the Bad Place together!'

Then, the cold shivers came over me, when I heard a ghost-like sound originatin' from the woods behind the widow's wood-frame house. 'That ghost is unhappy in its grave, and must go around grievin' while scarin' the shit outa' all Hannibal's citizens,' I reckoned. Next, a spider crawled up my shoulder, and I flicked the sucker into my candle's flame, incineratin' the bothersome bastard and pretendin' that its body was delightfully roastin' in hell along with Tom and me.

'That's a bad thing,' I realized. 'A mighty bad omen indeed.' I recalled the perfect remedy for the totally bad luck event of burnin' a damned spider, so I took-off all of my clothes, and ran stark naked backwards doing three complete rotations of the bedroom. Next, I crossed my chest three times for good measure, and I finally tied-up a lock of my long hair to keep witches from meddlin' into my personal affairs. 'Tomorrow, I gotta' find a lost, rusty horseshoe, and nail it up against my bedroom wall, just to neutralize the damned evil spirits that had been generated from me torchin' the damned spider in the candle flame,' I vowed.

I sat-down while havin' a bad case of the heebie-jeebies, and shook all over like I had one of those nasty adult sex diseases in the advanced stages. I removed my pipe, and lit it up to puff some satisfyin' tobacco, tar, and nicotine into the air to serve as incense to help cancel-out the evil spirits caused by the black spider's fiery death. The house was as still as silent hell, and so I wished that I was dead too, just like the friggin' lucky spider was. I then heard the bell in the town clock-tower thud twelve times. 'Midnight!' I uneasily thought. 'This is when death stalks everyone weak, or anyone nervous. I better stay strong and focused!'

Then, my ultra-sensitive ears detected a distinct snap, and something mysterious stirrin' outside the house down near the ground. I sat still as a statue waitin' to meet my imminent doom. My acute hearing then heard what sounded like a dying cat squealing "Meow, meow, meow!" directly below my window.

I immediately knew how to respond to the magnificent code bein' transmitted. I scrambled-out the opened window, and plopped my bare feet down on the shed's tin roof. Then, I shinnied-down the drainpipe, and hustled into a cover of trees and bushes. Sure enough, my good buddy Tom Sawyer was waitin' to greet me.

Without a moment's hesitation, Tom and I stealthily meandered around the dirt path to the Widow's back porch. We had to be careful how we were treading, because stray dogs and cats often took craps in that area alongside the house, and I was still barefooted. And I fully realized that getting shit on the soles of a person's feet is even worse than getting nasty-smellin' animal turds stuck to the bottom of a kid's shoes. I know because that disgustin' shit has happened to me more than once.

When we surreptitiously passed by the kitchen window, I stumbled over a root, and my tripping produced a noisy thump. Tom and I slinked-down and laid still as if we were mutilated corpses. Jim (Miss Watson's big human property) came-out from the kitchen in response to the sound his ears had heard. The big oaf craned his powerful, muscular neck out, and nervously called, "Hoo dare!"

'Doesn't that dumb black bastard know any damned verbs?' I thought. 'He's fuckin' speakin' American English in a different freakin' language!'

As I was sayin', Tom and I were camouflaged behind two bushes, and the big black jerk was standin' right in the middle of the backyard vegetation. The black giant was within touchin' distance, and I didn't dare breathe, fart, gulp, or sneeze. Jim stood there for a full five-minutes, until the frightened ogre got-up the gumption to again speak his type of jargon.

"Hoo dare?" Miss Watson's slave anxiously asked. "Hoo the hell dare? Is you a ghost?"

My ankle began itchin'; my ear began itchin'; my ass began itchin', and soon my balls began itchin' somethin' fierce, too. 'I'm gonna' die if I don't scratch my whole damned body pretty soon!' I uncomfortably reckoned. I recalled that I was not supposed to scratch anything, includin' my ass and my balls at a funeral, or at a church service, where quality people were congregated (besides the inferior hicks from the sticks). I only itched in the wrong damned places at the wrong damned time, and that's another freakin' reason I wanted no part of society's incomprehensible rules, customs, traditions, extraditions, and laws. My fertile imagination was rudely interrupted by Jim, who was neurotically speakin' his slave dialect of English-non-English.

"Say dar; hoo is you out dare? Whar is ya'?" the huge lummox called. "There're no dogs and cats takin' dumps out here right now! But I did hear somephin'. Well, I'm just gonna' set my ass-down here and listen 'til I hears it again."

Jim stretched-out upon the ground under the stars, in the area separatin' Tom's hiding bush from my hiding bush. All the while, I was thinkin' about lickin' Becky Thatcher's bush regardless of what her pappy the Judge would say about my perversion, which was actually a genuine need to-get-laid-or-blown that dwelled pretty deep in my heart. Soon, Jim stretched-out his massive body on the dirt, while the inside of my nostrils began itchin' like a son-of-a-bitch. I clenched my teeth and bit my tongue, makin' my mind focus on the damned pain rather than on rubbin' my damned snout right off my face. Luckily, Jim began breathin' heavily, and then the black monster dozed-off five minutes later. His loud irregular snorin' made the ground vibrate like there was a colossal earthquake in progress.

Tom Sawyer was a daring kid that loved danger, and made every adventure more-risky and complicated than it really had to be. My best friend gestured with his head, and winked with his eye, the dual motions signalin' for me to clandestinely follow him. We crawled back toward the quiet house on our hands and knees, and I felt a plethora of garden ants scurryin' all over my arms, legs and ass. Twenty-feet away from snoring Jim, my pal Tom had the enviable audacity to whisper something so preposterous that I thought it was humorous.

"Let's tie Jim to the tree he's lyin' near," my most-excellent chum inanely suggested. "I think that darin' task would make a great adventure, and would be another feather in our caps, right Robin?"

"I don't wear caps," I obstinately retorted. "And besides, Jim's liable to wake-up and cause a ruckus," I objected. "Then the Widow and Miss Watson would really bust my stones if the two wrinkled old ladies found-out I was leavin' the house against their will."

"Okay, I'll concede round one to ya'," Tom reluctantly stated. "But now, Huck, I gotta' tell ya' an even better idea. I'm gonna' sneak into your house up the drainpipe, and enter through your bedroom window. Then, I'm gonna' visit the Widow Douglas's bedroom and steal those three candles ya' was braggin' about yesterday. I need 'em to have my first official gang meetin'."

"But the widow is sleepin' in her bedroom?" I vehemently balked, not realizing that I almost woke-up snoozing Jim. "The Widow's awake, and she'll think you was me stealin' her sacred candles that she lights when reading her damned *Bible*."

92

Tom called me a "cowardly yellow-bellied snake", and then my determined pal silently set-out for the aforementioned drainpipe. My devious companion demonstrated a chimpanzee's agility, as the brave kid maneuvered up the fixture, eventually clambering onto the green tin roof, and next climbing through the window into my bedroom. I waited in the dark listenin' to the irregular rhythm of Jim's dissonant snorin', forty or so feet away. Five minutes later, my loyal comrade returned down the flimsy drainpipe, carryin' his purloined three candles.

"Huck; I left a shiny nickel on the bedroom table to cover the candle expenses," my courageous associate informed. "An honest kid always pays his debts! I think I'm gonna' write my own Commandments after we get the gang started!"

"But the Widow will think it was me that took the candles and left the stupid five cents," I distressfully answered. "And then I'll get bashed and battered around like I was fightin' one of those ferocious bears or kangaroos that come around once a year with the circus. Who needs that shit?"

"Guess what Huck?" Tom asked while snickerin' and gigglin' his rear-end off.

"I haven't a clue," I disgustedly replied. "What's so vital ya' got to say?"

"When I entered the Widow Douglas's bedroom in the dark, she was havin' some wild sixty-nine session with her seventy-three-year-old sister. The Widow was lappin' away on the bottom and Miss Watson was munchin' away on top."

"You're bullshitin' me!" I gasped. "Their pussies must be drier than the Sahara Desert to begin with!"

"I seen it all with my own eyes, and heard the lustful sounds with my sharp-hearin ears," Tom adamantly insisted. "Those two old bitches were so into it that I had no trouble exchangin' the nickel for the three candles, and then hightailin' it out of the damned bedroom. That had to be the most surprisin', and the most disgustin', raunchy thing I ever did see or hear."

Tom and I promptly left the property in the opposite direction, and soon marched-up a familiar steep hill. "Miss Watson's slave knows plenty about witchcraft and black magic spells," Tom confidently related. "Tomorrow, if you're still alive, you be sure to ask the Widow and Miss Watson if Jim detected anything strange happenin' around her house."

"That's right Tom," I concurred. "Jim always keeps a magic five cent piece tied to a necklace around his neck. Other blacks come from miles around just to marvel at the cheap piece of shit. Jim claims the necklace could fetch witches and demons," I added, "but he never told the other darkies the exact words that would successfully summon *them* to Hannibal."

"But the visitin' superstitious Negroes was afraid to even touch the nickel," Tom indulgently laughed. "They thought the devil was inside the silly five cent piece. That's what I need now, Huck," Tom facetiously remarked. "A girl that's a five-cent-piece! Even Becky Thatcher would do!" Tom added while deliberately breakin' my vulnerable balls.

"Jim sure knows how to scare the shit out of his fellow slaves," I admitted, while pretending to ignore my juvenile colleague's allusion to my beloved girlfriend. "His balls at times must be bigger than blown-up balloons! I gotta' admit, Tom, that Miss Watson really owns an interestin' slave there, that's for damned sure!"

Well, when Tom and me ascended the hilltop on the fringe of the Widow's property, we looked-down into the village and noticed three or four oil lights and lanterns twinklin' where the sick people were takin' medicine, or where the dead folks were bein' mourned. The constellations were shinin' and beautiful, and the moonlight allowed the old faithful, mile-wide Mississippi River to sparkle next to the somnolent hamlet. The overall illumination was so awe-inspiring that Tom and me even forgot about Jim inhalin' green-headed flies while snorin', and about Miss Watson and the Widow naughtily doin' perverted senior-citizen lesbian sixty-nine.

My intrepid buddy and I descended the steep hill and proceeded down a well-worn path, which was a pretty nifty shortcut into town that we always used. Joe Harper (who was very *bizarre*) and Ben Rogers were hiding in the old tan-yard waitin' for us. The four of us then trekked to the riverbank and unhitched a skiff belongin' to the already-sleeping town mayor. Then, we competently rowed-out into the channel, not realizin' that our combined weight might sink the damned small, weatherworn boat right into the muddy Mississippi. The prospective gang members took turns rowin' the skiff, and finally, about two and a half miles downstream, we went ashore exactly where a big exaggerated scar marked the site of our pre-planned hillside destination.

"This is the secret hideout," Tom proudly informed the two other assholes and me. "It's my favorite place to come and jerk- off!"

"Shouldn't ya' jerk-off and then *come?*" Ben Rogers cleverly challenged.

"Shut your damned trap, if ya' wanna' see tomorrow morning!" Tom angrily answered our idiot friend. "I'm supposed to be the only goddamned comedian in the gang!"

The four of us carefully climbed the precarious hill, and crawled between several treacherous sticker bushes; and then our gang's bossy leader made us all take an oath of allegiance to *our* organization's clandestine cause. "Ya' gotta' promise to keep this all meeting a big secret, and not even tell your girlfriends, your wives, or your consciences," Tom sternly commanded. "And if one of ya' assholes squeals, I'll personally beat the shit out of ya', even when I only was suspectin' that ya' would be squealin'.'"

My best pal then led us through a narrow hole that existed in the rocky terrain, which was situated right behind the thickest growth of bushes. Then, we lit our four candles and crawled on our hands and knees like escapin' prison convicts. Twice, out of reacting to the suspense, I stupidly almost-swallowed my candle flame and wick. That particular dumb military-like crawling maneuver continued for almost two-hundred-yards, until the four participants reached the mouth of a really swell cave (that didn't look that swollen).

The inductees followed Tom through several tight passages until we ducked under a wall, and wriggled into a well-concealed hollow. On the other side was a chamber where we could all finally stand-up without havin' to look at someone else's ass while crawlin' like a procession of hypnotized infants. It was really damp, cold and sweaty inside the "cavern' room" as Tom had so loquaciously labeled the rock chamber.

"Now we're gonna' start this band of robbers called Tom Sawyer's Gang," my idol began his splendid explanation. "And everybody that wants to join my gang must solemnly take an oath and write his name in blood."

"But what if I don't want to use blood?" Ben Rogers foolishly objected. "What if I wants to use somethin' else?"

Tom Sawyer was one smart cookie. My pal knew that him and me had already gone through puberty, and could squirt semen all over the damned place, but that Ben and Joe couldn't, because the two punks were younger, and didn't even have hair under their arms or on their tiny balls to be able to ejaculate. "Okay Ben," Tom austerely replied. "If ya' all are afraid of usin' blood to sign your name, we'll all then use our own semen. That way we can all jerk-off and use our body fluids to do the trick. Since semen is almost transparent, it'll be just like usin' invisible ink!"

"No thanks!" Ben Rogers mildly protested. "On second thought, blood's perfectly fine with me."

So then, Tom whipped-out a folded sheet of paper from his pants' pocket, and marvelously read a historic oath he had written during a recent moment of inspiration. "Every kid must stick to the band and not tell anybody any of our sacred secrets," my closest friend proclaimed like a colonial town crier, or a loudmouthed somebody like that in olden days.

"What does ya' mean by secrets?" Joe Harper questioned.

"I popped my thirty-first load yesterday," I bragged, "so I guess the fact that *you,* Joe, doesn't yet have hair around your pecker would be one of the club's secrets too, along with Ben bein' a disgustin' gay virgin."

"Good example, Huck," Tom agreed and complimented, showing a degree of admiration. "In fact, it was a perfect example. Now let me continue with what we're gonna' swear to do, and also not to do. Now, if anybody tells anyone in Hannibal any secret of our gang, then that kid will not eat, drink, sleep, piss, or shit until *he* kills everybody in his friggin' family as a penance. Is that simple fact fuckin' clear?"

"As clear as I can piss my bladder empty without any yellow appearin' in the fluid," I appropriately stated. "Yellow definitely shows cowardice!"

"And the sign of our gang is gonna' be a double cross, because-that's what we're goin' to be doin'; we're gonna' trick, rob and double-cross everyone else in Hannibal. Now then, you three genuine, non-religious assholes know exactly how we're goin' to keep the goddamned devil away from snoopin' on our fraudulent activities," Tom emphasized. "And if an unfaithful gang member squeals on anyone else, that dirty rat must carve the cross deeply into both breasts of all his family members, after he kills 'em off, one by one."

"Isn't that rule a little harsh and cruel?" Ben Rogers nervously questioned.

"Well Ben, if ya' don't kill your family in twenty-four hours, then Huckleberry and me is gonna' cut your dick and balls off, and use 'em as fish bait. Ya' got any more asinine, nonsensical objections to raise?"

"Er, none at all!" Ben amiably agreed with a worried expression showing upon his face. "After I pop my first big load, I wanna' still have a dick and balls left to do it at least twice a day!"

"And anyone else outside the band that uses our adopted symbol, which is the Sawyer Cross, must be sued," Tom proceeded with expressing his extraordinary bullshit. "And that includes the damned preacher, and the fucked-up town undertaker. too. Do ya' country-bumpkin shit-heads all understand that pertinent bullshit?"

We all mechanically nodded our heads showin' our fathomin' of Tom's infallible declaration, and totally affirming our dumb-ass, wholehearted endorsement of his fallible insanity.

"And furthermore," Tom dramatically read from his prepared written oath. "Any kid in the gang that tells any confidential secrets, in addition to havin' his dick and balls cut-off and used for fish bait, then that stupid-shit will have to also have his throat slashed at the jugular; his carcass burned in the blacksmith's furnace, and his cursed ashes scattered all over this here secret cave," Tom pompously lectured. "Then, the craven asshole's name will be blotted off the club's list, and the dishonored fuck-head will be forgotten by the remainder of the members in-good-standin', until the day *they* officially die."

"Is that all?" Joe Harper incredulously inquired before taking a deep gulp that made his Adam's apple do an involuntary yo-yo routine three times.

"There's one more important particular I gotta' mention," Tom haughtily continued. "If a member reveals any secret of the gang, an evil curse will haunt that evicted and disgraced member's family for the next thousand generations."

Everybody agreed that Tom had orchestrated one fantastic oath to swear by, because next to playin' with our miniature erect dingles, we all loved to indiscriminately curse and swear.

"Did ya' think of all that neat bullshit all on your own?" I asked infallible Tom Sawyer. "Or did you find-out all of those terrific ideas in a library book?"

"No, Huck, you dumb-ass fuck!" our gang leader defensively answered. "I read some of the things outa' stolen pirate books, and others from certain robber journals. But actually, every high-toned gang here in Missouri has a similar damned code of ethics!"

Ben Rogers then thought of an irregularity that could have been embarrassin' to me. "Huck Finn here ain't got no family to kill, if *he* tells any of our confidential secrets," the conniving, little bastard declared. "What's ya' gonna' do about *him?*"

Tom contemplated the potential conflict for a moment. "Well, ain't Huck got a father?" our fearless leader retardedly retorted.

"Sure, he's got a biological father, but the deadbeat's abandoned Huck," that detestable little prick, Ben Rogers, maintained. "Huck's pappy is always lyin' drunk and wallowin' with Farmer Gray's hogs every time I see him in town. But he's been missin' from civilization for over a year now, either dead, or gallivantin' all over creation."

"Isn't Ben tellin' one of *my* secrets?" I yelled and balked.

"Yeah, but he's tellin' it to gang members, so that don't violate any of our oath!" Tom objectively clarified.

The fellas' discussed my unique predicament concerning a lack of family to kill, and the guys were going to leave me out, sayin' that everybody in the club ought to have a family, or a legitimate father to kill, or else the entire scenario would not be fair and equitable to each of the other members. Everyone was *stumped* without even having a damned sawed-off tree-trunk anywhere nearby, so we all sat there like moronic jerk-offs. I felt like I was about to burst into tears, or go into a hysterical tirade, and violently beat the shit out of Joe and Ben, and then make them suck my dick, when all of a sudden, a flash streaked across my mind, and I was miraculously enlightened.

"Hey guys," I ecstatically yelled. "What about Miss Watson to offer for sacrifice? You guys would have fun executin' an old formal nasty *Bible*-totin' bitch like her!"

"Oh, she'll do!" Tom defended my suggestion in direct support of my desperate-but-creative proposal. "I ain't never killed no eighty-year-old practicin' lesbian before. But I guess I gotta' stab or shoot her from behind, before the queer old lady turns-around and gets her *licks* in with the Widow Douglas!"

Then, upon Tom's very excellent instruction, the four of us all stuck a pin in our dicks and squeezed the blood into a small cup that our leader had brought along just for consummating the formal initiation ceremony. And with the accumulated blood extracted from the four members' dangling peckers, we then had sufficient red ink to sign our names to the official document. My limp penis really badly hurt, because Tom said the blood had to be obtained from the heads of our sensitive dingles, and not from the damned shafts.

"Now," Ben Rogers articulated in an adult-like mellow voice. "What the hell's the line of business for this damned gang? Are we gonna' rape and screw grandmothers, or are we gonna' terrorize dispensable senior-citizen lesbians like Miss Watson and the Widow Douglas, and possibly even our leader's wonderful Aunt Polly."

"Well, to start off with, until we get some valid operatin' experience," Tom replied while chewing on a length of straw extending-out from his mouth, "we're gonna' rob rich people, and hold them hostage. And if the captured aristocrats give us any verbal shit, we're gonna' murder them, real savage like."

"But there ain't many really rich folks in Hannibal to keep the gang busy for more than a week!" Joe Harper ridiculously argued.

"And if we only steal cattle and rob houses," Ben Rogers interrupted, "we will be…"

"Look turd-head!" Tom yelled at the obnoxious kid, who was tryin' to impress us with his general ignorance and arrogance. "Stealin' cattle ain't robbery, and breakin' into houses ain't robbery, either. Those damned juvenile practices are only examples of burglary. Burglars ain't got no damned style or class. We're desperados, daring highwaymen," Tom eloquently editorialized. "We're gonna' stop stages, and buggy carriages on the road while wearin' masks, and then we'll first kill all the men and shave the women's pussies just for fun."

"Must we always shave women's pussies and then kill them?" Ben Rogers declared. "I don't think we oughta' kill women with fine hairy pussies; especially beautiful blondes; that's what the hell I'm thinking! We could glue the pussy hairs together, and sell them as men's toupees!"

"Well," Tom elaborated. "We could bring the women with the hairiest pussies here to this cave and hold 'em for ransom. That would be a lot of fun I suppose."

"Ransom?" Ben Rogers innocently asked. "What the hell's that?"

"I really don't know for sure," Tom insincerely replied. "But that's what the hell pirates and gangs do in those damned books I was tellin' ya' about, so naturally that's what the hell we've gotta' do to have any style and decent class."

"But how can we do it if we don't know what it is we gotta' do?" the apprehensive Ben Rogers queried with a very confused look on his damned grotesque-looking face. "This gang is gonna' be doin' some illogical things!"

"Look, Asshole. Have ya' ever gotten laid and popped a heavy load inside a pretty girl or lovely lady?" Tom challenged.

"Er, no!" Ben admitted in pure humiliation.

"Well then, virgin Asshole. I've done that damned easy thing many, many times," Tom boasted. "But the first time, though, I didn't know what the hell I was doin'. But it all came naturally to me after I got started. The same thing's gonna' happen with ransomin'. It's gonna' come natural to ya', once ya' start, I guarantee it!"

"If ya' say so," Ben conceded with his head crestfallen. "If ya' say so!" the asshole obediently reiterated.

"And furthermore," Tom elucidated. "Since ransomin' is all done and already explained in books, we can't do anythin' any damned different, or else things will get all muddled-up. We gotta' believe what the books say, whether we think the published words are fucked-up, or not! That is, we gotta' believe every damned book except the damned *Good Book* that the fucked-up Widow and Miss Watson always read like their worthless lives depend on it."

"Oh, Tom, that's all quite grand and wonderful," Joe Harper butted in. "But how in tar-nation are these hostages goin' to be ransomed if we don't know how to ransom them? That's the thing I want to get at. Now, what do *you* reckon this ransomin' bullshit really is?"

"Well Shit-head," Tom angrily answered. "If we keep the prisoners until they're officially ransomed, it probably means we keep them hostage until they're officially dead. Now stop annoyin' and aggravatin' me with your trivial horse-crap!"

"Now, look who's talkin' bullshit!" Ben intrepidly chimed-in. "Those hostages will drive us broke, always havin' to be fed and attended to. They'll be eatin' up all our food, and then always tryin' to escape our custody. I say we just kill 'em and save ourselves plenty of money and aggravation."

"Okay Ben," Tom said with a wide grin. "As commander of this here gang, I'll appoint *you'* official executioner, so that *you* can kill all the adults we capture and take hostage."

"Er Tom," the neurotic Ben Rogers stammered. "I was only suggestin' that one of us would have to stay-up all night and all day guardin' the captives. But if that's what's necessary until we figure-out exactly what *ransom* means, then I guess we'll have to do it before decidin' to kill or execute our friggin' captives."

"Tom's right!" I interrupted, sticking-up for my closest chum before we ever attempted our first stick-up. "If it says in books that we gotta' ransom people, then that's what the hell we're gonna' do before we kill anybody. I mean," I stipulated. "Don't you silly assholes think that the people that wrote and made the books know what the hell they're talkin' about or doin'?" I rhetorically argued. "And besides; the Widow has a dictionary in her living room, and I'll look the word 'ransom' up, and then report its definition at our next damned meetin'."

"Okay, with me," Ben Rogers enthusiastically subscribed to my fantastic proposition. "And if 'ransom' means shavin' ladies' hairy pussies, I'm gonna' ransom as many of 'em as I can get my hands on. I mean; women have much more hair on their cookies than girls our age do; I'm pretty certain that *that's* for damned sure!"

"That's a great idea!" Joe Harper acknowledged. "We'll have Ben kill all the damned men, and then we'll ransom all the women and have enough fine curly pubic hair to go into the wig business. Other than that, I ain't got nothin' exceptional to say or report."

"I don't want to kill nobody!" Ben squawked. "I just wanna' shave and lick the ladies' hairy pussies! But first though, I think I should practice shavin' and lickin' my mom's pet housecat!"

"But ya' joined my gang, and you'll have to abide by *my* rules!" Tom screamed at the puzzled and disenchanted squirming kid. "And I aim to kick *your* ass black and blue, and black again, if ya' dare defy my authority! Get the message, Asshole!"

Ben shut his mouth tight, and Joe and Tom really gave *him* the raspberry, even though a kid named Huckleberry was present. And poor Ben Rogers had to suffer Tom and Joe's perpetual tormentin', or else the annoying brat would have to be beaten-up (by them) in front of me for my distinct pleasure.

So, then Tom Sawyer was unanimously elected President of the gang, and Joe Harper was installed as Captain. I was appointed Vice-President, and Ben Rogers was elected "Three to one" as "Chief Wimp and Sissy". And we all were elated when Tom announced that each of us would get to be "Sergeant-at-Arms, Legs, and Pussies" on a wonderful weekly rotating basis.

"The Jumping Frog"
Mark Twain

When Samuel Langhorne Clemens (a.k.a. Mark Twain) was a barefoot lad growing-up in Hannibal, Missouri, the boy worked as a typesetter for his older brother Orion's newspaper, the *Journal*. Later, the master storyteller ventured-out onto the muddy *Mississippi River* and learned the challenging trade of riverboat pilot under the expert tutelage of Horace Bixby.

Then, the tragedy of the *American Civil War* broke-out, so the mighty *Mississippi* was closed-down to commercial navigation in 1861. Out of his piloting job, Mark Twain packed his bags and headed west, seeking a new career as possibly a gold prospector, or an aspiring newspaper journalist. In May of 1864, Twain left the Nevada Territory and journeyed to San Francisco, where the industrious journalist penned his first (and most famous) classic tall tale, "The Celebrated Jumping Frog of Calaveras County". The innovative, satirical work appeared in the New York *Saturday Press* on November 18, 1865, and the cynical humorist Mark Twain became an overnight sensation. Herein, lies a vain retelling of the literary giant's inimitable landmark story.

A stranger rode his horse into Angel's Camp, an old dilapidated mining village situated in Calaveras County, California. The visitor was seeking information about a friend of a friend of his, and the former Angel's resident was reputed to be one Leonidas W. Smiley.

The traveler tied-up his horse at a hitching post and entered the nearly deserted Angel's Saloon, where the visitor came across an old geezer sleeping and snoring in a rickety, antique, wooden chair that looked as if it indeed had rickets. Upon waking up, the fat, elderly bald-headed, gentleman introduced himself to the itinerant eastern guest as the Honorable Simon Wheeler.

"Where can I find Leonidas W. Smiley?" the visitor to the camp inquired. "He was a boyhood friend of a close friend of mine, and supposedly, later became a devout minister of the Gospel; and that's the Gospel truth, and not random bullshit. Last reports indicate that this Smiley character was prospectin' for gold right here in Angel's Camp, Calaveras County."

"Well, howdy there, stranger," old garrulous Simon Wheeler casually greeted his unexpected visitor. "We don't get too many easterners visitin' us out here in fool's gold country. That gold rush everyone's in heat about is nothin' but a big bust. Yessiree stranger; that's exactly what the hell it is. A big bust!" Simon Wheeler emphasized as his dilated pupils turned to a wall calendar and intensely scrutinized a big-breasted nude woman massaging her impressive, huge tits, featuring big brown succulent nipples.

"Well, Sir, what about Leonidas W. Smiley?" the eastern dude with a distinctive New England accent asked Mr. Wheeler. "That is to say, the Reverend Leonidas W. Smiley."

"You must mean old Jim Smiley!" the bald-headed, slightly addled old codger exclaimed. "I've known cucumbers and eggplants that are smarter than him. Well anyway, Stranger," Simon Wheeler disclosed. "Jim Smiley's the only Smiley I've ever had the pleasure of knowing here in Angel's Mining Camp, so just sit back and relax while I tell ya' all I can think of about that stupid asshole."

The friendly stranger pulled-up a chair and sat-down between a cracker-barrel and a hot potbelly stove, politely listening to the exaggerated tale manufactured and presented by the pot-bellied old whiskerando, Simon Wheeler. The old feller' leaned forward in his creaky chair, corralling and blockading the visiting dude in one trapped corner of the cobweb-infested saloon.

Old Wheeler never smiled or frowned, nor did his voice vacillate or waver one iota. The camp orator began his contrived narrative without any noticeable enthusiasm or animation, as if his utterances were of some worldwide significance or academic profundity. The stranger dared not interrupt the loquacious speaker by stating any declarative or interrogative sentence, preferring to absorb the total impact of the preposterous story that *he* suspected was being facetiously fabricated and related.

"Reverend Leonidas W., well now, yes; Reverend Leonidas. Well Sir," Simon Wheeler began with a forced smile, "in the winter of '49, or maybe in the spring of '50, I ain't no goddamn historian ya' know; so, I don't recollect the time and date exactly. But I remember the giant mother-humpin' water flume that existed back then wasn't finished being built yet, when Smiley took his first half-hour piss in Angel's Swamp, and nearly killed all of the brave pike and the shiners swimmin' around in there. Smiley was the most curious jerk- off ya' ever wanted to see or meet, but above everything else, the asshole loved to bet and gamble on anything and everything."

"Bet and gamble?" the visitor challenged. "But I had deliberately said that Reverend Leonidas W. Smiley was a minister of the…"

"That's right, Stranger," Simon Wheeler asserted and stubbornly maintained. "This pud-puller Smiley was only happy when he was gamblin', playin' poker, or rollin' the friggin' dice. But the young bastard was lucky, uncommonly lucky," the old storyteller continued. "And that freakin' ball-buster would bet on anything from whose wife had the biggest knockers, to whose dick was the longest, either when soft or hard. Smiley would take any side he pleased, and when he wasn't bettin', he was always scratchin' his pimply ass or rubbin' his hairy balls; whichever happened to be closest to his overanxious right hand."

"Sir, in all due respect," the all-too-polite visitor earnestly insisted, "your description doesn't seem to match the Reverend Leonidas W. Smiley I was asked to...."

"Never mind that nonsensical, stupid bullshit!" Simon Wheeler exclaimed as if the chatty storyteller was a renegade mental patient exclusively hanging out at Angel's Saloon. "Now if there was a horse race, the lucky shit would either be flush, or be a big fuckin' loser at the end. Smiley even bet on which mare would have the most colts or fillies, claiming to be a sort of a *stud'* meister himself. But let me tell ya' Stranger," the old, whiskered fellow indiscreetly added, "I ain't never seen him stickin' his tiny dick inside of the old gray mare that ain't what the hell she used to be; now that she's authentically dead. And if there was a ..."

"Now just wait a minute," the sophisticated eastern Yankee visitor passing through Angel's Camp objected. "I come from a genteel Atlantic Coast town where all the folks are mannerly and docile, and I'm not used to hearing this sort of slang language being..."

"That's fuckin' perfectly all right!" reasserted old Wheeler as the accomplished speaker shoved his astonished guest back into *his* squeaky wooden chair. "Now, as I was stipulatin', this shit-head Smiley would bet on dog fights, catfights, chicken fights, female mud wrestlin', and on jerkin-off and female masturbation contests to see who would come to an orgasm first, or who would pop the biggest load the farthest. That son-of-a-bitch was the luckiest son-of-a-bitch I've ever..."

"I think I've heard enough!" the appalled visitor decided, and as the insulted guest attempted to rise and to vacate the premises, old Simon Wheeler roughly pushed him back into *his* chair to continue his remarkable dissertation.

"Now Sonny," the bawdy, risque narrator proceeded, "once there were two birds sittin' their asses on a fence, and instead of bettin' which one would fly away first, old Smiley bets the mayor which bird would take the first crap. Then, this fella' Jim again bets the mayor which bird would shit the most turds in the first half-hour. And once a straddle-bug was skitterin' all over the shit-eatin' wood-planked floor, right here in this armpit saloon, and old Smiley bet the visitin' governor of Vermont where the bug would eventually skitter to. Well," Wheeler elaborated. "The bug skittered its way right up the governor's wife's stockings, and tickled her crotch and aroused clit really good, until the cultured bitch wiggled and wriggled her fat fanny all over this here crowded saloon lookin' like a drunken hooker. The damned governor laughed so fuckin' hard that he gladly paid old Smiley the fifty dollars *he* had bet just to..."

"Now Sir, I believe I've heard enough of this barroom vulgar conversation coming from your filthy mouth," the embarrassed stranger balked. "So, if you don't mind, I'll be on my…"

Old Simon Wheeler forcefully knocked the red-faced guest back into *his* rickety chair, that actually looked like it had a worse case of rickets than the storyteller's flimsy rickety chair had. "Now Sir, like I was pertinently sayin', this bitchin' bastard guy named Jim Smiley would bet on anything. Once he bet Parson Walker when the preacher's wife took sick that she would die of malaria, and when she did pass away, the grievin' Parson had to pay Smiley a hundred dollars, and Smiley insisted that the bet be mentioned in the woman's obituary in the local *Gazette*. Smiley was a lot smarter than your average everyday ass-wiper, that's for damned sure. And also, when he…"

"Please Sir," the new arrival angrily-and-bitterly protested. "I have an important appointment in San Francisco and I must be on my…"

"Never mind about trivialities!" Simon Wheeler yelled in a very contrary tone as the saloon proprietor manhandled the thin, weak dignified visitor back into *his* creaky, rickety chair. "Ya' ain't leavin' until I get to finish the whole damned friggin' story. Now, this here Smiley had a mare he called the fifteen-minute nag, that reminded Smiley of *his* dead wife that he had shot in the head six times with a revolver because the nasty bitch always *nagged* the hell out of him. Anyways," Wheeler editorialized, "this female horse always would lose the goddamn race because she was pregnant and had distemper and asthma, and everything' else; so, Smiley had it all figured-out. The genius at betting used to give the old gray mare that wasn't what she used to be a hundred-yard head start, and the goddamn bitch would win the race every time by a lousy cunt hair; yes, she would. And the curious folks around these parts…"

"Sir, please excuse me, but I must take my horse to the livery station because he needs a new…"

"Now just a cotton-pickin' minute," chastised old Simon Wheeler as the aged control freak twisted the stranger's arm and thrust him back into *his* unstable wooden chair. "I thought you eastern guys was notorious for courtesy and for manners. You is actin' mighty uncivil and rude by wantin' to leave this here cozy room before I'm done with my intriguing tale. Now then," Wheeler commented and transitioned, "this asshole Smiley has this here bull hound dog pup he owned, and to look at the freak, ya' wouldn't want to give two red cents for his leash and collar, let alone for him. But Smiley had the vicious pecker-headed pup trained, ya' understand. As soon as money was placed down on the table in the form of a bet," the long-winded speaker elucidated, "the mutt's under-jaw, nose, and impressive dick all stuck-out straight ahead, and then the energized canine was a totally different *animule* altogether."

"What did Smiley call this weird-looking dog?" the stranger asked, exhibiting s degree of mild curiosity.

"I'm getting to that important detail," Wheeler mildly scolded. "Smiley named em' Andrew Jackson as a joke, because *he* knew his dog would do something *unpresidented (unprecedented).* When Andrew Jackson would get into a mean dogfight that was bet on, the old rascal would win every time by latchin' on with his choppers to the other dog's hind legs, and then bullyraggin' the other mongrel all over the damned place, until the other dog was whimpered into fuckin' submission," Simon Wheeler explained. "Andrew Jackson really knew how to kick ass really swell, and if his sharp teeth missed the other dog's hind legs, then the mutt would viciously bite the other cur's dick off, and swallow the tasty morsel just like it was a little hot dog wiener."

"Did Andrew Jackson ever lose a dogfight?" the stranger wanted to know. "I hope that this is the end of the Leonidas W. Smiley story!"

"Now I was getting to that prominent detail when *you* so rudely interrupted me," old Simon Wheeler reprimanded. "One day, Andrew Jackson got shucked-out bad, because the shaggy mutt the critter had to fight was as ferocious as a grisly grizzly bear. And besides that rather fairly-pertinent fact, the new dog everyone was bettin' on against Smiley had no friggin' hind legs; and when old Andrew Jackson went to bite the bitchin' freak, he didn't know what the fuck to do!" Simon Wheeler described in detail. "So, the other damned dog took the initiative, and bit and beat the shit out of old Andrew, and then bit *his* tender loins off and chewed them up good. Then, Smiley's dog just curled-up and died, and it always makes me feel remorse for old Andrew Jackson; yes, it does, the way it all ended for him and the way his fightin' career was radically terminated."

"Well, then," the totally dismayed stranger interrupted. "Did Smiley change his evil gambling ways after what had happened to his precious dog, Andrew Jackson?"

"No indeed!" Simon Wheeler testified. "Smiley became even more intent on bettin' and riskin' the damned odds. This here Smiley had rat terriers, and chicken cocks, and tomcats, and all them kinds of dip-shit varmints, and the addicted gambler would throw all of the nasty cantankerous *animules* into this here cock fightin' pit, which was really like a fuckin' *animule* sports' arena. The seven or eight species would have a big brawl," the storyteller expounded, "and everyone would put their dollars-down and bet which one would be the last creature standin'. That's how fucked-up Smiley was, and how fucked-up he had made everyone else stayin' here at Angel's Camp, preposterously prospectin' for fools' gold."

"Look Mr. Wheeler, I appreciate your fine hospitality," the uneasy visitor mentioned and exaggerated, "but I think I've heard enough equivocation about your Jim Smiley when I really need some tangible biographical data on the Reverend Leonidas W. Smiley."

When the visitor attempted to rise and escape *his* captivity inside Angel's Saloon, Simon Wheeler kicked the newcomer in the testicles, and then punched the stranger in the gut, knocking the air out of *his* lungs. Then, the eastern traveler had to sit there in excruciating pain and listen to the remainder of corpulent, bald-headed Simon Wheeler's stellar description of Jim Smiley's immoral and illicit betting exploits in Angel's Camp.

"Well Stranger," the old talkative fellow proceeded. "This here Smiley catched a frog down at the swamp one day, which was easy to do, because the swamp was swamped with frogs. The obsessed gambler then took the creature home and taught him how to jump great distances, even though it wasn't fuckin' leap year anywhere in Calaveras County. Old Smiley educated that frog in all the basics of jumpin', settin-up a pole, and next increasin' the pole's height each time. That fantastic frog even whirled in the air like a dizzy doughnut, doing somersaults and tumble-saults, and table salts, and the like, and the critter always came-down flat-footed like a smilin' Cheshire cat that intentionally falls outa' a tree."

Although the exasperated stranger was still in agony from the flurry of blows that had been administered to his solar plexus, which the decent gentleman had received from the incomparable Simon Wheeler, *he* still had the wherewithal to ask a rather relevant question. "Did Smiley's frog have a name?"

"I was just getting to that pertinent point, so don't fuckin' *jump* to conclusions!" the senile storyteller bristled and acknowledged. "Old Smiley would train this friggin' frog by makin' the thing leap-up and catch flies the master would dangle above the jumpin' poles. The two practiced the art and the science of jumpin' every single mornin', noon, and night until the fuckin' frog was the most skillful *hopper* in the whole damned area, even though he didn't look anything like a goddamned toilet!" Wheeler amusingly ascertained.

"But did the frog have a damned fuckin' name?" the frustrated fit-to-be-tied visitor, also a dedicated minister of the Gospel cursed.

"Well, Sir; I saw Smiley place old Daniel Webster down on the planked floor of this here dusty saloon: incidentally, Daniel Webster was the fuckin' flyin' frog's name, and then Smiley would yell out, 'Flies, Daniel, flies!' Well Sir," Simon Wheeler euphorically pointed out, "there weren't any damned flies around anymore to reward the damned hungry frog, but old Daniel Webster would jump-up a storm anyway, and break all existin' records, and win lots of cash for everyone interested in bettin' on *his* phenomenal leapin' ability!"

"Look Shit-head!" the virtuous, self-righteous minister turned ordinary person in and around Angel's Camp yelled. "How did the son-of-a-bitchin', mother-fuckin, cunt lappin' frog ever lose a turd-eatin'-bet for Smiley?"

"Well, Stranger; now you're finally talkin' my language!" Simon Wheeler answered and commended without even using a single curse word. "Ya' never did see a frog so modest, so humble, so gifted, and so straightforward as this fucked-up Daniel Webster was. Yes siree; when it came-down to fair and square jumpin' on a dead level plane," Wheeler boasted, "Daniel could cover more ground in one leap and hurtle over any obstacle better than any other non-royalty frog of his mediocre breed. Smiley would ante-up two twenty-dollar bills, and everyone else in attendance would cough-up and bet the incredible sum of forty dollars against Daniel, just to attempt bankrupting Smiley, so that *he* would quit gamblin' and bustin' everyone's friggin' stones all the goddamn time."

"Well, you crazy old, demented mother-fucker; what the fuck happened next?" the irate and now belligerent traveling minister demanded in a totally out-of-character rant.

"I'm getting to that particular highlight," Simon Wheeler promised. "But Stranger, ya' gotta' oblige me with some old-fashioned western patience. Old Smiley was monstrous proud of his special frog, and he kept it in a latticed box', I guess more of a cage than a goddamned box. One day, a feller,' a real wise-ass in the camp came across Jim Smiley carrying his box containin' Daniel. The braggart asked Smiley rather matter-of-factly, 'Say, what the fuck does ya' got in that peculiar box'?"

"Look Mr. Wheeler, I really have to…"

"Just sit-down and fuckin' relax your testicles before ya' make me have conniptions!" Simon Wheeler insisted, as the saloon owner smashed the visiting minister back into *his* rickety wooden chair. "And Smiley answered the feller' sorta' indifferent like, saying, "It might be a parakeet; it might be a mongoose, or it might be a castrated canary, but it's not. It's a goddamn fuckin' ordinary, non-fancy frog sittin' quietly inside this silly box!' And then the camp newcomer looked at the frog careful-like, slowly turning the latticed box all around this way and that, and the jerk-off starkly says to Smiley, 'Say, Buddy; so it is a goddamn fuckin' ordinary, non-fancy frog. What's he good for'?"

"And what the fuck did that stupid asshole Jim Smiley say in response?" the almost-livid visitor to Angel's Camp asked from his imprisonment in the rickety wooden chair.

"Oh well," Wheeler genially replied. "Smiley says rather easy and carefree. "He's good for one thing, I should ascertain; and that is he can out-jump any other goddamned frog in Calaveras County'."

"This story is absolute bullshit!" the visitor-minister vociferously objected. "I'm getting' the hell outa' here right now!"

Old Simon Wheeler administered a frenetic flurry of expert karate and judo' chops to the parson's neck, diaphragm, groin, penis, and ass, and soon the stranger was once again seated, slouched-down in his all-too-familiar squeaky, creaky, rickety, wooden chair.

"Now then," the tale's principal narrator proceeded speaking to his now unconscious audience of one, "the rookie passin' through Angel's Camp peered-inside the latticed box and cleverly says to Smiley, 'I don't see any points about your asshole frog that's any better than any other asshole frog I've ever seen'!"

"Maybe ya' do, and maybe ya' don't know didley-squat about frogs and am-fib-ians," Smiley said to the limp and listless injured stranger. "Maybe ya' don't understand the science of frogs, or maybe you're still a rank amateur just like most local assholes are. I'll risk ya' forty dollars sayin' that old Daniel Webster here can out-jump any other frog in Calaveras County. Well Stranger, the new fellow studied the latticed cage and its sole occupant for a full minute, and then aptly answered Smiley, 'Sir, I'm only a dumb greenhorn here in Angel's Camp, but if I had a healthy frog, I would surely bet ya'!"

After a brief pause, old Simon Wheeler continued his expository narrative. "Then Jim Smiley felt compelled to favorably respond to the suave man's blatant challenge. 'That's okay, that's all right!' the native resident said. 'If you'll hold this lattice box for a minute, I'll hustle-down to the swamp and catch ya' a comparable frog that will jump against old Daniel'!"

The listless stranger that had been brutally assaulted, mugged and molested by Simon Wheeler was now regaining full semi-consciousness. The parson shook his head and reacquired some semblance of sensibility. "What the fuck happened?" the groggy minister asked in reference to *his* recently administered pain and suffering, and not requesting more details about Simon Wheeler's hyperbole involving Jim Smiley and Daniel Webster.

"Well Sir," Wheeler characteristically blustered, "the feller' put-up his forty dollars next to Smiley's bet, and then he sat-down to wait for Jim to return from the pond with a capable specimen to jump against Daniel Webster. Then the wily jerk-off got a most brilliant idea," Simon Wheeler indicated with great admiration. "He took a teaspoon out of his coat pocket, filled it up with quail shot, and meticulously poured the special ingredient down Daniel's throat. The guileful asshole repeated this deceitful act with the spoon at least twenty shit-eatin' times, until Daniel finally weighed at least five more pounds than usual!"

"Look Asshole!" the stranger-minister defiantly blurted-out. "I don't give a shit about Jim Smiley or his mother-fuckin' frog. I only came here to fuckin' find-out some information about the Reverend Leonidas W. Smiley."

"I'm getting' to that essential idea, so just mind your p's and q's, and I'll tell ya'. My God, Mr.! I ain't never met somebody as rambunctious and as spoiled rotten as you are, and with such a goddamned short attention span! Anyway," Wheeler snorted after spitting a large green lunger into a floor spittoon. "Smiley stepped out to the swamp and slopped-around in the mud like a happy pig in shit. Jim catched a nice-lookin' frog, and brought it back to this here saloon where the thrillin' jumpin' contest was goin' to be held."

"If you don't tell me about Leonidas W. Smiley soon," the perturbed Reverend threatened, "I'm gonna' tear this fuckin' saloon apart and crush your goddamn balls into mince-meat!"

"I'm tellin' ya' about Leonidas in a minute, so stop threatenin' my ass," Simon Wheeler pledged and demanded. "Smiley hands the new frog to the stranger and commands, 'Now when you're ready, set your critter alongside Daniel, and I'll give the startin' numbers.' Well, the greenhorn did exactly as Jim had dictated, and then Smiley yelled out 'One, two, three-jump!' The new frog from the pond hopped off lively-like, but old Daniel had indigestion and couldn't budge an inch; just like he was anchored into the floor planks. Smiley was surprised and disgusted, but Jim didn't have no clue as to what the fuck was wrong with old Daniel!"

"I wanta' know exactly what the fuck ever happened to that evasive bastard Reverend Leonidas W. Smiley!" the visitor-Preacher screamed like an incensed maniac.

"Just hold your damned horses, and I'll tell ya'!" wildly exclaimed Simon Wheeler. "The scamming feller' took Smiley's forty-dollars and paced to the swingin' doors over yonder, and turned and bellowed, 'I don't see any points about your asshole frog that's any different or better than any other asshole frog I've ever seen before'!"

"Damn it! What about fuckin' Leonidas W. Smiley, or I'll rip your balls right out of your scrotum and then fanatically choke you to death with my bare hands!" the normally passive Minister deliriously boomed at Wheeler.

"Now then," the master storyteller calmly proceeded, "Smiley just stood there scratchin' the damned dandruff out of his scalp; lookin' at Daniel Webster for the longest time and sayin' over and over again, 'What the hell's wrong with this fuckin' frog!' at least five hundred times. Jim catched and lifted the fat frog by the neck and saw that the critter weighed at minimum five pounds, and understood that Daniel couldn't leap worth a damn if *his* hopping-mad life depended on it. And then," Simon Wheeler paused as the old codger inhaled a large quantity of air. "Jim Smiley turns the frog upside-down, and the *animule* belched-out two handfuls of heavy quail shot. And then Jim became madder than all hell that's being full of aggravated hornets. Smiley threw the frog onto the planked floor, and sprinted-out through the swingin' doors, runnin' hard after the abominable, clever feller' that sneakily tricked him; but Smiley never catched-up with him and…"

"But what about that stupid jerk-off asshole, fuckin' Reverend Leonidas W. Smiley?" the traveling Preacher insisted.

"Well, Stranger," Wheeler tersely added. "The greenhorn with the victorious frog happened to be your Reverend Leonidas W. Smiley. He's the one that broke Jim Smiley's balls but good with the quail shot trick, and also in the process, broke Smiley of his terrible gamblin' habit, too!"

Just then, wrinkled-face Simon Wheeler heard a saloon patron calling his inglorious name from the other end of the bar. "Just stay where ya' are, Stranger. I'll only be gone for a second once I serve that drunken lush a double-shot bourbon. I just gotta' tell ya' about this here mother-jumpin', one-eyed, quill-less porcupine that didn't have no tail or testicles, but only a short, stumpy projection, and a nose that was a weird cross between a very green banana and a very ripe watermelon."

At that junction, the traveling-Minister became so fed-up with, and so pissed-off at old Simon Wheeler that the itinerant Preacher reached his right hand down to the old timer's huge testicles, and squeezed with all his might. The man effectively and literally crushed the storyteller's balls, as those nuggets had never been crushed before. "There Fuck-head!" the traveling Parson triumphantly hollered. "Just like Jim Smiley had been cured of gamblin', I hope that you're balls bein' busted will ultimately cure you of your idiotic exaggerated storytellin', you obnoxious, arrogant, egotistical asshole!"

And with those magnificent words, the self-satisfied Preacher limped-out of the almost-empty western saloon, unhitched his black stallion, and climbed atop *his* faithful horse, leaving old Simon Wheeler bent over in sheer agony inside Angel's Saloon.

The recipient of the minister's vengeful wrath was wishing that he had the balls to tell the old drunk seated at the bar the fascinating story about the quill-less porcupine without a tail and having a nose that was a weird cross between a green banana and a ripe watermelon. Fortunately, discretion prevailed, and old, agonizing Simon Wheeler remained perfectly silent as the bullshitting Western bard poured the old drunk a delicious double bourbon.

"Perseus and Medusa"
Nathaniel Hawthorne

Acrisius was king of Argos, and the tyrant was so full of shit that the mental case daily sat on a golden toilet instead of upon a golden throne. Besides always taking lengthy craps, slapping his monkey, and scratching his royal ass most of each day, the king (just like all other ancient rulers of Argo) was notorious for telling anyone and everyone who asked about his city-kingdom, "Ar-go fuck yourself'!" The worst part about the entire fiasco was that chronically constipated King Acrisius thought that *his* single redundant hundred-year-old joke was actually funny.

The King of Argos had a beautiful daughter named Danae, who had a bad habit of walking in the woods and then dreaming about getting laid by some horny forest god having multiple sex organs. One day Danae was picking daffodils near a grotto when Zeus, king of the gods, happened to be sauntering by on his way to Ethiopia to visit his fellow Olympian Apollo, who had recently had a new magnificent temple erected in *his* honor in that distant African land below Egypt.

Upon seeing Danae's many charms, Zeus immediately got a gargantuan hard-on, and felt that he had to plant his rod inside the nearest mortal vagina. Danae was mesmerized by the King-god's magic wand, which of course was erect, huge, long, thick, and throbbing. The pretty nymphomaniac then made a major mistake in judgment. Instead of giving Zeus a super-duper excellent blow-job, she got on her back, opened her hairy eager beaver, and had the royal poop pumped out of her until her face nearly turned as purple as Zeus's pulsating bazooka.

A month later, Danae missed her period and discovered that she was indeed pregnant. Her child would be half-*divine* and half-human; whereas, grapes are totally "the vine" fruit, and her child might also be *divine fruit of the womb* if he or she (the potential fruit) turned-out to be gay, either homo' or lesbian.

Danae rushed to her constipated father, Acrisius, seated upon his golden hopper, and told the monarch the bad news. The thoroughly upset full-of-shit king instantly got severe diarrhea, and almost died from a bad case of dehydration.

"Danae, first Lord Zeus screwed the crap out of you in *the forbidden mating woods,* but now he's going to screw me really good, too!" the king lamented while awkwardly wiping his smelly ass with rough cabbage leaves.

"I don't understand exactly what you mean, father?" Danae replied.
"I didn't know you had a vagina!"

"Danae, I don't have a goddamned vagina, and if I did, I'd pour cement in the hole, and seal the fucker up! Anyway, my dear daughter," Acrisius continued. "A few years back, I had journeyed to *Delphi* to visit Apollo's *Oracle* there, and find out my future!"

"That was more stupid than being screwed by Zeus!" the daughter abruptly answered. "The Oracle always predicts gloom and doom, and never augurs happy tidings. You would've been better off, father, seeing Medusa's face and being turned into stone. Then, you wouldn't have to shit into your golden hopper and suffer dehydration all of the damned time!"

"Anyway, dear daughter," the king went on as the imbecile wiped his fat ass with red onion peels, since he had used-up all the coarse cabbage leaves, "I asked the Oracle if I would ever have a son, but the prophetess predicted that I would only have a daughter, who would eventually bear a son who would eventually grow-up to kill me! And now it's fuckin' happening in real time!" the king insanely screamed. "That blooming seed planted inside your womb is half divine, and when the boy grows-up, he's gonna' eliminate your old man's shittin' ass right off the fuckin' planet!"

"How do you know the sex of the baby that has not yet been born?" Danae challenged. "How do you know I'll definitely have a boy?"

"Because I trust the Oracle a lot more than I trust you and your promiscuous snatcheroo!" the king countered. "And besides Danae, the Oracle has cement up *her* crotch, and wouldn't bull-shit me for sex, or anything else cheap and vulgar, just to get her freakin' rocks off like you've always desire doing!"

Nine months quickly passed. Acrisius became extremely distraught and disconsolate, and not wanting to have Danae executed by the royal hangman, the cruel king placed his daughter and her child in a large chest, and had the pair cast out to sea. The indiscriminate waves carried the floating, waterproof box to the island of Seriphos, where a handsome fisherman named Dictys retrieved Danae and her crying baby from the pounding surf that was violently smashing into treacherous rocks.

Dictys shared his home and possessions with the lovely disowned princess, and with her strong-lunged crybaby son. The fisherman never had sex with the attractive woman because once Dictys learned the boy's father was the chief *Olympian*, the discreet fellow didn't want to be shafted up the ass by one of Zeus's dazzling, electrified billion-volt lightning bolts.

Seventeen-years elapsed, and the boy had matured into a young strong sailor, who journeyed to many islands in the vicinity to engage in trading whores for harlots, and bartering prostitutes for hookers. Danae had named her son Perseus, but all of the natives of Seriphos believed the lad to be "son of Zeus" because of his terrific biceps, his firm chest, and his cute compact butt.

Perseus was adept at boxing, wrestling, bullshitting, and javelin throwing, but the accomplished athlete also possessed admirable social qualities that engendered courtesy, virtue, humility, and justice. But trauma was certain to accompany drama in Perseus's life on the small island of myriad idle gossipers, along with mentally-sick, perpetual masturbators.

Dictys' brother was Polydickdees, ruthless king of Seriphos, who incidentally had three uncircumcised penises. The ruler was extraordinarily evil, cruel, villainous, conniving, greedy, and arrogant. And when Polydickdees saw Danae, his *privates* began *publicly* throbbing and pulsating, like a divining rod, or like Zeus's divine rod. While Perseus was at sea and unable to defend his mother's welfare at home on Seriphos, Polydickdees took Danae away from Dictys' jurisdiction and said to her, "If you will not be my wife, then you'll most-certainly be my servant. What is your response, woman?"

"I wouldn't marry you if you had the only dick and the only set of balls in the whole wide world!" Danae snottily retorted, not knowing that the freak-of-nature king had three uncircumcised peckers and seven uncircumcised testicles. "I'd rather fool around with bananas, squash, and cucumbers than have any kind of sex with you, oral or otherwise, you big, selfish, dumb, braggart asshole!" Danae lambasted Polydickdees.

Meanwhile, on the island of Samos where Perseus's ship was taking on a cargo of harlots, hookers and slaves, the handsome sailor stepped into a nearby woods to take a long leak. A twelve-foot-tall woman approached with a bronze helmet on her head, and the female figure was carrying winged sandals, a bronze shield over her shoulder, and a bronze spear in her right hand.

'When the hell are we Greeks ever going to get out of the damned *Bronze Age?*' Perseus thought. 'There must be more to this stupid age than ridiculous copper and tin alloy!'

The tall luscious babe then spoke to the young sailor, who blushed as the young man tucked his pecker, still dripping urine, back under his tunic. "Perseus, you must perform a special errand for me," the tall deity requested.

"Who are you, giant lady, and how do you know my name is Perseus? Are you a glamorous spy, or are you a gorgeous woodland prostitute? If you want my opinion about woman that put out," the young sailor mentioned, "I'd prefer if you were a gorgeous woodland harlot, for I have no money to pay for a vivacious woodland prostitute!"

"I am neither," the voluptuous goddess disclosed. "I am Pallas Athene, daughter of Lord Zeus, and goddess of *Olympus.* And I can read goodness in a man's heart, and I've readily detected *that* abstract quality in yours. Tell me, dear Perseus," Pallas Athene continued. "Would you rather have a soul of fire, or would you truly prefer a soul of clay?"

Perseus considered the enchanting goddess's proposition, even though Pallas Athene was not trying to proposition him. "Definitely a soul of fire," the lad wisely answered. "For it's a lot better to know adventure and die in the flower of youth than to be like a cow chewing its cud in the field for an entire boring lifetime. For fame and honor go to those possessing souls of fire," the youth eloquently elaborated, "even though those with souls of clay often become rich kings; live in colossal palaces; get laid every night, and can afford all of the best hookers and prostitutes available in the whole damned ancient world!"

"You've chosen wisely," Pallas Athene commended while holding up her bronze shield so that Perseus could view an image that was being reflected from it. "See here, Perseus; do you have the courage to slay *this* terrible monster, Medusa the Gorgon? She has vipers for hair; formidable talons and claws for hands and feet, and the creature bites men's dicks off when giving very bad unprofessional blow-jobs. What do you think of the ugly bitch?"

"She's the most hideous creature my eyes have ever beheld, and I'll certainly cross my legs and eat a pound of saltpeter before I ever confront her," Perseus promised the heavenly goddess. "Where can I find the ugly thing?"

"You're too young at present, and not yet ready to assassinate her," Athene politely chastised. "So, kindly return to Seriphos, and when the time is right, you shall answer the challenge, and be equal to the task," the beautiful goddess promised.

"Okay, I'll be glad to kill Medusa as long as I don't have to lose my virginity, along with my sensitive dick, screwing the venom out of her," Perseus agreed. "For all I know, the Gorgon might have metal jaws planted up her snatch, and that fate might even be worse than receiving a damned fatal blow-job from her ravenous lips, and from her poisonous, dagger-like fangs!"

The goddess then instantaneously vanished *into thin air,* because goddesses, like magicians, wizards and sorcerers, hadn't yet mastered the technique of vanishing into thick air, since factories with smokestacks didn't exist back then to lethally pollute the atmosphere. So, ambitious Perseus obediently returned to Seriphos, where his ears heard gossip that his mother had become a lowly slave in ostentatious King Polydickdees's opulent palace.

The livid young sailor dashed the full mile to the pretentious king's residence, and darted from room to room, desperately searching for his mother. The muscular sailor came across Danae turning a hand millstone and crying her tits off. Evil Polydickdees then entered the chamber, followed by his brother, the benign-but-poor Dictys.

"Craven tyrant!" Perseus recklessly and imprudently shouted at the always-scheming king. The enraged *Adonis* quickly lifted up the simple hand-operated machine that Danae had been rotating. "Mom!" the incensed sailor yelled. "Has *this* mother-fucker been screwing you against your will?" Perseus bellowed as *he* raised-up the run-of-the-mill basic everyday grindstone to use to split-open the suddenly fearful king's cranium.

"Please, my son. Show tolerance and restraint!" Danae begged. "We are but lowly strangers in this hostile land, and must act humbly and not haughtily, although I wish you could break Polydickdees' head, ass, and balls open before I have to again diligently *put my nose to the damned grindstone!*"

"Your mother is right!" counseled passive and wise Dictys. "If you do to my wicked brother what we'd all like to do to my wicked brother," the honorable fisherman noted, "then all of the ignorant people of Seriphos will fall upon us, and then viciously kill us. That's because all of the fucked-up people of Seriphos love being governed by my fucked-up, evil, reprehensible brother. How could I ever explain it to you more logically?"

Polydickdees had been trembling as if the repugnant despot had been experiencing a one-man earthquake. Perseus lowered the heavy hand mill that had been elevated above his head, set it upon the stone floor, and then quickly ceased being so *mill*itant. The son of Zeus grabbed his mother's hand and conducted her to the island's temple of Pallas Athene, where Danae was accepted by the resident priestess as a floor and altar sweeper, along with being a temple marquee scrubber, and a dust and ass wiper, because vacuum cleaners, feather-dusters, and utilitarian toilet paper hadn't yet been invented.

Now, pernicious Polydickdees was a cunning old bastard, and the son-of-a-bitch plotted to somehow get Danae back in *his* custody, and permanently removed from the temple's safe sanctuary. Of course, the king could have sent his soldiers to kidnap Danae at the temple, or to kill the impudent Perseus and the benevolent Dictys at their home, but the sinister distator had never endorsed simple solutions to complex problems, and preferred living and anguishing with difficult decisions.

So, the nefarious king schemed-up a rather complicated trap to send his chief nemesis on "an impossible mission of no return". Polydickdees organized a massive feast, and invited all of the island's nobility and dignitaries, including Perseus, to the grand banquet, designed to pay homage to the king and to *his* very prosperous land.

Every guest brought an expensive gift, and presented his or her item to the ignoble monarch. Then, the villainous royal asshole summoned

Perseus to *his* throne for everyone to witness a contrived confrontation, and the shrewd ruler cunningly asked the embarrassed lad, "Perseus, I have invited you to my splendid celebration, but where is your' gift to present to your honorable king?"

Perseus was unaware of such a custom, and stood humiliated before the curious assemblage of pompous aristocrats. The very embarrassed mariner blushed, and then was so nervous when the youthful sailor stuttered, "I have not brought anything because I'm an impoverished mariner, who can barely provide for my own basic needs, which incidentally don't include expensive hookers, risqué couch dancers, and kinky prostitutes."

"This insolent young man," the king preached to the pride and flower of *his* corrupt realm, "had been washed ashore onto our peaceful island. We've dutifully given him asylum and residency, and now the ungrateful fool demonstrates his thanks by not bringing his king a worthy gift. You even claim to be the son of Zeus! I say, Perseus; you're simply an illegitimate vagabond pretending to be of divine descent! How do you' account for yourself, you ludicrous, ridiculous, fabricating fucked-up simpleton?"

The insulted young sailor grew angry with abundant shame and pride, and cried-out for all of the shocked audience of prominent guests to hear, "I shall bring your majesty a present nobler than any you have thus received at your feast!" Danae's son pledged without having any specific idea of what such a gift might be, or even what the hell he was talking about.

"Well then," Polydickdees pressed on. "Exactly what might this superior gift be? Pray tell, Perseus. Let the people of Seriphos know its description and its true value!"

Everyone in the crowded throne chamber boisterously laughed at the king's derision of the almost-destitute young sailor, who boasted that he was indeed the son of the chief-god of the universe. The young attendee then vaguely remembered the beautiful tall woman he had encountered on Samos, and reckoned that now was the time to exhibit the courage her powerful words had instilled in him.

"King Polydickdees," Perseus uttered in a stronger voice than he had exhibited before. "I shall bring you the head of Medusa the Gorgon. That awesome prize will be my special gift to you!"

All the guests in attendance gasped at the young man's bravado. The naïve sailor had played right into the king's plan to get the boy off the island, so that Polydickdees could then permanently capture Danae from the temple, take her to his palace, and then screw the shit out of her ten times each night with his incredible three dicks and seven swollen testicles. "You have foolishly promised to bring me Medusa's head?" the king wildly chuckled and sneered. "Well then, junior jerk-off; leave

Seriphos immediately to engage in your dumb-ass, frivolous quest. And don't come back to this island until Medusa has given you some head! Ha, ha, ha, ha!"

The son of Zeus and Danae finally realized that the sly king had cleverly tricked his ass, and the insulted young man left the great feast being jeered and mocked by the five-hundred jovial guests, who all loved being governed by the cruelest and most deplorable king east of the *Pillars of Hercules*.

Perseus was disgusted with his own gullibility. The troubled youth ambled out to the island's high cliffs overlooking the sea, and prayed that Pallas Athene would come to assist him in undertaking *his* extremely dangerous exploit. Three times the youth wept and begged for the goddess to appear, and when despair had virtually saturated his soul, a wonderful mist was discernible upon the eastern horizon, and soon drifted-over to the cliff where the hoodwinked adolescent had been standing. A sparkling, celestial figure slowly-emerged from the illuminated haze.

"Perseus," Pallas Athene greeted. "Raise your head up high and be proud of the noble virtues that inhabit your heart. Take this bronze sword, shield, helmet, along with these winged sandals, and wear them proudly on your daring quest. Now, it is time for you to achieve honor, and convincingly slay Medusa the Gorgon," the goddess announced. "Then, you'll promptly take her head back to Polydickdees as you have so valiantly promised. Your will shall be vindicated by beating the shit out of Medusa, and then turning Polydickdees to stone at his palace!"

"Gee, Pallas Athene. I really made a complete asshole out of myself at my opening act at the palace!" Perseus admitted with an innocent smile. "Please show me how I can redeem my lost credibility."

Athene further explained that her hero had to venture-out on a perilous seven-year-journey to the end of the known world, and that if Perseus was ever overcome by cowardice, then the youth would surely perish with a *soul of clay* in the shadowy "Unshapen Land".

"But how can I slay Medusa if her despicable face will turn me into stone?" Perseus insisted on knowing. "It's bad enough that I now have rocks in my head, let alone a petrified matching stone face to boot!"

"All of that crazy information you'll learn in due time," the goddess sincerely pledged. "This unique expedition of yours must be accomplished in many small steps. First, you must go north and visit the three Gray Sisters, who'll give you specific directions to the Three Daughters of the Evening Star, who dance around the *Golden Apple Tree* like sex-starved, horny lesbians. The daughters will provide you with the correct directions on how to find Medusa's diabolical lair!"

"But how the fuck can I ever kill Medusa if one brief glance at her despicable face will simultaneously freeze my ass, dick, balls, and sperm into solid stone!" Perseus demanded.

"You shall see her reflection in your invincible bronze shield, and then smite the detestable monster with this magic bronze sword," Pallas Athene divulged to her fascinated listener. "Then, you'll stuff her shit-ugly head inside this shit-ugly goatskin sack, and transport it to King Polydickdees for *his* personal inspection."

"But how can I fuckin' cross the seas without a sturdy ship?" Perseus inquired. "I can't even swim a stroke, even though I'm a goddamned experienced sailor!"

"Put these divine winged sandals upon your feet. They'll guide you across the winds to your particular destinations," the goddess patiently explained. "Wear the sandals proudly, along with the bronze shield, bronze sword, and the bronze helmet. Now venture-out into mythology, and start kicking some enemy ass!"

"Can't I at least say goodbye to my mother and to kind Dictys?" the soon-to-be hero asked. "The two have done much to develop my character!"

"No, you may not!" Pallas Athene imperatively stated. "It's now time for *you* to trust the will of the gods, and to discard aside mortal emotions and human associations. Cast your fate to the winds, Perseus. Aspire to a higher power, and then glory and fame will be your legacy forever!"

The glittering cloud descended from the stratosphere, and again enveloped the celestial goddess, and it soon glided out over the sea, and disappeared over the eastern horizon from where it had come. Perseus adorned his feet with the splendid winged sandals; placed the bronze helmet upon his head; lifted-up his new sword and shield, and then gently floated-up into the air. Soon, the airborne hero became adept at regulating both his flying speed and his altitude, and after an hour of assiduous practice, the prospective champion set-out on his great quest, possessing a joyful stout heart.

The lad was thoroughly enjoying the thrill of flight, and after beating several falcons in several impromptu sky races, Perseus buzzed the cities of Athens and Thebes, scaring the shit and the piss out of the daily pedestrians, who were distracted from shopping in the busy marketplaces. And after several months of showing off his aerial skills all over Greece, brave Perseus came to an ominous moor, which after a hundred-miles, gradually converted into a vast sheet of ice.

The courageous fellow then followed an obscure mountain trail through an intense blizzard until the excited adventurer finally reached the isolated cave of the notorious Three Gray Sisters, who were too ugly and wicked to ever be ancient nuns, or to even be over-the-hill hookers.

118

The three old, blind bitches were grotesque-looking, warty-faced witches that were preoccupied passing their single eye amongst themselves, and arguing incessantly about *its* possession. The illustrious young hero pitied the Three Gray Sisters, who actually didn't give a shit or a damn about pity for each other, or for that matter pity toward anyone else on the whole goddamned planet.

"Oh, noble Three Gray Sisters. I am Perseus," the young stud formally introduced himself to the hideous hags. "And I need some vital information. Please tell me the directions to find Medusa the Gorgon, for I don't have a map, or even a compass!"

"You have the voice of a child of man," the first perceptive ugly sister answered. "Who are you really, oh intrepid mortal?" the witch asked, for in her heart, the old bitch really wanted to get laid because she hadn't had any decent sex from a stiff cock in over five-thousand-years. "Holy Hera! I haven't been pumped since I had 'menopause' over five-millennia ago," the hoary whore remarked. "And the *men* have *paused* porking me, ever since my once juicy love canal dried-up!"

"The rulers of *Olympus* have dispatched me to find the repulsive Gorgon, and to gain knowledge of her whereabouts from you Three Gray Sisters," Perseus claimed. "Don't you three 'sisters' have a *Mother Superior* I can speak with?"

"Look, jerk-weed!" the second cantankerous sister's voice boomed. "You might have to eat all three of our ancient dried-up, smelly, lice-infected cunts if you don't cooperate with our easy demands. We are kin to the Titans, and also to the Gorgons, and to the Monsters of Antiquity, too," the second cauldron guardian laboriously explained. "And we want *you* to know that we despise the new rulers of *Olympus,* and also their fucked-up human worshipers!"

"Listen, twisted Sister," the bold young adventurer answered the most horrible-looking hag of the three. "I would rather jerk-off naked in *that* wicked blizzard out there than eat or screw any of your raunchy, smelly, dried-up, arid, useless pussies. Now then," Perseus adamantly continued. "Tell me the way to Medusa!"

"Who is this insolent pecker-head who dares invade our privacy?" the third withered, pallid-faced Gray Sister insisted on knowing. "Give me the eye so that I may evaluate *his* appearance, and admire his muscular physique, and imagine and fanta*size* the 'size' and length of his hairy pussy plunger!"

As the three ugly, warty, ashen-faced sisters grappled and groped for the singular magical eye, which the gruesome trio had been passing and sharing amongst themselves, Perseus reached-out his free hand, and grabbed *their* only window to the world. "Now then, you ugly, ingrate bitches. I now have your sacred eye in my possession. I insist that you please tell me where the Gorgon resides, or I shall confiscate your most-essential eye; I will fly to the moon, and deposit your' seeing device inside an active volcanic crater," the angry traveler threatened. "And try pissing me off some more with your stupid rhetoric, and I'll cut off your distorted heads, along with your flaccid tits, with my magic bronze sword, and I'll gladly donate the amputated relics to the *Athenian Mythological Museum of Unnatural History*."

"You wouldn't dare!" the first wretched-looking old hag exclaimed. "You haven't the testicles or the sperm to attempt that!"

"If you don't cooperate and give me accurate directions," Perseus emphatically predicted, "then I'll make all three of you pathetic, stubborn, miserable blind bitches' lick and suck on my stenchy hemorrhoids, until the suckers disappear right out of my hairy, infected asshole!"

"Okay, you win this time, you conniving young bastard!" the first disgusting witch acknowledged and compromised. "Go south toward the sun, and you'll arrive at the *Golden Apple Tree* with three young maidens merrily dancing around it. The beauties are the *Hesperides,* daughters of the Titan Atlas's brother, and they'll give you the necessary directions to Medusa's secret island," the old bag disclosed. "Now, give us back our vital eye, so that at least one of us can view your form, and fantazise about having hot sex with a young stud-meister such as yourself!"

The hero returned the portable eye to its rightful owners, left the dismal, isolated ice cave, and continued southward, flying over desolate mountains and weedy meadows until the skilled aviator observed a tremendous form in the distance, holding-up the sky, and separating it from the earth. 'That is Atlas,' Perseus reckoned. 'And some day he'll be relieved of this important duty, and then finally go into the lucrative business of manufacturing reference books for libraries and for school classrooms.'

Then, the young champion heard sweet angelic female voices harmoniously singing, so he descended from the clouds and viewed the *Daughters of the Evening Star* prancing and dancing around a magnificent apple tree, featuring large golden fruit suspended upon its wonderful limbs.

The beautiful, cheerful *Daughters of the Hesperides* held hands and enthusiastically danced-around the fabulous *Golden Apple Tree,* which had a listless, lazy dragon coiled around its base. The blithe nymphs ceased their merriment upon detecting the arrival of the valiant crusader against evil injustices.

"Who the hell are you?" the first blonde-haired beauty asked with half of her golden bush, and all of her firm tits hanging out of her loose-fitting tunic. "Are you *Hercules* come to steal golden apples from our incomparable tree?"

"No, fair maidens," the young champion candidly replied. "My name is Perseus, but you're positively right about one thing. The goddess Pallas Athene has sent me on a *Herculean* labor. You must show me the way to Medusa the Gorgon's secret lair!"

"Not just yet!" the second blonde-haired and blonde-bushed maiden imperatively answered. "Come dance with us. Then, we'll let you play with us, too!"

"Well, I must admit, that's a mighty big temptation you've offered me!" Perseus exclaimed as he licked his lips while thinking about *those* other lips between the comely girls' perfectly-structured legs. "You just aren't paying *lip service* to what we'll be doing, are you?" Perseus begged for positive verification.

"No, but you can masturbate any and all of us," the third horny nymph informed. "But you cannot penetrate our maidenheads, because we must remain virgins in order to perform our monotonous function. But we do give good blow-jobs that are guaranteed to make you come again!" the *comely* nymph confidently stated.

"Well, that's all very nice and proper," the hero aptly agreed. "But I'll have to take a rain-check on your generous offer. I'm obligated by promise to perform a vital errand for the Immortals, but after I'm finished the *Promethean* chore," Perseus elaborated, "even though I am not Prometheus, I can then also lose *my* virginity, and even my maidenhead too, if I have one near my prostate!"

Then, the fair damsels cried and slobbered all over the place, and also all over each other, whimpering, "Medusa will surely turn you into stone. Then, you'll never have the pleasure of massaging our hot, wet, pink, blonde fluffy beavers, or sucking on our firm erect succulent nipples," the first nymph regretted. "Won't you please reconsider? That scumbag Medusa lives in an alien *cunt*ry."

"I assure you, fair maidens. I'll not be converted into stone by some ugly hussy!" Perseus warranted. "Now, if you presently tell me the precise directions to her remote lair, I can then be on my way. The sooner I can leave, the sooner I can return here and learn some fine hands-on hedonism."

"Very well, then!" the second blonde damsel agreed as she scrutinized the impressive bulge protruding below the center of Perseus's sexy, orange tunic. "The knowledge you seek is not within our scope of experience, but if you request that same information from the Titan Atlas, who can see far into the distant Unshapen Land from his position of holding up the sky, he'll probably gladly help you."

The favorite of Pallas Athene accompanied the luscious blonde knockouts up the side of a steep mountain where their uncle was busy keeping the sky separated from the Earth.

"Uncle, please assist this young man," the first maiden yelled-up and requested. "He requires knowing the location of Medusa the Gorgon's den. Is it somewhere in Denmark?"

"I can see in the distance the Gorgon resting in the shade of a primitive island, but kind stranger," Atlas cautioned, "you cannot approach the island unless your identity is cloaked by the *Hat of Darkness*. Then, Medusa might be able to smell your presence, but won't be able to see you, even with *her* keen eyesight."

"Well then, kind Atlas," Perseus wondered and asked. "Where is this unique *Hat of Darkness?* Where could I locate it?"

"*The Hat* is hidden in the depths of *Hades*, but my immortal nieces could easily retrieve the cap for you. But in payment for rendering that favor," Atlas continued, "I must receive one in return."

"What would you like me to do for you?" the bronze-helmeted champion curiously asked. "Would you like me to scratch your balls, or massage your ass?"

"No, Perseus. This fuckin' task of holding up the sky is far too tedious and boring for even a Titan to perform," Atlas persuasively complained. "So, if you are successful in butchering Medusa's head off, show it to my face, so that I may be turned to stone. Then, my horrible gruesome assignment will be that much less difficult for the remainder of eternity!"

"That's a deal!" Perseus euphorically acceded. "You can be the envy of every drunk's most passionate desire. Atlas my friend. I want you to just think about your future status for a second. You will be *stoned* for all eternity!"

The *Daughters of the Evening Star* took a secret passage leading into the side of the mountain; which led to a macabre tunnel; which gradually descended fifteen-miles into the Earth's core. A full week transpired, until the three blonde dolls finally completed their perilous mission, and ascended to the Earth's surface, carrying the inimitable *Hat of Darkness* as their prized trophy.

"Thank you, kind sisters of mercy, for obtaining this terrific gift," the young adventurer from Seriphos declared. "And I'll be thinking all about your hot, wet, pink, blonde pussies, and your firm, erect, succulent nipples all the way to Medusa's lair, I assure you."

And then the young stud placed the extraordinary *Hat of Darkness* on top of his bronze helmet. In seconds, the sailor-turned-hero vanished from sight, laughing like a maniac as the jolly crusader cavorted-around in his invisible state, tickling the fair maidens under their arms, and then feeling and squeezing their firm tits, featuring very erect, succulent nipples.

Perseus flew onward toward the Unshapen Land that had been alluded to and indicated by Atlas. Ahead, the hero could see the three sleeping Gorgons' talons glistening in the morning sunlight, and the on-a-mission champion instantly forgot about contemplating the fair damsels' blonde pussies and firm tits, while concentrating all of his mental dynamics on the immediate task at hand. 'Pallas Athene suggested that I fly aloft and glance at Medusa's image in my bronze shield,' the daring fellow remembered. 'If my back is to the sun, then I could more easily accomplish *her* expectation.'

The hero's invisible form furtively flew above the three lethargic, inattentive Gorgons, all sleeping and basking in the sunlight as if the monsters were lazy dinosaurs grazing in grassy lands, unaware of a meteor hurtling through the atmosphere, ready to destroy their existence. Perseus's hand trembled as the encroacher held his bronze sword aloft, for the ferocious Gorgons looked rather invincible, even while resting in their non-aggressive state. Medusa was rolling and tossing back and forth in her sleep, perhaps having a premonition of impending disaster.

Pallas Athene's champion gazed into *his* bronze shield, which served as a reliable mirror, and the trespasser viewed the beast's horrendous locks that were now identifiable as moving, living serpents. The monster's sharp fangs protruded out of the sides of her evil mouth, and even as she slept, the creature hissed intermittently. Medusa was so foul and so wicked-looking that Perseus felt inspired to immediately initiate his "supernatural errand". Looking into the immortal bronze shield, the determined assassin savagely swung his sword, and his aim and effort had been true to the mark. In one mighty twist of the arm and wrist, the repulsive creature had been decapitated.

The victor reached-down, and without directly looking, grabbed the bloody head, and adroitly inserted it into the goatskin sack. 'Now, I gotta' get the fuck outa' here in a hurry!' the triumphant hero anxiously thought.

Medusa's body flipped, flapped, and flopped all over the rugged terrain, instantly waking-up her savage sisters from *their* slumbers. In a second, Perseus was again airborne, and as the perplexed sisters searched in vain for the invisible assassin, the murderer was entirely hidden from their scrutiny by the very effective *Hat of Darkness*. The enraged Gorgon sisters flew-off, and four times circled the rocky ledge where the surprise assault had occurred, but no evidence of any culprit was anywhere to be seen or found. Only a flying goatskin bag could be detected in the far distance, speeding-away toward the western horizon.

"Serve me well, my swift winged sandals," Perseus implored. "Give me the lightning speed of Hermes to escape the vindictive beasts on my trail, lusting for sour revenge."

The intrepid assassin flew south across the Mediterranean Sea, and soon Perseus arrived at northern Africa, the land of the *Golden Apple Tree,* and also the *Daughters of the Evening Star.* The two determined

Gorgons finally abandoned their futile pursuit, with the approach of evening and the nearby Mediterranean Sea marking both time and geographic boundaries for *their* exhausted bodies to honor.

After landing on the African peninsula bordering the spectacular *Golden Apple Tree*, Perseus gallantly trekked over to the vicinity of beleaguered Atlas to finally fulfill his grateful promise made to the grieving Titan.

"Satisfy your pledge to me!" Atlas urged the successful youth. "Show me the bitch's fuckin' ugly puss, so that I can escape my *Olympian* punishment, and be transformed into stone for all eternity. I demand you turn me into an inanimate mountain crag right now!"

And Perseus honored his responsibility to the melancholy, woeful giant by removing the bloody Gorgon's head from the goatskin bag, and then showing its' cursed horrible face to the colossal figure. Instantaneously, the Titan changed into a jagged mountain peak, and the surrounding northern African ridges still, to this day, bear the giant's familiar name, the *Atlas Mountains.*

Then, Perseus enclosed the Gorgon's head inside the thick goatskin sack, so that no further damage or transformation could accidentally result from its accidental exposure. The three blonde maidens came sprinting-up the mountain trail to inspect their uncle's new radical, rock-hard appearance and sang several verses of: "Turn to stone; turn to stone; Uncle Atlas has turned to stone!"

"He's now as solid as *Gibraltar,*" the first nymph attested.

"Uncle Atlas can now be one of the *Pillars of Hercules*," the second golden-hair vixen marveled.

"Uncle is finally out of his misery!" the third *Hesperides'* daughter gleefully shouted. "Now Perseus, just point Medusa's head at your' pecker so that it might turn hard, too!"

"Sorry, ladies," the chaste-hearted champion idealist answered. "I promise to come back some day with a huge erection to satisfy all three of you young horny bitches. But right now, I must consummate my important journey."

"Perseus, take with you *this* wonderful fruit," the second nymph insisted as the blonde maiden held out one of the lustrous golden apples. "It has sufficient energy to sustain you for a full week!"

"And don't forget to come back to northern Africa so that you can fondle our tits and do anything you'd like to our eager-beaver pussies!" the third young maiden reminded.

"Now, fly eastward over the drab Libyan shore, and from there, zoom north to the land of Greece," the first lovely damsel instructed. "And please, Perseus; retain your sacred virginity and save it for *us* horny young broads to claim!"

124

The three blonde maidens then all kissed Perseus upon his lips and face, and the enthralled favorite of Pallas Athene ascended into the air, and followed the three daughters' explicit directions, heading straight to the Libyan coast. From there, the son of Danae would continue his flight odyssey to Seriphos, where the returning hero would discard the goatskin sack outside the palace and then nonchalantly present vile Polydickdees with Medusa's grotesque face and head.

"Rappaccini's Daughter"
Nathaniel Hawthorne

A young man, named Giovanni Guasconti, came, very long ago, from the more southern region of Italy, after the novice had graduated last in his class from Mafia Regional High School. The greenhorn's principal aim was to pursue his important studies at the prestigious University of Padua. Giovanni, who had but a scant supply of gold ducats inside his shallow, ripped pocket, took lodging in a high and gloomy chamber of an old edifice, which certainly wasn't the palace (or even the servant's quarters) of a Paduan nobleman.

The dust-laden dump exhibited atop its single entrance the armorial bearings of a fucked-up, rather indigent family long since extinct. The youthful impressionable stranger, who was not unstudied in the abundant pornography poems of his antiquated country, recollected that one of the ancestors of *that* loser family, and perhaps once an occupant of that very inferior domicile, had been pictured by Dante as a partaker of the immortal agonies of the Italian author's rather legendary, diabolical Inferno.

These reminiscences and associations, together combining with the tendency to experience heartbreak, being natural to a young man alone for the first time, venturing-out of his familiar native sphere, caused Giovanni to sigh heavily, and inadvertently inhale three huge green headed flies. After nearly coughing and choking his lungs out onto the rickety floor, the distraught young traveler sneezed convulsively a dozen times to clear his nostrils, and then with bloodshot eyes, sadly looked around the rather desolate and ill-furnished apartment.

"Just what I don't need for inspiration!" the new big city arrival exclaimed to the apathetic, drab blue ceiling, with both his arms extended upwards. "A primitive, pathetic piss-poor pad in Padua!"

"Holy Virgin, Signor!" cried old Dame Lisabetta, who had been readily won by the youth's remarkable beauty and obvious bulge in his leotards; the hag kindly endeavoring to give the chamber a habitable air. "Your evaluation of this nasty apartment was wrong. This abominable rat-hole is nothing to sneeze about! Now Giovanni, do you find this old fleabag room gloomy? For the love of platonic intercourse being enjoyed in Heaven, then, just stick your grease-ball head out the window, and you'll see as bright a sunshine as you've ever witnessed since you had left Nipples, er, I meant to say, Naples."

Young callow-minded Guasconti mechanically did as the old promiscuous retired whore had advised, but could not quite agree with Lisabetta that the Paduan sunshine was as cheerful as that of southern Italy, where sultry nudist camps and hot sex farms abounded. Such as it was, however, the sun's radiant rays fell-upon a lush garden situated beneath the window, and expended its fostering warm energy upon a variety of healthy plants, which seemed to have been carefully cultivated with exceeding care.

"Does this garden below belong to the house?" Giovanni asked. "Where I come from, there are plenty of naked girls and nude women in gazebos and in spas, sunbathing in places just like the one below. In Naples, we jokingly call an area such as that one beneath this window Bush Gardens!"

"Heaven should forbid such vulgarity occurring, Signor. Unless the garden you've mentioned is fruitful and contains better pot herbs than any that grow below us now," answered old Lisabetta, slowly rubbing her enlarged clit, "I'd say you're trying to bull-shit me. No;" resumed the old lowlife bitch. "That garden you've observed below is cultivated by the hands of eccentric Signor Giacomo Rappaccini, the famous plant doctor, whose reputation has been heard of as far away as your native erect Nipples, er, I mean Naples. It is said that the doctor distills these plants into medicines that are as potent as a charmed aphrodisiac. Oftentimes, you may see Signor Rappaccini diligently at work, and perchance the signora, his virgin daughter, too, meticulously gathering the strange flowers that grow and thrive inside the gorgeous garden."

The old kinky hag had now done what she could for the drab presentation of the less-than-mediocre chamber, and then after commending the young man to the protection of the saints, along with the horny Roman and Greek goddesses Venus and Aphrodite, the hoary, no-teeth, former hooker took her departure.

Bored Giovanni still found no better occupation than to curiously look-down into the garden beneath his one and only window. From its general appearance, the student judged the setting to be one of those unique botanical gardens which were of an earlier date in Padua than currently present elsewhere in Italy, or in the whole wide world, including famous and risqué Bush Gardens in Naples.

'Perhaps it might once have been the pleasure-place of an opulent family that valued sex and more sex; for down there is the ruin of a marble fountain in the center, sculptured with rare artistic flair,' Giovanni speculated. 'But the fountain is so woefully shattered that it's impossible to trace the original design. Even the cherub on top has had his marble balls busted. The flowing water, however, continues to gush and sparkle from the Roman boy's erect penis, and then arching high into the sunbeams. God, that's exactly how I piss!'

A low gurgling sound ascended-up to the young man's window, and the sensation made Giovanni feel as if the fountain were an immortal spirit that was echoing its dissonant song unceasingly, and without heeding the myriad vicissitudes (obviously caused by humans) around it.

All about the pool into which the water subsided grew various plants, all of which seemed to require a plentiful supply of moisture for the nourishment of gigantic leaves, the necessary liquid being provided by the accommodating pissing cherub.

In some instances, banks of flowers gorgeously grew in magnificent arrays near the side stone walls. One shrub in particular, set in a marble vase inside the pool located next to the residence's cesspool, bore a nice profusion of purple blossoms, each of which had the luster and royalty of a splendid gem. Every portion of the rich, fertile soil was populated with a variety of plants and herbs, which, if less beautiful, still showed tokens of assiduous care. 'The lucky son-of-a-bitch who owns this nifty-garden could start a floral delivery service with the god Mercury as its emblem logo,' Giovanni mused and considered. 'That kind of flourishing business could make my imaginary partner Hermes and me quite wealthy!'

Some flowers had been placed in urns, rich with old carvings, and others in common garden pots, some of them growing cannabis; several thick vines crept serpent-like along the ground, or climbed high upon faded bricks, using whatever means of ascent was offered them, reaching right up to the roof of the garden's solidly-built outdoor shithouse. One plant had wreathed itself around a statue of Lesbos, which was thus quite veiled and shrouded in a drapery of hanging foliage, which covered her exaggerated tits and shaved crotch, so happily arranged that the figure might have served as a sculptor's LBGTQRS art study.

'That hard-looking cold statue down there can't be Venus de Milo, because it's not disarming enough. Oh, I see now!' Giovanni then realized. 'That tough-looking lady upon the pedestal is the sexually-disoriented dyke Sappho, supposedly the first lesbian living on the Greek Isle of Lesbos. Her crack seems all it's been cracked-up to be,' evaluated the lad, as his devious imagination mentally separated from the abundant greenery, while his perceptive eyes closely examined the statue's twat from the overhead window. 'It's too bad that frowning Greek bitch was a goddamned lesbian! I mean, at least she could've been a kinky bisexual instead!'

The knowledgeable student paused while still peering-down from his elevated vantage point. Then, the aspiring medical doctor keenly noticed three white round balls lying upon the verdant lawn. 'I never learned in any of my art texts back in Naples that Sappho was constipated, and only shit perfectly circular hard marbles!'

While Giovanni stood at the window, his ears heard a rustling originating from behind a screen of dense green tree leaves, and the viewer soon became aware that a person was busy at work 'fucking-around' in the north end of the huge garden. His noticed figure soon emerged into full view, and the previous phantom showed himself to be a tall, emaciated, sallow and sickly-looking man, who incidentally had been dressed in a black academic scholar's robe, the same type of ridiculous black garb that professors wear at ridiculous kindergarten and college graduations.

The laborer was beyond the middle term of life, actually being an old fart with long, gray, curly hair; a thin gray beard, and a classic face singularly marked with age marks and wrinkles. But in truth, the codger inside the garden possessed a singular countenance, which could never, even in his more youthful days, have expressed much warmth of heart. Basically, the old coot looked apathetic, selfish and totally fucked-up.

Nothing could exceed the intentness with which this scientific gardener examined every shrub which grew in his path: it seemed as if the old asshole had been looking into the plants' innermost nature, making salient observations in regard to their creative essence, and discovering why one 'Who gives a shit?' leaf grew in *this* shape, and another developing in *that* 'Who gives a shit?' form.

On the contrary, the garden proprietor avoided their actual touch, or the direct inhaling of their odors, with a certain caution that impressed Giovanni most disagreeably; for the old man's demeanor was that of one walking among malignant influences, such as savage beasts, or deadly snakes, or evil spirits, which, should *he* allow them one moment of license, would wreak upon him some terrible fatality.

All this bull-shit was strangely frightful to the young man's imagination, to witness that air of insecurity in a person cultivating a garden; that most simple and innocent of human toils, and which had been like the joy and labor of the unfallen Biblical parents of the race. Was this garden, then, the Eden of the contemporary world? And this maniacal man, with such a perception of harm in what his own hands had caused to grow; was he the modern Adam?

The distrustful gardener, while either plucking-away the dead leaves, or busily pruning the two most-luxuriant shrubs (without also wearing a tu-tu), protected his hands with a pair of thick gloves that in the past, the garden fanatic had probably used to participate in senior citizen boxing matches at the nearby Montague Rectangular Sports Garden.

When ambling in his current walk through his botanical paradise, the crazed experimenter eventually came to the magnificent plant that hung its purple gems beside the about-to-crumble marble fountain. The determined geezer then placed a kind of mask over his wrinkled mouth and nostrils, as if all the environmental beauty surrounding his skinny ass concealed a deadlier malice than himself. But then, finding his started task still-too-dangerous to perform, the potential geriatric hospital patient drew back, removed the mask, and called loudly, but yelling with a horribly hoarse voice that even a miniature pony wouldn't recognize.

"Beatrice! Beatrice!" the diseased throat vociferated. "Shit! Because of my malignant cancer, I can't even mutter a fuckin' utter, even though I'm a Leo wearing leotards!"

"Here I am, my ice-cold parent. What would you need?" cried a youthful feminine voice from the window of the opposite house. Yes, a delicate girl's voice as rich as a tropical sunset, and such a sweet intonation that quickly made Giovanni think of deep penis penetration into a wet pink love tunnel. "Are you screwing-around again in the garden, Father? Why the hell do I call you Father? You're a freakin' mad scientist, and not a lost pedophile priest just aimlessly walking-around down there!"

"Yes, Beatrice," the apparently frustrated gardener answered. "And I need your help right this minute. I've forgotten how to use the scissors, and can't find my heavy-duty cutting shears."

Soon, there emerged from under a sculptured portal the figure of a youthful, voluptuous, big-breasted girl, whose tits were too damned large for even the most expansive double-breasted woman's suit to accommodate. Beatrice looked stunningly vivacious, and her blithe spirit seemed filled with life, health, and energy. And most all of her physical female attributes were tensely girdled inside the damsel's tight-fitting azure-blue dress, which beautifully covered her most-alluring, virgin pleasure hole.

Yet Giovanni's fancy must have grown morbid, as his engorged-with-blood reproductive snake began throbbing, and then slowly uncoiling, inside his tarnished brown leotards, which instantly needed major mending. The powerful impression which the fair maiden made upon his erect pecker was as if here was an extraordinarily special flower, the human sister of those vegetable ones thriving over yonder; more beautiful than the richest red roses, or the finest yellow tulips, which then automatically made Giovanni Guasconti think about two lips; not the ones upon the luscious girl's mouth, but the pair of hairy ones between her lank legs.

'Who needs to masturbate when I could get laid in the shade!' the new university student excitedly concluded. 'I'd like to deflower that hot-looking doll right this instant! Oh no! I'm having a goddamned premature ejaculation! It's not a nocturnal wet dream! It's a damned daytime nightmare!'

As comely Beatrice descended the garden's four stone steps, and soon sauntered-down the familiar flagstone path, it was observable that the knockout teen honey had been inhaling the perfumed scents of several of the plants of which her boxing legend father had most carefully avoided contact.

"Here, Beatrice," the apparent parent indicated. "See how many needful clips require to be done to our chief purple treasure. Yet, shattered as I am, my vulnerable life might pay the penalty of approaching our prize, me standing dangerously close as this most difficult circumstance demands. Henceforth, my true-blue assistant, I fear that this precarious plant must be consigned to your sole charge. Oh shit, Beatrice! You again forgot to bring your office clipboard to record the clippings!"

"And gladly will I undertake the cutting," the splendid young lady answered, as the daughter bent towards the magnificent purple flowered plant, and opened her arms as if to lovingly embrace it. "Yes, Father. I promise to use cutting-edge technology! The shears will be sheer pleasure!"

As Beatrice ardently and gingerly clipped-away, in fact much better than a Yankee clipper (New England barber), Giovanni, positioned at his lofty window, rubbed his eyes, and next removed with a convenient frayed cloth, the sticky semen that had just filtered through his retarded leotards.

'She speaks to the flowers as if they are her human sisters,' the now non-aroused onlooker marveled. 'I wish I could play an instrument like the guitar or mandolin. Then, I could be the flower of the music world, and easily win over dear Beatrice's affections in a Roman minute.'

The interactive scene below soon terminated. Whether Dr. Rappaccini had finished his labors in the garden, or that his watchful eye had caught the young stranger's covetous face observing above, the old curmudgeon now took his daughter's arm, and swiftly retired into their residence. Night was already closing-in; but oppressive oxygen exhalations seemed to proceed from the plants, and steal upward past the apartment's open window. And Giovanni, closing the lattice, experienced cold shudders while maneuvering the shutters.

Immediately, the romantic fool paced to his couch and dreamed of a rich flower, and of a beautiful girl, amazingly both one and the same integrated species. The nouns flower and maiden were quite different, and yet the same entity, and fraught with some strange peril in either shape. Beatrice's more-than-scary aged father, Professor Giacomo Rappaccini, might get pissed-off at the adolescent's flirtation with his treasured daughter, and quickly and violently 'pistil whip' vulnerable Giovanni to death.

But there is an influence in the light of morning that tends to rectify whatever errors exist in a young jerk-off's quixotic love fancy, or even in his exercise of poor social judgment. We may have observed during the sun's decline, the naïve adolescent dreaming and fantasizing about intrepidly giving Beatrice a full-moon on that night, which was to reveal only a half-moon.

Giovanni's first movement that evening was a lengthy bowel movement. Then, gaining essential intestinal fortitude, the university student rose from his tawdry couch, advanced to the window, opened the shutters, and gazed-down into the garden which his dreams (and not his gushing semen) had made so fertile. Young Guasconti was surprised (and a trifle ashamed) to discover how real his vicarious, fucked-up, voyeur love affair had proved to be.

The young idealist rejoiced that, in the heart of the barren, now-tranquil city, the new arrival had the privilege of overlooking that sacred spot of lovely and luxuriant vegetation. The garden scene would keep horny Guasconti in communion with Nature before jealous Dr. Rappaccini would savagely excommunicate Giovanni from the enthralling 'Garden of Eden' for avariciously pumping both the hard and soft poop out of his virgin daughter's ass.

Neither the sickly, thought-worn, very decrepit Dr. Giacomo Rappaccini, nor his brilliant enticing daughter, was now visible (or for that matter, invisible). Giovanni could not determine how accurate were his observations about 'obsessive and compulsive' Dr. Rappaccini, and the botany scientist's hot-looking daughter, indeed without obsessive and compulsive Guasconti ever being introduced to either garden visitor.

'I got to somehow meet and shack-up with that Beatrice babe,' the sex-starved eighteen-year-old thought. 'Maybe, I'll successfully steal some money, take her on a Grand Canal gondola ride over in Venice, and then plow my erect fadorkenbender straight into *her* grand canal!'

* * * * * * * * * * * *

In the course of the next day, Giovanni paid his respects to Signor Pietro Baglioni, distinguished professor of medieval medicine at the university, and without dispute, a physician of eminent repute. Giovanni had brought a fine letter of introduction to the elderly professor, who apparently was a genial, out-of-touch, out-of-the-loop academic suffering from Lupus disease. The erudite scholar invited the young man for dinner, and then the medical pedagogue made himself' very agreeable by the freedom and liveliness of his bull-shit conversation, especially when warmed by a flask or two of Florentine Tuscan wine, which had been prepared by Dr. Baglioni's eighteen- year-old girlfriend, Florence.

Believing that men of learning in and around Padua knew about each other's reputations and myriad contributions to art and science, Giovanni took the opportunity to mention the name of Dr. Giacomo Rappaccini. But the renowned professor did not respond with so much cordiality as young Guasconti had anticipated.

"Unfortunately, ill evil would become a teacher of the divine art of medicine," Professor Pietro Baglioni criticized, in answer to the impertinent dumb-ass question of the brash student. "I wish to withhold due and well-considered praise of a physician so eminently skilled as

Giacomo Rappaccini, but on the other hand," the medical guru aptly qualified, "I should answer your stupid-shit inquiry carefully, because in my irresponsible youth, I used to be a fraternity drinking buddy of *your* old man over at the Palermo Spaghetti Institute, so I don't want to have you interpret any erroneous ideas originating from my loquacious commentary. The truth is that our worshipful Dr. Rappaccini possesses as much science as any member of the revered Padua faculty, where most of the instructional staff members have lost their faculties. Now then, Giovanni. Despite Dr. Rappaccini's myriad eccentricities, I must confess that there are certain grave objections concerning his professional character."

"And what are those disturbing challenges to which you allude?" the inquisitive young man audaciously asked. "Is he a Lotus Eater? Has he invented giant-sized carnivorous man-eating lilacs? I promise you, Professor Baglioni. Whatever you disclose to me about the baneful botanist, mum's the word!"

"Has my new-found friend Giovanni any life-threatening disease of body or heart, that he requires the services of an accomplished physician?" the medical professor oddly asked, with a forced smile. "My advice is to stay away from the Padua horse and mule cart carriage station, or else you might get a terminal illness! Ha, ha, ha!"

"Very funny, Professor!" the extremely interested student acknowledged. "But please Signor, divulge to my ears more about this perverse Dr. Rappaccini."

Dr. Baglioni paused for a minute to awkwardly organize his disheveled, fleeting thoughts. "It is said of him, and I, who know the man fairly-well," the distinguished physician prefaced. "I can attest and answer, for it's quite true that the demented fanatic cares infinitely more for *his* plant science than the same insane asshole does for mankind. I must speak frankly here Giacomo, er, I mean Giovanni. Dr. Giacomo Rappaccini doesn't give a mouse's shit about either you, or me, or mankind. He only cares about his cherished plants," Baglioni orally continued, shaking his bald head in a negative fashion. "When I say the word 'plants', I'm not speaking of factories or manufacturing facilities. I'm referring specifically to flowers and vegetation, and also to other fucked-up products of nature like that. Rappaccini's half-dead patients are interesting to him, only as subjects tailored for some new botanical experiment of some peculiar and dangerous sort."

"Methinks he is an awful man indeed to detest humanity so obnoxiously," visiting Guasconti remarked, mentally recalling the cold and purely intellectual aspect the student had evaluated of conniving Rappaccini fucking-around in the family garden. "And yet, my worshipful Medical Professor, is it not a noble spirit to be so dedicated to the study of tropical and non-tropical topical vegetation? Are there other scientists capable of so spiritual a love of Botany? Is Dr. Rappaccini an avowed vegetarian; an avid vegan?"

"God forbid," the palsied professor, somewhat-testily answered. "Have you lost your cognitive thinking, Young Man? I don't believe that you're a gay fruit, but are you instead an incompetent brain-dead vegetable? I insist that your atrocious rhetoric makes no fuckin' common sense whatsoever!" Dr. Baglioni vehemently asserted. "Listen carefully, you aspiring asshole! It is better for me to heal a baby's illness in a nursery than for Rappaccini to save a dumb-ass flower or shrub in *his* nursery. Giovanni, I find your excessive curiosity to be more academically honest. You're a facetious, shallow-minded asshole, just like your old man was back at the glorious Palermo Spaghetti Institute. Do I make myself fuckin' perfectly clear?"

"Thanks for giving me the worthless rap on Dr. Rappaccini," the vernal dinner guest half-apologized. "Only tell me more damaging gossip, if you desire to do so!"

"It is *his* absurd theory, which hypothesizes that all medicinal virtues are comprised within those substances which we term and catalog as vegetable poisons," Dr. Baglioni very angrily related. "These miscellaneous toxic plants the totally-insane maniac mischievously cultivates with his own diabolical hands. And mendacious Rappaccini is believed even to have produced new varieties of poison; yes, new toxins more horribly deleterious than any other chemical compounds normally prevalent in Nature."

"Holy shit, Professor!" Giovanni exclaimed. "Your descriptive account of Dr, Rappaccini's bizarre, radical experiments not only defines the colossal problem; it fuckin' *compounds* it!"

"Yes, Giovanni. It's an absolute miracle that the deranged Signor Doctor does less mischief than might be expected," Dr. Baglioni maintained. "Now and then, it must be considered by the educational establishment that the zealous charlatan has effected, or seemed to have effected, a marvelous cure for shingles by ingeniously using hay from British thatched roofs and straw from African huts, amazingly combining the melted-down ingredients' mixture to create a viable vegetable compound, that evidently, fully alleviates the disease's symptoms."

"I see," the university student comprehended and declared. "Dr. Rappaccini probably contemplated that shingles on roofs might be the key clue to solving the shingles condition in asshole humans. And so, the botanist had wondrously invented a fantastic compound consisting of boiled straw and hay!"

"Exactly!" the pissed-off, envious Medical Professor verified. "Now, the lousy son-of-a-bitch is trying to create an intelligent, thinking, problem-solving cucumber, and then transfer his results to increasing the intelligence of mentally-challenged humans. Tell me Signor Giovanni, is *that* fucked-up idea of his insanity, or genius?"

"I don't know, Professor, for you see," conveyed young Guasconti, "I'm not too much smarter than a radish, let alone a sophisticated cucumber earning a doctorate degree!"

The youth might have taken Dr. Baglioni's opinions with many grains of allowance had the teenager known that there was a history of academic warfare of long continuance, the rivalry occurring between the Medical Professor and the oddball Dr. Rappaccini, in which the latter was generally thought to have gained the professional advantage because of the much-heralded shingles cure discovery.

"I honestly know next to nothing about the important information you've just explained," Giovanni admitted, after musing on what had been said of Dr. Rappaccini's exclusive zeal for plant and vegetable science. "I know not how dearly this strange scientist may love his art; but surely, there is one mortal object that is dearer to him than botany, a certain gender item that might fascinate and motivate him. The narrow-minded asshole does have a beautiful daughter."

"A-ha!" the Medical Professor exclaimed with an indulgent, hardy laugh. "So, now my friend Giovanni's sexual-desire secret is out and exposed. You *have* heard of this pulchritudinous daughter, whom all the semen-shooting young straight men in Padua are positively wild about, although not half-a-dozen of the immature idiots have ever had the good chance to ever inspect her flawless face."

"So, tell me, Professor. What the hell do you know about lovely Beatrice! I'm rather anxious to learn all the horny details!"

"I detect that you wish to make Rappaccini's Daughter into Giacomo's Rape-accini's Daughter," naughtily jested and laughed the university's chief surgery lecturer. "Even before I had developed my bad case of Parkinson's disease, and had to abandon my practice of lobotomy neurosurgery for the sake of performing basic autopsies," Dr. Baglioni elaborated, "I've learned little of the Signora Beatrice, save that Rappaccini is said to have instructed her deeply in his clandestine plant science, and that, young and beautiful as local fame reports her, she is already-qualified to fill a professor's chair at the university. Perchance her influential father destines her to occupy *my* faculty seat, the dirty, envious bastard! So now, with those confidential opinions being shared, Signor Giovanni, drink-off your fifth glass of cabernet, so that you can get the hell out of here, and begin studying your easy-to-read, large print medical textbooks!"

"Anything else to tell me Professor?" the very annoying first-year anatomy student asked.

"Yes, Giovanni! Cease being a fucked-up gullible dickhead. Start thoroughly thinking with your' human brain, instead of with your goddamned reproductive fadorkenbender!"

* * * * * * * * * * * *

Young Giovanni Guasconti decided to return to his modest lodging, somewhat-heated with the wine he had voraciously quaffed, and which now caused his tender brain to swim with strange fantasies in reference to Dr. Rappaccini and the beautiful, big-titted Beatrice. On his way to his apartment, happening to pass by a florist's stall, the drunken romantic purchased a fresh bouquet of flowers.

'After I had bought the cheap bouquet of daisies, several gay pansies (or perhaps petunias) had strolled by my staggered gait, the inordinate queers walking hand-in-hand,' the inebriated student remembered. 'Holy crap! A faggot is another designation for an effeminate homo', and a *fagot* is a bundle of gathered sticks. I hope that Beatrice doesn't prefer having intercourse with LBGTQ-plus faggots, because of the unique tree fagot reference.'

Ascending the creaky steps up to his lofty dismal chamber, the dizzy occupant soon seated himself near the room's single window, but his body was within the shadow thrown by the depth of the wall, so that the junior spy could look-down into the garden below with little risk of being easily-discovered by potentially antagonistic, possessive Dr. Giacomo Rappaccini. All observable objects beneath his eyes existed in a totally serene solitude. The random strange plants were basking in the early evening sunshine, and now and then, nodding gently to one another in the weak breeze, as if in acknowledgment of mutual sympathy and kindred fraternity.

In the midst, situated alongside the shattered marble fountain, grew the magnificent shrub, with its purple gems clustering all over it; botanical jewels glowing in the evening air, and gleaming back again out of the depths of the adjacent water fountain pool. Soon, as half-intoxicated Giovanni had half-hoped, and half-feared, a fabulous female form majestically appeared beneath the antique sculptured portal, and casually ambled through the central path of the now moonlit garden.

On again beholding the sight of magnificent Beatrice, the young man was startled to perceive how much her beauty exceeded his recollection of it; so brilliant, so vivid, and so desirable was her tantalizing hourglass figure.

'Beatrice could easily be Miss Italy in any national beauty contest,' assessed the greedy-hearted medical student. 'She makes Juliet Capulet look like the ugly Mother Superior at the now-defunct Lasagna School for Orphaned Girls over in Bologna!'

Approaching the central shrub, Beatrice threw open her arms, as with a passionate ardor, and drew the bush's branches into an intimate embrace, indeed administering a firm hug so personal that her features were hidden inside its leafy bosom, and her glistening ringlets all intermingled with the aromatic flowers, as if the exotic broad had been erotically initiating an abnormal sexual encounter.

"Give me thy breath and all thy energy, my dear sister," Beatrice weirdly exclaimed. "For I am faint with common air. And give me this purple flower of thine, which I separate with gentlest fingers from the short stem, and am placing the bloom close beside my most-appreciative heart."

'Jesus Christ!' Giovanni imagined. "Not only is Beatrice a lesbian like Sappho of Lesbos was, but the crazy chick thinks that the shrub is another female to adore and caress. If this post-medieval Renaissance world isn't completely fucked-up, then I don't know what the hell is!'

With those most-peculiar words spoken, Giacomo Rappaccini's beautiful daughter plucked one of the richest purple blossoms off the shrub, and was about to fasten the petal onto her bosom. Just the thought of the girl wanting to make love to a stupid-assed shrub flower made the eager voyeur's dick shrink and shrivel-down inside his tight brown leotards.

'What utter bull-shit!' the light-headed, hiccupping viewer critically thought. 'I wonder if they're about to rub bushes.'

But now, unless Giovanni's five hefty draughts of red wine had bewildered his senses, a singular incident next occurred. A small, orange-colored reptile, of the lizard or chameleon species, creeped (crept) along the path and jumped forward, just at the feet of Beatrice, also giving Giovanni the creeps. Beatrice had observed the remarkable phenomenon transpire, and the girl crossed herself in the traditional Christian sign. Sadly, but without surprise, did she act; nor did Rappaccini's daughter, therefore, hesitate to arrange the fatal flower situated upon her bosom.

"Leaping lizards! Am I awake? Have I lost my reliable senses?" the student protagonist whispered to himself. "What is this odd-behaving being up to now? 'Beautiful', I shall warmly call her, or inexpressibly 'terrible', a complete, psychologically disturbed, sexually confused, Italian princess goddess? That's what the hell this virgin vixen is!"

Beatrice now strayed carelessly through the colorful garden, approaching closer beneath Giovanni's window, so near that the whimsical jackass was compelled to thrust his head quite out of its concealment in order to gratify the intense and painful curiosity which she had involuntarily excited. At that dramatic moment. a huge two-toned insect happened to crawl over the side garden wall, and the aggressive creature truly-frightened the bug-eyed, drunken, horny university student.

138

Beatrice gazed at the speedy insect with childish delight, and in an instant, the animated spider grew faint and fell at her feet, the thing becoming quite dead from no reasonable cause, unless the queer event was a result of the atmosphere exhaled from her faint breath. Again, Beatrice crossed herself in the standard Holy Trinity Christian sign, and sighed heavily as she bent over to thoroughly examine the motionless dead insect.

An impulsive shocked movement of Giovanni's arms and head immediately drew Beatrice's eyes to the overhead window. There, Rappaccini's Daughter beheld the skull and face of the young fellow, rather possessing a Grecian urn cranium shape than an Italian head, with fair, regular features, and a glistening of gold among his recently acquired fake yellow earrings. Not knowing exactly what else to do, Giovanni instinctively threw-down the inferior bouquet which he had hitherto held in his hand.

"Signora," the idiot said. "Those are pure and healthful uncostly flowers for you to smell and savor. Wear them in your fluffy tresses for the sake of me, Giovanni Guasconti of Downtown Naples."

"Thank you, Signor," a somewhat-alarmed Beatrice replied, with her rich melodic voice that came forth as if it were magical music. And then, with a mirthful expression, half-childish and half-woman-like, the smiling girl announced, "I accept your gift of cheap withering daisies, and would fain recompense it with this precious purple flower. But if I toss it into the air, it will not reach you. Som Signor, I strongly suggest that you get your ass out of here before my old man shows-up and summons the constable for you to spend the whole night sobering-up in the nearest jail."

Beatrice lifted the frail bouquet from the ground, and then, as if inwardly ashamed at having stepped aside from her maidenly reserve in order to respond to a stranger's unexpected surprise greeting, the fair damsel passed swiftly homeward through the bountiful garden. But few as the moments were, it seemed to Giovanni, when the beauty was on the point of vanishing beneath the sculptured portal, that *his* beautiful bouquet was already beginning to uncannily wilt within her loose grasp.

"I just blew my golden opportunity to plant my erect pickle smack in the center of Beatrice's weedy garden," Giovanni sobbed and lamented. "God! When am I ever going to get laid in Padua!"

* * * * * * * * * * * * *

For many days after that daisy bouquet incident, the young man avoided the window that looked into Dr. Rappaccini's garden, thinking that the mad scientist would incessantly endeavor to decapitate Guasconti with his hand shears, or viciously and repeatedly stab him with his sharp scissor blades.

'Maybe I should evacuate Padua, along with this rat-trap apartment, and forget about the bewitching Beatrice and her positively lunatic old man,' Giovanni surmised. 'Sometimes rank cowardice is a better option than fucked-up valor. Oh well, maybe tomorrow I can catch a glimpse of Beatrice sunbathing nude upon the cesspool lid.'

Sometimes, the greenhorn university student attempted to assuage his fever spirit by initiating a rapid stroll through the streets of Padua, or by ambitiously taking his gait beyond the city's gate: his measured footsteps kept time with the throbbing of his brain, and the pulsing of his excitable dick, so that the brisk saunter was apt to accelerate itself soon into a mild sprint. One day, the trekker found himself arrested, but not by the police; his arm had been seized by a portly personage.

"Signor Giovanni! Fat chance of meeting you on the piazza!" the corpulent, baldheaded gentleman commenced his narrative. "Stay calm, my' young friend. Have you already forgotten me? I'm the guy who had beaten the shit out of your wimpy old man on fraternity pledge night."

Yes, it was envious Professor Baglioni, whom Giovanni had deliberately avoided ever since their first meeting, honoring a gut feeling that the medical instructor's shrewd sagacity would look too deeply into the callow student's secret love desires concerning Beatrice Rappaccini. Endeavoring to recover his composure, Guasconti stared forth wildly from his inner world, into the outer one, and spoke like a romantic fool lost in a passionate dream.

"Yes, I am Giovanni Guasconti. You are Professor Pietro Baglioni. Now leave me the fuck alone! Let me pass!"

"Not yet, not yet, Signor Giovanni Guasconti," brashly answered the perceptive, smiling Medical Professor, but at the same time, scrutinizing the youth with an earnest-but-suspicious glance. "I did grow-up side by side with your delusional father, and knew all of his peculiar proclivities. And shall his son, an incredible ditto of *your* dumb-ass parent, in both appearance and behavior, pass me like a complete stranger in these archaic streets of metropolitan downtown Padua? Stand still, Signor Giovanni; for we must have a word or two before we part."

"Speedily, then, most worshipful Professor, speedily," Giovanni nervously responded with feverish impatience. "Does not Your Worship see that I am in serious haste? Must I now have to tell you that I'm suffering from a bad case of advanced diarrhea?"

While the two acquaintances were speaking, a sinister-looking man in black approached along the street, stopping and moving feebly like a person in deleterious health. The pedestrian's face was marked with a most sickly and sallow hue, but yet so pervaded, with an expression of piercing and active intellect that a casual observer might have easily overlooked.

As the infirmed old fogey passed, the afflicted person exchanged a cold and distant salutation with Dr. Baglioni, but then the feeble walker fixed his frightful eyes upon Giovanni with an intentness that seemed to bring-out whatever negative emotion that was within him to absolute contempt. Nevertheless, there was an extremely weird quietness represented in the stern evil look, as if taking merely a speculative, scientific acknowledgement of the lad's presence, and then concurrently not exhibiting any particular human interest in the young man whatsoever.

"It is Dr. Rappaccini!" the Medical Professor whispered to his student when the sickly, pallid-faced stranger had finally passed. "Has he ever seen your face before? Don't be surprised if he wants to vilely poison your ass tomorrow."

"Not that I better know his identity," Giovanni affirmed. "All I wish to do is screw his daughter into total euphoria. What the hell's wrong with that?"

"He has seen you now! He must have seen you before! Using relevant botanical terminology, your delicate ass is grass!" Baglioni emphatically claimed. "For some purpose or other, this demented man of science is making a case study of you. Be prepared to be squeezed into a test tube for future analysis. I know *that* nefarious look of his quite well! It's the same blank expression that coldly illuminates his face as he bends over a bird; a mouse, or a butterfly, which in pursuance of some obscure experiment, the cruel investigator then kills his targeted subject by administering the noxious perfume of an innocent-looking flower. That Botany pedagogue possesses a hideous stare as deep as Hell's Nature itself, but certainly, indeed without Nature's kind warmth of propagating love. Signor Giovanni, I will stake my life upon it! You're the subject of one of Rappaccini's major experiments! If I were you, I'd get the fuck out of Padua right this instant, or else risk being emulsified, or possibly wholly vaporized right into oblivion."

"Will you make a fool of me?" Giovanni passionately asked. "Listen Signor Professor Baglioni; you've maliciously described an untoward experiment in speculative detail. On the contrary, I believe I should implicitly trust Dr. Rappaccini. He looks about as harmless as a pet boa constrictor."

"Doomful naivete! If you exhibit cooperative patience, you shall be promptly executed and delivered to the afterlife; that is, if you believe in the hereafter, then you gotta' understand what Dr. Rappaccini is *here after.* Get my general gist, Asshole!"

"And the Signora Beatrice; what role does she have in this unfolding mystery play?"

"Don't be surprised if she winds-up being the alluring bait, and you the captured hooked fish," the grim-faced medical teacher declared. "Beware of my dire prediction coming to fruition, er, I mean coming to vegetation! If the charming bitch you have the hots for looks too good to be true, then the charming bitch *is* too good to be true!"

But impetuous Guasconti, finding sanctimonious Baglioni's pertinacity excessively intolerable, forcefully broke-away from the bothersome conversation. Soon, Giovanni was fast gone into the darkness of night before the well-intentioned, gossipy professor could again roughly seize his arm. The very aware medical instructor looked after the young man's departure with worried eyes, and then the honest trouble-warner shook his head in absolute disgust.

"This must not be," greatly disappointed Dr. Baglioni said to himself. "This fucked-up youth is the son of my old fucked-up friend Antonio, and I vow that Giovanni shall not come to any harm from the crazed lunatic's planned botanical destruction. And besides," Pietro continued his personal mumble, "I'll not permit this fanatical madman Rappaccini to 'snatch' the lad out of my own hands, just because Giovanni desires entrance into beautiful Beatrice's snatch. And besides, I have yet to collect Giovanni's medical school tuition. Perchance, most learned Giacomo Rappaccini, I may intelligently foil your nefarious scheme precisely where you least dream of being checkmated! I shall not allow my friend's son to be a lousy pawn on your scurrilous botanical chessboard!"

* * * * * * * * * * * *

Meanwhile Giovanni, intrigued with the geometric concept of circumference, had pursued a circuitous route home, and at length found himself staggering at the door of his inferior lodging. As Master Guasconti crossed the dilapidated threshold, the resident was met by old Lisabetta, who smirked and smiled, and the ugly wench was evidently desirous to attract his attention onto her lackluster, sagging tits, and flabby wrinkled ass. After ignoring the old witch's puckered lips, the seasoned dame laid her grasp upon his cloak.

"Signor! Signor!" the housekeeper whispered, still with a hungry smile dominating over the whole breadth of her grotesque, wart-faced visage. "Listen Signor! Stop being a fuck-headed Neapolitan! There is a private entrance into the garden you don't know about!"

"What did you say?" Giovanni returned, reeling quickly about. "Did you say that there is a private entrance into Dr. Rappaccini's exclusive garden?"

"Hush! Hush! Not so damned loud!" Lisabetta softly spoke, putting her age-spot, mole-laden hand over his mouth. "Yes; it wends into the worshipful doctor's garden, where you may see and admire all his fine shrubbery. Many a young man in Padua would give a year's gold simply to be admitted among those most-excellent, rare flowers."

Giovanni put a piece of gold into her trembling greedy hand. "This coin is for your espionage information, and not for sex. You'd have to work a lifetime to earn enough money for me to even consider having any kind of regular or oral sex with you. Even if I was blind, I would vomit at the mere thought. Now Lisabetta, I demand that you show me the fuckin' secret way. And you better not be involved in a goddamned conspiracy with Dr. Rappaccini against me. If so, I promise I'll hastily shove a watermelon up your plump ass, and a saguaro cactus up your raunchy cunt, both objects simultaneously!"

Giovanni's withered, haggish guide soon led the distraught young man along several remote passages, and finally undid an obscure door, through which, as it was opened, there came the sight and sound of rustling leaves, with the broken sunshine rays glimmering among them. Giovanni stepped forth, and forcing himself through the entanglement of a shrub that wreathed its prickly tendrils over most of the hidden entrance, and amazingly, soon stood beneath his own window inside the open area of Dr. Rappaccini's exotic garden.

Giovanni recognized but two or three separate plants in the collection, one a gigantic watermelon, and the second being a large saguaro cactus. "See the melon and the cactus, Lisabetta," the medical student pointed-out and verbally indicated. "Now get the fuck out of here before I decide to sodomize you with the two unorthodox dildos."

Several moments later, while busy with those contemplations and garden observations, the intruder heard soft rustling, and turning rapidly, his eyes beheld Beatrice emerging from beneath the sculptured portal.

After Lisabetta had scampered out of the forbidden garden into a side portal, Giovanni searched-around and suspected that several plants in his immediate vicinity were indeed poisonous. Suddenly, Beatrice approached the then-discovered lad, and the sweet doll's quiet, placid demeanor immediately put his apprehension at ease. There was a look of surprise expressed upon Rappaccini's daughter's impeccable face, but her overall grace seemed vastly brightened by a simple and kind engenderment of endearing pleasure.

"You are an accomplished connoisseur in rare flowers, Signor," Beatrice commenced with a smile, specifically alluding to the cheap daisy bouquet that her new amorous neighbor had flung from the high window. "It is no marvel, therefore, if the sight of my Father's special collection has tempted you to take a closer inspection. If he were here right now," elegant Beatrice eloquently stated, "Father could tell you many strange and interesting facts as to the nature and habits of these most stellar shrubs; for he has spent a lifetime engaged in such studies, and this garden is truly *his* small world."

"And as for yourself, fair Lady," Giovanni replied, "fame says true that you likewise are deeply skilled in the virtues indicated by these rich blossoms and by these spicy erotic effervescent plant perfumes. Would you deign to be my instructress? I should prove to be an eager beaver scholar studying your eager beaver, er, I meant to say, I would be an eager beaver if personally taught by the famous Signor Rappaccini himself."

"Are there such idle rumors circulating about me?" Beatrice asked, with the musical tone of a pleasant laugh. "Do people in the outside world beyond these high walls actually say that I'm skilled in my father's science of plants? What a jest is *that* erroneous hearsay! No; although I've grown-up among these splendid flowers, I know no more of them than their hues and perfume; and sometimes methinks I would fain rid myself of even that same small knowledge," the auburn-haired, silk-dressed goddess articulated. "There are many flower varieties represented here, and those not the least brilliant, neither shock nor offend me when the blooms meet my curious eyes. But pray tell, Signor, do not believe those radical stories about my science achievements. Believe nothing of me save what you see with your own eyes. Have you visited an optometrist lately? You hardly seem a man of vision!"

"And must I believe all that I have seen with my own eyes?" Giovanni pointedly asked, while the recollection of recent former snooping scenes made him fully recollect. "No, Signora; the pupils in my eyes are really your pupils to learn and master Botany, along with other impertinent academic bull-shit. You demand too little of me. Bid me to believe nothing, save what comes from your own divine crotch lips. Er, I mean from your own divine mouth lips."

It would appear that Beatrice vaguely understood the impulsive university student in a fantasy sort of manner. There came a deep flush to her cheeks, although her ass was fully covered; but the "*human deity*" looked directly into Giovanni's eyes, and responded to his gaze of uneasy suspicion with a queen-like haughtiness.

"I do so bid you, Signor, although I am not running an Italian or Dutch auction here," Giacomo Rappaccini's Daughter oddly replied. "Forget whatever you may have fancied in regard to me. If true to the outward senses, still it may be false in its internal essence; but the words of Beatrice Rappaccini's lips are true from the depths of my vulnerable heart, and then extending outward. Those truths you may believe, although I have yet to say anything especially pertinent or significant."

Beatrice's voice and attitude suddenly became gay, and the daughter appeared to derive a pure delight from her incidental communion with the horny youth, a meeting not unlike what the maiden of a lonely island might have felt conversing for the first time with a voyager from the civilized world. Evidently, the girl's experience of life had been confined within the limits of that isolated garden.

Rappaccini's Daughter talked now about matters as simple as the daylight; and about common summer clouds, and now the strange maiden asked elementary questions in reference to the city, and then inquired about Giovanni's distant home; his friends; his mother; and his sisters, with each of the odd questions indicating an incredible lifelong seclusion.

Then, the maiden picked-up a purple flower and gently held the stem and petals to her pallid nose. Immediately, Giovanni realized that the rare purple flower and Beatrice's fragrant breath amazingly smelled identical.

"For the first time in my restricted life," Rappaccini's lonely daughter murmured while eerily addressing the purple flower, "I had forgotten thee while conversing with this young man."

"I remember, Signora," Giovanni accurately recalled, "that you once promised to reward me with one of these living gems in return for the bouquet which I had the happy boldness to fling toward your bare feet. Permit me now to pluck it as a memorial of this most fortuitous meeting."

The callow romantic briskly made a step towards the aforementioned shrub with extended hand, but Beatrice darted forward, uttering a shriek that pierced through his heart like a dagger. The concerned girl anxiously caught his hand, and drew it back with the whole force of her slender figure. Giovanni felt her mere touch, the sensation instantly thrilling his throbbing testicles.

"Touch it not!" the maiden exclaimed in an agonized voice. "Not for thy life! It is fatal, and will be lethal to your body, including your hyperactive genitals!"

Then, hiding her very embarrassed face, the upset girl fled from her suitor's company, and quickly vanished beneath the dull sculptured portal. As Giovanni followed her escape with his melancholy eyes, the youth beheld the emaciated figure and pale intelligence of Dr. Rappaccini, who had been warily watching the recent garden encounter. Master Guasconti knew not how long the crazed botanist had been spying on his ass from within the eerie shadows of the secret garden entrance.

* * * * * * * * * * * * *

No sooner was Giovanni Guasconti alone in his gas chamber (lots of farting being done) that the image of Beatrice came back to haunt his passionate musings, her mental manifestation invested with all the witchery that had been gathering around her form, ever since his first dynamic glimpse of her fantastic body. Whatever formerly had looked ugly (including Lisabetta's scuzzy face and horrendous body) was now beautiful; or, if incapable of such a change, half-decent anyway. Thus, surrendering to the need-to-get-laid, the class-cutting university student spent the night, neither falling asleep nor dropping-out of bed, until the kiss of dawn had begun awakening the slumbering flowers flourishing inside Dr. Rappaccini's fucked-up botanical garden.

When thoroughly aroused in a none sexual manner, Giovanni suddenly became aware of a burning and tingling agony in his right hand, the very one which Beatrice had grasped in her own palm when the naïve dumb-shit was at the point of plucking one of the gemlike flowers. On the back of that swollen hand was now a purple print showing an explicit design of four small fingers, and the likeness of a slender thumb upon the young fool's aching wrist.

"What the fuck's this shit?" the afflicted youth shouted to no one but himself. "I think I'm turning into a goddamned purple pansy or lavender petunia! Perhaps I'm even changing into a shrinking violet violet! If so, I hope I'll be a straight pansy or petunia, and not a gay faggot shrinking violet that had fallen off a Sicilian shrub!"

Giovanni rambunctiously wrapped an unkempt handkerchief about his color-changing hand, and wondered what evil creature had mysteriously stung him, but the chronic dreamer soon forgot his pain with his mind in a tranquil reverie of Beatrice; the dumb-fuck romantic wondering if she was really a Purple People Eater.

After the first encounter with the inimitable beauty, a second was in the inevitable course of what is generally called "fate or destiny". A third; a fourth; and next, another intentional meeting with Beatrice in the garden was no longer an occasional incident in Giovanni's daily life, but within that whole green open space. in which the lover might be compelled to live a monotonous. insular existence as a shunned purple human.

Being accustomed to Giovanni's predictable return each morning, Beatrice expectantly watched for the youth's appearance, and the damsel flew to his side with confidence, even though the girl lacked the luxury of wings upon her angelic back. If, by any oddball chance, the smitten-by-Cupid's-arrow dumb-fuck suitor failed to come at the appointed moment, Rappaccini's Daughter faithfully stood beneath the now-familiar apartment window, and sent-up the rich sweetness and flagrant fragrance of her thick flowery breath, the strong aroma floating around the medical student in the middle of his personal *gas chamber,* and the emitted warmth would then metaphorically echo and reverberate throughout the four chambers situated inside the young fellow's captivated heart.

146

"Giovanni! Giovanni! Why tarry thou? Calm-down and come down!" And down the wooden steps the already turning-purple asshole hastened, with the infatuated dumbbell descended into that seemingly magnetized Eden trap of very poisonous purple flowers.

On the few occasions when Giovanni had seemed tempted to overstep the social limits and grab Beatrice's firm tits, or reach for her hairy bush, Rappaccini's Daughter instantly grew so sad, and so stern, that the pristine doll wore such a look, scaring the accumulated feces out of Giovanni's increasingly purple rectum. At such times, the suitor was so startled at the horrible suspicions inhabiting his addled mind that his love grew thin and faint, and soon Master Guasconti's once potent sex organ shrunk-down to thimble-size in the gloomy morning mist.

A considerable time had passed since Giovanni's last confrontational meeting with eminent Dr. Baglioni. One morning in late October, however, the lazy dunce was disagreeably surprised by a prompt visit from the ax-to-grind professor, whom the concerned lad had scarcely thought of for several whole weeks, deliberately playing hooky, and being absent from the esteemed university.

The visitor chatted carelessly for a few moments about the unreliable gossip abounding in the city and around the university, and then after his small-talk subsided, Dr. Baglioni took-up what the revered college lecturer considered to be a pertinent topic.

"I've been reading a work written by an old classic author," the somewhat-literate medical man revealed, "and my weary eyes met with a story that strangely interested me. Possibly you may remember the sage tale. It is of an Indian prince, who sent a beautiful woman as a present to Alexander the Raisin, er, sorry Giovanni, I had meant to say Alexander the Great. The gift princess I've just mentioned was as lovely as the dawn, and as gorgeous as the spectacular sunset. But what especially distinguished her was a certain rich perfume evident in her breath; a hypnotic scent richer than a garden of Persian roses," the professor impressively described, all the while curiously staring at Giovanni's peculiar purplish skin. "Alexander the Grape, er, I mean to say *Great,* as was natural to a youthful conqueror with an oversized ego and comparable penis, fell in love at first sight with this magnificent female; but a certain sage physician, happened to be present, causing much trouble and chaos, discovered a terrible secret in regard to her."

"And what was that terrible secret?" Giovanni asked, turning his eyes downward to avoid those of the garrulous professor. "Would the Indian princess be crushed like a soft grape in a wine press because of Alexander's obvious crush on her? Did Alexander buy her a grape jelly sandwich at a new deli in India?"

"That this lovely woman," continued Professor Baglioni with austere emphasis, intentionally ignoring Giovanni's stupid drivel, "had slowly-but-surely been nourished with poisons from her birth upward, until her whole nature was so imbued with toxins that she herself became toxic to other humans. Poison was her dominant element of life. With that rich perfume saturating her breath, the lethal princess blasted the very air around her with noxious gas, more horrible than a bull elephant's two-minute-long reverberating fart. Her love would've definitely been poison; her embrace certain death. Is not this a marvelous tale parallels your horse-shit infatuation with Beatrice Rappaccini?"

"A childish fable, and nothing more," Giovanni maintained, nervously squirming in his chair as if to expel from his own asshole a bull elephant sized lengthy fart. "I marvel how Your Worship finds time to read such nonsensical fiction, scattered among your more-important medical studies."

"By the by," the wily professor added, looking uneasily about the dingy, dismal apartment so as not to stare at his absent-to-class student's purple-hued epidermis. "What singular fragrance is this odor that drenches the air within your apartment? Is it the perfume of your grimy gloves? It is faint, but positively delicious; and yet, after all, by no means, is it one iota agreeable. If I were to breathe it for long, methinks it would rot my lungs and make me ill. It is like the breath of a condemned, contaminated flower; but despite my poor vision, I see no *fuckin' flowers* anywhere in this repulsive chamber."

"Nor are there any," Giovanni verified, "and besides, flowers don't have sex like humans do, so there can't be any damned *'fuckin' flowers'*. Now Professor, I urge you to leave the practice of medicine, and then become an expert in agriculture, because in my acute judgment, I think you're ready for the fuckin' funny farm!"

"Yes, Lad; but in truth, my sober imagination does not often play such wicked tricks as yours does," Dr. Pietro Baglioni sarcastically declared. "And were I to fancy any kind of putrid odor, it would be that of some vile apothecary drug, and not a fucked-up artificial flower fragrance, just like the one depicted in the popular Italian love song *Arrivederci Aroma*. Now, in regard to our worshipful friend, Dr. Rappaccini," the university medical teacher lucidly elucidated, "as I have heard from hearsay, there are tincture formulas with foreign alien odors richer than those of Alibaba's Araby. Doubtless then, my dumb-ass medical disciple, the fair and learned Signora Beatrice would administer to her patients with draughts as sweet as an Indian maiden's breath; but extreme woe to him that sips or smells the highly potent intoxicant!"

Giovanni's face soon evinced many contending emotions. The tone in which the mentally-feeble and physically-frail Professor Baglioni had alluded to in regard to the pure and lovely daughter of Dr. Giacomo Rappaccini was an overwhelming torture to the student's sensitive soul; and yet the intimation of an adverse view of her character, an evaluation opposite to the student's own perception, gave instantaneous distinctness to a thousand dark demonic suspicions to inhabit Giovanni's mind.

"Signor Professor," the aggravated purple-skinned lover stated. "You were my father's friend; perchance too, it is your purpose to act in a similar friendly disposition towards his now-perplexed son. I would fain feel nothing towards you, save respect and deference. But I pray you to observe, Signor, that there is one subject on which we must not speak a fuckin' vowel or consonant. What you know or hypothesize," distressed Giovanni editorialized, "is not the true virtue, or the pure character of Signora Beatrice. You cannot, therefore, estimate the wrong, the blasphemy, the false witness, and the verbal injustice that your toxic words have regrettably characterized about the Indian princess's, er, I mean to say, about Beatrice's benign attributes."

"Giovanni! My poor ignorant hollow-minded Giovanni!" the worried medical professor exclaimed with a dire expression of pity. "I know this wretched girl far better than you do, for obviously I am *not* turning purple and you evidently are. You shall hear the truth in respect to the malicious poisoner Dr. Rappaccini, and his equally poisonous not-so-innocent daughter; yes," Baglioni proceeded with his rambling piercing discourse. "The young bitch is just as poisonous as she is beautiful. Listen carefully, you' human purple mushroom; even if you should clobber me on the head with a violin to do violence to my gray hairs, it shall not silence me one iota. That old fable of the Indian princess has become a veritable truth performed by the deep and deadly science of Dr. Rappaccini, and also evident in the alluring person of lovely Beatrice. Be aware and wary of her distinct detrimental odors Giovanni, especially the enticing one being emitted by the girl's wonderful hot love tunnel!"

Mixing humiliation with mortification, shocked Giovanni groaned and defensively hid his violet-toned purple face.

"Her crazed and incensed father loved the smell of incense," Baglioni continued, "and the compulsive lunatic was not restrained by natural affection from offering-up his only child in this horrible manner; yes, offered as the sacrifice of his insane zeal for science. The botanical alchemist who Beatrice admires is indeed a medical fraud, a most dangerous medical fraud at that! And the nut-job will offer his daughter on his botanical altar of contempt, just to vindicate his diabolical theories in addition to his mendacious pursuits."

"It is a horrid, dreadful dream," Giovanni muttered. "And surely, it's a veritable nightmare you're presently dictating to my dubious, disbelieving ears."

"But heed my prosthetic, er, I mean 'my prophetic' words, my callow juvenile Asshole," the obdurate professor resumed, "and attempt to be of good cheer, son of my illustrious former college fraternity drinking friend. It is not yet too late for your rescue and to salvage your endangered life. Possibly we may even succeed in bringing back this miserable flower child before she winds-up in San Francisco protesting constructive things like war and capitalism."

"You're a chemist besides being a medical doctor," Giovanni complimented his talkative guest. "What's your solution Professor?"

"Behold this little silver vase I've removed from my pocket! It was inspirationally wrought by the creative hands of the renowned Benvenuto Cellini, and the vessel is quite worthy to be a love gift to the fairest dame in Italy," Baglioni optimistically explained. "But its fabulous contents are invaluable. One little sip of this antidote would've rendered the most virulent poisons of the Borgias innocuous. Doubt not that it'll be as efficacious medicine against those wretched mixtures of the scurrilous Giacomo Rappaccini. Bestow the vase, and the precious liquid within it, upon your fair Beatrice, and hopefully await the beneficial result."

Dr. Baglioni laid a small, exquisitely-wrought silver vial upon the table, and soon withdrew his hands, leaving what he had said to produce its effectiveness upon the young man's mind.

"Holy hallelujah!" the instantly-relieved student yelled without farting. "First, I listen to your ridiculous Indian princess anecdote, and now I've learned about your fantastic Beatrice antidote! How dually remarkable can a solution get!"

"We will yet thwart Rappaccini and his formidable insanity," the adamant Medical Professor promised, as the ancient scholar decided to finally descend the squeaky stairs.

* * * * * * * * * * **

Throughout Giovanni's whole acquaintance with Beatrice, the suitor had occasionally been haunted by dark surmises as to the beauty's dark-side character; yet so thoroughly had Rappaccini's Daughter made herself appear as a simple, natural, most-affectionate and guileless creature, that the negative image of her now, espoused by Professor Baglioni, seemed so strange, uncanny, and incredible.

"I gotta' institute some decisive test," Giovanni attested, as the infatuated fellow incredulously peered at his purple image being reflected from his grubby apartment's sole mirror. "The lizard, the insect, and the flowers have continued to bug me about Beatrice's chameleon nature, and about her flagrant perfumed breath that makes me' fume inside with purple rage. I know what the fuck I'll do!" the love-struck student decided. "If I can witness one purple flower instantly wither within Beatrice's elegant hand, that'll prove Professor Baglioni's outlandish theory to be true. I'll venture-out to the florist shop, avoid the pedestrian pansies and petunias sauntering by, and purchase another bouquet of daisies to give my precious doll-baby buttercup. Otherwise," Giovanni enunciated to his purple hourglass image, "I'll have to be a lonely purple wallflower at the upcoming freshman hop!"

After purchasing the rather ordinary daisies with his last gold ducat, the romantic fool comprehended that it was now the customary hour of his daily secret rendezvous with Beatrice Rappaccini. Before descending the steps leading to the secret portal that gave access into the precarious botanical garden, Giovanni mumbled, "At least her poison has not yet insinuated itself into *my* system. I'm not yet a blooming idiot; a victimized purple flower in the process of being perilously perished within her witchy grasp."

After returning to the stranger-than-fiction garden, and after recovering from his most recent fantasy stupor, the besieged boyfriend began watching with curious eyes a spider that had been busily at work artfully hanging its networked web. Giovanni bent towards the insect, and soon emitted a deep, long breath. The spider suddenly ceased its toil, and the web vibrated with a tremor originating within the body of the black arachnid. Again, Giovanni sent forth a breath, deeper, longer, and imbued with a venomous feeling, seemingly emitted out of *his* now-viperous heart: the experimenting novice knew not whether he was a wicked wizard, or perhaps only a clumsy nincompoop desperately in love. The affected spider made a convulsive grip with its limp limbs, and soon hung dead upon its intricate web.

"Accursed! Fuckin' accursed!" Giovanni lividly cursed and muttered. "Have thou grown so poisonous that this deadly insect perishes by thy own lethal breath?"

At that moment, a rich, sweet voice came floating-up from the opposite end of the evilly-enchanted garden. "Giovanni! Giovanni! It is past the hour! Why tarry so tardily thou? Come to me! Come in your wonderful, filthy, white-stained leotards!"

"Yes," Giovanni courteously replied. 'She is the only being whom my breath may not slay! Would that it might!' the gallant, infatuated jerk-off silently concluded.

After meeting and briefly greeting, the unlikely pair ambled-on together, sad and reticent, and came thus to the marble fountain and to its accompanying pool of water, recently deposited by the night rain, still, several puddles remaining on the ground. Nearby grew the shrub that bore the incomparable, gemlike, outstanding purple blossoms. Giovanni was affrighted at the eager enjoyment, the sensational appetite so to speak, with which the youth presently found himself inhaling the fragrance of the "condemned flowers", so as had exactly been esoterically depicted by sagacious Professor Pietro Baglioni.

"Beatrice," the university freshman abruptly asked. "Whence came this shrub?"

"My Father had created it," the girl responded with untainted simplicity. "My Father thinks and believes *he* is the Creator!"

"Created it! Created it!" Giovanni indignantly repeated. "What do you mean, Beatrice? Stop worshiping your reprehensible old man as if he's God Almighty!"

"He is only a wise, dedicated little man fearfully acquainted with the secrets of Nature," Beatrice expressed. "And at the hour when I first drew my initial breath into my infant lungs, this peculiar plant sprung from the soil, the offspring of his weird science, and of his extraordinary scientific intellect."

"Tell me more malignant malarkey," the befuddled suitor implored. "My insufficient, hapless brain now requires less-cerebellum and more-cerebrum!"

"While I was but *his* earthly child," Rappaccini's curvaceous daughter continued her singular narrative, now alertly observing with terror that Giovanni had been drawing nearer to the shrub. "Approach not that plant!" Beatrice imperatively commanded. "It has supernatural qualities that you can little dream of. But dearest Giovanni, I eventually grew-up and blossomed with the remarkable plant, and was later mystically nourished with its potent breath. I soon comprehended that *it* was my twin sister, and I loved it with a human affection; for, alas! Hast thou not suspected it; an enveloping awful doom that looms in the gloom from womb to tomb?"

Here Giovanni became overly vexed, and the exotic garden visitor frowned so darkly upon Beatrice that she paused from her unusual pronunciation and trembled. But her faith in *his* almost-tangible tenderness reassured her, and made her blush, regretting that she had doubted his sincere veracity for even an instant.

"There was indeed an awful doom," the girl continued her recollection, "that is, upon the effect of my father's fatal love of science, which coincidentally estranged me from all society of my kind. Until Heaven sent thee, dearest Giovanni, oh, how lonely I was. I now implore you! Plant your purple plum inside my purple pussy garden right now!"

"Was it a hard doom?" Giovanni asked, fixing his eyes upon her while rearranging his hard, swelling, purple erection, which was pulsing-around inside his only pair of brown, white-stained leotards.

"Only of late have I known how hard it truly was," the puzzled daughter commented, tenderly glancing at his hyperactive boner. "Oh, yes, but my heart was torpid, and therefore quiet about excessive emotional excitement."

"Accursed one!" the boyfriend shrieked, with venomous scorn and heightened anger prevalent in his tone of voice. "And finding thy solitude, thy wearisome, thou hast severed me likewise from all the warmth of life, and hast enticed me into thy dangerous region of unspeakable horror! I don't need a piece of ass so badly as to die for it! Hell no! Fuck that shit!"

"Giovanni!" Beatrice exclaimed, turning her large bright brown eyes upon his purple face. But the force of his honest words had not found its way into her impregnable mind; Rappaccini's Daughter was merely thunderstruck six-full-hours after the day's heavy rain had fallen.

"Yes, poisonous thing!" repeated Giovanni, beside himself with passion. "Thou hast vilely done it! Thou hast blasted me! Thou hast filled my veins with toxins before I could die from lustily filling your crotch with purple semen! Thou hast made me as hateful, as ugly, as loathsome, and as deadly a creature as thyself; a world's great wonder of hideous monstrosity! An emotional freak without a frivolous circus sideshow! Now, if our breaths be happily as fatal to ourselves as to all others, let us join our lips in one lethal kiss of unutterable hatred, and so die together!"

"What has befallen me?" Beatrice murmured, alarmed with a low moan generating out of her hurting heart. "Holy Virgin; pity me, a poor heart-broken child about to get laid by a bouncing, hard, throbbing purple pickle!"

"Thou-dost you pray?" Giovanni bellowed, still with the same fiendish scorn being expressed upon his countenance and in his voice. "Thy very prayers, as the strange words come from thy celestial lips, taint and corrode the atmosphere with shades of death. Yes, yes; let us pray!" yelled the hysterical suitor. "Let us go to the local church and dip our fingers in the holy water at the portal, and then together perform the Sign of the Cross! The insane fanatics who will come after us will perish, being plagued by a predatory purple pestilence! Let us jointly sign crosses and articulate our inconsequential prayers into the apathetic air! The contaminated atmosphere will be scattering curses abroad in the likeness of holy symbols! According to our fucked-up Christian customs and traditions," the lad argued, "all this stupid religious shit must first happen before we can acceptably get laid, and then mutually and simultaneously die!"

"Giovanni," Beatrice nervously answered, for her grief was ascending far beyond common passion. "Why join thyself with me in communicating and enacting those terrible sinful words you've mentioned? It is quite true that I am the horrible thing thou hast named me. But what hast thou to do, save to only shudder at my hideous misery; to go forth out of this garden and mingle with the remainder of thy lackluster race, and forget that there ever crawled on Earth such a monster as poor diseased Beatrice? Have you never screwed a Gorgon before?"

"Do you pretend or feign ignorance?" Giovanni interrogated, scowling upon her as if she was Medusa reincarnated. "Behold! This strength, this incredible power called love I have gained from the pure and pristine daughter of Dr. Rappaccini. Blessed is the fruit of thy womb, and I can't wait to lick it after you diligently suck upon my throbbing grande banana!"

A swarm of summer insects began flitting through the air in search of the food promised by the fragrant floral odor emissions of the fatal garden shrubs. The hungry bugs circled around Giovanni's head, and the creatures were evidently attracted towards his presence by the same influence which had drawn the bugs from the sphere of several of the aromatic shrubs. The suitor issued forth a purple-tinted breath among their flying colony, and Guasconti smiled bitterly at Beatrice when a score of the besieged insects fell dead upon the wet turf.

"I see it! I see it now!" Beatrice shouted. "It is my father's fatal science at work here! No, no, Giovanni; it was not I! Never! Never! I had dreamed only to love thee and be with thee for a little time, and so to let thee gradually pass-away into my past, leaving but thine image in mine heart, and the splendid memory of your throbbing erection in my firm hand; for, Giovanni," Rappaccini's Daughter convincingly added, "believe it or not, though my body be nourished with poison, my spirit is God's adventurous creature. And my famished soul craves love as its daily food. But my avaricious and cynical father has ironically united us in sharing this fearful sympathy. Yes; spurn me; tread upon me; kill me, if need be, but first screw me into high ecstasy before either or both of us die! Oh, what is death after such eloquent words as thine have spoken? But it was not I. Not for a world of bliss would I have ever killed, even a tiny ant, either deliberately or by accident."

Giovanni's passion had virtually exhausted itself in its most recent outburst from his purple lips. There now came across him an odd sense, mournful, but not without tenderness; his comprehension was a valid and true interpretation of the intimate relationship between Beatrice and himself.

"Dear Beatrice," Giovanni addressed the gorgeous girl while she shrank-away as always at his erection's waving approach. "Oh, my dearest Beatrice; our fate is not yet so desperate. Behold! There is a medicine, a very potent mixture of profound ingredients, as a wise physician has persuasively assured me, and the magical formula is almost divine in its efficacy."

"Well, what the hell is this miracle cure?" the frustrated girl demanded knowing. "We can sell it at the piazza mart and make ourselves a propitious fortune!"

"The compound is composed of elements and benign drugs that are the most opposite to those by which thy awful-awesome Father has brought this insidious calamity upon thee and me. It is distilled of blessed herbs, blended with life-giving vitamins, fruits, and special minerals, all the items hardly available at the corner Health Apothecary Shop, let alone at the discount piazza mart. Shall we not quaff the elixir together, and thus be mutually purified from evil?"

"Give it to me before you give it to me!" Beatrice demanded, first pointing to her boyfriend's bouncing erection, and next extending her hand to receive the little silver vial which handsome Giovanni had taken from his bosom, while thinking about Beatrice's bosom. "I'll drink this miracle antidote, but do thou await the result."

The anxious girl put Baglioni's antidote to her lips, but at the same moment, the figure of Dr. Giacomo Rappaccini emerged from the side garden portal and maneuvered slowly towards the deteriorated marble fountain. As the vile villain drew near, the pale man of science seemed to gaze with a triumphant facial expression at both Giovanni and the pristine virgin maiden, as might an artist, who should spend his life in achieving a magnificent statue, finally becoming fully satisfied with his success.

The gaunt-faced botanist stopped and paused; and next, the mad experimenter's bent form grew erect with conscious power. Dr. Rappaccini spread-out his ancient hands over the lovebirds in the attitude of a benevolent gracious Patriarch imploring a blessing upon his cherished children; but indeed, those were the same vile hands that had thrown poison into the stream of *their* lives. Giovanni trembled and Beatrice shuddered nervously, and the petrified girl instinctively pressed her hand upon her heart.

"My daughter," Dr. Rappaccini announced. "Thou art no longer lonely in the world. Pluck one of those precious gems from thy sister shrub, and bid thy bridegroom wear it in his bosom. I promise you that it'll not harm him now. My science and the sympathy between thee and him have so wrought within his system that he now stands apart from common men, as thou dost, daughter of my pride and triumph, apart from ordinary women. Pass on, then, through *this* world, with your new-found love becoming most dear to one another! The young man's purple semen shall turn to white sperm juice once more!"

"My Father," Beatrice courageously answered, with her demeanor feeble-and still, as the daughter spoke with her quivering hand upon her heart. "Wherefore didst thou inflict *this* miserable doom upon thy only child?"

"Miserable!" Giacomo Rappaccini's voice boomed. "What mean you, foolish girl? Do you deem it misery to be endowed with marvelous gifts against which no human power or any mortal strength could rival or conquer; to be able to quell the mightiest opponent with a single potent breath; to be as delightfully terrible as thou art beautiful? Wouldst thou, then Daughter, have preferred the condition of a weak woman, exposed to all evil and capable of none yourself?"

"I would fain have been loved, not feared by quixotic purple lovers," Beatrice sadly stated, sinking her desirable body down upon the garden's ground. "But now it matters not. I am going into eternity, Father; departing to where the evil which thou hast striven to mingle with my being will pass-away like a fleeting dream; yes, like the fragrance of these poisonous purple flowers, which will no longer taint my breath among the flowers of your accursed Eden. Farewell, Giovanni! Thy words of hatred are like toxic lead within my heart; but they too, will fall away as my soul either ascends into glorious Heaven, or descends into diabolical Hell."

And thus, the poor victim of man's ingenuity, and also the innocent product of thwarted nature, a sweet girl needlessly sacrificed for the cause of perverted scientific knowledge, had fatefully perished there, at the feet of her father and of her dearest love, Giovanni.

Just at that moment Professor Pietro Baglioni appeared inside his medical student's overhead apartment window. The agitated university pedagogue called-down loudly, in a tone of triumph mixed with accompanying horror.

"Rappaccini! Rappaccini! Is *this* tragic result my eyes are witnessing the upshot of your evil experiment gone fatally wrong! You perverted monster!" the incensed medical professor loudly exclaimed. "You've selfishly sacrificed your own flesh and blood daughter upon your contemptible altar of botanical science!"

"The Catbird Seat"
James Thurber

Mr. Erwin Martin had made a lucky strike and had bought the last pack of *Camels* on Monday night in the most crowded cigar store on bustling Broadway. It was theatre time and seven or eight men were inside the establishment pretending to be buying cigarettes while cunningly bartering money and contraband for marijuana and meth' cocaine. The clerk, whose real job was being the local illegal drug czar, didn't even offer a single glance at Mr. Martin, who surreptitiously put the seventy-five cent pack into his overcoat pocket, furtively left a dollar upon the dirty counter and then inconspicuously ambled outside.

If any of the staff members at F & S Market and Merchandise Distributors had seen Erwin Martin buy a pack of cigarettes, that observer would have been quite astonished by witnessing the subtle transaction, for it was generally known that Mr. Martin did not smoke, and never ever had acquired the nasty habit. No one in or around the store premises even noticed his presence, nor did anyone in the vicinity desire to know, or for that matter, anyone who had been one of Mr. Martin's few paranoid acquaintances gave a Sixth Avenue shit whether the stealthy fellow had lung cancer or not.

It was just a week to the day since feckless Mr. Erwin Martin had decided to 'rub-out' Ms. Vagine Barrows. The somewhat interesting terminology 'rub-out' pleased the gentleman exceedingly because the little phrase suggested nothing more than the correction of a typographical error on office copy paper--in this case, an unfortunate error of his vastly demanding and tyrannical boss, Mr. Filmore Feitweiler.

Self-conscious Mr. Martin had spent each night of the past week meticulously working-out the complicated details of his vile plan and then incessantly examining and rehashing them on paper and also in his distrustful mind. As the neurotic *Camels'* customer ambled hastily in the eastward direction of his home-sweet-home, now the obsessive/ compulsive fanatic conscientiously reviewed his complex homicide scheme again.

For the hundredth time the potential felon resented the element of imprecision, the margin of guesswork that entered into the highly competitive business of retailing, and coincidentally, imprecision also contaminated the business of committing the "perfect murder crime." The file manager, as the key F & S department project employee, had worked it out, and his methodology was casual and fairly bold, but the risks were too considerable to even contemplate the remotest chance of failure. Something unforeseen might go drastically wrong anywhere along the line. And therein lay the cunning of the plotter's rather devious scheme.

No one on the outside would ever see inside his cogent sagacity the cautious, painstaking clandestine hand of one Erwin Martin, head of the filing department at F & S, of whom grumpy Mr. Filmore Feitweiler had once obtusely said, "Man is fallible in fucking-up somewhere along the line, but shrewd and thorough Erwin Martin isn't." Yes, up to now no one in the company would ever suspect or detect Erwin's elusive hand since no asshole working for the firm ever suspected or detected Martin of being involved in any wicked skullduggery, that is, unless any part of the genius's concealment were to presently be accidentally exposed and the wily culprit foolishly getting caught in the act. 'I can't fuck-up! I can't fuck-up!' the man worried as he sneakily approached his Manhattan residence.

Sitting in his nondescript apartment's recliner, drinking a glass of his favorite beverage milk, mediocre Mr. Martin carefully reviewed his case against Ms. Vagine Barrows, as the mastermind had monotonously done thrice every evening for seven consecutive nights. Naturally, he reviewed his critical analysis at the beginning.

The lousy bitch's quacking voice and braying laugh had first profaned the halls of F & S on March 7, 1941 (Mr. Martin had a head for remembering dates, all except female ones that he never had). Old Roberts, the bullshitting personnel chief, had introduced her as the newly appointed Special Adviser to the President of the firm, the lady martinet reporting only to Mr. Filmore "Fill More Positions" Feitweiler. From the outset the reprehensible amazon had greatly appalled normally tranquil Mr. Erwin Martin, but the experienced-in-conflict veteran office trooper hadn't overtly shown his dissatisfaction to anyone. His sole reticent response was giving his new nemesis his dry hand, a look of studious concentration, and a faint insincere smile.

"Well," Vagine had melodramatically complained to hard-working Erwin, looking at the pile of papers accumulated upon his desk. "Are you attempting to lift the proverbial oxcart out of the ditch?"

As Mr. Martin recalled *that* non-inspirational "Road to Damascus" epiphany office moment over his milk, which he instantly spilled but did not cry over, Erwin squirmed slightly in his recliner chair and inaudibly farted. 'I must keep my mind concentrated on her unethical back-stabbings cavorting around as a special adviser to good old F.F.; but not so much not on her fucked-up peccadillos as being a despicable personality,' Erwin wisely and secretly contemplated.

Inside the downtown office building, Martin's special strategy design he had found difficult in doing, despite his considering entering an abrupt written objection to his new superior and then sustaining it. The many faults of the contemptible 'dyke' kept reverberating upon his mind like the outbursts of an unruly courthouse witness. Ms. Vagine Barrows had, for almost two years now, baited him, all the while endeavoring to initiate an argument to then report the hostile confrontation to good old F.F.

In the halls, in the elevator, even in his own office, into which the surly bitch romped now and then like an apocalyptic circus horse, Ms. Barrows was constantly shouting those same fucked-up ludicrous questions at him. "Are you lifting the oxcart out of the ditch? Are you tearing up the pea patch? Are you hollering down the rain barrel? Are you scraping around the bottom of the pickle barrel? Are you using enough toilet paper to clean-up your colossal mess? Are you sitting in the damned catbird seat?"

It was Joey Hart, one of Mr. Martin's two dependable assistants, who had explained what the gibberish coming out of Vagine's foul mouth actually meant. It took the aspiring felon a while to fathom that everything the nasty office 'dyke' would utter in his direction generally meant just about the same goddamned thing: a magnified trite criticism on steroids.

"Vagine must be an avid Dodger fan," Joey had concluded. "Red Barber announces the Dodger games over the radio and he uses those precise stupid-shit expressions--picked 'em up doing baseball games down South, I believe."

Hart had gone off the record to explain the trivia to Martin. "I think the clichés are simpleton, silly remnants left over from the goddamned Civil War. For example Erwin," Joey confidentially indicated, "the term 'tearing-up the pea patch' basically means going on a rampage; and 'sitting in the catbird seat' means sitting pretty, like a Brooklyn batter with three balls and no strikes on him. Don't get your' irritable bowels in a gaseous uproar Erwin, but it appears as if Vagine Barrows is out to fuckin' detonate and destroy your ass!"

Mr. Martin dismissed all this office sensationalism with an effortless shrugging of his wimpy shoulders. True, the persistent female harassment had become annoying, it had driven the recipient near to on-the-job distraction, but Erwin was too solid a man to be moved to murder by anything as childish as to being grossly verbally abused by a selfish 'dominant lesbian.' It was fortunate and necessary, emotionally molested Erwin assessed and reflected, that the aggrieved office manager should accumulate facts and then pass on the important charges against Ms. Barrows to good old F.F., but next Martin would on the Q.T. consult with another trusted key assistant to volatile Mr. Filmore Feitweiler.

"Despite her uncouth rudeness," Erwin told old maid associate Miss Helen Paird, "I always try to project the outward appearance of amiable tolerance. That's my biggest problem and my best attribute Helen. I'm too damned polite when encountering an avowed enemy."

"Why, I even believe you sort of like the woman, maybe even love her enough to shack-up with that dominatrix Vagine," Miss Paird, F.F.'s other reliable assistant, said to Erwin. He had simply smiled. "You'll have a few S & M tricks with the dominatrix!"

* * * * * * * * * * * *

Erwin Martin's mind would often drift-off into fantasyland where the beleaguered fellow would imagine a courtroom judge's gavel rapping a case of alleged corporate negligence to order. Ms. Vagine Barrows stood charged with willful, blatant, and relentless attempts to maliciously destroy the efficiency and the operating system of reputable F & S Market and Merchandise Distributors. The in-place program was competent, material, and relevant evaluation to review her detrimental advent upon the work scene along with the witch's ambitious ballistic rise to power.

In his daydream, Mr. Martin had gotten the story from Miss Paird, who seemed always able to find things out through perceptive observation and discovery. According to Helen, Ms. Barrows had cordially met Mr. Feitweiler at a Las Vegas convention party, where the domineering woman had mercifully rescued vulnerable F.F. from the embraces of a powerfully built drunken man who had mistaken the burly F & S president for a famous retired Middle Western university football coach.

According to the dream's evolution, Vagine had led Filmore to a soft leather sofa and somehow worked upon him a monstrous magic. The ageing company president had hastily jumped to the horrendous conclusion right there and then that this 'dyke' was a woman of singular attainments, equipped with nice knockers who also could professionally bring-out the best in F.F. and in the then failing firm.

Now venturing back to reality, Helen Baird's version of the dyke's history was that to show his gratitude for the Las Vegas scenario, Filmore Feitweiler had introduced Vagine Barrows into the financially troubled F & S Company functioning as his special adviser. On that non-momentous day, confusion got its gigantic foot caught in the door. After Miss Tyson, Mr. Brundage, and Mr. Bartlett had been fired for no legitimate reasons, and after forty-year-employee Mr. Munson had taken his hat and vehemently stalked-out of his office, mailing in his official written resignation later, old Roberts, the ground level shipping manager, had been emboldened to speak and confer to Mr. Feitweiler.

"Sorry to bother you from your paramount duties F.F.," Roberts prefaced his grievance, "but your loyal dedicated Mr. Munson's department had been a little disrupted by Ms. Vagine Barrows interference in standard day-to-day decision making. Boss, hadn't they,

160

sorry Sir, by the pronoun *they* I mean the wounded firm, so therefore, hadn't *we* perhaps better resume the old safe and successful system instead of us implementing this crazy woman's bizarre hare-brain changes?"

"Certainly not!" F.F. stubbornly maintained. "I have the greatest faith in Mrs. Barrows' tits, er, I mean in her wits. They require a little seasoning, of course, a little hot seasoning, yes, that's all they really need. Especially around the nipples, er Roberts, I meant to say especially around the various ripples!"

After the brief personnel conference involving Vagine Barrows as the subject of debate, Mr. Roberts had given-up his crusade to get the bitch fired or demoted. Mr. Erwin Martin now took the task upon himself of reviewing in detail all the destructive changes wrought by big-breasted Ms. Barrows, and the middle management employee determined that "the dyke" had begun chipping away at the cornices of the firm's edifice and now she was swinging at the foundation stones with a sharp pick-ax.

'Could it be that Vagine has Indian blood flowing in her cold veins?' Erwin speculated, 'If so, she must be one of those unhappy lesbian Chipp-away (Chippewa) squaws!'

Mr. Martin came now, in his mental-recall summing-up of the workplace dilemma, the office conflict could be traced to the afternoon of Monday, November 2, 1942-just one pathetic week ago. On that infamous day, at 3 P.M., petulant Ms. Barrows had bounced into his office unannounced. "Boo!" she had yelled like a fucked-up trick or treat Halloween ghost. "Are you scraping around the bottom of the pickle barrel?"

Mr. Martin had been staring at the office intruder from under his green eye-shade, saying nothing but angrily thinking, 'My damned pickle doesn't need any fuckin' barrel bottom right now!' The female invader then had begun to nonchalantly wander about Erwin's sacred little office, taking-in all the minor defects with her great nit-picking, popping eyes, the quick inspection being performed all the while with her erect tits protruding like two huge torpedoes that had been welded to her massive chest.

"Do you really need all these filing cabinets cluttering-up the damned place?" the uncivil lady had demanded like a Parris Island no-nonsense female Marine drill sergeant. "There must be plenty of dumb-ass duplication existing in all these disorganized cabinets."

Mr. Martin's heart had jumped to attention without any particular desire of saluting his (rank) superior rank office officer. "Each of these files," Erwin diplomatically emphasized, keeping his voice low, steady and even, "plays an indispensable part in the overall smooth-working distribution systems of F & S."

Vagine then deliberately brayed at him. "Well, don't tear up the pea patch!" And then, the unlikeable troublemaker sauntered over to the door. From there Ms. Barrows nastily and sarcastically bawled, "But you sure have got a lot of fine scrap in here!"

Mr. Martin could no longer doubt that the finger of persecution was being pressed upon his beloved department. Her notorious pickaxe was on the upswing, was in fact transforming into a chainsaw, a dangerous tool poised for the first lethal slice directed exactly toward Erwin's vulnerable neck.

The advance written letter warnings had not come yet; Martin had received no blue memo' from the still-enchanted Mr. Feitweiler bearing nonsensical job performance recommendations pertaining to a negative evaluation originating from the mahogany desk of the obscene woman fault-finder. But there was no doubt in Mr. Martin's astute mind that one would be forthcoming rather soon.

"If the abominable witch wants to be a faultfinder," Martin mumbled to himself, "Vagine oughta' buy a goddamned Geiger counter, study seismology and then move-out to sunny California in the vicinity of the goddamned San Andreas fault!"

The victim decided that he must act quickly and vengefully make Vagine his victim. Already a precious week since the difficult office encounter had gone by. That very night, employing his vivid imagination, Mr. Erwin Martin stood-up in his apartment living room, still holding his sixteen ounce glass of milk. "Gentlemen of the jury," he said to himself while projecting his daydream into the pretend apartment courtroom, "I demand the death penalty for this most horrible fucked-up individual, Ms. Ugly Vagine Barrows."

* * * * * * * * * * * *

The next day at his work office thorough and efficient Mr. Erwin Martin followed his usual routine, polished his eyeglasses more often than usual (five times in the first half hour) and then assiduously sharpened an already sharp pencil four more times. But not even Miss Helen Paird noticed him paying extraordinarily special and nervous attention to all of the irrelevant detail. Only once did the prospective assassin catch sight of his targeted victim, who had smugly and unsuspiciously swept past him in the hall lavatories' area, Vagine greeting Erwin with a patronizing and perfunctory very brief "Hi!" salutation.

At five-thirty the vexed candidate for the nightly Action News main story walked home, as usual, and anxiously swallowed-down two tall glasses of milk instead of the normal one. Erwin had never drunk any liquid stronger that Grade A milk in his life--unless you count an occasional ginger ale on New Year's Eve and the annual Fourth of July celebration.

The late Sam Schlosser, the S letter of F & S, had praised Mr. Martin at a staff meeting several years before for *his* exercising commendable temperate temperance habits. "Our most efficient worker Martin Erwin, er, I mean Erwin Martin, neither drinks nor smokes," the corporation's co-founder praised the loyal employee, inadvertently getting his simple-sounding name reversed. "The tangible results speak for themselves." Bald and fat Mr. Filmore Feitweiler had been sitting next to his bald and fat corporate partner, nodding his noggin in tacit approval.

That evening Mr. Erwin Martin was still meditating about that impromptu Sam Schlosser moronic speech along with the firm's "red-letter day." As usual, Erwin walked over to Schrafft's Restaurant on Fifth Avenue near Forty-sixth Street at precisely 8 p.m. The faithful patron finished his usual meal of steak and potatoes and after dinner read as usual the financial pages of the *Sun* up to a quarter to nine. It was Erwin's 'like clockwork' custom to take an after dinner stroll around bustling Times Square at 42nd and Broadway.

This particular time, however, the disgruntled F & S worker, with plenty of grievances on his mind, walked down Fifth Avenue at a casual pace, but then his lazy gait quickened. Erwin's gloved hands felt moist and warm, his forehead cold, and most significantly, Martin's bowels were constipated. His self-awareness caught himself transferring his pack of *Camels* from his overcoat to an inner jacket pocket. As he did so, the potential criminal wondered if the cigarettes represented an unnecessary element of stress to his grand murder plan, for Ms. Vagine Barrows smoked only *Lucky Strikes.* 'If I get in a *Lucky Strike* to her head with a blunt instrument like a crowbar, well, that surprise blow oughta' do the bitch in!' Martin hypothesized. 'Too bad I forgot my fuckin' crowbar and sledgehammer back at my apartment.'

It was the wimpy office manager's idea to haughtily take a few puffs on a *Camel* (after the rubbing-out had occurred), stub it out in the nearby ashtray holding her lipstick-stained *Luckies,* and thus drag a small red herring across the investigation trail.

Perhaps it was not a good idea to demonstrate such arrogant bravado after intentionally committing a major murder felony. Once lighted, it would take valuable time to finish 'the weed.' Erwin might even choke or cough too loudly, causing a nosy neighbor to investigate his telltale throat being clogged with smoke, nicotine and carbon dioxide.

Mr. Martin had never seen the house on West Twelfth Street where Ms. Barrows lived, but Erwin had a clear enough stereotype 'mind-picture' of the brownstone structure in his very orderly and organized cerebrum. Fortunately, Vagine had haughtily bragged to everybody she knew about her "perfectly ducky" first-floor apartment in the "perfectly darling three-story brownstone." There would be no doorman or other attendants to worry about; just possibly several eavesdropping tenants of the second and third floors, probably already listening and hoping for the thump of Ms. Ugly Vagine Barrows' big hard firm tits and ass hitting the floor.

As the Action News candidate meandered and veered along through pedestrian traffic, Mr. Martin realized that he would get to his anticipated destination before nine-thirty, an inconvenient forty-five minutes prior to his already mentally arranged time of arrival. He had considered walking north on Fifth Avenue from Schrafft's Restaurant to a point from which it would take him until ten o'clock to reach the house. At that hour people were less likely to be coming in or going out of various residences in the designated crime vicinity.

But in order to competently honor the forty-five minute time adjustment, fastidious Erwin would have made an awkward loop in around Herald Square, pace around the entire Empire State Building on 34th Street, and then amble his non-routine route all the way down to West 12th Street.

It was impossible for Erwin to accurately figure when people would be entering or leaving the upscale apartment house, anyway. Indeed, the permanent elimination of despicable Ms. Vagine Barrows represented taking a great risk at any hour. If Martin ran into anybody listed in his telephone address book, or for that matter met any casual acquaintance while patrolling Greenwich Village on his vital 'commando mission', the scheming perpetrator would simply have to place the 'rubbing-out' of Vagine Barrows in the inactive file category box until the golden opportunity for a new strategic situation again developed.

The same circumstances would hold true if there was someone visiting the obnoxious bitch inside her luxurious apartment. In that case Erwin would just say that he had been coincidentally passing by, had recognized her often bragged-about charming house, and thought he'd drop in for a tall glass of milk and some much-needed social gratification.

Feeling compelled to act as soon as possible, Erwin decided to abandon his original plan and to immediately get his fat ass in gear. It was eighteen minutes after nine when Mr. Martin confidently turned his steps into Twelfth Street. A tall fellow passed him, and then another preoccupied man and a woman, exchanging essential gossip about "how to cheat on your spouse."

Erwin made sure that there was no one within fifty paces when he came to the desired house, located halfway down the block. Martin was up the steps and inside the small vestibule in no time, pressing the bell under the appropriate card that appropriately read: "Ms. Vagine Barrows".

164

When the clicking in the lock started, on impulse Erwin skillfully jumped forward against the door. Like an accomplished private investigator on the hunt, the scrupulous visitor got inside the safety zone rather fast, cautiously closing the door behind him. A bulb in a lantern hung from the hall ceiling on a long chain seemed to illuminate a monstrously bright light.

No one was standing, ascending or descending on the stairway, which went up ahead of him paralleling the left wall. A door opened down the corridor in the wall on the right. The brave guest approached it swiftly on tiptoe, when suddenly it instantly shocked Martin by swinging open.

"Well, for God's sake, look who the hell's here!" bawled the pretentious Ms. Barrows, and her classic braying laugh rang-out like the report of a loud shotgun. Feeling threatened, Erwin rushed past her like a football tackle, bumping her in his confused haste.

"Hey, quit the damned shoving!" she sassily exclaimed, forcefully closing the door behind them, automatically making Erwin thinking that he had been trapped in a kill zone. The unlikely pair was now standing inside Vagine's well-appointed living room, which seemed to Mr. Martin to be lighted by a hundred lamps, tiffany mostly, but definitely not from Tiffany's.

"What's after you?" the female despot promptly asked. "Have you changed your name to William? You're as jumpy as a Billy goat."

Erwin found that he was unable to speak or even fart. His thumping heart seemed to be wheezing in his throat. "I--yes," Martin finally brought-out in a befuddled reply. "I mean, er no! My first name's still Martin!" the ruffled visitor stammered.

Vagine was jabbering and laughing as the accommodating hostess started helping him off with his coat. "No, no," the addled assassin insisted. "I'll put it here." He took it off without Ms. Barrows' expert assistance and placed his coat on a chair near the door.

"Your hat and gloves, too," the villainess added, indicating her command with her two hands. "Please remember, you're informally present in a lady's house."

Erwin reluctantly put his hat on top of the coat. Ms. Barrows seemed even larger in stature inside her apartment than she did standing and barking at Martin inside his diminutive F & S office. The fellow kept his gloves on in protest to her imperative tone of voice. "I was just passing by," he uncreatively mentioned. "I recognized—say, is there anyone here?"

The hostess laughed louder than ever. "No you fool," she typically disagreed, "we're all alone. You're as white as a KKK sheet, you funny man. Whatever has come over your sensibilities? I'll mix you a hot toddy or get you a tall glass of *Southern Comfort*."

The presumptuous woman started toward a cabinet door across the room. "Will scotch-and-soda be all right? But say now, you don't drink alcohol, do you?" She next turned and gave Erwin her amused look, feigning disappointment like a 1940s' female Hollywood movie actress would.

Mr. Martin pulled himself together. "Scotch-and-soda will be perfectly all right," he courageously answered. Erwin could hear her mockingly and annoyingly laughing in the kitchen. His eyes searched quickly around the living room for the best murder weapon to utilize, for in his machination, Martin had counted on finding one there to improvise during his brutal extermination. There were andirons and a poker in place next to the attractive brick fireplace, and something large was leaning in a corner, the object looking like an Indian clobbering club. None of them would do. The murder act couldn't be done exactly that way. He began to pace around the living room while Vagine was still mixing the scotch and soda concoctions in the adjacent kitchen.

'Oh no,' Erwin thought while fearfully considering a terribly hideous prospect. 'Possibly Vagine plans to get me drunk and then use the poker or the Indian club on me.'

During his cursory living room observation, Erwin speedily came to an expensive-looking French provincial desk. On its slate lay a metal paper knife with an ornate handle. 'Would it be sharp enough to slit her throat?' the neurotic man wondered. The jittery fellow reached for the miniature item and in the process clumsily knocked over a small brass jar. Stamps spilled out of it and the heavy object fell to the hardwood floor with a disturbing clatter. "Hey Cement Hands," Ms. Barrows boisterously yelled from the nearby kitchen, "are you' again tearing-up the pea patch?"

Erwin managed to emit a strange laugh, sounding like an oddball Munchkin from the *Wizard of Oz* movie. Picking up the dropped knife, the coward tried its piercing point against his left wrist. It was blunt and pathetically dull. The decorative knife wouldn't do, even to open a thin envelope.

When Ms. Barrows reappeared, carrying two highballs, Mr. Martin, standing there with his gloves on and his intimidated balls high inside his scrotum sac, became acutely conscious of the gross exaggerated fantasy that his overactive imagination had wrought. Cigarettes in his pocket, being alone with Ms. Vagine Barrows in her plush Greenwich Village apartment, a potent liquor drink especially prepared for him by his prospective victim--it was all too incredibly improbable to ever fully comprehend. It was more than incredibly improbable; it was incredibly impossible. Somewhere in the back of his overmatched mind a vague idea stirred as the visitor continuously stirred his cold scotch and soda.

166

"For Heaven's sake, take off those damned gloves," commanded Ms. Barrows in her Parris Island Marine tone. "Are you pretending to be the head waiter at the goddamned Stork Club?"

"I always wear them in the house," Mr. Martin fretfully declared. "If I owned a car, I would definitely put them in the glove compartment." The ideas of strangulation and of leaving no fingerprint evidence began to bloom, strangely and wonderfully inside his already abused mind.

Vagine put her mixed drink glass on a coffee table in front of the sofa and sat on the couch, motioning for Erwin to duplicate her maneuvers. "Come over here, you oddly peculiar chubby little man," she unromantically beckoned and insulted. "Let me try and evaluate your true masculine gumption!"

Mr. Martin gingerly stepped over to the grouch on the couch and sat nervously beside her. It was extremely difficult removing a cigarette out of the full pack of *Camels,* but showing true grit and awkward determination, Martin luckily managed to accomplish his goal.

Vagine adroitly held a match for him, laughing. "Well," she lustily announced, handing him his not-yet-used cold scotch and soda from the coffee table, "this visit of yours is indeed perfectly marvelous. You with a drink in one hand and a cigarette held in the other. Too damned bad you have only one mouth for both."

Mr. Martin puffed away indulgently, but amazingly, not too awkwardly, and then the guest took an adventurous gulp of the rather dark-colored highball. "I drink and smoke all the friggin' time," he lied and boasted. Erwin then clinked his glass against hers, imitating what he had often seen in dumb-ass theater movies. "Here's nuts to that old windbag, Feitweiler," the imbiber brashly proclaimed, and then hardily gulped another mouthful. The stuff tasted awful, but Erwin made no grimace out of sheer dread of being royally reprimanded and humiliated.

"Really now, Mr. Martin," Vagine challenged and disagreed, her polite voice and posture suddenly changing to one of sternness, "you are pissing me off by irresponsibly insulting *our* esteemed employer." Ms. Barrows was now designated "All Special Adviser to the President," and the imperial bitch proudly coveted that prestigious corporate title.

"Vagine, er, I mean Ms. Barrows, I've had a dynamite idea. I'm preparing a powerful bomb in a secret laboratory location," related Mr. Martin restively, "which when exploded will blow the old goat higher than Hell, perhaps blasted into Purgatory, and if fucked-up Feitweiler is lucky, his dead ass will zoom right past St. Peter's desk and then right through the goddamned gold gilded Pearly Gates, directly into Downtown Heaven."

Erwin had only had a little of the potent dark-tinted drink, which was not quite as strong as that of the muscular big-titted hostess.

"Do you take dope or something like heroin?" the non-heroine Ms. Barrows coldly asked.

"Yes, heroin," said Mr. Martin. "I'll be coked to the gills when I finally bump that old fuck buzzard off. The dirty conniving bastard deserves such a rotten fuckin' fate."

"Mr. Martin!" Vagine apprehensively shouted, getting to her feet in a hurry. "That will be all of that fantasy violence talk from you. You must go away at once. Your defiant rebellious rhetoric has upset me greatly!"

Mr. Martin took another swallow of his scotch and soda. He then proficiently tapped his cigarette out in the rectangular red ashtray and next confidently put the pack of *Camels* on the coffee table. Then the failed assassin stood erect with his corpulent chest valiantly sticking-out to deliberately rival Ms. Barrows' impressive dual breast torpedoes.

The agitated hostess mimicked his rapid activities and angrily stood-up, glaring and frowning at Martin, who without instruction, walked over and put on his hat and coat.

"Not a word to anyone about this confidential conversation," the semi-intoxicated office manager austerely requested, and then the emboldened Greenwich Village visitor laid an index finger against his closed lips. "Honestly, Vagine," the suddenly intrepid guest quipped, "I think you oughta' move to Holland. That's where all the goddamned dykes are! Maybe the next time you take a leak, another fucked-up lesbian companion of yours could stick her middle finger up your cunt to stop it!"

All the appalled Ms. Barrows could yell out was "Really! What a dumb-shit request you're begging of me! You weak, insubordinate, impudent fool! Your insolence will soon learn your ass that I'm still the one sitting in the catbird seat! I'm gonna' get your lard-ass rear end outa' S & F, er, that is to say you're gonna' be fired like a Cape Canaveral rocket from F & S headquarters!"

Mr. Martin put his right gloved hand onto the doorknob. "I'm the one sitting in the catbird seat," he cockily vociferated. The F & S employee, completely out of character, then stuck his tongue out at the astonished bitch, expeditiously stepped out the door, staggered down the steps and soon left the property. Nobody saw him go.

In less than an hour of steady walking, Mr. Erwin Martin eventually arrived at his small midtown apartment, well before eleven. Much to his satisfaction, as usual, no apathetic neighbor ever noticed him entering. The relaxed resident had two glasses of milk after brushing his teeth, and for once in his lackluster life, felt greatly elated. Anyway, the invigorating sixty-minute trek had satisfactorily worn-off all effects of the imported scotch whiskey he had consumed. The audacious fellow climbed into his familiar bed and attentively read a porno' magazine for a brief while before falling fast asleep before midnight.

* * * * * * * * * * * *

Mr. Martin promptly arrived at the F & S company office at eight-thirty the next morning, punctual as usual. At a quarter to nine, an infuriated Vagine Barrows, who had never before arrived at work before ten, swept into his office like a ferocious University of Miami lady hurricane.

"I'm reporting your fat rear end to Mr. Feitweiler right now!" the contemporary amazon shouted. "If the Chief turns you over to the police on one-man conspiracy charges, it's no more than you deserve, Asshole!"

Mr. Martin gave the belligerent trespasser into his sacred realm a look of shocked surprise. "I beg your pardon?" Erwin mildly admonished the encroaching dyke. "This isn't Amsterdam, but at one time New York was called New Amsterdam! We don't have many dikes here in the city, but perhaps you'd like to inspect the Holland Tunnel!"

Ms. Barrows snorted and bounced out of the room, leaving Miss Helen Paird and Joey Hart staring after her wiggling firm ass. "What's the matter with that old Medusa now?" asked Miss Paird.

"I have no idea," calmly answered Mr. Martin, resuming his deluge of work heaped upon his desk. The other two lower office officials looked at Erwin and then flanked at each other. Miss Paird got-up and went out toward the ladies' lavatory at the end of the hall to sit on the toilet, which was her version of the catbird seat. On her way Helen walked slowly past the closed door of Mr. Feitweiler's revered office.

Mrs. Barrows was adamantly yelling inside, but she was not braying in her typical condescending tantrum style. But in her rush to get to the bathroom, Miss Paird could not interpret or decipher exactly what the emotionally disheveled supervisor was saying to the receptive boss. Upon returning to the tiny office the unmarried woman shared her discovery with Joey Hart and with Erwin Martin. In short, Helen disclosed her information about the "big personnel discussion" transpiring "in F. F.'s bailiwick."

Forty-five minutes later, Ms. Barrows left the president's office and sped into her own enclosure, slamming rather than shutting the door. It wasn't until half an hour later that Mr. Feitweiler sent for Mr. Martin. The usually meek and modest head of the filing department, neat, quiet, and cooperative, stood at attention like a Parris Island recruit in front of the old man's empty desk.

Mr. Filmore Feitweiler was pale and nervous. The corporate executive slowly removed his bifocal glasses and for a half a minute twiddled them without enunciating a syllable. But then the boss's vocal cords made a small low grunting sound within his throat, roughly clearing his allergic voice-box.

"Martin," he said, "you have been with us more than twenty years and never caused the firm any trouble. In fact," F.F. resumed his disciplinary narrative, "I've always viewed you as being a quiet troubleshooter as opposed to being a loud-mouthed troublemaker!"

"Thank you, Sir. I've been with F. & S, for twenty-two years, when it was then D & R," recollected and said Mr. Martin.

"In that time frame," further pursued the pompous president, "your work and your--uh—manner, yes, your demeanor have both been notably exemplary."

"I trust so, Sir," stated Mr. Martin. "I try my best to fit in. Nothing's worse than a square peg attempting to squeeze into a round hole; that is, except maybe a round peg searching for an available trapezoid to adequately accommodate its mathematical three-dimensional shape!"

"I have understood from trustworthy sources, Martin," expressed Mr. Feitweiler in a solemn, more serious tone of voice, "that you have never taken a drink or smoked a legal cigar or cigarette. Is that office bullshit correct?"

"That is correct, Sir," answered Mr. Martin with relative certainty. "I even detest a chimney smoking!"

"Ah, yes," Mr. Feitweiler acknowledged, polishing his glasses with a desk tissue. "You may now comprehensively describe exactly what you did after leaving the office yesterday, Martin."

"Certainly, Sir," Erwin agreed with a degree of poise. "I walked home because I never dash or sprint, ever since I injured myself doing cross-country in middle school. Then I ambled over to Schrafft's for my usual dinner. Afterward I walked home again as I do every damned evening. I went to bed early last night, Sir, and then I read an *Argosy* man's adventure magazine for a while. I was fast asleep before eleven."

"Ah, yes," said Mr. Feitweiler again, since those two words were the boss's favorite exhortation. The chief company administrator remained silent for a moment, searching for the proper words to orally convey to the "bean-counting head of the filing department".

"Mrs. Barrows," F.F. said finally, "Mrs. Barrows has worked hard for the firm, Martin, very hard, just like her firm tits and ass. Now it grieves me to report that dear Vagine has suffered a severe mental breakdown. The attack has somehow taken the form of a severe persecution complex, which is accompanied by horribly distressing hallucinations."

"I'm very sorry to hear the bad news, Sir," Erwin prevaricated. "I never knew that she was capable of breaking herself down, but the dyke, er, I meant to say 'the woman' was positively superb at doing *that* sort of devastation to other people working here on the fifth floor!"

"Mrs. Barrows is under the delusion," continued a more somber Mr. Feitweiler, "that you had visited her abode last evening and had behaved yourself in an--uh—unseemly manner." The boss then raised his hand to silence Mr. Martin's expected little-pained outcry. "It is the nature of these aggravating psychological diseases," Mr. Feitweiler elaborated, "to fix their wicked malady upon the least likely and most innocent party as the--uh—principal source of persecution. These obscure matters are not for the layman's mind to logically grasp, Martin. I've just had my own psychiatrist, Dr. Fitch, on the phone. I wanted Fitch to fetch me a sketch about the bitch's, er I mean the afflicted woman's condition, but of course, the ingrate asshole wouldn't commit himself," Feitweiler explained, "but old Bitch, I mean by *that* reference good old Fitch made enough professional generalizations to substantiate my grave suspicions about the suspected lesbian dyke."

"What is Dr. Fitch's prognosis?" asked Erwin.

"During our confidential conference, I had suggested to Ms. Barrows, when she had completed her-uh--story to me this morning, that she should visit Dr. Fitch for consultation and for gender-identity sex therapy, for I suspected a condition, or perhaps several detrimental conditions existing at once. In my office, the dumb cunt flew off, I regret to say, into a panic rage, and demanded--uh—that is, requested that I call you on the carpet for a rugged reprimand and demotion. You may not know, Martin," F.F. ignorantly summarized, "but Ms. Barrows had planned a reorganization of your department—subject to my authority and approval, of course. This brought you, rather than anyone else, into her frustrated and overworked mind--but again, that is a gray-area phenomenon for Dr. Fitch and not for us to evaluate. So in conclusion, Martin, I'm afraid to report that Ms. Barrows' usefulness here at S & F, I mean 'F and S' is at an end."

"I'm dreadfully sorry, Sir," the euphoric file department manager falsely declared. "I had suspected that Ms. Barrows was obediently giving you a good blowjob under your desk and also a decent hand-job once in a while too, that is, until you've just ingeniously revealed that the bitch is a certifiable lesbian dyke possessing a heightened persecution complex that could have put the entire company in grave sexual jeopardy!"

It was at this point during the weird interview that the door to the office blew wide open with the suddenness of a gas-main explosion, and instantaneously a fit-to-be-tied Ms. Vagine Barrows violently catapulted through it.

"Is the little rat denying my story?" she screamed like a hysterical banshee suffering with agonizing hemorrhoids. "The lying son-of-a-bitch can't get away with that shit! That lousy little fat prick standing in front of your desk is a disingenuous, fucked-up story fabricator!"

Mr. Erwin Martin moved his body discreetly to a point directly beside Mr. Feitweiler's black soft leather swivel chair.

"You drank scotch and soda and smoked a *Camel* cigarette at my Greenwich Village apartment last night," the enraged female bellowed at Martin, "and you know it too! You called Mr. Feitweiler an 'old windbag' and vowed you were going to blow him up to Kingdom Come when you got coked to the gills on your fucked-up heroin habit!" The incensed accuser stopped yelling to catch her breath, and a new glint sparkled in her popping eyes. "If you weren't such a drab, ordinary, little dicked man," she ranted like a maniac, "I'd think you'd planned it all. Sticking your tongue out, facetiously saying you were sitting in the catbird seat, because you thought no one would believe me when I would repeat your fucked-up bullshit! My God, this nightmare is all really too perfect for a total asshole like you to scheme-up and employ!"

The prosecuting employee with the alleged persecution complex then brayed loudly and deliriously, and the fury prevalent in her vengeful heart was again quite evident in her indignation. The fired amazon then glared at Mr. Feitweiler. "Can't you see how that pinheaded weasel has tricked us, you' old frivolous full-of-yourself Fool? Can't you see his little bait and switch game?"

But Mr. Feitweiler had been surreptitiously pressing all the concealed buttons hidden under the top of his clean-slated empty desk, and within thirty seconds dozens of F & S employees began pouring into the stately walnut-paneled main office.

"Stockton," said Mr. Feitweiler, "take stock in what I have to say. You and Fishbein will escort Mrs. Barrows to her home, although lesbians like her prefer to have a female escort. Mrs. Powell, you will go with them. Just please pretend that you're an experienced lesbian escort."

Stockton, who had played a little football as a third string nose tackle in high school, blocked Ms. Barrows as she made a livid charge for the still-serene Mr. Erwin Martin. It took him and Fishbein together with a headlock administered by Mrs. Powell to force the hostile woman out the door and into the hall, which had become overcrowded with a bevy of eavesdropping stenographers and horny office boys.

The hubbub pandemonium of the forced evacuation finally died-out down in the corridor. "I humbly regret that this regrettable incident has happened," apologized Mr. Feitweiler. "I shall ask you to dismiss it from your overburdened mind so that it does not interfere with the dispensation of your work duties, Martin."

"Yes, Sir," affirmed Erwin, anticipating his chief's "That will be all" commentary by gradually moving toward the one and only escape door. "I'll certainly dismiss it as soon as I use the emergency bathroom facilities."

Erwin Martin proudly exited the fancy office and gingerly shut the door, and his step was light and quick in the hall. After spending thirty minutes inside the men's room crapping and then wiping his chubby ass,

172

Martin cavalierly entered his department with an ostentatious gait, and the victorious, bureaucratic F & S file manager paced quietly and narcissistically across the cluttered room to the W20 file, wearing all the while a look of studious concentration.

"The Secret Wife of Walter Witty"
James Thurber

"This baby's going through hell iced over!" the grim Commander's voice thundered like thick ice cracking away from an Arctic glacier. The frightened flight veteran of fifty-three combat missions was clad in full-dress uniform having an impressive array of battle medals and campaign ribbons and the brave man also sported a heavy '*white cap*' pulled down over one none-functioning "cold right eye." The hydroplane Commander's left pupil looked down at the nearly frozen ocean and observed thousands of ominous 'white caps' waving in rhythmic concert amidst a slue of small and large jagged icebergs.

"We won't make it to the base because there's a nasty friggin' blizzard dead ahead between headquarters and us!" the co-pilot exclaimed.

"Sew your lips shut Captain Berg!" the determined Commander loudly volleyed back as he glanced out the plane's window and glimpsed an immense iceberg that didn't look like a round head of lettuce. "I do the goddamned talkin' in this freakin' cockpit! Are you a fuckin' dunce or what?"

"Throw on the auxiliary power lights!" the now-quivering and perturbed Commander bellowed to his petrified crew. "Rev her up to ten thousand big ones! We're gonna' penetrate those Arctic virgin storm clouds and if we don't, we'll go down in aviation history like bona fide true-blue American heroes!"

Just then a voluptuous naked blonde entered the cockpit from the cargo compartment and much to the astonishment of the already dumbfounded crew the doll zipped down Walter Witty's fly. The buxom-bombshell got Witty's diminutive wick erect into a firm thick dick in a matter of fifteen seconds and then began lustily performing oral sex.

"She's goin' down! She's goin' down!" the one-eyed Commander boomed to his totally distracted crewmembers that had suddenly forgotten all about their overwhelming potentially disastrous hydroplane crisis.

Before Walter Witty prematurely popped his weasel the gorgeous naked blonde got off her knees, stood up, and much to the other six still flabbergasted observers' astonishment sat on top of Witty's now enormous red throbbing tool and began riveting up and down like a hyperactive jackhammer. Witty's pale blue eyes bulged out of their sockets and as the happy fellow fantasized his highly pleasurable reality the lucky man's parched tongue slowly vacillated like a grandfather clock's pendulum back and forth, licking his dry lips.

"She's no longer goin' down!" Captain Berg screamed to his don't give a shit fellow crewmates. "She's no longer goin' down! She's now on top of the storm I tell ya'! She's now climbin' on top all right!"

Every other male in the huge hydroplane's '*cock*pit' watching the horny blonde pumping her lusciously wet hairy pink slit up and down on Walter Witty's huge erection began rubbing the pit of *his* own cock. The engines' cylinders increased to the wildly wonderful sound of *pocketa-pocketa-pocketa-pocketa* as the blonde beauty squirmed and gyrated atop Witty's erect dick with even greater intensity than she had exhibited moments before. The entire crew (including the Commander) was virtually mesmerized and completely distracted from their very imminent danger.

"We're gonna' explode! We're gonna' explode!" Captain Berg yelled. "If *she* goes any faster we're gonna' fuckin' burst like Vesuvius!"

The now very alarmed Commander momentarily directed his attention away from Walter Witty and his kinky secret blonde wife. "Ice is forming on the pilot's window!" the one-eyed martinet shrieked like an obsessed maniac. "This baby can't become *frigid* right at the climax of this great adventure! Rev them up to twelve thousand and max' this sucker out! We gotta' get this flyin' crate out from behind the proverbial eight ball!"

The non-frigid blonde bombshell began pumping and pounding her fantastic golden snatch even harder and faster upon Walter Witty's sensational sticky dick-stick. The hydroplane's engines increased in volume even more as the aircraft rocked and vibrated to the familiar noise of *pocketa, pocketa, pocketa-pocketa* as the very aroused Witty's eight-inch-long erection slid in and out of his secret wife's luscious crotch' *pocket* making the identical set of sounds as the hydroplane's failing engines. Click-clack, pocketa-pocketa, click-clack, pocketa-pocketa was the redundant chorus of exciting reverberations coming from the wild sexual activity and from the strained roaring engines.

"Damn it Witty!" the Commander screamed at the top of his lungs while Walter was about to cream at the top of his enlarged pecker. "Can't I even touch and pinch one of *her* erect brown nipples! Just only one little feel is all that I desire, pretty please Walter?"

"Go fuck yourself!" Witty nonchalantly and insubordinately answered his chagrined superior in a half-trance as his plenteous pleasure rapidly accelerated onward toward its much-anticipated crescendo.

"Full strength in Number Four turret!" the Commander ordered to Captain Berg, who was preoccupied working his own swollen stick. "Full strength I say Berg!" Then the one-eyed envious son-of-a-bitch again pleaded something relevant to Walter. "Please Witty, can't I just rub my thumbs and forefingers against her erect nipples before we fuckin' crash into the ice-cold Arctic! I need a gratifying final thought to end my frustrated prudish Puritanical WASPish existence!"

"Suck my dick after I pop my twelve-ounce-load!" Witty defiantly replied to his sexually frustrated superior. "Ah! Eight inch dick into the side pocketa-pocketa-pocketa hole! I'm ready to shoot my essence on cue! I'm ready to shoot on cue! Break my goddamned balls you luscious sex machine! Go on bitch, break my fuckin' balls!"

The plane's crew (with the exception of the totally appalled and pissed off normally prudish Commander) all removed *both* hands from the controls and began to vigorously and enthusiastically work their poles as Witty and his secret blonde wife approached mutual orgasms.

"Fuck the goddamned world! Fantasy is much better than harsh reality! The Old Man will get us through the dangerous blizzard!" Captain Berg hollered at Lieutenant Waters as the two men worked their sticks with both their hands while simultaneously watching Witty and his secret wife get it on. "The fuckin' by-the-book Old Man can do it all by himself too!"

"Not so fast Walter! Slow down! You're too excited!" the real Mrs. Witty chastised her timid henpecked husband. "Why are you driving this car so damned fast?"

Walter Witty briefly glanced down at the bulge in his white summer cotton pants he was wearing during the height of winter. "Hmmm!" the shy husband answered with obvious disappointment in his voice. Witty looked at his shrew of a wife's haggard wrinkled face. Mrs. Witty (with her gray-streaked auburn hair and snotty sanctimonious attitude) seemed to be a distant cold female that hadn't been laid (or enjoyed being pumped) in twenty years', which happened to be very close to the actual truth.

"Walter, the speed limit is forty and you were zooming away up to fifty-five!" *his* real nightmarish small-titted wife reprimanded. "Slow down and enjoy the roses."

'Bullshit!' the usually meek driver thought in mental defense of his doomed ego. 'I wasn't up to fifty-five! Damn it, the gorgeous blonde and I were skyrocketing up to twelve thousand fuckin' revolutions a minute!' Walter imagined with a smile.

"You know you don't like to go over forty," Witty's un-witty mundane wife sternly criticized her besieged husband after a short silent interval. "You were dangerously speeding this car up to fifty-five in a thirty-five mile per hour zone!"

'Can't I just go down with the blonde in a blaze of glory on a crashing hydroplane!' Walter regretted in that singular moment of self-sympathy. 'I couldn't pop a load into my bitchin' bitchy wife's stenchy snatch in a hundred years!' Walter mentally lamented as he felt his formerly huge erection shrinking down to a diminutive wiener between his sweaty legs. 'Damn it! Now I feel like taking a freakin' piss! If I could orgasm while takin' a leak, I would deliberately piss my damned pants all day long!'

Walter Witty drove onward toward Waterbury, thinking all the while about the joy of happy dick burying inside the cockpit of a diving hydroplane. The roaring of the SN202's engines through the worst Arctic storm in naval aviation history faded in Witty's mind as the intimidated Connecticut driver tried dismissing the thoughts of his wife's small tits and of her oppressive Victorian sexual mores from his now-devastated fragile mind.

"Walter, you must be tensed up again, all revved up!" his domineering wife concluded and expressed. "It's one of your anxious days. I wish you'd let Dr. Renshield give you a physical, a blood test and a much-needed urinalysis."

An image of a female Dr. Renshield with solid non-silicon blimp-like tits and a juicy wet pink blonde-haired slit with a delightfully rigid but squiggly clit' entered the fickle man's fabulous imagination.

"Stop right here alongside the curb!" Mrs. Witty ordered. "Slow down or you'll have passed the hairdresser's! Learn to follow directions Walter!"

All Walter Witty could do was contemplate the fantastic blonde's golden hairy bush when his nasty wife barked-out the non-magical word "hairdresser." The husband fantasized giving his secret wife's exotic blonde bush a nice pubic-hair shampoo and subsequent trimming.

Walter Witty obediently stopped his old black *Ford* in front of the designated Waterbury, Connecticut beauty parlor where his bossy wife had to have her wiry scraggly hair done. "Remember to buy those very important overshoes while I'm having my hair done!" the bitchy dame reminded her tamed docile domesticated tortured husband.

"I don't need overshoes!" Witty insolently answered back while the man was creatively thinking of buying *rubbers* for the next time he mentally screwed his secret blonde wife. 'I wish they did major plastic surgery inside that beauty parlor. Mildred needs work all over her damned ugly body, especially her pathetic face, chest and pubic bone area!'

"Walter, we've been through this debate many times before," the austere wife chastised. "First and foremost you need your overshoes! You're not a young man any longer and your reflexes and your memory are failing!"

'That's because of you, you wicked fuckin' bitch!' Walter impulsively and instinctively thought. 'I would definitely feel younger if *you* knew how to give decent head or if you opened your legs once in a while and invited me to get my hungry dingle wet!' Walter raced the car's coughing engine in neutral gear to symbolically demonstrate his restive rebelliousness coming to the surface.

"Why don't you wear your gloves? Walter, have you lost your gloves?" Mrs. Witty mercilessly interrogated.

Walter reached his left hand into his overcoat's side pocket and removed the gloves his stuffy old hag wife had been alluding to. He submissively put them on as directed, but after Mrs. Witty had exited the black *Ford* and entered the beauty parlor the driver defiantly removed the objects from his hands.

'Please make her into a knockout blonde and inject some silicon into her flabby breasts,' the beleaguered husband wished to certain imaginary miracle-working beauty shop personnel. 'And above all else, work on her fuckin' bad bossy attitude!' the disgruntled spouse pondered after subconsciously stopping his *Ford* for a red traffic signal.

"Pick it up bro'! Get it on now!" a groovy black cop yelled while waving his hand directing traffic.

Walter Witty hastily put his gloves back on, getting his mental commands confused between his stern wife and the serious Afro-American police officer. The old black *Ford* jerked forward and Witty fancifully drove around the streets and avenues of metropolitan downtown Waterbury, Connecticut looking for a decent house of prostitution in what his fertile mind had labeled the "*red light* district." On the way to his familiar standard parking lot destination, the driver motored past the city's main hospital and his mind quickly tripped into another dimension.

In his daydream Walter stepped into a shoe store and bought the first pair of overshoes he came across. "Would you like a bag?" the courteous male attendant asked Witty.

"Why should I want a bag?" Walter Witty humorously challenged the clerk and then winked. "I've been married to *an old bag* for the past goddamned thirty years!" the purchaser laughed knowing full well that the store clerk was not acquainted with either his 'old bag wife' or with him. As Walter imagined leaving the retail shoe outlet he began thinking about his upcoming visit to Dr. Renshield's office.

"It's the multimillionaire professional golfer, Wesley "Lynx" Mulligan!" exclaimed the beautiful built-like-a-brick-shithouse brunette nurse.

"Yes," answered Walter Witty while systematically removing his *gloves*. "I've just coincidentally dropped into the local clinic for my annual *HIV* screening and to obtain my bi-annual sperm count results. Who has this particular case you're referring to?"

"Dr. Fairway and Dr. Foreiron, but there are also two specialists consulting the surgeons every procedure. Dr. Greensfee from New York and Dr. Caddy-Teaoff from London are contributing their inputs," the blonde bombshell Dr. Renshield disclosed. "Dr. Caddy-Teaoff just flew over the big pond to this crazy American cuckoo nest and Dr. Greensfee took the *A-Train* subway down from Harlem with Duke Ellington's band all the way here."

Swinging doors opened at the other end of the short corridor and Dr. Fairway came out from the main operating room with a solemn expression on his florid face. The world-renowned neurosurgeon looked visibly drained and exhausted. "Hello Witty," Fairway matter-of-factly greeted the hospital visitor. "We're havin' a very challenging time with Mulligan in there. Things are not up to par, so to speak. My golfing friend Lynx is a good friend of Tiger's, and we think Wesley Mulligan had suffered 'three strokes' while getting a triple bogey on the fourth hole. Besides that," Dr. Fairway elaborated to Walter Witty, "poor Mulligan has a large food divot stuck in his small intestine and a mammoth shit divot blocking his large intestine and we're afraid to operate on those life-threatening encumbrances right now. Witty, want to take a look at the tremendous obstacles we're facing?"

"I'll be glad to inspect Mulligan's 'handicap' and explicitly render my opinion of his intestinal fortitude," Walter agreed. "You might have to make *a hole in one*."

Whispered introductions abounded in the crowded operating room: "Dr. Caddy-Teaoff, Dr. Witty. Dr. Greensfee, this is Dr. Witty. Dr. Foreiron, Dr. Witty'."

"I've read your trilogy on erratic cardio-vascular pulmonary effects on cerebral dysfunction and mental disintegration," Dr. Caddy-Teaoff informed Witty as the eminent surgeon vigorously shook Walter's hand. "The books contain some of the most brilliant bullshit I've ever read!"

"Why thank you Dr. Caddy-Teaoff!" Witty gratefully acknowledged. "When I write bullshit it's got to be brilliant! And incidentally Dr., I react favorably to praise and flattery!"

"Didn't know you were in the States," Dr. Greensfee jealously muttered to Witty. "I thought you were in Nigeria collecting snake venom or somewhere in Egypt researching a cure for the East Nile virus coming from the Israeli West Bank."

"I like to keep you stupid jerk offs guessing as to my specific whereabouts," the infamous Dr. Walter Witty haughtily chided his world-famous colleagues. "With assholes like you fellas' in charge of important operations, no wonder why the friggin' funeral business is booming. Do you imbeciles want me to be the lead surgeon is this rather commonplace set of incisions to be performed?"

"Why yes, now that you've mentioned that scenario," Dr. Fairway acceded while absolving himself of responsibility for Mulligan's almost-certain death. "That would be the ideal venue to ensure Wesley Mulligan's miraculous survival and smooth recovery."

180

Muscular male nurses rolled a colossal complex-looking machine over to the operating table. Two-dozen tubes were expertly inserted inside Mulligan's mouth, ears, nose, penis, rectum, well, into every conceivable orifice his damned body had. The electrodes connected to Wesley's arms, legs and penis were instantly activated, and a sudden smile beamed from the unconscious duffer's face as his pleasure senses rose above and transcended the high anesthesia dosage that had been administered. Mulligan was unconsciously fantasizing that he was merrily jerking off and popping a tremendous load into the cup of the ninth green in *Palm Springs.*

"More anesthesia," Dr. Caddy-Teaoff instructed nurse Goodhead, who then conveyed the important request to Walter Witty, a world-famous anesthesiologist in addition to being a world-famous neurosurgeon and acclaimed frog dissector. The skilled nurse then knelt down, lifted Dr. Greensfee's and Dr. Caddy-Teaoff's operating gowns and began massaging their sexual equipment. Dr. Fairway and Dr. Foreiron caught on to the non-golf 'foreplay' immediately. They sauntered over to the opposite side of the operating table and started removing Nurse Goodhead's gown, blouse, bra and pink panties.

Meanwhile Dr. Witty's secret naked blonde wife (alias Dr. Renshield) gently pushed Witty to the tiled floor, opened his fly, mounted his erect tool and began pumping away like a hyperactive piston on *his* engorged salami. Nurse Goodhead abandoned the more sexually inferior doctors, crossed the operating room and sat her bountiful bare ass down on Witty's face and then nearly rubbed her vulvas off over his sniffing nostrils.

Five minutes of the operating room orgy had elapsed, and then the other prominent demented surgeons found themselves vigorously masturbating while watching Walter Witty's secret blonde wife and the vivacious Nurse Goodhead intensely fulfilling Walter's most cherished secret sexual fantasy.

Wesley Mulligan began moaning and groaning on the operating table, his subconscious mind fabricating a form of intense sexual arousal while being stimulated by sensory sensations filtering into his brain from the real-life participants' ecstatic panting and gasping. Mulligan's dick grew into a massive hard-on, but no one in the operating room even noticed or cared because the horny surgeons were wildly jerking off and the sawbones were too preoccupied watching Witty get his rocks off from his secret blonde wife Dr. Renshield and the fantastically built Nurse Goodhead's lustful activities.

As everyone in the operating room (including the unconscious Wesley Mulligan) approached orgasms the complicated operating room machine began going *pocketa-pocketa-pocketa* as it exploded and sputtered to a halt. Walter Witty was fully cognizant of the in-progress-dilemma so he nonchalantly removed a ballpoint pen from his pants' pocket as his kinky secret blonde wife Dr. Renshield was riveting the hell out of his pulsating dick and as Nurse Goodhead was smearing fragrant pussy juice all over his face with her moist pink snatcheroo.

Witty blindly reached up to the sophisticated non-functioning machine and deftly snapped out a circuit board and then clicked the ballpoint pen between two connectors, and the fancy newly repaired anesthetizer immediately resumed operation. Just as sexual juices were about to squirt all over the normally professionally managed O.R., a vexing voice interrupted Witty's reverie by saying, "Back your cruddy old *Ford* up, Mack. And watch out for that green *Buick LeSabre!*"

Walter Witty slammed on his raunchy *Ford's* faulty brakes and the impatient parking lot attendant loudly yelled, "Wrong lane, Mack!"

"Er, sorry, gee, yeah!" Walter anxiously replied as he finally made the transition from his fantasy world back to the stark impersonal reality he knew all-too-well. The embarrassed driver cautiously backed out of the "Exit Only" lane and redirected his weatherworn black *Ford* automobile into the proper "Entrance Only" driveway.

"Ya' gotta' get laid more often!" the ill-mannered parking lot attendant gruffly joked. "You'd be a better driver if ya' got sex over with and then ya' could keep your friggin' eyes on the goddamned road!"

"Er, you might have said something significant there!" Walter readily admitted as his former donkey dick shrank down to around three centimeters in length. 'That's only the third hard-on I've had in over a month,' he lamented feeling sorry for himself.

"Leave your piece of junk right there," the attendant commanded. "I'll put her away for ya'. Ya' don't have to worry about anybody stealin' that piece of crap you're drivin'. It's nothin' but worthless scrap metal!"

Walter felt like telling the fellow to 'Get bent you slimy pond scum!' but didn't have the testicles to communicate those particular vitriolic words.

A defeated and humble Walter Witty climbed out of his ancient vehicle. "Hey, Mack, better leave the key in the ignition in case I have to move that baby. Or," the now-jaunty parking lot employee added, "I might drive that sucker out to Indianapolis to see if that mean black monster qualifies for the big *500'* race." The parking lot attendant then leaped into the lackluster old *Ford*, started it up, backed up displaying arrogant adroitness, and put Witty's "venerable black machine" precisely between two parallel white lines exactly where it belonged.

'These antagonistic parking lot creeps are so damned cocky,' Walter thought as he began walking along downtown storefront windows on Main Street. He trudged through the February slush that covered the Waterbury sidewalks. 'That fuckin' reminds me. I gotta' buy my overshoes or else my sharp-tongued real wife verbally castrates me in the town square!'

A half-hour later Walter stepped-out onto Main Street with the box of standard-looking overshoes tucked under his arm. 'My wife wanted me to buy something else besides these shitty overshoes,' Witty recalled. 'What the fuck was it?' he wondered. 'The bitch told me twice too just before we set out for Waterbury, but what in the world was it? Was it soap pads? Toilet paper? Aspirin tablets? Dandruff shampoo? A triple-x' porno movie?' Witty delightfully mused.

A newspaper boy passed by shouting information about the ongoing Waterbury trial and that news sent Walter's mind journeying back into his marvelous fantasy world.

"Perhaps this evidence will rekindle your suspect memory," the Prosecutor declared as he showed Exhibit A to the unfazed reticent person occupying the witness stand. "Have you ever seen this weapon before?"

Walter Witty received the gun from the District Attorney and inspected it thoroughly. "This is my favorite Colt .45," the collector suavely stated. "I can tell by the galloping horse engraved on the wooden handle!" the man seated on the witness stand expertly testified.

The crowd in the courtroom's gallery began to buzz so the judge banged his gavel to reestablish order. "Order, order in this court!" he judiciously yelled an important phrase he had learned in *Harvard Law School 101.*

"You're an expert shot with any sort of gun, aren't you Mr. Witty?" the *DA* dramatically challenged the modest and soft-spoken defendant.

'Fuck off asshole!' Walter thought. 'I'd like to shoot this baby up my real wife's crotch and finally bust her cactus-like cherry!' After mentally deliberating for a moment, Walter Witty calmly and convincingly answered, "I'm the best shot in all of New England and can easily beat in a contest any marksman blindfolded if I wanted!"

"I object!" Witty's shocked defense attorney vehemently bellowed. "We've already amply proven that Mr. Witty could not have fired the fatal shot. His right arm was in a sling on the night of July 24th because his ulna had been fractured from falling out of bed while reaching for a bedpan!"

Walter Witty casually and defiantly raised his formerly injured right hand and the stunned opposing attorneys ceased their harsh debating and stood with their mouths agape. "I could have easily murdered Marvin Gardens at four hundred feet using my left hand. In fact Your Honor, I could very easily shoot *you* dead standing on my head with my eyes closed!" Witty assured as he pointed the murder weapon at the judge, who immediately ducked down under his mahogany desk podium.

Turmoil broke loose in the courtroom as the bailiff, attorneys and the gallery all ducked down under tables, chairs and seats. "I control your goddamned destinies whether you shit-faces like it or not!" Walter gloated and cited. "I take nothing but shit from people like you all my fuckin' life and where does it get me? On trial for a murder I never committed!"

A woman's scream pierced the tense courtroom atmosphere. The shriek originated from the rear of the chamber and a dis*robed* buxom blonde female dashed up to the defendant on the witness stand and threw her arms around her hero. The District Attorney attempted to fondle Walter's curvaceous blonde secret wife's tits but then Witty let the prosecutor have a vicious right cross to the jaw that sent *him* reeling across the courtroom, over the railing and tumbling into the jury box. "You dumb fuck! You stupid *cur!*" Walter shouted at the vanquished District Attorney as the gallery stood and gave the champion of justice a hearty and well' deserved round of applause.

"*Puppy dog* biscuits!" Walter said out loud. "I have to buy puppy biscuits or Mildred will castrate me!" he reminded himself. A woman passing by chuckled and said to her female companion, "He said he had to buy puppy biscuits! His wife probably doesn't cook and makes him eat puppy biscuits! What a wimp that stupid asshole must be! Ha, ha, ha!"

Walter Witty felt intense humiliation as he quickened his pace to the nearest downtown grocery store. Fatigued from his four block walking' ordeal, the slightly befuddled hapless man entered the food emporium. "I want some biscuits for a small puppy dog," Walter mentioned to the apathetic lady clerk.

"Any particular brand?" the miserable woman wearing the white apron replied as she aggressively chomped down on a wad of chewing gum while reading about the super-dramatic Waterbury trial in the local newspaper.

The greatest pistol shot, the best neurosurgeon and the bravest hydroplane navigator thought deeply for a second and then gave the clerk an appropriate response. "It's the one and only box that reads 'Puppies Pop Their First Load For It'," Witty proudly and authoritatively related.

Walter examined his wristwatch and determined that his bossy critical real-life wife would be finished with her hairdresser appointment in ten minutes. 'I better hurry,' he advised his better judgment. 'Mildred is to meet me at the hotel and she despises if she gets there first and has to wait ten seconds for me. I'd be much better off if I had married an obnoxious sex-starved male orangutan without any friggin' teeth!'

The customer thanked the clerk for the requested dog biscuits, paid for the boxed product at the cash register and then hastily paced the three city blocks to the hotel. At the designated rendezvous an exhausted Walter Witty plopped himself down into a comfortable mint-green lobby chair facing a window. Witty placed the box of overshoes and the bag of puppy biscuits on the red-rose carpet directly underneath his lobby chair.

The relieved husband casually reached over to an end table and picked up a wrinkled copy of *Liberty Magazine* to peruse its patriotic contents. The headline read, "Can Hitler's Forces Defeat the Free World through the Air?" The very intrigued reader scanned several photos of German bombers and of devastated London streets. Those graphic stimuli kicked Walter's imagination into high gear.

"The flak is blasting all around us Captain Witty," the extremely frightened Sergeant urgently declared. "Sir, your copilot's losing a lot of blood and there's nobody else aboard that can help you fly this metallic orange crate!"

"That's perfectly all right, Sergeant," Captain Witty readily acknowledged. "Drag Winston Churchill into the back compartment with the other wounded and petrified diplomats and then return up here in an instant. I'll fly this friggin' tin can solo if I have to!"

"But Sir," the alarmed Sergeant nervously countered, "that's impossible. It takes two skilled men to pilot this monster and the Archies are pounding the hell out of the air."

"Tell the friggin' Archies to start singing 'Sugar, Sugar'!" Witty wittily remarked. "Somebody's got to destroy the enemy ammo' dump and that special somebody's goin' to be me!"

"But Sir, enemy fighters are closing in and the flak that's bein' shot is getting closer and closer!" the paranoid Sergeant protested. "We'd be safer inside a Kansas tornado funnel!"

"Get the fuck in the back of the plane with that idiot Churchill or I'll have ya' court-martialed after I finally land this baby!" Captain Witty threatened his subordinate. "Just remember wimp, danger, adventure and victory are reserved only for the bold-hearted!" the Captain ranted while addressing his shell-shocked listener.

Witty unscrewed the cap on a metal flask of blackberry brandy and gulped down the entire contents for good luck. Then the intrepid man-in-command threw the empty container onto the cockpit's holey shrapnel-ridden floor.

"I never saw anyone that could drink brandy like you can," the Sergeant admiringly complimented as a burst of flak sent more shrapnel splattering through the copilot's side window.

"Get the fuck in the back compartment with Churchill or I'll crash this freakin' plane into the ammo' dump rather than me bombing the ammo' dump from here to eternity!" Witty wildly whooped. "Obey my command or die!"

"Yes sir! Yes sir!" the Sergeant dutifully replied, dragging the unconscious and seriously wounded copilot into the rear of the beleaguered bomber. Flak was bursting all around the crippled flying fortress and the ratta-tat-tat of enemy fighter machine guns could be discerned in the distance. The straining engines were making the distinct familiar sound of *pocketa-pocketa-pocketa*. The courageous pilot looked to his right and his new copilot was an attractive naked blonde with succulent brown erect nipples and natural hard tits the size of very mature cantaloupes.

Something rigid hit against Walter Witty's shoulder. His body immediately stiffened-up inside the mint-green hotel lobby chair. The meek man slowly turned and raised his head to view his scornful real-life tiny-titted dry-crotched bossy wife.

"Walter, I've been searching all over this mediocre hotel for you," the real Mrs. Walter Witty balked, "so why do you have to hide inside this old tarnished faded chair? How did you ever expect me to locate you slouched down in this very remote section of this dull lobby?"

"Things close in and I tend to get claustrophobic," Witty apologetically confessed. "You're absolutely right dear, this lobby could use more illumination."

"What on Earth are you talking about, you silly man!" his real wife spouted out. "Did you buy the puppy biscuits?"

"Yes Mildred," Walter answered with his head crestfallen.

"Did you purchase your overshoes?" his relentless wife demanded.

'Overshoes,' Walter imagined. 'Another name for overshoes is *rubbers*. Oh yes, I bought rubbers but I'll never get to use them on you, you frigid, bossy, fun-less leeching ruthless bitch!'

"Well Walter, I'm waiting for a reply!" his brutal real-life wife insisted and kept lecturing. "Are you going to answer me? I detest the silent treatment, you know!"

"Yes, I did buy my overshoes," Walter politely responded, "but did it ever occur to you Mildred that sometimes I enjoy being alone? I value and cherish solitude and isolation sometimes! Sometimes I wish I was a hermit living in a cave."

Mrs. Witty stared at her spouse disbelievingly. "You're too torqued-up for some obscure reason. You *are* indeed acting quite erratically today," she observed and stated, "so when we' get home, I'm going to take your temperature."

'Oh Lord, please have her give me a rectal thermometer up my asshole,' Walter wished and hoped. 'I really could use the anal stimulation!'

The odd couple strolled through the hotel's revolving doors and ambled two blocks south toward the familiar Waterbury parking lot. Mrs. Witty stopped in front of a corner pharmacy and remembered something she had forgotten to purchase. "Oh Walter, just wait here a minute! I need to get you some rectal salve for your tricky hemorrhoids you're always complaining about!"

Walter Witty stood impatiently in the cold February morning air and decided to light a cigarette. He placed his box of overshoes and his bag of dog biscuits on the cold pavement. Sleet began showering down from the lower atmosphere to add to the poor man's dismal mental anguish. The abused husband sullenly leaned against the drugstore's brick wall imagining that he was standing in front of a Pancho Villa firing squad.

"To hell with the handkerchief blindfold!" Walter boisterously yelled as a passerby stopped and chuckled at *his* rather bizarre exclamation.

'Mr. Witty,' the chief Mexican bandito said with a heavy accent, 'you already have your cigarette you are smoking. Think of a last wish before we execute you and if it's within reason and if it involves sex, we shall grant it!'

Witty thought and thought about his imagined predicament. Then a wonderful inspiration entered his all-too-fertile mind. Ten seconds later Walter's well-stacked buxom-blonde secret wife ran naked towards her long-lost lover. The exotic erotic doll got down on her knees, pulled Witty's zipper down and began fondling his limp organ until it became engorged with warm blood. The thoroughly enchanted members of the Mexican firing squad dropped their weapons and promptly began jerking off.

"Walter! Walter!" Witty's dominant wife yelled. "Why didn't you come into the pharmacy out of the cold? You could've been 'blown' away!"

"Mildred, I wish I had been 'blown away' *twice!*" the formerly henpecked husband courageously answered his totally unbearable spouse.

187

"Rip Van Winkle"
Washington Irving

Whoever has made a pleasurable boat voyage up the Hudson River will automatically be impressed with the Catskill Mountains, especially if the observer previously and exclusively believed and thought that cats kill mice. The Catskills are a segment of the great Appalachian Mountain Chain, and yes, as everyone who studies American geography is quite aware, the Appalachians are parallel to the equally magnificent Peachalachians. And in truth, the magical hues characteristic of the Catskills often change from season to season, and the promiscuous wives of elderly, impotent male residents are perfect weather barometers, even though few of these sex-crazed nymphomaniacs have any lethal measure of mercury in their un-prudish-but-fully-covered hourglass bodies.

When the daily air and wind pattern is fair and tolerable, the Catskills are cloaked in a majestic blue and purple haze, but when the sky is remarkably sunny and cloudless, the wondrous mountains will accumulate a hood of gray mist around their loftiest summits, a peculiar vapor that simply mystifies (mistifies) the casual observers randomly taking peeks at the peaks, making the apexes appear to be akin to the stellar gleaming of the Crown Jewels of England.

At the base of these fairy (but not gay) fabled mountains, the visitor could, on a clear autumn day, notice smoke billows swirling-up from various chimneys situated throughout the somnolent village, a hamlet of great antiquity, having been founded by conscientious early Dutch colonists. The houses themselves had been built of small yellow bricks that had been carefully imported across the *Atlantic* from the Netherlands, the construction materials never ever passing through the famous Holland Tunnel. The mediocre village homes featured latticed windows, gabled fronts, and un-circumcised weathercocks adorning the roofs, which were used for the sole purpose of gauging wind direction.

Within this aforementioned nondescript village existed a certain dwelling that was rather shabby and weatherworn, and inside the hideous-looking eyesore lived a lazy, indolent asshole named Rip Van Winkle. Several decades before the "Great Revolutionary War", un-industrious Van Winkle resided in the grotesque-looking abode with his shrewd shrew of a wife, Dame Van Winkle, along with his toddler daughter Judith, and seemingly comatose infant son Rip Junior.

As for lethargic Rip Van Winkle, the unmotivated bumpkin claimed to be a direct descendant of the noble Van Winkles of yore, a noteworthy clan that had audaciously battled against savage and peaceful Indians alike in the chivalrous days of valiant Peter Stuyvesant, the last Dutch

Governor of New Netherland, before the province became New York under notorious British dominion.

But poor Rip Van Winkle was neither a fighter nor a wife lover. And much to his nasty spouse's chagrin, Rip was beloved by the lackadaisical men along with the horny women of the commonplace village, despite the fact that even Rip's listless donkey was a totally lazy ass, also. So, whenever Van Winkle either tilled his potato garden or disked his small field to plant assorted summer and fall vegetables, it was indeed a *harrowing* experience for the pleasant peasant to endure.

But popular Rip Van Winkle was a kind and humble neighbor, and an obedient henpecked husband, who obviously never had ever read and comprehended William Shakespeare's supreme classic masterpiece "The Taming of the Shrew," for Van Winkle was illiterate and never even learned the twenty-six letters of the standard alphabet.

Despite these rather glaring shortcomings, the benevolent man possessed an enormous penis that remained erect for hours on end, several centuries before Viagra, Cialis and Levitra were ever commercially produced by greedy drug companies, and then vastly distributed by avaricious left-wing, liberal pharmacies, along with immoral profit-minded apothecaries.

And without a doubt, the good kinky, adulterous village wives, all of whom were infatuated with Rip Van Winkle's superb perpetual erection, unanimously sided with the Pauper's "accursed position" against the frequent railing of his dominant shrew, and their abundant gossip always laid the ultimate blame for any one-sided family dispute squarely upon sharp-tongued Dame Van Winkle.

"Poor Rip! If only his nasty-tempered wife knew what the hell she was missing," the village wives would marvel and chatter during afternoon quilting bees. "But unfortunately, she's a reprehensible frigid bitch who absolutely hates her own damned cunt! God! Rip's eight-inch-long tongue is almost as delightful as his fantastic foot-long pussy stuffer! How the hell that venomous, bellicose, frigid witch ever had two kids I'll never know!"

And psychologically defeated Rip often assisted the younger village boys in making miniature outhouses and massive dildos, and also flying kites exhibiting artistically-drawn nude women. And the innovative experimenter occasionally demonstrated to the hamlet's youth the proper manner in which to be licking wet pink hairy pussy, how to be shooting square marbles in the thick mud, along with proficiently exploding large quantities of putrid sperm juice into the lower atmosphere.

And finally, Van Winkle was proudly adept at telling the more superstitious male urchins all about dangerous Iroquois Indians; about weird witches possessing three hairy-crack slits, and also about vile pedophile ghosts that ironically raped and tortured unprepared priests, ministers, bishops, parsons, imams, popes and rabbis. So naturally, when Rip was preoccupied napping or slumbering under a secluded tree, the inspired acne-faced juvenile delinquents would obsessively masturbate each other when the perverts weren't privately jerking-off inside their family's smelly wooden outhouses.

But truly, benign Rip positively despised any form of toil or labor for himself, or more specifically, for his own monetary advancement, but the good-natured loser would gladly help any of his neighbors plow their fields, and as a wonderful reward, the appreciative farmers would allow Van Winkle to sexually service their nympho' wives when they themselves were too pooped to pop their already-overworked weasels. And when the accommodating fellow wasn't intensively porking the kinky neighborhood sluts, wily Rip would carry his foul fowling piece upon his shoulder into the local woods and shoot squirrels, foxes, rabbits, lemmings, cockroaches, and even pet pigeons named Walter.

But regrettably, Rip farted-around so much that there was a tremendous gaping gash in the crotch part of his very baggy pants. Van Winkle's favorite attire was a pair of ancient galligaskins, similar to the oddball garb that the first Hudson River Dutch settlers had worn in the early 1700s. And formidable Dame Van Winkle's persistent oral tirades made Rip think, 'My wife's uncouth mouth is too big even to suck on my gigantic dick! If she were any respectable ordinary woman,' Van Winkle sadly considered, 'my spouse could administer a superior blow-job much more adequately than any sex-skilled whore, harlot, or hussy residing in the entire Hudson Valley!'

Rip's truest domestic friend was his sole canine Wolf, who also feared Dame Van Winkle's wrathful diatribes much more than the trained predator was intimidated by hostile area Indian tribes. However, Wolf was a ferocious attacker of docile pet dogs, often behaving like a fierce cannibalistic sadist, habitually biting-off little puppies' wieners as well as those belonging to wildly bullying bulldogs, compelling the vanquished victims into licking their own disgusting-looking, mangy-furred peckers, which were shaped sort of like lengthy Z-formed lightning bolts. And in regard to his psycho' dog, grateful Rip earned many a shilling having Wolf lick various old men's dicks, especially those limp danglers attached to elderly geezers who hadn't enjoyed either an erection or a decent ejaculation for several decades.

As years of difficult matrimony rolled by, Rip became extremely disenchanted with Dame Van Winkle's perpetual litany of threatening remarks. 'She's got the only adult pussy in the village that I've never both licked and screwed on the same night,' Van Winkle lamented in reference to his lambasting partner for life. 'I think I'll head over to the village inn and see what the fuck my loyal buddies Nicholas Vedder and Derrick Van Bummel are bullshitting about. We three assholes really relish sitting together in the shade around and beneath the hanging sign of His Majesty King George the Third. At least the cozy tavern is one placid spot for me to relax and escape my cruel woman's chronic ridiculing.'

Nicholas Vedder was the inn's revered proprietor, whose favorite St. Bernard Barf-thalamew would always vomit whenever all-too-aggressive Wolf was busy patrolling and prowling the immediate vicinity. Rip's thoroughly-obnoxious mutt would (without warning) deliberately stick his pecker into a bowl full of vinegar, and then force poor Barf-thalamew to lick the sour taste off. This was particularly humiliating to Vedder's exploited pooch, because Barf-thalamew happened to be the only Muslim animal in the entire Christian hamlet, and the abused cur secretly desired celebrating Ramadan year-round without licking any sour meat.

Erudite Derrick Van Bummel was the sagacious village schoolmaster who had the distinct reputation during every school day of teaching his illiterate students a boring classic that would make the class sick. Each sultry summer and fall afternoon Vedder, Van Bummel, Van Winkle along with three of their undistinguished cronies, would sit on the splintery, circular bench constructed around a tall oak tree and loudly gossip about local news and current politics, and to make their physical existence more comfortable, there were six square holes hollowed-out upon the rudely-fabricated, rickety round bench, each senile man sitting upon a separate one, so that if anyone had to take a serious crap during an intriguing group dialogue, the aged fellow in question, not wanting to miss any important conversation being exchanged, so quite fortuitously, the curious gent didn't have to rise and stroll over to the inn's rear outhouse; but instead, just made a fecal deposit right then-and-there in front of the inn while sitting upon his own private hopper.

And flamboyant Derrick Van Bummel would daily fascinate his proletarian audience of five morons from early June until late September, adroitly and impressively employing his enviable vocabulary, articulating certain significant dictionary words like "cunnilingus," "bordello", "pornography", "harlot", "copulation", "ejaculation", "brothel", "fellatio", and incredibly, the perverted schoolmaster's mesmerized listeners really never fully fathomed one iota of what the fuck the knowledgeable pedagogue was adroitly orating.

"You know Nicholas," garrulous Van Bummel prefaced, his skinny ass seated upon his square hopper hole located beneath the really tremendous oak, "you preposterously verbalize your mediocre, lackluster concepts like you're a combination of a contemporary Sophist and a sacrilegious Pharisee-turned-Sadducee."

And then next, a rather bewildered Nicholas Vedder indignantly answered, "Derrick, speak normal Swahili, so that maybe I could fuckin' understand your dull, dumb-ass bull-shit better!"

192

"Nicholas, don't you know what the esoteric nomenclature 'coitus' means?" Van Bummel deliberately asked his very flabbergasted inn acquaintance.

"Yes, I happen to have a bad case of *colitis,* and have to pass gas every time I hear you speak your totally ridiculous drivel," Vedder all-too-honestly replied, just as the zany innkeeper loudly propelled a large amount of fecal matter down into the wide, square hole his fat ass had been hovering over, much to the general amusement of the five other fucked-up Dutchmen. "I lack the intestinal *fart*itude to comprehend or endure any of your fucked-up insane gibberish. Every time I listen to your lingo, Van Bummel, I nearly shit my brains out!"

Just then an enraged Dame Van Winkle showed-up in front of the inn, lifted an embarrassed Rip Van Winkle up from his familiar bench by his ears, furiously kicked her appalled husband in the testicles three times, and then after dropping her humiliated spouse into the nearby high weeds, grabbed both Nicholas Vedder and Derrick Van Bummel by their exposed necks, hoisted the surprised nitwits up off their square thrones, and then violently plunged their heads precisely into their two pungent square shitholes, whose never-cleaned storage drums were situated directly beneath.

Then, without any evident hesitation, the incensed hag latched onto her already-stunned husband's right ear, and forcefully yanked Rip out of the high weeds, dragging him off the friendly premises, cursing and screaming vehemently during the whole bizarre enterprise.

* * * * * * * * * * * *

On a most excellent autumn afternoon, seldom-motivated Rip Van Winkle, accompanied by his faithful companion Wolf, initiated an arduous ramble high-up into the interior of the scenic Catskill Mountains, the challenging excursion occurring immediately after petulant Dame Van Winkle had brutally scolded her husband, telling Rip to "Take a long hike off a short crag!"

The crestfallen Dutchman reckoned that he should scramble as far away from oppressive "Petticoat Tyranny" as the persecuted soul possibly could wander. 'I dare not lie down here,' the disconsolate trekker realistically thought, 'or else Wolf will certainly piss on my face as is the nasty scoundrel's distasteful habit. My neurotic mutt must have some sort of major urinary or kidney problem. I just gotta' maintain my spunk and keep ascending. Too damned bad I'm not ascending up into Heaven instead of up from that raunchy village below! Oh well. I suppose this rugged mountain just has to satisfy my weary emotional needs for the time being!'

193

From a narrow opening positioned amidst the dense tree growth, Rip's eyes again detected the sleepy village far below, and his keen pupils also perceived the incomparable Hudson River glittering like a silver stream off in the distance, shining from the bright sunlight's weakening reflection. Several small fishing boats (that had learned how to catch pike and shad all by themselves) were recognizable to the south, the vessels obviously heading towards New Amsterdam (New York) where the ambitious fishermen would sell their daily catches at market.

To Rip's immediate right was an ordinary mountain glen, with steep ridges, and now the overhead crags were gloomily shading that part of the lofty ravine from the fearful adventurer's eyes. 'I hope I can shoot a squirrel or two with my trusty fowling gun,' Rip wished and prayed. 'I gotta' remember to string those fur-babies over my shoulder and conceal them underneath my tawdry wool jacket, or else Wolf will wolf-down those luscious suckers before I could ever say 'That gay faggot Attila the Hun' just once.'

As bedraggled Van Winkle was about to reluctantly descend the precarious incline, his cold ears detected a squeaky voice hallooing from a distance, "Rip Van Winkle! Rip Van Winkle!" Thirty-seconds later Rip's surprised eyes discerned a freakish-looking midget of sorts, the queer-looking bloke struggling to carry a heavy cask through a tunnel that nature had (over the eons) carved through *that* remote side of the picturesque mountain.

'That little twerp in desperate need of help is wearing a jerkin that the short piss-head more than likely wears when jerkin'-off!' Rip mused and smiled. 'And what's with the wild, grizzled beard and the shabby galligaskins the puny asshole is wearing, quite similar to the ones I have on my bony rear-end right this minute; yes, they're just like the tarnished ones I had inherited from my great-great-great grandfather! Maybe this gay-looking son-of-a-bitch elf is really masquerading as a fucked-up female transvestite in disguise.'

The diminutive, wrinkle-faced dwarf gestured for Rip to approach and assist him in enacting and completing *his* seemingly-difficult task. Thinking that he might earn a cup of rum or gin as a reward for his solicited cask-transport employment, Rip readily complied with the strange imp's tacit hand-signal. The unusual pair clambered-onward with their difficult burden, laboring up a narrow, shadowy gully, and as the encumbered duo awkwardly ventured-on, Van Winkle heard certain long, rolling peals of thunder originating a mile or so up the desolate rustic trail.

'That peculiar noise sounds a lot like people playing a game of ninepins!' Rip recollected. 'I have no money, so I hope I can participate in their merry gambol without having to gamble! Come to think of it,' Rip nostalgically reminisced, 'bowling's definitely up my alley! But even without a map, I'm aware that we're perilously climbing just east of Tarrytown! We're certainly not anywhere near friggin' Bowling Green, Ohio!'

Soon, the un-dynamic twosome emerged from the thin dark tunnel, and next ventured into a second hollow that was surrounded by high precipices along with towering coniferous trees that understandably shrouded the glaring sun, and made all visibility almost opaque. 'This little asshole companion of mine must have a mild case of laryngitis because the wimpy knucklehead hasn't spoken a damned word since he first beckoned my name! How did the little jerk-off know my full name to begin with?' Rip wondered. 'Oh, now I get it!' Van Winkle comprehended, his inquisitive mind swiftly shifting gears. 'Another name for being a bowler is *kegler,* and now I've been helping this annoying, mute pipsqueak deliver this keg of liquor to some sort of mysterious mountain party! Shit! I hope they have plenty of marijuana and drunken whores there, too!'

The exhausted transporters slowly entered a natural pristine environment that handsomely formed a remarkable sylvan forest amphitheater, and in the center of the surreal phenomenon stood a company of odd-looking, serious-faced, miniature gentlemen actively playing an intense game of ninepins. The extraordinary chaps were dressed in the quaint-but-ancient fashion of revered Dutch fellows who had lived several centuries before, all sporting behemoth-sized breeches having decorative rows of buttons down each pant side. 'Those idiotic jerk-offs are wearing jerkins just like my anonymous guide. Holy Hades! I now feel just like Alex in Fantasyland!'

The tiny corpulent 'Dutch leprechauns' all possessed stone-cold, melancholy expressions upon their visages, suggesting that the keglers were fundamentally bored and unhappy with life and with living, and if the oddball phantoms were indeed three-centuries-old as it initially seemed, one could easily sympathize with their remarkably tired plight.

A stout, little, gray-haired asshole, sporting a short shiny sword dangling from his waistband, appeared to be the contingent's supreme commander. And the entire astonishing assemblage reminded Rip of smaller versions of characters in an old Flemish painting the dolt had once viewed while touring a prominent New Amsterdam Museum, and when the speechless, elaborately festooned personages began coughing-up and spitting disgusting green lungers all over the damned verdant meadow, alert Van Winkle accurately concluded that the diminutive, repugnant freaks were indeed 'phlegmish'.

'Those portly Lilliputian Dutchmen must all bathe their cats in vinegar because they're all showing sour-pusses, exactly where natural human smiles oughta' be displayed upon their faces!' Rip creatively imagined. 'These frightening petite ghouls oughta' have been dead two-hundred-years-ago! At least, that's what my inferior education is tellin' me!'

Suddenly, upon noticing the arrival of their impoverished native human guest, the pint-sized, ancient Dutchmen ceased their bowling activities and then concentrated their full attention upon incredulous Van Winkle, whose eyelids immediately began to neurotically flap and winkle. The alien celebrators then emptied the contents of the heavy keg into a sturdy flagon, and next the eccentric group gestured for Rip to wait upon and serve the designated alcohol to them, and upon clumsily completing the obliging servant's duty, the sad-faced entourage motioned to Van Winkle to indulge in sampling the potent beverage himself.

Rip was delighted to acknowledge that the wonderful drink tasted exactly like the Holland gin that old tavern owner Nicholas Vedder secretly kept as 'inn's secret treasure' down inside his cobweb-infested 'wine cellar'. But being extremely thirsty, Rip 'Let it rip!' and promptly gulped-down two additional cups of the abominable intoxicant, and soon thereafter, the dizzy and giddy imbiber's sensibilities had been egregiously conquered, and a few seconds later, victimized Van Winkle's body collapsed upon the wet, soggy turf, and soon poor Rip's vulnerable mind drifted-off into a deep, intoxicated sleep.

* * * * * * * * * * * *

Upon waking-up from his extended, drunken siesta, Rip found himself' lying upon a damp knoll, strangely enough, the exact spot where he had first observed the old hobbled dwarf carrying the heavy wooden cask upon *his* shoulder. Birds were busily hopping, chirping, and twittering-around the tangled bushes, with several rude sparrows zooming-down from tall pine trees, and then prodigiously crapping upon Van Winkle's exposed, scruffy head.

'Surely, I've not accidentally slept here for a full night!' Rip's fuzzy mind evaluated. 'Dame Van Winkle will barbarically castrate me. and gladly feed my shriveled-up testicles to hungry Wolf, who will surely voraciously devour them without any particular regret. Say, where the hell is old Wolf anyway? I hope my miserable mutt hasn't run-off with some dominant Doberman bitch. Perhaps he's been attacked and eaten by those ravenous black hawks from Chicago that migrate here to the gorgeous gorges every autumn.'

Then, the awoken sleeper further speculated for a moment. 'How could I ever again say 'Fleas Navidad' to my psychotic dog on Christmas if Wolf's permanently abandoned me up here in the Catskills? Oh, that flagon! That certainly was a terribly lethal vat of Holland gin!' Rip remorsefully remembered. Without any more pondering, confused Van Winkle moved his hand down inside his tattered galligaskins. 'Thank goodness I still seem to have my dependable balls and scrotum sac somewhat intact!'

Lying flat upon the ground, Rip anxiously rummaged-around, and soon frantically searched the immediate proximity for his well-oiled fowling gun, but instead, the anxious fellow discovered a rusty old firelock that had apparently experienced better times. Van Winkle now suspected that the reveling roisters who had been partying the night before had cast a mischievous black magic spell upon him, and that the inane rascals had cleverly traded the well-maintained fowling piece for the "useless piece of junk" the beleaguered fellow now held in his hands.

"Woe is me!" the distressed man exclaimed to his apathetic surroundings. "Woe is me!" Van Winkle repeated to the empty and uncaring forest. "I had been sleeping on cruddy algae and upon slimy ferns, but at least I wasn't resting on my goddamned laurels!"

After weakly rising from his former prone position, the disenchanted explorer noticed that his aching back was suffering from severe rheumatism! 'This raunchy pain is absolutely excruciating!' Van Winkle thought, successfully utilizing an academic word he had learned from all-too-vociferous Derrick Van Bummel. 'Holy shit! I've lost my formerly reliable hard-on! Now, only if my flaccid dick can get stiff again from my new-found advanced arthritis condition. In truth,' Van Winkle fearfully conjectured, 'my shrew of a spouse won't give a flying shit about this exceptional deficient predicament of mine, because we never have had oral, kinky, or even standard straight sex. To this very day, I don't know how the hell we ever had two repulsive biological children. But I don't know if the horny town wives, and the equally horny village kids, will be able to adjust to and appreciate me suddenly becoming Mr. Softy!'

Cautiously descending from a series of treacherous mountain slopes, fatigued Rip next slipped, tripped, and tumbled several times among birch-wood and sassafras trees, and after slowly rising to his feet, moments later, the confused wanderer trampled through random dense growths of witch hazel and poison oak. Wild grapevines also impeded Van Winkle's downward progress, the dense brush abruptly interrupting one rollicking downhill roll, but still, the stubborn and perplexed fellow stumbled, and his frame again rotated round and round, culminating in another prolonged, frenzied descent.

After eventually smashing into an enormous elm tree, and now fearing the looming prospect of starvation, the famished squirrel hunter courageously persevered and doggedly (without Wolf) continued pursuing his ill-fated destination. 'I can't die up here plum in the middle of nowhere!' the troubled trekker worriedly assessed. 'I need to visit Nicholas Vedder's wife's fucked-up, erotic tattoo and body mutilation parlor at least one more time before I fuckin' die!'

After finally locating the huge mountain's base, a half-hour later, the encumbered ambler approached the *outskirts* of the village, which was easily identifiable, since all of the gay-looking hamlet homosexuals were appropriately dressed in short red kilts with accompanying matching pink brassieres.

'Shit!' Rip instinctively hypothesized. 'I know just about every straight and homo' asshole cavorting-around the whole countryside, and yet, I can't recognize a single one of these nauseous, degenerate jerk-offs, who are all staring at me like a gaggle of homos' as if I'm some sort of LBGT ghost! If this is an innocent dream, it's rapidly transforming into an intolerable nightmare!'

And then, the busy-body village residents followed the new arrival's path in what actually constituted an improvised parade. One of the Village People, a goofy goon named "Tonto from Toronto", was imaginatively dressed as a savage Indian warrior, and another outstanding faggot wearing tight black leather was indeed a modified backwoodsman, while a third village personage was in the costume of a city policeman, and upon Rip's baffled scrutiny, the fourth associated fruitcake (prancing-around within the unorthodox singing group) voluntarily described Van Winkle as being an out-of-the-closet British Redcoat "going full-musket".

The abnormal, un-religious procession eventually reached the village center, and not one friendly dog, or unfriendly child, pretended to know who the hell the formerly notorious Rip Van Winkle was. But the returning lazy farmer imagined that *he* was a victorious General leading a triumphant phalanx of soldiers into ancient Rome, but then on second thought, the strange new homes, the unfamiliar names painted upon overhead shingles, along with the fully-indecipherable new-town scenario further addled Rip's already-disoriented thought processes.

And upon managing to rub his grimy, cold right hand under his chaffed chin, flustered Rip Van Winkle made a rather startling discovery. 'Holy tits' flying all-around in Satan's Hell! My beard's grown a foot! Thank the Lord it's a foot without five or more fucked-up toes!'

Indeed, the new arrival was under mental duress, and his now-anemic mind was rapidly encountering a wicked identity crisis. Rip's deteriorating brain was indeed thoroughly disheveled.

'Who the fuck am I?' the groggy refugee futilely guessed and self-interrogated. 'I feel horribly bewitched without my witch of a wife ever being involved! Of all the lousy, fucked-up negative luck! Why couldn't damned Dame Van Winkle take-up squirrel hunting, and get herself lost up in the alluring Catskills, instead of poor, old me?'

* * * * * * * * * * * *

The still-restless vagabond gradually and finally made his journey to his treasured home, but much to his mounting apprehension, Van Winkle observed an abode existing in abject decay with the windows shattered, the doors unhinged, and the roof and shingles half caved-in. An ugly cur that somewhat-resembled Wolf (but having protruding rib bones) skulked-around, wagging its ruffled mangy tail between its hind legs, and growling incessantly from misery, while moving among the knee-deep weeds, and then the despicable beast very pathetically managed leaving the greatly neglected front yard. "My very dog finds me quite avoidable!" Rip softly muttered. "Even without the aid of a mirror, come to think of it, I do smell like shit in addition to probably looking like shit, too!"

Upon very deliberately stepping into the ramshackle house, Van Winkle instantly determined that the hideous place was far beyond repair. Staggering through the dilapidated shack's most accessible zone, Rip called-out for his wife and children, but only morbid echoes could be heard bouncing off the decrepit walls, and then ringing like ghostly whistles throughout the more distant chambers.

The frustrated fellow next exited his former modest bungalow and made his way to the prior scene of Nicholas Vedder's Inn, which now displayed a unique shingle reading, "The Union Hotel: Owned by the Honorable Mr. Jonathan Doolittle".

"Jonathan Doolittle," whispered Rip to himself. "He sounds like a worthless, indolent asshole, just like I am and was. We oughta' get along famously, he and I."

And then, Rip perceptively noticed a shoddy flagpole, but the attendant banner atop seemed rather alien to his vague memory, the fluttering cloth characterized by a circle of stars and supplemented with thirteen alternating red and white horizontal stripes. "What the hell's that weird eyesore?" Van Winkle yelled to a crowd of astonished pedestrian bystanders.

"Why that's the Flag of the States!" shouted back an astounded citizen. "Where the fuck have you' been hiding your ass? In fuckin' Siberia?"

And next, Rip peered at the overhead portrait of King George, who was no longer garnished in a bright red, aristocratic jacket, but now was proudly wearing a blue coat with buff trim, and instead of a scepter in the monarch's palm, the impressive military figure now held a gleaming sword. "Who's *that* strange soldier portrayed up there?" Rip hollered-out. "Who the hell is this new guy General Washington, as that alien sign up there reads?"

"Why it's George Washington, of course! He was instrumental in inspiring the American Continental Army in defeating the dreaded British at Yorktown in the last battle of the Revolutionary War!" a local politician rather boisterously bellowed. "You musta' slept through the entire major conflict, you dumb old fuck Geezer! And by the way, are you trying to conduct some kind of local revolt here with that rusty old piece of shit you're toting, and are you mischievously leading a disorganized rabble of rebel women and children at your heels? Tell me, Old Codger. Are you a Federal or a Democrat?"

"I think this senile jerk-off is a riot, even with his mob of women and children!" a Second Politician arrogantly boomed as everyone else hardily laughed aloud. "I'm willing to wager that this near-dead Methuselah's real name is Arthur Wrightis! Ha, ha, ha!"

Meanwhile, throughout the entire stranger-than-fiction spectacle, a third egocentric politician, a laconic African named Maliko Akimbo, stood there reticent in the middle of the clamorous throng, and quickly flashing a broad grin, the gaunt Kenyan, indiscriminately wearing tight leotards, was deftly standing semi-erect with his left arm akimbo, and with his right hand leaning against a long silvery cane.

"Alas, assembled Ladies and Gentlemen," cried-out Rip in a timid and rather dismayed tone of voice. "I'm a simple, poor, quiet asshole, and yes, a foolish native of this fucked-up place, and quite confidentially, I must admit that I'm also a loyal disciple and a true-blue bona-fide subject of His Majesty, King George. God bless his mortal soul!"

"This crazed nutcase intruder is a bleepin' Tory!" a male voice in the crowd screamed. "This senile Old Fart is a contemptible Tory, a spy, a despised British supporter! Let's lynch his wrinkled ass from that tall oak tree right here and now!"

"Yes indeed, the reprehensible King had all of the Tories on his side except one," the opinionated First Politician loudly yelled above the din. "And that asshole's name was Vic Tory! Ha, ha, ha!"

"Folks, truly I mean no-one any harm," Rip all-too-candidly testified. "I merely came here to the center of town looking for some old friends that I used to bull-shit with."

"Well then, who the hell are these imaginary chums of your?" snobbishly demanded the cocky Second Politician. "I hope that your old pals aren't fucked-up, hangable Tories, too!"

"Where's my good buddy Nicholas Vedder?"

After a moment's silence, an elderly curmudgeon stepped forward and replied in a shrill piping voice, "Holy fuck! Nicholas Vedder! That gabby shithead's been deceased and buried these last eighteen-years. A wooden tombstone that's now rotted-away in the graveyard told of his date of birth, and also of his date of death! But," the pencil-necked geek qualified. "Nicholas Vedder's very shrewd wife still operates the extremely profitable tattoo and body mutilation shop on the corner, and she's even selling myriad volumes of immoral pornography down in Mr. Doolittle's dank cellar, which used to be her perverted husband's personal sex and sadism clinic that most people thought was a mere gin and whiskey storage area!"

"Well then," apologetically continued Rip. "Where the hell's my favorite drinking crony, Brom Dutcher?"

"Brom Dutcher!" exclaimed a fairly delirious woman standing in the raucous crowd. "Why, he was killed in the great siege that had been fought at the base of Antony's Nose! Old Brom was shot in the face by a musket ball, and instantly lost both his enlarged nostrils. The poor bastard couldn't breathe anymore, and his lungs soon expired from a lack of air!"

"Well then, where's my old talkative pal Derrick Van Bummel, the wise-assed schoolmaster, who knew more impractical educated bull-shit than either Miguel Shakespeare or William Cervantes?"

"Derrick Van Bummel?" yelled-out an old destitute prostitute who could no longer hump and pump upon either a soft or hard mattress. "That imbecile jerk-off went-off to fight in the war, became a fabulous general, and now the disliked windbag is incompetently serving in Congress way down south in Washington."

Rip's puzzled mind was swimming in sheer quandary with the amount of new complicated terminology being divulged and delivered to his oversized dirt-laden ears: Revolutionary War, General Washington, Stony Point, Antony's Nose, Congress, along with the vague allusions 'Federal and Democrat'. "Does nobody here know a very unfortunate, hen-pecked fella' named Rip Van Winkle?"

"Rip Van Winkle!" hooted a loud-mouthed lesbian standing in the volatile mob. "Why, that's lazy Rip Van Winkle leaning against that tree over yonder. Yes, the detestable dunce is as idle as a sleeping turtle! This unbelievable tale you're spouting, Old Man, can only be described as the bull-shit of all bullshit!"

Rip turned his head and gingerly glanced to his right. His bloodshot eyes beheld an acne-faced punk frenetically scratching his testicles, and then alternating to vigorously rubbing his scrawny ass in public. The ragged wretch was indeed as lackadaisical and as phlegmatic as his obedient, biological father had always been.

"Hey, Old Fuck!" the First Politician haughtily commanded. "Who the hell are *you* anyway? Tell us your legitimate name, or else I'll summon the town constable and have your butt mercilessly tossed into the clinker!"

"God only knows who the hell I am," Rip complained with an indication of genuine concern. "I'm at the limit of my wits, to be sure. I'm somebody else other than who I thought I was. No, that's me screwing-around, scratching my ass over yonder, but no, that juvenile delinquent is somebody else that's gotten into my shoes."

Rip then felt compelled to look-down at his feet, and with a degree of worry, confirmed to everyone in his doubting audience the fact that he was now barefooted. "I had been my old happy-go-lucky self just last night, but soon, I fell fast asleep very fast, and those little trouble-making morons evilly switched my gun, and then the naughty creeps also stole my splendid dog, and now everything's radically changed for the worse. I mean," Rip lamented, "I'm changed, and now to be perfectly honest, I can't tell who the fuck I am!"

* * * * * * * * * * * *

The still somewhat-interested village witnesses now began looking at each other, impulsively demonstrating a variety of winks and nods, the aggregate of folks simultaneously circling their index fingers around the sides of their foreheads. Some of the more suspicious inhabitants even schemed to secure the rusty gun by wrestling it away from the itinerant old codger, who then un-persuasively prattled-on with his erratic narrative.

At that most critical juncture an attractive young lady frenetically pushed her way through the jabbering crowd, simply to obtain a better peep at the bizarre bearded newcomer. The young female was holding a chubby baby in her arms, the alarmed infant crying at the sight of the aged man inadvertently possessing "the rough gray crocodile skin". "Hush Rip! Hush you little whimperer! The old hysterical asshole won't harm you one bit!"

The child's singular name along with the air of the mother's tone of voice magically caught Rip Van Winkle's addled attention. "Who might you be, my Fair Woman?" the undesirable-looking village visitor nervously inquired. "What is your formal married name?"

"Judith Gardener," the young mother stammered. "I'm as good as divorced right now from my irresponsible husband. But on the positive side of things, I do own and operate a small-town landscaping business titled: 'Do your gardening with Gardener'."

"Do you also have a nursery?" Rip inquired.

"Yes," Judith eagerly answered. "That's the back room in my house where I breast-feed my infant son!"

"And your father's name?"

"Ah, the poor bad-luck slug; Rip Van Winkle was his name. But it's been twenty-years since the frivolous fool marched-up into the mountains with his dog and gun," Judith sadly disclosed. "His pooch Wolf returned home the following morning without my father. Some gossipers say that my pop had been shot by a tribe of inebriated Indians from Cleveland or from Atlanta. But I was only a naïve little girl at the time, excitedly looking forward to experiencing the highly-anticipated glory of entering puberty, and getting violently raped and laid!"

Rip then sighed heavily, for the distraught geezer wanted his parched tongue and dry lips to produce one more salient question. "Where's your mother?"

"Oh, she had died several years back," Judith divulged without any sign of sorrow. "She broke a blood vessel in her throat while excessively yelling at a traveling peddler from Boston."

'What a marvelous *stroke* of luck!' Rip automatically thought. And then the sentimental codger couldn't control his rampant emotions any longer. Van Winkle aggressively grabbed and gathered his daughter along with her shrieking offspring into his grimy arms and boldly announced, "I *am* your derelict father! Young Rip Van Winkle once! Old Rip Van Winkle now! Does nobody here in this fucked-up lesbian and gay community remember Rip Van Winkle?"

A debilitated, hoary, old whore nonchalantly stepped forward and raised her withered hand up to her brow, her movement quite closely and methodically surveying and inspecting the old squirrel hunter's haggard-looking countenance. The gruesome-looking wench paused for a pregnant moment and then succinctly proclaimed, "Sure enough, it is truly Rip Van Winkle! Don't you recall? You had screwed me three times in your stenchy outhouse, and twice more upon a neighbor's haystack, all in the same day!"

Rip's implausible story was told and retold a plethora of times, for amazingly, the whole two decades being fast asleep had been to Van Winkle as but one crazy, sinister, mysterious night. Virtually every settlement along the Hudson from Tarrytown to Albany soon knew the exotic tale by heart, and Rip gracefully evolved into an overnight sensation, lecturing at esteemed, prestigious colleges and universities such as West Point, Harvard, Princeton and Yale, already quixotic safe havens where the new savant's inimitable oratorical presentations were much in demand and coincidentally, immensely received and savored.

But the authentic and highly-regarded village historian, one venerated Peter Vanderdunk, who was renowned for dipping doughnuts into huge cups of gin-spiked tea concocted by irascible Nicholas Vedder Jr., was well-versed in the various Dutch fables and legends that were prevalent throughout the resplendent Hudson River Valley. Peter immediately corroborated and confirmed the validity of Rip's totally spectacular tale.

"Every twenty or so years," dementia-suffering Vanderdunk commenced his recitation, "noble explorer Henry Hudson and his crew of tiny sailors come up the river, and together the disgruntled immortal assholes haunt the royal Catskills. Their ship is still called the *Half Moon*, meaning that Henry Hudson and his goofball midget mariners were, at best, only half-assed sea-goers. In fact," Peter loquaciously communicated, "my delusional father once came upon the four-foot-tall zany shit-heads playing ninepins up in the mountains, and the disturbing noise of their balls crashing into bowling pins resulted in frightening blasts of thunder radiating throughout the indigenous ravines and valley passes. I mean," Peter proceeded with his' informative exposition, "nobody's ever goin' to roll *my* friggin' balls down a fuckin' rocky ravine, that's for goddamned sure! How the fuck could I ever have a wild and miraculous orgasm screwing some receptive tramp at age ninety-nine without any goddamned testicles merrily bouncing-around inside *my* shriveled-up scrotum sac?"

Eventually, the tragic anachronism affectionately known as "Rip Van Winkle" was able to reunite with several of his old inn companions, and most of them (including a rejuvenated Rip) could still respectively achieve super erections, and consequently squirt sticky sperm juice all over the round wooden outhouse table still-situated in front of Mr. Doolittle's totally ghetto hotel.

And Rip was unanimously accepted as the principal patriarch of the now-bustling town, ingeniously chronicling certain hazy-minded events that had occurred in the Hudson River vicinity years before the all-important American Revolutionary War had evolved.

Despite his now-honored regional reputation, Rip Van Winkle could never fully fathom how he was presently a free citizen of the United States, but in reality, *that* new-found special liberty meant little to his ultra-sensitive psyche. Losing twenty-years of a person's life while still aging *that* length of time would certainly represent a massive dilemma characterizing anyone's general mental and emotional development.

The abusive dictatorship of King George the Third of England was now truly diminished in Rip's scattered mind when in essence, the onerous debacle, when compared to the vicious "Petticoat Tyranny" of the all-too-diabolical Dame Van Winkle, was of minimal significance to the now-eminent Sir Rip Van Winkle. And whenever the vengeful shrew's awful name was incidentally mentioned outside Mr. Doolittle's Hotel, Rip's contemporary cronies would all reflexively piss their pants soaking wet, and likewise, amused Van Winkle would concurrently crap a mammoth load directly into his two-century-old galligaskins.

Washington Irving (1783-1859)

Named after George Washington, author Washington Irving was America's first internationally recognized literary figure. Irving started-out as a lawyer, but from the very start of his career, fully resented the monotony of his chosen profession.

In addition to authoring his first huge success titled *Knickerbocker's History of New York,* Washington Irving later achieved tremendous popularity with the publishing of *The Sketch Book,* which included his classic American stories "Rip Van Winkle" and "The Legend of Sleepy Hollow".

In later years, Washington Irving had built a beautiful mansion on the Hudson just below Tarrytown, the estate being named *Sunnyside.* The famous writer also is credited with creating the still-used cliché, "the almighty dollar".

"A Legend of Sleepy Hollow"
Washington Irving

Author Washington Irving (1783-1859) lived and died in the great American transformation period between the *Revolutionary War* and the *Civil War*. Irving witnessed the phenomenal growth of the *Industrial Revolution* that radically changed the United States from a colonial agricultural economy to a manufacturing dynamo, as the nation's population shifted from rural towns to rapidly expanding cities. Washington Irving was given his first name in honor of George Washington, and the renowned "Father of American Literature" even wrote a widely-acclaimed biography on the distinguished First President's life.

Washington Irving's famous *Sketchbook* contained two classic tales that became his most famous works, "Rip Van Winkle" and "The Legend of Sleepy Hollow". The popular character Ichabod Crane appeared in the latter novella, and Irving cleverly named the tall slender fellow appropriately, because 'Crane' obviously possessed an "Icky Bod". Here's a new rendition of the benchmark tale that definitely warrants the title *Sick Tasteless Classic.*

Tarrytown lies on the eastern shore of the *Hudson River* about twenty miles above New York City. It was regarded as a lazy, somnolent place both before and immediately after the *Revolutionary War* had been fought. Its citizens were mostly of Dutch ancestry. The inhabitants habitually *tarried* to mingle, gossip and exchange anecdotes with friends, acquaintances, pimps, gays, and promiscuous prostitutes. Several miles from the dull village was the quietest place in all the area, a hamlet known as Sleepy Hollow, and the cranky- pranky children of the tiny neighborhood were often referred to by wary adults as Sleepy *Hollow-wieners.*

The garrulous residents of Sleepy Hollow were uneducated, superstitious retards that still believed in witches, wizards, goblins, ghosts, the Easter Bunny, the Gay Tooth Fairy, and jolly old Santa Claus. The general countryside had been discovered and explored by Henry Hudson, who was really searching for a place to leave his notorious ship the *Half Moon* to take a good healthy shit somewhere on forest land. Some older residents claimed that an old Iroquois Indian Chief held his war council powwows there, and the redskin's spirit still haunts the villagers, wearing a raunchy multi-colored hairy toupee to keep his "wig wam" during the height of winter.

The whole *Hudson Valley* hinterland abounded with local tales and legends of haunted spots, haunted rivers, haunted houses, haunted whorehouses, haunted male homosexuals, and also haunted horny lesbians. A shooting star or a glaring meteor sighted anywhere in or around Sleepy Hollow meant only one thing: the end of the world was imminent, so everybody had to immediately get laid and start screwing each other like there was no tomorrow. But since everyone in the lazy hamlet was God-fearing and deathly afraid of dying in sin, the residents all stayed inside before nightfall so that the insane imbeciles would never observe a comet, a shooting star, or a blazing meteor soar across the evening sky over Sleepy Hollow or over Tarrytown.

The principal specter that haunted Sleepy Hollow was an awesome figure on horseback without a head, and the grotesque terror was also missing a dick. Area amateur historians believed that the ghost was that of a Hessian storm-trooper without any ante-Nazi trench coat. According to legend, the apparition's head had been amputated by an errant *Revolutionary War* cannonball, and the riding soldier's jaded estranged wife had cleanly sliced-off her husband's pecker before his unfortunate encounter with the colonial army's cannon blast. The unearthly Hessian and his galloping black horse are sometimes heard by paranoid and neurotic country folk huddled together in their wood-framed houses, all afraid to view comets, meteors, and *shooting stars,* aiming muskets at their sinful existence.

The dominant theory pervading the region was that the wandering ghost was instinctively *head*ing back before dawn to a churchyard where his headless and dick-less body had been laid to rest in an unmarked grave. The unfortunate specter is known at all evening fireside chats as the acclaimed and inimitable "Headless and Dickless Horseman of Sleepy Hollow".

In that fucked-up place called Sleepy Hollow once lived Ichabod Crane, who happened to be more fucked-up than the fucked-up place was. The lanky schoolmaster claimed that he "tarried" in and around Sleepy Hollow for the purpose of educating and molesting the area's children in an effort to learn how to practice being a professional, card-carrying, dangerous pedophile using a schoolteacher's identity to disguise his very plausible M.O. (modus operandi).

Ichabod was a tall thin jerk-off that looked very much like a featherless crane. The nutjob had narrow shoulders, a gaunt face, long appendages, feet that could have easily served as shovels, and an enviable curved twelve-inch-long dingle that looked something like a combination featherless flamingo's head and a semi-circular German sausage.

Crane's own head was small and flat upon its crown. The buffoon had huge ears, enormous green glassy irises, a very long, snipe snout, a midget's ass, and a set of balls that actually needed a second scrotum. Ichabod's head looked like a weathercock, and as has already been mentioned, his enormous hose-length-cock looked like a featherless flamingo's throat that could easily station and house at least three-thousand disgusting cockroaches. The schoolmaster often looked like an itinerant scarecrow walking at a distance on top of a hill with his loose overcoat and baggy pants fluttering all about his silhouetted figure.

Ichabod's schoolhouse was a one-room, dilapidated building constructed mostly of rotted-out logs. The broken windows were stuffed with old copybooks to keep-out the wind, and to prevent area voyeurs the privilege of watching Crane sodomizing some innocent young male student with *his* erect donkey dick. The schoolhouse was at the bottom of a woody hill, and a babbling brook (without legs) *ran* close by. The stern pedagogue's philosophy was quite simple and Bible-based. The ludicrous-looking instructor believed in and always practiced the golden maxim: "Spare the rod and spoil the child!" That is why Ichabod disciplined all his students with a stiff birch switch, and also why he sodomized and 'gomorrahized' the young boys with his impressive erect rod, which the abuser never spared but always shared. In fact, most of the young assholes that were sodomized in the ramshackle schoolhouse actually liked the experience and wanted to be porked up the ass again.

When school hours were over, Ichabod was both the companion and sexual playmate of the larger boys, who all envied his foot-long erect penis, which always required three hands to jerk-off. Crane was also a horny bisexual that had never gotten laid with a female, either human or sheep. The molester often visited the homes of students who happened to have pretty sisters and big-breasted mothers, but after showing his fantastic flamingo-headed pecker to a semi-interested girl or lady, she would invariably shout, "You'll never squeeze that ugly headed *bird* into my limited love nest, so don't even fuckin' try!"

The visiting academic instructor had a gargantuan appetite, and was reputed to possess the dilating powers of a famished anaconda. Ichabod often boarded at the homes of farmers' children whom he had taught, living a week at a time helping with domestic chores like mending the fences, watering the horses, milking the cows, chopping wood for chimney fires, hustling the available wives and sisters, and sodomizing and 'gomorrahizing' naughty little boys inside red barns and inside diminutive, smelly outhouses.

In addition to his myriad community responsibilities, Ichabod was the notorious singing master of the village, earning many a bright shilling by instructing psalm-singers while desperately searching for his true sexual identity. The conversant pedagogue was also an avid gossiper, a sort of traveling gazette, spreading insidious lies and half-truths about philandering husbands and whoring wives, just to try and get his first piece of ass, or his first *boner*-fide blowjob from a jealous blind wife, or from the spouse of a jilted, blind husband.

Ichabod found great pleasure in spending long winter nights by the fireside with old wrinkled Dutch wives, while everyone in the house was distracted smelling succulent apples roasting upon the fireplace hearth. The educated guest would nervously listen to their scary tales of goblins and ghosts, and especially to the retelling of the Headless and Dickless Horseman of Sleepy Hollow, who could no longer get any *head* because he didn't have a fuckin' dick. Then, Crane would delight in frightening the good Dutch wives with imaginative and exaggerated stories of comets, meteors, shooting stars, sun spots, and zooming asteroids that looked like hemorrhoids, and next proudly show his listeners his gigantic erection with its grotesque flamingo-like head. And the appalled, hysterical, horny bitches would then become even more terrorized and traumatized, would shriek rather deliriously, and would finally dash outside bare-assed naked to take a much-needed shit in the nearest outhouse, or hanging their raunchy asses over the nearest cliff.

Among Ichabod's loyal musical disciples was a blooming blonde lass named Katrina Van Tassel, the daughter and only child of Sleepy Hollow's wealthiest farmer. The psalm instructor quickly became infatuated with Katrina after surveying and inspecting Old Baltus Van Tassel's huge, prosperous estate. The wily teacher thought that he could live in an elite manner (manor) as an idle aristocrat for the remainder of his days, if only he could marry and pump Katrina, share the large farm's rich bounty, and then fuck-around with some old blind bitch that wasn't afraid of big ugly dicks. To say the least, Ichabod Crane was a lazy, gold-digging goldbricker, possessing lofty, clandestine ambitions. Katrina, though, was a bit of a flirt who loved to cock-tease any local man, and after the victimized fellow would become hot and horny, the young lady would abandon his company and then mesmerize another gentleman with her abundant feminine charms, which included a set of rock-solid, fantastic tits that couldn't fit inside any bra.

Ichabod frequently visited the Van Tassel castle, which was majestically situated atop a high cliff overlooking the radiant *Hudson River*. The gullible cad wrongfully thought that Katrina's random flirting was specifically directed toward him, not realizing that *that* was how the ditzy blonde with the humungous knockers acted with any interested male, either potent or impotent, bald or 'balled'. 'If only I had a normal-sized dick,' Ichabod sadly lamented, 'I could've gotten laid at least a thousand intercourses by now, and could've been sucked and blown at least twice as many times. I fuckin' hate flamingoes!' the ultra-sad instructor sullenly grieved.

One day, Ichabod visited the splendid Van Tassel mansion, stepped into the barnyard, and then ambled into fenced-in pastures to view fleets of duck, regiments of turkeys, scads of domesticated guinea fowl, and flocks of snowy-white geese. When Crane saw a dozen sleek porkers screwing each other inside the pen beside the red barn, the avaricious observer instantly became aroused. Ichabod then tried making some time with Katrina, who was reputed by male scuttle*butt* to give the finest facial *butt* rub and also "the best lickety blowjob" in and around Sleepy Hollow.

"Katrina," the always-horny, virgin, big-dicked bisexual began. "Do ya' think you could ever learn to love me?" the naïve schoolmaster asked.

"Why certainly Ichabod!" the Van Tassel broad sarcastically answered. "But never quite as much as I love the taste of apple cider vinegar on my broccoli, or the sight in my hand mirror of the seven sickening vaginal warts that are clogging-up my prodigious love tunnel! The village doctor says I'll never be able to have children, because of my wart-infested pump tube!"

Ichabod was not thwarted or discouraged by Katrina's frank admission. The marriage pursuer thought that if he could eventually wed the girl, the couple would never have any offspring because of *her* confounded vaginal wart condition, and then lucky Crane and his beautiful wife would be the exclusive heirs to her aristocratic father's very profitable estate.

"Well, Katrina," Ichabod stated in a slightly-disappointed tone of voice. "Sorry to hear about your terrible slit hole problem. Maybe we can get a highly skilled *wart*hog with sharp tusks to surgically remove your stubbornly attached vaginal warts!"

Ichabod however did have some *stiff* competition for the soft hand and the hairy blonde pussy of Katrina Van Tassel. Brom Bones was a boisterous, broad-shouldered, triple-jointed, big-dicked bully with short curly black hair and ante-Nazi tendencies a full hundred-years before Adolph Hitler ever knew *he* had an asshole. Brom was a skilled horseman, whose most difficult stunt was to stand on his head and successfully take a crap while his sleek black steed was galloping twenty-two and a half miles-an-hour through a woodland swamp. No one in Sleepy Hollow could duplicate that sensational feat. because no one else ever dared attempt it.

Brom Bones was indeed always ready for any frolic, festivity, feud, frolic, or fornication opportunity, and was motivated more by mischief than by malice. The brawny yeoman had four loyal companions that comically imitated his uncouth example, and the fellow's bullying posse would beat the shit out of anyone that Brom had specifically targeted for assigned molestation. Ichabod did not know exactly how to neutralize the hostile Brom Van Brunt, along with his cadre of wild, hooligan, equestrian apostles.

Van Brunt was aware of Ichabod's intention of courting Katrina, so the devious trickster devised several "fanciful torments" to aggravate his prime rival. Brom and his gang of "neo-Hessian storm troopers" once clambered up onto the log schoolhouse's cedar-shake roof, and mischievously stopped-up the chimney with a small barrel full of smelly horse manure. When Ichabod endeavored lighting a fire inside the hearth to make his Sunday afternoon psalm singers more comfortable, the whole interior of the building became clogged with dense, stenchy smoke, and then the remote schoolhouse soon smelled like a gigantic, foul crock of shit to boot.

On another occasion, Brom and his fearsome troublemakers broke into the schoolhouse at midnight, turned all the desks topsy-turvy, and quickly constructed an outhouse in the center of the building's only room. The following Sunday afternoon Brom Bones and his posse of delinquent uncouth rebel-rousers brought their trained hunting dogs to the vicinity of the old schoolhouse and stood behind a clump of birch trees. Every time that Ichabod raised his right hand and endeavored to start singing "Crock of Ages" with his choir, the nefarious bullies gave the trained hunting dogs the signal to bark incessantly, until finally prompted with the command to stop. The beleaguered schoolmaster suspected that every ghost, every witch, every rabid canine, and every avowed arsonist living in and around Tarrytown was vilely interrupting his "valuable transmission of culture and civilization to Hudson Valley's knowledge-hungry, ignorant masses."

One autumn afternoon, Ichabod was lecturing his students on the merits of having a fresh mouth, a rinsed penis, and a super-clean asshole, when a courier delivered an unexpected message to the schoolhouse door. A kind of buzz reigned throughout the formerly quiet classroom, because one of Ichabod's more imaginative disciples had brought a beehive for "show and tell", and had placed the object inside the unwary teacher's desk while Ichabod was preoccupied receiving and reading *his* letter. Crane anxiously opened the "Surprise Invitation" requesting him to attend a "local quilting frolic" that evening at the venerable Van Tassel estate.

"Okay students, I have some bad news for you!" Ichabod austerely communicated in a contrived, raised voice, which momentarily camouflaged his true joy. The perverted teacher's out-of-the-ordinary declaration was met by a mumble of low groans being emitted by his thoroughly-bored, horny students.

"I have to attend a special meeting later today, so school is dismissed an hour earlier than usual!" the austere schoolmaster matter-of-factly announced to his usually apathetic disciples.

"Hooray!" the jubilant kids all euphorically yelled. "We can finally get the fuck out of this fucked-up shit hole!" Flying triangular paper airplanes were tossed into the air, almost a full century before Orville and Wilbur Wright did their Kitty Hawk experiment.

212

When all of the "little son-of-a-bitchin' urchins" ecstatically evacuated the premises, Ichabod sat down at his desk to again touch and read the invitation that had been written by his trampy, big-busted dream girl. The recipient opened his desk's top right drawer, and a thousand antagonized bees came flitting-out in a violent frenzy. The agitated creatures swarmed all around the exasperated teacher's face, kneecaps, head, dick, and vulnerable ass. Ichabod (a minor WASP himself) tried waving his arms to chase-away the irritated insects, and failing to do so, rushed out of the schoolhouse, dashed to a nearby stagnant pond, and then dived into the dirty, polluted water, which the school's naughty boys and girls often used as a convenient outdoor lavatory. Every time Crane would come up for air, a squadron of attacking bees would spot his exposed head, and make a beeline for it. So, Ichabod had to involuntarily practice being a human submarine for two whole hours until the incensed flying insects lost their motivation to sting the shit out of the already-tormented and much-maligned schoolmaster.

At his humble apartment, situated above a Dutch farmer's ramshackle barn, Ichabod spent two whole hours preparing for Katrina Van Tassel's "very special quilting frolic". The excited invitee brushed his scraggly, unkempt hair at least a dozen times, put some medicinal snakebite lotion on his three dozen bee stings (located all over his swollen body), and then entered his only rusty black suit that was ordinarily reserved for Sunday church services, for psalm singing lessons, for circumcision ceremonies, for weddings, and for occasional formal funerals.

"Jesus Aloysius Christ!" Ichabod exclaimed while watching the October sun set on the western horizon. "I gotta' be at Katrina's place in a damned half an hour! I don't even have enough time to jerk-off!"

Ichabod borrowed an old beaten-up plow horse named Gunpowder from his apathetic landlord, who was an elderly, senile, incontinent mass-murderer and serial killer named Hans Van Ripper (now reputed to be one of Jack's diabolical ancestors). The shagged stallion had definitely seen better days. The mangy horse possessed a knotted mane, a tangled tail, and an inverted inside-out dick that looked like it had recently taken its last piss. Gunpowder's left eye had lost its pupil and was glaring in the late autumn afternoon sun, but the creature's right eye was completely blind, and therefore it was certainly much better off than the left one was.

Wearing his morbid black outfit, highlighted by moth-infested black knickers, Ichabod was a *suit*able figure to appear riding the aged, disintegrating stallion all around the countryside, over hills and dales in a very roundabout route to Katrina's party. The short stirrups had his knees rising up to the saddle's pommel. Crane's sharp elbows stuck-out like weathervanes, and the ungainly rider carried his whip in his left hand, as if the control-device was a classroom ruler to measure some little boy's dick.

But worse still, as Gunpowder moved as quickly as the weak animal could through that section of the already-shadowy *Hudson River Valley,* Ichabod's arms crazily flapped up and down like an uncoordinated, ungraceful pair of turkey wings. And since the ridiculous idiot never wore underwear, Crane's flaccid, foot-long salami got tucked underneath his bouncing frame, directly between his asshole and the pommel, and his abused pecker was smashed every time his buttocks violently collided with the ancient saddle. 'This is one time I wish I had a tiny two-inched dangle!' Ichabod regretted as the rider clumsily bounced up and plopped down upon the saddle, attempting to control brain-dead Gunpowder's reins.

It was just before dark when Ichabod (mounted atop old Gunpowder) finally arrived at Baltus Van Tassel's fabulous mansion, lording over the tranquil *Hudson.* Everyone who was anyone from Tarrytown to Sleepy Hollow was in attendance, including Ichabod's most formidable competitor for Katrina's abundant affections, Brom Van Brunt. The bellicose bully had ridden to the affair upon his favorite jet-black steed, Daredevil, a creature that loved adventure and cherished excitement and conflict much like Brom did.

Tables in the tea-room abounded with foods, pastries, and taste-tempting delicacies that inspired Ichabod to gorge his stomach by sampling a bit of everything that was on display. The famished visitor ate at least one slice of seven different types of cakes, and then rambunctiously consumed doughnuts, biscuits, muffins, strawberry shortcakes, strawberry long-cakes, ginger cakes, and then apple, peach and pumpkin pie slices that had already been meticulously cut. Ichabod glanced-over at Brom Bones, and instantly became intimidated when *he* noticed Van Brunt devouring a French 'cruller', which he feared would naturally make the nasty bully even *crueler* than he already was.

A variety of delectable meats were also exhibited on various tables for the purpose of being viewed and swallowed by the party's seventy blithe-mooded guests. Heaps of smoked ham, smoked beef, smoked marijuana joints, broiled shad, roasted chicken breasts, and capon legs, along with pig's knuckles, pig tails, pigskins (that looked like miniature footballs), and pig's balls were all availably stacked on the large central table, all ready to be ravenously chewed, gobbled, munched-on, and digested.

The sound of music produced by a local amateur hick band originated from the parlor, which had been converted into a dancing room, with all of the expensive furniture removed and temporarily stored in the wonderful mansion's attic and cellar. Ichabod prided himself on his dancing prowess, so he asked Katrina to "cut a rug and a floor" with him, and since the blonde broad was the hostess, and no one else was out on the planks bopping-around, the comely Van Tassel damsel accommodated his request, which would have been certainly denied under other circumstances in any other place.

Crane was a rather awkward dancing partner during the lively fiddle tune, and the clod clattered-around the floor in a terribly cumbersome manner like a true klutz. Ichabod drew chuckles from most folks witnessing the bizarre demonstration with the exception of Brom Bones, who thought that dancing was a stupid activity, especially designed for faggots, lesbians, and transvestites. Van Brunt was smitten by extreme jealousy, and stood brooding all by his lonesome in a far corner of the noisy parlor room.

After the lively dance number had finished, Ichabod stepped to the refreshment table to cool-down and enjoy a glass of homemade eggnog. Brom Bones made it his duty to look for a drink, and the ruffian intentionally bumped into the feckless schoolmaster, who thought the contact with his chief rival was just incidental.

"Fancy meeting you here, Crane," Van Brunt began his calculated intimidation. "Do ya' give fucked-up dancin' lessons in addition to fucked-up singin' lessons?"

"Why no!" Ichabod stammered as nervousness surged throughout his emotions. "I can sing a lot better than I can cavort-around on a dance floor."

"Well then, you gay, pedophile son of a bitch," Brom calmly but effectively stated. "The next time I see your skinny ass flirting in any way with Katrina, I'm goin' to grab your dick and then savagely twist it into beef jerky, and you'll never to able to jerky your dangle again! Ya' friggin' understand!"

Ichabod quickly remembered his pecker being crushed by the weight of his haunches and by Gunpowder's saddle on the ride over to the Van Tassel castle. "Er Brom," the naïve teacher innocently and defensively answered. "My reproductive organ already feels like beef jerky!"

"Don't get wise with me, you stupid-assed academic fuck!" Van Brunt robustly exclaimed. Everyone in the room suddenly became quiet as the distracted spectators became aware of the ensuing argument. Noticing that the other guests had become reticent in order to eavesdrop on the escalating dispute, Brom Bones whispered into Ichabod's ear. "You'll be on a slab at the undertaker's tomorrow if ya' give me any more of your stupid fuckin' bull-shit tonight," the area bully threatened. "Now lay off of Katrina so that I can *lay on her* and get my precious noodle wet! Get the vital message, you narrow-assed slime-ball!"

Later, during the "quilting frolic", some old-timers gathered their chairs in a circle in front of the huge, warm hearth and began reminiscing about several memorable *Revolutionary War* battles that had been fought in the surrounding vicinity. Since many soldiers had been killed in various raids between the warring Colonial American and British armies, the conversation soon switched from military conflicts and victories involving dead soldiers to the region's myriad haunting ghosts and spirits. Ichabod apprehensively listened to the retelling of the Headless and Dickless Horseman of Sleepy Hollow legend, and the neurotic coward nearly pissed himself during the tale's 'climax'.

The Van Tassel revelry finally broke-up just before midnight. The cheerful farmers gathered their families into wagons, and had a procession of rattling buggies that led right through Tarrytown Proper, with the remaining carriages making it safely into neighboring Sleepy Hollow. Ichabod foolishly lingered behind to have a few parting words with the always-flirtatious Katrina, who normally enjoyed attention, praise, and approval from horny male companionship.

"Katrina, will you marry me?" Ichabod rashly asked when the rich young dame only wanted to hear sweet nothings whispered in her ear, and then bust Ichabod's balls by being a bitchy cock-teaser (or in Crane's case, a flamingo-head teaser).

"Fuck off, asshole!" Katrina yelled at the top of her lungs. "I wouldn't marry you if you had the last human dick in the entire universe! I'd rather get it on with old Gunpowder!"

Disappointed and disconsolate from being so candidly rejected, Ichabod sallied forth with dispatch atop old Gunpowder, swiftly exiting from the opulent Van Tassel stronghold. Sulking and melancholy, the rejected rider sobbed and moaned the first full mile on the lonely dark trail that wound its way through dells in the direction of distant Sleepy Hollow. It was the dead hush of midnight with a new moon making the sky appear completely black and foreboding. A fierce watchdog was heard barking from the opposite shore of the famous river. The only detectable sounds that the dejected schoolmaster could discern were the chirping of sex-starved crickets, and the twanging and croaking of horny bullfrogs.

All of the various stories of goblins and apparitions that had been discussed near the Van Tassel stone fireplace now ascended into Ichabod's memory from his turbulent subconscious. Shadows from tall trees made the night sky appear darker and darker. The constellations gloomily sank deeper into the morbid-looking sky. Dark clouds negated all celestial illumination. Worse yet, Gunpowder was slowly approaching the very scene where many of the eerie ghost stories had their original setting.

A slow-moving brook intersected with the narrow dirt trail, and both embankments on either side of the small creek were soft and marshy. A few muddy, splintered logs served as a bridge across the dreary stream, and Ichabod finally mustered-up sufficient courage to urge his decrepit horse to cross the dangerous span. The ominous bridge had been widely recognized as a haunted place by authoritative Sleepy Hollow senile elders and storytellers, and it was greatly dreaded by anyone that had to cross it alone after dusk.

As Ichabod and his ancient plow-horse approached the sinister bridge, the blood vessels in his neck expanded, and the teacher's heart incessantly pounded inside his chest. The unskilled rider gave Gunpowder a dozen kicks to the ribs with his stirrups to advance forward, but the stubborn, nearly comatose horse was reluctant to budge an inch. Ichabod's anxiety increased with the delay, and he desperately jerked the reins in the opposite direction. His uncooperative steed reacted to *his* nervous prodding, and quickly stumbled into several patches of briars and brambles. The frail horse stopped directly in front of the rudimentary bridge.

Just at that frightful interval, a tramping noise was discerned to Ichabod's immediate left. At the edge of the swamp, in the center of a dark grove, the shocked rider beheld a huge, towering shadow on horseback, menacingly facing the flabbergasted novice night traveler.

The terror-stricken schoolmaster's hair bristled and rose up on his head. "Who are you?" Crane demanded in a stammering voice. "What do you want with me?" the anxious fellow apprehensively stuttered with a very parched tongue.

The immense figure on horseback articulated no reply. Ichabod repeated his futile questions in a very intimidated and craven voice.

The great black-robed figure finally answered Ichabod's plea. "I am the Headless Dickless Horseman of Sleepy Hollow!" a very powerful bass voice bellowed. "And I intend to sever your head from your neck, but more importantly, I want to slice off your dick and use it for my very own!"

Shutting his eyes, the more-than-worried country pedagogue nervously began singing a familiar psalm tune as Ichabod imagined he was fatefully entering the legendary Valley of Death. The shadowy figure sitting atop its jet-black stallion trotted directly alongside old Gunpowder, who was about to have a heart attack and be benevolently carted to the Tarrytown glue factory.

"I want you to give me some head!" the Headless Horseman imperatively bellowed in the direction of the petrified schoolmaster. "Give me some head, I say!"

Ichabod gave old Gunpowder two swift kicks with both feet, and the old, mangy animal ungracefully made it across the crudely-built bridge of logs. Crane managed to quicken his horse's gait, hoping to leave his determined tormentor behind. The relentless stranger advanced the pace of *his* black thoroughbred to match Gunpowder's burst of acceleration. Every time Ichabod and Gunpowder moved forward faster, the pursuing rider and his magnificent black equine effortlessly matched the increase in velocity.

When Gunpowder managed to rise to the crest of a hill, Ichabod turned around and caught a horror-stricken glimpse of his anonymous, audacious pursuer. The mysterious equestrian's head, which should have been attached to the rider's neck, was being carried upon the pommel of *his* horse's saddle.

Ichabod frantically whipped and kicked Gunpowder, but his efforts were to no avail. The highly-skilled Headless Dickless Horseman easily stayed directly behind the very petrified schoolmaster. Sparks flashed upon the ground from the impacts of the galloping horses' hooves. 'I'm so fuckin' scared I can't even fart or shit!' Ichabod thought in dire distress, just when his flimsy tailcoat fluttered before his scared eyes, and temporarily obscured his field of vision.

'My cock could use a sock as a jock!' Ichabod wished as his frame mercilessly pounded and bounded up and down, crushing his sick wick-dick against the very hard saddle. 'I can think of a much better way to beat my meat!',

Despite Ichabod's great hysteria, Gunpowder's present panic had given *his* rider an initial advantage in the wild and woolly chase, but then, the already-stunned schoolmaster's saddle snapped-off *his* horse's underbelly. Poor 'Crane' *whooped* as he frenetically clasped his arms around Gunpowder's neck while holding-on for dear life. The fierce pursuing black horse trampled over the fallen saddle, as Ichabod frightfully heard the powerful steed panting and snorting close behind him.

The Headless Dickless Horseman's speedy animal pulled-up alongside Ichabod, and much to the schoolmaster's horror and dismay, the phantom rider rose up in *his* stirrups and violently flung *its* head at Crane. The terrified fellow ducked-down to avoid being hit by the circular missile, which to *his* misfortune had been accurately thrown. The object smashed into Ichabod's cranium and sent the schoolmaster reeling off of Gunpowder, and then propelling into the air onto the forest's ground. Gunpowder, the black thoroughbred, and the ghastly rider passed by in a blur, leaving a hurricane-type gale in their wake.

The following morning, old Gunpowder was discovered saddle-less, and casually munching on some clover in front of Hans Van Ripper's modest farmhouse. Several days passed without any indication of Ichabod Crane's existence in or around either Sleepy Hollow or Tarrytown. Curious citizens appointed each other scouts, and the searchers set-out on exploratory expeditions to investigate the haunted brook, but only during the safety of daylight hours. The day rovers found a trampled saddle in a shallow ravine off one part of the dirt road, and deep hoof tracks were evident in and around the supposedly haunted log bridge. At another dismal location along the narrow, dirt trail, a schoolmaster's triangular black hat and remnants of a shattered pumpkin were also discovered.

An old Tarrytown farmer visiting New York City several years later brought home news that Ichabod Crane was still breathing and teaching "young urchins" somewhere in the Harlem section of that mostly Dutch city. The informative farmer additionally reported that Ichabod had left Sleepy Hollow out of fear of the vindictive goblin; out of the embarrassing loss of Katrina Van Tassel, and out of debts owed to Hans Van Ripper for the broken saddle and for three months tardiness on *his* rent.

Brom Bones triumphantly accompanied Katrina Van Tassel to the local church altar to share the Holy Sacrament of Matrimony. And when asked about the disappearance of his main rival for the hand of Katrina, the notorious bully, Brom Bones, jokingly replied, "Who gives a flyin' shit about that square-dicked horse's ass? He ain't fit enough to have a dick or a pussy, let alone havin' the privilege of instructin' Sleepy Hollow's younger generation of juvenile delinquents about fuckin' sex education!"

The jilted pedagogue's body was never found along the aforementioned Sleepy Hollow dirt road in order to provide tangible evidence that would substantiate proof of the frequently discussed encounter's occurrence. The missing teacher soon became the subject of rampant and rabid local gossip, and in due time, Ichabod Crane became a distinct local legend, whose fame soon rivaled and eventually surpassed that of the Headless Dickless Horseman of Sleepy Hollow. Much to Ichabod Crane's utter chagrin, Brom Bones and Katrina Van tassel lived happily ever after inside her deceased father's enchanting mansion.

"The Red-headed League"
Sir Arthur Conan Doyle

Sir Arthur Conan Doyle (1859-1930) created one of the most famous characters in British literature, the inimitable private detective Sherlock Holmes. Holmes makes his friend Dr. Watson (the narrator) feel like *he* has the mental prowess of a pre-kindergarten kid throughout each story, and the reader sees all the clues and all the evidence from the narrator's limited and somewhat uninformed perspective.

Arthur 'Conan' Doyle certainly was no barbarian. Born in Edinburgh, Scotland, the great author was educated in the medical field and practiced that profession in 1882. It is not that coincidental to connect the idea of the narrator Dr. Watson being a physician when the author had extensive training and background as a *medicine man*. Altogether, Sherlock Holmes appeared as the main character in fifty-six short stories and novellas and also in four novels. A classic Sherlock Holmes story is "The Red-headed League", where the incomparable private detective outwits an accomplished Scotland Yard sleuth and amazes Watson by using observation, reason, and some good common sense to solve a rather baffling crime in progress.

* * * * * * * * * * * *

I had walked to Baker Street and visited my distinguished friend, Mr. Sherlock Holmes one morning in the autumn of last year, and found the master detective in deep communication with a corpulent, florid-faced old fart having fiery red hair. I apologized for my intrusion, and both Holmes and the aforementioned old fart with the blazing red hair ignored my salutation while expressing minor concern for my presence. I was about to withdraw from the room with my embarrassed red face, and with my head crestfallen, when Holmes roughly tugged me inside his private quarters and adroitly shut the door behind us.

"My dear Watson, you could not possibly have arrived at a more propitious time," my friend cordially whispered with a feigned prodigious smile upon his countenance. "Certainly, you're welcome to hear me bullshitting with a client anytime."

"I was afraid you were engaged," I amiably replied.

"I'm not engaged and I never intend to marry," Holmes jested. "And if I was engaged, it certainly would not be to a fat, red-headed old shit," my crime-solving acquaintance engagingly answered, so that only I could hear his rhetoric.

"Then, perhaps I should wait in the next room," I suggested. "The window has an excellent view of the active house of prostitution just across Baker Street."

"I admit that this street is rapidly becoming a rather sleazy neighborhood," Holmes declared while shaking his head in disgust as he tugged my arm into his apartment. "And I must confess that I enjoy voyeurism as much as you do. Now Mr. Wilson, I'd like to introduce you to my partner and key assistant, Dr. Watson, who has been instrumental in solving some of my more difficult cases, and perhaps can render valuable input concerning *your* unique dilemma."

The stocky, red-headed gentleman half-rose from his chair and nodded his head as a gesture of greeting, with a trite, little glance from his beady, fat-encircled eyes that looked as if the pupils required leech liposuction surgery ten years ago back in 1880.

I had always felt awkward upon first meeting a Sherlock Holmes' client because the master detective was so perceptive and so astute at interpreting clues and information, which *he* always made me feel like I was a stupid asshole.

"Try the settee Watson," Holmes congenially directed, reclining into his favorite armchair and putting his fingertips together to form a perfect triangle. "I'm fully cognizant, my dear Watson, that you share my enthusiasm for all that is deviant and outside the predictability of routine mundane existence. I appreciate the manner in which you've documented and if I may say so, often amateurishly exaggerated and distorted all over London many of our past investigative escapades into the world of crime."

"Your bizarre cases have always fascinated me," I politely answered, as I noticed in the window behind Mr. Wilson a big-chested blonde hooker entering the house of ill-repute located directly across Baker Street. "Yes Holmes, you have a way of exploring and penetrating the deepest dark hole and keeping 'abreast' of even the most minute illicit developments," I concluded and praised. "You very much enjoy the little game of tit for tat."

"Now Watson," Holmes continued, "Mr. Jabez Wilson here has been good enough to trek through the nondescript rabble on the London avenues and venture here to Baker Street to tell us a most singular story. As you know," Holmes emphasized before lighting his pipe, "the queerest detective stories are usually concerned more with the smaller crimes and not with the larger ones. Mr. Wilson, will you be kind enough to review your narrative for Dr. Watson's sake?"

The chubby, red-faced client proudly puffed-out his broad chest, alternately scratched his balls, and next his ass several times, and then pulled-out a wrinkled, oil-smeared newspaper from inside his greatcoat. As the client scrutinized the first column of the advertisement page, I

222

took a good look at Mr. Jabez Wilson and attempted to discern peculiar characteristics that might coincide with those that Mr. Sherlock Holmes would soon assess and subsequently elaborate upon.

My initial inspection of Mr. Jabez Wilson allowed me to deduce very little. I keenly observed that the man was probably just an ordinary tradesman, a fat slob blob in need of a serious diet, pompous and self-centered, and remarkably slow with an *IQ* somewhere between that of a dull dog and an alert llama. Jabez wore baggy gray, shepherd-check, tight-fitting pants that looked as if the apparel hadn't been washed in at least three decades. The visitor wore a somewhat tawdry black frock coat that was unbuttoned in the front; a heavy Albert chain, and a square pierced metal symbol of sorts dangling down, as either a charm or ornament. A frayed top hat and a shiny brown overcoat with faded velvet collars had been placed upon a side chair. As I completed my hasty cursory examination, I could distinguish nothing exceptional about Mr. Jabez Wilson other than his extraordinary, fire-engine-red hair, and a definite pissed-off expression upon *his* face, similar to one a constipated person has when he or she can't initiate a much-needed shit.

Sherlock Holmes was keenly aware of my preliminary visual evaluation of Mr. Wilson's unimpressive general physical appearance, and the egotistical ingrate shook his head to slyly mock my overall incompetence at attempting to do *his* work. "Watson, I believe that Mr. Jabez Wilson has in his lifetime done plenty of physical labor; he takes snuff; he is a loyal Freemason, and he has been to China. Also," Holmes elucidated, "outside of the obvious facts that Mr. Wilson has done a lot of writing recently, and that he scratches his balls and ass quite often, I can determine little more just upon initial observation."

'Mr. Wilson doesn't have athlete's feet,' I suspected. 'The buffoon has athlete's body. Or maybe he suffers from a dermatitis condition.' I was amazed at Holmes' perceptions of our mediocre-in-appearance guest, and my mind remained in a quandary as to how my friend had made *his* seemingly brilliant deductions.

Mr. Jabez Wilson promptly sat-up in his chair, and still had his forefinger upon the first column of the newspaper advertisement page while staring incredulously at my enigmatic but sagacious companion.

"Holy shit, Mr. Holmes! How did you ever know all that pertinent bull-crap about me?" the red-haired gentleman admiringly inquired. "I mean, for example, how did you know I did plenty of shitty-assed manual labor? It's as true as any of the gospels, for I began my fucked-up work history as a dysfunctional ship's carpenter."

"Your ugly callused hands, my kind sir," Holmes indicated. "Your slightly deformed right hand is quite a bit larger than your highly deformed left one is. Now either, Mr. Wilson, you masturbated eight hours each day of your adult life, or worked exclusively with that right hand eight hours a day, five days a week. The muscles in your right hand are much more developed than those smaller ones in your opposite palm, which incidentally looks like a crab claw," the somewhat all-too-frank genius related. "I took a chance on *that* observation, and bet that you were more of a dedicated laborer than you were a stupid jerk-off with nothing better to do since age ten."

"Well, Mr. Holmes," Jabez Wilson gasped in utter astonishment. "What about the accurate snuff' theory, and what about the fantastic Freemasonry determination?"

"Well, sir, snuff powder is evident all over your shabby, smelly clothes," Holmes informed. "And I noticed that you're sort of a maverick by choice because against the strict code of your Masonic Order, you stubbornly insist on wearing an ordinary arc-and-compass breastpin."

"Ah," Mr. Wilson excitedly realized and uttered. "And how about your keen detection that I've done a lot of goddamned writing recently? I can't understand in my wildest imagination how in the hell you remarkably figured-out *that* obscure fact?"

"Mr. Wilson," Holmes indicated while pointing to the visitor's jacket. "Your scruffy-looking right cuff is so damned shiny for five inches, and the tawdry-looking left cuff has a smooth patch up near the friggin' elbow where you had rested it upon the writing table."

"I see, you really know your shit!" Wilson admiringly complimented Holmes. "You oughta' go into waste management. But how did you know I had spent time in China, where I was screwing horny harlots with slanted beaver cracks?"

"The disgusting fish that had been tattooed above your right wrist has a certain dye and tint that is only blended together and applied in such a manner in China. I've done extensive research on Chinese tattoos, preferring to study academic manuals and texts on the matter rather than getting laid or eating suspect foreign pussy," my brilliant colleague explained. "I've even contributed to the literature of pornographic representations especially evidenced in Chinese tattoos. That delicate pink on the fish scales is also used to portray a woman's pink vagina when she has her glorious beaver open in certain suggestive and graphic Chinese tattoos."

Mr. Jabez Wilson gave forth a most hardy laugh that nearly shook the entire room. "Well, I've never been exposed to such incredible fascinating chicken-shit interpretation in all my life!" our lackluster guest exclaimed. "I thought at first you had made some incredible magical deductions, but now I understand that you've noticed simple everyday chicken-shit, and somehow managed to make it into wonderful chicken salad!"

"Mr. Wilson," Holmes imperatively replied. "Can you produce the slick advertisement that got you started on your little expedition into the criminal mindset?"

"Yes, I have it right here," the slightly-chagrined tradesman answered. "This rather enticing newspaper ad is what gave me a hard-on about the *Red-headed League*. You might want to read it for yourself, Dr. Watson," the befuddled fellow persuasively urged. "It's especially slick as Mr. Holmes has already described, but not just because of the oil stains smeared all over it. Oil stains are more desirable than shit stains, that's what I always say!"

I eagerly 'snatched' the newspaper from Mr. Wilson (while simultaneously thinking about my wife's stenchy-smelly silver-haired *snatch*eroo), and avariciously read the following very curious advertisement:

To the Red-headed League

In compliance with the stipulations of the will of the late Ezekiah Hopkins, of Lebanon, Pa., USA, another vacancy has now opened for a deserved candidate to be admitted into the privileged *Red-headed League*. The work is purely nominal for phenomenal compensation (4 pounds per week). All red-headed men twenty-one years of age or older, of intelligent mind and sound body, are eligible for admission. Apply in person at eleven' o'clock to Mr. Duncan Ross, at the League's London offices at 7 Pope's Court, Fleet Street.

"What on Earth does all this crazy horse-shit mean?" I ejaculated, after reading over the announcement twice and nearly popping a load while watching two more really stacked slutty prostitutes enter the sleazy bordello situated across the street.

Holmes chuckled at my obvious inability to decipher the cryptic message hidden inside the goddamned advertisement. I was becoming equally as pissed-off and petulant as Mr. Wilson had been up to that point.

"Watson, it's all a little arcane for the average amateur or novice detective to decode?" the champion ball-buster stated. "You might be in over your head."

"No shit, Sherlock!" I defensively and lividly answered.

"But first, Watson, Mr. Wilson will tell us about himself and his very regular household," Holmes countered, successfully pulverizing my sensitive balls after efficiently breaking them, "and exactly how this strange newspaper ad has affected *his* life and business. Make a note

Watson, you oddball clod, the paper is the *Morning Chronicle*, August 9, 1890, just two months ago."

"Well, Mr. Sherlock Holmes," said Jabez Wilson, wiping his forehead with an old, sooty handkerchief he must have gotten as a gift from a repulsive tramp. "It's just as I had been repeating to you. I have a little pawnbroker's shop at Coburg Square on the fringe of the city's business and retail district. It has not been doing too terrific as of late, and several times I've even contemplated suicide as a viable alternative to financial failure."

"Do you have any assistants?" I asked Mr. Wilson, showing Holmes that I did indeed possess an element of intelligence despite my shoddy, dismal track record functioning as a master detective's faithful apprentice.

"I used to be able to keep two reliable assistants, Dr. Watson, but now I can barely afford one," the still-sulking fellow confessed. "But this young man I now have is willing to learn the simple trade at half wages, so the current arrangements have been working-out rather satisfactorily for the both of us."

"What's the name of this self-motivated, ambitious youth you've alluded to?" Holmes automatically asked Wilson. "He's either very naïve, or very slippery. My first inclination leans toward the latter."

"His name is Vincent Spaulding," Mr. Wilson revealed. "And contrary to my first impression, he never worked in the USA manufacturing American sporting goods. I know Spaulding could do much better working somewhere else, but since he's satisfied with his meager compensation in order to learn pawn-broking from the inside-out, I figured that our relationship has been mutually beneficial."

"Your assistant Mr. Vincent Spaulding sounds as unique as your puzzling *Red-headed League* advertisement," Holmes concluded and shared. "Does your apprentice possess any special faults or any deviant habits?"

"Vincent absolutely loves photography. He's always taking photos, and then scampering down the steps to the cellar to develop them," Mr. Wilson confided. "Sometimes, I think he's got some tough-looking vixen down there that either gives him a good lay or a fantastic blow-job."

'Hmmm,' I thought. 'Maybe he's got one of the bitches from the bordello across the street down Mr. Wilson's basement,' I delightfully mused. "Is this Vincent Spaulding still in your employ?" I asked.

"Yes; he and a girl of fourteen that does a bit of cooking and cleans-up my establishment, making it presentable to prospective customers," Jabez Wilson communicated. "I'm a lonely widower and don't have any damned children, and I consider myself much the better-off to not be burdened with such an earthly curse. But I still manage to pay my debts, and keep my nose above water, so to speak."

'Hmmm,' I amusingly considered. 'Vincent Spaulding is molesting a fourteen-year-old girl, and the punk's probably pumping her wet pink well dry. I wonder if I could get this girl's address so that I could seduce this young chickadee myself'.' Then, my wandering mind broke-away from my daydreaming fantasy, and I asked Mr. Wilson, "How did you come across the particular *Morning Chronicle* advertisement?"

"Two months ago from this day, Spaulding entered my office and said, 'Look here Mr. Wilson. I wish in the Lord's name I had red-hair, the young fellow persisted in an excited manner'," Jabez indicated. "My assistant showed me the strange ad, which I intensely read. Vincent told me that the *League* had more vacancies than there were eligible redheaded men. And also, gentlemen," Jabez Wilson proudly stressed before loudly farting. "The four-pounds a week published stipend was mighty-tantalizing to a parsimonious old geezer like myself. I never have enough money for street hookers, and as you can plainly tell, I'm too fat and ugly to get a bona-fide whore to fulfill my sexual needs and fantasies."

"Did this Vincent Spaulding know more details about the *Red-headed League* than had been disclosed in the very curious newspaper' ad?" Holmes shrewdly asked.

"Why hell yes!" Mr. Wilson verified. "My eager assistant told me that I was quite eligible to get an appointment into the League since I possess fiery red hair. Spaulding told me that the deceased Ezekiah Hopkins was an eccentric American millionaire that had bright red-hair, and since the entrepreneur had originated from London, the old coot wanted to share some of his wealth with red-haired gentlemen from the London area."

"What the hell happened next?" I asked, while thinking that this Mr. Jabez Wilson was the biggest, most stupid jerk-off I had ever seen, or heard, or had the displeasure of meeting in my very boring life.

"I ordered Mr. Spaulding to shut-down the pawnshop and accompany me to Pope's Court on Fleet Street so that I might apply for the coveted vacancy formally announced in the newspaper ad," our un-illustrious guest stated. "Well, gentlemen," Jabez proceeded after again loudly farting. "Every red-headed dip-shit in London was standing in a longer line than the one outside the gates of hell. It looked like a fuckin' roosters' convention. Every color of red was represented from orange to clay, but few heads possessed the blazing red hair that firmly grows from my grimy scalp."

"Your experience with this *League* has been a most entertaining one so far," Holmes assessed and commented. "It sounds like you're being expertly set-up to have both your anus and your colon surgically removed."

Jabez Wilson then vociferously described how Vincent Spaulding had dragged him to the front of the line and then cut in front before three-hundred protesting, boisterous red-headed men. Wilson next stated that the *League's* office was bare, except for several tables and chairs, and that Vincent Spaulding had casually introduced the pawnbroker to a certain Mr. Duncan Ross.

'This Wilson is so dumb that the fool deserves to be violently fucked up the old a-double-scribble,' I reckoned. "Tell me Jabez," I piped-up. "What was your conversation with Mr. Duncan Ross like?"

"Well, Mr. Ross had bright red hair, and immediately commended me on my fiery red crop, and said that I was the most qualified for the *League* that he had interviewed all morning. The fascinating *League* representative then did something outrageously peculiar. The agent vigorously pulled my hair until my damned eyes were tearing, and the uncouth bastard nearly tugged my brains right out of my skull," Mr. Wilson described in an animated manner. "Mr. Ross then vigorously shook my hands, and apologized for *his* impolite, aggressive act. He persuasively commented, 'We've been deceived in the past by imposters having red wigs glued to their scalps, so I had to confirm that you possessed remarkable, genuine, blazing red hair,' the representative told me, expressing ample appreciation."

"What did Mr. Ross do with all the other three-hundred red-headed imbeciles that showed up to be interviewed?" I incisively asked our bewildered guest.

"He stepped over to the window, raised it up, and yelled to everyone impatiently standing in line outside that the vacancy to the *League* had been filled," Wilson informed us. "The red-headed idiots were highly disappointed, and all three-hundred of the dunce-like bozos simultaneously gave short-in-stature Mr. Duncan Ross the royal middle finger while petulantly shouting-up a series of unsavory descriptive expletives."

'This Jabez Wilson is even more of a moron than the three-hundred disillusioned, red-headed nincompoops,' I generalized. 'I'm glad that Vincent Spaulding probably sodomized *his* fat dumpy ass daily.' "Tell me, Mr. Wilson," I said regaining my skeptical focus. "Did Mr. Duncan Ross ask you any additional irrelevant questions?"

"Mr. Ross asked me if I was married, and when I told him 'No', he seemed a little uneasy. The administrator declared that the *League* preferred married men because *those* individuals tended to be more responsible and stable," Jabez nervously informed. "But then, Mr. Ross made me feel a bit more comfortable when the evaluator told me that I appeared to possess noble qualities that happened to offset the important married-man requirement."

"Did you ask Mr. Duncan Ross any significant questions about this rather incredible *Red-headed League!*" Sherlock Holmes calmly interrogated.

"Why yes," Jabez Wilson anxiously answered. "I found-out that the hours of my service to the *League* would be from ten in the morning until two in the afternoon, Monday through Friday. Since most of my pawn business is done at night, I was very receptive to me making four pounds a week performing nominal work for the phenomenal *League.*"

'This Mr. Wilson must eat a lot of bird food to keep his fucked-up brain going,' I conjectured. "And exactly what were your duties at the *Red-headed League* in order to receive the handsome stipend of four pounds a week?" I coyly asked.

"My assignment was to copy the *Encyclopedia Britannica* word for word starting with the 'A Volume'," Jabez told Holmes and me in an almost-apologetic tone of voice. "I had to provide the pen, ink, and writing paper, and the work was to be done in the *League's* almost empty Pope's Court office. It all seemed too good to be true!" Jabez exclaimed as Holmes and I had to cross our legs to stop from pissing our underwear and our pants right-off our thoroughly amused bodies. I also squirmed around on the settee as I released three consecutive silent but pungent-smelling killer farts.

"Was that all you can remember from the strange interview with Mr. Ross?" Holmes indulgently laughed while choking on his pipe from heavy smoke that must have accidentally gone down the wrong bronchial tubes.

Wilson then related that Duncan Ross had congratulated him for admission to the incomparable *Red-headed League*. The red-hair manager had related to Jabez that *he* was to report to duty the next morning at ten. "I thought that the entire enterprise was at first a colossal hoax, but despite my mounting skepticism," Mr. Wilson embarrassingly continued, "I bought pen, ink, and paper, and directly proceeded to the *League's* office at Pope's Court. My employment continued for eight wonderful weeks, and every Friday afternoon at two p.m. Mr. Ross entered the *League's* office and plunked-down four shiny gold sovereigns upon the table. I never dared leave the room, fearing I might jeopardize my rather lucrative salary."

"What kind of paper did you use to write on?" I asked, trying to impress Sherlock Holmes with my investigative acumen.

"I used 'foolscap," Mr. Wilson informed, "but it just as well should have been *dunce-cap*, pardon the pun. Eight weeks had elapsed rather quickly, and I learned plenty about Abbots, Archery, Architecture, Assholes, Artichokes, Astronomy, Acronyms, and Attila, and I was all euphoric about finally getting to the B words when suddenly the whole dick-headed business of copying the encyclopedia books came to a halt."

"To an end?" I laughed, half-amused and half-surprised at our client's extraordinary revelation.

"Yes, Dr. Watson," Jabez Wilson seriously and solemnly affirmed. "The next morning, I enthusiastically walked to Pope's Court on Fleet Street as usual. The *League's* office door was locked, and a cardboard sign had been tacked onto it. Pretty tacky, huh? Here's what the damned sign read," Jabez disclosed to us as the perturbed man held up the flimsy piece of white cardboard.

The *Red-headed League* is Dissolved, October 9, 1890

"Dissolved!" I marveled and exclaimed as a picture of a medicine tablet disintegrating inside a glass of cold water flashed across my vulnerable mind. "What a goddamned bummer!" I sympathized with Mr. Wilson, who along with Spaulding never made American sporting goods.

Sherlock Holmes and I then gazed upon Mr. Jabez Wilson's pissed-off, hurt-looking face, and we both nearly split our guts open as all sorts of farts (some of which were wet) were emitted from our very active assholes.

"I cannot see where there's anything at all funny about the *Red-headed League* being dissolved!" Jabez Wilson peevishly objected. "It certainly is nothing to giggle and fart about! If you two gentlemen cannot do anything better than rudely scorn and ridicule me, I can indeed go elsewhere!"

"No, no, Jabez," Holmes chuckled as the master detective let-out one more rather atrocious gas bomb. "Your exceptional case is most refreshing, and Watson and I had spent last night eating jalapeno peppers and hot tomales at a Mexican Taco and Burrito bar manned by incompetent illegal aliens. Tell me, Mr. Wilson," Holmes continued while still incessantly giggling. "What measures did you take after you had discovered the note tacked onto the door?"

"Well, as you can imagine, I was in quite an extended stupor," Jabez informed us as Holmes and I couldn't stop farting alternately between lusty gasps of laughter. "I hastily checked all the building's neighboring offices, and no one had ever heard of any such legitimate organization as the *Red-headed League*. I then asked the landlord if he knew a certain Mr. Duncan Ross, and the gentleman maintained that he had never heard of him, but once knew a fellow named Duncan Doughnutter."

"What happened next?" Holmes demanded knowing.

"Well then," I begged for clarification from the landlord, "the redheaded gentleman in Number 4," Mr. Wilson recollected and said as Holmes and I had to cross our legs to prevent us from doing #1 and #2 all over the expensive rug and polished planked floor, while Jabez told us all about #4.

"Oh," the building's landlord answered. "His name was William Morris, a solicitor that was using the room as a temporary surrogate office until his new premises would be available," Jabez elaborated. "He moved out just yesterday."

Holmes and I could not stop laughing.

"Where could I locate the dirty bastard?" Jabez Wilson recollected and reviewed his conversation with the landlord for *our* benefit.

Holmes and I had never laughed so hard in our lives as we had at that moment.

"His new offices are at 19 King Edward Street near St. Paul's Cathedral,' the office owner had told me," Wilson stated.

Holmes and I were getting more and more giddy with each passing second.

Then, the perturbed, re-headed man continued his odd narrative. "St. Paul's Cathedral!" Mr. Wilson exclaimed while remembering for *our* benefit his conversation with the landlord. "That's not owned by St. Paul. He's been dead for centuries. The archbishop owns the damned cathedral!" Jabez recalled and preposterously commented as Holmes and I continued exchanging loud noxious odors from our A-holes while laughing indulgently at the nonsensical bad luck skein of *our* highly-perplexed client.

"Now, Mr. Holmes and Dr. Watson," our guest pontificated in a very annoyed tone of voice. "When I had arrived at 19 King Edward Street, I found nothing more than an old, dingy factory that manufactured artificial kneecaps; female breast and male penis prosthetics. and ribbed two-headed wooden dildos. No one at the remarkable factory had even heard of either Mr. Duncan Ross or Mr. William Morris."

"And what did you do then?" asked Mr. Sherlock Holmes as my associate quickly rose, walked-over to the window, and violently shut it directly upon a bulge in the front of his pants, so that he wouldn't piss himself and flood the whole damned polished floor and expensive rug with stinky yellow fluid.

"I went back to my pawnbroker shop at Saxe-Coburg Square and consulted with my assistant, which was like trying to communicate with a deaf, dumb, and blind person," Mr. Wilson stated. "Vincent Spaulding advised me to stay put and that I might hear from the *League* by mail. I became impatient waiting for an explanation by post, so to expedite matters, I then decided to contact *your* reputable expertise."

"Well, Mr. Wilson, you had done the proper thing in coming to me," Holmes answered with a trace of conceit in his baritone voice. "But I suspect that more dangerous matters are at stake here than might immediately meet the eye or ear."

"Dangerous enough!" Jabez emphatically balked. "I've lost four pounds of splendid income a week! Now I have to hustle cheap, fat ugly whores, and not have the extra cash to pay for ritzy expensive prostitutes!"

"You have no exact complaint against this very interesting phantom *League*," Holmes explained to our disappointed-but-livid visitor. "You've been generously recompensed for peculiar labor done, and have received over thirty-pounds for your unique employment. And," Holmes convincingly added, "just look at all of the fantastic knowledge and trivial facts you've gleaned from the fabulous A Encyclopedia! You now are an expert on about one'-twenty-sixth of all immaterial academic bull-shit known to mankind! Ha, ha, ha!" Holmes and I mutually laughed as Sherlock pressed down even harder on the window frame to prevent himself from taking a really long messy leak.

"But, Mr. Holmes," Jabez stubbornly replied. "I want to find-out who this scoundrel Duncan Ross really is, and why the rogue played this horrendous hoax on me, a rather costly prank if I might add over its eight-week duration."

"A few final questions," Holmes emphasized while still indulgently laughing. "How long did Vincent Spaulding work for you before your youthful employee brought the odd newspaper ad to your immediate attention?"

"About a month," the red-haired gentleman snorted like a miniature bull. "Yes, about a month, indeed!"

"How did Spaulding come to be in your employ?" Holmes deftly asked our distraught visitor.

"In response to an advertisement," Wilson disgustedly stated, angrily shaking his head. "Perhaps I should stop reading newspapers and the reprehensible ads published inside them."

"Was he the only applicant for the sole position you had available?" I interrupted.

"No, I had over a dozen inquiries, but since Spaulding would work for only half salary," our addled guest related, "I chose him over the other possible candidates."

"What does this fellow Vincent Spaulding look like? Describe his general appearance," Holmes demanded and probed.

"Short, stocky, nervous in his habits, and no beard or mustache on his shaven face," Mr. Wilson recalled and articulated. "And yes, he's definitely not a day over thirty."

"Are his ears and penis pierced?" Holmes countered. "Does the fellow wear earrings?"

"I don't know about his penis, but his ears certainly are pierced. Yes, he told me a gypsy had done it for him as a favor for giving the woman a colorful cave tattoo around her shaved pussy," Mr. Wilson remembered and uttered.

'Pierced earrings!' I thought. 'This Vincent Spaulding not only sounds like a prick! He sounds like a friggin' double prick, maybe even a double prick with a pierced dick!'

"Is this asshole assistant Vincent Spaulding character still with you?" Holmes definitively asked our already-agitated client as the master detective finally felt it was safe to raise the window.

"Oh yes, sir," Jabez articulated. "My faltering business is not too extreme in the morning hours, so that's why I've found the time to discuss this matter with you."

"Thank you, Mr. Wilson," Holmes emphatically declared and then chuckled. "I'll be able to render an opinion on your singular case in a day or two. By Monday, I'll get in touch with you, and convey my acute insights."

After our neurotic guest swiftly exited the premises, Holmes dashed to the lavatory, and upon his departure ten-minutes later from that enclosed sanctuary, I next utilized the facilities rather extensively. When I returned to my settee, Holmes asked me what I thought of the unusual set of weird circumstances that had been experienced and expressed by Mr. Jabez Wilson.

"I make nothing of the bizarre puzzle," I confessed. "It's a most 'queer' fairy tale, even for these gay nineties."

"As a rule," Holmes philosophized and shared, "the more incredible and eccentric a story originally seems, the less mysterious it becomes once the veneer is systematically stripped-away. Watson, the everyday commonplace simple-assed crimes are the most difficult ones to crack-open."

"Are we going to do any challenging detective work this afternoon?" I innocently inquired. "My stomach is growling for some more jalapeno peppers and hot sauced tacos."

"It's amazing that you didn't defecate your spleen and your pancreas out while in the washroom," Holmes said with a smile. "We'll have lunch, attend a splendid violin concert at St. James Hall, and then amble out to Saxe-Coburg Square to investigate Mr. Wilson's mediocre business establishment."

"Oh *fiddle*sticks! A monotonous violin concert, you say?" I cautiously protested. "I adamantly hate 'violins' almost as much as I abhor violence!"

"Watson, stop acting like a big, sulking crybaby," Holmes admonished. "Pablo de Sarasate doesn't fiddle-around, and the virtuoso plays second fiddle to nobody!"

That afternoon (after suffering through the "disconcerting" violin concert), Holmes and I traveled by the London underground to Aldersgate, but Mr. Alder was not anywhere around or near his gate. We then took a short stroll to Saxe-Coburg Square, and soon found Mr. Jabez

Wilson's shabby little store, among a block of shabby little stores, not far from a dismal-looking railroad yard. Three gilt balls and a brown overhead shingle identified our client's struggling pawn-broking business.

Holmes was acting quite peculiarly, and I couldn't figure-out his modus operandi. My eminent friend first sauntered up and down the filthy street, keenly inspecting the appearance of each residence or business. Finally, my clever companion returned to the vicinity of the pawnbroker's shop, tapped the pavement five or six times with his ever-present cane, obviously looking for some *concrete* clues; then ascended the stone steps, and loudly knocked on the door. An intelligent-looking, clean-shaven young man asked Holmes to enter.

"No thank you," my devious partner courteously responded. "I only need directions on how to get to the Strand?"

"Third right and then the fourth left," Mr. Wilson's sole assistant efficiently and promptly answered.

Holmes descended the in-need-of-repair steps and nonchalantly approached me. "Shrewd fellow," my colleague melodramatically claimed. "He's definitely the fourth smartest fellow in all of London, and certainly the third most audacious."

"What affiliation does Vincent Spaulding have with this *Red-headed League?*" I automatically inquired. "Why were you looking at his pants? Were several of his buttons unfastened? Did he have an erection?"

"No, you' dumb dork!" Holmes chided and rebuked. "I was staring at the knees of his ancient trousers."

"Stop intentionally withholding valuable information," I aggressively criticized. "Why did you beat the pavement a half-dozen times with your cane?"

"Let's take a little educational trek around the block," Holmes deliberately suggested. "I wish to explore every single inch of enemy territory."

Behind Saxe-Coburg Square was one of London's major traffic *arteries* teeming with horses, carriages, and delivery wagons, all acting as if they were blood cells flowing-around inside an 'artery'. Pedestrians were preoccupied, milling-around, traveling to their designated destinations, and stylish flourishing businesses (that incidentally abutted the dingy stores on Saxe-Coburg Square) abounded on the more-prestigious avenue.

"It's a hobby of mine to remember all of the businesses in and around London," Holmes confidently indicated. "Over there Watson is Mortimer's Tobacco Shop; the *Coburg Gazette* Building; the Vegetarian Gourmet and Epicurean Restaurant; the City and Suburban Bank, along with McFarlane's Urban Carriage Depot. That just about does it, Watson," Holmes concluded and disclosed. "Now let's evacuate the area before we're accosted, deluged, and solicited by some classy prostitutes. You know how I enjoy being frugal, and absolutely prefer the company of free harlots and whores."

"You're right Holmes," I instinctively agreed. "They're a lot more expensive on this swanky avenue than the slutty whores soliciting patrons on Baker Street, or the hare-lipped harlots looking for all sorts of sex in the vicinity of Saxe-Coburg Square."

"I believe that this oddball business at Coburg Square is most dangerous, and it requires *our* immediate attention," Holmes cryptically stated while evasively concealing specific knowledge that would shed much-needed light upon the mysterious *Red headed League's* function and purpose.

"Why do you regard it as a 'grave' matter?" I asked as we strolled past an old city cemetery on our way to the 'underground', where some notorious London mobsters often hung-out and aggressively mugged unwary pedestrians.

"Today is Saturday," Holmes reminded me. "And I believe we'll have adequate time to stop a rather bold crime from occurring. I shall require *your* dependable assistance tonight at ten, and don't forget to bring along your army revolver. Now Watson, you might need its essential services."

I had seen the exact same evidence and had witnessed the precise same settings as my astute colleague had observed, and yet, from *his* enigmatic words, Holmes had deciphered the crime, while I was still groping for more pertinent clues. I wondered what the nocturnal expedition that my evasive friend had proposed was all about. I soon gave-up my random speculations in frustration and despair. I decided to hustle a cheap hooker on Baker Street rather than annoy myself with wondering about the enactment of a stupid, nebulous crime about to be committed.

By 9:45 my gonads had replenished the semen I had squirted into the cheap hooker's hairy, wet, pink vagina, so I obediently reported to Holmes' residence on Baker Street. Two handsome hansoms were parked at the curb outside the familiar brownstone building. Upon entering my partner's interior office, I found the inimitable Sherlock Holmes in deep conversation with two gentlemen, one of whom I immediately recognized as Peter Jones of Scotland Yard. Holmes' favorite pastime was making government detectives feel like complete idiots, often calling the bungling sleuths "Incompetent Scotland Stock Yard Amateur Investigators."

"Our raiding party is now complete," Holmes summarized as the inimitable sleuth buttoned-up his pea jacket, and pulled his small hunting crop out of one of the pea jacket's pods. "Watson, I know you're remotely acquainted with Detective Peter Jones of Scotland Yard. Allow me to introduce you to Mr. Merryweather, a key metropolitan banking official, who will accompany us tonight on our ambitious little adventure."

'Mr. Merryweather would probably look gay in any kind of weather,' I thought, but soon dismissed my initial mental reaction in deference to more objective analysis. By virtue of studying the gist of our ensuing conversation, it was quite apparent that both Merryweather and Jones were quite cynical of Holmes' intended crime bust.

"Sherlock Holmes is rather theoretical and his deductive reasoning is quite extraordinary, and sometimes luckily accurate," Jones attested to Merryweather, who was preoccupied checking-out Peter's impressive peter bulge. "Sometimes, Holmes is more on target with his wild generalizations and conclusions than is the regular police force, that always uses proven conventional methods."

"It's all extraneous bull-shit unless you, Holmes, can prove otherwise," Mr. Merryweather cynically stated as *he* checked-out my pubic area hidden beneath my thick wool trousers. "But I must warn you that I miss my rubber," Merryweather complained while referring to a common game of cards, and not to wearing a prophylactic during homosexual anal insertion. "This is the first Saturday night in twenty-seven years where I've missed my damned rubber!"

"Mr. Merryweather," Holmes stressed to the disgustingly pompous and nauseating faggot. "The stakes will be high tonight, and I conjecture they'll be somewhere around thirty-thousand-pounds. And for you, Mr. Jones," Holmes elaborated, "you'll have the distinct opportunity to put the shackles on a criminal you've been conscientiously trailing for quite some time."

"True, John Clay is a problematic, high-profile murderer, thief, counterfeiter, check forger, and voyeur," Peter Jones concurred and claimed. "That slippery bastard has taken pictures of me pumping several bitches in the bordello across Baker Street, and then selling the shocking and incriminating photos to my dyke of a wife. I can't wait to arrest and beat the shit out of that brazen little mother fucker!"

"Wasn't Clay's grandfather a royal duke?" Merryweather academically asked. "Clay indeed has royal blood flowing inside his veins, and the villainous rascal is quite intellectually gifted too, attending and dropping out of *Eton* before he ever learned how to manufacture shoes at *Oxford.*"

"Okay, let's get this traveling clown-show on the road," Holmes forcefully recommended. "Mr. Merryweather and Mr. Jones; you two take the first hansom, and Watson and I will follow in the second. And Merryweather," my partner and mentor further instructed. "We're going *straight* to the scene, so no deviant homosexual activity or immoral advances towards Jones, who is an avowed heterosexual and homophile that will eliminate your fat faggot ass in a hurry if necessary. I strongly urge that *you* should also go 'straight' tonight."

The hansoms' wheels rumbled and rattled through a labyrinth of gas-lit avenues until we diverted into Farringdon Street, the red gaslight district where expensive bitches practiced their sultry and salacious trade.

"Jones is really not a bad fellow," Holmes evaluated and uttered inside our carriage. "Although he's an absolute moron in his chosen profession, and also quite a philanderer, who incidentally, absolutely despises gays and their lifestyles. I hope we don't have a homicide on our hands involving Merryweather before a great in-progress-larceny is ever attempted."

The four of us exited our respective cabs at a prescribed agreed-upon location, and then Mr. Merryweather cautiously led us down a narrow alleyway where I was sure the faggot would try to proposition either Jones or myself with his demented gay bull-shit. The bank executive then opened a small door that led to a not-so-wide corridor. We passed through several grated gates that had been swiftly opened by Merryweather's trusty master key. After passing through a maze of right-angled and left-angled halls, Merryweather lit a lantern and guided us down a huge passageway that led to a cellar, or vault, with a good number of wooden crates and sturdy cartons loaded with thirty-thousand-pounds of lustrous gold bullion.

"We're not vulnerable from either above or from below," Peter Jones determined and disclosed. "We're safe from detection now!"

Then, Mr. Merryweather disproved Peter Jones' contention by tapping with his cane upon the stone floor. "Why, it sounds quite hollow?" the financial administrator noticed and exclaimed.

"Please refrain from any loud exclamations or exhortations!" Holmes sternly advised Merryweather. "Every damned high-pitched sentence you utter sounds as if *you're* in the midst of having some perverted gay orgasm!"

"Oh, you say the sweetest things, just like Big Benny!" the gay bank director (like clockwork) sweetly complimented Holmes, as Merryweather frivolously and seriously waved his right hand back and forth like an authentic faggot in my scrupulous partner's direction.

"We have at least an hour until the attempted heist," Holmes estimated. The veritable genius got-down on his knees to inspect the cracks in the floor's stones, and I cleverly stepped between Sherlock and Mr. Merryweather, because I suspected that the bank director's first impulse was that Holmes (on his knees) could administer an improvised blow-job to the multimillionaire sex deviate.

While still on his hands and knees looking for cracks in the floor stones, Holmes explained the whole situation regarding the infamous *Red-headed League,* while Merryweather seemed fascinated by my partner's tight firm ass. "French gold has been stored in the Coburg Branch of the City and Suburban Bank," the master detective informed me. "The bank just happens to *abutt* Mr. Jabez Wilson's pawnshop, and I believe that Vincent Spaulding, alias John Clay, and his partner Duncan Ross, alias William Morris, are going to emerge from their tunnel and try and rob the gold Napoleons from Mr. Merryweather's bank."

I could detect that Mr. Merryweather became aroused when Sherlock Holmes again used the term *"abutt"* while the bank director was being thoroughly intrigued by the sleuth's solid firm ass. "So," I finally understood and chimed-in, "Clay and Ross paid Mr. Wilson the four pounds a week to copy the encyclopedia while *they* were busy digging the tunnel from the pawnshop's cellar to this bank vault."

"Yes," Holmes reflexively concurred. "And that accounts for Mr. Vincent Spaulding's love of photography, always going into the basement to develop his fictitious photos! Watson, I'm glad you've finally gotten the total picture! Ha, ha, ha!"

"And why do I have to have my army revolver?" I asked, trying to change the subject to camouflage my overall stupidity about not figuring-out the now very obvious tunnel scheme.

"If *they* are armed," Holmes surmised and declared, "then Watson, have no compunction about shooting first and blasting their bad-sperm testicles right off their criminal bodies if need be! That'll save our always-bitching taxpayers the expense of costly court procedures and case appeals."

The four of us silently sat in pitch darkness inside the cold, damp, dank cellar. I was getting very apprehensive about the prospective crime about to be initiated, and also about Merryweather putting his hand on my knee as I sat in the dark on a wooden crate loaded with gold Napoleons.

"The culprits have but one means of escape," Holmes observantly whispered, "and that is back through the tunnel to the adjacent pawnshop. Do you have that route covered?" Holmes asked Inspector Jones.

"Yes, I have one of my best inspectors and two bobbies there to apprehend the villains should that occur," Jones assured. "Two of the policemen used to be professional wrestlers, and as you know, there is nothing quite as effective in a hairy situation as two bobby pins!"

It was very unnerving sitting there in the cold, dark, concrete room for the next half-hour. At one point, I heard Jones snoring, and Merryweather panting incessantly, as the excited homo began rubbing my thigh with his sweaty palm, and soon, my keen ears heard Holmes farting from his most recent jalapeno pepper and spicy taco meal. The overall coldness made me contemplate a new-fangled Mexican treat, a frosted *burr*ito.

Suddenly, in the dim stillness, a glimmer of light outlined the perimeter of a large rectangular stone cemented into the floor. Soon, the lurid spark transformed into a bright yellow line. Next, the stone was gently pushed-out of place, and it made a dull thump next to the former hole it had concealed. A white hand appeared, reaching-out from the shadowy hole, apparently ascertaining that the criminals' eventual egress from the shallow cavity had been secured. Then, a lantern's light was visibly discernible, protruding out of the gaping hole above the pit. A young man placed the lit lantern aside, and then pulled and elevated himself right into our illustrious trap.

"It's all clear," the short fellow erroneously called-down to his accomplice still inside the hollow. "It was a lot harder coming through my mother's hole when I was born than exiting this one," the imbecile laughed. "Great Scotland Yard! What the fuck is this!" the unsavory robber screamed as Holmes and Jones roughly grabbed the trespasser by the collars and started beating the living shit out of him. The surprised interloper's hand held a pistol, but before the weapon's trigger could be pulled, intrepid Holmes's handy hunting crop spanked-down upon the young man's wrist, and the handgun clanked and slid across the cold stone floor.

"It's no use John Clay! Surrender!" Holmes yelled at his principal adversary involved in that most sensational crime. "I've already broken your right wrist, and if I have to do the same to the left one, you won't be able to jerk-off in prison for at least the first three months!"

"First you break my wrist and now you got to break my delicate balls!" John Clay, alias Vincent Spaulding, yelled and protested. "But my red-headed pal is gonna' get-away to fight law enforcement another day!"

"Three policemen are waiting for him at the other end of *your* imaginative tunnel," Holmes informed the frustrated crook. "You fell right into our snare, you idiotic, diabolical, punk thug! I suspect you got the tunnel idea by gazing at a wet pink split beaver centerfold in an expensive porno' magazine!"

"That's none of your damned business!" our unhappy captive hollered.

Detective Peter Jones quickly applied the 'derbies', which had been imported all the way from Kentucky, USA.

"Hey, easy with those damned handcuffs!" John Clay strenuously objected. "I have royal blood flowing in my veins, so please, exhibit some fuckin' aristocratic courtesy towards your noble prisoner, and kindly address me by saying *sir* and *please*."

"Please, sir," Holmes suavely stated. "Get your ass in gear and prepare to spend the next twenty-years of your fucked-up life in jail."

"Please, sir," Peter Jones sarcastically added. "You're gonna' wish you had tits and ovaries after I eventually get through with you!"

"Please, sir," Mr. Merryweather said to Clay as the notorious faggot tucked an object into the criminal's shirt pocket. "Here's my business card. When you finally get released from jail, be sure to look me up!"

After the daring thief had been taken into custody, and quickly escorted out of the building, Holmes had some final remarks for Mr. Merryweather's astute ears to absorb. "I have had several important scores to settle with that very cunning, craven individual," my friend and hero divulged. "And I believe that the bank should pay me a standard fee for my services. I shall send an itemized bill in the mail."

The following morning, I met Sherlock Holmes inside the parlor of his neat and tidy Baker Street home. "How did you know that the attempted bank robbery was to occur on Saturday night?" I pleaded for Holmes to answer.

"I noticed that Vincent Spaulding had grime all over his pants at the knees when we had visited him at Saxe-Coburg Square," Holmes casually lectured. "So, I hypothesized that the young man was digging some sort of tunnel. After I had pounded the sidewalk in front of Mr. Wilson's pawnshop with my cane," the master sleuth proceeded with his comprehensive explanation, "I determined that a tunnel could not be under the street in front of the business. That's when we walked around the block, and I observed that the City and Suburban Bank was directly behind Jabez's humble pawn store."

"But Holmes," I answered while still a trifle flabbergasted about recent events. "How did you know the robbery was to be attempted Saturday night?" I curiously repeated.

"When the *League's* office was suddenly closed, that was a telltale sign that *their* tunnel had been completed, and that Mr. Wilson's occupation, cleverly being diverted to copy the encyclopedia, was no longer needed," Holmes matter-of-factly revealed. "I reckoned that Saturday would be the best day for the robbery to occur because it would allow the sly culprits two full days to escape London with the pilfered gold bullion and Napoleons."

"Okay, Holmes, you have my sincere admiration for another job well done," I admirably praised. "But what are we to do now?"

"I don't frown upon *all* crime," Holmes affably admitted. "In fact, Watson, some illicit activities are even tolerable. So, let's abandon my stuffy residence and go across Baker Street and see if Madame Honeywell has any new big-busted, red-headed girls in her employ. I hear that Mr. Merryweather's former wife works there, and that she's a hot red-headed bitch just waiting to be humped and pumped!"

240

"Terrific idea, Holmes!" I agreed and congratulated. "Let's hurry over to Madame Honeywell's right now, and have our throbbing weasels popped!"

"The Speckled Band"
Sir Arthur Conan Doyle

I have studied seventy or so cases of my dear friend Sherlock Holmes over the last decade and now realize that he is the master detective of the century, and that I'm basically a stupid shit wanna' be sleuth. Some of his remarkable exploits have resulted in human tragedy; some are so comical that I've laughed my ass off thinking about them, and a large number of his investigations have been mere inquiries into the bizarre. But none of Holmes' weird cases have been as commonplace as London's abundant street corner pimps, hookers, and Cockney drug hustlers.

My mentor didn't give a shit about money. He worked because he loved finding-out about the secret lives of the mundane assholes he was representing, comprehending, and apprehending. But quite peculiarly, all of my friend's major cases had to be as fantastic as Siberian blow-jobs among Arctic nudist nomads in the height of a severe blizzard.

And one of the most spectacular cases that I recollect involved a renowned Surrey family, the Royletts of Strokes-Moron. At that time, Holmes and I were still sharing our bachelor room at 221B Baker Street, and we had bachelor parties almost every night with the hookers that lived across the hall, and who sometimes practiced their most necessary trade at the bordello across the street. In fact, we were *their* best customers, so the horny bitches seldom had to leave their rooms and street walk. That's why neither Holmes nor I ever had enough money to live alone in our own accommodations and pay individual rents.

Widespread rumors abounded about the death of the notorious Dr. Grimesby Roylett. Most of the scuttle*butt* involved Roylett suffering a slow death sitting on an outhouse toilet seat. I know for certain how the ignoramus happened to die, and will reveal the particulars in this unprecedented chronicle of events.

April 10, 1883 was when the extraordinary adventure began. I woke-up with a gorgeous hooker from across the hall wrapped in my arms, and my blurry eyes suddenly found Sherlock Holmes standing directly above us with an enormous erection protruding out of his underwear. Holmes always got his biggest hard-ons when being challenged by a new exciting detective case, so I immediately knew that something was up besides his huge erection. As a rule, the master sleuth was a late riser, but as indicated with his stiff rod, that specific early morning, my illustrious friend was indeed an early *bird rising.*

I glanced at the clock on the room's mantelpiece, and it indicated a quarter past seven. I felt awkward, since the chunky bitch I was in bed with was still sleeping and snoring-away, so I stared-up at Holmes and his erection in surprise, and I truthfully experienced a degree of chagrin. I was quite regular in my habits, but sudden irregularity made me feel like taking a royal crap in one of Roylett's old toilets.

"Sorry to disturb you, Watson," Holmes began in a serious tone of voice. "Mrs. Hudson-on-Avon has just informed me that we have a beautiful young client waiting in my office to be interviewed. So naturally, I felt it incumbent upon myself to disturb you!"

"Is the building on fire?" I angrily protested while greedily fondling the sleeping woman's gigantic breasts. "What in blazes is happening Holmes?"

"It seems that a young lady has appeared in my office in a panicky state of excitement, and *we* have to determine whether her arousal is sexual or not," Holmes matter-of-factly clarified. "She insists upon seeing me naked with my huge tool extending out," Holmes facetiously laughed and boasted. "The woman's presently impatiently waiting for us, and she's standing in the sitting room."

Now, when attractive young ladies wander about our sleazy section of London so early in the morning and subsequently wake-up sleepy, horny men, I always presumed that either the dolls had something important to communicate, or their vaginas needed to be probed and penetrated. I also immediately began growing an erection, and it was not because of the *comely* snoring red-haired slut snoozing in my embrace. I almost had a premature ejaculation just thinking about the newly-arrived, pretty lady restlessly waiting in Holmes's office for us to appear there and mutually render our essential services.

"My dear fellow, I would not miss this new case for all of the prostitutes on Baker Street," I euphorically answered. "I assure you that my testicles, in addition to my bowels, are in an uproar!"

I had always respected Holmes' keen insights, and envied his rapidly developed exploratory hypotheses in the art and science of detective investigations. His intuitions were always impeccably accurate, and their foundations were always extraordinarily based on flawless logic. What I admired most about Sherlock Holmes had also always caused me to be thoroughly pissed-off, with my pride, always having to endure unparalleled jealousy of his sagacity on all-too-many occasions.

I regretted hopping out of bed because the red-haired hooker I was sleeping with began provocatively licking her lips in her deep sleep. After hastily donning my formal clothes, I accompanied Holmes down to his cheaply-decorated office. An exotic lady was dressed in black, wearing a heavy veil. I immediately observed that the well-endowed woman was standing in the sitting room.

"Good morning, madam," Sherlock Holmes genially greeted our surprise visitor. "My name is Sherlock Holmes, master detective, and I love probing into women's problems, ever since I was a childhood orphan when my name was changed from Master Bates. This is my companion and associate, Dr. Watson, who is also a master detective who, when he was young, changed his name from Master Bates to Master Watson. So, madam as you can plainly recognize, Watson and I are actually formerly orphaned biological brothers. Miss Stoner, I believe, according to your card of introduction," Holmes expressed, "you may speak freely in front of Dr. Watson, just as you intend to do with me."

"Glad to meet you," I said to the nicely built woman, totally clad in black. "Sherlock Holmes has taught me how to be quite an Inspector," I added as my greedy eyes closely and covetously examined the attractive young lady's round firm tits'.

"Please forgive us," Holmes apologized. "My housekeeper, Mrs. Hudson-on-Avon has had the foresight to light a hearth fire, so please come closer Miss Stoner. My maid really knows how to light my fire, pardon the expression. Now, Miss Stoner, I shall happily order you a steaming cup of coffee, or perhaps tea, because I notice that you're shivering."

"It's not the cold weather that's making me shiver, Mr. Holmes," our distressed female guest revealed. "It's fear and terror that compels me to tremble."

Then, the knockout broad raised her black veil, and I could feel my tool simultaneously raising-up, too. Obviously, the attractive woman was in a miserable state of anxiety. Her young face was most pallid, and her stunning features appeared highly agitated. And Miss Stoner's eyes were melancholy and reflected fright, just like the pupils of hunted animals usually did. I was most intrigued about all of that very irrelevant bull-shit, which I have just boringly described. The pathetic-looking lady appeared to be around age thirty; her hair was prematurely graying, and her tresses thoroughly accentuated her weary, disconsolate expression. Sherlock Holmes studied Miss Stoner introspectively, while I closely scrutinized her hourglass figure along with her large, firm knockers.

"You must not fear anything or anyone in this screwed-up world," Holmes soothingly related to the disenchanted beauty. "Dr. Watson and I will soon amazingly set matters straight for you, won't we Watson?"

I felt my growing erection throbbing between my legs and instantly replied, "Er, yes Holmes. We'll soon set matters *straight* all right!"

"Now, Miss Stoner," Holmes proceeded with apparent purpose and confidence. "I detect that you've come into the city this morning by train."

"How do you know that?" the lady astonishingly inquired. "Are you a swami?"

"I've been *trained* to make such appropriate observations way down upon the Swami River," Holmes unflinchingly joked, and then the sleuth/guru lustily laughed, which was his singular bad habit. "For you see Miss Stoner, you have half of a return train ticket tucked inside your left glove's palm. And you must've started-out on your rail excursion quite early. You must've endured an intense drive in a cart along a series of rough roads before you finally reached your local friendly train platform."

The gorgeous lady jumped-up, spilling her hot coffee all over my pants, and the lovely bitch instantaneously scalded my wonderful super-hard erection. Helen Stoner stared in bewilderment at my illustrious associate and ignored my great humiliation. "Are you some kind of perverted voyeur?" she instinctively accused Holmes. "Have you been stalking me?"

"There's no mystery to my knowledge of your most recent activities," Holmes disclosed with a forced smile. "Your jacket's left arm is sprinkled with perfectly fresh tiny mud deposits in at least seven minuscule places. Now I know you aren't a mudslinger Miss Stoner, so I naturally deducted that a country cart throws-up mud onto clothing, making *that* type of random splattering array possible. And the cart only performs such a disservice when its occupant sits on the left-hand side of the driver."

"You're perfectly correct in your analysis," the lady commended, exhibiting both surprise and admiration. "I started my little expedition into London from home well before six. I reached Leatherhead at twenty past the hour, and managed to catch the first scheduled train to Waterloo."

I had meant to ask Miss Stoner if Napoleon Boner-part was at Waterloo, but then judiciously refrained from advancing such a stupid pun to a new female acquaintance. I also thought about 'Leatherhead' being a good blow-job given to an inflated rugby ball, but decided that *our* first meeting was not the time or the place to be so indiscreet and jovial.

"Sir, I'm extremely disturbed and suffering from great distress," the young lady intimated to Sherlock Holmes. "You're the only one I could turn to for competent help and advice. Only one gentleman really cares for me, but unfortunately, he can be of little help. And my cousin, Mrs. Honeywell, has spoken highly of your professional skill, and I had obtained your business address from her," Miss Stoner elucidated. "You've kindly assisted her in the past with your notorious probing, and I know from your stellar reputation that you, Mr. Holmes, could shed light on the mysterious dense darkness that presently envelops me."

The quivering woman paused for a moment to compose her fragile spirit, so that Helen could commence with her story's intriguing preface. After regaining her poise and confidence, Miss Stoner then felt compelled to proceed with her amazing narrative. "I cannot pay you for

246

your services until six weeks from now. Then, I shall be married and have some control over my own income," the disturbed young lady embarrassingly reported.

Holmes was thinking the same damned thing I was. The woman didn't need money to repay us, but could pay for our services by other more pleasurable means. The master detective turned to his desk and unlocked the top *drawer,* where my comrade usually kept his drawers and undershirts and his (legal) briefs. My colleague removed his casebook, and then reviewed his work schedules along with his most compelling past cases. "Honeywell," Sherlock Holmes recalled. "Ah yes! Her situation involved a missing opal crown. Watson, that exceptional case had been solved before *our* stellar association materialized, and I don't mean before the *British Bar, Pub and Tavern Association*, which of course, both you and I aren't yet qualified or honorable enough to join."

Holmes then promised our newest client that he would give her case the same meticulous care and effort as had been devoted to Mrs. Honeywell's case, which *he* couldn't accurately remember five minutes before to save his blessed life. "And now, I beg you Miss Stoner," Sherlock Holmes smoothly proceeded, "please tell us everything about the mystery that brings you to us this morning."

"Mr. Holmes, the very grief of my terrible situation lies in the fact that my fears are so hazy and nebulous," the woman emotionally conveyed. "My suspicions are based on some very small details that might seem quite trivial and insignificant to the casual listener."

"What does your prospective husband think of these trivial details?" I asked, as I stared at the woman's not-so-trivial breasts, suggestively expanding and contracting because of her great duress.

"My fiancé thinks and believes that I'm imagining all of this horror to which I allude," the stunning woman dramatically informed us. "He doesn't directly say *that* opinion to my face, because I'm always wearing this stupid black veil, but I can tell by his body language, and by his elusive conversations, that Percy doesn't give a horse's rear end about my very upsetting dilemma. My future husband naively believes it's all of a picayune nature!"

"You may begin your story by first officially identifying yourself," Holmes stated. "I always like knowing to whom I'm employed, so that I may formally send you an itemized bill for my highly-skilled services."

"Well, Sir, my full name is Helen Mary Stoner, and I live with my erratic and unpredictable stepfather, Dr. Grimesby Roylett, who is the last survivor of one of the earliest Saxon families in England," our newest client informatively added. "The Royletts have lived at Strokes-Moron, a former house of prostitution for stupid country bumpkins and backwoods' hicks. The estate is on the western border of Surrey, yes *siree* it is!"

"Those particular names are very familiar to me," Holmes nodded. "Many hick idiots and hack aristocrats have lost their money in addition to their sperm at Strokes-Moron during its gory glory years. I have several uncles that were all pumped-up every time they were to take the train out to Surrey, because they couldn't afford a surrey to get laid in," Holmes related and chuckled. "The numbskulls had spent all of their meager earnings on beer and prostitution, and couldn't afford their own means of transportation, just like Dr, Watson and I can't, either."

"Royletts' Toilets was a very profitable business, and the family was at one time one of the wealthiest in all of England," Miss Stoner reluctantly divulged. "Their land holdings sprawled into neighboring counties: Berkshire to the north, Hampshire to the west, and New Hampshire to the far west. But in the last century, four Roylett heirs were totally immoral, and their frivolous misfortunes squandered the entire family fortune. An addicted gambler just about ruined the family wealth in the beginning of the 1800s," Helen recalled and shared. "Only a few acres where the original whorehouse-homestead was located were left. And ever since prostitution was legalized in Surrey, Strokes-Moron has fallen into debt, and presently carries a heavy mortgage. The last Roylett before my stepfather lived the life of an aristocratic beggar, longing for the profits and the luxuries of yesteryear."

"Tell me more about Grimesby Roylett," Holmes insisted. "I understand that Royletts' Toilets went into bankruptcy, shortly after a fellow named Thomas Crapper invented the flush toilet."

"That's very true, and you're most perceptive," Helen Stoner complimented my garrulous and erudite partner. "My nasty stepfather was Nebuchadnezzar Roylett's only son. Grimesby Roylett borrowed some money from a rich relative that wanted to see *him* leave England, and woefully get killed overseas. My stepfather obtained a fraudulent mail-order medical degree, and then lived in Calcutta near the internationally famous cow slaughterhouse situated there. He soon established a large practice in India as a quack doctor, and also as a soothsayer rip-off-con-artist giving his medical patients bogus crystal ball readings."

"Did Dr. Roylett's patients ever get impatient with his scam techniques?" Holmes incisively asked.

"No, but several robberies had occurred in his house after my stepfather had bilked the local peasant population of their life savings," Miss Stoner sadly admitted, "and in a fit of drunken anger, Dr. Roylett blamed his Indian butler, and then mercilessly beat him to death before the poor fellow had a chance to return to his Apache reservation in New Mexico."

"Your stepfather sounds like he's quite a violent man possessing a nasty temper!" Holmes critically opined. "Did the Calcutta authorities prosecute him? It sounds like Dr. Roylett should be persecuted instead of prosecuted!"

"My mercurial-tempered stepfather barely escaped the death penalty when the exhibitionist appeared nude before the Calcutta judge," Helen embarrassingly told us. "But somehow, he won the court's sympathy for committing the heinous murder, and served only ten-years in prison. Then, the crazed lunatic returned to Strokes-Moron, a disappointed and hostile man."

"Tell us about your mother," Holmes requested as if he was a devout disciple of Sigmund Freud. "Was she British?"

"My mother was the daughter of Major General Stoner of the Bengal Artillery," Helen explained. "Dr. Roylett married her when he was practicing medicine in India. And after General Stoner got tired of killing tigers and elephants with heavy artillery shells, we all moved back to England."

"Do you have any brothers or sisters?" I inquisitively asked, simply to impress my genius detective partner with my sophisticated interrogation techniques. "And if so, do your siblings share your great grief?"

"I *had* a twin sister, Julia, and we were only two-years-old when my mother regrettably married Dr. Roylett," our client recollected and declared. "Mother had a handsome trust that she drew out of to the amount of a thousand-pounds a year. She willed the fund to my stepfather with one stipulation. An annual sum would have to be given to Julia, or to me, in case we should marry," Helen confided. "But my dear mother specified in her will that my sister and I could not marry each other, if we wanted to profit from the inheritance."

"I take it that your mother is no longer living," Sherlock Holmes assumed and relayed. "This inheritance business of a thousand-pounds a year seems to be a big factor in your problem. I mean, I once lost fifty-pounds in one day at a slim-fast London speakeasy/casino, and quite frankly, I've been thoroughly pissed-off ever since!"

"My dear mother was killed in a terrible train wreck near Crewe eight-years-ago," Helen sobbed. "And ever since then, Dr. Roylett has had a one-track mind, and has been trying to railroad me into a dark mystery I cannot fully comprehend."

"Did Dr. Roylett practice medicine upon his return to England, or did he finally learn how to do doctoring, and not have to employ his profession in pretend situations?" I cleverly and cynically asked. 'I wonder if Helen and Julia slept in twin beds?' I mused, but kept my rumination to myself.

"My stepfather took Julia and me to live in the old abandoned bordello at Strokes-Moron," Helen sorrowfully sniffed. "The sizable inheritance from my mother's will covered all of *our* basic needs. Julia and I were quite happy being lazy, and not having to work for material comforts like common laborers must do. But my stepfather became very introverted, and never talked to neighbors or to outsiders. He isolated himself inside his room, and would bitterly quarrel with any human who ever bothered casually saying 'Good Morning!' to him."

"Is Dr. Grimesby Roylett the only crazy man in your family tree that has fallen out of *his* tree?" I amusingly asked the troubled and flustered lady.

"Temper tantrums and physical altercations are prevalent traits common among the Royletts of Strokes-Moron," our melancholy client related. "In my *step*father's case, I think it had something to do with those dancing lessons he took during several long stays in the tropics. Julia and I both suspected that Dr. Roylett had contracted jaundice when his wrinkly forehead turned an orange-ish color from several horrendous bouts with yellow fever."

"You said that your stepfather's mendacious vituperations were rather acrimonious," Holmes declared, as I abruptly scurried to the bookshelf to find the nearest dictionary. "Did he *verbally* insult anyone besides you or Julia?"

"Dr. Roylett used mostly nouns rather than actually verbally assaulting us," Helen corrected. "He was indeed the terror of Surrey. People would disperse and scatter at first sight of his approach. Last week, my stepfather picked-up the local blacksmith and hurled the strongest man in Surrey over a wall and into a pigsty. And up until then, I thought that only humans got sties in their eyes, and not hogs accompanying the sties. Anyway, Mr. Holmes, I had to pay the blacksmith all of my savings as passive extortion to stop him from suing *our* estate, and consequently jeopardizing mother's dwindling inheritance."

"Do any traveling salesmen or Jehovah's Witnesses ever trespass onto Strokes-Moron and knock at the front door?" I intelligently and sarcastically queried.

"No, Dr. Watson, but Dr. Roylett allows wandering gypsies to camp on a few thorny acres of the estate," Helen sobbed with a handkerchief held up to her bloodshot eyes. "He lets them stay in exchange for gypsy mothballs that he stacks and stores in the bedroom closets. Then, my eccentric stepfather ventures-off with the itinerants, and doesn't return for weeks on end from his stealthy secret expeditions."

"Does your stepfather keep any pets?" I profoundly asked. "Someone like him might have to be reported to the *Animal Protection Society for the Prevention of Cruelty to Canines, Felines and Parakeets.* I once knew a Scotch terrier that was harbored with a sailor in the society's witness protection program."

"Yes, my stepfather does have pets of the non-traditional variety," our knockout woman visitor softly and sadly uttered. "He has a hungry cheetah and a vicious baboon roaming all around the property, terrorizing any wandering traveling salesman or *Bible*-toting Jehovah's Witness who accidentally meanders anywhere around Strokes-Moron. Dr. Roylett likes to intimidate everyone in town that is wary of the wild animals scavenging and patrolling about the estate. My stepfather exhibits quite a passion for ferocious Indian animals."

"Do you have any servants?" I methodically read from my amateur detective checklist.

"No servant ever stays too long in the house without being terrified by my vile stepfather's unpredictable temper, and also because of the vicious baboon and the unfed cheetah roaming about," Helen Stoner ruefully answered. "Julia and I were terrified right up to the time of *her* sudden and unexpected death, just two years ago."

"How did your *twin* sister die?" I keenly asked. "Did the two of you ever live in the Minneapolis-St. Paul area?"

"Julia was thirty at the time of her mysterious passing," Helen cried. "My twin sister and I never associated with peers our own age, since we feared our stepfather's wrath and were deathly afraid to share his behavioral eccentricities with friends. However, we did have an aunt, my mother's *maiden* sister, Miss Honoria Wesphail, who lectured for small stipends at colleges and universities, and who incidentally never lost her maidenhead. She lives over in Harrow, where as you know, the natives make horse plows."

"Did you ever have any harrowing experiences over in Harrow?" I ingeniously asked.

"Julia visited my aunt at Christmas three years ago. Aunt Honoria's neighbor delivered her Christmas tree to her door. The gentleman was a retired major in the marines," Helen remembered and irrelevantly informed. "Julia then went over to his place and helped him erect his tree, and next assisted him in decorating the Douglas fir with his balls."

"Did your stepfather approve of the proposed wedding?" Holmes skeptically asked. "Did he give Julia his blessing?"

"Dr. Roylett had no objection and went along with the wedding idea," Helen confirmed between intermittent sobs. "But then, Julia inexplicably died two weeks before the marriage day. I suddenly lost my best friend."

Sherlock Holmes had been leaning in his chair with his back turned toward us while his eyes watched customers and prostitutes enter and leave the popular brothel across from our residence, the illicit activities occurring opposite his inelegant office on Baker Street. Then, the master detective swiveled-around and intently stared at our beautiful-but-anguished guest.

"Please be very precise about Julia's death," Holmes seriously indicated. "I need to evaluate every minute detail!"

"Only one wing of the old manor-house is currently used," Helen commented while weeping. "The bedrooms are all on the ground floor, and the sitting rooms are all located in the central block of the building. Dr. Roylett occupies and sleeps in the first bedroom; Julia slept in the second, and I had my bed in the third consecutive room," Miss Stoner shared. "The rooms do not connect by means of doors, and the narrow corridor is the only means of entrance and exiting. Do I communicate these facts plainly enough to your satisfaction?" Helen asked Holmes.

"Perfectly so," my mentor replied as the crime-solving guru swiveled back around in a full circle to check-out the well-stacked hookers entering and exiting (in *broad* daylight) the very active whorehouse across Baker Street, which incidentally had no bread or pastry shops.

"The windows to the consecutive bedrooms open-out upon the lawn, which is really only a smattering of crabgrass and dandelions," our distraught client elaborated. "The night of Julia's death, my stepfather retired to his room early. My twin sister complained that she smelled harsh Indian cigar odors permeating from *his* quarters and into hers. I know that fact because she left her bedroom and came to visit me to vent her grievance. We chatted about Julia's soon-to-be nuptial, and then cheerfully discussed the prospect of my sister losing her cherished virginity. Julia rose at eleven p.m. to leave, when she paused at the door and asked me a most peculiar question."

"What was it?" I excitedly inquired. "Did she want to sell you her chastity belt?"

Helen Stoner deliberately ignored my stupid drivel. "Julia asked, 'Helen, have you ever heard a strange whistle in the middle of the night'?"

"Well, did you?" I impetuously asked. 'It must've been that dirty bastard Dr. Roylett summoning a dark gypsy woman up to his bedroom,' my naughty mind conjectured.

"Never," I answered my twin sister. "Are you sure it wasn't our frightful stepfather heating a whistling tea-kettle on the stove?"

"The last few nights, I've heard a low, clear whistle and the train station in Surrey is just too far away," Julia fearfully disclosed to Helen as retold to Homes and me. "I'm sure it came from our stepfather's bedroom, or perhaps from the poorly-maintained lawn. I thought I would see if you, Helen, had also heard the very unsettling sound."

"Maybe it has something to do with those devious gypsies," I earnestly suggested to my concerned twin. "But I must confess, I sleep more heavily than you do," I consoled my beloved sister. Then, Julia returned to her room, and I distinctly heard her key lock the door," Helen remembered and stated.

"Was it you and your sister's habit to always lock yourself in?" I analytically asked. 'How the hell are either of you ever supposed to get laid?' I snidely thought.

"We both always kept our doors locked because of the menacing cheetah and baboon terrorizing the vicinity," Helen maintained. "Neither Julia nor I ever felt secure roaming-around under those most difficult circumstances. Dr. Roylett's a control freak of the worst kind!"

"Please continue your intriguing exposition, Miss Stoner," Holmes declared with his back still to us. "Your story is now becoming most interesting, and I want to be there during its climax!" the famous detective snickered as my friend watched (through his window) a fat hooker punch a dissatisfied, frugal patron in the testicles.

"I felt that danger was somehow imminent on that bleak, eerie evening, and I could not fall asleep," Helen continued her description. "I always believed that twins shared a common genetic bondage, and when one of us was in trouble, the other one felt the anxiety. The wind started howling outside, and a torrent of rain was wildly smacking against the ancient house," Miss Stoner testified. "Suddenly, I was scared out of my wits by a horrifying scream that nearly made my massive breasts fall right off my chest. I knew I had heard my sister's terrified voice shrieking like a banshee."

"What did you do next?" I reflexively asked. "Were you afraid of leaving the safety of your room?"

"I rushed-out into the hallway, and my ears heard an ominous whistle, just as Julia had described to me a few hours before. Then, I discerned a clanging noise, as if a heavy anvil had fallen several times upon the floor. And next, Julia appeared before my very eyes, crouching-down near the light of the hall lamp. Her hands reached out to me for help, and I saw extreme terror seemingly molded on her alarmed face. My sister swayed to and fro like one possessed."

"Did your twin keep any liquor in her room?" I recklessly inquired. "Perhaps she was a little intoxicated!"

"Don't be ridiculous!" Helen sternly admonished. "My sister was not an alcoholic. A casual drug and tobacco user, maybe sometimes, but definitely not a whiskey fanatic or a wino!"

"What did you do when your sister was behaving in such an unorthodox manner?" Holmes perceptively asked with his back to Helen Stoner and me. "Were you momentarily paralyzed?"

"I ran to Julia and threw my arms around her, even though neither of us were lesbians," Helen qualified and sobbed. "She fell to the floor in a dazed state of mind. My sister then writhed and wriggled-around like a possessed soul, helplessly trapped in an obscure elusive dimension between this world and the next."

"Did your sister see and talk to you before she collapsed and expired?" I incompetently interrogated. "Did your afflicted twin eat a quantity of sushi that wasn't prepared properly before she had retired for the night?"

"At first, I thought that Julia was hysterical and did not recognize me, but then she shrieked-out a strange riddle that I couldn't quite fathom. 'Oh my God, Helen!' she screamed like a raving mental patient. 'It was the band! It was the speckled band!' Julia quickly faltered and then pointed directly to Dr. Roylett's room, but soon she choked to death before my very eyes, as if an evil invisible person had been strangling her."

"The Speckled Band?" I curiously asked. "I think they were once booked for a concert at the *Albert Hall*."

"I rushed down the narrow corridor calling for my stepfather to render assistance, and Dr. Roylett came darting from his room in his bathrobe," Helen whimpered with her wet hanky in front of her mouth. "Julia was already unconscious when *he* came upon the tragic scene. Our stepfather poured a pint of brandy down her throat, but Julia slowly faded-off into oblivion."

"It sounds like your sister might've drowned from excessive brandy rather than dying from the indecipherable Speckled Band, although I too think that *the group's* killer music is both hideous and abominable!" I proposed and remarked.

"Quiet Watson, or I'll send you back to Hannibal, Missouri to live with your spinster cousin Miss Watson," Holmes reprimanded. "Now, Miss Stoner, are you absolutely certain about this whistle and about that metallic sound you heard? Would you swear to it in a court of law?"

"The county coroner asked me those same questions at my sister's inquest, and I testified under oath that I had heard those queer noises," Helen verified. "But please remember, Mr. Holmes, that a wicked storm was in progress, and *that* loud distraction could've altered my perception of normal household sounds."

'Hmmm, Stoner,' I whimsically thought. 'Perhaps Helen's rock-throwing male ancestors eliminated religious zealots and made them into martyrs during the days of the *Roman Empire,* which of course really never moved around at all!' I fancied.

"Was your sister nude at that moment?" the dirty old rascal Holmes subjectively asked.

"No, Julia was clad in her bikini nightgown, but she had her panties on underneath," Miss Stoner affirmed. "She had a burned match inside her left hand, and a matchbox with its striker in her right palm."

"Ah!" Holmes enthusiastically gasped. "I'm now enlightened by the additional information about the match. That's very significant evidence, Watson! The burnt match is actually quite illuminating. Ha, ha, ha!" my partner laughed as he adroitly swiveled his chair around again, facing Helen and me. "Exactly what did the coroner's inquest determine?"

"Nothing special!" Helen disgustedly replied. "My testimonial evidence indicated that her bedroom door had been locked from the inside, and therefore Julia's room was inaccessible from the corridor. And dense shutters totally concealed the old-fashioned iron-barred windows from outside intrusion. There was no secret trap door on the floor. And the brick chimney was too narrow for anyone to enter or escape."

'I still think Julia had inadvertently died by brandy drowning,' I mentally maintained.

"What about the walls?" Holmes wanted to know.

"The walls and the ceiling were solid with no secret hatches," Helen remembered and reported from the official inquest report. "They were solid as *Gibraltar*. And my sister had no outstanding body marks that suggested violence. The coroner was completely befuddled, since it was quite apparent that Julia was alone in her locked room."

"What about poison?" I rudely interrupted. "For example, did she put too much iodine on an athlete's feet infection?"

"The county doctors examined my sister's blood and body tissues, and found no trace of such a despicable devious substance," our perplexed, grieving client answered. "I think that Julia died of pure fright that instantly sent her weakened heart into cardiac arrest. But exactly what phenomenon had exasperated her, I cannot imagine, and have no clue."

"Yes, your *exasperation* was certainly exacerbated by your emotional travail!" I nonsensically contributed.

"Watson, you just gave me a very good theory," Holmes conceded, "but I must first perform my own information gathering before I dare share my complicated hypothesis with either you or with Miss Stoner. Were itinerant gypsies gallivanting on the estate at the time?"

"Yes, they're always fiddling-around, dancing, gambling, and causing a general ruckus," Helen admitted with frustration quite evident in her demeanor.

"Do you suppose the term *speckled band* refers to the handkerchiefs the gypsies wear around their heads?" I impetuously asked. "In that case, Julia, should've shouted 'It's the Speckled Bandanna! and not 'It's the Speckled Band'!"

"My sister was delirious at that traumatic final moment!" Helen wept. "Sometimes, I mentally relate her 'speckled band' shriek to the traveling band of gypsies, and especially to their alluring Chinese vagabond dancer, Gypsy Rose Lea, who by the way, was married to another Oriental gypsy voyeur, Peking Tom. The weirdo pair were both pretty friendly with my stepfather."

Sherlock Holmes shook his head in disagreement and enunciated, "These are deep treacherous waters we're *currently* swimming in. I hope that there's only one shark named Dr. Roylett circling us. Now, Miss Stoner, please continue with your fascinating dissertation."

"Two lonely years have elapsed since Julia's unexplainable death," Helen inconsolably divulged. "Then, a man I've known for many years asked me to be his bride. His name is Percy Armitage, the son of a policeman over in Crane Walter, over near Reading. My demented stepfather reluctantly said that our marriage would have his blessing."

'His blessing sounds more like a damned Pharaoh's curse,' I suspected. 'Dr. Roylett makes Jack the Ripper seem like Jack the Rapper.'

"Two days ago, my crazy stepfather hired workmen to do some general repairs on the bedroom wing of Strokes-Moron," the unnerved woman related. "A gaping hole was made in my bedroom wall, and I had to temporarily move into Julia's former quarters. I had to sleep in my dead sister's bed. What a bummer!"

'Maybe the ghost or spirit of a prostitute that had been brutally murdered in Strokes-Moron when it was a flourishing whorehouse had terrified Julia to death,' I stupidly speculated.

"Imagine the terror I endured last night when I heard the same low whistle along with the same metal sound that Julia had claimed to know," Miss Stoner wailed without a harpoon. "I leaped-out of bed and lit the lamp, but my eyes saw nothing irregular in the shadowy room. I put on the black clothes I'm now wearing, and waited for the rooster's call. At daybreak, I rented a dogcart at the nearby Crown Inn, and arrived in the beastly device at Leatherhead. Then, with dispatch, I took the morning train to London to confer with you, Mr. Holmes."

'Next time you ride the train, I'd like to ride *you* Miss Stoner in a special berth,' I mischievously and ravenously thought.

"You've done quite wisely," my eloquent partner commended our vivacious client. "But I'm very much afraid Miss Stoner that you're deliberately protecting your stepfather from withholding vital information from my scrutiny."

"What do you mean?" our lady visitor strenuously balked. "I believe I've been most open and cooperative with you!"

Holmes aggressively latched onto Miss Stoner's sleeve and pushed back its frill. Five small black and blue marks that represented four powerful fingers and a thumb had been impressed upon her milky-white skin, just above Helen's right wrist.

"You've recently been abused, Miss Stoner," Holmes accused. "And I strongly suspect that Dr. Roylett was trying to intimidate you about something."

The abashed lady blushed, and then quickly covered her exposed wrist. "He's a very rough and uncouth man who is used to having his own way," Helen answered in unexpected defense of her hostile stepfather. "Sometimes he doesn't know his own strength when he's overwhelmed with anger."

Holmes rubbed his chin and stared intently at the sizzling fire in the hearth place. "We don't have a moment to hesitate," my enigmatic associate articulated. "A thousand additional details must be ferreted-out before I can hypothesize a professional opinion. I warn you, Watson, that we're bravely embarking into a very dangerous and dark enterprise. Miss Stoner, if we visit Strokes-Moron later today, could we inspect the bedrooms without your stepfather's knowledge or suspicion?"

"He's scheduled to be in London today, conducting private business," Helen declared. "He'll probably be away all day, so he shouldn't interfere with your important detective work. We do have an Arab housekeeper, but I'll easily divert her attention to another section of the estate."

"Splendid opportunity!" Holmes exclaimed. "And Watson, you have no objection to this unscheduled trip out to Surrey?"

"Not at all," I readily replied. "I once had a little affair on the train platform there. That was the first time I had ever gotten involved in public affairs, and it was all rather embarrassing having sex in front of a captive audience at the station."

"Do you have any other errands to run in the city?" the *private* investigator (who often unofficially checked men's peckers in public restrooms) asked our guest.

"I have two small items I intend to purchase near the Strand," Miss Stoner told us. "But I promise to catch the twelve o'clock train back to Leatherhead. I'll return by dogcart to the Crown Inn, and be back at Strokes-Moron just after noon."

"And we'll also be there around one," Holmes predicted. "Will you stay and have some breakfast with us? We're having some Japanese sushi!"

"No thank you," Helen sniffed as the voluptuous broad finally got over her very annoying bawling. "I must attend to my shopping. But I want you to know that I feel quite relieved after telling you my nerve-racking concerns. And if you men come through for me, there might be some special favors and fringe benefits connected with our personal relationship." Miss Helen Stoner then flipped her veil over her goddess-like features, and slowly sauntered out of Sherlock Holmes's cluttered office.

"Well, Watson," Holmes said while looking-down and then buttoning his fly. "What the hell do you think about all that impertinent bull-shit we just heard?"

"This Strokes-Moron affair seems to be a very formidable and sinister case that has me *baffled* like the entrance to an underground septic tank," I imaginatively and humorously replied. "Helen Stoner is certain that the walls and floors of Julia's room were as dense as Dr. Roylett's best toilet, and obviously, the chimney and the windows prevented any human entrance or egress. Julia must've been alone at the time of her freakin' mysterious demise."

"Watson, what do you make of the strange night whistles and the very arcane words of the dying girl?" Holmes objectively inquired.

"I can't imagine, although to tell the blasted unadulterated truth, I never had a very good imagination, even in grade school," I honestly confessed.

"But Watson, let's take the effort to consolidate the relevant known ideas," Holmes academically recommended. "First, Doctor, think of the night whistles. Obviously, the noises weren't Julia indiscriminately farting. Second, consider the introduction of the gypsies into the formula. The roving foreigners were on close terms with Dr. Roylett, and must've occasionally used his outhouse toilet. Third, Grimesby Roylett had an ulterior embezzlement motive for wanting to see Julia dead," Holmes sagely indicated. "The fourth salient factor is Julia's reference to the damned elusive and perplexing notion of 'the speckled band'. And finally, my dear Watson, Miss Helen Stoner also heard the metallic clang that Julia had alluded to."

"Perhaps *that* peculiar phenomenon has something to do with the metal bars between the windows and the shutters," I theorized and presented.

"Don't be an asinine nincompoop," Holmes aggressively chastised. "Those damned vertical bars cannot be moved or altered. Why the fuck' don't you spend the rest of your worthless life inventing how to breathe underwater through human gills? Anyway, Watson. I'm rather convinced that this adventure of the speckled band can be easily solved if we simply take the time to combine and synchronize all of the friggin' elements I had just enumerated."

"But what did the fucked-up gypsies do?" I asked while almost being totally flabbergasted.

"These speculations are precisely why we're heading-out to Strokes-Moron early this afternoon," Holmes reviewed. "There might be some super porno' magazines stashed-away somewhere in the mansion to add to your excellent collection of split beaver photographs. I can't wait until scientists finally develop colored film! Watson! What the hell is this?"

The door to Holmes's office was slammed open, and a monstrous oaf stood in the portal. The ogre's clothing was an odd mixture of country farmer and that of a professional scam artist's apparel. The huge creep wore a black *top* hat that did not spin around, a long coat, and a pair of high gaiters (lower leg coverings) made from crocodile hides. His right hand brandished a hunting stick, and the enraged giant had to duck-down to enter the doorway. And worst of all, the colossal bastard's width blocked the entire area. The intruder's ugly countenance was yellow as if burned by another planet's sun, and a thousand wrinkles along with a grimacing facial expression suggested a definite malicious intent. The trespasser's deep-set eyes accentuated an almost-fleshless, red snout. 'This incensed man is a goddamned maniac-predator looking for vulnerable prey!' I surmised.

"Which of you two assholes is Holmes?" the awkward, grotesque-looking Goliath belligerently asked.

"I'm Sherlock Holmes, and quite proud of my dual appellations," my un-rattled urbane partner suavely answered.

"The fuckin' Appalachians are in America!" the livid intruder vehemently scoffed while getting names mixed-up with mountains. "Well, anyway, I'm Dr. Grimesby Roylett of Strokes-Moron," the arrogant encroacher informed us. "My stepdaughter has recently been in your fucked-up company. I had traced her to this scumbag office of yours. What the hell has Helen told you?"

"It's a trifle cold for the spring of the year, wouldn't you agree Dr. Roylett?" Holmes responded as my partner effectively and deftly broke our uninvited visitor's balls.

"I insist that you fuckin' tell me exactly what she's been sayin' to you?" the gargantuan old brute boisterously screamed like a senior Bedlam asylum patient holding court in the lunacy ward.

"The spring flowers are budding a little late, you obnoxious bloomin' idiot!" Holmes shrewdly and coolly remarked.

"Ha, you dare insult my intelligence and ignore my demands!" Roylett arrogantly bellowed, as I almost crapped and pissed my pants. The crazy dick-head then approached and threatened us with his hunting crop. "I know your widespread reputation as being Holmes the scoundrel, Holmes the meddler! Holmes the butt-in-ski!"

Sherlock Holmes did not pursue the argument any further, but only defiantly and courageously smiled at the incensed interloper.

"You are Holmes the Scotland Yard jerk-off puppet!" the crazed, relentless, demented doctor insanely mocked.

My associate further goaded his new-found opponent by smiling and saying nothing to the instigator with the alligator-like gaiters. "I feel a draft, even though there's no war in progress at the moment," Holmes commented while conveying one of his typical, intellectual, non-amusing riddles. "Please be kind enough to close the door on your way out!"

"I'll depart after I've had my day in law court," the madman ironically hollered. "I've tracked my stepdaughter here. I warn you, Mr. Holmes, that I'm a very dangerous man to either cross or double-cross!"

And then, the infuriated Dr. Roylett swiftly advanced to the fireplace and seized the poker from the vertical stand. With a frowning poker face, the incensed madman bent the black metal object into an oval to demonstrate his impressive great strength. "See that you keep your fuckin' necks out of my grip!" the irate visitor threatened with a wicked-looking snarl upon his gruesome countenance. Then, the livid ogre tossed the poker into the fireplace and stepped-out of the humble Baker Street office.

"He seems like a rather cordial and congenial fellow!" Holmes sarcastically remarked with an exceptionally wide grin. "I'm not quite as stocky as Dr. Roylett is, but if the loudmouthed asshole had stayed to pursue his intimidation, I would've proven to the imbecile that my grip is virtually as powerful as his." Holmes then swiftly stooped-down, removed the hot poker from the blazing fire, and showing little strain, my crime-solving companion straightened the object out as I saw the flesh in his palms bubbling, and heard his skin sizzling from the stoker's extreme heat.

"Then, you were not at all intimidated by his physical prowess?" I automatically asked for the lack of anything better to say. "As for myself, I must find some toilet paper immediately, because I've felt that my life indeed was in serious jeopardy!"

"That petulant shit-head had the audacity to equate *me* with the standard idiots over at *Scotland Yard*. Scotland Stockyards is what it ought to be named!" Holmes boomed as the sleuth finally realized he had scorched and blistered his hands with second-degree-burns by straightening-out the very hot poker. "I only trust that Dr. Roylett doesn't get to Helen Stoner before we do. His little cameo appearance inside my office has added zest to our intricate case, Watson, wouldn't you agree?"

"I don't know too much about adding zest, but it's certainly added piss and shit stains to my underwear, that's for damned sure!" I attested with a degree of certainty. "I gotta' use the facilities right now!" I added.

"Go right ahead!" the detective/shaman answered. "While you're wiping your smelly ass, I'll order our sushi breakfast. Then, I'll take a stroll down to Doctors' Commons where I must research some registered property deeds that'll aid me in cracking-open this most difficult and intriguing case wide-open."

Well, I nearly wiped the anus out of my asshole until I eventually got my butt spanking clean. I changed my underwear just in time to greet Sherlock Holmes returning from Doctors' Court, which was really a nomenclature-misnomer, because *it* was in reality a London lawyers' dominion. We ate a very sumptuous sushi meal so that I would have more feces to shit-out of my chubby ass the following day. Then, Holmes showed me the Doctors' Court' data that he had retrieved. The document was a blue legal paper, and on it were scrawled some fascinating notes and numbers.

"I've seen Julia's mother's will," the incomparable private detective profoundly related. "I had to perform some complex mathematics to determine the worth of the present investments in Dr. Roylett's inherited portfolio. At the time of the Doctor's wife's death," Holmes paused, and then continued his discovery. "The twins total yearly income was a whopping 1,100 pounds. But now, as inflation has risen, and stock prices have fallen, the value is only 750 pounds a year. So if Julia and Helen both married, then…."

"Then, Dr. Roylett's windfall bonanza would've diminished to a mere 250 pounds a year," I estimated while proudly sporting a perfectly clean asshole. "That sum's a mere pittance, and is hardly above the poverty line."

"And now Watson, let's not loiter here and dawdle the day away," the master detective advised. "As you know, I'd rather reconnoiter than loiter, ha, ha, ha! Roylett now knows that we're interested in his personal affairs, so we must intercept the reprehensible prick if he has malignant intentions of harming Helen. We must rapidly get to Strokes-Moron, Watson, before the villainous brute does!"

* * * * * * * * * * * *

My partner and I entered a Baker Street cab to Waterloo Station, before we eventually realized that the lazy driver had been standing outside on the sidewalk, buying bagels from a Baker Street vendor. Then, Holmes was glad that I had remembered to bring along my service revolver in case I had to plant a few bullets into Dr. Roylett's thick skull, or in case either of us out of sheer fright had to commit a sudden suicide.

"A pistol is an excellent argument to persuade anyone that can twist a poker into an oval," Holmes casually reminded me. "And just think, Watson, of how his superior grip could pulverize *your* testicles. I also hope you've brought your treasured toothbrush along, just in case we discover a discarded incisor or molar in Miss Stoner's bedroom! Ha, ha, ha! Oh, good. The driver finally observed that he has two passengers sitting in his cab!"

Twenty-minutes later, Holmes and I caught the train at Waterloo Station, and soon were heading out toward Leatherhead, where rugby helmets, in addition to rugby balls, are manufactured. We next rented a cart and drove five-miles through the magnificent Surrey dales on a perfect April day, with a sky that featured a bright sun and a few cottony clouds. Green buds were just sprouting-out from the dirt lane's hedges, and from its majestic flowering trees. The earth smelled fresh and sweet, and it struck me like a ton of shit that there was a distinct contrast between nature's pristine spring beauty and the sinister elements awaiting us at Strokes-Moron.

"Did you bring along your pistol as I had recommended?" Holmes annoyingly inquired for the fifth time. "And do you have bullets in it?"

"Yes," I affirmatively replied. "I've tucked the weapon safely inside my jacket."

"Good!" my partner answered with a straight face. "Even the damned flowers have *pistils* this invigorating morning! Ha, ha, ha Watson!"

'Fuck you, Holmes!' I thought but did not verbalize. 'Fuck you with your straightened hot poker shoved all the way up your ass to your goddamned tonsils!'

Then, my inimitable acquaintance folded his muscular arms under his chest, pulled his cap-down over his eyes, and dozed-off to slumber-land. But soon, just as quickly as he had fallen asleep, Holmes suddenly awoke. He tapped me on the shoulder and directed my attention to several meadows off to our right. "Look there!" he commanded.

I observed that a heavily wooded park was situated on a sylvan slope laden with clover and grass. Next, up the incline, a shaded grove partially hid the gray gables of a very old and disreputable former whorehouse.

"That's Strokes-Moron over there," my knowledgeable mentor indicated. "More screwing has been done there than in the *London Metropolitan Nuts and Bolts Factory*. For all we know, Watson, *you* and I might've both been conceived in *that* very infamous place! Ha, ha, ha!"

'Fuck you, Holmes!' I again thought. 'But this time I ought to shove Strokes-Moron up your ass, instead of your goddamned red-hot fireplace poker!'

"Yes sir, that's presently the residence of Dr. Grimesby Roylett," our alert eavesdropping cab driver added.

"I see that there's some construction going on there," Holmes mentioned, while pretending to make an observation of what he already knew. "That's indeed our destination over yonder!"

"There's the local village over to our left," the conscientious driver pointed-out. "You can exit, climb the stile (a footbridge over a fence or wall), and then proceed on the footpath over the glen to where that woman is pacing back and forth."

"That's Helen Stoner waiting to greet us," Holmes claimed while shading his eyes from the glaring sun. "Watson, we'll do as the helpful driver has prescribed!"

We hopped-off the cart, and as usual, I paid the driver because Holmes always was habitually derelict in carrying money around, being too preoccupied and focused on the case at hand in addition to being a parsimonious son-of-a-bitch. The driver turned the cart in the opposite direction, and headed back toward Leatherhead to take (as he had mentioned to us) some influential rugby executives to the city train station.

As Holmes and I climbed-up the verdant grove to the glen, Helen Stoner dashed over to greet us. "Welcome to Strokes-Moron!" the beauty yelled.

"Good afternoon, Miss Stoner," Sherlock Holmes amiably stated. "You now see that Dr. Watson and I always honor our word, especially each and every cuss word, ha, ha, ha!"

"I've eagerly been waiting for your arrival," Helen exuberantly announced. "All has turned out wonderfully. Dr. Roylett has gone into London to conduct confidential business. He probably won't be back until evening."

'That's great news!' I thought. 'I might be able to get laid in my clean new boxer shorts that I had bought from a former middleweight champion. I'm sure glad I'm not fuckin' friendly with any goddamned midget jockeys!'

"Dr. Watson and I have already had the pleasure of being introduced to your volatile *step*father, who incidentally looks more like a staircase," Holmes jested and laughed. My comrade then described to Miss Stoner what had transpired with Dr. Roylett's rude visitation to Baker Street.

Helen's lips turned pale as she listened to my partner's in-depth narrative. I immediately lost my partial erection when I then thought about receiving a blow-job from Miss Stoner's ghoulish, pallid-looking lips.

"Good angels in heaven!" our latest client gasped. "Did that ill-tempered beast follow me all the way to your office?"

"So, it appears," Holmes plausibly confirmed. "He knows that someone more cunning than he is hot on his trail. Our next encounter might have *this stud* beating *him* in a game of strip poker, ha, ha, ha!" my obnoxious friend guffawed and jested.

"What should I do?" Miss Stoner asked. "He's definitely an obsessed maniac with a capital M!"

"Lock yourself inside your bedroom tonight," the great private detective suggested. "If Dr. Roylett shows any hostility toward you, we'll quickly intervene and escort you away to your aunt's place in Harrow. So now, Helen, give us a brief tour of the bedrooms at Strokes-Moron. And Watson, don't get any perverted bourgeois boudoir ideas while we're engaged in our objective professional investigation!"

The archaic-looking residence had been constructed of *gray stone*, which at first led me to fancifully believe by association that the moron Tarzan of Greystoke had once stroked his mistress Jane at Strokes-Moron. The façade was covered with lichens, and I remember thinking, 'I better not take my shoes and socks off and rub my bare feet against the external wall, or else I might get algae and fungus between my toes, and be exposed to the possibility of dying to death from too much iodine as poor Julia Stoner might have accidentally done!'

The wings of the old manor house were shaped like a crustacean's extended claws, and I mused that I might *get the crabs* if I pumped Helen's bush too vigorously inside the dilapidated mansion. The large structure had a high central section with two curving wings, formed like a spread eagle, which immediately made me ponder about Helen Stoner's juicy pink beaver slit. The decrepit mansion's roof was partially *caved* in, and I then fully understood why Dr. Roylett behaved like a total *Neanderthal*. In one wing, the windows were broken, and the interior had been separated from the elements by thick cardboard sheets, which I hoped were not also found on the bed beneath the blankets. The old home's central portion was in better shape than the west wing, which I believe is also true of the American *White House*.

By virtue of comparison and contrast, the estate's east wing looked much more maintained than the ramshackle west wing did. The windows had blinds, and dark smoke billowed-up from the chimneys and wafted into the sky, wonderfully polluting the atmosphere and the overall environment. A wooden scaffold had been built against the east wing, and the dwelling's external gray stone had apparently been penetrated and partially demolished by sledgehammers. But no workmen were doing any masonry or carpentry repairs at that particular moment.

Holmes paced up and down the poorly-kept, shoddy-looking lawn, and closely examined the outside dirty windowpanes. "This room I presume is where you used to sleep before the repair-work had commenced," the crime-solving wizard perfunctorily asked Miss Stoner. "And the center room is your dead sister's, where you're presently staying, and the end chamber is Dr. Roylett's sleeping quarters."

"Exactly," Helen Stoner verified. "But there never seemed to be any explanation for these radical repairs that aren't the least bit urgent. All that my perverted stepfather ever emphasized was not he wanted to expand his carbon-footprint on the local environment."

"There're no rational reasons for your present sleeping accommodation," Holmes confided, "because I believe Dr. Roylett wanted to move you from your old room into Julia's. Now all we have to do is figure out why. We already know about the loss of inheritance for being *his* probable cause, but we don't know exactly how Julia had perished."

"Correct!" Helen agreed.

"Now, Miss Stoner," my erudite idol proceeded with his analysis. "The hallway runs parallel to these three consecutive bedrooms. Are there windows in the corridor?"

"Yes, but they're very small and narrow, and not even the tiniest dwarf or midget could squeeze through any one of them, let alone an adult's fat rear end," Miss Stoner answered while closely peering at my big corpulent ass.

"Now Helen," Holmes said while getting more personal. "Your new bedroom's door is locked at night, so entrance could not be achieved from the hallway. Please go into your new room and bar your shutters."

264

Holmes and I stepped outside the dilapidated mansion, and then examined the rusty hinges with his trusty magnifying glass. "They're of solid iron, and deeply implanted into the stonework," the genius detective observed and described. "I shudder whenever I think about rusty shutters. Hmmm!" the wise fellow interjected as his lengthy fingers rubbed his chin in mild frustration. "Watson, my original theory is being tested and negated by my most recent sterling observations. If the shutters were bolted as Miss Stoner claims, then not even Sampson or Hercules could've gotten in from outside, regardless of the vertical iron bars. Suddenly this damned challenging case is now fuckin' drivin' me crazy!"

My brilliant companion and I entered Strokes-Moron via a small side-door, which gave us access to the aforementioned narrow, whitewashed corridor. Holmes declined to walk into Miss Stoner's former bedroom, so we passed it, and stopped outside Julia's room where Helen was presently sleeping (until the unnecessary repairs were to be completed).

Julia's former bedroom (Helen's present living quarters) had a low ceiling and a wide gaping fireplace, which was the distinct custom with late eighteenth-century mansions. A utilitarian brown bureau with a chest of drawers was in one corner, and a small bed with a white cotton spread was situated in another. An ordinary *dressing table* (that wasn't putting-on any clothes) was stationed on the left-hand-side of the windows. Two nondescript wicker chairs and a lackluster square red carpet completed the bedroom's utilitarian furnishings. The wall panels were of worm-eaten *pin oak* wood, with queer-looking *Pinocchio* cartoon drawings artistically painted on each of the vertical planks.

Holmes plopped-down into one of the *wicker* chairs, and appeared to be temporarily *bamboo*zled. All the while, I stood and thought about Dr. Roylett's yellowish *rat tan*.

The master detective's eyes scanned the entire bedroom, and his keen mind evaluated every particular detail in it. "Where does that pull-bell communicate with?" my partner finally asked our hostess as Holmes pointed to a thick velvet bell-rope that hung down beside the bed. "Its tassel is actually touching the pillow."

"It goes to the Arab housekeeper's room," Helen ascertained and stated. "It looks newer than the other items in this room. The rope only was installed several years ago."

"Did Julia request the bell-rope?" the all-too-inquisitive clue gatherer asked.

"Why no, Mr. Holmes," Helen replied, shaking her gorgeous head. "She and I always got whatever we wanted all by ourselves."

"Well. Watson. It looks like the old rope-a-dope trick," Sherlock idiotically laughed while leaving Helen and me completely bewildered. "A rope has been installed without ever being asked for, and it had been suspended from where it shouldn't be. Watson, that's probably the greatest clue I've so far uncovered in this bizarre case."

"Do you suspect that the murderer is from *Hemp*stead, New York?" I stupidly inquired regarding the dangling rope. "I once visited there, and explored Coney Island, too! Man, you should see all the voluptuous bitches wonderfully promenading on that damned fine boardwalk!"

Holmes ignored my juvenile bull-shit, and then rapidly threw his body onto the floor, looking as if he was about to do some strenuous pushups, or pretending to be getting laid with an invisible ghost. My companion examined the cracks between the boards as if he was a dedicated gynecologist, looking for the perfect clitoris. Then, he rose and did the same with the pin oak paneling on the wall, as if he were searching for either the ideal vulva or the perfect labia formation. Finally, Holmes stood-up and grabbed the velvet bell-rope and gave it a hefty tug. "Why it's a dummy, just like you are!" my colleague haughtily exclaimed to me.

"Won't the damned thing ring?" I curiously asked, just like any other dumb asshole would have responded.

"Hell no, Watson, and it's not even connected to a wire," Holmes discovered. "And look up there, you confounded dolt! The rope's tethered to a hook that's conveniently situated just above the ventilator aperture."

"How extremely absurd!" Helen exclaimed. "And I never noticed *that* fantastic puzzling construction before. I must be just as much a *moron* here at Strokes-Moron as Dr. Watson is!"

"Very extraordinary indeed!" Holmes acknowledged as the renowned sleuth again jerked the rope in amazement twenty-seven times in succession, as if it was his stiff erection. "Now, only a foolish dunce-headed builder would ever put a ventilator shaft between two rooms. If he was less creative and more practical, he should've put the ventilator on the outer wall, so that it brought in fresh air from the outside."

'Hmmm,' I nonsensically thought. 'Julia had a ventilator when she really needed some sort of respirator during her last minutes! What a coincidental irony!'

"The ventilator is also quite recently installed," Helen added to our quandary. "And it was done about the same time as the dummy bell-rope had been put into place."

"Don't you see, Watson, this is the very essence of our little mystery of the speckled band?" Holmes alerted me. "We have an ornamental bell-rope that doesn't pull, and a decorative ventilator that doesn't need to ventilate. Miss Stoner, let's now inspect Dr. Roylett's bedroom."

The medical doctor's room was larger than the one Helen had been sleeping in, and was plainly furnished with a mediocre-looking cot; a small wooden shelf of academic books (that were mostly technical in nature); an armchair in need of new upholstery situated beside the cot; a plain wooden chair, and a commonplace circular wooden table. However, the most interesting object inside the mundane bedroom was a large metal safe. Holmes meticulously examined everything in the room, except Helen Stoner's marvelous tits and pussy, and my rather ordinary dick and balls.

"What's in this metal vault?" Holmes inquired as my inspired mind thought about a valuable short gold *pole* to be used to vault over a bar at college track and field contests.

"Oh, just my stepfather's business papers and some rare collectible pornography magazines," Helen answered with a blushing face.

"You've actually seen those items inside the safe, or is that only what Dr. Roylett had told you?" my best chum requested knowing.

"Only once I saw them by accident, five-years-ago," Miss Stoner replied. "Yes, I recall that the safe was full of legal papers and naughty magazines."

"Your stepfather doesn't keep a cat in this safe, does he?" the clever, snooping bloke desired knowing. "Cats obviously need to be occasionally fed, you know!"

"No! Why what amazingly strange ideas you have Mr. Holmes!" Helen responded, probably thinking about imaginative perverted, hedonistic sex, just like I was.

"Well then, just look at this!" Sherlock Holmes excitedly remarked as if he had luckily discovered a lady's authentic shaved pussy. My fellow detective curiously lifted a small saucer of milk from under the safe, which stood on four metal legs.

'Dr. Roylett still drinks breast milk and has never gotten off of weaning on mother's milk!' I foolishly hypothesized. 'So that's why the shit-head is so fucked-up!'

"We don't keep a cat here at Strokes-Moron, but there are a cheetah and a baboon!" Helen cautiously explained.

'And your pussy is a second *purr*fect cat you've failed to mention!' I fancied.

"Ah yes@" Holmes exclaimed with an elated chuckle. "A cheetah is really a very large cat. Yet, a small saucer of milk cannot satisfy its drinking needs. I dare say, there's another important thing that I've neglected to investigate."

'Is Holmes going to ask to examine her love tunnel?' I mused. 'I hope he doesn't ask me to go into the other bedroom if he does!'

Sherlock Holmes stooped-down, and his squat made the master detective look as if he was taking a royal shit with his pants on. He closely scrutinized the chair with the greatest curiosity. "Thank you for your terrific cooperation, Miss Stoner!" the unrivaled genius commended. "The matter is quite settled!" the felony expert finished as the crime-solving magician placed his magnifying lens inside his vest pocket. "Wait a minute!" the master sleuth uncharacteristically shouted. "Now here's something exceptionally fascinating!" Holmes then removed a small dog leash that had been hidden under the cot. "What do you make of this rather novel discovery, Watson?"

"I probably could make the leash into a functional whip!" I frivolously guessed and declared 'And then, I could have some terrific *S and M* with Helen!' I automatically personally thought.

Sherlock Holmes laughed indulgently at my general ignorance. "You totally inane simpleton!" he scolded. "It's really a very cruel and savage world out there. An imaginative madman who has used his intelligence to commit an egregious crime is the most detestable human being wandering about on this very treacherous planet. Your stepfather is most duplicitous," Holmes announced to Miss Stoner with a very grim expression upon his countenance. "Let's now return to the lawn while I carefully engineer and fit the entire puzzle together in my active mind."

Neither Miss Stoner nor I had the courage to disturb Holmes when he was so evidently engrossed in deep concentration. So, we followed him around in circles on the unkempt lawn for a full forty-five minutes without daring to interrupt his intense meditation. Finally, the great clue analyzer broke-out of his self-induced trance and spoke.

"It's very essential, Miss Stoner, that you follow my explicit directions precisely to the letter," Holmes imperatively instructed. "The matter is too inherently dangerous for you to either hesitate or falter. Your life may hinge on your compliance with my demand. Do you fathom the gravity of the situation?"

"I don't even understand the gravity of the earth," Helen cutely answered. "But I assure you, I shall do whatever you insist."

"First of all, Miss Stoner," Holmes vaguely enumerated with austere emphasis. "Dr. Watson and I must spend the night in your bedroom."

'Wow!' I thought. 'It's been a long time since I've been involved in a pleasurable threesome!'

Helen was quite mortified at his absurd suggestion, and skeptically gazed upon Sherlock Holmes in sheer astonishment. "What kind of perverted expression is that you just uttered?" she glibly objected.

"Let me thoroughly explain and elaborate," Holmes countered. "I believe that the village's only public accommodation existing over there is called the Crown Inn, is it not?"

"Yes, and the Crown Inn still uses the original outhouse manufactured by Royletts' Toilets, Incorporated, which it had been purchased from old Nebuchadnezzar Roylett," Helen academically recollected and related.

"Your bedroom windows are visible from certain rooms inside the Crown Inn," my illustrious teacher pointed-out. "When Dr. Roylett returns, lock yourself in your new bedroom, and use the old excuse that you have a throbbing headache because you're having your period. Then, when you hear your stepfather going to bed for the evening, place your lit lantern inside the bedroom's window as a signal to Watson and me. Next, leave your door unlocked, and frantically scurry over to the Crown Inn where you can stay in the second upstairs room facing Strokes-Moron, which according to standard mathematical logic, should be Room 23. If not 23, then Dr. Watson and I will rent either 25 or 27. We'll leave the door unlocked so that you may gain entry," Holmes specifically instructed. "Watson and I will come from the Crown Inn to Strokes-Moron, and enter your room after we see your flashing lantern signal in the window. And be sure to leave the small side door to the bedroom wing open."

'Shit!' I thought. 'I knew the possibility of a threesome was too damned thrilling-good to be true. And I wanted to be on the goddamned bottom, too!'

"Watson and I shall spend the remainder of the night inside your bedroom and determine the cause of what's been positively frightening you," my famous friend finished.

"Mr. Holmes, if you've already made up your mind about what's going to happen," Helen begged, "please tell me what has caused Julia's death, and what is currently egregiously haunting my maligned sanity."

"I require a trifle more evidence to prove my far-fetched theory," Holmes regretfully communicated.

"Well then," Helen humbly pleaded. "Could you at least tell me if you think my dear sister had died from fright?"

"No, I don't believe so," Holmes laconically answered. Then, my erudite friend paused a full minute to pensively ponder a notion. "I strongly suspect that there's foul play connected with Julia's unexpected departure from this Earth. And now, Dr. Watson and I must hang-out at the Crown Inn before your pernicious stepfather returns and wraps either crowbars or fireplace pokers around our vulnerable necks!"

Holmes and I registered and had no trouble renting Room 23 at the Crown Inn, facing Strokes-Moron. At dusk, we observed Dr. Grimesby Roylett drive-up to his partially renovated estate in his horse and buggy. The suspected villain guided his means of transportation into an adjacent in-need-of-repair barn. A few minutes later, a light went on in the old mansion's parlor.

"I forgot to tell you a vital detail," Holmes commented as we peered out of our rented room's window. "There's much danger associated with this particular adventure. Watson, did you take any salve for your sensitive hemorrhoids?"

"No, but I can lick a clean handkerchief and use it as a soothing blotter," I smartly and creatively responded. "You've apparently discerned more than I have from the clues we've mutually gathered and assessed. I saw nothing' unusual, Holmes, except maybe the dummy pull-rope. And it would be almost impossible for a rat to squeeze through the diminutive ventilator."

"It is wise that you stick to medicine and not make a career out of difficult detective work," my astute companion diplomatically advised. "Now Watson, I had conjectured that we should find a narrow ventilator even before we toured Miss Stoner's room at Strokes-Moron," Holmes confided. "Helen had told us in my office that she had smelled cigar smoke, remember?" my partner rhetorically asked. "So therefore, Watson, I naturally concluded that some sort of small opening connected Julia's room and Dr. Roylett's sleeping quarters."

"But what harm could such a small cavity bring?" I questioned. "I couldn't even fit my erect dick into it, if I could find a table, and somehow stand on my head like a goddamned circus contortionist!"

"You figure it out, my good comrade," Holmes encouraged, sounding a little like socialist Karl Marx. "First, a ventilator is installed; second, an unnecessary cord is suspended from the top of the wall near the ceiling, and a lady that was sleeping in the bed suddenly dies. Doesn't the convergence of those three odd facts strike you as being quite irregular?"

"Forgive me for being a stupid, ignorant asshole, but I see no connection between those three peculiar facts," I honestly stated in a very confused state of mind.

"Well then, Watson; didn't you observe anything extraordinary about Helen's bed?"

"No, none other than the sexual fantasy that you, Helen and me could be playing advanced sex games inside it," my lips most-candidly answered.

"The damned bed had been bolted and clamped to the floor!" Holmes explained. "Neither Julia nor Helen could ever move it. The bed had to always be stationary, directly under the unnecessary, never-used pull-rope, which was almost-connected to the also very unnecessary horizontal ventilator shaft."

"Holmes!" I gasped. "I can now dimly see what your inspired cerebrum has known all along. When a medical doctor goes astray from his professional ethics, then *that* devious bastard is the most horrendous and most malevolent criminal with whom to cope. Dr. Roylett could deviously use his medical knowledge to accomplish his nefarious ends," I gasped. "I knew right along when he screwed Helen and Julia's mom that the rotten son-of-a-bitch was a no-good mother fucker!"

"Now Watson, let me smoke my pipe in solace while you achieve an erection, and work *your pipe* just like you ordinarily do before getting involved in deep criminal activity," Holmes casually recommended.

At nine o' clock, all lights and lamps over at Strokes-Moron had been extinguished. Two additional hours passed upon my fob-chained timepiece. Then, at the stroke of eleven, a lantern glow was seen emanating from Helen's new bedroom.

"That's our prescribed semaphore," Holmes indicated. "And it's originating from the middle window."

We swiftly departed the inn, and then scrambled-up the incline leading to the former infamous whorehouse. A chilly breeze blew in our faces, and it suggested the coldness of death that I apprehensively suspected was looming over our heads. The yellow light still glared and twinkled ahead of us, as *we* rushed with dispatch through the gloomy trees and eerie bushes.

I gripped my handkerchief tightly when I considered the prospect of my hemorrhoids acting-up as they normally did, whenever I became scared shitless and farted empty blanks or wet blasts out of my sensitive asshole. We finally reached the estate's disheveled lawn and began crossing it diagonally.

Holmes and I had almost arrived at the old mansion when out from the high yew bushes charged what appeared to be a grotesque-looking, deformed child. The creature hissed menacingly and leaped around upon the dark landscape, with its nimble-but-writhing appendages. Then, the fierce, wretched, twisted creature quickly darted into the shadowy shrubbery.

"My God, Holmes!" I panted in extreme alarm. "Did you see that miniature monster?"

"Quiet you, pathetic numbskull!" my friend warned. "That was Dr. Roylett's baboon that you had just gone ape over! Ha, ha, ha!" my friend lowly chuckled.

"I hope the cheetah doesn't outrun its spots and chew my buttocks off!" I neurotically exclaimed. "Carnivores tend to like munching-on men that have fat meaty asses!"

I then slipped off my shoes, following Holmes's stellar example. We silently entered the small door that Helen had left open for us, and soon we slowly stepped down the dimly-lit, narrow corridor to the familiar second bedroom. "The room is presently not occupied," my clever partner informed. "Helen has gone to the Crown Inn via the main road, just as we had arranged."

"Do we have to sit in the dark?" I begged. "I'm afraid of the damned dark."

"Then, you should never die, Watson," Holmes whispered and ridiculed, "because there' isn't going to be any damned lights inside your closed coffin. And don't you dare go asleep. Sit in the chair by the table, and have your pistol ready for any emergency that might develop. And make sure you don't accidentally blast either yours, or my balls off!"

I removed my revolver and laid it upon the table, with the loaded weapon coincidentally pointing directly at Holmes' ass. My partner turned down the lantern light Helen had left behind, and my perceptive associate laid his long cane on the bedspread. 'This is going to be a terribly dreadful vigil; I just know it!' I lamented.

The next thing I knew, the room was in total blackness, as if Holmes and I had suddenly time-voyaged back to the *Dark Ages*. Then, I heard the wild cheetah screeching outside the window, and I reached for my handkerchief to jam up my asshole, should I become besieged with a severe and flagrant hemorrhoid attack.

The Surrey church bell boomed every quarter-hour, and each fifteen-minute interval seemed an eternity. We impatiently waited without exchanging conversation from midnight to three a.m. Then suddenly, there appeared a glimmer of light reflecting from the ventilator. The startling spectacle quickly vanished from sight, but its awareness was followed by a pungent, noxious odor, smelling much like metal burning. 'That monster Dr. Roylett has lit a dark lantern!' I presumed.

All was again silent, and I could feel my bowels churning, and my stomach growling. I soon discerned a soft sizzling sound, akin to a jet of steam being released from a stove tea-kettle. Holmes sensed that the sound meant something significant, so the mastermind quickly sprang-up from the bed. I thought that my hero had gone crazy when he instantly lit a match, and began violently wielding, and then wildly, thrashing his cane.

"Do you see it Watson? Do you see it?" my mentor repeated, as he furiously swung away.

I noticed nothing and actually believed that Holmes was becoming certifiably delusional. Then, I heard a low clear whistle similar to what Helen Stoner had previously described. And still, Holmes was lashing savagely with his cane at some obscure object that had escaped my vision. I detected that my comrade's normally calm behavior had suddenly transformed to one of ultimate horror and absolute fury.

Holmes finally stopped his fierce mania. Then, his scrutiny gazed-up at the ventilator shaft, and next the stillness was shattered with the most dreadful, hideous shriek I had ever heard.

"What can that screaming possibly mean?" I asked in complete astonishment. "It's fuckin' coming from Roylett's room!"

"It means that our adventure of the speckled band is now over," Holmes curtly summarized. "And I'm quite sure it's ended for the best in regard to Miss Stoner's future. Watson, please take your pistol to Dr. Roylett's room just to be certain!"

Holmes re-lit the lantern, and we carefully and furtively stepped next door. Another dark lantern rested on the table with its shutter only half closed. The illumination projected shafts of light upon the iron safe, the door of which was wide open.

Dr. Grimesby Roylett was sitting stationary in the wooden chair, and the victim was wearing a long gray robe that made him appear to be a mad scientist. His bare ankles were protruding from the robe's bottom hem. Red Turkish slippers adorned the evil man's huge, foul-looking, ugly feet. Roylett's chin was elevated, and his wicked eyes were fixed and staring at the ventilator aperture located at the corner of the ceiling.

"Christ Holmes! What the hell is that?" I yelled as I noticed a weird yellow band with brownish dots serpentine-around the demented physician's forehead.

"It's the band Watson!" Holmes victoriously exclaimed. "It's the goddamned speckled band!"

I nervously took a step forward, and much to my consternation, the fantastic headband began slowly moving. On top of Roylett's gruesome forehead I saw the poisonous viper's puffed neck, head, and lethal fangs.

"That particular small serpent is known as a swamp adder," Holmes triumphantly declared. "It's the deadliest snake in the entire south Asian continent, including India. Roylett probably died ten seconds after being bitten by the venomous creature."

Before I had an opportunity to answer, my brilliant partner leaned-over and withdrew the leash from the dead man's lap. He carefully tossed the noose around the lethal reptile's neck, and quickly withdrew the slithery scaly creature from its temporary residence upon Roylett's bald-head. Then, carrying the viper at arm's length, my partner quickly and adroitly tossed the snake into the metal safe, and instantly closed the door. "Violence usually backfires on the violent!" Holmes loftily and philosophically proclaimed.

My associate and I escorted Helen to her Aunt Honoria's home in Harrow, where Miss Stoner thanked us for our successful intercession into her personal dilemma. As Holmes and I traveled by train back to London, I needed to learn several missing particulars about the cryptic speckled band mystery.

"I had reached an entirely incorrect conclusion," Holmes honestly admitted. "One should never reason when supplied with insufficient data. Those gypsies and the usage of the word *speckled band* initially put me on the wrong trail."

"What put you' on the right track?" I curiously inquired. "You seldom are derailed!" I aptly noted as the train sped towards London on its own parallel rails.

"When you had inadvertently used the word *exasperation* in one of our casual conversations," Holmes amazingly told me, "I divided the word in my mind up into five syllables, and from the second one, I immediately associated the word *asp*. An asp is a snake similar to a swamp adder."

"Well done!" I simultaneously commanded to the car steward as I ordered how I wanted my steak prepared.

"Thank you!" Holmes said in response to a compliment he believed I had rendered. My mentor continued puffing-away on his signature pipe, and incessantly talking to me staring at the whizzing town lights our carriage was passing by.

"I knew that whatever had killed Julia could not have come from the hall, the windows, the ceiling, the regular walls, or the floor," Holmes reviewed and reiterated his fundamental clues.

"No shit, Sherlock!" I humorously commented. "But please reveal to me your additional evidence!"

"My attention, Watson, then focused on the bell-rope, the ventilator, the anchored-down bed, and the word *adder* being a synonym for asp," Holmes indicated. "I knew that Dr. Roylett had lived in India, and had brought a menagerie of native animals back to England. British coroners are not familiar with a swamp adder's poison, principally because those snakes are not indigenous to our fine homeland. God save the Queen!"

"The snake should be called a subtractor instead of an adder because it eliminates people," I idiotically injected into the bizarre conversation. "Weren't the bite marks noticeable on Julia's body?" I wondered and asked.

"There would only be two tiny fang prick-holes, hardly evident to the human eye," Holmes explained. "British coroners aren't trained to look for that sort of almost microscopic bite."

"But what of the whistle and the milk?" I asked, still trying to shore-up loose ends in the complicated mystery. "Please be kind enough to explain those queer factors."

"The whistle was blown to signal the snake back from Julia's room to be rewarded with a drink of milk from the saucer," Holmes disclosed. "The snake would descend from the ventilator to the bell-rope, and then stop at the victim's neck. It might bite Julia, or it might not. Dr. Roylett's experiment might've been conducted a dozen times before the serpent finally killed Helen's twin sister."

"Then, Helen was fortunate not to be bitten," I realized and then stated. "And the clanging metal sound must've been Dr. Roylett anxiously closing the snake with its toxic fangs back into the steel safe," I concluded and remarked.

"And I lashed at the viperous creature with my cane to force it back up the bell-rope into the ventilator," Sherlock Holmes revealed. "The snake must've been hurt during the fracas, so it incidentally took its anger out on its surprised master, patiently stationed at the other end of the ventilator tube."

"Then, you're actually indirectly responsible for Dr. Roylett's death," I declared with my eyebrows raised high.

"Yes Watson, and I assure you that the extinction of that dirty rotten bastard will not weigh heavily upon my conscience!" Sherlock Holmes proudly announced. Then, Holmes handed me a paper bag. "A present!" he excessively laughed.

I opened the bag, and to my utter happiness, I delightfully found a dozen collectible pornographic magazines that Holmes had marvelously pilfered from Dr. Grimesby Roylett's safe.

"HOMER'S ILL ILIAD"
Chapter 1
"Achilles and Agamemnon"

Brain-dead-but-awesome Ancient Muse, amuse and speak to me now of those intrepid heroes who had pillaged and looted the corrupt bordellos and brothels of Troy. You can begin your unique narrative with the verbal dispute occurring between King Agamemnon, leader of the Greek armies against Troy, and the mighty hero from antiquity, Achilles.

"Agamemnon, you' totally obnoxious bastard," Achilles brazenly insisted. "You've caused plenty of anger from Lord Apollo for insolently yelling-up to high heaven, 'A-pollo is a chicken! A-pollo is a chicken'!"

"Get real, Achilles," Agamemnon vehemently maintained. "True, I have been a trifle irreverent. All I did was create a minor crisis by mildly offending Chryses, Apollo's favored high priest, who is only four-foot-tall!"

"We have been plagued with various plagues ever since your mounting arrogance had insulted Phoebus Apollo," Achilles screamed, almost rupturing his tonsils and adenoids. "Lord Apollo had heard Chryses' pleas for retribution, and the dispassionate god shot thousands of arrows of death and disease down-upon our afflicted Achaean armies. You're to blame for all of the recent destruction and devastation to our apprehensive troops," alleged Achilles. "For nine whole days and nights, Apollo's silver arrows came-down like torrential rain, killing good warriors, and having us cremating the corpses upon makeshift funeral pyres. The bodies were easy to burn because your defiance of Apollo and his lethal arrows had already scared the shit out of thousands of our brave warriors, making our enemy, the Trojans, both jealous and envious of the sky chariot god's awesome shooting ability. No mortal in his right mind wants to have Apollo as an enema, or, I meant to say 'as an enemy'!"

On the tenth day of massive death, Achilles called all of the Greek captains to a general council and firmly stated that under Agamemnon's dangerous leadership, the Achaean military campaign against King Priam and his Trojan minions was doomed to utter failure. "The Trojans cannot defeat us, but Apollo's wrath very easily can slaughter our' frustrated soldiers. I suggest that we forget this unproductive siege upon Troy, unless one of you morons can reveal to this assembly exactly why the immortal gods have apparently sided against us!"

"I'll tell you precisely what you desire learning," Calchas calculated and volunteered a viable answer to Achilles' imperative request. "But first, you must guarantee me safety from the wrath of a bitter rival. I need inclusion in your secret government protection program."

277

"Look, Calchas!" Achilles yelled. "Even if your alluded-to foe happens to be King Agamemnon himself, I'll kick his royal ass good, along with easily crushing his tiny testicles bouncing-around inside his miniature scrotum sac!"

"Lord Achilles; Phoebus Apollo is especially angry on two counts," Calchas anxiously disclosed. "First, our leader against Troy called all-powerful A-pollo 'a chicken', rather repeatedly; and second, your adversary Agamemnon refused to surrender his handsome ransom Chryseis, high priest Chryses' beautiful daughter. Apollo will not stop shooting silver arrows into our vulnerable assholes and puncturing our' delicate scrotum sacs until Chryseis is safely returned to Chryses! It's that plainly simple! What a fully fucked-up situation this Chryses/Chryseis crisis is! After you return Chryseis to Chryses to avoid further crisis, I suggest that we alter our errant ways and make abundant sacrifices to Lord Apollo upon a newly constructed altar!"

But Agamemnon, king of Mycenae and the Achaean leader against Troy, became infuriated at Calchas' Chryses/Chryses commentary. "Look, fuckhead Chryses," the king of Mycenae bellowed. "All of your prophecies are basically doom and gloom in nature. Chryseis is a tremendous piece of ass, and she's better in bed than my wife Clytemnestra is at daily humping and pumping. And as you know, my captains. My brother King Menelaus of Sparta had married that cold-hearted bitch Helen, and I have regrettably married Helen's frigid sister, Clytemnestra!"

"Do you value this religious-freak girl Chryseis over your entire army of fifty-thousand men?" Achilles audaciously challenged Agamemnon. "Surely, you should not jeopardize all of us simply over a well-endowed whore. But first, you must scream-up to the sky, 'A-pollo is *NOT* a chicken! A-pollo is *not* a chicken!'"

"I shall surrender my pride and obey Apollo's greedy will," Agamemnon reluctantly agreed. "But then it would look like I am weak if I must surrender my prize at a belligerent underling's prompting. Now Achilles; I assert that I must be given another horny harlot in the place of me giving-up Chryseis."

"What woman do you wish to pump the poop out of?" Achilles demanded of Agamemnon. "You might just lose your confused head over a stupid piece of ass!"

"I might just consider possessing your prized concubine, Briseis, Achilles, or perhaps instead, I'll decide to confiscate Ajax's prized hussy. I can't emphasize how terrific it is for me being the chief chauvinist with absolute authority on this military expedition. There's plenty of time for my' heart to determine which sexy bitch I'll choose for my personal gratification! But first, I must avoid future crises by appeasing Apollo by giving that excellent piece of ass Chryseis back to that lunatic dumb-dick priest Chryses."

"You dare belittle super-strong Ajax, the great warrior who had cleaned-out several Trojan platoons like an ivory-skinned white tornado!" Achilles loudly challenged.

"As leader of the forces against Troy, I can do whatever I please," Agamemnon articulated, using the rank card. "Your might is no defense to my acclaimed and established wisdom!"

"You're a very greedy bastard," Achilles accused the Mycenae King. "Quite truthfully, I have no particular grievances or quarrel against the Trojans. I had led my troops here to Troy to help your brother Menelaus retrieve your sister-in-law Helen from the clutches of Prince Paris. In fact, I've contributed more to this battle than you have. Just look at all the cities I've sacked, and all of the promiscuous whores I've bagged! Yet, you; you stubborn asshole, get to keep all of the plunder to your own avaricious self! Frankly, I've had enough of your abusive bullshit!" livid Achilles screamed. "I'm inclined to gladly sail for home and return to Phthia in my native Thessaly, and leave you to fight Paris, Hector, Priam and the rest of the Trojans over the stolen wife of Menelaus, who is reputed from Greek gossip to be a third-class piece of ass!"

Agamemnon then accused Achilles of being an emboldened coward, and to demonstrate his supreme authority, deliberately belittled the greatest of Greek warriors. "Achilles; enough of your snarky innuendo; now hear me out! You cannot defy the will of the Lord King, namely myself, captaining this formidable armada! Since I shall give Chryseis back to the short high-priest Chryses, I demand that you make a reasonable concession before this military council and give me your prized female, Briseis, to compensate for Chryseis, in order to avoid more crises with Chryses, the dwarfish high-priest of Apollo."

When Achilles and Agamemnon were about to commence dueling with bronze swords, Hera, wife of Zeus, urgently dispatched Athena, daughter of Almighty Zeus, to whisper powerful words into enraged Achilles' ear.

"Hold your hand from your' sword, dear Achilles, and I urge you to forget about using your bronze weapon at this moment," Athena softly and discreetly recommended. "For your exhibition of self-control, I assure you, brave warrior, that soon you'll be fully rewarded with endless fame and glory, if you just wisely practice self-control and restraint against Agamemnon. Slice the garrulous asshole with your clever language, but not with your awesome sword!"

"As is our tradition, the meeting scepter has been passed along to me, and as you all know, I am the only one entitled to speak at this moment," the Phthian prince insisted. "Now Agamemnon; here my general evaluation of our' impasse! I've concluded that I shall refuse to fight on your behalf," Achilles boldly addressed Agamemnon while standing erect before the other noble captains attending the assembly. "As Hector and Paris courageously lead their soldiers against *your* invading armies, I will not participate any further in *your* futile battle!"

Elderly Nestor was then handed the scepter by Achilles, and the old fart slowly addressed the aggregate of Greek commanders. "I am the oldest one here, and had once fought with the hero Theseus, slayer of the Minotaur on the island of Crete. But I must confess to you, King Agamemnon, that this is indeed a black day! I advise that you give-up Chryseis to Chryses and not take Briseis from Achilles. And I say to you, Lord Achilles; I further extend this fair compromise as a viable solution to this ongoing argument. Please help us to defeat the Trojans and not sail back to your homeland with your battle-proven Myrmidons!"

"Well said, Nestor," Agamemnon complimented the distinguished philosopher from Pylos. "But Achilles is obviously extremely envious of my prowess, and the covetous fool evilly wishes to pilfer my authority! I shall never relinquish my newly acquired prize Briseis to *his* jealous disposal, and if the son-of-a-bitch dares to double-cross me, *his* pathetic blood will soak my trusty sword!"

Fearing the infamous wrath of Achilles, double-talking Agamemnon quickly relented from his demand, and the King of Mycenae instructed Odysseus of Ithaca to transport Chryseis back to her father, the midget high priest Chryses, in order to avert continuing crisis involving Apollo's revenge. But soon thereafter, Agamemnon instructed two guards, Eurybates, brother of Eurabadass, and Talthybius, father of the pygmy-runt Tallthebes, to escort Briseis from Achilles' tent and transferred into *his* personal custody.

"Lord King; can't I sail to Lesbos instead and eagerly watch some kinky lesbians in action?" Odysseus begged and asked Agamemnon. "I understand that there are some tri-sexuals living on that bizarre island, in addition to the notorious female homos!"

Meanwhile, aggrieved and thwarted Achilles, suffering from emotional distress, ventured to the distant seashore and beckoned his petulance to his mother, the sea nymph Thetis.

"Why do you sorrow so extensively, my dear son?" Thetis curiously inquired. "Did that antagonistic heel Apollo castrate your exposed testicles with one of his silver arrows? I've heard that the chariot sky rider's major beef is when a mere mortal like yourself yells-up to the clouds, 'A-pollo is a chicken'!"

"You already know the reason for my demeanor being quite disconsolate," Achilles replied to his immortal mother. "I've been horribly disgraced by Agamemnon, and have currently lost my slave girl Briseis to *his* imperial command. Now mother; I understand through hearsay that Almighty Zeus owes you a colossal favor. I'd like you to intervene for me and ask Lord Zeus to side with the home-team Trojans against the visiting Achaeans, and let all the Greek Captains finally realize the abundant crazed madness of Agamemnon! The Trojans must temporarily gain the upper-hand in the ongoing conflict! Then, the Greek Captains will finally comprehend exactly just how important I am, and just how unimportant Agamemnon really is!"

"My son, I see on the horizon a dim future for you as a mortal being. Confidentially, you have so little sand left falling inside your hourglass. Zeus and several other Mt. Olympus gods are presently attending a major feast in Ethiopia, but when they return from their merry festival, I'll plan to speak to him on your behalf."

Fulfilling his vital errand, Lord Odysseus reunited Chryseis with her father Chryses, and in the process, the current ever-escalating crisis with vindictive and arrow-gant Apollo had been successfully averted.

"In the future," the midget high priest/prophet commended, "I see you, Odysseus, going-down in history and standing next to fantastic contributors to world civilization such as the great Michelangelo, the magnificent Leonardo da Vinci, and a political genius with the weird appellation Thomas Jefferson," Chryses articulated and informed.

"Who the hell are those three anonymous assholes that you've just mentioned?" the King of Ithaca instinctively asked the tiny high-priest. "Those jerk-offs you've just indicated don't sound like ordinary Greeks or Trojans to me! Are the three others you've just mentioned distrustful Etruscans, or perhaps itinerant, fucked-up Chinese cavemen?".

Chryses ignored Odysseus's dumb-ass comments and solemnly proceeded with his preferred reverence to *his* adored god, Lord Apollo. The senile priest then offered monotonous prayers, dissonant songs, and cheap libations in the form of watered-down wine to satisfy the god's enormous ego.

"Odysseus, I bless you, valiant hero, in your gallant pursuit of evasive glory," Chryses advised. "The future of civilization depends on your genius in bringing the Trojan War of East versus West to a reputable end! Go now, oh illustrious champion; go in quest of your honorable destiny!"

And then Odysseus, with his essential mission of delivering Chryseis to Chryses being fully accomplished, sailed back to the shores of Troy with his crew upon his reliable Bireme.

On the twelfth day after the initial argument between Achilles and Agamemnon, Zeus had merrily returned to Mt. Olympus and granted an audience to Thetis, obsessively representing her tantrum-plagued son Achilles. But learning of the sea-nymph's visit, Hera, wife of Zeus, boldly confronted and challenged her husband's fidelity.

"I had witnessed you submissively bowing your head to that sea-whore Thetis, so what the Hades did you ever promise that conniving strumpet? I think, husband, that I already know the correct answer.

You'll create a convoluted scenario where the Trojans will drive the Argives back to their anchored black ships upon the shoreline, just to satisfy the will of that over-ambitious heel, Achilles, son of Thetis."

"Leave me the fuck alone, wife!" Zeus boomed. "If you continue goading my sensitive ass, I'll turn you into a horny frog who is de-evolving-down into an insignificant tadpole. Depart from this chamber immediately, or else woman, you'll most certainly feel my tempestuous anger when I become excessively pissed-off!"

Upon Hera existing the Mt. Olympus throne room, Zeus snapped his fingers and suddenly, his devout attendant Dream appeared to honor his master's imperative command, which happened several dozen times a day atop Mt. Olympus.

"Dream; I want you to take a brief trip to the distant shores of Troy and visit beleaguered King Agamemnon while the idiot's still sound asleep. Instruct the dumb-fuck to wildly attack the city with his entire force. Whisper into his defective brain that the day of the Achaean victory will soon arrive. This activity, meaning the power of suggestion as enacted by you, will be phase one of my most recent war game scheme. Now Dream, I hereby insist that you get your shit together and complete your assignment in forty-winks!"

"Yes, Master Zeus. I see much merit in your most-recent canard. As always, your imaginative wish is my loyal instruction!" Dream obediently declared. "But honestly, my dear Lord Zeus. You could call me by my other popular name if you'd like: Mr. Sandman!"

"HOMER'S ODD SEA ODYSSEY"
Chapter 1
"Goddess Athena Visits Ithaca"

Brain-dead-but-awesome Ancient Muse, speak to me now of that intrepid hero who had wondered and wandered all over known creation after pillaging and looting the corrupt bordellos and brothels of Troy. This major mage explored many cities and citadels around the Mediterranean Sea, where Odysseus learned their unique cultures, and while sailing upon the treacherous waves, the brave explorer suffered many torments from mentors and tormentors alike, as the Greek mariner struggled to save his own existence and lead his crewmen (warriors and worriers) back home.

But though the courageous King of Ithaca desired to salvage his doomed sailors, Odysseus, swimming in his own frustration, could not rescue or salvage his rowers from either drowning or from being devoured by famished monsters. The obstinate jerk-offs all died from their own stupidity; the totally greedy and ambitious imbeciles. As a pertinent example, the avaricious dumb-fucks feasted upon the sacred cattle of Helios Hyperion, who was the jealous god of the sun. And so, the vindictive, small-dicked giant snuffed-away their slim opportunity of ever safely arriving back to Ithaca. So now, Athena, the well-endowed virgin daughter of Zeus, will explain to us the entire epic adventure of Odysseus, beginning anywhere her egregious mind wishes.

To supplement this lengthy poem's mystery that pertains to Odysseus, the other more-obedient Greek kings and warriors, including all those who had escaped being utterly destroyed while plundering Troy, were now safely returned to their island homes, facing no more wicked dangers from engaging Trojans in battle, or devastating threats from the unpredictable, and sometimes belligerent sea.

But regrettably, dim-witted Odysseus, who after two decades being separated from Ithaca, still-longed to be reunited with his gorgeous, sex-starved wife Penelope, and the plagued fellow was quite determined to reach his ever-deteriorating palace. Currently, in this wholly truthful account, the daring adventurer was being held captive in a hollow, dank cave by that mighty, sex-starved nymph Calypso, the immortal bitch being a hormone-driven, ignoble goddess, who vindictively desired to vicariously screw Odysseus every single hour of every single day as her enslaved, infidel paramour.

But as the various annual seasons progressed and advanced in succession, the correct year finally arrived in which, according to what the mentally-retarded main Olympian gods had once secretly ordained, the journeyman King was scheduled by Zeus's decree to venture back to his native home in Ithaca; not that the bad-luck-merchant would be free from troubles even there, especially among his horny, rebellious, straight and gay island residents. To add to the drama, most of the normally apathetic Olympian gods pitied troubled King Odysseus; that is, all except contemptuous Poseidon, the sea deity who characteristically maintained his disreputable anger against mortal, ambitious Ithacans. And to amplify the ongoing dilemma, the trident-carrying sea god did not relinquish in demonstrating his ruthless animosity until valiant and persistent Odysseus eventually, through sheer human determination, stubbornly reached his native island destination.

"What the Hades is my brother, Poseidon, King of the Sea doing, pretending to be a pathetic landlubber in Ethiopia?" Zeus (Jupiter) asked his don't give a shit Olympian family. "Does he have water on the brain? Is he learning to dance the Wah Watusi? Why is my wet-behind-the-ears sibling being so pedestrian, behaving like a very lost human ambler?"

"No, Father. Forget all about the Watusi! Our sea god relative, my uncle Poseidon, is learning the essential step gyrations from local African crab trappers as to how to expertly dance 'the Fish'!" Athena (Minerva) maintained. "Your just-mentioned account indicates that you're into the art of anachronism, and your ridiculous statements are living proof that you've been gloriously time-traveling into the decadent future."

But simultaneously, at *that* momentous moment in classic mythology, zany Poseidon was preoccupied and engaged in partying like Dionysus (Bacchus) somewhere in remote Africa; the sea-god's thrilling expedition taking him amongst the wild-and-crazy Ethiopians, with Poseidon's illustrious presence being a long way off from the magnificent temples atop sparkling Mt. Olympus. The other bored and intoxicated gods had already gathered inside the great white marble hall of their Olympian King, Omnipotent Zeus.

Among all the arrogant, self-centered potentates, the mentally-challenged father of gods and men was the first to address the obnoxious, insolent audience. In his immoral, immortal heart, Zeus was momentarily recalling the recent murder of royal asshole King Aegisthus. Insane Orestes, King Agamemnon's celebrated son, had conveniently killed and butchered mentally unstable Aegisthus. So, with the deceased mortal ruler's memory kept in mind, Omnipotent Zeus now addressed his fully lethargic kin.

"It's excessively disgusting how these puny humans blame us kind-hearted gods for everything from their mild skin rashes to their lethal venereal diseases," Zeus lectured inside his mansion's radiant throne room. "The wily knuckleheads residing down on Earth falsely state that their abundant maladies originate from us innocent Olympians, when in fact, the pure truth is that the ludicrous nincompoops, through their own adulterous foolishness, bestow upon themselves harsh difficulties and

284

consequences, most of which incidentally have not been officially devised by the reliable dictates of infallible Fate," Zeus unclearly emphasized. "Now then, my fellow Olympians; there was an absurd numbskull who had existed down on Earth named Aegisthus, but the sex-driven ignoramus selfishly possessed for himself the gorgeous wife of King Agamemnon of Mycenae. Aegisthus wound-up brutally murdering acclaimed Agamemnon, the pure-hearted son of all-too-kind Atreus. And then, Orestes, son of King Agamemnon, murdered Aegisthus, with the abominable assassination transpiring right inside Atreus's atrium."

"Father, what happened next in that ongoing saga of hate and murder?" insisted curious Athena. "It is my understanding that tragedy often begets more tragedy in continuous, redundant cycles among the devious mortals!"

"And to add more detail, my beautiful Daughter; sex-addict Aegisthus had maliciously butchered Agamemnon's corpse into tiny fragments, immediately after the renowned leader of the Greek navy triumphantly arrived home to the mainland from miraculously conquering Troy over in Asia Minor. That very deliberate kill and mutilation violation definitely was not prescribed by the potent whims of infallible Fate. Aegisthus knew all along that his vile and demented evil act would ultimately establish the idiot's total ruin. The morally deficient dip-shit was then soon butchered by Orestes, the deranged son of King Agamemnon, who, as you all know, had gallantly led the Greek expedition against Troy!"

"Did you have any personal enmity towards the slain Aegisthus?" Athena inquired of her Almighty Father. "Was the aberrant king on your personal elimination list?"

"I resented the fact that *that* weird-fuck mental case occasionally wore purple garments during important palace events, and as you're well-aware Daughter, purple is the chosen color of the gods and is limited to *our* use only," Zeus verbally related. "Other than that intolerable behavior of wearing the color purple, I conceded and allowed Eternal Fate to decide Aegisthus's final demise."

"Who gives a canine's crap about these miniscule, insignificant and mundane human affairs?" challenged the handsome chariot god, Apollo. "A deplorable human butchery enacted in imitation of a previous deplorable human butchering. Lord Zeus; in all candor, I have more nobility in my little pinky than does the brightest and best of that terribly deranged mortal species residing down on Mother Earth!"

"You are more than *a chicken,* Apollo, so stop acting like a foul fowl! So now, back to my history lesson," Zeus gruffly replied, resuming his lengthy exposition. "Yes, my inattentive heavenly family. That silly earthly fool, regal Aegisthus, has satisfactorily paid in full for everything he had deserved in the form of revenge. First, the power-hungry villain had viciously crushed Agamemnon's balls with a heavy sledgehammer. And next, the vile aggressor had painfully castrated the aged victim with his already-bloodied rusty sword!"

Athena, possessing gleaming eyes promptly answered Lord Zeus.

"Son of famed Titan Cronos (Saturn), and genetically inferior and brain-dead father to us all; you who rule on high from your high-chair, er, I mean throne; yes indeed, Father; I now understand the story. Thanks to Orestes's need for retribution, deceased Aegisthus now lies stone-cold dead, experiencing a personal destiny he had initially himself caused. May any other guilty man who does similar to what Aegisthus had evilly attempted also be quickly destroyed!"

A copycat murder!" Zeus interrupted Athena. "Aegisthus killed King Agamemnon, and Agamemnon's son Orestes killed Aegisthus in quite a similar manner!"

"But dear Father; my vulnerable heart remains tremendously tattered. I remain worrying about the fate of wonderful Odysseus; my very special, ill-fated, and extremely confused explorer, who has had to endure and struggle with a frustrating series of horrible disasters for so many years; my mortal champion's defiant activities are still occurring far away from his former friends, and also far-removed from certain often-visited amorous prostitutes. I adamantly believe that faithful Queen Penelope is unaware of her husband's adulterous conduct practiced over his twenty-year absence from Ithaca. Yes, Father; ten years fighting like a valorous Spartan against the Trojans, and ten years being punished by your cruel, heartless brother, Lord Poseidon!"

"Get to the point, Daughter Athena," Zeus angrily replied. "Or else, I'll gladly dry-up your virgin pubic love garden for all eternity! In *my* dominant Universe, might makes right, and quite apparently, Athena, I happen to control all of the might."

"Maybe so, Daddy. But you and Uncle Poseidon savagely punish ethical Odysseus while you completely ignore the other less-moral Greek inhabitants who constantly call you a dizzy dumb-dick and a flagrant fuck-head! Why are you so ambivalent? Can't you see that you are biased against certain mortals, but you tolerate multiple misdeeds from others?"

"Daughter; describe your defense of this primitive caveman Odysseus whom you so admire, while I still enjoy a degree of patience," Zeus nastily retorted. "Honestly, I have less patience than the average mortal physician does, ha, ha, ha! In the future, a low-intelligence asshole named Hippocrates will certainly envy my incredible patience!"

"Well, Pop. The itinerant King of Ithaca is now being held hostage on a little-known island; its topography being surrounded by the moody Mediterranean Sea," Athena informed the assembly of gods. "The extensive body of water forms the mythological ocean's naval navel. And there, Big Daddy, within the lush semi-tropical forest landscape, lives a voluptuous, minor goddess, Calypso, who intentionally prevents her disconsolate captive, my stellar hero Odysseus, who is being egregiously held against his free will, from ever escaping or leaving her rather obstinate authority."

"So, Athena, in a million words or less, what's so damned special about this very ordinary fellow, Odysseus, King of Ithaca?"

"I absolutely adore brave Odysseus," Pallas Athene adamantly answered. "My favorite hero yearns to once again see the smoke and pollution rising from Ithacan chimneys. And the weary victim's spirit presently longs to be immediately defeated by imminent death. Yet, despite *that* overwhelming, grotesque adversity, Great Olympian Almighty Zeus, your occasionally sympathetic heart does not adequately respond to the punished Greek King's incessant pleas and appeals. Now Father; did not Odysseus obediently and respectfully offer, in honor of your immense glory, spectacular sacrifices that had been exhibited upon Troy's arid desert plain, situated beside the moored Greek ships. If so, Father Zeus; why are you so fuckin' angry with afflicted and beleaguered Odysseus? Are your enormous hemorrhoids again acting-up, or what?"

Cloud-gatherer Zeus then answered his recalcitrant Daughter and cynically declared: "My beloved child. How could I ever forget god-like Odysseus, pre-eminent among all mortal men for his reputed intelligence and for his benign offerings to us immortal gods, *we* who hold dominion over wide Heaven and inferior Earth? But my vengeful brother, Earthquake-shaker Poseidon, the stubborn and powerful sea god, is still furious about *that* injured Cyclops, the monstrosity known as Polyphemus, the mightiest of the Cyclopes, whose singular eye Odysseus had violently destroyed during a brief physical encounter."

"But Father. Why is the ogre Polyphemus and his missing private eye so important to you?" Athena detected and asked. "It is true that Odysseus had made a spectacle out of the hideous villain!"

"Thoosa, the notorious and promiscuous sea nymph, bore ugly Polyphemus in childbirth," Zeus recalled and stated. "The minor deity was a radical daughter of that irresponsible Phorcys, who commands the restless deep seas. Sex-craving Poseidon, down in those dark hollow caves, often had twenty-four-hour daily social and physical intercourse with the sultry bitch."

"I wish that Thoosa should have had genetically damaged Polyphemus aborted," Athena sternly argued. "That Cyclops has been a menace to civilization, and also to any seamen who might get shipwrecked on the monster's formidable island. The death of all intruders and trespassers is the only special justice that vile Polyphemus ever administered!"

"The blinding of Polyphemus is the principal reason why Earthshaker Poseidon, father of the Cyclops, makes Odysseus futilely wander and squander his impotent life all over my creation, venturing from island to island," Zeus articulated. "But vindictive Poseidon has not yet released your hero, the hard-headed voyager. So, Pallas Athene, who doesn't own a palace; I insist on this strategy; come now, my subordinate Olympic family; let's together consider the King of Ithaca's eventual return, so that the perplexed leader can successfully journey back to Ithaca and reunite with Queen Penelope and his only son, Telemachus. I predict that Poseidon's notorious animosity will soon relent. My ocean brother can't successfully fight me, along with my allied Olympian family, all by himself; not with all of us aligned against his mounting wrath."

Athena, goddess with the sensational gleaming eyes, proudly and quickly replied to her father's monotonous oration.

"Son of Cronos and father to us all; your enviable wisdom vigilantly rules the stars and constellations of heaven above. Let's urgently dispatch the swift flying Hermes (Mercury), killer of Argus, as our personal courier, sending our messenger god over to the island of Ogygia, so that our trustworthy postman can quickly tell that fair-haired nymph Calypso of our firm decision; which is that bold Odysseus will now leave and complete his extraordinary voyage back to Ithaca."

"Well now, Daughter. Your solution must end, as usual, in a satisfactory, fairy tale conclusion," declared Zeus. "If your imaginative plan fails, and this witch Calypso does not cooperate, then I promise that I'll further punish Odysseus by having the addled blockhead shit out of his pecker and piss from his asshole. Or, in another scenario," Zeus threatened, "I might shoot a bolt of lightning up your favorite hero's fat rear-end and effectively cauterize his colon and also his large intestine. Then, your mortal champion could neither shit nor piss out of his sealed-up anus!"

"I'll deftly zoom-off to distant Ithaca and urge the King's son Telemachus to initiate action. I'll instill admirable courage inside the young man's heart," Athena informed, "so that the son of Odysseus will call those long-haired Achaeans destroying his property to assembly. Telemachus will then intrepidly address the bevy of covetous suitors, who keep on butchering his father's flocks of sheep, and also keep randomly slaughtering the King's bent-horned cattle. I'll soon surreptitiously send vernal Telemachus on a secret mission to sandy Pylos, and then off to Sparta, where the pure-hearted lad can learn all about his brave father's remarkable exploits along with his new-found journey home."

After Athena convincingly spoke, the gorgeous goddess gracefully tied her lovely sandals upon her dainty feet; the famed immortal, golden sandals, which reputedly carry Zeus's daughter as fast as stormy winter wind gusts across the ocean seas and over endless tracts of land masses. Athena raced-down from Mount Olympus's lofty peak, sped across the land and sea to Ithaca, and then just confidently stood there, at Odysseus's outer gate, located before the in-need-of-repair palace.

Standing erect outside the musty structure's threshold, the resolute goddess's right hand was still firmly gripping her gleaming bronze spear, imitating the general appearance of Mentes, a noteworthy foreigner who ruled the fierce Taphians. At her position before the dilapidated palace, audacious Athena encountered the egocentric suitors still pursuing the hand of enticing Queen Penelope, the devoted wife of King Odysseus, whose fidelity remained strong, despite her beleaguered husband being away for twenty long years.

Those narcissistic, competing troublemakers, all cowardly parasites, were obviously enjoying themselves playing ancient checkers, and arm-wrestling right outside the huge wooden entrance doors, and all the while merrily sitting-down and laughing upon soft, thick hides of cattle skins. Little time was left for abandoned Queen Penelope to willfully surrender to gruesome reality, and agree to marry one of the malignant suitors, since her nomadic husband had been away from Ithaca for twenty long years.

"The Gay Tailor Who Became King"

"The Gay Tailor Who Became King" is an imaginative piece of children's literature based on a Polish folklore tale about the delusions of a jolly old homosexual clothes' adjuster, whose wild and unrealistic expectations are told in such a manner that they seem almost logical and ordinary.

Once upon a time, people wore so many clothes all year round that the imbeciles couldn't distinguish what sex they were, and the general situation was just like today, when folks wear so few clothes and still have the same problem identifying males from females, from neuters. A gay, little, thin tailor named Mr. Nodicka lived in those mysterious ancient times, and the merry fellow had a scrawny beard that contained exactly three-hundred-and sixty-five hairs (representing the number of days in a year), along with a rather sparse pubic patch with the same number of active growth follicles.

Mr. Nodicka was very gaunt; in fact, so slender that his appearance resembled a needle and thread, and many of his most loyal customers attested that the tradesman could pass through the eye of a needle much easier than a pregnant camel could. And on holidays and on special occasions like anniversaries, Mr. Nodicka braided his beard so that he could look as fucked-up as every other asshole in the tiny village of Stitchylvania.

One gloomy dismal day, a sinister-looking Gypsy entered the modest tailor shop, and she specifically requested some important work to be performed. "I have no money to pay for your wonderful services, but I'll gladly read your fortune in return for your work," the wench told the mild-mannered Nodicka.

"What has to be done?" the zany tailor asked. "Do you need your crotch or asshole sewn-up? What about zippers installed under your hairy armpits? I used to work part-time at the hospital's emergency room, you know!"

"You're actually on the right track," the old conniving Gypsy related. "I cut my left foot on a shattered mirror that my ugly face had accidentally broken, so I need a surgical *knit*wit like you to darn the damned wound. But be careful how you sew-up the flesh, and don't leave any scar. Otherwise, I'll return to this shop and fiercely suffocate you with my lousy, smelly cunt!"

Mr. Nodicka rendered his essential services, and two weeks later, the Gypsy returned to his humble shop to fully compensate him. "Leave Stitchylvania this Sunday and walk due West," the fortuneteller advised the little gay tailor, who was more than a little gay. "In time, you'll arrive at a place where there is a shrinking nobility among the wacko population, and then you'll soon be appointed King."

"I've heard some incredible bull-shit in my time, but this fantastic tale of yours appears to be the best," the gay tailor scoffed and laughed. "And since your extremely fucked-up story has made me even more cheerful than I usually am, I'll accept it as a valid payment of debt. Ha, ha, ha, ha!" the faggot tailor chortled. "It's so humorous that I feel as if I'm about to grow a square dick with cubic balls! Ha, ha, ha, ha!"

The following morning, Mr. Nodicka closed his nearly bankrupt tailor shop, and left *his* debt-ridden place of business carrying a bundle that included a thousand needles (some of them from pine trees); a dozen brass thimbles; ten-thousand-kilometers of light-blue thread; seven lucky irons, and three pairs of sharp scissors of various sizes.

"Which way is West?" Nodicka asked a fellow pedestrian that happened to be blind.

"The two-hundred-year-old senile gent wearing a ten-gallon hat full of rye whiskey, along with matching brown cowboy boots with heavy spurs answered, "Over there, Asshole! West' is where the people say the sun sets. But I warn ya' young fella' that there ain't too many saloons with swinging doors over in that fuckin' direction! And also, partner, make sure ya' don't fuckin' get shot at the *OK Corral*. That *OK* is not okay with me!"

Mr. Nodicka began walking in the direction that the old Polish whiskerando had recommended. Just outside Stitchylvania, the jolly tailor encountered a strong gusty wind, and it was a good thing the happy-go-lucky gentleman was carrying his heavy bundle, or else he would have been sucked-away with real gusto. The merry gent laughed exceedingly as the blustery blasts pushed him along until he heard someone shout: "Who' the fuck are you over there trespassing into my field?"

Nodicka looked-around during the turbulent windstorm, and noticed a frail Scarecrow standing in the middle of a wheat field. The elegantly dressed figure, wearing an Abe Lincoln stovepipe hat and a navy-blue jacket, was composed of five sticks: two arms, two legs, and a long erection upon which assorted blackbirds landed and pecked-away at the figure's much abused pecker.

The traveling tailor momentarily dropped his heavy bundle, removed his tiny cap, and bowed as if he were addressing high-browed Polish royalty. "Sorry to intrude upon your territory," the gay tailor apologized to the Scarecrow. "But I too live just a *sew-sew* life!"

"I'm very pleased to make the acquaintance of such a retarded asshole as yourself," the simple-minded Scarecrow answered. "I'm Baron Scarecrow, and I'm genuinely bored out of my mind watching various birds fly overhead attempting to raid this precious wheat field.

But I would prefer fighting tigers or panthers rather than simply scaring birds away," the depressed figure divulged. "And besides that' very relevant truth, Mr. Nodicka; I'm the best in my field because as you can determine, I'm the only Scarecrow in my field. Ha, ha, ha, ha! Where are you heading kind sir, if I may ask?"

"Mr. Nodicka was entirely too courteous and naïve for his own good, so the wandering tailor respectfully bowed and then hopped like a gay robin (or in this case like a silly jerk-off) three steps backwards, and inadvertently smashed against a tall oak tree. "That's the way well-bred men in Stitchylvania show their honor," the skinny tailor informed as the ignoramus got-up off the ground and dusted himself off. "Everything except the collision part with the tree is the customary acknowledgement. Now Baron Scarecrow," the traveling tailor continued his prattle. "I'm really on a bold journey to a distant place where I will become King. I suspect that you're a clairvoyant Scarecrow, for you knew my name without me ever disclosing my identity to you."

"Is it possible that a complete insignificant fool like yourself could ascend the complicated bureaucratic-aristocracy ladder and ultimately become a King?" the Scarecrow rhetorically argued. "On the other hand, most Kings I've ever heard about are indeed fucked-up Assholes, just like you are."

"Of course, I was born with a destiny and a certain propensity to become a King," Nodicka pompously stated. "And I believe that if you accompany me on my royal ramble, you'll be all the merrier. What do you say about my splendid designs, Mr. Strawbrains?"

"All right, Mr. Nodicka. I wholeheartedly accept your stupid invitation to join your silly folly," Baron Scarecrow replied. "I'm very weary of this monotonous job I've been maintaining for over a century. But first, you must mend my torn trousers," the good-natured Scarecrow requested. "I might meet someone prettier than you along the way, and decide to marry him or her, so I must appear handsome and debonair to everyone I encounter."

"I'll sew-up your pants and even re-do your zipper, despite the fact that you can't possibly piss out of a normal dick like ordinary male humans do," the tailor chuckled in a blithe tone of voice. "I can identify with what it's like being dick-less, so don't feel so fuckin' sorry for yourself."

In an hour, the jaunty tailor had mended the Scarecrow's hat and trousers, and after Mr. Nodicka completed his rigorous enterprise, a dozen ravens showed-up, expressing their disdain for the two conversing idiots. The meddling black-birds flew overhead and egregiously crapped on the two royal imposters' heads, and also violently begrimed their colorful clothes.

On the arduous journey West to nowhere, the two companions gradually became close friends. The thin tailor tethered himself to the Scarecrow in various "Rest Stop Fields" along the way, when it was time to sleep, and also when being viciously attacked by wild rabid dogs. The loyal Scarecrow would protect Nodicka by kicking at the growling curs and loudly yelling, "That'll be the last straw, you fuckin' beastly, mangy mongrels!"

While passing near the hamlet of Slowvodka, where all of the residents were chronic alcoholics and drank Sloe Gin, Mr. Nodicka suggested to his itinerant colleague in an appropriate oxymoron, "There's a heavy light originating inside that house. Let's knock on the door, and perhaps the intoxicated resident will provide us with adequate food and shelter to pass the night."

"I sincerely agree," the now-chilly Scarecrow declared. "I know this place can't be legendary Chicago, because it's but a mere windy village and not a slum-laden *Windy City*. Say, my good friend; what the hell's wrong with this fucked-up dwelling? It's slowly turning around, and the structure must have legs, ankles and feet!"

"The owner of this house must also be gay like us, because I see him dancing and jumping-about inside," the tailor observed and related. "Let's wait until the front door makes a complete rotation, and then we'll surreptitiously enter. I don't know if you've ever noticed it or not," Mr. Nodicka pontificated, "but it's pretty hard walking in through a damned window, especially when it's closed. That's why fuckin' houses have doors. I just figured *that* pertinent bull-shit out!"

After the front door made a full revolution (without guns, rifles, muskets or cannons), the two interlopers furtively entered the abode without first knocking on the portal. The roving duo viewed an exhausted, elderly Nobleman warming himself next to a log-filled fireplace, even though it was the height of summer, and a hundred and ten degrees outside, ever since the intense windstorm had passed through the area. Then, the two trespassers were astonished when the Nobleman clearly and plainly articulated, "Welcome eminent Mr. Nodicka and honorable Baron Scarecrow. Welcome to my humble domicile."

The tailor hopped back three times like a gay robin while Baron Scarecrow removed his tall stovepipe hat out of courtesy to their rather weird-looking host. The two guests then listened intently to the Nobleman's extraordinary oratory.

"Stay with me for dinner, and tomorrow you two morons can continue your fucked-up odyssey," the strange host deliberately suggested in a low tone of voice. "I'll contact my wife, my daughter and my relatives, and we could all participate in a major gang bang, even though you gay Mr. Nodicka are impotent and devoid of a penis, and you Baron Scarecrow should really be Barren Scarecrow because you only have a wooden stick for an erect dick. Ha, ha, ha, ha! What a pair of retards you two shit-heads are!"

Then, the bizarre Nobleman sternly clapped his hands, and suddenly thirty new people appeared without ever entering the room through doorways, portals, ceilings, or windows. When the Nobleman's daughter talked, she sounded exactly like a horse whinnying and neighing, and when the ugly young lady informed Mr. Nodicka that she'd like to have him for her husband, the tailor humorously responded to the unattractive, unpleasantly-plump girl, "Quit horsing around, because I'm both gay and dick-less! Find yourself another stud, preferably an Italian stallion, or a goddamned horny mustang."

A gigantic hanging cauldron with steaming soup inside was taken from the fireplace's metal rack, and soon the hot, foul-smelling food was served to everyone. The nutcase Nobleman then had something significant to disclose to his two gullible guests. "Mr. Nodicka and Baron Scarecrow," the austere aristocrat prefaced. "For some inexplicable reason my family is always cold, even during the height of summer. And so, every evening we eat this ill-flavored hot soup for supper, but we really get *stewed* by drinking hundred-proof-vodka from eight p.m. until midnight. Ha, ha, ha, ha! That's basically all we ever fuckin' do each and every evening in Slowvodka."

"I guess, then, you often resurface your walls and really get plastered too!" Mr. Nodicka cleverly added. "And next, dear Nobleman, you probably stick baked dough and sliced apples inside your pupils, and really get pie-eyed! Ha, ha, ha, ha!"

Soon, a queer-looking servant resembling a macabre, ghoulish zombie entered the dining room, and brought a large dish of fried rats garnished in a rich black sauce, and the valet quickly returned with bowls of broiled locusts, baked worms, and raunchy fillet of salamander. And for dessert, the odd assemblage ravenously devoured sour ovary eggs along with testicle meatballs, but the gay tailor and the impotent barren Baron Scarecrow alternated tossing all of their hideous, despicable food under the very long wide table.

"I'm quite impressed with your noteworthy ambition," the Nobleman said to the preposterous tailor. "I happen to be a proficient mind-reader, and am quite aware that you desire to ascend from Gay Tailor to Gay King, without even becoming a totally queer Gay Lord. Did you know, Mr. Nodicka, that King Hineymunch of Warsaw just passed away? He had been killed by his subjects after the terrorist people *saw war* in Warsaw."

"I understand completely," Baron Scarecrow rudely interrupted. "Since Warsaw is the city where the country's central government is located, the unsuspecting King was ludicrously killed by the effective administration of *capital* punishment. That's all very rational and logical.

Now is Warsaw very far from Slowvodka, or is it closer to the village of Sloe Gin?"

"A *crow* that is not *scared* or frightened can fly from here to Warsaw in two days, Baron Scarecrow," the knowledgeable Nobleman joked. "And I hear that the bellicose people of Warsaw are all clamoring to elect a new King. And I must candidly tell you, Mr. Nodicka," the phony aristocrat emphasized, "anyone who marries *my* weirdo daughter and shares her bridal honeymoon suite will automatically be nominated as the next Polish King of Warsaw."

When the Nobleman's daughter heard the word "*bridal*", the insane bitch automatically thought '*bridle*' and again began neighing and whinnying like crazy. Then, the hideous-looking lass amorously threw her arms around the surprised tailor's neck, and kept pretending to be and sounding like a filly from Philly' in heat.

"Let's run-away from this ridiculous madness!" barren Baron Scarecrow demanded to his befuddled traveling companion. "Now, I definitely know that this loony, unkempt house is really a barn when the owner's daughter acts and sounds like an absolute night *mare!*"

The bewildered tailor looked-around the expansive dining room, but could see not a door nor window from which to escape. The beleaguered gent then lowly whispered to the neurotic Scarecrow that the two weirdos should jolly their erratic hosts until the opportune moment arrived to swiftly hightail their scrawny asses out of the seemingly-dangerous premises.

"We'll all now salute and drink to your good health, dear tailor," the very disciplined fake Nobleman insisted. "But first I must insist; do you know the lyrics and melody to any particular song?"

"Yes, indeed!" Mr. Nodicka cooperatively answered. "I shall sing the first and worst verse, and then have everyone in the room mimic my lunacy and poor taste." The very thin guest removed his cap and began inharmoniously singing a most terrible tune, while saluting the Nobleman's daughter--wannabe'-equine.

"Sing praise to the lovely Slowvodka whore,
Sing praise to her wondrous snatch.
Let her juicy slit pump and hump some more,
And then, I'll greedily eat her hairy patch!"

All of a sudden, the entire insulted, perverted, extended family arose and loudly cursed and next wildly chased Mr. Nodicka and Baron Scarecrow twelve-times around the long, wide dining table; and next pursued the pair out of the oddball house. And upon exiting the extremely queer place, the two haunted escapees turned-around and were astounded to see the house and its peculiar occupants instantly vanish out of sight.

The two confused and addled journeymen trekked to a distant meadow in order to evaluate their circumstances and options. Both numbskulls shared common opinions about the rather spectacular, unnatural episode that had just transpired.

"I believe that the Nobleman and his fucked-up relatives were actually terrible transmigrating demons," the tailor bizarrely theorized and articulated to Baron Scarecrow. "And his ugly, fat daughter that falsely thought she was a horse, who incidentally, also wanted to be the Queen of Warsaw, was even more drastically fucked-up than her totally fraudulent fucked-up father was!"

"If you had a dick and wore jockey shorts," the Scarecrow imaginatively responded to the gay tailor, "then you could've ridden the Nobleman's daughter all night without a friggin' saddle."

The pair of disenchanted adventurers intrepidly continued on their merry way, and again sauntered West for seven more days until the jerks finally reached the outskirts of metropolitan downtown Warsaw. But inside the city limits, the rain came down in torrents in what was aptly described by Mr. Nodicka as "a unique combination hurricane and monsoon."

"I refuse to enter the city because then my stovepipe hat will get wet," the Scarecrow confided to his already-drenched companion. "Then, the straw in my head will become saturated, and I'll have a nasty case of water on the brain."

"And I refuse to enter the city and come into contact with so many people who are wet behind the ears," Mr. Nodicka confidentially conveyed to his totally nonsensical associate. "This heavy rain has indubitably already-dampened my spirits!"

A crowd of disgruntled, irate Warsaw residents approached, and quickly confronted and then accosted the two visitors. The city's temperamental Burgomaster next conducted a rather hasty and harsh impromptu interrogation.

"Who the hell are you two foreign freaks, and why have you come to Warsaw?" the angry Mayor asked the perplexed intruders. "You both have unfortunately arrived during a very ominous time!"

"What the fuck has happened here?" Mr. Nodicka asked the volatile Burgomaster. "What's all of this inane bull-shit deluge all about? Has the venerable Noah been reincarnated and is soon coming to town in his acclaimed ark?"

"The city's destruction seems to be inevitable," the gloomy Mayor predicted. "King Hineymunch had died a week ago, and ever since his passing, it has not stopped raining. The chimneys in our houses cannot sustain adequate fires, and soon our affected homes will be floating on water all the way to the evil crack houses over in Krakow."

"That's too bad!" Mr. Nodicka exclaimed. "Jimmy cracks corn over in Kansas, and I don't care; and dope addicts' crack houses in Krakow, and I don't give a shit about *that* crap either."

"But the worst part of the dreadful situation involves the King's ugly, obese daughter," the fully-pathetic Burgomaster related as the miserable crowd of onlookers became even more rowdy, hostile, and rambunctious. "The grotesque-looking Princess has promised to marry any man, either native or visitor, who can stop the relentless rain from falling."

"Baron Scarecrow!" the gay tailor enthusiastically yelled above the din of the increasingly belligerent throng. "Let's go into Warsaw and stop this friggin' downpour from completely flooding the city. I think I know exactly how to control this heavy rain, and tame the raging downpour into a *baby shower*! Ha, ha, ha, ha!"

After walking through savage torrential hail and continuous gusting gales, the two itinerant dreamers finally arrived at the city's Royal Palace. The disconsolate Princess opened the door and reluctantly let the dual do-gooders inside. "Oh, what a handsome man you are!" the royal, young, ugly, corpulent lady declared to the likeable tailor. "But please don't turn sideways. You're so damned skinny that you're liable to disappear from sight!"

The extremely slender Mr. Nodicka hopped backwards three times like a timid gay robin, and then respectfully addressed his new regal acquaintance. "Is it true, Your Grace, that you will marry the one that stops the rain?"

"I publicly pledged that I would do precisely that!" the alarmed Princess conceded and verified. "Do you know any original Indian rain dances?"

"And if I do stop it?" the clever, cunning tailor proposed while indirectly also proposing marriage.

"Then, I will keep my solemn promise, no matter how tiny your dick or your balls might be!" the lard-ass, ugly girl confirmed.

"Very well, Your Highness!" the determined tailor amiably agreed. "You will see beyond a shadow of a doubt that I shall stop the fuckin' rain, and unilaterally salvage your city from despondency, ruin and total eradication!"

The all-too-thrilled thin tailor nodded to his irascible Scarecrow confederate, and the dynamic duo subsequently left the regal palace. As the pair privately conferred, the entire pissed-off population crowded around them holding pebbles, stones, and rocks, intended to hurl and hammer the new arrivals, should the two ludicrous imbeciles fail in completing their proclaimed endeavor.

"How are you going to bring back pleasant weather amidst such a wet and unpleasant mob?" Baron Scarecrow apprehensively asked his all-too-confident mentor. "These nasty, uncouth morons will light a match to my exposed straw, and set me on fire right out here in the middle of the fuckin' flooded street!"

"I know where the rain comes from!" the tailor confidently bragged. "From the damned sky! And I also know that it always falls-down, and does not ascend up!"

"No shit Sherlock!" the Scarecrow attested. "You're about as smart as your last wet fart!"

"I have an hypothesis to offer," Mr. Nodicka intellectually stated. "When the great King Hineymunch died, he went directly to Heaven and made a hole in the sky from which to look-down on his city. The Monarch felt saddened leaving his subjects, predicates, and family down on Earth, so the deceased monarch continually weeps like an infant. He chronically and relentlessly cries right through the dismal opening in the sky!"

Baron Scarecrow saw much merit in Mr. Nodicka's fantastic conjecture. "You're either the smartest tailor that ever lived, or the world's biggest fucked-up asshole!" the impractical, straw-headed companion commented. "Why can't we just initiate building a duplicate, dry Warsaw ten-miles East of here! Or, we could even lead all of the city's ruffian residents to Stitchylvania, and make the village a thousand times larger than it is now, and we'll call the new fuckin' place Warsaw II!"

"Here's what we'll need from the fair citizens of Warsaw," the determined tailor instructed the Scarecrow without ever considering his partner's useful suggestions and opinions. "Have a hundred men carry a hundred ladders to the Warsaw Royal Palace. We'll then tie them together, and make a vertical path leading straight-up to the dark sky. And then I'll use the needles, thimbles, and thread from my bundle, and I'll stitch-up the opening that poor, melancholy King Hineymunch had formed, and consequently stop the troublesome rain from falling," the creative tailor predicted. "Now, Baron Scarecrow. I believe we'll require only about two-hundred-kilometers of thread to successfully perform the difficult labor."

The drenched, disgruntled, grumpy Warsaw men helped assemble and lift the huge connected ladder, and then the valiant Mr. Nodicka climbed-up the myriad rungs with his heavy bundle of useful materials. After two full wet days of assiduous sewing-together the badly torn piece of sky, the gap had been satisfactorily repaired, and the now-jubilant Warsaw' citizens all rejoiced when the rains finally ceased. Finally, the triumphant tailor descended the multiple-ladder to the applause of the appreciative peasant and serf Warsaw residents.

The now-ecstatic Princess exited her Royal Palace, and wiped her eyes, forgetting all about wiping her fat, smelly, ugly ass. She threw her arms around the blushing tailor's waist, and repeatedly kissed his wet, red face. Then, the deceased King Hineymunch's daughter drew Mr. Nodicka's hands to her enormous breasts, and allowed the trembling tailor to gently massage and fondle her erect nipples, and next his quivering hand was led to her wire-brush bush, where the grotesque-looking Princess permitted the hero tailor to softly rub her horrendous, pungent, brown pubic garden.

Mr. Nodicka was exceptionally happy and almost became sexually aroused as numerous male hormones surged throughout his skinny dick-less body. Then, the horny Princess made a rather shocking revelation. "Dear tailor from afar; it's a good thing you have no penis, because I am very allergic to sperm juice," she honestly disclosed. "Sperm juice rots my uterus and intestines from the inside out! I know this basic truth, because sometimes I masquerade as an old fortune-telling Gypsy woman and other times, I pretend to be a Nobleman's daughter with a terrible crotch infection living out in the countryside."

"What the fuck are ya' talkin' about, ya' ugly insane bitch?" Mr. Nodicka boisterously exclaimed. "I thought that when King Hineymunch's *rain* stopped, then my *reign* would begin!"

"That's what the fuck you think, new Kingy!" the now-livid Princess imperatively exclaimed. "In truth, I'm really a repugnant witch with supernatural powers. And so, while you and Baron Scarecrow obey my every command and whim," the new Queen of Warsaw declared, "I'll just pretend that I'm a horse, giving you plenty of fuckin' irrelevant instructions and prodigious directives."

And much to Mr. Nodicka and Baron Scarecrow's exasperation, the new Warsaw Queen began neighing and whinnying incessantly, sounding exactly like a filly from Philly' in exaggerated heat.

"The Flashing Elves"

Once upon a whim, in the lazy somnolent village of Bustercherrie, in the land of Bustdarebawls, there lived a poor shoemaker named William with his wife Meredith. Times were extremely harsh for Willy Shoemaker and his wife, the former Meredith Rottsi. In fact, William Shoemaker was so impoverished that the laborer was on a starvation diet, and just owned enough leather to make one more pair of shoes.

"Perhaps I shouldn't gamble, drink, smoke, philander, and buy pornography all the damned time!" Mr. Bill Shoemaker admitted to Meredith. "Being old is much worse than *getting* old!"

"Your bad luck better change for the better soon, or else I'm outa' here for good; I'll be going back to live with my wealthy parents and having to put-up with their verbal bull-shit!" the wife sarcastically replied. "They always said that you, dear husband, were a non-entity with aspirations of amounting to absolutely nothing," the wife critically chided. "Now let's have some lousy sex before we go to bed, because I don't like having lousy sex in bed!"

So, after the dejected shoemaker and his sex-starved wife had another lousy sixty-nine session, Meredith retired for the evening; her husband returned to his cruddy workbench, and cut-out the pattern for his next, and maybe last, set of woman's work shoes. Then, after sentimentally completing his mundane enterprise, William hobbled into the home's only bedroom. And after committing his soul to the Devil for the hope of obtaining personal gain, the totally fatigued pauper went right to sleep without even passing through drowsiness.

In the morning, after again praying for earthly reward and eternal damnation, William "Willy" Shoemaker entered his humble shop only to discover that the leather for the pair of lady's shoes he had laboriously cut-out had already been magically manufactured into a finished product on the worktable. William was so astonished, and his mind was so addled, that he couldn't even think crooked. The shoemaker lifted the splendid shoes up to his eyes to examine them more closely. '

To hell with heaven!' the impoverished tradesman marveled and thought. 'I'm going to pray to hell every night and also every single morning, if this is what the fuck's gonna' happen! These shoes are so well stitched that they appear as if a master-craftsman had painstakingly fabricated the pair. In fact,' William further imagined, 'they're stitched much better than my damned appendix and double hernia scars! That doctor who performed the operation was a real shoemaker, who had somehow turned into chief hospital surgeon!'

That same morning a wealthy gentleman came into the modest shop, scrutinized the newly produced shoes, and declared that he wanted to purchase them at any cost. William was quite thrilled at the good news, for now the old codger would have sufficient funds to purchase leather for two pairs of ladies' dress shoes, and then have enough money left-over to buy a bottle of wine, a used condom, and a loaf of bread to boot.

"Are these shoes for your wife or daughter?" William innocently asked the ecstatic wealthy customer. "They're very expensive, you should know."

"Mind your own damned business," the rich stranger caustically answered. "But if you really have to know the truth, you nosy bastard, they're being ordered for me to wear. I'm the proud new stripper and lap dancer at the local gay and lesbian inn."

After again having lousy unorthodox sex with Meredith, William cut-out the material for two new pairs of women's shoes, prayed to Satan for eternal damnation, and then retired for the evening. The next morning, the inspired shoemaker again pledged his soul to hell, and then cautiously entered his humble workshop.

Two additional pairs of women's shoes had remarkably been manufactured, and were amazingly waiting for William's scrutiny upon the aforementioned worktable. The shoemaker was positively thrilled to death, although still quite ill-prepared to die and go to hell. Later that morning, two customers came into the formerly unpopular shoe shop, and the new patrons merrily bought the two new pairs of women's exquisite footgear.

"And they weren't even couch dancers at the local gay inn," William euphorically disclosed to Meredith. "By the end of the month, if production keeps doubling daily, I'll own the biggest shoe factory in all of Bustercherrie, and also in all of Bustdarebawls."

"You're saving more soles than the freakin' Pope or the freakin' Devil is doing!" Meredith commented and indulgently laughed. "There's no business, like shoe business! Ha, ha, ha! Now let's go have some bad upside-down oral sex!"

One evening, three days before *Christmas,* the local citizens were all out at the village gay and lesbian inn, getting drunk celebrating the Winter Solstice, because none of the homos' and lesbians in the gay community (here a gay hamlet) were too religious or especially "morally insane". William had spent the entire previous day assiduously cutting-out the patterns for sixty-four pairs of women's shoes, and his multiple venereal disease wife was so excited at the prospect of not having to return home to her strict arrogant "I told you so!" rich parents that she industriously assisted William in his dedicated endeavor.

"Meredith, what do you say we sit-up tonight and observe who is performing this wonderful workshop service for us?" William cleverly suggested. "After he or they complete his or their wonderful task, we, and the stupid heels doing the labor, whoever the hell they may be, could have a wild orgy to celebrate *with a bang* the upcoming Winter Solstice!"

"Yes, William, that type of variety could really spice-up our boring sex life," Meredith promptly agreed. "We could have a fantastic orgy, and I could wear your new leather jock strap, and you could wear my newly-acquired pink bra, corset, and matching fish-smelling panties."

"You must confess," William articulated to his exuberant wife. "This nightly doubling of shoes at exponential proportions is rather extraordinary. By *New Year's Day,* we'll be the wealthiest people in all of Bustercherrie, and by the *Epiphany,* we'll be the richest couple in all of Bustdarebawls! At last, dear wife, I'll have enough money to pay for a goddamned circumcision!"

"You're absolutely correct," Meredith amiably concurred. "And wonderful things like this never happened to Mama and Papa Rottsi! My greedy parents never enjoyed such phenomenal magical occurrences! Soon, we'll be able to thumb our noses at the meager inheritance the demented shit-heads have planned for me!"

That evening, the couple shrewdly set a rusty lantern burning in the far corner of the workshop, and then furtively hid in a closet so that the duo could observe the benign intruder or persons performing the fabulous craftsmanship. At midnight, William and Meredith observed two little, naked, dwarfs enter the shop, each benefactor having an exceptionally long, limp hose hanging out of his clothes, reaching all the way down to his knees. The short, half-naked, stocky, cocky visitors quickly organized the various tools and materials that William had conveniently left at the workbench to their own fancy, and then the dwarfs industriously went about their business without conversing or even looking at one another. And in a mere three-hours, the two nude trespassers with the impressive sexual apparatus jointly and hastily *flashed* out of the premises.

"Did you see their fabulous tools?" the wife marveled after she and her husband, feeling gay for a moment, and came out of the nearby closet.

"No, I didn't!" William Shoemaker remarked. "The elves didn't use my little tool to make the damned shoes, that's for damned sure! But I must believe you that the two dwarfs did have tremendous donkey-like fadorkenbenders, though!"

The following morning, the shoemaker's wife explained to her lethargic husband, "Those little men with the big, long, limp dicks have made us the richest people in Bustercherrie," Meredith Rottsi euphorically related. "And we ought to show them our gratitude. The tiny fellows must be very cold running around this part of Europe all half-naked in the beginning of winter. I'll make them little pants, shirts, waistcoats, and huge jock straps, and since you always say that I'm a 'nitwit', I'll even knit both the miniature assholes a really neat pair of green stockings."

"I hope these damned fat elves, or whatever the hell they are, don't switch allegiances, and start working for jolly old St. Nicholas in *his* workshop!" the husband warned. "But I'll cooperate and make each of the little fellows a pair of shoes to do clubbing at either the local popular gay and lesbian inn, or at the local straight tavern, which has only three nightly patrons!"

By dusk, all of the clothes, underwear, and shoes had been made for the two short, half-naked men, and William worried if he and his spouse's gratefulness might backfire-on, or jinx their recent good luck skein. When midnight arrived, the two zany dwarfs (having the sexual equipment of veritable giants) entered the workshop as usual; faithfully performed their much-appreciated service, and then enthusiastically donned the garments and shoes that had been laid aside for them. Next, the effervescent dwarfs hopped over tables, jumped all about, and did cartwheels all over the damned place to express their general excitement and jubilation at finally having decent clothes to wear. Then, one zany dwarf said to the other:

> "What spruced-up dandy boys are we,
> No longer poor cobblers, we will be.
> Now that we've got clothes and underwear,
> Let's get our fat asses, the fuck out of here!"

And then, the diminutive-but-chunky talented dwarfs sped-out of the shoe-shop as if both had suddenly been afflicted with severe diarrhea, or had been feeling a desperate need to rush to either the local gay inn or to the local straight tavern.

The exuberant dwarfs were never again seen in Bustercherrie, but reports in the form of honest gossip from other villages in Bustdarebawls maintain that two highly-skilled dwarfs, clad in the finest of green clothing, hang-out at gay and lesbian inns in those other highly respected gay and lesbian communities, and the well-to-do, handsomely clad little men revel in eating "corn on the cobbler" at various area taverns.

And as for William and Meredith Shoemaker, the remarkable couple now own the biggest chain of gay and lesbian whorehouses in all of Bustdarebawls, and the married couple have been currently attracting investors' attention by issuing an *IPO* to float the current prototype for the first straight-sex brothel in the entire land.

"Jack's Magnificent Beanstalk"

Once upon a stupid time, when moronic people abounded and haphazardly frolicked-around upon the pristine earth just like they do today, a poverty-stricken widow, abandoned by her indigent husband, had a donkey-brained son named Jack, and also a fairly decent cow appropriately called Milky White. Each and every morning, Jack brought and sold fresh milk at the marketplace, which the naïve lad and his invalid mother then used the compensation to purchase food, porno' magazines, sexual aid devices like vibrators and penis and tit enlargers, along with other basic sundry, everyday necessities.

But one gloomy, gray, morning, Milky White got pissed-off at being his owners' exploited property and produced no milk, which to Jack and his mother, was not any *utter*ly ridiculous matter. The perplexed, avaricious mother and her numbskull gullible son were in an absolute quandary, and naturally considered how the pair might mutually solve their sudden unexpected dilemma.

"What shall we do Jack?" the distraught mom implored her doltish son. "Jack, my boy, stop jumping over that friggin' candlestick and listen-up for a second! What the hell should we do, son? It looks like no more nudie flashcards for you, and no more spectacular breast implantations for me!"

"Don't get overly depressed, Mother," Jack confidently suggested. "I'll read the want ads posted in the town square, and get a job in a brothel, or in a nightclub that features acrobatic nude couch dancers. I've been practicing some complex maneuvers on our shoddy sofa, and I believe I'm ready to try some davenport dancing for wealthy faggot clientele at the local gay bar!"

"Jack, you're underage and must still attend elementary school," the distressed mother chastised, while giving her silly son a much-needed reality check. "We have no alternative other than to sell Milky White and use the money to start an adult bookstore, or some other business enterprise of *that* profitable nature. Porn' is definitely the best way to go, if we gotta' start from scratch!"

"All right, you've convinced me, mother," the easily influenced son cooperatively acceded. "I'll regretfully take Milky White to the main marketplace and see what kind of offers I can receive from one of the merchants, before you even know that our cow has *passed your eyes.*"

Jack went-out to the dilapidated barn and grabbed the cow's halter-top, which had always been too small to fit as a makeshift bra around Milky White's prodigious udders. The lad hadn't yet reached the village marketplace when a peculiar-looking fellow having a long, curled nose, and no visible teeth, accosted the impressionable boy escorting his non-functioning, on-strike milk dispenser.

"Good morning, Jack!" the bizarre stranger began. "Where are ya' headin' with your fancy albino cow?"

Jack had forgotten to ask how the weird-looking fellow knew his name, not realizing that the stranger was indeed his estranged father. "I'm heading toward the marketplace to sell Milky White for cash on the barrelhead," the lazy, callow teenager honestly explained. "Mom needs the dough to start an adult porno' shop, even though the village has twenty-seven similar businesses already servicing a population of eighty-nine horny, sex-starved residents. When your house is a money pit, you need a cash cow, ya' know!"

"You seem to be most competent and experienced at selling cows," the seemingly newcomer to Jack's life flattered. "But young man, I'm curious if ya' know how many total beans make the number five."

"Ha, ha, ha; that's an old schoolyard riddle," Jack laughed, as if the adolescent had feathers tickling under his armpits. "Even my retarded father that I've never known would comprehend the answer to *that* simple ditty. Two in each hand and one additional bean in the mouth! What an absurd, asinine question you've asked!"

"You're quite a remarkable youthful mathematician, and ya' might someday give Isaac Newton some serious competition," the goofy-looking huckster laughed as the street hustler reached deep into his pants' pocket and retrieved several ugly, irregular-shaped beans. "Now since you're so intelligent at computing arithmetical answers," the garrulous, scruffy-looking gentleman continued his drivel, "I'll make a difficult sacrifice and barter these five miraculous beans for possession of old Milky White there. It's all over the village square that your cow's value has significantly declined because she no longer is producing abundant milk, just like your mother's tiny tits aren't either."

"Do ya' actually think that I'm some kind of mentally-deficient jackass?" the insulted boy defensively challenged. "You can shove those ridiculous beans up your ass, and then mistake them for small hemorrhoids that are piling-up."

"Ah, my lad, but in your haste to judgment you've not truly recognized the potency of these fantastic magical beans," the stubborn conman suavely maintained. "If ya' take them home and conscientiously plant them right now, when you wake up tomorrow morning, they'll have sprouted and grown all the way up to the beautiful blue sky."

"You're more-full of feces than the overflowing village cesspool ever was!" Jack loudly replied. "How do I know that you're not a disreputable con-artist like my derelict deadbeat old man was, trying to take advantage of my lack of experience at the esoteric art of cow trading?"

"Well Jack, my boy," the gullible kid's irresponsible father, role-playing as an honest deal-making cow-trader, declared. "If the beans don't grow vines up to the clouds, then I pledge that you'll get your cow back dead and butchered by noon tomorrow. What do ya' have to say about my very interestin' proposal? Good bargains are hard to come by these days."

"Okay, I've always enjoyed being a born loser and a living dumb-shit sucker!" the boy confessed. "Folks say that's exactly how my disingenuous father was often victimized. I guess that being hosed is embedded in my family genes on both sides."

Jack returned home before twilight, and reluctantly told his mother about his preposterous negotiation with the total stranger, who in *his* recollection, was a stranger, stranger-than-fiction.

"You should've gotten at least fifteen-pounds for that two-thousand-pound heifer," the knucklehead's mother appropriately criticized. "Now, because of your general ignorance, my wonderful adult porno' bookstore won't be worth a hill of beans, let alone a mere handful of five silly seeds. When it comes to gross stupidity," the mother caustically admonished, "your gullible nature outrivals that of your deadbeat father, whom you never knew, or never want to be introduced to."

"If I sow the five beans right now, which I must do to follow the salesman's specific instructions," the dipshit son insisted, "they'll grow right up to the sky overnight, and then we could have a big public attraction right here in our backyard. We could even charge admission, and sell insurance to anyone who dares climb the glorious beanstalk up into the stratosphere. We'll also probably have to buy a big safety net to put around the beanstalk's sturdy base."

"How could you be so futilely fucked-up?" the mother boisterously screamed. "Why must I be so blessed by having an absolute dingbat for a son? Milky White was the best milk provider in the entire county, and her beef would've been worth a small fortune. We should've moved to London and sold her to a rich Beefeater at London Tower."

"But mother, the man said he would quarter our cow and give us the meat if the seeds didn't grow into a magnificent beanstalk," the mentally-deficient son ineffectually argued. "What's your beef?"

"Where's the beef! That's my beef!" the irate mother ranted. "Take that and that you dumb little asshole!" the livid matriarch shrieked as the livid woman smacked Jack's face silly while indulging in self-satisfying child abuse. And then, the disgruntled mom disgustedly threw the solid beans out the window, which thank goodness was open at the time. "And now get your wise ass up to bed, and no supper for you, you pitiful, pathetic son of a worthless, good-for-nothing bastard!"

So, Jack dejectedly climbed the squeaky steps up to his pauper's bedroom, and throughout his steep ascent, was wishing that he were a prince possessing a really big pecker. 'I'm so upset I can't even get a miniature hard-on to slap and smack around to relieve my accumulated tension!' the despondent juvenile idiot regretted. 'I'm more disappointed for my mother's sake, because I had been conned into doing an extremely foolish deal. I hope that friggin' phony seed-hawker gets piss into his bloodstream, if those magic seeds turn-out to be duds after all.' And next, the young punk dozed-off to sleep without ever achieving a satisfactory erection to smack around, to fondle, and to wildly manipulate.

When the foolish kid woke-up the next morning, Jack's bedroom had a rather different appearance. Sunlight was now gleaming inside only part of his sleeping area, but dark shadows were prevalent everywhere else. And so, Jack dressed, and next sauntered-over to his window, which any normal intelligent, curious boy would have done in the opposite order. The immature dreamer gazed outside the shabby shanty, and his eyes observed a tremendous beanstalk that had risen all the way from the ground all the way up to the magnificent, azure sky.

'It looks like that shady jerk-off I met yesterday was actually telling the truth about the magic beans!' Jack thought. 'Oh well; I guess that's the end of poor old Milky White. Say, that's what I also call all my damned ejaculations!'

Since the colossal beanstalk had grown right past Jack's window, all the boy had to do was climb outside and latch onto the tremendous vine, and then carefully clamber-up to the majestic clouds. And so, the intrepid lad initiated his great adventure.

'I gotta' remember to first open the window before I grab onto the beanstalk,' the not-too-bright kid considered. 'If I'm not careful, I could break at least one window a day ascending and descending this extraordinary piece of vegetation.'

So, Jack hastily opened the window, gripped the beanstalk with both hands, and then the dimwit closed the window with his right palm and fingers. The anxious explorer shinnied and shinnied up the abnormal plant until the ascender arrived at the cloudy blue sky.

Jack discovered a wide cumulus road that had somehow fluffily accumulated there, so the juvenile nutcase walked-along the wide cottony path, not realizing that he might accidentally plummet down to earth at any time. Soon, the blockheaded dunce reached a gigantic house, and was instantly greeted by a huge woman that could have been an ogre herself, if she had a penis and a set of testicles between her legs instead of a pair of disgusting sagging tits (whose flabby nipples touched her toes) attached to her massive chest.

"Good morning, Mrs. Whoever the hell you are," young Jack audaciously articulated without a trace of normal courtesy. "Could I have some breakfast? I haven't eaten in eighteen long hours so I would like to break my fast."

308

"So, my young illustrious, mischievous trespasser, it's breakfast that you want!" the mammoth Amazon answered. "I assure that you'll be breakfast yourself if ya' don't swiftly get your ass off of this private property at once. The last boy up here disguised himself' as a tax collector, and wound-up chopped-up in my husband's bowl of stew. My spouse Stuart is indeed a formidable ogre, and there's not a thing up here that my hubby savors more than little dismembered English boys mixed into his stew, especially when my unpredictable husband is stewed after drinking two-hundred-gallons of potent red wine."

"Don't give me your standard line of bull-shit!" Jack haughtily squawked. "Your husband obviously discriminates against English boys, especially when the big lunk thinks he's *eatin'* young lads from *Eton!* What an absolute, total disgrace! And if that's the damned case, I'd rather be dead and eaten than have to starve to death before being eaten. Do ya' get the message I'm sayin', ya' nasty old dragon-faced bitch?"

"Well, if that's your attitude, come into my kitchen, and I'll give you some putrid goat's milk, a stale slice of bread I've made into junk toast, and a big chunk of rancid cheese, so that when you fart, my greedy husband will be able to easily determine your cheesy hiding place, and then squeeze the livin' shit out of your foul intestines with his brawny bare hands!"

When Jack was just finishing about half of his not-so-exotic feast, the obnoxious impish fool heard a very loud and disconcerting "Thump, thump, thump!" and instantly felt the enormous home's floor and walls vibrate and tremble as if an unprecedented skyquake were in progress.

"Is the moon crashing into the earth's atmosphere?" Jack yelled in horror. "What the fuck's goin' on out there?"

"Holy stromboli!" the warty-faced, immense, alarmed bitch hollered. "It's my old man come home to have his daily main meal. Quick Junior Asshole; hop into the oven where you can safely hide."

"Do ya' think I'm some sort of a mini-brained dunce?" Jack vehemently protested. "I might just as well hop into a meatgrinder, or perhaps into a steaming, scalding cauldron! I might've flunked nursery school thrice, but I'm nobody's fool when it fuckin' comes to recognizin' danger!"

"Do ya' have a better fuckin' idea?" the twenty-foot-tall, vitriolic old bitch staunchly argued. "Hop into the oven, and I guarantee you that you'll feel home on the range."

Jack caught a glimpse of the fifty-foot-tall giant approaching, just as the bellicose ogre's hoary wife swiftly closed the oven door. The gargantuan husband had three calves strung around both of his calves, which added up to six about-to-be slaughtered baby cows all together. The awesome Goliath unhooked the squealing animals, cruelly smashed their heads-down against the mammoth table (until each had been knocked unconscious), and then strongly bellowed, "Here Martha Stuartess; broil me some delicious meat for my breakfast. How come we never eat lunch or dinner in this damned story? Hey, what's that odd smellin' odor I'm keenly detectin' with my nostrils?

Fee-fi-fo-fum,
I smell the perspiration of an Englishman,
Fingers, toes, ankles, thumb,
It's not a man, but a British boy' scum,
Be he alive, or be he dead,
I'll soon eat his friggin' head, inside my bread!"

"You must be dreaming my dear!" the wife unconvincingly replied. "Or perhaps you smell the remains of the little boy from Liverpool you had eagerly devoured yesterday. Now please go wash and tidy-up, and don't forget to brush your teeth, because your mouth and throat smell like a Birmingham garbage dump. I've left out a thousand-gallon bottle of rubbing alcohol for you to gargle with," the nervous wife communicated. "And by the time you freshen-up and take your daily morning shit, your delectable breakfast will be ready and waiting for you upon the table."

So, the monstrous giant paced-off to the only downstairs' lavatory where he kept water in the closet. Then, the wife opened the oven door and instructed her trembling captive, "Wait in here you little scamp until he's asleep! He always dozes-off right after consuming a satisfying breakfast."

"Don't ya' have another death chamber I could hide in?" Jack strenuously objected. "Do ya' have a razor blade I could leap onto, and slice myself' in two, balls and all? Such an imaginative suicide would be quick-but-messy, but cleaning-up the messy part would be *your* damned problem!"

The suspicious giant returned from his bathroom activities, and Jack noticed through a crack in the oven wall that the behemoth had stepped-over to a massive chest, and removed several bags of gold. Of course, the boy just assumed the sacks were bags of gold because the imbecile couldn't see inside them, and the cloth objects certainly weren't transparent.

Then, the titanic homeowner counted his numerous shiny coins until his head began to nod, and his mouth started yawning, and at that particular moment, Jack thought that *he* was going to be sucked right out of the oven by the strong vacuum caused by the behemoth's inhaling. And soon thereafter, the immense sky resident began sleeping until the walls shook, expanded and contracted with every rhythmic exhalation and inspiration.

Next, frightened Jack slid past the now partially opened oven door, and deftly leaped-down onto the wood-planked floor. And when the fearful interloper came to the ogre's foot, the youth stooped-down and picked-up a fifty-pound bag of gold coins, his behavior following a genetically transmitted social trait, because the kid's ancestors on both sides of his family were notorious bandits, burglars, purloiners, thieves and robbers. The anxious boy briskly dashed out of the enormous dwelling with his precious plunder tucked under his left armpit; his bold actions transpiring right before the old antagonistic Bitch returned from taking a hefty shit herself.

When the boy again arrived at the beanstalk's summit, the young robber tossed-down his heavy bag of gold, hoping that it would land on his mother's noggin, so that he could enjoy the new-found wealth all to his greedy self. And then, the naughty lad laboriously climbed-down for a full half-hour, and when his exhausting descent finally reached his bedroom window, the junior larcenist methodically rolled himself into his room, forgetfully breaking the closed glass pane in the process.

"Well Mother," Jack stated upon entering the shack's filthy kitchen. "Wasn't I correct about the fantastic beans? The things were really magical, and I'm glad I hadn't eaten them. Holy shit! I could've been killed, and I could've died instantly from internal bleeding when that son-of-a-bitchin' beanstalk would've begun to wildly sprout inside my tender stomach."

So then, Jack and his now-grateful mother happily lived-off of the stolen bag of gold for around a year, but when the last coin had been spent on vegetables and dildos, the avaricious boy decided that he should again ascend the awesome beanstalk and rob the formidable giant one more time. On the one-year anniversary of his first grand larceny, Jack daringly clambered-up the impressive beanstalk (which incidentally no one else in the village ever noticed, marveled at, or cared, or gave a peasant's shit about) until the juvenile delinquent again located the cloudy white path, and on that second daring jaunt, Jack nonchalantly approached the giant's monument-sized abode.

The ogre's grotesque-looking wife was busy sweeping the front doorstep when the trespasser again solicited her with another dose of his insincere, inane, juvenile bull-shit. "Good morning again, Mrs. Stewartess!" the trespasser began rather brazenly. "Could you possibly be inclined to give me something good to eat?"

"Hit the road, Jack!" the despicable, humungous, bitchy bitch coincidentally yelled. "My husband does not take kindly to impudent, over-curious English boys investigatin' around his house. But I must say, you do look awfully familiar! I do believe the last time you had visited us, my lax husband reported one of his bags of gold missing," the erratic wife related. "Killer Bob was so pissed-off that the ignoramus filled the entire fifty-foot-deep cesspool while taking an hour-long leak!"

"That's really pretty weird, lady!" Jack audaciously replied. "Your husband sounds like a real pisser. Perhaps I can clarify matters if ya' cordially invite me in for a little chow." And then, the boy ruminated, 'Perhaps I should change my name from Jack to Rob!'

The grotesque bitch was so interested in Jack's valiant words and in his confident, egotistical demeanor that the humongous Amazon invited the intruder inside to enjoy and savor a scrumptious meal. But the diminutive visitor had hardly started swallowing his hot soup when his ears discerned a most frightening "Thump, thump, thump!" So according to past practice, Jack once again obediently concealed his tender body inside the wife's drafty oven.

The next events were a rerun of what the predictable giant had done before. The inimitable Bob Stuart Stewartess sat-down, scratched his cannonball-sized testicles, and then killed and ravenously ate his booty of six calves that had previously been strapped to his leather boots. And next, the monstrous hulk boomed, "Wife; fetch the hen that lays the golden eggs!" as if Mrs. Martha Stewartess was a faithful hound-dog commanded to retrieve a simple stick. And when the especially-talented, unique chicken had been brought into the kitchen, the powerful human anomaly yelled-out "Lay!" with his voice sounding a lot like ear-shattering, verbal thunder. And after the intimidated hen produced a beautiful golden egg, the appreciative giant nodded his head in approval a dozen consecutive times, and then dozed-off into dreamland.

Jack immediately sprang-up out of his hiding shelter and dashed to the giant's chair, and much to the astonishment of Mrs. Stewartess, the inhospitable little thief snatched-up the unique hen. And before one could say Jack Samuel Richard Philip George Jeffrey David Stephen Robinson, the junior felon was fleeing-out the front door, and his legs were soon sprinting-down the clouded road with the cackling hen still in his tight grasp.

"Wife!" the awakened giant vociferated. "Where is my ordinary-looking hen that lays the lustrous golden eggs?"

"I had placed the magic hen at your feet, just before you began your daily napping!" the wife casually answered from the adjoining room. "Maybe you ate it by accident in your dream, thinking that the hen was a savory calf. Have you ever considered Transcendental Meditation as a viable therapy for your failing memory?"

In the meantime, Jack frantically dashed to the now-familiar beanstalk, and carefully-but-speedily exited the sky path, and was soon headed in the direction of good old terra-firma. Upon entering his shack's front door, the pilferer showed his new possession to his astounded mother, and much to her astonishment, every time the lad yelled-out the word' "Lay!" the ordinary-looking chicken produced a shiny golden egg, even though everyone from here to Jupiter is aware that a hen only lays one egg per day.

The productive hen supplied enough eggs for Jack and his mother to acquire all new furniture and kitchen appliances for their modest domicile, and soon the two shanty residents both forgot all about how wonderfully resourceful Milky White really had been. Then one morning, while being bored (as most rich kids usually are), Jack determined that his life needed to experience another exciting exploit. 'I think I'll return to my old *bean-stalking grounds,* and risk my fabulous luck one more time! Who the hell knows what other marvelous things *that* belligerent-but-stupid ogre keeps inside his house besides gold coins, a very skilled chicken, and a repulsive-looking wife that could scare the living and dead shit out of a colony of adult gorillas?'

The following morning, Jack followed his inclination and again ascended the wonderfully-sturdy beanstalk. But the boy was clever to bypass the giant's wife when she had stepped outside to fetch a pail of water, instead of searching for another highly-talented hen to amuse her obnoxious, demanding husband. The brave youth stealthily hid behind several tall bushes, and when the tall, bulky wench had her back to him, the bold lad sneaked into the house, and then surreptitiously hid inside the pantry. Soon, Jack's ears detected the familiar "Thump, thump, thump!" that signaled the approach of the incomparable giant, who was being accompanied by Mrs. Stewartess. The horrible ogre addressed his subordinate wife by saying:

"Ho-ho-ho! Fi-fi-fo-fum,
I smell the flesh of an Englishman,
By tit, by testicle, and by prized gonad,
This English cad smells like, a British lad,
Little puppy dog, tiny pussy cat, the typical runt,
This lousy English punk smells worse than your cunt."

Although quite offended, the giant's tolerant wife feared that her husband's wrath might be next directed toward her, so she deftly switched the focus of her spouse's vehemence to a more favorable subject. "I believe that the little rogue was hiding in the oven the last time when he had stolen the magic hen from you!" the wife claimed. "The punk delinquent had left a wet, snotty handkerchief in there, just before your gifted chicken had been maliciously purloined."

The immense ogre was terribly disappointed upon inspecting the oven's vacant interior. And then, in an effort to prevent the gruesome monster from flogging the eggs out of her vulnerable ovaries, the fearful wife invented some rather credible fiction.

"Husband, I believe that the Leatherhead boy you had sampled for breakfast was the one that your excellent olfactory nerves still smell," the huge, towering wife imaginatively fibbed. "Your keen nasal and mouth taste buds are simply detecting lingering residue from the boy's already-eaten body. That problem generally comes with the territory of you being a dedicated cannibal."

And so, the prodigious giant sat-down at his enormous table, scratched his psoriasis infected crotch seventeen times. and uttered, "Well Martha, I could've sworn I smelled a boy's sweaty skin along with also his dirty asshole." And thereafter, the colossus stood and opened the cupboard to examine its burgeoning contents, but fortunately for Jack's sake, the suspicious investigator failed to remember to search inside the pantry.

Feeling frustrated and depressed, the fatigued ogre called for his enslaved wife to feed him his standard high-protein breakfast, and after the husband swallowed-down three more cooked calves, the husband insisted that Mrs. Martha Stuartess fetch for him his Golden Harp, which also sang opera, besides playing (music) with itself.

And within a half-hour after the melodious musical medley had commenced, the master fell *fast* asleep, which actually here means *slowly* into a deep-sleep. And when the subservient wife left the room to take her morning crap in the outhouse (she preferred an outhouse to the giant's abominable-stinking bathroom sanctuary), Jack leaped-out of the pantry, swiftly confiscated the Golden Harp, but the worried, inanimate instrument hysterically cried-out, "Master! Master! Please save me from this thoroughly delinquent, rather dysfunctional, junior jerk-off!"

The callow felon bolted left and dodged right, hurrying as fast as his bony legs could, but the visiting thief's strategy proved to be ignorant, because Jack had to remain on the twenty-foot-wide, white cottony road all the way to the infamous beanstalk, still a distant three hundred (parking) meters down the gray lane.

And then, the pursuing monster witnessed the young desperado disappear down into one of the large clouds where an arrowed sign read: "Porno' Shop: Giants Only" had deliberately been planted by the ogre's whoring wife (who had been secretly having an affair with another little, horny oven boy from the village below).

"Help me, Master! Save me from this arrogant little thug!" the Golden Harp frenetically cried-out. "This little perverted rogue is more than a little perverted, and I think that the lunatic creep wants to fondle my G-string!"

The incensed giant awkwardly maneuvered himself down from the beanstalk's summit, and upon peering-downward toward the ground, his covetous eyes perceived his screaming Harp being held in the boy's obstinate clutches. But the rascal was by then only several-hundred-feet above the ground when Jack neurotically hollered, "Mother! Mother! Get me my axe, you old battle-axe!"

And the escaper's diligent mother, who had been impatiently waiting for the anticipated "axe command" for hours, came rushing with the dangerous cutting tool in hand, and when she arrived at the beanstalk's base, the woman looked-upward with her mouth agape as if she were about to administer a super-blow-job to the rapidly descending ogre.

Jack jumped the last five-feet to the ground, with not a moment to 'spare', or even a propitious moment to make an incredible bowling strike. The boy quickly handed the harping Harp to his stunned Mother, pulled the axe from her clutches, and began industriously chopping-away at the beanstalk as if he himself' were a European Paul Bunyan. The vertical vegetation shook and vibrated from the first ten blows, because it was an inferior quality plant, despite the fact that it had been both magical and stupendous in size.

After two-dozen walloping hacks, the beanstalk finally severed, its unbelievable form toppled, and then collapsed to the ground, generating a tumultuous thud. The ogre also fell off the plummeting vine, and soon landed upon his head, breaking his crown, even though he had never been a king, and had never aspired to be one.

Jack then enthusiastically presented the paranoid singing harp to his now-enthralled mother, and the wondrous instrument shrieked-out: "Fuck this goddamned shit! I'm not singing one fuckin' note for either of you two retards!"

And in the end, Jack and his proud Mother became very rich from selling the golden eggs from the phenomenal plain-looking chicken, and by touring all of England (including Leatherhead), and exhibiting the totally amazing "Bitching and Foul-mouthed Harp" to applauding crowds at circus sideshow venues.

People, with nothing better to do, gladly paid a pound apiece to listen to the Golden Harp's incessant cursing and continuous condemnations, which made the audience members feel good about their own major and minor aggravations that were prevalent in their own miserable, mediocre lives.

"The Bishop's Candlesticks"
Victor Hugo

Victor Hugo (1802-1885) was born in Besancon, France. The acclaimed author was a connoisseur of fine wines and cheeses, and Hugo often recommended that booklovers drink and eat merrily while concurrently digesting the contents of his works.

Contrary to popular belief, Victor never invented new methods to tie shoes that were called French "Hugo knots". Victor's brother Eugene was very jealous of his sibling's success, and spent much of his miserable life in an asylum, while Hugo was also happily institutionalized in marriage. Victor felt guilty about Eugene's diagnosed insanity,, and many of his stories reflect hatred and rivalry between brothers. Hugo had *not* been elected president of the *Reading Comprehension Association* as many literary advocates believe, and consequently, the eminent French author missed the opportunity of acquiring the nickname *RCA Victor*.

Victor Hugo never wanted to be interrupted while writing, or when having either straight or oral sex. In the morning, Victor took his shower standing nude on a sundeck, and the exhibitionist had been honoring *that* same very interesting practice ever since his first baby shower. Tourists noted the author's curious morning bathing habit, and the nosy gossipers included *their* welcomed voyeurism as one of the most curious stops on their Parisian itinerary. *Les Miserables* and *The Hunchback of Notre Dame* (who later never played professional football for Knute Rockne) were Hugo's most famous classic novels. "The Bishop's Candlesticks" is one of the distinguished author's best-known novellas.

A loud knocking at the French Bishop's front door quickly got his attention. "Come in!" the pedophile church official yelled. "The door's unlocked!"

The front door was instantly slammed open, and a fierce-looking man with dazed eyes stood in the foyer. A tattered knapsack was hanging from the intruder's shoulder, and a stick that looked more like a club was held in his right hand. The encroacher's face had a weary-but-surly expression, and the glassy-eyed fellow looked both hideous and bellicose.

The Bishop's enlarged pupils studied the man's violent-gruesome-looking appearance with *his* mouth agape. "What is the purpose of your visit?" the high church official asked. "Do you wish to make a confession? Is your troubled soul absolutely in need of absolution?"

The vile-looking street-person placed the bottom of his intimidating club to the floor, and leaned both hands upon it while supporting his upper body. "My name's Jean Valbluejean," the unexpected visitor announced. "I was recently released by the French government as a falsely-convicted galley slave, and I'm finally free after spending nineteen-years of forced labor and demonic drudgery, all sacrificed, at my personal expense, for *our* esteemed, fucked-up lunatic government."

The startled Bishop was rather flabbergasted with his visitor's lowlife background along with his acerbic attitude, and the religious official's two attractive female companions (seated at the supper table) were also in a mild state of shock.

"Your Warship, er, I mean Your Worship; I was finally liberated four damned days ago, and am now heading toward Pontarlier," the released convict explained. "I've been trekking four days from Toulon, and today, I'm roving the vicinity alone. I've walked about fifty-five freakin' kilometers. As you can plainly see, I'm totally exhausted, emotionally unstable, somewhat fucked-up, and I hereby personally request your hospitality."

"Will not any of the inns take you in?" the frightened Bishop curtly inquired. "The greedy proprietors usually don't turn anyone away in exchange for money."

"I had stopped at several inns in town, but I was sent away because I carried a yellow passport," Jean Valbluejean answered. "The hostile landlords told me 'Be off!' and no lodging proprietor would have anything to do with me, once he examined my damning credentials."

"Couldn't you stay in the town jail?" the feckless Bishop incredulously asked. "My parishioner's taxes help support that excellent institution, you know."

"I went to the local prison, and the keepers rejected me because their records show I haven't committed any major crime in the area," Jean sadly articulated. "And so, a policeman took me to the municipal dog kennel. I was placed in a cage with a rabid, mean-assed mongrel that viciously bit me twice on my delicate rear end. And I must say, Your Worship, that my sore, mutilated ass is really aching and throbbing right this minute!"

"Couldn't you just sleep out in a farm field?" the problem-solving, apathetic Bishop curiously queried. "I mean it's not such a cold and nasty spring night."

"I was lying in a farmer's weed garden, but the stars were covered by *dense clouds* that were not too intelligent," Valbluejean joked. "I thought it would rain, but since no God was in the vicinity to prevent a downpour, I came back to town to seek shelter and sustenance."

The Bishop pensively contemplated what Jean Valbluejean had stated. 'Hmm,' he thought. 'A non-believer whose soul it is my duty to salvage from hell's infernos.' Then, the on-a-mission Bishop (who was not standing on a mission) loftily and sanctimoniously replied, "Jean Valbluejean; God is both ubiquitous and omniscient. He is everywhere, and He knows everything. How did you get to arrive at my door?"

"I was lying on the pavement in the town square when a good prostitute, perhaps Mary Magdalene reincarnated, directed me to seek sanctuary at your superb home," the ignoble traveler fabricated. "She told me, 'Go and knock on *that* door, and you'll meet a noble man and two women with nice knockers of their own hanging on their chests.'"

"Well, the alert streetwalker gave you some stellar advice," the man of the silk (who was formerly a man of the cloth) reading admitted. "The good woman must regularly attend my church."

"What sort of house is this?" Jean Valbluejean asked. "Is it an inn or a bordello? I have a hundred and nine francs and fifty sous to show for my damned nineteen-years of forced government service. I'll pay for a room, whether this is a cheap inn or an expensive bordello," the hardcore criminal said as he glanced and smiled at the avaricious Bishop's two beautiful servants. "And needless to say, I'm very exhausted and hungry. Will *you*, kind sir, out of the goodness of your humble heart, allow me to stay here for the night?"

"Madame Magliore," the demanding Bishop imperatively ordered. "Set the table with an additional knife and fork for our un-distinguished guest. Have a seat Jean, and tell us all about your exploits."

"Madame!" Jean Valbluejean exclaimed to Madame Magliore. "I've hit pay-dirt! I've hit the super-jackpot! I knew this fabulous place was a friggin' authentic, swanky bordello!"

"Please refrain from utilizing vulgar nomenclature in *my* blessed domicile," the sanctimonious Bishop haughtily admonished. "I personally find your choice of ghetto terminology rather abhorrent and obscene."

"Wait a damned minute!" Jean interrupted his eminent host. "Have you not comprehended that I said I was a despicable galley convict and have just been released from incarceration? You're dealing with a fucked-up maniac here!"

"I told you that you must exercise discretion in your choice and utilization of reprehensible words," the insulted Bishop again chastised. "Must I remind that you're also in the presence of reputable women?"

"Sure, reputable women whoring-around in a typical house of ill-repute!" Jean shouted and laughed. Then, the ex-convict hastily removed a yellow, wrinkled sheet of paper from his pants' pocket. "Here's my yellow passport that verifies my lowly status in society," the obnoxious and offensive rogue emphasized. "I learned how to read from my gay roommate on the galley ship. I orally recited passages from romance novels. while the gay faggot orally gave me head each and every night until my testicles could manufacture no more sperm."

Madame Magliore and her companion Mademoiselle Valisshon started squirming in their chairs, and then began rubbing their horny crotches, and touching their tender nipples in response to Jean Valbluejean's vivid sexual description.

"This is what my yellow passport reads," Jean continued his mediocre revelation. "I was born in 1805. As a young boy, I kicked the shit out of my neighbor, whose last name was Bonaparte, and gave the nasty little dick-head a Napoleon complex. As a result of my errant ways, I served nineteen-years laboring in the horrible galleys. Five of those years were for breaking and entering a virgin countess's pussy. Now, Your Worship; you figure that bullshit out! And then, the additional fourteen-years were allotted and tacked-on for attempting to escape the galleys four times," Jean informed with a noticeable frown upon his grimy-looking countenance. "This abused man you're presently peering at is very dangerous, and will screw anything, either male or female, that walks on either two or four legs. That's exactly what the goddamned document states, if you have time to read it."

The faggot Bishop began sweating profusely, as fresh blood surged to his penis for the first time in three hours, while both Madame Magliore and Mademoiselle Valisshon began licking their lips with their tongues, and gently rubbing their swollen clitorises.

"All the friggin' world has frowned upon me and turned me away," Jean whimpered and sobbed. "My deranged mind is still in a quandary. Is this an inn or is it a brothel? Will you be courteous enough to provide me with some food and a bed? Have you a stable with a strong horse in it? Do you have any valuables in this domicile worthy of pilfering? Do you two gorgeous, voluptuous, horny women always masturbate in public?"

"Madame Magliore," the astonished Bishop said to the deep-breathing climaxing woman. "Put some clean sheets on the bed in the alcove so that our fine guest, Jean Valbluejean, can stain them up good with his multiple ejaculations."

"Yes! Yes! Yesssssss!" the aroused, sophisticated, aristocratic lady gasped as she got her rocks off.

Then, the high-ranking church administrator turned to Jean. "Sit down and warm yourself at my table," the astounded Bishop politely directed. "Your crummy bed shall be made while we're eating and conversing. Madame Magliore, you may use the hammer, wood, and nails in the tool shed to make Jean's bed. Ha, ha, ha!"

The visitor's gloomy, sullen face suddenly transformed into one' expressing joy, anticipation, and curiosity. The dastardly rascal began stammering and spouting-off like a delirious madman. "This can't fuckin' be true! You'll let me stay at this cozy house without ever incurring any debts? You will not reject me, a former convict that possesses an erection that could keep a mare in heat happy! What a fuckin' bonanza I've fallen into!"

320

"Sir, I again caution you to moderate your scurrilous language," the holier-than-thou Bishop firmly reiterated as Madame Magliore re-entered the room. "When I was your tender age, I too was screwed-up in the head and made myriad *lewd*icrous remarks, but then, with the help of God, managed to reform my errant ways."

"You called me the distinguished title of *Sir,* and yet you did not mortify me in the least," the avowed crook uttered. "I told you the truth about my true identity, and yet you did not banish my ass from being a guest in your fine house."

"That village slut you had met out in the square works on a commission basis, and the hooker sends all itinerant riffraff here," the affluent Bishop divulged and explained. "And I shall see that *you* sleep in a fine bed for the first time in nineteen-years. And I'll even give you the bed with the mattress that doesn't squeak if you're lucky enough to shack-up with either Madame Magliore or Mademoiselle Valisshon, or maybe even hit the jackpot and sleep with both exotic erotic nymphomaniacs."

Both ladies were again enjoying multiple orgasms, as Jean suggested that he would definitely sleep with one or both of them. "Yes, that would undoubtedly be the *climax* to my most recent adventure!" Valbluejean jubilantly stated. "By the way, obliging landlord, what is your name?" Jean innocuously asked.

"Quite frankly I'm a low priest who enjoys getting high and living like a pauper in this ordinary nondescript house," the prevaricating Bishop modestly answered and jested. "For your information, I'm a reformed pedophile who now actively recruits members for the boys' eunuch choir at my church."

"A goddamned priest!" Jean laughed while slapping his left knee. "Then I could make a modest donation to your church instead of being charged a fee for food, lodging, and whatever else might happen in the line of carnal pleasure for me at your residence. I'm sorry Your Worship," Valbluejean apologized. "I didn't take notice of your enchanting robe. Confidentially, I only pay close attention when women or men disrobe!"

"I shall accept no payment from a sturdy individual that has endured such hardship as you've unfortunately experienced," the merciful Bishop sympathetically promised. "Keep your precious money, Jean. How long did it take you to fully accumulate your hundred francs?"

"Nineteen-years of blood, sweat and tears," Jean dramatically reiterated. "I still have it all. Yesterday, I spent the twenty-five sous I had earned helping invalids at the Grasse Hospital wipe their smelly asses'. What a shitty job that was, especially when I ran out of toilet paper and dry grass!"

"Did you keep the sacraments when you were laboring on the galley?" the inquisitive Bishop curiously inquired. "It seems to me that you need a lot of grace to negate all of the disgrace that apparently exists in your totally warped life!"

"Since *you* are a religious personage," Jean acknowledged while arching his eyebrows, "we did have an accomplished chaplain named Charlie at the galleys. One day, a Monsignor visited the ship, and gave me his blessing; I think he was a Monsignor or a high Cure. Forgive me, Your Excellency, because as you've already identified, I'm a trifle deficient when it comes to using the right fuckin' vocabulary."

"Did this low-level-bishop say Mass on your ship?" the religious hierarch asked his peculiar visitor. "Most bishops have *cardinal* reasons for doing things. Those cardinal reasons confirm *their* psychological marriage to their noble motivations and ambitions."

"The alluded-to bishop had a pointed hat on his head, and I figured that his head, which was hidden underneath, must've been shaped like a friggin' pyramid," Jean nonchalantly declared. "But when the moron said his sermon and read the gospel, I was too far away to even hear his flagrant bull-shit. I just remember thinking that I hoped his dick wasn't also cone-shaped like his friggin' oddball head was, situated underneath that weird-looking, triangular hat."

"Madame Magliore," the formal Bishop austerely-but-courteously commanded. "Please set Mr.Valbluejean's knife and fork on the side of the table nearest the hearth. The night breeze originating from around this section of the Alps is colder than a frigid Eskimo woman's rectum." Then, the very strange bishop paused for a moment to garner and express his scatterbrained thought. "This inferior table lamp gives-off a very dim light," the embarrassed Bishop noted.

Madame Magliore caught the concerned Bishop's hint, and stepped to the cleric's bedroom to fetch two very familiar silver candlesticks that were ordinarily used to decorate and to illuminate the wooden table.

"The candlesticks that Madame is obtaining are indeed multi-functional," the haughty Bishop confidentially told Jean with a wink. "Few can hold a candle to either Madame or Mademoiselle with what *they* skillfully do with those fascinating objects."

'Mademoiselle Valisshon and I use these candlesticks for sexual gratification,' Madame Magliore remembered with a broad smile directed toward Jean. 'We take the candles out of their bases, and then replace them with beautifully-shaped, smooth-studded, wooden dildos. Then, we straddle our hairy crotches directed above the simulated vertical hard-ons, and simultaneously start pumping up and down until we both experience fantastic mutual orgasms,' the Madame bizarrely recollected as the promiscuous lady finally returned to the kitchen, and began setting the candlesticks and candelabra (candle*labia*) down on the table.

"Monsieur la Cure," Jean addressed while fantasizing having group sex with the two vivacious ladies. "You don't despise me, do you? I'm indeed a disadvantaged fellow who just might enjoy shoving dildo candelabra up beautiful ladies' furry slit tunnels. My motto's always been "Screw everyone, before they have an opportunity to screw me."

The gay Bishop seated at Jean's side gently touched his guest's warm hand. "Sir, you need not feel obligated to inform me who you were," the Bishop elaborated with an envious smile. "Sometimes touch is the best communication without the use of words. God! Am I getting a wonderful hot flash that won't quit! Spill and share your soul, dear Jean Valbluejean, while I imagine an appropriate gratifying solution. Please begin your penetrating remarks, so that I may have intellectual *intercourse* with you!" the faggot Bishop ejaculated. "Now relate to your captive audience your most trying problems," the Cure expressed, as the covetous homo softly massaged Jean's muscular tattooed left arm. In the meantime, Madame Magliore and Mademoiselle Valisshon again began rubbing (like crazy) their erect, squiggly, pulsating, crotch buttons.

"I wore the French red jacket designated for galley slaves, because only the gay jerk-off convicts wore yellow jackets, that neither came out of nests nor hives," Jean disclosed as he became more sexually aroused watching the two horny ladies. "My bright uniform was accompanied by a ball and chain around my foot, and my fucked-up companions and I futilely tried breaking each other's balls with mallets in order to escape, but all of our efforts were to no avail. Each of us had a splintery plank upon which to sleep, and to dream of two big-breasted ladies wildly masturbating simultaneously," Jean disclosed as his eyes watched Madame Magliore and Mademoiselle Valisshon temporarily lost in another dimension while furiously rubbing-away in sheer ecstasy.

"Nineteen-years I wore a double chain around my ass and balls, which dragged on the floor of the ship's dungeon whenever I shuffled my feet to take a healthy shit or a needed piss," Jean commiserated with his empathetic listener. "And now, I must carry this fuckin' yellow passport around that hauntingly reminds me of the gay, degenerate faggots sodomizing each other in their homosexual yellow jackets, all happening on that disgusting galley ship."

"You've indeed escaped a place of extreme sorrow and despair," the understanding Bishop gasped as he began rubbing and massaging Jean's dirty hairy chest. "There'll be more joy for all of us in heaven when sinners remorsefully repent both their trivial and their heinous transgressions," the self-righteous Bishop continued his impromptu sermon. "Until that special moment of triumph arrives, we all must deal with the sinful pleasures, lusts, and temptations that inherently afflict and overwhelm us mere mortals."

Madame Magliore and Mademoiselle Valisshon were now rolling all over the floor, and were both panting and moaning in fantastic euphoria. Finally, the two bitches wrapped their arms around each other and embraced in sharing one positively-culminating, fabulous release of dual elation.

In another minute, the Madame and the Mademoiselle gracefully stood, dusted themselves off, and adroitly served the soup that had nearly boiled on the wood-fed-stove. The appetizer was both watery and salty, and had several strips of raunchy bacon floating on its surface. The soup was served with mutton, figs, country cheese, and a loaf of *pump*ernickel bread in honor of Jean Valbluejean's stiff erection. A bottle of cheap wine (that was the favorite of local vagabonds and hobos) was next placed in the center of the table.

"Well Jean," the garrulous Bishop grunted with an element of regret. "It's my adherence to hospitable gaiety that compels us to voraciously eat our sumptuous mutton and our delectable soup."

'Well, you bullshitting church faggot,' Jean Valbluejean thought as he sipped the putrid hot soup. 'Keep acting gay around me, and you'll certainly wind-up in the fuckin' hospital or in the local morgue. I only tolerate your homo' bull-shit because I'm greatly hungry and sleepy.' Then, Jean considered the prospect of enjoying his un-nourishing meal. "Okay my illustrious host," the dangerous criminal responded while feigning cordiality. "Just don't slurp your soup, making it sound like a dozen pigs sucking slop from a dirty trough."

Mademoiselle Valisshon sat-down next to Valbluejean and began rubbing his muscular legs, and soon his stiff, inflated crotch for most of the meal's duration, while poor Jean had to respectfully listen to the delusional Bishop's extended bull-shit litany. 'These crazy people are even more fucked-up than I am!' the amazed dangerous guest concluded. 'Civilized society is far more treacherous than the hold of any fuckin' galley slave ship, that's for fuckin' sure!'

After saying a perfunctory grace (while Jean was devouring his edibles), the considerate Bishop then served himself an ample helping of soup. "It *strikes* me that something is missing from the table," the Cure yelled at Madame Magliore, who was also very busy massaging Jean's testicles and the base of his swollen fadorkenbender.

'I'd like to *strike* you right in the center of your big fat mouth,' Jean thought in regard to his obnoxious host's stupid drivel. 'And then I'd like to sever your glib tongue.'

"Madame Magliore, you've arranged the silverware in too simple of an order," the very fastidious gay Bishop criticized. "A fine table is like a fine story. They both start with a good *setting*. Ha, ha, ha!"

'Go fuck yourself faggot!' both Jean Valbluejean and Madame Magliore simultaneously thought. 'And may your tiny dick rot inside your gargantuan asshole!'

Madame Magliore reluctantly got-up and located the missing additional spoons and forks that the very meticulous Bishop had specifically alluded to. But Jean Valbluejean almost choked to death on a mouthful of mutton when the uncouth visitor reflexively gasped (as he popped a load in his pants) in reaction to Mademoiselle Valisshon vigorously jerking him off. After clearing his throat of meat particles, Jean again avariciously swallowed-down his remaining food. Madame Magliore soon returned to the table with the glistening formal silverware.

After the lackluster supper, the odd guest and his homosexual priest-host had a candid conversation about conservation. Then, the shrewd itinerant adroitly changed the subject. "Monsignor Cure; you seem to have a cure for my biological needs," Jean began his weird statement with a weirder compliment. "Yet, I must criticize that the cart drivers that pelted my ass with cobblestones and bricks out on your street late this afternoon ate better goddamned food than you've served me here. Why the fuck don't you open a sleazy greasy spoon bistro and poison everybody in your fucked-up community?"

"I enjoy the company of Madame and Mademoiselle so much that we scarcely have time to venture-out to the grocery store and buy decent victuals to consume," the slightly-chagrined Bishop explained to the wayward derelict. "When they're redundantly eating each other out all-day-long, the beautiful ladies have no time left to buy or eat basic foods! Quite frankly, Jean, I'm tired of their monotonous, hedonistic, lesbian proclivities."

"This place of yours is more like an insane asylum than an inn or a bordello," Jean verbalized and protested. "It's like a nightmare residing inside of a friggin' nightmare! Aren't there any normal bastards and bitches around anymore for me to rob?" the thief lamented and complained. "I absolutely hate having any interaction with queers and LBGTQMPRAF weirdos. I even despise stealing from them!"

The often-aloof Bishop picked-up one of the silver candelabra with its burning tallow flaming away at its base. Then, the high church official handed its twin to Jean. "*Come,*" the sexually frustrated Bishop implored, not realizing that Valbluejean had already just popped a serious load. "I shall now lead you to your room."

The former convict followed the Cure through the Bishop's bedroom in order to reach the designated alcove situated near a small chapel. Jean observed that Madame Magliore was removing the used candles and inserting the rounded smooth dildos into the bases of the dual candelabra.

Inside the aforementioned alcove, a clean bed and fresh-scented sheets had been prepared for Jean Valbluejean, who was still trying to figure-out if he was staying at a stranger-than-fiction whorehouse, or patronizing a very unprofitable, fucked-up inn.

"I trust you'll have a decent night's rest," the sexually disappointed and perverted Bishop commented. And next, the pedophile/homo' slowly left the vagabond fellow's makeshift accommodations before Jean ever had a chance to say, 'Thanks a lot for your generosity, you gay faggot fuck!'

Four hours later, at two-hours past midnight, Jean was awakened by the nearby cathedral bells tolling the precise time. The journeyman could not restfully sleep, because his mattress was too comfortable compared to the hard plank upon which the mendicant had dutifully slept-upon for nineteen-years. 'I'll lie here until the bell strikes three. Then, I shall complete my clever. devious mission. and quickly hightail it the hell outa' here.'

The cathedral bells predictably rang again sixty-minutes later. Jean rose up in his bed; scratched his ass and his balls; paced to the window; opened it, and took a lengthy piss, wetting a drunk bum sound-asleep, lying on the cobble-stoned sidewalk below. The outside temperature was very chilly. Valbluejean listened intently, but could not discern even the slightest movement in the demented Bishop's house. 'There're no bars on this window,' Jean observed as the dedicated thief tucked his dingle and testicles back into his grimy underwear. 'I could escape by leaping out of this opening down into the courtyard. Then, I could clamber-over that whitewashed wall, and get the fuck outa' this dump with my purloined plunder intact. There's a street on the opposite side of that wall. Christ! That sharp wind almost blew my dick and balls off!' the smalltime-villain thought while slowly and quietly closing the window.

Jean slowly ambled toward his knapsack, and removed a metal tool. The short iron bar resembled a device often used by French miners to pry and remove loose rocks from lofty hills and from various cave walls.

Holding his breath and employing soft footsteps, the nefarious guest surreptitiously stepped toward the next room, peeked inside the quarters, and observed a bizarre three o'clock ritual being performed in the perverted Bishop's bedroom. The wacko Bishop was lying on top of a faced-down doll that resembled the body of a thirteen-year-old choirboy. He soon was alternately staring at Madame Magliore and at Mademoiselle Valisshon, who both had their dresses rolled-up while they straddled their brown beavers and their wet pink cave-slits over the two dildos that had been inserted into the pair of candelabra.

When the Bishop gave the signal, the two women (standing on the floor) squatted down onto the vertical dildos, burying the objects deep into their hairy, pink slits. Then, the kinky ladies began riveting their haunches and hips up and down in piston-like fashion. Getting aroused, the gay Bishop achieved a meager erection, and immediately began sodomizing the young choirboy manikin up its ass.

As the outrageous, intense, deranged phenomenon progressed, Jean Valbluejean also became aroused. The observer wedged his huge erection into the crack of the door, closed it gently, and as the rascal voyeured the explicit activities going on inside the maniac Bishop's bedroom, the excited guest began instinctively thrusting his ass and erection back and forth.

The incredible sex orgy grew in intensity, and the remarkable event proceeded for fifteen glorious minutes. All four participants climaxed simultaneously, and Jean Valbluejean's ejaculation flew from the door crack. clear across the room. and splashed directly into the maniacal Bishop's face.

"That was the most realistic orgasm I've ever had," the delighted Bishop commended his two very promiscuous women companions. "But I didn't know that one of you had any testicles that could produce and zip a humungous load of sweet semen clear across the room. Well, I guess I can learn something new every day, if I dutifully paid more attention," the cleric stated before wildly licking his ugly tongue around his wet sticky face and lips.

Jean Valbluejean returned from the hall to the alcove, and impatiently waited for the cathedral bells to toll five. He again rose and stealthily stepped toward the warped-minded Bishop's sinful bedroom. The cleric, the two women and the artificial choirboy were all piled in one heap, with the three humans snoring-away in what appeared to be tranquil ecstasy. Moonlight was filtering through an overhead window/skylight, and dimly lit the bedroom, exactly as similar shafts had done during most of the extraordinary sex orgy that had transpired earlier. Total satisfaction beamed from the visages of all three sleepers, as the vulgar assholes mutually and securely enjoyed their serene reposes.

Jean Valbluejean stood there above the slumbering imbeciles with his miniature crowbar in his right hand, but the self-centered crook was terrified at perceiving the gigantic, luminous halo that seemed to eerily surround the sleeping Bishop and hover-above his two unorthodox female colleagues. 'Those hot bitches and that fucked-up bastard don't deserve such celestial illumination,' Jean readily determined. 'The three buffoons should be roasting in hell for their sinful lusting, just like I'll most certainly be doing after *Judgment Day*. At least, I'm perceptive and know when a goddamned mortal sin is actually a goddamned mortal sin!'

But despite the angst his heart held toward the crazed Bishop and toward the horny, kinky women, Jean still felt a degree of guilt as the wandering criminal considered the design of his planned theft. He briefly hesitated in indecision. The obstinate criminal felt inclined to mash the Bishop's brains out because he thoroughly loathed self-righteous, pompous, asshole, homosexual pedophiles that feigned having culture and civility. But then, Valbluejean figured he would have to also kill Madame Magliore and Mademoiselle Valisshon, who were peacefully sleeping in the same pile as the perverted religious figure, all three lying amidst *his* most-unique, juvenile male doll.

Jean proceeded directly to the cupboard, and was surprised to see that the key had been left in the lock. 'I don't even have to use my tool to pry open the freakin' door,' the exploring thief thought and smiled. ''Instead of fuckin' stealin' valuable silverware and candelabra, I should be kidnapping the Madame and the Mademoiselle. I could certainly make a handsome fortune promoting their fantastic dual candelabra sex routine, played to rapid classical music, to receptive theater audiences all over fuckin' France.'

Valbluejean first seized the sleeping Bishop's silverware. Then Jean grabbed the pair of candelabra, distinctly smelled them for any pussy-juice-residue and next carefully placed the objects into his tattered knapsack alongside the silver forks, knives and spoons. The villainous rogue then furtively paced past the three dozing slumberers; nostalgically passed through the portal, and next prudently advanced past the small chapel.

After reaching the alcove, the scrupulous criminal raised the window, and soon swiftly leaped, accidentally falling upon the same sleeping bum he had pissed-on several hours before. Jean rose from the cobblestone sidewalk; savagely kicked the drunken indigent in the head; dashed to the whitewashed wall, and then climbed-over the temporary barrier. The former convict quickly fled the vicinity like a frightened gazelle.

The next morning, the refreshed Bishop was strolling about his courtyard garden, searching the premises for the drunken vagabond to give *him* his decent early blow-job. Suddenly, a very disturbed Madame Magliore sprinted towards the horny homosexual/pedophile, who habitually persisted in committing *cardinal* sins, even though he was only still a damned bishop.

"Why are you so alarmed Madame?" the Bishop wondered and asked. "Did your dildo again get stuck up your divine pink crotch, and you can't get it out?"

"Monsignor, Monsignor!" the worried woman hysterically screamed. "Does Your Grandeur know where the magnificent silverware and the silver candelabra are?"

"My Grandeur hasn't gotten hard since last night!" the dim-witted Bishop stupidly laughed. "And my penis, erect or otherwise, does not have a brain where it can know anything!"

"But Your Excellency, the silverware and the candelabra are missing!" Madame Magliore distressfully cried. "Mademoiselle and I now have no appropriate dildos of equal size to stick into our most-cherished love tunnels!"

"I suspect it's the renegade man staying in the alcove that has probably purloined those valuable items," the Bishop logically theorized and declared. "Go to his room and see if he's still occupying his bed. I must have *confirmation* before I can baptize the unscrupulous culprit by savagely drowning the no-good-bastard in the holy water dunking fountain."

Madame Magliore bolted inside the stone house and rushed through the Bishop's room, and then through the small chapel to the alcove. Yelling all the while for the chief occupant, Madame Magliore next hustled through the remainder of the residence and out to the courtyard to convey the bad news to her concerned benefactor. "The man is gone!" she loudly panted as if she were having one of her extended candelabra orgasms. "He's stolen your valuable property."

The craven Bishop sniffed some snot back into his deepest sinuses, and remained reticent for a moment. "We must get those silver items back, especially the wonderful candelabra," the distressed Bishop insisted in a resolute tone of voice.

"What'll Your Worship eat his supper with now?" the woman asked. "The silver forks, knives, and spoons are missing, too!"

"We can use the pewter utensils I've stashed under the altar in the chapel," the irritated Bishop promptly related.

"But metal made out of tin and lead smells lousy, and is not a worthy substitute for silver," the woman eloquently argued and sobbed. "But Sir Cure, you do not have any pewter candelabra!"

"That's right!" the forgetful Bishop realized and gasped. "Without the silver candelabra, I'll be without entertainment, because you and Mademoiselle won't be able to use your magnificent dildos. Then, I won't be able to achieve an erection to energetically sodomize my young choirboy doll up the ass. This dilemma is indeed a much greater problem than I had originally imagined!"

A half-hour later, the dejected Bishop was devouring breakfast at the same table where Jean Valbluejean had sat the previous evening. "I don't need a silver spoon, fork, or knife to dip a piece of bread into my cup of milk," the church official jested to his two thoroughly pissed-off female companions.

"That's true, but without the silver candlestick holders, Mademoiselle and I can't get our rocks off properly, and you won't be able to penetrate your adolescent male doll with your tiny erect pecker!" Madame Magliore growled. "You'll too suffer from *their* absence!"

"In retrospect, villainous Jean Valbluejean was quite a unique man," the disenchanted Bishop phlegmatically answered. "And the interesting idiot never stayed to have untraditional sex with any of us. I mean, we never really found out his true sexual disorientation!"

"What corrupt and asinine ideas you have!" Mademoiselle Valisshon protested to her demoralized superior. "You trustfully received a stranger into this house. He confesses that he's a desperate convict just released from a galley. And then, the crook stole our irreplaceable candelabra that had much more than sentimental value. That brazen rascal barbarian could've killed us all, *you* gullible, degenerate asshole!"

"Coulda', woulda,' shoulda'," the distraught Bishop ridiculed and mocked. "But I gotta' admit that my sexual appetite cannot be satisfactorily fulfilled without those treasured candelabra!"

As the three complainers were finishing their rancid meal, a loud knock was heard at the front door. The three cowards sat mum at their breakfast table for a moment.

"Come in. The door is open for any and all perverts, as usual!" the melancholy Bishop yelled.

A rather unusual and fierce-looking group appeared in the portal. Three uniformed men were restraining a fourth at the foyer's threshold. The trio of antagonistic men clad in denim blue happened to be city gendarmes, and their unhappy captive was none other than the conniving Jean Valbluejean.

The sergeant in charge of the local vice and advice squad respectfully saluted the imminent Bishop and bellowed, "Monsignor! Monsignor! Er, I mean esteemed Cure. We have apprehended this slippery culprit trying to flee our non-violent and reputable straight and gay community."

"Ah, so there you be!" the apprehensive Bishop boomed back without the aid of a boom box. "Jean Valbluejean, I'm so happy to see you again!"

"Then, you know this dirtball thief!" the thoroughly-confused sergeant asked the Cure.

"Why certainly officer!" the shrewd Bishop answered. "I had given this intrepid man the silverware and the candelabra to fetch himself three-hundred-francs for services rendered."

Jean Valbluejean opened his eyes and stared at the naughty, haughty Bishop. 'Services rendered?' he thought. 'What the fuck is the stupid-assed, dumb-fuck talking about?'

"Your Worship," the astounded sergeant stammered. "Then what this scumbag fellow told us was the absolute truth! The conniver insisted that *you* had gratefully given him the silverware and the candelabra. Then, he had walked to the marketplace and..."

"That's correct," the highly-respected cleric interrupted the stunned policeman. "And you've dutifully brought him back here to my humble residence as a terrible mistake. I had no available cash, so I gave Jean the equivalent amount in silver as just compensation for vital services rendered. I'm sorry that you fine gentlemen have been inconvenienced by an absurd misunderstanding."

"We sincerely apologize, Your Excellency!" the embarrassed sergeant formally stated. "Then, we can let him go so that we can search for vice in *our* very fine straight and gay community?"

"Of course!" the sharp-minded Bishop facetiously concurred. "Jean Valbluejean is an *outstanding* member of French society, and that's probably why you incompetent idiots caught him *out standing* near the marketplace. Ha, ha, ha!"

The bewildered gendarmes loosened their grips on their suspect, and then their former arrestee awkwardly tottered backward.

"But if you catch Jean again, be sure to capture and bring him directly to me for prosecution," the coy Bishop plainly articulated. "I need more vital services from him that he must obediently perform."

The three puzzled policemen saluted the Honorable Bishop and immediately left the premises. The three residents of the household then stared at the grateful felon.

"I owe you my life," Jean appreciatively stated. "As a former convict, I could've been hung for foolishly committing grand larceny that didn't turn-out too grandly."

"You owe me much more than your damned life," the always-scheming Bishop wryly stated and then smiled.

"What did you mean by 'services rendered'?" Valbluejean curiously asked his new master.

"You'll see later tonight," the now-gleeful Bishop predicted. "Until then, enjoy some mediocre breakfast with the three of us!"

That evening, Jean Valbluejean discovered that "services rendered" pertained to *future obligations* that had to be completed in return for the plotting Bishop's most benevolent favor. The exploitive church superior introduced Madame Magliore, Mademoiselle Valisshon, and Jean Valbluejean to a third silver candelabra that had been cunningly concealed inside the tabernacle above the small chapel's altar.

"Here, Jean Valbluejean, is *your* personal candelabra," the devious Bishop declared. "Each evening, *you* are to perform between Madame Magliore and Mademoiselle Valisshon. You shall efficaciously grease-up your anus, and then deftly squat-down and rivet upon *this* third dildo apparatus that I've been exclusively saving for such a special occasion."

"Why you dirty son-of-a-bitch!" Jean Valbluejean boisterously balked. "I would've been better-off staying in the galley and being sodomized by faggot convicts with the same fuckin' sexual fantasies that *you* practice, and in the process, *you* enjoy what's wrongly described as self-gratifying biological pleasure in our totally-perverted 'French *civilized* society'!"

"Exactly Jean," the insane Bishop agreed. "And as a distinct reward, you'll even get to screw the Madame and the Mademoiselle once a month while they're having their messy periods! I guarantee you, my new servant, that you'll have, as the British say, 'a bloody good time' staying here, attending to my needs for the remainder of your damned, miserable life! Ha, ha, ha!"

"The Fourth Voyage of Sindbad"

The Voyages of Sindbad are part of a body of literature known as *The Arabian Knights*. A big-crotched queen had betrayed her little-dicked husband by being unfaithful. The monarch was not a good lover in bed, but had keenly economically screwed everyone in his sleazy realm, especially ruining the horny queen's family's wealth. According to oral (sex) tradition, the angry small-peckered ruler had murdered his wife because of her gross infidelity, and the rich monarch then vowed never to keep another marriage partner longer than a single day.

And so every morning, the paranoid, self-conscious king married a new woman, porked her with his minuscule beef injector in the afternoon, and then killed her the following dawn before randomly marrying another promiscuous female. Then, a courageous lady named Shahrazad married the crazy king with the incredible inferiority complex, and to prevent herself' from being killed, the new wife would tell the insecure monarch a wonderful story each night so that he did not execute her, and wanted to hear the next tale in the amazing bull-shit saga.

After a thousand and one thrilling nights, the loony king decided to keep Shahrazad as a wife, especially when the woman told the neurotic emperor that she was really married to the notorious Sindbad the Sailor, and that her notorious husband would castrate and systematically dismember the wimpy king should *he* dare lay a hand on her in an uncouth manner in one of his uncouth manors. Here is one of the tales about *her* alleged spouse Sindbad that captured the king's imagination, and also intensified his fear. Shahrazad narrated the story in the first person while pretending to be her very famous husband telling the tale.

* * * * * * * * * * * *

Being stranded in a foreign land really sucks. The territory and its alien inhabitants seemed more fucked-up than I was, and I persistently cursed and muttered as I trekked onward toward a faint glimmer in the distance, which I suspected to be a 'mirage', even though I knew that I wasn't anywhere near *Caesar's Palace*. My illusion turned-out to be a dozen men gathering pepper from plants growing wildly along the rugged coastline. The bastards were sneezing all over the damned place every time they tried talking, and the twelve men were covered from head to toe in hideous snot and mucus globs.

As soon as the pepper gatherers saw me approaching, the laborers instinctively hastened in my direction, while discharging an abundance of mucus all over the goddamned place. "Who are you and where the fuck do you come from?" the pepper-pickers all amazingly chanted simultaneously.

'Either these sneezing, spitting jerk-offs have a limited vocabulary, or the dunces all think the exact same thoughts!' I naturally imagined. "I'm a poor stranger to this extraordinary land, and I'm allergic to pepper, so I want to warn you erratic assholes to keep your damned distance, or else I'll have to surgically cut your balls off with my scimitar," I sternly answered.

"That's nothing to sneeze about!" the twelve idiots all stated in unique unison.

"But I want you imbeciles to know that I'm simply a poor unfortunate, simpleton, shipwrecked sailor stranded in this very desolate land," I articulated. And then, I felt compelled to relate my sensational adventures to the *nosy* gasping pepper gatherers, and the dolts listened intently to my intriguing stories while disgustingly wiping their sticky nostrils onto each other's clothing. The hunched-over pepper-pickers were astounded by my revelations, and almost sneezed their tracheas and lungs out at the climax, instead of jerking-off at the climax as normal men would surely do.

"By Allah's grace, your tales are absolutely marvelous!" the dunderheads all chanted while coincidentally sending wet green boogers spraying in all directions. But apparently, one of the morons had a mind of his own.

"But Sindbad, how did you manage to escape the cannibals on the far side of this island, who devour anyone that trespasses into their off-limits territory?" the curious snot-nose nicknamed "Sergeant Pepper" asked, before spitting-out a large green lunger onto the hot beach sand to watch it sizzle like an egg being fried. "No one ever escapes the savages' *clutches,* or their incredible, automatic thought transmissions."

I told the sloppy sneezers about the other ship survivors' unlucky fate. My sailor colleagues had come under the cannibals' witchdoctor's peculiar spell. The pepper-gatherers felt sorry for *my* cruel plight, and provided me with adequate food (two pepper sandwiches), which I immediately washed in a nearby stream, even though I knew nothing about such harmful things as germs and bacteria. I noticed some blackbirds flying and cawing overhead, scavenging for food morsels, so I rather *raven*ously ate the lousy pepper berries sandwiched between bread slices I had been given.

The pepper-gatherers then escorted me to their small ship, lifted anchor, and skillfully sailed toward their nearby island home. The nosy men with large, grotesque, gorilla-type nostrils led me to their King, who looked somewhat like a hamburger, and whom the natives humorously called Burger King, because he was the chief authority in their burg. The

Burger King asked me about my history, without me learning anything about *his* geography, science, mathematics or sociology.

I described to the Ruler all that had happened to me in my voyages since leaving Baghdad, my home city of mystery and enchantment. The King's advisers also listened to my profound recollections. One in my audience was the weirdo Emperor's wife, who had big tits, and had grown up on a prosperous milk farm, so I mentally dubbed Her Majesty 'the Dairy Queen'.

I dined with Burger King and Dairy Queen and ate their delicious foods as if I was the main guest at a Boston market. Then, we all gave thanks to Almighty Allah for all His glorious gifts and favors, none of which I could think of at the damned time. After the sumptuous meal had been consumed, I left the Burger King and the Dairy Queen's strange company, and strolled-around the avenues of *their* rich, populous city. The market places were well-stocked with food and utilitarian items, and whores and male-prostitute slaves were being aggressively and openly bartered for coins and paper currency.

'Ah, this is indeed a very pleasant city just like the Baghdad I remember!' I thought. 'I shall make friends with the people, and perhaps they'll provide me with a beautiful slut that I could screw and sodomize until *we* could forget all about the mundane screwing part.'

All of the citizens of this weird land rode exotic thoroughbred horses that had no saddles and bridles. I was curious about *that* particular fact, so I inquired about my perceptive observation, sharing my introspective concerns with the vociferous Burger King. "Oh, your High Ass, er I mean Highness," I began. "How come your riders' horses do not have saddles or 'saddle lights'. A saddle definitely increases the rider's control and ease; it loosens-up constipation when one bounces up and down, and a saddle also gets a woman's pussy wet and juicy when her crotch continuously rubs and bumps against its hardness."

"What is a saddle?" the King incredulously asked. "I never saw or used one ever in my restricted aristocratic life, but since I always have trouble taking royal shits, and since my wife's crack is as dry as the Arabian Desert in the height of summer," the King confided, "I think I could've used one of those saddles you're alluding to forty or fifty years ago."

"Your Highness, I'll make you a splendid saddle so that all the dumb-shits in your asinine kingdom can accurately and proudly call you Your High Ass just like I do," I jokingly replied. "And after you try it out on a real horse, you'll undoubtedly say that *it* is definitely much better than having either gay or straight sex."

"Anything is better than sex with my wife's juiceless, useless pussy," the Burger King admittedly regretted. "And if this saddle can alleviate my chronic constipation, I'll be able to sit on the hopper every day like a commoner, and not just once a week like a suffering Monarch while excreting little hard turds that are indeed more than a *little hard.*"

After His Excellency furnished me with some needed wood, the King introduced me to an imaginative carpenter that had colonies of carpenter ants inside his pants. I sketched-out a basic saddle design onto the wood for the carpenter, who was wiggling-around all over the damned workshop, and after he saw the stirrups, the itchy man told me, "I think I made similar objects for the local gynecologist and for Madame Saddam de Sade that owns the popular local *S and M* parlor."

I sheared some wool from a sheep, and then crafted it into felt that even felt like felt. I next covered the saddle with a rich leather exterior, which I vigorously polished even better than I ever polished my sandals with my feet in them. Next, I attached the belt, the buckle, and the stirrups, as five-hundred horny women gathered-around asking me embarrassing questions about getting laid with their open legs in the stirrups, so that their husbands and lovers could be back in the saddle again.

"You're right," I chuckled and stated to my female audience. "These splendid, helpful stirrups can be best used when something goes into your pussies, and also when something like a crying baby comes out! Ha, ha, ha!"

Next, I commissioned a non-union blacksmith (at the ignorant King's expense) to manufacture bridle bits to my exact specifications, which naturally would complete the prototype saddle's general properties. And so, the highly-versatile blacksmith (whose name was Mohammed Negro-Jones) forged the metal stirrups, buckles, and bits that were eventually incorporated into the kingdom's first official saddle and bridle combination.

I asked the King for one of his finest royal Arabian stallions, and after I attached the saddle to the marvelous beast, I led the good-tempered animal over to the 'Royal Pain-in-the-Ass'. The Ruler thanked me for my ingenuity, and then he rode the beautiful white creature all around his capital city, bouncing up and down, and happily taking royal diarrhea shits all over the formerly immaculate metropolis. "All systems are go!" the merry Ruler kept screaming like a maniac. "Especially my fuckin' hyperactive digestive/excretory system!" the fool kept deliriously repeating like a retarded parrot having dementia.

The King finally had flushed-out his colon (and his semi-colon) while farting most of his hemorrhoids right off his now-hyperactive rectum ring, and the quack was so thrilled with his fecal discharges that he rewarded me handsomely for my illustrious major contribution to his backwards civilization. And then, the King's chief adviser examined the saddle, and it reminded him of his paramour's fat ass, so the counselor wanted me to make a special one for him, too. And when the other nobles in the court had inspected the Monarch's impeccable saddle, which resembled a butterfly, the object also reminded them of Dairy Queen's fat ass (which *they* had been frequently porking), so I immediately had more customers that paid me rather prodigious prices for their custom-made saddles.

So then, I hired the blacksmith and the carpenter, and *we* were merrily busy, day and night, assembling saddles for all of the brothels and maternity delivery rooms in the whole damned land. Soon, the commoners gave me their life' savings so that the natives could screw their lovers more satisfactorily, and I even gained three-hundred lady customers (most of them dykes) that preferred being on top of their mates during their peculiar brand of sexual intercourse. After a month of our assiduous labor, little was accomplished or was produced in the kingdom, because everyone in the population was fucking-around, but no one (including me) really cared or gave a shit about anything else except getting laid, blown, or sodomized.

Then, one day, I was reading an illustrated pornographic book to the illiterate Burger King when the idiot said to me, "Sindbad, you really know how to sin bad, ha, ha, ha," the faggot ignoramus profusely and repulsively laughed. "I hold you in great affection. Now, you can either receive a wife from me or be my personal lover!" the Gay Lord exclaimed. "I demand your total obedience in this regard, or else you'll be swiftly and promptly executed at dawn."

You can imagine the great consternation and the tremendous pressure I felt at that unique moment, when I had to immediately make a serious decision. "Oh, my great Gay Lord," I nervously prefaced. "By Allah's invincible will, I owe you much praise and kindness. Indeed, I'm one of your humble servants that prefers screwing and sodomizing women, rather than to sodomize or be sodomized by fat bald men," I reminded the asshole Emperor. "Therefore, I would prefer to marry a gorgeous lady, and take her as my sex-starved wife, rather than to have my ass dilated ten times a day by *your* very mediocre salami that looks more like an abbreviated, shriveled-up, ancient hot dog."

"Oh Sindbad; I'll see to it that you marry a lovely, intelligent, stunning woman, and next you'll automatically become a noble citizen of my land," the garrulous King explained. "Then, you can be in the saddle, so to speak, for the rest of your adult*ery* life in my magnificent kingdom that has only a few major laws, the most prominent one being freedom of sex."

"Is this woman I've been selected to marry wealthy, and does she bring me a fantastic dowry?" I innocently asked. "I don't wish to wed a pauper or a wench."

"She's my wife's fucked-up sister, and the woman likes straight sex even more than I enjoy perverted sex!" the talkative King indicated.

"And my screwed-up sister-in-law is not a virgin, and she already has had her maidenhead broken on a maiden voyage to Baghdad," the emperor roared as the knucklehead slapped his bony knees in glee. "You, Sindbad, being a roving sailor, would appreciate that fucked-up *naughty-*cal joke! Ha, ha, ha! And after you and she marry, then you both can live with us here in *The Palace,* which as you know, at night is converted into a terrific and spectacular burlesque and vaudeville orgy theater."

I was so flabbergasted I could not speak. I nodded my head in tacit approval of the King's extraordinary proposition, even though that was the first time I had ever been propositioned by a demented Gay Lord ruler. Finally, I carefully answered, "Oh great Faggot King, your fantastic wish is my command!"

So, the fickle Gay Emperor summoned a Kazi (and a Kamikaze) and told the two judges to marry me to a charming woman that had already been tested for venereal diseases, and who had been found to have only two lethal types. The woman (like her sister the Queen) owned many dairy farms, estates, and very profitable whorehouses throughout the land, that were all exempted from paying taxes and tribute to the Imperial Gay Emperor. As a result, all competing houses of prostitution had been forced out of business because the establishments had to pay the hedonistic Burger King ninety-percent of their profits as excessive taxes.

I really enjoyed humping and pumping my lovely prearranged spouse, whom I must admit, also gave me fabulous blow-jobs and exotic massages, too. I soon forgot about all of the myriad hardships and travails I had experienced as a struggling merchant sailor on my many exceptional voyages. The strange Gay King was so grateful sodomizing his faggot advisers in the saddle (that I had made for *his* white Arabian horse) that the horny fellow had provided me with my own miniature palace, along with a loyal staff of eunuch slaves and bisexual regal officers that I was allowed to discriminately screw economically, physically, and intellectually.

I promised myself, 'When I finally return to Baghdad on the majestic Tigris, I'll *bag* a few whores for my *dad* from this fucked-up land. Also,' I selfishly thought. 'I'll take my pretty wife to Baghdad to live with me, so that I won't be between Iraq and a hard place for the remainder of my goddamned existence on this insane maniacal planet.'

But destiny eventually governs cruelly over every man, and unfortunately, my fate was no exception. One morning, I learned that Almighty Allah had taken the wife of my neighbor. However, the information I next found-out really scared the shit out of me! I visited next door to comfort and mourn with my neighbor, who naturally was very despondent and disconsolate over his loss.

"Your beautiful wife is presently with Allah," I distinctly noted to the inconsolable husband. "And now she's enjoying His mercy, eternal sex, and suave kindness. Allah will surely in time grant you another wife with a wet, pink, juicy pussy," I assured the saddened fellow. "So, you should now be rejoicing rather than weeping, you stupid sentimental asshole!"

But then my sobbing neighbor revealed something rather perverted that almost made my swollen balls pop right off of my body. "Oh my friend," he sadly declared. "How can I ever enjoy another wife when I only have one more day left to live? That's not even enough time to jerk-off six times, and be lucky ejaculating five delightful sticky loads!"

"What the fuck's the matter with you!" I criticized quite out-of-character for my normally-tranquil demeanor. "You're as healthy as a bull, or as potent as a studhorse in heat. You're strong, rich, powerful and bisexual!" I elaborated. "Surely you can acquire another attractive wife in a jiffy, and then give her many jiffy lubes!"

"My dear, straight friend," the sorrowful bisexual man ruefully continued. "I swear to you that tomorrow, I'll be sentenced to die, and that you'll not again see me until *Judgment Day* when we'll both be presented with our virgin harems at that great brothel in the sky!" the moron stated as my neighbor pointed to the heavens, which just at that moment happened to be his bedroom ceiling.

"Stop speaking in moronic, ludicrous riddles, you fucked-up hysterical buffoon!" I boisterously yelled. "Explain yourself more precisely."

"It's a custom in this Gay Faggot King's land that when a married person dies, his or her spouse will also be buried the next day, so that neither may enjoy life after losing his or her mate," my thoroughly upset, fucked-up neighbor divulged. "Only the royal Faggot Burger King is exempt from this heinous law, so that's why he allows all of his advisers, and every other *burger* with *ham* on his dick muscle to screw *his* wife the Dairy Queen to death."

"By Allah," I shrieked in amazement. "This wretched tradition that you describe is a most horrible law that borders on being bizarrely grotesque. Not one of the Gay King's insubordinate subjects should ever be subjected to it!"

Soon, other mourners arrived at my melancholy neighbor's residence, even the pregnant women that were suffering from *mourning sickness*. Some of the sympathizers were skilled morticians that prepared the woman's limp body for proper burial. After setting her perfumed corpse upon the funeral bier, everyone in attendance drank three funeral beers each, and then we carried her body outside the city to "the cemetery". At a mountainside near the island's end, we stopped, dropped the funeral bier onto the ground and hardily imbibed three more funeral beers each while bullshitting and listening to the eternal sea beat its relentless surf upon the rocks.

Then, I was directed to help roll a huge stone, which was designed to secretly conceal a deep pitiful pit. I peered-down into the dark hollow, and its bleakness reminded me of a death tunnel. My perverted mind immediately imagined the vertical tunnel to be a giant perpendicular birth canal in reverse. On the count of three, and with the absence of ceremony, the pallbearers tossed the woman's corpse into the deep pit and we all heard her body smash against the rocky floor of the shadowy cave below.

"We save more funeral bier and cemetery plot expenses that way," one of the more parsimonious funeral attendees confidentially told me. "One must be frugal nowadays, so that one can save his money for good prostitutes, because good whores that want to do it for free are really fuckin' hard to find."

Then, the zany entourage tethered a rope around the fearful husband's waist, and soon lowered him down into the odd subterranean graveyard to be with his dead wife. As was *their* oddball custom, the mourners afforded the sentenced husband a jug of fresh water along with seven biscuits to sustain him, until his soul finally would reach the outskirts of heaven.

When the crying fool reached the bottom of the inescapable pit, the victim obediently untied himself. The mourners drew-back the rope, sealed-up the mouth of the burial grounds with the mammoth stone, drank three more funeral beers each, and then the drunken fools returned to the sprawling city. I stayed behind to pray for my dear neighbor's soul, and to study the awesome eternal sea.

"By Allah," I cried and protested. "This certainly is a terrible way to die." 'Holy tits!' I thought and realized. 'If my wife the Dairy Queen's sister dies, this same incredible bullshit is gonna' fuckin' happen to me!'

I ambled-back into the King's exotic city and sought-out His Majesty, who was sitting upon his palace bathroom throne, taking a standard royal dump. At that moment, I was quite disenchanted with the marriage/death law that *his* imperial government had been requiring and enforcing. Finally, I broke his serious concentration and asked the pecker-head a germane question.

"Oh, my Faggot Lord. Why do you bury the living with the dead?" I asked.

"It's a lot cheaper that way," the sanctimonious, Gay King glumly remarked. "We don't have to maintain two separate cemeteries; one for the dead, and one for the living. I must balance my friggin' fiscal budget every damned year, ya' know! I need more annual expenditures specifically earmarked for royal pleasure and for regal entertainment!"

"No, Your Highness," I attempted to clarify. "Why does an implausible law exist in your land where the living spouse must be buried with his or her dead marriage partner? The law seems to defy all conventional morality!"

"Sindbad," the Gay Monarch very deliberately answered. "You're of course referring to an ancient custom handed-down from my island's sacred *dead* ancestors. When a husband or wife dies, the spouse must die too, leaving the entire estate to the King. How the fuck do ya' think I can stay so rich and maintain such an opulent and decadent lifestyle?" the avaricious Emperor maintained. "And besides, Asshole. The husband and wife can obviously be reunited in the afterlife. It works-out well for them, too, but most of all, it works-out for me!"

"Oh, noble Faggot King; if the wife of a foreigner such as I Sindbad should fall ill and perish," I hypothesized and articulated, "would I then predictably be buried the same day with my wife, even though I come from another land?"

"Sure as hell, yes, you would," the King abruptly indicated. "And why not? Why should a dumb ass like *you* inherit my sister-in-law's great wealth when you weren't even born anywhere near my wondrous kingdom? Sindbad; are you some kind of ambitious, parasitic, gigolo, or what?"

When I heard the Queer King's verification of my worst-case scenario, my nuts shriveled-up to the size of raisins, and my dick nearly turned inside-out. My mind became dizzy and dazed, and I felt trapped in the horrid jail cell known as my Gay Emperor's kingdom. I left the opulent palace in an absolute stupor, wishing that I had never dreamed of owning a chain of fucked-up hamburger taverns in the fucked-up Burger King's shitty-assed, regal country.

'I don't want my fat-assed wife to die, and then have to be buried alive next to her,' I feared. 'Who the hell wants to have sex with his dead wife? It's bad enough to have it when she's fuckin' alive. Maybe I'll get my dick and balls caught in some kind of machine having moving parts,' I speculated, 'and I'll luckily die first, before my wife gives-up the ghost! Oh Allah; please show me such a splendid God-sent mutilation machine when I'm ninety-nine years old, and am an old handicapped fuck too old to fuck!'

I then intentionally distracted my already-confused mind from further contemplating the uncivilized marriage/death law by occupying myself performing certain daily tasks and mundane chores. But a month later, my native-born, obese wife became ill while having her bloody period, and then she unexpectedly died inside a cow pasture two days later.

Now, I was scared, anxious, paranoid, neurotic, and pissed-off beyond belief (all at the same time). The Burger King and his wife the Dairy Queen came to my small palace to console me in regard to the death of my spouse, and in regard to my awaiting fate. I felt like cutting all of their balls, dicks, and tits off with my trusty scimitar, but there were two-dozen distressed mourners present for me to successfully kill everyone, without eventually sacrificing my already doomed life, too, during the melee.

The women then cleansed and perfumed my wife's corpulent body, which remarkably was still having its period even hours after her untimely death. She was lavishly dressed in a white gown, and expensive golden necklaces and bracelets adorned her neck and arms. Then, the contrite trite mourners all drank beers, lifted her bier and next transported my dead spouse to the mountain having the aforementioned macabre, deep-cave cemetery. The funeral procession halted, dropped the bier onto the ground, and the participants predictably drank three more beers each, but I wasn't the least bit thirsty. I felt like I had to verbally condemn the assholes for wanting to lower my valued ass into the morose death pit.

"Almighty Allah had never instituted such a disgusting law as the one you totally-despicable shit-heads evilly practice and adhere to," I futilely protested. "And I absolutely hate your wicked custom. Had I known about it, I would've remained single, and would've been content screwing the Dairy Queen's rich sister, along with ten-thousand other horny whores soliciting sex on this damned, remote, Allah-forsaken island!"

"Ha, ha, ha!" the thoroughly-amused Burger King laughed, inspiring his entire funeral procession entourage to imitate his inane insane zaniness in a "Chameleon Effect Behavior". "Only stupid men find out too late that marriage is always a death trap, no matter who the hell dies first!" the repulsive Ruler cruelly ridiculed.

After apathetically dumping my wife's chubby body into the pit, the muscular funeral bier carriers then grabbed my arms, tied me up against my will (I didn't actually need *a will* because the Burger King would automatically acquire my small palace and savings anyway), and then lowered me into the dark hollow with a jug of fresh water along with seven dry biscuits. When I finally had been descended to the bottom of the hundred-foot-deep cavern, the attendees yelled for me to untie myself', so that my executioners, by default, could pull-up the rope.

"Fuck you, you cheap niggardly bastards!" I screamed-up. "The fuckin' rope stays down here with me!"

"Up your peasant-class, lowlife yazoo, Sindbad!" the infuriated Burger King hollered-down. "You're at the end of your rope anyway, you dumb, misguided, idealistic jerk-off!"

The heavy rope was tossed-down, and it nearly knocked me unconscious when its mass landed directly onto my head. Next, the jolly sadists rolled the enormous stone in front of the pit, sealing me inside the dank, morbid graveyard, without a damned hint or clue as how to escape.

Sufficient dim light existed for me to peruse my immediate surroundings, which were very unpleasant to see and to smell. The stenchy cave was full of decayed and decaying bodies, with many male skeletons situated on top of (what I believed to be) female anatomies. Apparently, the husbands had endeavored screwing their deceased wives, or their outside-of-marriage former girlfriends, one final time. The underground cavern's air was full of a putrid odor from the numerous rotting corpses, and I heard the groans and moans of the dying off in the distance, instinctively electing to enjoy sex with new-found partners one final time, before expiring into the dreaded, opaque afterworld.

'By Allah,' I apprehensively thought. 'I deserve such an ignoble death, since I've undoubtedly been a complete fucked-up asshole my entire life!' I penitently concluded. 'I'm so depressed that I don't even feel like penetrating my wife's cold, perfumed, cleansed pussy, still having its period. And to think of how totally fucked-up I've been all my damned errant life before ever arriving at this entirely fucked-up place! It's the absolute pits!'

I sorrowfully meditated on my unbearable misfortune for a long time. 'Oh, Allah the Glorious, oh Allah the Great!' I courageously prayed. 'You've graciously allowed me to escape one catastrophe after another, and I now beseech You to permit me to survive this inhuman tribulation, so that I may escape this abominable land, and screw normal women with hairy pink pussies back in Baghdad! Please spare me of this impending miserable, demoralizing, uncivilized, and humiliating death!'

My mind cursed the Devil and praised Allah, hoping for either a miracle, or for instant salvation. I threw myself onto a heap of bones, rubbed my crotch against them, and could not even get a decent boner. I prayed for Death to envelop me, but even The Fiend appeared to be on vacation. I was besieged with hunger and thirst, so I felt-around for the biscuits, ate one of them that happened to be covered with insects, and surprisingly the damned bugs tasted much better than did the small cake I had swallowed. I quenched my dire thirst by greedily gulping-down several mouthfuls of water from the leaky jug I had been provided.

I stood, and then in the shadowy recesses, explored the extensive cavern, discovering many small side caves, but none leading anywhere except to Death. Hideous corpses, skeletons, and raunchy-smelling, decaying flesh were present everywhere. Many now-brittle bones from ancient times had broken-off from their owners' frames. I finally crawled into a small, secluded cave where I gingerly curled-up into the fetal position, and soundly slept from sheer exhaustion.

After my food supply had become depleted three days later, I desperately searched-around and pilfered several cakes from other more feeble victims that had also been doomed to be buried with their wives. 'I hope my supplies don't run out before I die,' I solemnly prayed. 'I don't want to die from starvation. Perhaps Allah will mercifully rescue me from this horrid relentless Devil's environment!'

After I had consumed my final cake, a startling thing happened. The stone was again rolled-back, and a deceased man was thrown down to his grave. Then, a gorgeous woman was lowered along with fresh biscuits and a new water jug. I carefully watched her weeping from my secluded corner of the cave, and the beautiful lady did not suspect my presence while enduring her burdensome grief. Soon, the huge stone was rolled-back into place, and the accursed cave was dark once more. 'This part of the King's burg is the absolute pits!' I despairingly reckoned. 'Maybe its original name was Pittsburgh.'

Next, I inexplicably turned into a wanton madman. I rapturously raped the frightened, grieving woman, and pumped her pussy dry before irrigating her hot receptive hole with warm semen from this lustful seaman. Then, when the woman asked me for more sex to comfort her great grief, I reached for and lifted a huge thighbone, and banged her over the head three consecutive times with the solid femur. The despondent wife moaned, groaned, and then went unconscious.

I found a nearby corpse buried in a sack. I removed the covering, and then lustily gathered-up all of the necklaces, bracelets, rings, gems, trinkets, and jewelry that the deceased had been wearing when the rich bitch had been buried. I conveyed my new food supply and my pilfered acquisitions to the nearby remote side cave, where I ate and covetously felt my booty sack, and alternately rubbed my scrotum sac. 'I must survive, escape, and live, so that I can be a wealthy nasty bastard,' I pondered. 'Then, I could tell the damned Devil to go fuck himself' up the ass with his jagged, ugly, long, red dick!'

Every time a live spouse was lowered into the repugnant mass tomb, I killed him or her, and confiscated the jewelry, the biscuits and the damned water. I was going insane from greed, murder, and an obsessive lust for life and sex. I humanely rescued the first beautiful woman I had knocked unconscious, and shared my biscuits, dick, and water (and she shared her biscuits, buns, pussy, and tits) in exchange for standard straight, subterranean sex. I promised the still-dazed, disheveled and distraught wife that I would find and kill the scumbag bastard that had knocked her silly with the solid femur bone.

"How do you know that someone hit me over the head and knocked me silly with a solid femur bone?" the confused spouse boldly and surprisingly asked.

"I saw the nefarious, brutal bastard's shadow do it to you," I instinctively lied. "But at the time, I was too damned weak and disabled to stand upright, let alone fight him to the death."

"Okay, show me *that* nifty sixty-nine position again!" the woman pleaded, entirely forgetting about her dead husband, his dead dick, and about the phantom molester wielding the solid femur bone.

One night, I was awakened from my slumber by something mysteriously scratching and digging inside the cavern. I raised my trusty femur bone, left my snoring female companion sleeping soundly, and then cautiously advanced toward the noise's origin. I perceived a wild beast (similar to a wolf in its mannerisms) and pursued the animal to an extremity of the cavern. Suddenly, I noticed points of light from the night sky, and I immediately recognized the celestial objects as twinkling stars in the *Orion* constellation, which I knew from my knowledge of sailor astronomy, would be at that particular position in the firmament. There were crevices formed in the cave's rocks, and never before had I enjoyed a mere hole in the earth more than I cherished a woman's hairy love tunnel.

The cavern's crack was indeed better than a woman's pussy, and the hungry wolf-like creature had penetrated it with its entire body. I assiduously labored, making the newly-discovered opening wider, and soon the space was big enough to allow a human to crawl through. Then, I proceeded back to my secret hiding place, caressed the sleeping woman's tits, but regrettably, squirted discharge all over her face in a premature ejaculation when she (in her rapturous sleep) thereafter sucked on my stiff, wet, pulsating erection. The gorgeous lady instantly awakened, and next, I carried my booty sack, and led her to the newly located and expanded cavern aperture, which we each individually and easily squeezed through.

My lady companion and I rested upon the mountain's slope overlooking the inviting, salty sea. We were fatigued, but overjoyed at our escape from the disgusting pit.

"Look," I revealed to the attractive female. "There's enough jewelry in this sack to buy a chain of hamburger joints, or barbecue beef greasy spoons, anywhere on this Allah-forsaken planet!"

"You've stolen from the dead?" my wonderful woman companion asked and maintained in a shocked but rather sanctimonious voice.

"Why should I not? These gems and expensive golden items would only go to waste and rust underground back there in that hideous mass cemetery!" I adamantly argued. "If you're smart and practical, you'll permit me to share them with you."

"You're smarter than the average wolf or bear, I must say," the knockout doll complimented. "Just give me back the articles that originally belonged to me, and I'll verify your complete story, whatever your crazy story may be, to anyone in authority that challenges or disbelieves it."

"We'll camp-out on this campy mountain under the eternal stars," I suggested to my new-found female comrade. "Perhaps a passing ship will spot us before the smallpox will spot us."

I committed numerous other ungodly atrocities short of cannibalism just to stay alive. Each week I re-entered the cave and used my trusty femur weapon to club a recently buried-alive victim. Then, I would eagerly steal his or her biscuits and water for sustenance, along with his or her jewelry for prospective wealth for both me and for my grateful lady accomplice.

One late spring day, I observed a ship sailing on the eastern horizon. I removed my woman companion's dirty white tunic, and waved it in the air, realizing that the sailors would come in response to a naked woman's body first, and to my animated distress signal second. The mariners quickly noticed us perched upon the steep mountain slope, and sent-out a salvage boat to investigate.

"Who are you?" the bewildered crewmen bellowed. "We've never before seen any human standing on this treacherous slope!"

"I'm the famous Sindbad of Baghdad," I proudly replied. "And this is my humble wife. We had been stranded here by ruthless road bandits, but then I killed them all with my bare hands, cut their testicles off with my scimitar, and tossed their scumbag bodies and balls into the eternal sea."

"Holy shit!" one of the rowers hollered-up to us. "Sindbad the Sailor! You're very acclaimed all over the world! Your fabulous reputation and exploits precede you! You're more famous in these parts than even fuckin' Popeye the Sailor! You even make Popeye seem wimpy!"

My new wife and I hopped-down into the sturdy rowboat, and we were speedily transported to the sailors' merchant ship. Once the captain found-out my identity, he warmly shook my hands, and out of sheer fear, forgot all about his diabolical intentions of fondling, porking, and sodomizing my "new virgin wife".

"Could I offer you some pearls and diamonds in exchange for safely being conducted to Baghdad?" I inquired as I jiggled my sack containing valuable rings, necklaces, trinkets, and bracelets into the thoroughly-amused captain's face.

The captain rose above the strong temptation I had offered. "Sindbad, I would never fuck with anyone of your tough international repute," the honest fellow indulgently laughed. "And if we're attacked by pirates near this dangerous place known as Pittsburgh, I'm sure that even their swollen hemorrhoids would shrink-back once the lawless buccaneers learned of *your* noble name."

"Thank you, my lord, for safely rescuing us from the gruesome mountain overlooking the sea," I gratefully acknowledged. "And if you please, show my wife and me to a quiet room where we can get washed-up and have some decent food along with some frantic sex in absolute privacy."

"It's our fucked-up custom that whenever we find a shipwrecked man, it's our duty to feed and clothe him, and then take the lucky prick free-of-charge to his native port," the captain confidentially disclosed. "But quite truthfully, this is the first time I've ever picked-up a stranded man and a stranded woman! I must pray to Allah for some new instructional guidance!"

My new wife and I graciously thanked the cooperative captain for his diligent assistance, and also for his benign generosity. We entered our cabin, ate a decent meal, had fantastic sex, and when I exited to fetch a pitcher of water, I witnessed eight sailors eavesdropping with their left ears against inverted glasses on the side of our ship's quarters, while simultaneously intensively jerking-off with their right hands. When I returned to the room with the fresh water, my new mistress and I prayed to Allah on behalf of the captain and his sex-starved crew, and then we got it on again.

As we sailed by the Burger King's coastal metropolis, my new mistress and I both gave the pompous Gay Emperor of the land and his arrogant Dairy Queen wife the royal double middle fingers. The ship voyaged to the Island of Bell, and next the vessel sailed onward to Kala near the land of Hind, where *hind*sight was always better than foresight. Hind was famous for its rattan and camphor marketplace, which incidentally had been constructed out of those particular rare materials. The next stop on our journey was Al Basrah, and finally the sturdy ship sailed up the Tigris and docked and anchored at Baghdad.

"What are you going to do with your magnificent treasure trove?" my very curious mistress asked.

"I'll give a ten percent donation to all of the Fakirs and to all of the mangy Mother-Fakirs in Baghdad," I honestly informed her. "And some of my fortune I'll use to establish a viable hamburger restaurant chain just to spite the deplorable Gay Burger King. And when I've exhausted the remainder of my fortune on you and me Shahrazad," I continued with a wry smile, "I shall sell you into slavery to a tiny-dicked king, and soon return to the sea for more superb adventures, wild sex, and valuable plunder."

"Don Quixote Fights the Windmill"
Miguel de Cervantes

Miguel de Cervantes (1547-1616) was born near Madrid, Spain. His family was indigent, and Miguel grew up in abject poverty. Seeking misadventure and escape from destitution, Miguel fought gallantly in a war against the Turks in 1570, and subsequently sustained serious wounds at the battle of Lepanto. The ship carrying Cervantes was returning to Spain when Mediterranean pirates captured the vessel. Everyone aboard was transported to Algiers, and imprisoned for ransom. Five-years later, Cervantes was released with the help of sympathetic friars, who didn't like to *monk*ey around.

Miguel de Cervantes was later appointed a tax collector, and when the maverick tried obtaining taxes from church property, the appointee was promptly thrown into jail. That is where Cervantes spent a great deal of his idle time authoring the classic novel *Don Quixote,* which was first published in 1605. As a tax collector, soldier, ghetto dweller, and prisoner, Miguel Cervantes studied the unique characters in his company, and in the process, learned an immense treasury of knowledge about human nature.

In Miguel de Cervantes' wonderful novel, Don Quixote was a valiant old knight that lived his withering adult life as an anachronism, who was constantly in conflict with the traditional-but-contemporary institutions of Spain. Despite his earnest efforts to right all social wrongs, the idealistic poor fellow thought that he was an adventurous knight errant, several-hundred-years *after* such crusading idiots had become extinct from human history.

With the aid of a corpulent neighbor, Sancho *Panza* (big stomach in Spanish), whom Don Quixote appointed as *his* noble loyal squire, the two fools journeyed throughout Spain from Granada to Barcelona to right all wrongs, and subsequently, interfere into, and consequently fuck-up, other people's lives. Don Quixote's battle with the windmill is a famous chapter from Miguel de Cervantes' inimitable novel.

* * * * * * * * * * * * *

While the Knight Errant and his faithful squire Sancho Panza were lost somewhere on a plain about a half-mile from their La Mancha homes, the fat assistant had something irrelevant to say to his most benign master.

"Sir Knight, remember that you had promised me that I'm to become governor of an important island," Sancho sincerely reminded and communicated. "I feel that I should achieve greatness and be respectfully and accurately recorded in history books, before my ass and my soul leave this totally fucked-up Earth."

"It is an excellent tradition among knights of yore, as well as with contemporary crusaders, to make their squires special emeritus governors over conquered islands," Don Quixote readily verified, "because certainly, a fool like you, my dear Sancho, could do a much better job than the asshole governors already incompetently governing over governed islands."

"When will I ascend to such a high responsibility?" Sancho curiously asked. "When will I trade in my donkey Dapple for a soft velvet throne? My hanging balls are getting crushed whenever I bounce up and down, riding this spotted jackass all over the worst parts of Spain, looking for fucked-up misadventures and fucked-up people to fuck-up some more!"

"As soon as *we* conquer our first kingdom, you'll get to become an illustrious emeritus governor, but the elusive kingdom must be an island," Don Quixote pledged and qualified to his irascible partner. "The propitious appointment might transpire in a mere six-days or it might require six decades, whichever unpredictable event happens to come first."

"But Senor Don Quixote; kingdoms, as I understand kingdoms to be, are usually always on land," Sancho argued in a very puzzled tone of voice. "And kingdoms around these fucked-up, forsaken parts aren't usually islands, or don't have any islands inside their kingdoms, which I've already fuckin' said when I specifically stated that kingdoms are always on land, meaning continents or peninsulas."

"Don't be silly, my corpulent, inquisitive squire," Don Quixote sternly emphasized. "For I foresee that you'll most definitely become ruler of an island, as soon as we two adventurers conquer a kingdom rampant with immoral infidels. My statement would not be less valid if it were either written or engraved on stones, just like the sacred *Ten Commandments* were."

"Just don't engrave all those fuckin' shit-eatin' words on *my* sensitive stones," Sancho comically insisted. "And Senor Don Quixote; would my raunchy wife, Joan, be a queen, and my six obnoxious children princes and princesses on this very special island you've mentioned?" Sancho wanted to know. "I mean, Master; the only goddamned reason I've foolishly accompanied you on this shit-head exploit was to get the fuck away from all seven of those fucked-up assholes!"

"There's no doubt in my mind that your *governorship* will be your major claim to fame," Quixote answered his squire with great certainty and moral clarity. "And if you wish to appoint your wife queen, and your children princes and princesses, then that'll be *your* exclusive executive privilege."

"Holy shit!" Sancho exclaimed. "Not only will I become a governor, but I'll have my own damned 'governor's ship' of state anchored in my harbor, too!"

"Is your humble family ready to become royalty?" Don Quixote sincerely asked. "With such supreme titles comes great commitment, along with tremendous duties and responsibilities!"

"My wife eats too many vegetables, and farts all the damned time, so I think she'll make a better countess than she would a queen," Sancho all-too-honestly answered. "And to tell you the truth, Senor Don Quixote, my dysfunctional sons and my flirtatious daughters would make better prisoners and prostitutes than the imbeciles would as functioning princes and princesses."

As the two erudite crusaders were conducting their ludicrous, meaningless, esoteric conversation, Don Quixote caught sight of forty-windmills in a row, rotating their blades on a distant open plain. The demented master announced to his fat squire, "Fortune is looking out for us today, dear Sancho. It's like a magnetic beacon of light guiding us in the direction of fame and international repute. Behold, my dear squire," Don Quixote seriously indicated with all his heart and soul. "At least; a hundred monstrous giants are defiantly aligning within our view, and all desire to do battle against us."

"But Senor Don Quixote," Sancho replied with amazement and apparent concern. "Those objects are only fuckin' ordinary windmills you're seeing, and not fierce, aggressive giants as you maintain."

"After we engage and defeat the intruders in honorable combat," Don Quixote lectured Panza, "their spoils will make us rich. We shall perform great service for the world in general, and for Spain in particular, if we could successfully eradicate those evil monsters from the face of the Earth."

"But Master, they're only commonplace rotating windmills," Sancho futilely insisted. "If those suckers are truly giants, then I claim that my dick is long enough to lap up water like Dapple's mouth does, and that my talented asshole can bite, chew and swallow just like *your* asinine mouth can do."

"Those awesome giants have very long arms, Sancho," Don Quixote erroneously observed and related. "And quite obviously, they're vile ogres indeed, for they each possess more than two arms, like ordinary humans and ordinary monsters do."

"Take special care, Master," Sancho Panza gasped in terror. "I've already told you that those things are ordinary windmills, and not the extraordinary threats that you perceive them to be. The arms are merely spinning sails being whirled-around by the strong wind," the squire articulated, "so therefore, *you* must be one fucked-up, mentally retarded sick-pup asshole if *you* think and believe that those windmills are what the fuck ya' say they are!"

Don Quixote cleared his throat to demonstrate to his assistant that the insane knight was ready to engage in violent battle. "It's plainly evident, Sancho, that *you* are deficient in matters regarding arduous adventure, and that you totally lack experience in evaluating the obvious circumstances associated with battle," the master chastised. "If thou art afraid to confront the giants, I assure you that your cowardice is completely understandable to me! I've spent decades developing both courage and audacity. It's unfortunate that I must take advantage of such weak foes as those that are presently impeding our forward progress. The upcoming brief confrontation will undoubtedly be one-sided in our favor."

So, saying those idiotic but most noble and wonderful words, Don Quixote applied his spurs to his ready-to-die old white plow horse Rozinante, which heeded his master's war cries, and lazily trotted-off at a speed of two-miles an hour.

"You'll regret being so goddamned *mil*itant!" Sancho yelled to his imaginative superior. "At least, you should get your stupid butt kicked by humans, you dumb, stubborn asshole!"

Don Quixote ignored Sancho's desperate pleas, and shouted insults to the distant windmills, which possessed no ears to hear him, and were too far away to ever hear him even if they did have ears. "Fly not away you heinous malignant creatures, for even though you're the plague of this sacred territory, I, Don Quixote, Knight of La Mancha, shall vanquish your malice, and you'll all pay a heavy price for your insolence when I decisively pound you into oblivion."

A heavy breeze sprung-up at that very moment, and the great sails on the forty-windmills began rotating faster than they had been revolving before. This new activity inspired Don Quixote to challenge, "Although you beasts wield more arms than the giant Briareus," the valiant, senile, old man in armor yelled to his imagined adversaries as he pointed his lance forward upon Rozinante, "this memorable, historic assault you'll not be able to recollect; for you parasitic despots will soon be dead and thoroughly eliminated from your wretched existence."

Sancho Panza was not quite as delusional as his crazy and bizarre master was. The impish, irascible, stocky squire was much more practical and worldly than his cavalier-minded leader could ever aspire to be.

"I gallantly dedicate this contest to Lady Dulcinea de Toboso, whose precious, pristine beauty is most sacred and esteemed within my tender heart!" Don Quixote nobly exclaimed as Rozinante strained to quicken his pace to a maximum speed of four-miles an hour.

"Senor Don Quixote!" Sancho screamed ahead. "Dulcinea is even a bigger whore than my lustful hog wife is, and *that* ugly, horny bitch you love was an admitted nymphomaniac when she was only eleven-years-old!"

But Don Quixote was resolute in demonstrating his inflexible stubbornness. Rozinante trotted-ahead toward the first windmill, and didn't know any better, because the poor creature was nearly blind, and certainly deaf and apathetic. The intrepid knight thrust his wooden lance forward with great vigor, and its tip amazingly penetrated one of the whirling sails, which then lifted the undaunted Don Quixote into the air, and the temporarily thwarted knight soon found himself being "manhandled by the giant", as his aged body made a quick rotation. The stellar knight was then un-gently deposited upon the dusty ground, where Don Quixote slowly rolled-down an embankment, and ten-seconds-later, finally stopped face-down with his entire body slightly damaged.

Sancho rushed to the battle scene as fast as he could upon old Dapple. The chunky squire leaped-down from his spotted donkey to assist his completely disoriented master. "Senor Don Quixote; I told you that those massive things were windmills and not giants!" the aide reminded his chief benefactor, whose mind at that particular moment was filled with swirling comets, asteroids, planets, stars, and galaxies. "Why can't you simply dedicate your fucked-up life to sex and whiskey, so that I then could see some merit in your asshole pursuits?"

"If that giant was a windmill as you say," the hoary, errant knight returned, "then my dear Sancho, it certainly was not your everyday run-of-the-mill windmill."

"Master, you must see reality for what it is, and not imagine it to be some twisted fairy tale," Sancho Panza asserted. "You need bed-rest very badly!"

"Peace be with your admirable spirit, my dear Sancho," Don Quixote uttered as the defeated cavalier managed to get to his knees. "The very complicated rules of combat engagements are constantly changing both in nature and in complexity, my beloved squire, and I'm thoroughly convinced that this insolent trickery has been the work of the evil sage Freston that had maliciously stolen all my books about knights and about heroism from my wonderful library shelves."

"What the fuck' are ya' talkin' about?" Sancho incredulously yelled. "The shit-head wizard Freston just exists in unpopular gaudy fantasy tales! Freston is about as real as are the giant pyramids over in England!"

"Sancho," Quixote obstinately argued. "It's an undeniable fact that Freston had changed those fifty formidable giants into windmills at the last second to deliberately deprive me of my decisive victory over *his* treacherous evil. For the vile sorcerer Freston is indeed the Devil's ally, and the heinous magician even has the power to move the great pyramids from Egypt to England if *he* wanted to. But also, dear Sancho," the noble sage concluded and vociferously stated, "Freston's black art will be no match for the swift justice that my trusty sword and lance will command."

"Master, you need a fuckin' exorcist, a fine enema, and then a good blow-job from Dulcinea de Toboso in that exact order," Sancho sympathetically advised. "But first, I must attend to your needs because you're all bruised-up and battered, and indeed Sir Knight, you actually look like both Freston and Briareus had conspired, and then together collaborated in really beating the livin' shit out of you."

At three o'clock the next afternoon, the dynamic pair journeyed along the Pass of Lapice, which was a popular spot richly recorded in romantic tradition. "Here Sancho," the inimitable master declared, "we may meet the wonderful challenges and quests of which I had previously alluded. But my faithful squire," Don Quixote continued his absurd prattle, "you shall not raise a sword and shall not come to my assistance, regardless of how abnormal or overwhelming the odds might appear against me. I must ultimately triumph, regardless of how many foes I'm called-upon to simultaneously vanquish."

"Senor Don Quixote," the squire answered. "Pardon my objection, but only vulgar lowlife assholes travel through *this* fucked-up valley, and they'll surely kick the organs and the shit out of you far worse than Freston and Briareus had just done yesterday, and then the greedy bastards will gladly rob you of your money; take you hostage, and hold you for ransom," Sancho pragmatically cautioned. "I know the ways of those shit-head jerk-offs, and believe me when I say that the best policy is to steer clear of the dangerous rabble. Fucked up people only know how to fuck you and me up, and that's the simple fuckin' truth of the whole fuckin' matter. Fucked-up people only know how to do fucked-up things!"

"That is why only I should defend *us* against their repulsive wickedness," Don Quixote proudly insisted. "So, my dear Sancho. You just stay in the background while I pound and trounce my craven-but-powerful enemies into submission with a vengeance never before seen on this sin-laden planet."

"I've always been a peaceful man, which others have falsely interpreted as cowardice," Sancho admirably admitted. "I have a strong dislike for quarrels and fights of any kind, for the longer I live, the more I can get laid and blown by ugly whores, and to me Senor Quixote," the squire indicated, "natural and oral sex are more important than even the very best foods, or even much better than shitting big brown, healthy-looking turds, after eating the very best fattening foods!"

While the pair of adventurers bickered and exchanged their standard nonsense, two friars affiliated with the *Order of St. Benedict,* mounted on large mules (big enough to be camels heading toward the pyramids in

England), appeared approaching the knight and his squire from the opposite direction.

"Look, Sancho," Don Quixote alertly noted. "Those simpleton bandits are wearing masks to terrorize those potential victims in the vicinity they intend to rob. This is a most fortuitous opportunity for me to defend the principles of right against the perversions of wrong! I absolutely despise meandering, pernicious individuals!"

"Senor Don Quixote," Sancho futilely challenged. "Those are merely traveling friars wearing masks to keep the dust from the ground along with the gross smell from their jackasses' asses' out of *their'* friggin' nostrils. They're only commonplace friars!"

"And look carefully, Sancho," Don Quixote proceeded with his absurd monologue. "The robbers are also kidnappers, who are accompanied by five confederates on horseback that have captured a traveling Queen or Princess riding in *her* coach! It's my imminent mission to free the fair maiden from her most-perilous, life-threatening custody."

"But Senor Don Quixote," the equally-alert squire balked. "Those are merely servants guarding the Biscayan lady heading for Seville to visit a renowned barber in that city to have her pubic hairs trimmed. The two asshole men on mules are separate traveling friars, who are not in her company."

But before the Knight Errant could evaluate and comprehend Sancho's perceptive observations, the self-appointed enforcer of justice sallied forth in haste to engage in his next preposterous conflict. "I can *plainly* see that those vile enchanters are holding that unfortunate Princess hostage against her will," the misguided knight shouted. "And it is my sacred duty to free the beautiful royal heiress from *their* ignoble capture."

"Senor Don Quixote, I beg you not to fuckin' interfere into the lives of ordinary people doing ordinary things!" Sancho loudly yelled to no avail. "Those muscular guards will do you more harm than the fuckin' windmill had done. Please listen to reason, and stop acting like an absolute dumb-fuck jerk-off!"

Even though Don Quixote was going as fast as the befuddled gentleman could upon Rozinante, Dapple was easily able to keep pace with the ancient plow horse, so Sancho was capable of still engaging in strange conversation with his crazy employer.

"I've told you several times," the knight repeated to his squire, "that thou Sancho are exceedingly ignorant in the matters of chivalrous engagement. What I tell you is the pertinent truth, and thou shall one day realize the veracity of my words."

"Go ahead and get your ass kicked and mutilated!" Sancho hollered in disgust. "Fools' like you deserve to get their stupid asses' kicked and savagely maimed, mauled, mangled and mutilated!"

When Don Quixote finally accosted the targeted friars, the encroacher surprised the priests by exclaiming in a booming voice, "Horrible and detestable villains! Surrender immediately the lovely Princess you vile scoundrels have captured and are carrying-away in that uncouth-looking jail-coach behind you! If you do not accede to my precise demand," the demented knight emphasized, "prepare to be the recipients of instant death, as my just and swift punishment of your sinful and criminal ways shall implement!"

The itinerant masked friars looked at each other in total amazement, and held tightly to their donkeys' reins. One of the monks realized that he had been stopped by a ludicrous old man, who was going through the cruel ordeal of enjoying *his* second childhood.

"Sir Knight," the friar amiably laughed. "We are not savage monsters as you've erroneously depicted, but only two religious men of the *Benedictine Order*, traveling about our business going from one city to another. We know nothing of the lady in the coach behind us and of her attendants, other than that they are fellow travelers."

"I recognize treacherous knaves whenever I see, hear, or smell them," Don Quixote obstinately maintained. "And I assure you that you'll certainly pay for your loathsome lies, in addition to your un-repenting pirate ways, unscrupulously holding innocent people hostage for ransom," the decrepit old knight audaciously declared. "Prepare to meet your doomed fate, you perverted rogues, as I methodically and conclusively administer earthly justice!"

The brave liberator did not wait for a plausible reply from the flabbergasted friars, and energetically applied his spurs to Rozinante. The deranged Knight lowered his wooden lance as the white plow horse again achieved its maximum speed of four-miles an hour.

Don Quixote attacked the astounded monks with great fury and ferocity, and if the two friars had not leapt from their beasts of transportation, the duo surely would have been injured, if not maimed, during the remarkable encounter. The two frightened clerics scurried in haste,, and finally made it to a canyon rock formation where the pair managed to quickly and neurotically ascend to safety.

Sancho Panza immediately dismounted from Dapple, and dashed-over to sincerely apologize to the awed friars, who were avidly praying to Heaven for deliverance from their most recent earthly trauma. After thanking God for their miraculous escape, the first out-of-breath priest removed his mask and initiated a conversation with the stocky squire.

"Are you taking that knight fellow to a prison, or conducting him to an advanced mental asylum?" the curious first friar asked.

356

"No, your Holiness," Sancho answered as if he were addressing a pope. "My master truthfully believes he's a knight, and that you two men were typical everyday road bandits. I admit that you priests *are* thieves that live lazy rich lives by robbing innocent people through generous church donations and contributions," Panza clarified, "but that's no reason for my master to go positively berserk, and attempt knocking the shit and piss out of you!"

The two friars were so pissed-off at Sancho for insulting their monastic way of life that the colleagues leapt-down from the jagged rocks, and pounded the living feces out of poor Panza, who as usual, paid a heavier price for Don Quixote's idealistic nonsense than the master did himself'. The livid monks tore every hair out of the screaming Sancho's mustache, nose, beard, ears, and sideburns; kicked and mauled the stout squire without exhibiting any Christian clemency, and then finally left their humiliated victim lacerated, senseless and breathing most irregularly upon the hot, sandy desert.

While the luckless Sancho Panza was getting the feces and urine pounded out of him by the two incensed friars, Don Quixote rode Rozinante parallel to the woman's coach. "My dear Lady; may I beg your indulgence by introducing myself'," the peculiar intruder aptly stated. "I am invincible Don Quixote, Knight of La Mancha, and I've emancipated you from your most dangerous hostage situation. I've most-bravely defended your honor in the name of Dulcinea de Toboso, the most beautiful virgin residing this side of the great China Sea."

The stunned woman sat in her coach with her mouth agape, trying to figure-out the mystery of Don Quixote's very unorthodox deportment. Then, the great itinerant champion completed his preliminary remarks.

"Now that you're enjoying the benefits that my benign intercession has produced," Don Quixote confidently exhorted, "I request that you go directly to Toboso and tell my beloved Dulcinea of my glorious triumphant deed, and how I've set you free from a pack of heinous villains in my latest fabulous escapade."

"Who the fuck are you?" the aristocratically-dressed woman in the coach asked. "Do you have worms or shit for brains?"

Before Don Quixote could resume his crazy discourse, one of the woman's Biscayan servants brazenly and arrogantly dashed-up to the hero; grabbed the knight's vest; then confiscated the knight's wooden lance, and next easily broke the pole over *his* knee. "Get your goddamned ass out of our path, or else I shall kill thee as sure as I wipe my ass at least once a week," the servant vehemently yelled at the temporarily-bewildered crusader.

"If thou were a gentleman instead of being the scurrilous hypocrite that thou art," the quixotic Quixote sarcastically criticized his new-found teen enemy, "I would be more inclined to vanquish you in mortal combat. But since your egregious conduct indicates that you're nothing but a callow, shallow-minded, subordinate fellow of inferior ilk," the old pretentious knight articulated, "I shall not hesitate to thrash and pulverize you brutally should I feel compelled to do so."

"What! You say that I'm not a gentleman?" the insulted servant angrily retorted. "Draw your sword, you stupid old fuck, and then you'll see that I've adequately mastered the standard gentleman's fighting skills that you profess to possess."

"That event shall transpire presently, for I see that you must be taught a good lesson in respect and decency," the wacky knight imperatively replied. Don Quixote then awkwardly drew his wooden sword, and holding it tightly the fine knight flung himself off of Rozinante and landed squarely upon the arrogant Biscayan servant. The two pugnacious fellows savagely crashed against the coach, and the lady occupant instantly leaped-out, fearing that the fracas might continue inside the confined passenger compartment.

The other servants accompanying the apparently wealthy woman attempted to separate the two brawlers, but the crazed Biscayan lackey was so infuriated that he obnoxiously screamed, "If any of you dare stop or hinder me from killing this old demented, fucked-up lunatic, then I shall also slay you, and conveniently leave your fuckin' carcasses out here in the remote desert for the scavengers to devour!"

The livid Biscayan servant then delivered a most powerful blow with his sword to Don Quixote's stomach, and if the knight had not had his metal armor worn over that vital area, the old crusader would have been vulnerable, and easily severed in two. After losing his helmet's visor and part of *his* earlobe to the angry attacker's mighty hit, Don Quixote boldly bellowed-out, "Oh Dulcinea; lady of my many dreams and queen of my humble heart, may thy beauty motivate me, and thy love give me sufficient strength to win this great contest!" And then the old crazed hero glared at the thoroughly-peeved lackey and boomed, "You are doomed to defeat, you tawdry, offensive contemptible vassal!"

Don Quixote then rushed the young molester, and collided into his adversary with such violence that the impact sounded like an intense thunder clasp. The young guard's own shield smashed him in the jaw and nose, and blood squirted-out of the dizzy fellow's mouth, nostrils and ears. The lady's protector fell to the ground, victimized by the old demented, lucky knight's rage and incredible exuberance.

The victorious dueler then pointed the tip of his sword at the shocked guard's throat and commanded the haughty upstart to "yield or be slain."

The wealthy lady that had been riding inside the coach ran forward, exhibiting great grief, and the aristocrat begged on her knees that Don Quixote spare the life of her secret lowlife lover, that was not so secret anymore.

"Fair Lady, I shall mercifully grant your plea," Don Quixote benevolently acknowledged. "But I insist that you immediately dispatch this rank amateur that I have just defeated to the town of Toboso, where he is to seek-out and present himself to my immaculate-hearted Lady Dulcinea. After this raunchy, unsavory, saucy individual appears before my beloved damsel and tells her of my excellent exploit and victory," the gallant knight uttered, "then my Lady will deal with this lousy pond-scum as she sees fit."

"Your Dulcinea is the biggest whore in all of Spain, and she doesn't even get paid for her goddamned services," the brash young vanquished man sitting on the ground declared. "I myself have porked her at least a dozen-times, and have received at least a score of decent blow-jobs from *your* fair maiden!" the insolent scamp screamed at Don Quixote. "I'll gladly execute your command and immediately go to Toboso, just so that I can pump Dulcinea's pussy dry once again."

"Shut thy foul mouth, or else I shall be inclined to dislodge your neck from your shoulders!" Don Quixote yelled like a maniac at the totally humiliated Biscayan that had been quite vanquished by a feeble old coot who believed that *he* had been engaged in brutal and lethal man-to-man combat.

"Do and obey exactly as this noble knight has commanded!" the rich woman directed her livid servant. "Dulcinea once worked in one of my bordellos, and I want *you,* Carlos, to see if she'll return and again work for salary plus commission!" the successful Madame instructed. "I need another experienced, veteran hooker in my Seville whorehouse!"

"Thank you, my kind Lady," Don Quixote commended the Madame without ever realizing the full extent of the conversation. "It is because of your courteous demeanor that I release this lowlife to your custody and servitude. Get-up to your feet right now, you dastardly, despicable clown!"

Sancho Panza managed to also rise to his feet near the ridge of rocks, and the beleaguered squire gingerly hobbled over to his remarkable master. "Oh, most cavalier neighbor and most dynamic knight," the squire commented, and then kissed Don Quixote's bloody and grimy right hand. "Now that *you* have decisively won your first great and terrible battle, please bestow upon me the wonderful island you had promised that I should govern."

"Brother Sancho," Don Quixote replied and then sighed. "Look around and perceive thy environment. These are not islands in our vicinity, but only desolate desert valleys and remote mountain crossroads. I've gained nothing except honor and a severed right ear in this most bitter-but-noteworthy recent altercation. But after *we* successfully conquer a magnificent kingdom, Sancho," the valiant Don

Quixote pledged, "then you can forget about being a governor, for I'll certainly make you an eminent prince or king."

"I now believe you, Senor Don Quixote, after I've witnessed *you* swiftly defeat that sword-wielding knave of a guard," Sancho informed his senile master. "And if *you* fuck-up the world the way you fucked up that ill-mannered, punk barbarian, then I say let's go and have some great fuckin' adventures together."

Sancho then helped the mildly-wounded Don Quixote mount Rozinante, and next he enthusiastically clambered on top of old Dapple. And then the thoroughly befuddled members of the Madame's traveling entourage shook their heads in total dismay, thinking that the predictable world that the spectators had known had now thoroughly gone amok. The gentle and bold Knight Errant waved to the Madame (whom he still believed was a queen), while Sancho gave the departing party the royal middle finger.

"Well Sancho, are you ready to have more fabulous adventures?" Don Quixote ambitiously asked.

'I myself' have screwed Dulcinea many times,' Sancho thought. 'That lucky guard is on his way to Toboso,' Sancho contemplated and smiled while shaking his head in disbelief. 'I'll bet he's going to get the best piece of ass, and the most fantastic blow-job, of his entire goddamned life!'

"Sancho, I detest silence, so please pay attention to me when I speak," Don Quixote imperatively admonished. "Now, I had just asked you if you were ready to experience some more extremely terrific adventures!"

"Yes, Master, as long as our next adventure is either in or around Toboso!" Sancho very succinctly answered.

"The Bet"
Anton Chekov

Anton Chekov (1860-1904) was born in Taganrog, Russia but (contrary to popular opinion) the author was never a minor character on the popular *Star Trek* television series. Anton's father was besieged with bankruptcy and the young man organized stories into pulp fiction and silly jokes and was remarkably paid a whole penny per line. When asked how he got his story ideas Chekov once told an acquaintance, "Show me an object and I'll write a story about it regardless whether it's an ashtray or an outhouse toilet seat." After Anton's friend joked that *he* often took craps in small ashtrays, the next day Chekov spitefully composed the tale "The Ashtray."

In the early phase of his writing career, Anton Chekov used various pseudonyms such as "Brother of My Brother" and "Rover." Eventually Anton realized that he had a real named that actually appeared in bold print on his birth certificate. "Motley Stories" published in 1886 was the Russian author's first claim to fame using his actual birth name. Chekov studied medicine and did become a doctor but since he treated most of his patients for gratis, that demanding profession proved to be too unsuitable and unprofitable for the benign humanitarian.

Perhaps Anton Chekov's most famous short story is "The Bet," an imaginative tale that involves a wager between a young idealistic lawyer and an aging wealthy banker.

Autumn had come early to Moscow. The tree leaves were of red and yellowish hues and each day the sun rose a little lower on the eastern horizon and set a little earlier in the west. On a dark night in October the banker nervously paced back and forth in his enviable library. The prominent investor was recollecting a particular conversation he had had with a young articulate lawyer on a similar autumn night exactly fifteen years before.

'I had invited many charming people that discussed major controversial topics,' the banker recollected. 'I wish I had never gotten into that damned nasty wrangle with the brash lawyer about capital punishment. That heated debate could now ruin my entire friggin' future.'

Many intellectuals, academics and newspaper chroniclers attended the sensational affair. The plurality of the guests deplored the principle of capital punishment and naively preferred to see wanton criminals immediately released from prisons to commit more heinous rapes, murders, terror, molestations and mass homicides. Moscow's elite cognoscenti generally considered the government's practice of capital execution obsolete, immoral and inhumane while the idealistic liberal critics ignorantly viewed assassinations, killing, slaughtering and massacres by psychotic felonious individuals as merely being an expression of wrongfully exercised free will of individuals that could be rehabilitated of their errant ways.

"Capital punishment is incompatible with the precepts of a genuine Christian state," the young attorney confidently declared. "I contend that life imprisonment with a maximum fifteen-year stay would be more than sufficient punishment for even the most egregious crime."

"I think you're quite full of shit!" the argumentative conservative-thinking banker bluntly maintained. "Certainly I've never experienced capital punishment or life imprisonment otherwise I would be too dead or too isolated to give this spectacular party. Capital punishment seems more benign to me than forcing someone to stay against his or her will in prison and it certainly is less goddamned expensive to honorable plutocratic tax evaders like me. Ha, ha, ha!" the financial tycoon sarcastically commented. "Fifteen years of incarceration is definitely not a satisfactory or cost-effective reprimand for a convicted murderer."

"Why do you find the notion of extended imprisonment appalling?" the brash attorney defiantly challenged. "Just because you're a rich old fuck doesn't mean that you're also a wise old fuck!"

"Executions eliminate societal scum instantly," the insulted banker indignantly insisted, "and life in jail kills a man's spirit inch by inch a day at a time. Which process is crueler? Killing a degenerate murderer by means of capital punishment or making him suffer and slowly decay in a prison? And young man," the monetary mogul continued his dissertation, "I resent you impetuously and indiscreetly calling me a rich old fuck when I'm actually and more appropriately a 'fuckin' wealthy intelligent investor'!"

"The state is not the Almighty," the adamant but callow lawyer countered like a competent defense attorney. "Only God can morally take away life. The state is not God!"

"You're totally fucked up and going nowhere with your' goddamned naïve liberal attitude!" the traditional-minded banker angrily criticized. "You're a sarcastic utopian dreamer, which happens to be a lethal combination that will guarantee you nothing more than an angry unsuccessful future. I happen to despise pompous young bull-shitters! Now say something realistic and practical or I'll be inclined to kick you the fuck out of my opulent mansion once and for all!"

The twenty-five-year-old lawyer seriously weighed the gravity of the banker's threatening comment and then answered, "In retrospect capital punishment and extended prison incarceration are almost equally immoral. It's better to live in even the most austere Spartan conditions than not to live at all. If given a damned choice however, I would definitely choose prison over death!"

The banker became exasperated and smashed his clenched fist onto a table, fracturing his ring finger. "You're a young stupid shit!" the established robber baron screamed at his youthful challenger. "I'll bet you two million American dollars that you couldn't survive in a simulated prison environment for fifteen years!"

The lawyer shrewdly considered the banker's tempting terms and promise and then smartly expressed himself. "But sir," he politely replied, "I don't have two million dollars to bet."

"Are you an ignorant asshole or what?" the infuriated banker retorted. "You don't have to have two million dollars to bet against me, you idiotic fool! You're betting your loss of a free life in the outside world for a decade and a half and I'm the gambling capitalist taking the financial risk of losing two million American dollars! Christ my dear fellow," the conceited mortgage fore-closer condescendingly complained, "in fifteen years it'll be 1885 and I hope to hell there's not going to be any major economic world recession between now and then!"

"Agreed!" the ambitious, greedy quixotic attorney exclaimed. "I wager my valued freedom against your two million! A fuckin' fool and his money are soon separated," the all-too-confident barrister boldly stated. "See ya' at your bank office for that sweet check in fifteen miserable years!"

And that's precisely how the extraordinary bet had materialized. The banker had accumulated more millions than the Duke of Luxemburg and the antagonistic lawyer had more guts than a bull elephant in heat. Both men were stubborn and egotistical (ego testicle), never compromising one iota and always acting impetuously on whim. Each man was enraptured with and dominated by his' own obstinacy.

At dinner the banker resumed his discussion with his forensic foe. "Come to your goddamned senses before it's too late," the wealthy man advised his callow acquaintance. "Two million American dollars doesn't mean a goddamned thing to me but you my reckless friend stand to lose the best years of your life."

"Grow some testicles!" the vernal lawyer chided. "You're now afraid of losing the extraordinary bet and having to pay me, you' covetous cantankerous old jerk-off!"

"You need a highly qualified psychiatrist," the reputable banker asserted. "Voluntarily going to prison for fifteen years is a lot more difficult than legally being forced to go. Just being aware of the idea that you could be free will gradually torture and poison your mind!" the experienced businessman pontificated. "I truly feel sorry for you! When you get out you'll be even more fucked-up than either baby Rasputin or the senile Czar is!"

The chagrined banker continued pacing back and forth in his library recollecting every detail of the debate that had transpired a decade and a half before. 'Why did I allow that inflexible asshole to bet me fifteen years ago?' he regretted. 'Both of us are now losers! What good is a bet if nobody fuckin' wins? And the capital punishment controversy is still in progress despite our individual losses! The entire fiasco was the caprice of a well-fed man and the greed for gold on behalf of a proud but lazy lawyer. The surly attorney and I are equally fucked-up, but in very different ways!"

The woeful banker then thought about how he and his nemesis had agreed that the lawyer should be locked in a garden wing of the banker's mansion. The detainee was not permitted to step outside his solitary confinement, could not have any visitors and could not receive any correspondence. He was allowed to read pamphlets, newspapers and magazines, play a musical instrument, drink wine and whiskey, smoke cigarettes and finally, to jerk-off a maximum of twice a day.

'It's too bad I had to squander a good deal of my fortune paying off the government officials after the czar's economy suffered through several devastating worldwide recessions and depressions,' the banker grieved and lamented. 'I've maintained my aristocratic lifestyle but have gone through most of my goddamned savings in the meantime. And the fucked-up attorney has to communicate with me by note through a window requesting his books, music and wine. Indeed,' the very worried banker evaluated, 'that brazen introspective bastard has experienced more psychological pleasure being insulated from the fuckin' hostile outside world than I have while suffering a terrible decline both in health and in my ever-shrinking bank account."

As mutually understood, the lawyer had contracted with the banker to remain confined for exactly fifteen years from October 15, 1870 to midnight on October 15, 1885. Any violation of the agreement on the attorney's part would liberate the banker from his obligation to compensate "the voluntary prisoner." The rich man had come to a plausible conclusion. 'We're all captives of our own wants, needs, dreams and greed!' the financial risk-taker evaluated. 'And now the goddamned moment of truth approaches! That young obnoxious prick is going to wind-up with the deed to my fabulous mansion!'

The first year of *his* garden-house confinement the lawyer suffered extreme loneliness. He craved human contact. The isolate was depressed, moody, bored and filled with contempt for society and indeed felt jealous animosity toward the prosperous banker. Daily he heard classical melodies being played on the piano inside the splendid mansion.

The disillusioned legal expert refused wine and alcohol that difficult first year. "Those fuckin' evil temptations are destructive addictions that arouse desire, and a prisoner like myself' determined to survive must abandon all selfish desires to avoid corrupting and then destroying *my* inner core. Drinking good vintage represents the pinnacle of boredom

364

and also the height of aristocratic decadence," the idealistic lawyer prudently wrote in his diary. "And tobacco pollutes the air and wickedly debilitates the lungs! Oh God, I really need a good smoke, a tall glass of potent vodka and a decent piece of ass!"

During that first year of his peculiar sentence the lawyer was provided with and read numerous adventure novels. He absorbed a myriad of complex love, detective, mystery, fantasy and comedy stories, which ultimately made him desire all of those sensational things ordinarily available in everyday life. During the second year of isolation the lawyer requested via a memo' that he wished for the mansion's piano not to be played because *he* wanted to fully concentrate and focus his remarkably hungry mind on reading and comprehending the complex plots and appreciating the colorful characters represented in classic literature.

'If it weren't for literature, I would have no motivation to live,' the lawyer realized. 'There's more unbelievable bullshit in the chapters of these books than there is in all of the world's cow pastures,' he candidly reckoned. 'I never really fathomed just how important certain bullshit is in maintaining the mind's stability!'

When the fifth year of his contract commitment commenced, the resolute prisoner sampled fine wines and again patiently listened to piano pieces originating from the mansion's great room. The banker's maid and butler spied on the attorney's activities and then reported their observations to their very curious employer. The snoopers told their superior that "the prisoner" had quit reading books and presently only ate, slept and drank wine.

'Good!' the banker thought and chuckled to himself upon hearing the news. 'The ornery prick is now trapped in a self-destruct pattern and is probably contemplating suicide. Let him stay scornful and sulk away his vital energy. I'm en route to winning the friggin' bet!' the banker thought with a grin upon his lips. 'What a bullheaded dunce that rambunctious middle-class nincompoop is!'

The attorney attempted writing an imaginative story of his own but soon became frustrated and then tore up his sketchy composition into shreds. He would weep and sob for hours on end, feeling sorrow and pity for himself and experiencing rage towards the stern banker and also towards the callous outside world. 'I can't possibly go insane because I had already been insane by accepting this outrageous bet!' the "crimeless convict" ruminated. 'And I can't stand shitting and pissing into a pot and then waiting for the butler to collect my stenchy body wastes. And I greatly miss taking baths and showers. Oh well, some people don't even have a cheap metal pot' to pee in,' the poor fellow consoled himself'. 'Why did I have to become an arrogant lawyer? I would've been much happier as a dynamic pimp or as an enterprising male prostitute!'

During his sixth year of segregation from civilization the unpretentious prisoner felt inspired to zealously study philosophy, history and foreign languages. In the next four years the accommodating banker was instructed to supply six hundred prodigious academic volumes, which the lawyer voraciously read. Then the multi-millionaire received a most bizarre letter from his 'demanding captive.'

"My dear jailor," the missive began. "I write these lines in six languages to demonstrate how educated and proficient I've become in the art of professional communication. Please have several experts examine my literary statement and if I've adequately mastered all six languages, I beg that you order a gun blast to resound throughout the garden. I shall become aware that my dedicated efforts have not been wasted by virtue of hearing the blast signal, which will definitely be rapturous music to my ears and certainly much more enjoyable than those fucked-up dissonant piano pieces I must involuntarily listen to."

The author of the request then continued his extended memorandum with an esoteric statement that was presented in the form of a fascinating metaphor. "The geniuses from antiquity up to the present era have spoken in various languages, but all of their voices and words burn to the same flame. I'll soon feel vindicated and have the emotional intensity to pursue other lofty more challenging endeavors that shall in the end emancipate my mind from monotony; thus, shall my endeavor victoriously transcend my cruel incarceration!"

The prisoner's wish was honored and two shotgun blasts were fired off in the garden, one of which ricocheted off of an awning and nearly accidentally assassinated the now exuberant attorney. 'Next time I'll simply request that a fuckin' firecracker should be exploded to verify a special request!' the lawyer creatively and practically decided.

After the tenth hellish year the prisoner idly sat in his enclosure reading the *New Testament* and he had virtually memorized every chapter and passage. 'What a fantastic book the *Bible* is!' the captivated captive marveled. 'Everyone screws everybody else, most of the time without even having sex!'

And next the lawyer occupied his time analyzing the history of theology and the origins of religions. 'Now I realize that society has gotten most of its wonderful bullshit from the terrific bullshit that religion has organized and indoctrinated over the centuries!'

The banker had a different perspective concerning the attorney's appetite for knowledge. 'The stupid shit is trying to out-psyche me,' the distrustful businessman theorized. 'The asshole's attempting to show me that he still has enthusiasm for life's pleasures despite his horrible deteriorating mental condition. He's even worn-out his shitting and pissing pot and I had to purchase a new one. Thank goodness his spirit has just about been eroded too!'

During the last two years of his contracted duty the newly inspired prisoner read more profound literary bullshit reflected in the works of William Shakespeare, Miguel Cervantes and Lord Byron. He requested (via handwritten notes) books on chemistry, biology, music, medicine and homosexuality. The attorney's eager mind was swimming in a sea of debris and he was drifting from one academic piece of flotsam to another attempting to attach meaning to a life he still considered worthy of salvaging. 'I'm really fucked-up after reading all of this fucked-up bullshit!' the lawyer hypothesized. 'Just imagine how fucked-up I'd be if I was actually living all that irrelevant bullshit in the outside world these past friggin' fifteen years.'

In the meantime, the banker paced back and forth in his library thinking about the strange contest he and the lawyer had contrived fifteen Octobers in the past. 'The caustic asshole will be free tomorrow at midnight,' the notorious investor thought as he stopped to scrutinize his wall calendar. 'Under *our* agreement I'll be compelled to pay the son-of-a-bitch two million American dollars. But if I cough up and honor the settlement, I'll be financially ruined forever.'

In October of 1870 the banker had more money than he could ever spend in seven lifetimes. But after making some speculative investments in world stock and commodities' markets that had gone sour and after suffering through several international economic crises, the banker's money ledger had as many debits as credits.

'If I didn't fuckin' gamble and lose big in the stock market,' the former tycoon sorrowfully recalled, 'my fortune would not have decayed into a meager bourgeois income. I was once audacious and confident. Now I tremble with each minor oscillation in world economic markets. That damned fuckin' bet I had made back in 1870 has returned to evilly haunt my mental health. Why didn't that haughty fuck-head die?' the banker wondered. 'The belligerent bastard's only forty years old, will obtain my life's savings and will leave my custody a rich man with every bitch in Moscow wanting to suck his tiny dick! I would happily trade places with the lucky bastard tomorrow night and would gladly sacrifice my left nut to do so!'

The very upset investment banker feared that he would have to endure shame and hardship should the two million American dollars have to be surrendered. 'And I must swallow my pride when *the altruistic fool* offers to help me pay my fuckin' ongoing debts!' the disgusted man concluded. 'There's only one practical solution to my dilemma. The fucked-up crazy fool must die!'

The banker impatiently waited until all of his servants were asleep. He then swiftly walked to his safe and removed the key to the garden-house door. Then he donned his overcoat and quietly stepped out of his mansion and into his cold dark wet garden. The damp hostile autumn wind howled and made the tree limbs dance to its gusty tempo. The banker peered into the bleak bitter darkness but could not see any of the familiar white statues or exotic shrubs that comprised his extravagant outdoor garden.

As the distraught man rounded the garden wing he yelled out "Peter! Peter!" for his caretaker, but there was no reply. 'My caretaker has taken shelter from the rain and is probably asleep in the greenhouse,' the banker surmised. 'This makes my homicide plan even more excellent and foolproof,' the haughty plotter congratulated himself. 'The authorities will first suspect that Peter had committed the despicable act and not me. But first I'll try to implement Plan A.'

The man felt for the garden-house steps using his feet and shoes as his sensors. After ascending the four brick steps, he opened the unlocked outside door and entered the botanical indoor structure. Then he lit a match. 'Peter's not here!' he observed. 'His bed is empty and there's nothing on *his* stove! He must be wandering around drunk as usual. My caretaker will definitely be the police's prime suspect if Plan A fails.'

The lit match then expired, burning the banker's fingertips. The anxious stalker peered through a small window into the interior chamber that housed the attorney. The light from a votive candle made the surroundings dimly visible. 'Ivan is docilely sitting in the chair and opened books are strewn all over the carpet and the table. The asshole's unkempt hair has grown all the way down to his knees. Ivan looks like a freakin' hermit in dire need of three barbers.'

The banker gently rapped on the window but the meditating occupant did not stir. 'Perhaps he's dead!' the renowned moneylender thought. 'I'll remove the seals from the door and then turn the lock.'

The ancient rusty lock seemed to groan and then the door finally squeaked open on its old reliable hinges. No one greeted the banker's entrance. The visitor stood for a full three minutes but the man with his back to the portal did not budge one inch. Then the evil-minded stalker approached the piteous sitting man and was surprised to perceive his generally disheveled appearance.

'He looks like a goddamned skeleton!' the banker gasped. 'Ivan's face is gaunt and his gray beard is grizzled. His complexion is yellowish as if he has jaundice. His eyes are sunken inside their sockets and his skinny hands look like they belong in a damned grave,' the observer noted. 'I've seen avowed mendicants in better physical condition. This emaciated excuse for a man is only forty-years-old yet he looks like a hundred and forty!'

Ivan Petrov sat still as if he was in a deep trance. A sheet of paper with letters in small script lay on the table. 'Poor creature!' the banker thought. 'I only have to knock him to the floor with one blow and then smother him with a pillow! The medical examiner will believe my testimony that Peter had performed the murder during a moment of drunken rage! But before I execute this idealistic fool first let me see what he had jotted down on this paper.'

Boris Gandov picked up the wrinkled sheet and carefully read: "Tomorrow at midnight I, Ivan Petrov shall be liberated into freedom and join society's malevolent ranks. But before I abandon this horrible lonely room and appreciate the sun and the earth once more, I must Mr. Gandov, address several pertinent facts."

Boris cleared his throat and thought, 'What' could this stupid bastard who is about to be slain possibly have to say to me after fifteen years of captivity? Has he hired Peter to kill me after this wretch receives *his* handsome stipend? What could possibly be inside this damned fool's mind?' Then the perplexed intruder interrupted *his* daydreaming by continuing his reading.

"I swear before God as my Witness that I despise freedom, health and life and I make this commentary with a clear conscience. I now have great contempt for everything in the universe that *your* books Boris Gandov describe as noble and worthwhile. I've assiduously studied this fucked-up world and its malignant knowledge for a decade and a half. I, Ivan Petrov did not directly observe the world or its people but only read about *their* goddamned vanities and their fuckin' mediocre shortcomings. My mind vicariously hunted women and deer while I sat and drank your vintage wine and listened to your asshole piano concertos."

The banker paused for a moment. 'Petrov's gone completely insane. What the fuck is *he* trying to say in this asinine letter? It's undeniably an ongoing travesty of the greatest magnitude!'

"And gorgeous well' endowed women visited my mind every night and their qualities and charms were aptly described by *your* goddamned famous poets and dreamers. The enticing women whispered marvelous stories into my ears, which incidentally have not been cleaned in over fifteen goddamned years."

'This scoundrel son-of-a-bitch needs to be institutionalized right away!' Boris concluded. 'His twisted perverted mind is swimming in a river that's murkier than the stagnant Volga.'

"Throughout your abominable books I ascended the peaks of Iranian mountains and next triumphantly stood on Mt. Blanc's summit. I witnessed the sun rising in the morning and then majestically flood the afternoon and evening sky with a spectrum of magnificent hues. I saw tremendous lightning bolts splitting dark gray clouds and reigning thunder down upon the derelict masses."

'This shit-head is beyond salvation! Why should I kill the dumb crazy mother-fucker when he's already residing in hell?' Boris Gandov assessed. 'If Plan A fails I'll immediately deploy Plan B!'

"I vividly envisioned an abundance of green woods and fields and sterling rivers, lakes and cities. I've heard beautiful sirens beckoning me while playing their lyres on treacherous rocks and I've listened to the demigod Pan playfully seducing my spirit with his enchanting pipes. I touched the evil wings of gargoyles and demons and those of beautiful angels that approached me to speak meaningfully of God."

'Jesus Christ!' Boris Gandov imagined. 'This fuckin' poor bastard has already given his soul to Satan! Must I join his soul in hell for my mortal sin of brutally killing the quixotic fucked-up son-of-a-bitch?'

"I have through *your* wicked books hurled my immoral immortal soul into the bottomless pit. I presently reside at the base of *Dante's Inferno*. I now casually perform numerous black miracles and burn cities to the fuckin' ground at whim. I randomly establish new religions and shrewdly manipulate the gullible masses. My damned conquests make Alexander-the-Great's most stellar achievements seem trivial and picayune. And yet my greedy will has not been fully satisfied."

'Don't infect me with any more of your contagious evil!' Boris implored the self-appointed 'Power of Hell'. 'Ivan, please save me from eternal damnation!'

"Your books made me wise to the inglorious pitfalls of human nature," the letter emphatically stated. "All human knowledge has been compressed and cataloged into my incomparable memory. I'm now cleverer and more detestable than the entire human race put together! And *you* Boris Gandov are absolutely clueless about the true purpose of human existence. You're but a tiny fraction of the evil that dwells throughout my mind and that resides inside the depths of my troubled heart!"

'Spare me of this vile lunacy!' Boris Gandov begged the heavens. 'Let me die before my mind diminishes to Ivan's vulgar decayed contaminated state of being!'

"And I wholeheartedly scorn all of your learning, your wisdom, your material-word-knowledge and your blessings," the letter attested. "Everything on this fuckin' earth is vacuous, contemptible, malignant, weak as flesh and as ethereal as a mirage. Death will easily wipe *you* Boris Gandov from the face of this sinful earth and then you'll be effectively exterminated, feeling like an insignificant timid mouse trapped in its hole. I offer eternal damnation to you, Boris Gandov!"

'I regret ever entering this garden-house bastion of evil!' Boris guiltily thought. 'Let me now finish reading this accursed letter and then I'll get the fuck out of here! Tomorrow at midnight I initiate Plan A!'

"You scheming bastard, you think that you'll be a benefactor to your daughter now living in Paris? Your posterity Boris Gandov and your inheritance will be melted down like frozen scum. And then your beloved doomed earth will burn as surely as your wicked soul shall blaze away alongside mine in the heartless eternal hell."

'This letter makes no goddamned sense at all! It's the fictional work of a crazy person feigning genius!' Boris concluded. 'It's fuckin' insanity at its worst moment! Ivan Petrov, I can now feel *your* fuckin' lunacy possessing and demonizing me!'

"You might consider me insane but insanity is an admirable quality that you've been practicing all of your goddamned adult life," the letter directly accused. 'You insist that lies are truth, argue that deceit is honesty and insist that ugliness is beauty. You cunningly pretend that goodness is naivete and that evil exists in the other exploiters and parasites of your wicked race. You Boris Gandov have effectively bartered heaven for earth and shall surely trade earth for hell."

'But what about our bet?' Boris mentally asked the letter as if it could magically speak for Ivan. 'What about our fuckin' bet? I want to live out my life in comfort and in luxury!'

"And now I shall exhibit my disdain for *your* evil way of life. Boris Gandov, prominent banker and financier, I hereby give up my claim to the two million dollars, which fifteen years ago I had dreamed to be heaven. I'll demonstrate my rejection of said sum by departing from this garden prison five minutes before the midnight deadline. You'll be able to consolidate and hoard your extensive fortune after I deliberately breach and violate the principal term of *our* contract."

Boris Gandov's hands trembled as he placed the 'accursed letter' back onto the table. Ivan Petrov sat like a neglected hideous-looking condemned man that had just visited and barely escaped the indiscriminate jaws guarding death's portal.

Gandov pivoted around and left the glass-enclosed prison weeping like a child. He returned to his ornately decorated mansion through the biting cold rain and ignored the howling swirling winds. The puzzled banker entered his bedroom thinking about Plan A, opened up a suitcase and stared at the two million dollars in worthless Confederate currency. 'Our deal just said two million in American dollars,' he thought. 'It did not specify what kind of American dollars they had to be!'

And then Boris lit a robust blaze in his master bedroom's fireplace and very deliberately tossed the bundles of bogus bills into the leaping flames. 'It's hard to trick the damned devil at *his* own game!' the deceitful greedy man acknowledged.

Early the next morning Peter came dashing into the mansion and had something important to share with his all-too-selfish employer. "I just saw Ivan Petrov exit the garden-house, stumble to the front gate and then disappear from the property. Master, it seems that you've admirably won the very odd bet after all!'"

The shocked banker sprinted to the garden-house to verify Peter's claim. Boris glanced down at the table and noticed that the letter was no longer there. "I'm not so sure I've won any bet at all," the banker cryptically stated to his already confused servant. "I've merely allowed a foolish man to discover the purpose for living on this repugnant planet and I've helped another man discover the true meaning of life. Here Peter," the banker indicated to his shocked employee. "Please gratefully accept these thousand Russian rubles for being such a loyal servant all these years. And by my newfound generosity," Boris Gandov said, "I shall give *you* your second well' deserved installment very soon indeed."

"The Interlopers"
Saki

Saki was the penname of Hector Hugh Munro (1870-1916). H.H. Munro's writing name was not derived from the popular Japanese fermented rice liquor. The pseudonym actually originated from the name of the gods' cupbearer in the poem *The Rubaiyat* by Omar Khayyam.

In 1896 H.H. Munro followed in his father's footsteps but had to give up his journey because a heavy rain had washed away all of the footprints in the mud. In 1897 Saki again followed in his father's footsteps and enlisted in the Burma police as a lieutenant because the Italian Mafia didn't need any additional lieutenants or Capos. The un-evolved Saki suffered from fevers and malaria and lasted little more than a year in the Burma police but the aspiring author did manage to construct many shaving cream signs along major highways.

Many of Saki's stories feature man's inhumanity to man on a personal level, but in real life H.H. Munro was reputed to be an understanding gentleman that despised brutality and callousness. Many of Saki's stories feature werewolves, is-wolves, was-wolves, am-wolves, are-wolves and vampires, reflecting his fascination with paranormal phenomena. Saki believed that animals were more compatible with nature than man was. He also believed that humans possessed powerful intelligence and advanced emotions, which gave the ascendant primate race the capacity to elevate itself high above the animal/physical world to allow men to harness, control and predict nature's behavior and also permitting them the wherewithal to invent flush toilets.

One of Saki's most famous stories is "The Interlopers," essentially meaning "trespassers" as ostensibly demonstrated in the *Lord's Prayer* "And forgive us our interlopes, as we forgive those that interlope against us." Also, "The Interlopers" is not to be confused with a popular southern New Jersey deer-hunting club, "The Antelopers."

The Carpathian Mountains *run* through Romania and Czechoslovakia and seldom do any walking, ambling or hiking. In an eastern Carpathian deciduous and coniferous forest, a man stood alone in the dead hush of winter listening and watching. The sentinel was waiting for detection of any moving object to come within rifle range.

'I'm not looking for any damned animal to shoot,' Ulrich von Gradwitz reminded himself. 'It's the blood of my human enemy that I'm in quest of. If I lived in America instead of in these forsaken Romanian Carpathian Mountains, I could just break into the nearest *Red Cross* office and steal the damned blood of my enemy!' Ulrich delightfully mused.

Ulrich von Gradwitz was a big landowner, standing six-foot-seven inches tall without his boots on. His land stretched for many miles (kilometers) in all directions and was well stocked with game. The narrow strip of land that Ulrich was presently patrolling bordered the property of his most dreaded enemy, Georg Znaeym. Their ongoing futile feud had been in progress since feudal times when their ancestors had proclaimed and vociferated to each other, "Put up your dukes!" "You're trying to rook me!" and "Shut up or I'll fuckin' crown ya'!"

A notorious area lawsuit had allowed Ulrich to confiscate the disputed land from Georg, and many incidents of *poaching* had resulted in various hard-shell *scrambles* because Ulrich liked his eggs sunny-side-up and Georg preferred his yolks over-light. The bitter futile feuding between the von Gradwitzes and the Znaeyms had been evolving over three generations and all local champagne labels featured the "sour grapes" going on between the two distinguished but proud battling men.

Ulrich hated Georg with a passion because Znaeym was suspected of conducting raids into the narrow formerly disputed territory and killing deer, bear, rabbits, squirrels, cockroaches, mosquitoes, lightning bugs and whores. Since both patriarchs hated each other, the feud never died down and kept the local Carpathian newspapers in business with front-page headlines of shootings, beatings, muggings' and also with providing published obituaries. When they were boys, Ulrich and Georg had wished that each other's dick and balls would rot off, and later as desperate men they desired to rape and sodomize each other's wives, midwives, sisters, aunts, female cousins, daughters, stepdaughters, stair-daughters, mothers, mistresses, concubines and horny mothers-in-law.

Ulrich had on that wintry night organized his men into teams of sentries to keep their eyes panning the dark forest for any signs of Georg Znaeym's men disguised as lost sojourners or as male prostitutes. "We're not on the lookout for four-footed quarry, for as you know men *the quarry* next to my manor house does not have four feet but only four feet of water!" Ulrich joked to his loyal hit men. "If you see any prowlers roaming around Romania assume and believe that they're thieves and shoot first and then ask unnecessary questions later. Now men, here are some goddamned *NRA* membership forms to fill out before you use your newfangled rifles! I absolutely loathe bureaucracy and am sure glad I'm not living in the twentieth century when things and government are bound to get a lot worse with plenty of irrelevant paperwork! Now go to your assigned stations!"

Ample deer were flitting about the forest and Ulrich presumed that Georg's men were responsible for all of the unnatural commotion. "Be on the lookout for interlopers and antelopers!" Ulrich reminded his lethargic don't-give-a-shit companions. "This is even worse than the damned American prairie where the deer and the antelopers roam, but now those woodsy suckers are doing it right here in Romania! I mean what the fuck would Count Dracula do with a stupid asshole like Georg Znaeym?" Ulrich asked his unmotivated sentinels. "Now men, stay here on this crest while I explore over yonder hill so that something exciting can happen to me in this story. I'm the main character," Ulrich indicated to his un-inspired hired help, "so something big has to happen soon. I mean what good is having great fuckin' characters with no goddamned plot? Do you shit-faced jerk offs follow what the hell I'm sayin' here?"

Ulrich left his dumbfounded confounded henchmen and meandered his way down several treacherous slopes and through a ravine cluttered with dense tangled undergrowth. He then stopped, for exhaustion had temporary dominion over his out-of-shape corpulent body. Ulrich listened for any sound suggesting the approach of marauders from Georg Znaeym's campy camp. Only the howling wind and the relentless movement of tree branches permeated the cold icy air.

'If only I could encounter Georg Znaeym alone face to face,' Ulrich fantasized. 'I wish to kill the bastard mano y mano with no witnesses and leave his corpse in this thicket for the damned scavengers to devour.'

As Ulrich von Gradwitz stepped around the gnarled trunk of a gargantuan barren beech tree, he was obsessed with the desire to eliminate Georg Znaeym's existence from the face of the earth. Suddenly the vindictive Ulrich was more than astonished to come face to face with his avowed foe', who incidentally also had been cautiously circumnavigating the same ancient beech tree from the opposite side.

The two opponents stood eyeball to eyeball for a very long moment, their pupils reflecting mutual disdain. Both men held rifles and each man's hate-filled heart' was overwhelmed with the tempting impulse to savagely fight to the death. But each man had been taught by civilization's stern school-marms to not kill an enemy in cold blood when facing that rival directly in the eyes. Word of such action would bring instant dishonor, infamy and a criminal reputation to the executioner and to his fucked-up extended family.

Before either Ulrich or Georg could utter a single derogatory syllable nature's violence accidentally intervened and made its presence known. A huge section of the ice-laden beech tree thundered down upon the two feuders before either Ulrich or Georg had the wherewithal to leap out of the way or before either repugnant neighbor could initiate any significant feuding.

Ulrich von Gradwitz found himself lying beneath the heavy limbs and branches of the severed beech tree. His right arm was numb and was stuck beneath his right hip. His left arm was surrounded by a dense tangle of branches and limbs. Both lower appendages had been trapped underneath the tremendous weight of the beech tree mass.

"Help!" Ulrich heard Georg pathetically plead. "My limp limbs are trapped underneath all these heavy limbs! I can't limber any of them up!"

Fortunately for Ulrich his thick leather hunting boots had spared his feet from being crushed in the accidental devilish 'Act of God!' 'I'm stuck beneath this tree limb until help arrives to rescue me!' Ulrich very intelligently realized. 'I can't even open a *branch office* underneath this horrible massive tree section! I think I've broken a leg without even being in any goddamned play! What a bummer this bullshit is!'

Ulrich felt warm blood rolling down the sides of his face and verified its identity by extending his tongue out of his mouth and licking his icy mustache. At his side lay the injured body of Georg Znaeym, who was still alive but his breathing was 'labored' even though it wasn't the first Monday in September. Ulrich realized that Georg was just as trapped and equally as helpless as he was. Each man had been a victim to the same extraordinary accident and had more scratches than a really bad pool or billiards' game.

Ulrich was struggling to have his rationality triumph over the spiteful baser emotions that were surfacing from deep within his heart. Von Gradwitz felt thankful that he had survived the possible catastrophe but the baron was deeply angered that he had to share his regrettable circumstance with his most intense and dreaded adversary.

Georg Znaeym surrendered his rigid obstinate disposition and ceased struggling with his irreversible predicament. The man had been virtually blinded by a puddle of blood into which his nose had been pointing. Then Georg felt compelled to render a most spine-tingling laugh. "So Ulrich, you're remarkably still alive but you're caught just like I am. Our souls share similar fates in that only the strong survive and only the good die young. What an ironic travesty!" Georg mocked. "Ulrich von Gradwitz snared by my men right in the middle of what *he* claims is *his* own forest! Your damned dick should fall off and be eaten by a goddamned hungry skunk!"

"And your damned balls and scrotum should detach from your pubic area!" Ulrich maliciously replied. "True I am temporarily caught in this bind and trapped in *my* own forest," von Gradwitz continued his bravado, "but when my men arrive *you* Georg Znaeym will wish that you had been caught poaching instead of scrambling. Shame has descended upon you; you dumb fuckin' egghead!"

Georg remained reticent for a moment while contemplating the essence of Ulrich's cruel words. "Are you certain that your men will find us first? As you might know Ulrich, I too have a contingent of able-bodied henchmen out searching for me right now!" Znaeym boasted. "I'm quite confident that my minions will be here first to release me from this most insulting and extremely embarrassing situation."

"When my men drag me out of this terrible snag," Ulrich stubbornly answered, "then they'll have little difficulty in rolling the heavy beech-tree trunk over on top of you! That ought to *stump* you for good, you dumb fucked-up asshole pecker head!" von Gradwitz arrogantly stated and crazily laughed. "Then Georg, your men will eventually find you dead underneath the heavy *trunk* that weighs as much as a hundred fleshy elephant snouts! Ha, ha, ha!" Ulrich shouted like a lunatic. "Then I shall have the courtesy to send a phony sympathy card expressing my condolences to *your* most ignoble family!"

"Fuck off Ulrich!" Georg ranted in pain while facing his chief rival. "My men had instructions to come searching for me should I not return in ten brief minutes from my little ramble. On second thought," Znaeym confidently stated, "I shall not send your family a sympathy card expressing my shallowest condolences because *you von Gradwitz* had been caught poaching when you brazenly scrambled onto my property! And now we've both been am*bushed* by a tree!"

"Good shit Georg!" Ulrich readily agreed. "We'll fight this feud out to its completion and to our deaths, if need be; you, me and our fucked-up foresters. And no interlopers will dare come between our wraths, not even fuckin' Satan himself! Agony, death and eternal hell to you, Georg Znaeym, or whatever your damned *z*-name is!" von Gradwitz deliberately mocked.

"The same to you Ulrich von Gradwitz, forest felon, game snatcher and homosexual rectum penetrator supreme! You aren't good enough to even lick my dick!" Znaeym exclaimed and then coughed.

Ulrich and Georg both acknowledged that it was futile and impossible to escape the fallen tree's entrapment. Each man prayed that *his* men would arrive first to then determine the vigilante sentencing of *his* avowed enemy. Ulrich still had the strength and the presence of mind to rotate half-of his free left arm and remove a wine flask from his coat pocket. It required five minutes of assiduous biting for von Gradwitz's teeth to finally unscrew the stopper and to eventually gulp down several ounces of the rich liquid. The swallowed wine had instantly revived Ulrich's mind from the momentary shock-stupor he had been experiencing from extreme duress and from loss of blood.

Ulrich was able to glance across to Georg and amazingly felt a pinch of pity for the man anguishing under *his* burden while keeping groans and tears back that would humiliate him in front of his mortal foe. "Georg, could you reach this wine flask if I tossed it over to you?" Ulrich uncharacteristically and mercifully asked. "You should fuckin' swallow and enjoy the drink before you might perish from your great travail!"

"No thank you Ulrich," Georg answered with a degree of decorum and sensitivity. "I have so much blood caked around my pupils!" he gasped. "And I don't want to start a new bad habit of drinking with a dangerous enemy!" Znaeym panted.

Ulrich evaluated Georg's antagonistic comment and remained silent for a moment. He pathetically lay there and was helplessly listening to the howling wind and to the weird sound of distant tree branches rubbing against one another. Both men were in awe of their now-eerie environment.

An idea was slowly expanding inside von Gradwitz's bewildered mind. Ulrich's eyes scanned the fallen form of his longtime enemy, now weak, fatigued, in excruciating pain and far more injured than *he* was. The prospect of Georg's death and the sensation of *his* own throbbing pains made Ulrich for the first time re-consider the gravity of *their* dual dilemmas.

"Neighbor, do as you intend if your men arrive first," Ulrich offered, "but as for me I've changed my attitude in regard to our relationship. If my men come here first," von Gradwitz proposed and compromised, "then I assure that *you* will be the first to be released and treated for your injuries!"

"What the fuck did you say?" Georg Znaeym incredulously asked. "Why in God's name have you suddenly become a saint instead of the fucked-up vile sinner that I've known and despised all these years? Is it because you now fear death and God's omnipotent judgment?"

"Georg," Ulrich calmly proceeded, "we've quarreled like silly school children over this stupid piece of woodland just because we happen to come from different necks of the woods, so to speak. I insist that we've both been fickle fools fighting over something so unimportant as a strip of forest," von Gradwitz retorted and maintained. "Now a good piece of ass, well that's a different story altogether than a mere insignificant piece of property! A good piece of ass is definitely worth fighting over!"

A very long pause prompted Ulrich to wonder whether his fellow sufferer had already died. "Georg, can you still hear me? I wish for us to bury our hatchets and end our long-standing quarrel!" von Gradwitz declared. "Georg, can you still hear me? For God's sake, answer me!"

Georg Znaeym had not spoken for so long that Ulrich wished that his former foe had only fainted from loss of blood and had not actually become deceased. Ulrich spoke penitently and remorsefully to his obstinate neighbor. "Just think Georg how the whole town would stare and gossip if we rode to the marketplace together on horseback!" Ulrich stated. "No jerk off living in Romania could ever remember a Znaeym and a von Gradwitz jointly showing comradeship and trust."

"Fuck you von Gradwitz!" replied Georg Znaeym after mustering every piece of strength in his body and then directing it to his vocal cords. "Fuck you, you shit-face asshole!"

"Just think Georg," von Gradwitz persisted, "what wonderful peace would descend on this vicinity if we would just end our senseless feuding tonight. No one would interfere with our arrangement for *we* are the leaders of the two most powerful families in the area!"

"Suck my dick!" Georg slowly and methodically uttered. "And then you can lick and swallow the millions and millions of sperm right out of my goddamned testicles!"

"And just think Georg," Ulrich maintained while ignoring his former foe's vitriolic remarks, "you can come and keep the Sylvester feast night before *New Years Day* at my residence and we could then party together upon splendid game killed upon *our* mutually-shared rolling lands!"

"And after you suck my dick and swallow my load," Georg Znaeym insisted to his remorseful neighbor, "you can then thoroughly lick my scrotum and my rectum too, you king-sized asshole!"

"And then," Ulrich continued while ignoring Georg's indignant prattle, "I promise to never fire a shot on your sacred land unless," cough, cough, cough, "unless of course Georg you've invited me as a welcomed guest to your noble estate," von Gradwitz elaborated. "And if you want, you could then shoot with me down in the marshes and eat marshmallows with me while we merrily pursue the foulest of fowl!"

"Get cancer in every fuckin' organ of your goddamned body!" Georg nastily replied. The man's voice was obviously strained with the excessive pain he was enduring. "And I hope your friggin' rectum falls off after your pecker and your gonads drop to the ground like acorns!"

"Georg," Ulrich continued his confession, "I never thought I was capable of doing anything else except hating your damned guts, but in this last half hour I've felt a genuine need to make amends and to terminate our perpetual conflict."

"Ulrich, I'm gonna' drink down the rest of your putrid wine right this moment just to spite your miserable ass and hopefully get fuckin' drunk," Georg optimistically predicted. "And I want you to know before you might die that I've screwed your ugly fat horny wife at a secret rendezvous at least a hundred and sixty-nine different times!"

"Georg, no matter what you say I'll truly be your friend forever!" Ulrich affirmed. "Even though I've truly clandestinely screwed your gorgeous well' stacked wife a hundred and seventy times, I still wish that we be comrades and allies."

Both men remained silent and listened to each other's heavy breathing for the next several minutes. Ulrich thought about their heartwarming reconciliation while Georg wished for the opportunity to pork Ulrich's hussy of a wife at least two more times at *their* secret rendezvous so that *he* could be one up on his sex-starved neighbor. The exhausted bleeding men waited in quiet desperation for a search party to finally discover their mutual perplexity. Soon rescuers would bring relief and warm brandy to revive their vital life instincts, at least that is what each man possessively hoped.

And Ulrich von Gradwitz and Georg Znaeym each privately offered sincere prayers to the Almighty, each victim wishing for *his* men to arrive first on the scene to have the honor of liberating the other man from *his* life-threatening plight. Then Ulrich was inspired to make a salient suggestion.

"Georg, let's both shout for assistance!" Ulrich sincerely urged. "In this quiet place certainly our two voices could be easily heard from afar!"

"And finally, I hope you get cancer of the voice box!" Georg Znaeym imperatively related to his newfound cohort. "Our voices will never carry far in this unbearable dense undergrowth," the neighbor doubtfully explained. "And besides Ulrich, we'll both grow tits and pussies before any of our incompetent foresters locate our whereabouts!" Znaeym cynically remarked.

Ulrich von Gradwitz overlooked his pessimistic colleague's comments and lustily shouted out, "Over here assholes! We're trapped over here underneath this shattered ancient beech tree!" he bellowed with all his vocal might. "Over here I say! Over here assholes!"

"I think my keen ears heard a rustling not far away," Georg stated, giving encouragement to Ulrich. "Yes, I definitely heard some movement originating from our right!"

"I heard nothin' but the persistent damned wind," Ulrich bluntly answered. "But if you insist your auditory perception had discerned something distinct, then Georg I shall again call for help! Over here!" Ulrich boomed as loudly as he could. "We're both trapped over here!"

"Oh, piss out a roaring fire!" Georg bitterly complained. "I hope you von Gradwitz aren't attempting to piss out a blazing inferno or that you aren't merely fartin' your ass into an absolutely full cesspool!"

A silence again reigned supreme for another full minute. Then Ulrich gave a most triumphant cry. "My eyes see figures crouched down and scrambling through the woods where *you* had been poaching," von Gradwitz said to the in-shock Znaeym. "The crouched figures are following the exact same path that I had taken to this horrible fate! I'll bet they must be my men coming to the rescue!"

"Suck your dead mother-in-law's cunt!" Georg vehemently protested. "Suck it Ulrich von Gradwitz like there's no goddamned tomorrow!"

Ulrich was motivated to again address the approaching crouched-down figures. "Over here idiots! Over here you dumb fuck heads!" he repeated. "Georg, I think they now hear me. They're descending the ravine and advancing down to our location. They heard me!" the man jubilantly yelled with his last bit of energy being expressed as enthusiasm.

380

"Fuck the world von Gradwitz!" Znaeym sarcastically ridiculed. "Fuck the whole goddamned world and all of the freakin' whores and homosexuals and priests and pedophiles in it!"

"They're in our proximity," Ulrich gleefully determined and conveyed to his totally negative and disgruntled neighbor. "The rescuers, they're running down the hill and responding to my plea!"

"How many shit heads are there?" Georg inquired. "And how many fuck heads are there in addition to the shit heads you can count?"

"I can't specifically identify how many," von Gradwitz candidly answered from his prone horizontal position on the cold frozen earth. "But conservatively, I estimate about nine or ten in the search party!"

"Are they your assholes or are they my valiant foresters?" Georg asked. "Yours or mine?"

"Don't you ever listen when I speak to you?" Ulrich admonished Znaeym. "I already told you nine or ten! You dumb mother fucker and wife porker!"

"Then, they must be your jerk-offs because I only had seven of my yeomen accompanying me," Georg informed his emotionally unstable neighbor.

"Whoever men they are," Ulrich added, "they're making admirable time and showing praiseworthy speed arriving to our mutual discomfort. Brave lads are they all, I say. Brave intrepid lads are they all!"

"Can you definitely recognize them as *your* men?" Georg asked. "If they're your men I'll buy them a harlot each to pump the poop out of while their wives are havin' their goddamned periods! A friggin' harlot each I say!"

Ulrich von Gradwitz did not answer. A sniffle and then a slight whimper were then discerned coming from his throat.

"Are they your clowns or mine?" Georg repeated. "Your goddamned clowns or mine?"

"Neither," Ulrich replied with an insane giggle and then with a perverted hearty laugh. "Neither yours nor mine!" he reiterated in a crazy laugh and a demonic utterance characteristic of a dying man possessed by grotesque trepidation. "Neither yours nor mine I say!" Ulrich ranted like a maniac.

"Well then Ulrich. Whose men' are they?" Georg entreated. Znaeym lifted his head and strained his eyes to observe what Ulrich had already seen and known.

"Wolves!" von Gradwitz shrieked like a demoralized demonized madman. "How fuckin' ironic Georg! Wolves I say!"

"Comedy of Errors"
William Shakespeare

Act I

"The Comedy of Errors" is a fairly crazy play about situational comedy scenes involving nutcase misadventures concerning sets of male twins. The setting is in an ancient Greek city-state during the First Century B.C. Aegeon, a dysfunctional Mediterranean merchant from Syracuse (city on the coast of what is now Sicily), foolishly arrived in Ephesus, a city of worm-brained renegades in Asia Minor that espoused ancient Greek culture.

The rulers of Ephesus and Syracuse were sullen, jealous idiots that fully hated each other, so a reciprocal law was in existence that if any citizen of Syracuse ever landed in Ephesus, then he or she would be put to death; and vice-versa, if any resident of Ephesus ever landed in Syracuse, he (masculine by preference) would die by having all of the sperm juice, urine, blood and other fluids removed from his or her body until that intruder expired; or, until the accused was administered an alternate cruel death method at the discretion of the extermination-happy Duke. One exception, or escape clause to the harsh law, did exist for the unfortunate captured Aegeon: the bizarre stipulation being stated that if the *Syracuse traveler* could in one hectic day raise the sum of one thousand marks to pay as ransom to the covetous Duke of Ephesus, then the seafaring trader could buy his freedom, and get the hell out of town with his testicles and rectum still attached.

"I appear before you, Duke Solinus, for being arrested for the picayune matter of visiting your fair city Ephesus here in Asia Minor," Aegeon of Syracuse prefaced his introduction to the royal court. "And I'm surprised to see that there're many adults and so few juveniles living here in Asia Minor."

"Dipshit Merchant of Syracuse," Solinus answered from his lofty throne position. "You act and speak more like a zany clown than a donkey-brained trader. This is serious shit, er, I mean serious business that you're involved in, and your expendable life is at stake, so I strongly suggest that you heed my important words. Your murderous Duke of Syracuse has killed many traveling citizens from Ephesus, and I'm here to remind you that your life is in jeopardy, because our government has established a parallel law pertaining to nosy spies with huge nostrils originating from Syracuse. Now tell me your fascinating story of how the hell you ultimately wound-up here," the Duke of Ephesus urged Aegeon. "You may receive my expressed token sympathy before I might have you brutally executed. Usually, we have a giant from the neighboring gay and lesbian community give those Syracusans sentenced to death a lethal injection of semen up the ass from his mammoth, log-sized sperm shooter."

Aegeon paused, took a deep breath, gathered his random thoughts, and then began reviewing his life's entire history, while Solinus rubbed his weary eyes, yawned prodigiously, and then became distracted by picking boogers from his snot-filled nose. "Now wait just a minute, Duke Solinus!" the wandering merchant/prisoner insisted. "Is there any way that I can escape such an abominable rectal torture and subsequent death?"

"You have one minuscule hope!" the death-sentencing Duke haughtily snickered. "If you can raise the sum of one thousand marks, then I shall set you free to return on your trading voyage. If you can't assemble the one thousand marks, then I'll personally see that you'll receive one thousand painful marks all over your ugly body, before the gay giant proceeds to sodomize your ass right up to your' larynx! Now let's get this show on the road, and initiate your reviewing of your asshole tale of woe, that much to your utter disenchantment, and much to your potential demise, has brought your dumb-ass to foreign Ephesus!"

Aegeon recounted how, many years before the present, the merchant had sailed to Epidamnum, located adjacent to Epididymis, situated on the *Adriatic Sea*. Several weeks later, the merchant's pregnant wife joined him in Epidamnum, where the joyful woman prematurely gave birth to twin boys.

"Now Duke Solinus," Aegeon (who liked to trade in the *Aegean* as well as in the *Adriatic*) told the apathetic ruler. "A remarkable coincidence happened approximately twenty-three years ago. A destitute prostitute named Epi simultaneously also gave birth to twin boys in Epidamnum, and Epi was damned numb after the double-breech delivery. Man, was that birth messy!"

"I know and recognize stupid-sounding bullshit when I hear it," Solinus warned the defendant, as the dastardly Duke simultaneously cleaned his ears with both of his booger-laden thumbs. "So, be careful, or I might be directly ordering you to be administered a thousand marks on your scoliosis-laden back, ha, ha, ha! Now, Syracusan Hostage, continue with your comical narrative!"

"Well, Duke," Aegeon stammered; "my wife Aemilia always wanted to have quadruplets, so she negotiated with Epi, the damned numb prostitute bitch, and as a result, I purchased *her* two male offspring almost as soon as the little suckers plopped from Epi's snatcheroo right onto the barn hayloft straw mattress."

"Your wife Aemilia sounds just as asinine and retarded as you do," Solinus ridiculed. "It sounds like you two low-level morons deserve each other! And that Epi bitch is obviously a third moron."

"Yes Duke," Aegeon agreed before clearing his throat and then swallowing some very thick phlegm. "On the way back to Syracuse, our trading vessel became shipwrecked during a turbulent tempest. My wife and I put the four screaming babies on wooden debris floating in the choppy sea, where *we* also desperately clung to several bobbing planks. Aemilia and two of the bratty kids, one her son and the other the prostitute Epi's little nipple-chewer, were rescued by a first ship, and I and the two remaining raunchy infants were miraculously salvaged from the heartless sea by another vessel. To this day, I don't know where my wife had been taken, and I've never seen those two little breast-fed suckers, whom Aemilia had escaped with from drowning, ever again," Aegeon disclosed. "Now I know Duke, that this crazy story sounds like fantasy fiction, but I swear to you it's absolute fact, definitely not short of truth. All of this amazing horse crap actually happened over twenty-three years ago!"

"But how the hell did you ever get here in Ephesus?" Duke Solinus inquired. "That's what the fuck I want to know. Please enlighten me, Prisoner, about those other juicy details!"

"Well Duke, when my son Antipholus reached the tender age of eighteen, the adolescent grew anxious and desired to find his twin brother," Aegeon explained; "mainly because Antipholus didn't like sleeping in a twin bed all those years without any twin brother there to give him comfort, and whatever else perverted young men do when the punk teenagers are not toying with their dingles all alone at midnight in the dark."

"Where was your wife's rescue ship heading?" the Ephesus Duke asked. "What was its destination?"

"I believe to Corinth," Aegeon remembered and related. "And *my* rescue ship eventually docked in Epidaurus, which as you're aware, is on the posterior ass side of Epididymis, not far from Epidamnum."

"But Prisoner Aegeon; I don't understand your fucked-up fallacious math'?" Solinus challenged the shuddering, nervous defendant. "Your son Antipholus takes-off from home at age eighteen, probably because he hates your guts, and right now, I can readily see why. And now it's twenty-three years later, from the original shipwreck. Is that correct?? What happened to those five omitted years? Was civilization erased? Did an epic calamitous event occur that I never knew about? Did the goddamned calendar makers go on strike?"

"Well Kind Duke, my son Antipholus has been roaming for five years now, and I'm worried about him and his servant Dromio. I fear that they've wandered into Asia Minor somewhere, and that's how the fuck by coincidence I had inadvertently wound-up here in Ephesus."

"No wonder why no fuckin' lawyer would take your case," the Duke of Ephesus rankled. "You're trying to tell and convince me that reality is queerer than fantasy and myth!"

"Sir Duke; I've lost my wife Aemilia, I've lost my twin sons, and I've also lost the missing twin boys that my wife and I had designated as *our* twin boys' servants," Aegeon revealed as the merchant from Syracuse languished in anguish.

"I've heard enough ludicrous insanity for now!" the half-drunken Duke declared. "Now Aegeon, or Aegean, or whatever the hell your screwball name is, I command that you walk your ass into downtown metropolitan Ephesus and see if you can collect one thousand marks from friends, misers, penny-pinchers, swindlers, prostitutes and merchants that you might meet or fight. That sum ought to buy your ransom, but I remind *you,* junior shit brains, that you have but a single day to meet your colossal debt obligation. And if begging and borrowing don't fuckin' work in your favor, you'd better learn how to cheat and steal in a goddamned hurry! Now, you Syracusan shit-head, get the fuck out of my presence before I change my erratic, ever-vacillating mind, which happens much more often than I change my damned expensive silk underwear!" the adamant Duke yelled. "Now Jailer, I command you to take this roving ignoramus into thy custody while the dumb-fuck frantically begs, borrows and steals!"

* * * * * * * * * * * * *

"The Comedy of Errors" is a play farce that is full of bizarre coincidences, as well as having its principal characters being full of abundant feces. Aegeon, the Merchant from Syracuse, had a son Antipholus of Syracuse, who has a servant, Dromio of Syracuse. Aegeon's wife Aemilia (who hadn't seen her husband for over twenty-three years) had a son Antipholus of Ephesus, who had a servant, Dromio of Ephesus. Naturally, the two mixed-up sets of identical twins were the exact same age.

Apparently, the boys' dysfunctional parents, Aegeon and Aemilia, got all four males mixed-up, and might have possibly even made the prostitute Epi's twins the masters, and Aegean and Aemilia's biological twins the unfortunate lowlife servants, each pair growing- up hundreds of miles apart. Or perhaps Aegeon and Aemilia really absolutely loathed one another, and used the near-catastrophic shipwreck incident as a good excuse to stay separated, without experiencing the public disgrace of becoming divorced, which was a major taboo of those fucked-up ancient times.

Now unknown to the itinerant merchant, Aegeon, his weirdo son Antipholus of Syracuse, along with Dromio of Syracuse (just

386

coincidentally), had arrived in Ephesus searching for Aemilia; the twin son *not* knowing that *his* long-lost psycho brother Antipholus of Ephesus already lived there in Ephesus, along with Dromio of Ephesus. (And *you,* Shakespearean reader probably thought that only *your* life was fucked-up!) The next scene opens with Antipholus of Syracuse and his servant Dromio of Syracuse conversing with a prosperous Merchant of Ephesus.

"You two stupid assholes better tell everyone who you meet in this city that you're from Epidamium, or Epididymis, or from Epidamnum, rather than from that den of iniquity, Syracuse," the Merchant strongly suggested to the new arrivals to Ephesus. "Or else, your goods and ship will be confiscated by our impulsive dock-master, Julius Seizure, and you'll be both taken before the Death Duke to be tried and executed by ungodly lethal semen injections professionally administered up your rear entrances. Now here's the money I owe you for your inferior products, and just play it cool until autumn arrives."

"Here Dromio," Antipholus of Syracuse demonstrably said. "Take this sack of money to the Centaur Inn that's in the center of town. Stay there, and I promise I'll show-up around dinnertime. I'll do a little touring, check-out where all the whorehouses and gay and lesbian bars are located, and then register as a guest into the Centaur," the Master Antipholus of Syracuse divulged. "Now servant, get the hell away from me before I sell half your ass into slavery, which is much worse than frolicking around in massive exploitive servitude for the rest of your doomed life."

"I'll make reservations for lodging at the disreputable Centaur Inn, and I'll await your arrival there," Dromio of Syracuse told his tyrannical master. "I'll even inspect the inn's coed outhouse, and the public piss, shit and regurgitation recreational gardens for you!"

After Dromio of Syracuse left to conduct his important errand in downtown Ephesus, Antipholus of Syracuse asked the wealthy Merchant if he'd like to have lunch with him at a loco local tavern. The visitor from Syracuse was mildly disappointed with the Merchant's response.

"Sorry to say, Antipholus, that I have a previous engagement with several other prominent area importers and exporters," the accommodating and affable Merchant apologetically explained. "We're getting into practicing hardcore whore and drug smuggling, and then conveniently blaming it all on unsuspecting merchants from Syracuse. Remember what I had mentioned about not disclosing your identity as a trader from Syracuse, or you'll be called and labeled a Syracusan traitor; you'll be splattered with rotten pumpkins in the public square, and then you'll look like a jerk-off Orangeman, and be ridiculed, scorned and humiliated for not having a buddy who looks like a fuckin' tangerine."

"Thanks for your helpful advice," Antipholus of Syracuse gratefully acknowledged. "Is that how your dock-master, the orange-skinned Julius

Seizure, got his extraordinary pigmentation? I honestly think that his unique skin color looks quite attractive."

"Yes, Orange Julius was bombarded with tons of rotten pumpkins until the elderly bloke finally convinced the dumb-dick Duke that he was from Troy, and not from Syracuse," the amused Merchant informatively explained. "I might see you, Antipholus, later this evening at the Centaur Inn, it behooves me to say. Ha, ha, ha! See you later, instigator. And my dear Friend; if you value your head and your dick, by all means, don't tell anyone you're from fuckin' Syracuse!"

'I'm really here in Ephesus to search for my mother and for my twin brother,' Antipholus remembered as the itinerant fellow strolled down the city's main street. 'This metropolis has a terrible reputation for atrocious felonies and enforcing arbitrary and questionable laws. But if my mom and my twin brother both work in an area brothel, then I might get lucky and accidentally discover them. And if they're both happily employed in a thriving gay and lesbian whorehouse, I'll be even luckier than ever!'

At that moment, Dromio of Ephesus was meandering down the street, and naturally Antipholus of Syracuse perceived the nutcase as being Dromio of Syracuse, *his* jaunty, rascally servant. The slightly shocked Master accosted whom the wandering merchant believed to be his loyal slave, who appeared rather dumbfounded and confused by his supposed Master's introductory commentary.

"Hello Dromio, you queer bait Imbecile, you!" Antipholus hailed the fat, runty stranger. "How come you've returned to this location so soon? I realize that you're notorious for your quickies, but this example of your shortening of time is truly absurd! Your shortening of time is even faster than the local baker's shortening of bread! Ha, ha, ha! Now Dromio, do you still have my goddamned money?"

"What the hell are you talking about?" Dromio of Ephesus asked Antipholus of Syracuse, thinking that the individual the dwarf was speaking with was his usually predictable Master, Antipholus of Ephesus. "I haven't seen your friggin' ass all morning, and now you lay this stupid nonsensical bullshit on me! And up to this moment, I had thought that I was the biggest asshole in town! Your wife wonders where the hell you are; why you had never showed-up for breakfast, and she's sent me out to learn who the hell you're screwing now!"

"What kind of illogical bullshit are you fabricating?" Antipholus of Syracuse lividly boomed. "I fancy that your fancy is a little too fancy. Now I repeat, where the fuck have you' left the money that I just gave you a half hour ago? And don't pretend to have amnesia! Tell me Dromio, or else I'll squeeze the stagnant shit right out of your anaconda-like intestines."

"Oh Master, you must mean the sixpence I had in my possession last Wednesday," Dromio of Ephesus recollected and articulated. "I spent it on a cheap jug of wine, and then sat mesmerized in an inn and watched the barmaid's jugs get bigger and bigger. What a set of knockers that well-endowed bitch had!"

"I'm not in a jovial, sportive mood Dromio," the visitor from Syracuse rebuked his servant facsimile. "Don't dilly-dally. Tell me where the fuckin' money is, or else I'll squeeze the blood, piss and shit out of your flabby, pygmy-like body! We're strangers in this fucked-up city, and the no-nonsense dock-master is suspicious of our conversation, and the loading and unloading supervisor is staring at us while standing next to a pile of stinking decaying pumpkins!"

"I advise you, Master, to return home immediately, or you won't get any decent sex from your wife until *Mt. Olympus* crumbles to the ground," Dromio of Ephesus emphasized. "If you value your limited sex life, I suggest you get the hell home immediately."

"What the fuck are you' talking about Dromio?" Antipholus screamed. "You know I ain't fuckin' married, and that once a day, habitually out of boredom, I screw a different intoxicated bitch every night, just for variety's sake! Now, for the last goddamned time Dromio, where is the sack of gold coins I had entrusted to you? I might need one of those coins to buy my first cheap piece of ass in Ephesus."

"What in shit's ugly name are you prattling?" Dromio incredulously asked the person whom he believed was his Master, Antipholus of Ephesus. "You gave me no gold, and you, like a totally focused human animal, pump the crap and the farts out of your wife every single evening, and at least twice a night when she's having her period. I know this to be fact, Master, because I hear your bedroom wall thudding every time your thick forehead, bed and skull bang into it."

"Look shit-head, stop jerking me around instead of jerking me off!" Antipholus shouted, getting the full attention of the gargantuan Julius Seizure, standing only fifty feet away. "You know for a fact that I'm not married! Quit being a knave knucklehead, and give me back my goddamned money."

"Look and listen, daft Master!" Dromio of Ephesus exclaimed in a bewildered tone of voice. "My mission is to take you home so that you can shack-up with your nympho' wife, and then have your standard mediocre dinner. I do believe that My Mistress and her sister both want a piece of you tonight!"

"Look Dromio, you frivolous, diabolical moron, even though we're the same age, I'm rapidly losing my damned patience and my remarkable tolerance for your juvenile quips and antics!" Antipholus of Syracuse yelled at the short, corpulent, dumpy fellow, as the mammoth Julius Seizure picked-up and then held two large rotten pumpkins in the distance. "Where are my thousand marks that I had entrusted to you? Stop trying to act goofy and aloof when you pretend to mistake me for a foreign comedy *talent* scout!"

"Look here, Master," Dromio of Ephesus argued in a startled and puzzled tone of voice. "I have marks from my bisexual girlfriend and from my male companion boyfriend's fingernails all over my neck, back, ass and shoulders. But I have not one mark from you, let alone the incredible thousand marks as you've indicated and insisted."

"You have no wife or mistress, or girlfriend, or sex-maniac male companion, Dromio!" Antipholus vehemently yelled and persisted. "You pathological liar! You're a gay son-of-a-bitch, and you know it! Who are you trying to deceive? Do you think that I was fuckin' born tomorrow, er, I mean yesterday?"

"Since when have you gone to live in Dementia Village, Master?" the astonished Dromio of Ephesus candidly asked. "I heard that too much jerking-off will make a fellow go blind, but obviously, too much sex and too many orgasms destroy the damned brain. I think that your present behavior and verbal utterances are proof of my bizarre theory."

"Now, I understand and fully fathom why people say that Ephesus is full of deceivers, fraud-peddlers, criminals, and psychopathic maniacs," Antipholus of Syracuse bellowed as Julius Seizure was busy frantically organizing a team of rotten pumpkin hurlers in the background. "The crazy citizens' trickery and conniving has already negatively influenced you, my gullible Dromio. The Devil dwells here in Ephesus, and Satan's evil has contaminated your vulnerable, weak mind in just a few short hours. Therefore, my only feasible recourse is to drag you into yonder alley and beat the shit out of you, well out of the visual range of that awesome-looking, orange-skinned dock-master, Julius Seizure!"

"No Master, no! What's gotten into you? Delirium I think!" Dromio of Ephesus objected in vain as Antipholus of Syracuse pulled the protesting slave into the side dark alley. "Did a venomous enchanted spider bite you on the ass, Master? Are your bowels working backwards? Stop this unwarranted physical punishment, Antipholus. Stop kicking me in the ass and groin! Are you having an epileptic fit like the ones that our psychopathic dock-master Julius Seizure always has?"

"Take that, and that, you thieving Asshole!" Antipholus of Syracuse's voice boomed as the amateur pugilist incessantly and repeatedly smacked the totally-confused and abused Dromio of Ephesus across the face and chest. "That'll be the first and last time you will ever lie to me, Dromio. So, disobedient knave; take that, and that, and that, and that, and…"

Act II

Adriana, the shrew wife of Antipholus of Ephesus, was angry that her normally dependable spouse had not returned home from downtown. The wife was venting her mounting angst to Luciana, the woman's teenage sister.

"Where is my derelict husband?" Adriana angrily asked. "Antipholus is probably checking-out the nude beach on the other side of Ephesus. I have a hunch that the pervert is secretly a voyeur."

"Your husband is probably with Dromio hanging-out at the docks, or at the mart, where the two boneheads usually stroll and chat," Luciana answered. "After a few glasses of wine, the inebriated dolts will come staggering home in typical fashion, leaning on each other's shoulder. Time is their master, so why worry about the idle dreamers, Adriana? They're safe and drunk, meandering around somewhere in Ephesus. Only visitors from Syracuse have to fear coming here and attempting to explore this perpetual combat zone for unwanted intruders."

"But how come privileged men have these ample liberties to avoid daily responsibilities, and we do not?" Adriana bitched. "Luciana; I have an idea. Let's have sex change operations. We'll get two lengths of sausages hanging from the butcher's rack to serve as dicks."

"Men's jobs and business transactions happen out on the streets, and women are restricted to the home," Luciana complained and pointed-out. "The only women that work outdoors and make good money in Ephesus are streetwalkers. Even barmaids and lap and couch dancers are confined inside, just like we are! This male chauvinism bullshit really sucks It's totally exploitive, Adriana!"

"I'm treated like a horse, Luciana. I reckon that I put on the bridle at my bridal," Adriana lamented and uttered with remorse. "Only horses, camels and asses wear bridles, so I guess I'm fuckin' suited to be just an ordinary domestic beast of burden for the remainder of my damned life."

"Men think they're masters of the universe, but please remember dear Sister," Luciana emphasized, "pussy and not money makes the world spin around as some of the more progressive astronomers, astrologers and scientists believe, but are afraid to say publicly because of probable persecution. Even that midget ape, your servant Dromio, thinks he's superior to either you or me."

"I'll either give my husband the benefit of the doubt, or the doubt of the benefit," Adriana spoke to her younger sister with seemingly blazing eyes. "If Antipholus is sleeping with another woman, I mean sleeping with another woman besides me, then I'll cut his balls off, and if the goofball is shacking-up with another man, then I'll sever-off my husband's balls *and* his dick before severing relations, sexual and otherwise with the adult dolt. Until then, Luciana, I'll suffer as a wretched soul that knows hardship and adversity all-too-well. Well, Sister; I've concluded that life's a bigger bitch than both of us menstruating, suffering females put together!"

"Well older married Sister, I shall marry a man and not a woman, I hope one day," Luciana replied. "And I'll trust that my future husband never forgets how to make love. My juicy pussy will always be his guiding beacon home. Say Sister," Luciana said with her head sticking out the front window. "Here comes your merry husband strolling down the street right this minute without a damned problem, concern, or grievance in the world. Wait a minute! I was mistaken. It's that fucked-up retard Dromio, and not *his* shit-for-brains master."

After Dromio entered the house, the zany nutcase attempted to explain to the ladies exactly what had transpired between him and Antipholus of Syracuse, whom the servant still thought was his same-age boss, Antipholus of Ephesus.

"Where the hell is your tardy master, my derelict husband?" Adriana demanded knowing. "Is he dating an alligator or a cobra?"

"I can't figure Antipholus out," Dromio of Ephesus testified. "The normally placid man smacked my face and ears silly, and nearly decapitated my head with a flurry of savage blows and judo kicks. I consider myself fortunate not dying from his devastating wrath! Your husband has never before treated me with such fucked-up animosity! I'll never go drinking with that crazy son-of-a-bitch, ever again!"

"Well, why did he almost box your ears off your noggin?" Adriana curiously asked. "You must've really pissed him off about something."

"Insane is too benign a word to fully describe your husband's ferocious actions," Dromio of Ephesus attested. "The crazy bastard is horn mad, I tell you. In fact, I mean stark-raving, horn-cuckoo mad. When I told your spouse that we should go home for dinner because you have assiduously labored all-day-long to prepare the meal, Antipholus asked me to surrender a thousand gold marks, which is ten times more money than I've ever seen in one place my entire life," Dromio disclosed. "Then, your mentally-ill marriage partner suddenly had the audacity to say that he wasn't married, had no house in Ephesus, and that I deserved to get the shit beaten out of me every damned hour! I never suspected that my master was so fuckin' mentally ill, if not mentally cruel. I think Antipholus is a goddamned psychopath on the loose, and I want no part of his erratic aggressive behavior! Your husband is turning into a beast, a monster!"

"Peasant jerk-off," Adriana yelled at Dromio in a rage. "Go and retrieve my out-of-kilter lazy louse of a spouse, and bring Antipholus home immediately, or Luciana and I will, with great satisfaction, practice some reproductive organ modification on you!" the enraged woman shouted as the wife raised a butcher knife high over her head to demonstrate her sincere intent to commit flagrant violence.

"I'll go, Madam, into the streets, and if I get brutally flogged, pummeled and pounded again, I only ask that should I die, that you collect donations to pay for my proper pauper's funeral and burial," Dromio requested. "I humbly hereby request that my mutilated and pulverized dead body will receive more respect than my live flesh does. But being a loyal servant, I shall honor your command."

"Damn it!" Adriana exclaimed to Luciana after Dromio stormed out of the house. "My face is getting wrinkled and showing its age, and my cunt is no longer moist and inviting. That's the reason why I suspect that my unfaithful husband's pleasurably screwing another younger woman! If Antipholus is merrily porking another wench into ecstasy, then I'll screw and nail the unfaithful cheater right into that massive ceiling timber up there! The rotten bastard is on the prowl searching for fresh pink tunnels to probe and examine. Sister, I feel like hard, stale, week-old bread, ready for the garbage dump! Married life really sucks, Luciana! Boo, hoo, hoo! Avoid it like the plague."

"Maybe the unlucky, horny woman was pursuing him, and not Antipholus chasing after her," Luciana intelligently suggested. "And despite his grotesque deformity, Dromio's actually kind of cute after all is said and done. I think I have the hots for the immature, hideous-looking simpleton!" Adriana's sister confessed. "Needless to say, I go for the different-type of guy. I really wonder if Dromio has a normal- sized male apparatus?"

"Don't make the same fuckin' moronic mistake that I did by getting married, and then being desperately trapped for the rest of your miserable life!" Adriana wept and sobbed. "Start tending to a year-round garden, Luciana, and begin growing crop after crop of cucumbers. That wonderful vegetable is not only good for eating', do you get my gist sister? Who needs an aberrant cheating spouse?" Adriana rhetorically asked. "Now listen to me Luciana, for I'm a woman of much dreadful negative experience, and I know what the hell I'm talkin' about. Grow fuckin' cucumbers and consistently use them for sexual gratification. Better yet, grow corn, but don't forget to husk it before doing the insertion. Now, let's get back to manufacturing those long, thick, smooth, wooden dildos, because unfortunately, I've already depleted my supply of damned hybrid cucumber and corn plant seeds."

* * * * * * * * * * * *

'This goddamned Ephesus is really a fucked-up place where fucked-up things happen to fucked-up people!' Antipholus of Syracuse seriously thought. 'The entire city must be under a wicked sorcerer's spell. And after I had maliciously slapped around that slapstick fool Dromio, I then remarkably discovered that my gold was safe at the Centaur Inn, which is the *inn* place to be here in this very peculiar city. Now I miss my droll servant and seek his singular company. Dromio, Dromio, wherefore art thou Dromio?'

Antipholus couldn't believe his dark blue eyes when the Syracuse native observed Dromio (of Syracuse) nonchalantly sauntering-down the cobblestone street. The Merchant from Syracuse felt guilty for beating the crap out of Dromio (of Ephesus), whom he had perceived to be Dromio (of Syracuse).

"How are you doing Master?" Dromio of Syracuse saluted his superior. "You look glum as a purple plum. Are you having a bad face day? Are you still constipated from three weeks ago?"

"I'm sorry that I recently assaulted and abused you," Antipholus sincerely apologized. "How could you be so merry and gay after being so brutally abused? Well, Dromio. Let's forget about the gay part for now. When you had jested just a half an hour ago that you had not known anything about the Centaur Inn; that my wife whom I didn't have wanted me home for dinner at a tenement house called the Phoenix, and that you know nothing about my hard-earned thousand marks of gold!" the master questioned and reviewed to his befuddled servant. "Why didn't you just tell me the damned truth, Dromio, and not answer me so goddamned crazily when I had simply asked you about those rudimentary, logical things! You could've avoided a savage beating, my faithful servant, if you hadn't been so fuckin' facetious with me! But dear slave, I must apologize for beating the crap out of you."

"What the hell are you talking about Master?" Dromio (of Syracuse) incredulously asked. "You must've contracted scarlet fever because your face and your sweating forehead are turning crimson!"

"Look Dromio; I slapped your face into pulp just a half hour ago because I thought that you were a villain that pilfered my gold, and that you were lying to me about other relevant matters," Antipholus answered while trying to hold back more negative emotion. "And now, you're acting fucked-up again, in this totally fucked-up city! What in Asia Minor is going on here? I think that both you and Asia Minor seriously need a psychiatric evaluation!"

"Master, I haven't seen a hair of you, you bald-headed Freak, ever since I departed your eminent presence to head towards the Centaur Inn in the center of Ephesus!" Dromio (of Syracuse) insisted. "Now I believe you're under the influence of either alcohol or an evil wizard's wand, and that *you'* require immediate psychological intervention, or maybe even some heavy-duty emergency brain surgery!"

"Villainous Dromio!" How dare you utterly speak so crazily!" Antipholus of Syracuse accused and screamed. "There you go again with this lousy denial bullshit! I suppose you're going to deny obtaining a receipt for my gold deposit at the Centaur Inn, and informing me that my wife, whom I don't have, has dinner ready for me! I think you deserve another severe beating, because you now lie and claim I hadn't pounded and pummeled you in the first place!"

"Stop joking around, Master! I've never seen you behave in such a peculiar, fucked-up fashion before!" Dromio (of Syracuse) exclaimed. "If I didn't fear your prolific temper so much, I'd say that you're fuckin' lying through your buckteeth! Stop being so surreptitious, and please cease declaring all of this weird jesting, seemingly in earnest! It's making my bowels act-up! My alimentary canal feels like an elementary sewer system. I've already just farted wet gas four times, and that's a very bad sign of far worse things to come!"

"Why am I, a gentleman, arguing with such a saucy-mouthed, certifiable Asshole?" Antipholus yelled at his one and only true subordinate. "I don't like your demeanor Dromio, because contrary to my normal damned easy-going disposition, your strange language is making me all aggravated and vitriolic. I believe you require another advanced lesson in common courtesy."

"Couldn't I wear a soldier's helmet before you decide to start banging your fists against my sensitive coconut?" Dromio asked in jest, still believing that his incensed Master was kidding around. "Perhaps you'll allow me to wear two soldier helmets; a smaller one inside of a larger one!"

"Okay you stubborn. lying son-of-a-bitch!" Antipholus hollered at his true, obedient servant Dromio. "Take that, and that, and that, and that! This beating I'm vigorously administering to you should refresh your hazy, lazy memory of your first thrashing!"

"Thank you, Sir!" Dromio surprisingly said as he wiped blood away from his mouth, nose and ears. "If I was a hanging dirty rug, I'd be beaten less!"

"Thank me for what?" Antipholus asked in amazement. "I can't fathom your very odd words!"

"Thank you for giving me something for nothing!" Dromio defiantly replied. "That deviant practice of giving me something for nothing goes against your ordinarily frugal and parsimonious habits! Your typical spending habits and generosity are usually cheaper than dirt; quite actually, dirt cheap!"

"Take that, and that, and that, and that!" Antipholus screamed like an incensed maniac as the livid master used poor Dromio's face as a suitable punching bag. "You lying little, fat Bastard! I'll knock your fuckin' teeth down your throat all the way to your fuckin' anus! Now then, you battered idiot," Antipholus briefly paused to give his arm muscles and fists a rest. "Are you going to insist on taking me home to my non-existent wife, and my non-existent house, for my non-existent dinner?"

"Certainly not, Sir!" Dromio answered, fearing additional damage and injury to his person. "I recommend that we have a delicious supper at the hysterical, I meant to say 'historical' Centaur Inn!"

"At last, you're coming to your senses!" the Master commended his bloodied victim. "You mentally handicapped Fool! Thank the gods that I didn't have to strangle or murder you with my innocent bare hands! Thank traditional ethical logic, Dromio, for me being so merciful in sparing your worthless life!"

Just as Antipholus of Syracuse thought that Dromio of Syracuse had discarded his whimsical daftness, and had satisfactorily returned to sanity, Adriana and Luciana speedily rambled up the cobblestone street in the men's direction. More wild chaos was about to occur.

"Ah Antipholus," Adriana sarcastically greeted the bewildered stranger. "You look odd, and apparently you're frowning at the sight of my appearance. You think I don't know that you're screwing every harlot and hooker at the Centaur Inn, that demonic brothel in a tavern's disguise! Today, I truly wish I wasn't your dedicated wife and slave. Why have you rejected my perpetual love and sacrifice?" Adriana demanded of the speechless visitor to Ephesus. "Your lustful, licentious behavior has thoroughly and permanently contaminated our marital relationship! Why have you estranged yourself from my loving embrace, you wandering playboy jerk-off! Why have you abandoned your one true bed and your horny, dry-holed wife?"

"Who the hell are you, Bitch?" Antipholus protested the idea of being falsely lectured to and admonished. "I know you not, and from your sharp tongue, I wish to never make your acquaintance. I've only been in this fucked-up city for two hours, and with every passing minute, the fucked-up inhabitants are growing more fucked-up by the second," the confused fellow balked and squawked. "I suspect that Hades is more fathomable than fucked-up Ephesus is!"

"Antipholus," Luciana loudly chimed in. "What the hell's wrong with your shallow mind? Has your brain swallowed your asshole, or what? My sister sent Dromio out to retrieve your ass from the streets to have your evening dinner, and now *you,* like an outrageous lunatic, claim that you don't fuckin' even know us! Have you fuckin' forgotten your own name and identity, too? Do you still fuckin' recognize your image in a mirror?"

"I don't know what the hell you two obnoxious Bitches are talking about, either one of you!" the bleeding Dromio (of Syracuse) contributed, adding a new aspect to the general madness. "Forgive my bleeding Ladies, but I'm having my period from my face!"

"Dromio, this bully, my arrogant and abusive husband, brutally bashed the shit out of you just for you telling him to come home for supper?" Adriana yelled and alleged. "The ruffian had to buffet you around just because you told him to return home for the buffet?"

"Dromio, before I go completely insane in this insane city, did you ever converse with this shrew of a woman before now?" Antipholus queried his equally-puzzled assistant.

"I never saw this bitch before in my life, and I've never had the displeasure of exchanging words with her grotesque-looking companion, either," Dromio confessed. "Stranger bullshit I have never seen or heard!"

"Dromio, I insist that you cease your deliberate lying, or your next destinations will certainly be the undertaker's residence, and then the pauper's cemetery," Antipholus (of Syracuse) vociferously threatened his usually truthful helper. "Now level with me my servant, or I'll proceed to systematically level you!"

"Master, I swear on my heart that I've never seen or spoken to either of these two strumpets before in all my days on this fucked-up planet, or roaming around this totally fucked-up city!" Dromio reluctantly answered with a tremendous dumbfounded expression on his countenance.

"Well then, how does this bitch that claims to be my lawful wedded wife know my fuckin' name, and yours too?" Antipholus questioned Dromio like a court prosecutor. "Is she a goddamned soothsayer acting by means of divine inspiration?"

"How dare you and Dromio conspire and creatively counterfeit your incredible stories," Adriana directly accused Antipholus. "You're both awkwardly covering-up for scurrilously and immorally cavorting around town, and casually consorting with don't-give-a-shit wanting-your-money whores at the abominable and disreputable Centaur Inn! I know when men are lying through their teeth, and this is one such all-too-glaring instance! Now accompany me home my straying Husband," Adriana insisted while pulling Antipholus's sleeve. "I demand that you come home for some reconciliation, a decent dinner, and some major league sex. Thou art an oak, Antipholus, and I a virtuous vine to wrap-around your strong, muscular anatomy, whatever the hell those remote analogies mean!"

'Is this a pathetic nightmare or a wonderful dream come true?' Antipholus imagined. 'I'm getting a free meal, and getting laid, too, by this insane woman in this insane city! Life is good, but my new wife makes it even better! Ephesus is not such a bad fuckin' town after all. In this bizarre city, the women pursue, solicit and proposition the men. In the future, I ought to visit this dangerous, enchanted fucked-up place more often!'

397

"Dromio," Luciana piped-up, completely breaking Antipholus's extended fantasy daydreaming. "Go tell the other servants to get dinner ready and the table set immediately, you snail, you slug, you turtle wannabe'!" Adriana's sister gruffly criticized who she erroneously thought was her house servant. "Get your ass moving, or else I'll be inclined to do to you more harm upon your obese, distorted body than your dumpy rear end has already sustained."

'This crazy bitch Luciana loves me, and strongly desires to be pumped by my erect miniature pussy stuffer!' Dromio (of Syracuse) hypothesized. 'I won't mind getting laid' in this fucked-up, fantasy city where nothing makes sense! Although I feel virile as a gorilla, I mustn't ruin everything by acting like the dumb ass that I am. But if I want quality ass from this enticing Luciana broad, I must not act like an ass, even if I *am* in fact, and in truth, a stupid ass. But how can I avoid procrastinating when I don't even know where Adriana and Luciana live?' Dromio (of Syracuse) wondered. 'I can't appear to be too uncooperative or too uninterested. This whole fantastic, convoluted scenario is too fucked-up beyond belief!'

"Okay Dromio; you can walk home with us so you don't have to scurry ahead alone," Adriana amazingly volunteered the servant's temporary salvation from being awkwardly embarrassed at not knowing where the designated home was located. "You can guard the gate while your master Antipholus, Luciana, and I ravenously devour our delicious dinner. We women temporarily forgive you two wandering imbeciles for the queer pranks that you've both pulled, as long as you two mental cases admit and confess to have actually committed them."

'Am I on Earth, or in Heaven, or in Hell? All three places seem merged into one entity right now. Destroy my fragile ego, you attractive Woman that wildly claims to be my wife. I just don't fuckin' care!' Antipholus mused and thought. 'Screw the Centaur Inn, and it's prolific number of kinky prostitutes! As long as I have a delectable supper and get laid to boot, without having to pay a hooker at the Centaur, I have nothing to complain about, and don't give a shit that I'm capriciously berated and belittled by these two female tigers.'

"Master, should I still be your porter while guarding the gate?" Dromio hesitantly asked in a whisper. "I can't get laid while watching the front gate! The act would be too embarrassing to do in public on the street! I do have my morals, you know!"

"Remember the cardinal rule of servitude!" Antipholus whispered back to his servant. "The Master's needs always *come* first!"

Act III

An hour later, the yet-to-be-involved Antipholus of Ephesus arrived home for dinner bringing along two close friends, Angelo the Goldsmith and Balthasar the Merchant. Dromio of Syracuse, who had been assigned to guard the house's gate by Adriana, had stepped into the back yard to piss into a rabbit hole. Antipholus (of Ephesus) was more than dismayed to find the front door locked, and the commonplace home's dirty curtains drawn.

"Signior Angelo, I hope that you will excuse this unfortunate embarrassment, but my bitchy wife gets her ovaries twisted when the belligerent shrew thinks that I'm evading eating her horrible-tasting supper food," Antipholus (of Ephesus) apologized to his goldsmith acquaintance. "If we ever get inside and converse with Adriana, please politely tell the wench that I had purchased for her a new golden necklace, and that you'll promptly bring the jewelry piece to my residence tomorrow. That way, I'll be able to get laid tonight, and we'll all worry about tomorrow, tomorrow."

"How come the friggin' door's locked Master?" Dromio of Ephesus asked. "This surprise is rather uncharacteristic of Adriana and Luciana, who usually allow all kinds of men and boys to enter for fun, games, pleasure and partying."

"Shut-up, Fuck-head!" Antipholus rudely disciplined his naughty assistant. "On the way here, you've falsely claimed to my friends that I beat the shit out of you at the mart, and also falsely claimed that I had stated I had given you a thousand marks, which I don't fuckin' have with all of my money accounts and property added together! How much vino have you been drinking Dromio?"

"Argue and persuade all you want, Master, but you did savagely beat the shit out of me at the mart, and your fingerprints and knuckle and hand laceration marks are all over my face, neck, chest and ass," Dromio of Ephesus insisted. "The bruise-like welts look just like ink smeared on paper. Those mothers ain't going away soon! It would be easier for a woman to grow tits and nipples on her elbows, than for these terrible welts to heal within a year!"

"I believe that thou art a confirmed Asshole liar, and when you aren't an ordinary simple ass, you're a double asshole liar Dromio!" Antipholus of Ephesus belittled Dromio (of Ephesus) for the amusement of Angelo the Goldsmith and Balthasar the Merchant.

"If you think I'm an ass, then that's perfectly all right with me," Dromio returned. "But please don't hop on my back and force me to carry you all around the damned city. It's bad enough that most people already believe that you're gay. I don't want the gossipers to generalize the same about me by association. Since I'm an ornery double ass, as you've just described, I ought to kick your lazy butt Master all over Ephesus and its suburbs!"

"Well anyway," Balthasar the Merchant interrupted the minor argument. "I was promised a great meal and have waited out here for five minutes now eating and swallowing just air and dust. What the fuck's the matter here? Do you need a new front door, Antipholus?"

"Dromio, yell inside for my' wife, and her sister, to let us in while I confer with Angelo and Balthasar about important business matters," Antipholus (of Ephesus) directed his irascible servant as the three businessmen descended the entrance steps. "And if you fail again as is your wont, for your deserved punishment, I'll make you lick my wife's smelly cunt!" the perturbed homeowner lectured and rhymed as his two prosperous friends indulgently laughed.

In the meantime, (after draining his kidneys' contents into the backyard rabbit hole cesspool), Dromio of Syracuse had entered the house from the back entrance, and swiftly paced to the front door. When he was about to open the portal and again guard the house, the twin dwarf heard Dromio of Ephesus speak from the outside: "Bridget, Maud, Marian, Ciceley, Gillian, Martha, Gin, open the door and let me the fuck in!" the facsimile servant weirdly said, pretending that the home was a familiar house of prostitution.

"Chicken capon, chicken without a cape on, malt-horse beer, I'm warning you to get the fuck out of here!" Dromio of Syracuse rhymed back from behind the closed door.

"Who talks in there?" Dromio of Ephesus asked. "Your voice sounds just like me! Are you a fuckin' fucked-up ventriloquist?"

Hearing the mild. ridiculous debate-in-progress, Antipholus of Ephesus climbed the steps and hollered into the closed door, "Look Asshole, inside my home! I've caught you screwing around with my promiscuous wife, and also flirting with my kinky sister-in-law! Now open the goddamned door! I'd break the mother-fucker down, but then I would have to explain to the police why I demolished my own damned front door, and then have to pay for a new one besides. I'm quite hungry and desire my supper, so open the goddamned door!"

"Come again some other time when the hosts and guests are not so preoccupied!" Antipholus of Syracuse barked through the closed solid cedar door at his Asia Minor counterpart and duplicate. "Come back tomorrow!"

"Holy horse shit mounds!" Antipholus of Ephesus exclaimed in astonishment to his two friends. "That masculine voice is identical to mine! It's as if I'm conversing with myself, which seems to others as if I'm talking to myself! I think my fuckin' house must be haunted, or possessed by insane demons and devils. Hey, you in there. Who are you that keeps me from entering my own house? Are you animal, vegetable or fuckin' mineral?"

"It is I Dromio, who has been assigned the important role of pretending to be porter for this entire afternoon," the idiot from Syracuse honestly explained.

"You see what I mean Master," Dromio of Ephesus said to Antipholus of Ephesus. "Someone has stolen my identity and my personality, and another fucked-up spirit or magician has pilfered yours, too. Maybe you beat the shit out of that other Dromio behind that door this morning, just like you had beaten the total shit out of me this morning. But the other Dromio on the other side of the door must have developed a huge brain tumor that prevents the dumb-shit from acting normal."

"I didn't beat the shit out of anybody this morning!" Antipholus of Ephesus screamed his tonsils out like a livid psychopath. "I'm the only goddamned pacifist in all of Ephesus."

Then Luce, the house's kitchen maid, and also the girlfriend of Dromio of Ephesus. approached the home. The domestic servant was immediately intercepted and detained by her confused beau, Dromio (of Ephesus).

"What's all the chaos in there?" Luce asked her clownish male companion. "It sounds like a damned orgy going on inside!"

"Let our Master in," Dromio asked Luce. "You have the spare key and carry it around inside your smelly girdle. You might also try the key on your chastity belt, the next time you want some hot and heavy action from me!" the silly fool jested.

"I can't do it!" Luce stubbornly stated. "Your owner has come too late for dinner, and Madam Adriana might throw a temper tantrum and fire my ass for violating her inflexible rules. I need this pissy job simply to live at a subsistence level. just the same way you need your lowly employment working in this lousy ghetto dumpster. Our damned alternatives, Dromio, are pretty limited."

"Now if that is you chunky Luce standing outside," Dromio of Syracuse barked through the closed door after hearing and learning the maid's name, "then kick your jerk-off faggot friend in the balls three times for me and then wildly yank his dick off."

"What the hell's your voice doing inside there if you're out here bullshitting with me?" Luce asked Dromio of Ephesus. "This must be a goddamned haunted house for sure! And I always thought that just the rest of Ephesus was fucked-up, and not only the raucous Centaur Lap Dance and Striptease Lounge!"

"Let me inside!" Antipholus of Ephesus ordered Luce the Kitchen Maid. "Or lend me your key, and I'll let myself in! After all; it's my fuckin' house being debated here! And whoever is inside is making a mockery out of me in front of my distinguished guests!"

"Pound on the door with your fists until your clenched hands bleed and ache!" Luce defiantly answered her infuriated Master. "I must obey Adriana's clear rules, and *you* know you're late for dinner, farting around outside the front door, and that your wife doesn't tolerate that kind of disobedient chicken-shit either, with or without a valid excuse."

"Wife Adriana, are you inside?" the now-mortified Antipholus of Ephesus yelled from the outside steps. "I must speak with you because I'm tired of speaking with myself!"

"You anonymous, very annoying, and very pathetic Spirit Knave. I don't know who the hell you are, but I advise you to leave the premises immediately before I open the door and scald your face with boiling hot water!" Adriana hollered outside through the closed door. "My husband is already inside, so stop trespassing on our property, and I demand that you abandon the front steps this instant. And if you're a door-to-door salesman selling spoons, forks, knives, tampons, dildos, and bed pans, you can shove them all up your asshole, and then lick your anal ring clean."

"Antipholus," Balthasar the Merchant objectively said while giggling in between words. "Maybe we should heed your wife's sage advice. Adriana may be having her period and taking it out on everyone else!"

"She acts like she has her damned period every minute of every day of every month of every lousy year," Antipholus (of Ephesus) disgustedly remarked. "That demented bitch is a real witch that belongs in a deep ditch contracting trench-mouth!"

"Yes Antipholus, I agree with Balthasar," Angelo the Goldsmith urged. "There's neither cheer nor welcome in your turbulent home-sweet-home this evening, so let's go somewhere else to have a sumptuous dinner. How about the infamous Centaur Inn? I hear that they have terrific food and bedroom entertainment there in the apartments upstairs. We can all be like kissing cuisines, ha, ha, ha! Quite frankly Antipholus, your ramshackle home the Phoenix seems to have disintegrated into being a psychological rubble of ashes!"

"If we were elephants, Master, we could fart the door down if our trunks proved ineffective!" Dromio (of Ephesus) imaginatively-but-irrelevantly commented. "Let us in!" Dromio of Ephesus yelled at the top of his lungs through the closed door.

"Fish will grow feathers, and birds will have fins, and elephants will fly by farting smelly air before that impossible event ever happens," Dromio of Syracuse screamed back through the shut door.

"Master; I find myself talking with myself, but not at all fuckin' agreeing with myself," Dromio of Ephesus related to his greatly

402

chagrined employer. "Tomorrow morning, I might wake-up and find myself dead!"

"Dromio, go to the neighbor's house, and fetch me an iron crow, er, I mean an iron crowbar, and I'll in a rage destroy this door, and then also obliterate the discourteous imposters or maniacs concealed behind it," the bent-out-of-shape homeowner ordered.

"Such quack lunacy will damage your reputation in the already fucked-up Ephesus community, including the totally fucked-up gay and lesbian community," Balthasar emphasized, advising Antipholus against committing senseless violence against his own property. "And if you go berserk and kill four or more people by your vengeful deed, then the Death Duke will have you hung in the gallows for indiscreetly eliminating four or more resourceful or potential stupid taxpayers."

"Perhaps Balthasar's right in saying reason should prevail over anger," Angelo the Goldsmith counseled and chimed-in. "A good meal and a fine courtesan will cure you of your fits of fury. Patience should guide your judgment, Antipholus. I suggest that we forget about the Centaur Inn and saunter-over to the Tiger. That rat-trap has great week-old food there, and the veteran whores at that disreputable establishment can do it all. Why stay here and get into a vulgar fracas with raunchy, saucy lowlife Ghosts that are hitting on your wife and sister-in-law inside your sacred castle?"

"Your impeccable reasoning Angelo has victoriously prevailed," Antipholus of Ephesus acceded. "I know a particular attractive wench at the Tiger Inn who always bats her eyes when passing me on the streets. I predict she'll soothe my ruffled, out-of-kilter emotions, and empathize with my current mangled sentiments and feelings of inferiority."

"I'm glad that you finally came to your senses," Dromio of Ephesus praised his Master. "Truthfully, I don't know who would win if we had to get into a brawl with our own Ghosts or Voices."

Antipholus (of Ephesus) ignored Dromio's prattle and addressed the goldsmith. "Angelo, go to your business and get me a gold chain to give to the comely prostitute over at the Tiger Inn. Meet us there in an hour. You might also want to bring along several larger rusty iron chains for S&M happy hour! Ha, ha, ha! Now make haste and lose some of that chubby waist."

"Why are you doing this absolutely crazy thing, Master?" Dromio of Ephesus asked. "It's so unlike you!"

"I'll spite Adriana by getting the most expensive piece of ass ever!" the often-impractical Antipholus of Ephesus snickered and then laughed. "My wife gives quality head when she's jealous!"

* * * * * * * * * * * *

403

Luciana was having a discussion in a side room of the Phoenix with Antipholus of Syracuse about his marital vows, duties and responsibilities, which all seemed to have escaped the wandering merchant's memory. Adriana's sister was not-too-pleased with the man's non-committal nature and character.

"How quickly, Antipholus, you've forgotten your sacred pledge to love, honor and obey," Luciana criticized, finding fault with the man whom she truly believed to be *his* twin brother. "I suppose that you think of marriage and sex like you evaluate roast of lamb. It tastes good in the beginning, but if you sample it every damned night, you then lustily desire to eat pork, steak, beef, chicken, bacon, and ham, instead. But your very evident infidelity is contrary to the sacred nuptial vows you had made to Adriana."

"What the hell are you talking about?" Antipholus (of Syracuse) challenged. "I'm not married to Adriana, or to anyone else, male or female. I've never before been to a crazy place like Ephesus, and after I blow this fucked-up town, I never want to return here again in this life or the next!"

"I believe that you had wed my sister for her dowry, and also for her meager inheritance," Luciana all-too-candidly insinuated. "Pretend to be sincere to her, even if your heart and motives are tainted. A shameful bastard like you ought to be able to slickly mask his extra-curricular activities with other more-promiscuous women over at the Centaur. Some men wear their damned emotions on their sleeves, but you Antipholus are a patented bold-faced liar who only wears short-sleeve shirts, even in the goddamned winter. And you guiltlessly lie and blatantly claim that you aren't married to my beloved sister. You've certainly somehow changed from a good man into a monstrous, hedonistic heathen!"

"What the hell are you insanely babbling?" Antipholus objected. "I love you sweet Mistress, despite the fact that I've forgotten your goddamned name. You're quite a remarkable orator, so therefore, teach me how to think and speak eloquently. Stop traducing my ego, and benignly build-up my confidence like a well-bred woman should," Antipholus (of Syracuse) insisted. "Transform me into the man you strongly desire, and motivate me to achieve grand titles and awards. But I must first oppose the idea that your bitchy sister is my wife! And neither am I her faithful wedded husband! Now crazy misguided Wench, give me a kiss and let me feel and caress your succulent breasts, and our relationship will be off to a most excellent start. Oh, beautiful dark-skinned Lady; I'm willing to sacrifice everything I have lost in the latest lottery just to hit on you!"

"You're certifiably insane!" Luciana strenuously objected. "I can't be your mate because you're married to my mercurial-tempered sister,

Adriana. Either you aren't playing with a full deck, or you fell out of your tree off the highest limb. You're the most fucked-up man I've ever known, and you claim I've only known you for fifteen minutes."

"I love to gaze into your dark, brown, shit-colored eyes and imagine that we share splendid and inspired bliss and good cheer," Antipholus (of Syracuse) awkwardly wooed.

"Look asshole, brother-in-law; you certainly aren't the sharpest knife in the kitchen drawer," Luciana rankled. "So, *gaze* into my dark brown shit-colored eyes all you like, but I suspect that you've been consorting with other kinds of *gays*, if you accurately interpret my implied allusion."

"Oh, my precious Love; learn to honor and revere me," Antipholus (of Syracuse) proposed on his knee to Luciana. "I deeply love you more than life itself, and desperately need to get laid, or I'll drown in semen from the inside-out!"

"Why do you refer to me as 'my Love' when you should be pumping and porking my sex-deprived sister?" Luciana exclaimed as the angry hussy swiftly kicked the kneeling Antipholus in the groin, making him keel over on his side, and then instinctively holding his testicles in excruciating pain. "And furthermore, horny toad, I ought to kick you in the scrotum even harder a second time for my wonderful sister's sake!"

"I'll endure agony and hardship for your constant love," Antipholus (of Syracuse) cried and moaned as the visiting wooer frenetically rolled-around upon the wood-planked floor. "Usually, I have my ass kicked by ladies, but this novelty anguish originating from a violent whore wench like you certainly represents an all-time first! You, my wondrous Woman, have no husband, and I no faithful wife. Give me your soft enticing hand, and elope with me to Syracuse."

Luciana got so pissed-off and wild-minded at the suffering Antipholus's audacity that the unfair maiden compulsively kicked the house guest a second time in the "family jewels" for her beloved sister's sake, and next the perplexed Antipholus of Syracuse again tumbled onto and rolled around upon the floor in total discomfort.

"I hope your balls never again descend into your testicle pouch!" the livid Luciana yelled. "I just sent your epididymis to Epididium!"

Luciana exited the small side room, and after a minute had elapsed, Antipholus (of Syracuse) finally struggled to his feet. Dromio (of Syracuse) entered the room to check-up on his master's romantic adventures and learn of their results.

"Dromio," Antipholus said, wincing with pain. "Why the hell are you running all over this confounded house? Are you looking for a place to take a quick unexpected shit? I see no animal holes anywhere inside this dump!"

"Behold a complete Asshole!" Dromio exclaimed to his Master while unaware of his boss's extended suffering. "We're both definitely getting old and need to find ourselves appropriate wives. I realize that I'm getting long-in-the-tooth, because I now have more hair on my ass than I have on my head, and you're an accursed victim to the same damned condition. I do believe, Master, that I'm now a woman's man!"

"What do you mean when you say you're a woman's man?" Antipholus (of Syracuse) asked as the recent kicking victim gently massaged his recently received hurting injuries. "And you can't possibly be beside yourself because that's impossible, and also because you aren't holding a goddamned mirror in front of your face while looking backwards into another goddamned mirror."

"I've just fallen in love Master, and I don't know exactly what to do with my throbbing hard-on!" Dromio (of Syracuse) declared and stated. "Hard-ons are a rare phenomenon for me!"

"Whatever you do, don't stick the infected thing up my ass!" Antipholus nastily replied. "That'll not only add insult to injury, but also injury to injury. Who is this improper hussy that has remarkably captured your heart? Does she work as a bearded tattooed freak in a traveling circus sideshow? Is she employed over at the Centaur?"

"She's a common wench that works in this home's kitchen," Dromio explained to his still-aching Master. "She's sort of like a heavenly lamp that's really lit my fire!"

"Asshole, you're supposed to stick your log in her fire!" Antipholus caustically replied. "What kind of friggin' skin color does she have, for in this day and age, *that* important situation could change the complexion of everything?"

"She has swarthy skin pigmentation, like a dark pig; darker than the leather of the shoes you're wearing," Dromio explained to his still-baffled and aching boss. "I'm telling you, Master. Noah's flood could not extinguish the fire I feel in my balls. Do you understand how it feels when your balls turn dark blue and ache?"

"I most certainly do perceive it from plenty of recent experience," Antipholus of Syracuse groaned and acknowledged. "What's the Bitch's first name?"

"She told me ''Nell', but everyone else in this fucked-up house inside this fucked-up city calls her Luce," Dromio related in a rather bewildered state of mind. "And the gargantuan, obese bitch weighs at least three hundred and fifty pounds, and could lift us both up over her head, and simultaneously, body slam the two of us right through this damned wooden floor."

"Luce sounds like a hefty, stocky, wide-bodied heifer!" Antipholus accurately concluded and expressed. "Can you handle all that porterhouse?"

"Yes, I think. Nell is quite spherical, just like a globe, and I imagine that I could find each and every country and sea somewhere on her rotund anatomy," Dromio lucidly agreed. "Nell, er I mean Luce, makes fat look like skinny, and corpulent look like thin, if you know what the fuck I'm communicating. Luce must have loose bowels, and her intestines must be clogged all the way up to her thick and dense medulla oblongata!"

"Well, if her body reminds you of a globe, on what part of her gargantuan body would Scotland be?" Antipholus asked.

"On her exceedingly big-ass buttocks," Dromio imagined and eloquently remarked. "And France is situated under her left hairy armpit, and Britain is located under Nell's, er I mean under Luce's right hairy armpit, all partially shaven and bleached the color of snow, just like the fucked-up White Cliffs of Dover. And Spain is in her right sprained ankle, and the Indies are in her nose, for her nostrils feature a gold ring; and a ruby, and an emerald pierced into both sides, with hot ballast steaming out of her dragon-like nasal passages."

"Well then, where on her rotund body could Belgium and Norway be located?" Antipholus inquired as his great testicular pain finally subsided.

"Just like in Denmark, something is definitely rotten in her stinking crotch hole!" amused Dromio loudly mentioned. "But Master, I do believe that the women of this house are all witches, and like Circe in Homer's *Odyssey*, the malicious lady vampires might change us into oinking swine if we aren't captured squealing pigs already!"

"I believe you're absolutely right Dromio, and you and I have to hastily scoot out of this fucked-up town as soon as possible," Antipholus of Syracuse concurred. "I don't want to be married to any damned bitchy witch that might turn my dick and balls into cement. This whole crazy city seems to be under an evil enchantment. Here's my sage plan, and listen carefully," the Master told his servant. "Go to the mart docks and book passage for two on any ship going to any destination, just to get the hell out of here'. Then, return to this insane asylum house, rescue me from its lunatic occupants, and we'll fuckin' dash as fast as our feet and legs can sprint to the awaiting vessel. I love Luciana, but she's likely to magically turn-out to be that bitch Adriana's nasty hundred-year-old great-great grandmother!"

After Dromio of Syracuse left the premises and made a beeline to the harbor docks, Angelo the Goldsmith, who was quite familiar with the Phoenix house, entered the premises via the back kitchen door, and soon the merchant came face to face with Antipholus of Syracuse, whom he naturally believed to be Antipholus of Ephesus.

"Sorry, I'm late Antipholus," Angelo apologized, "but it took me much longer than I had originally thought to fabricate this splendid golden necklace for your wife. I figured that you no longer would be dining and fucking around at the risque Tiger Inn, and I was right, because I caught you fucking around here at your home."

"What the fuck are you' blustering about?" Antipholus (of Syracuse) exclaimed. "You've gone absolutely bonkers, and I don't even fuckin' know who you are!"

"You have a terrific sense of humor that you've concealed all these years that I've known you," Angelo observed and shared. "Ha, ha, ha! You really crack me up as if I were a vulnerable chestnut, or a fractured walnut. Ha, ha, ha! Antipholus. Now here's the magnificent golden necklace I had promised to manufacture for you!"

"What the hell do you propose I do with it?" Antipholus asked. "Use it as a kind of anchor to keep my balls tucked inside my scrotum?"

"Ha, ha, ha," Angelo guffawed. "You're making me piss my pants! Now, please give it to your horny, dry-welled wife you always complain about, and you can pay me for my labor later on. And then, Antipholus, we'll reminisce old times and bitch about our marital bitches over tall mugs of ale, ha, ha, ha!"

'This goldsmith is totally fucked-up, just like all the other totally fucked-up people in this totally fucked-up house, in this totally fucked-up city!' Antipholus (of Syracuse) evaluated. 'I'll just jolly the old fuck, and be one golden necklace richer after I retrieve my thousand marks Dromio has securely deposited at the notorious Centaur Inn. Then, my mentally-ill servant and I will make a mad bolt to the docks, if they haven't already vanished into thin air in this totally fucked-up city of zany sorcerers and crazed madmen.'

Antipholus graciously accepted the golden necklace just to get rid of the meddling goldsmith nuisance. "Thank you for the delivery and I'll pay you sometime tonight after dinner," the Syracusan lied to Angelo, to whom he had never been introduced.

"You're a jolly, merry son-of-a-bitch!" Angelo complimented the necklace recipient. "Farewell until later on, and may you screw Adriana a hundred times between now and then! Ha, ha, ha! Antipholus, you blithe bastard; you really tickle my fancy and crack me up something fierce!"

"Goodbye, Sir!" the stunned receiver said as Antipholus stared in amazement at the very expensive golden necklace in his hand. 'I'll keep this wonderful gift and give it to Dromio after I propose to him!' Antipholus (of Syracuse) mused and then chuckled.

Act IV

Angelo the Goldsmith owed a sum of money to a second merchant, which was equivalent to the debt that Antipholus of Ephesus owed *him* for the golden necklace that had been especially handcrafted for Adriana.

The pissed-off furniture merchant accosted the goldsmith on a busy Ephesus cobblestone street.

"Look here, Angelo," the aggravated chair and table dealer began his complaint. "The money you owe me is overdue, and I've summoned a constable here to arrest your fat ass if you don't cough-up the loot. Now I have a ship bound for the Persian Coast ready to sail, and I need my best artisans and craftsmen on the voyage. Pay-up right now or this officer, who incidentally is on my under-the-table payroll, will apprehend your butt, and transfer you onto my ship to fuckin' work in my employ until your sizable debt is satisfied."

"Antipholus (of Ephesus) owes me the exact same amount for a golden necklace I've recently produced for his rich wife Adriana," the goldsmith neurotically explained. "I shall retrieve that enormous debt shortly, even though I'll still be the same height that I am right now. I urge you, kind merchant, to walk with me to his Phoenix residence, despite the fact that we're preoccupied standing here in Ephesus in Asia Minor. Wow! Your threat proposal of tax-free income sounds interesting. Maybe I *will* work for you on the ship!"

"I don't give a shit what the pendant, or necklace, or whatever the hell the item you've mentioned costs!" the custom furniture merchant reprimanded Angelo. "You've owed me the fuckin' money ever since *Passover,* and before I know it, it'll be summer!"

"Look, Angelo! Here is your salvation!" the impatient Officer of the Law having arrest authority noted. "It is Antipholus (of Ephesus) and his asinine servant approaching us now. You can collect your debt that you claim that moody, unsavory fellow owes you!"

"While I go to the goldsmith's shop to confer with Angelo," Antipholus (of Ephesus) told Dromio (of Ephesus), "I want you to go and purchase, obtain, or steal a rope's end. I'm going to beat the shit out of my whoring wife Adriana, and her immoral confederates for having a sex orgy, and locking me out of my own house; thus preventing me from being an entertained voyeur. Now, take off Dromio! There's the goldsmith Angelo up ahead, and I'll shoot the shit with him while you venture forth and procure my rope of discipline. And don't fuckin' fool around, and do the rope-a-dope, you fucked-up dope, or you'll be at the end of your fuckin' rope as far as I'm concerned! Now get your ass in donkey-cart gear!"

Dromio (of Ephesus) sped off to obey his Master's peculiar instructions. Antipholus (of Ephesus) cheerfully greeted Angelo, but the worried goldsmith was much less jovial than his ordinarily and presently happy-go-lucky friend.

"What the hell happened Angelo?" Antipholus bluntly asked. "I never received that gold chain you had promised me to give to the pig prostitute over at the Tiger Inn! Did you give the gold chain to your corpulent boyfriend lap dancer over at the Hippopotamus, instead? Ha, ha, ha! Do you always renege on your given word?"

"Save your fuckin' bad humor for on stage amateur comedy night at the wild and crazy Centaur Inn," Angelo nastily grumbled. "Now Antipholus, I owe the money for the gold chain to this fine merchant standing next to me, and if you don't pay your debt in full, I'm assigned and commissioned to voyage on *his* ship to the Persian Coast to make cheap costume jewelry, desks, smooth wooden dildos, and curios; and also, I'll be forced to administer blow-jobs to all of his gay crew of perverted mariners every single day. Now, I implore you," Angelo begged his friend. "Pay your debt to me, or else I guarantee that serious legal proceedings against your ass will be initiated, and you'll be treated as if you are a violating Syracusan! My cousin, the City Duke, will handle your case. Is my statement perfectly clear?"

"What the hell are you talking about Angelo?" Antipholus (of Ephesus) questioned his normally-complaisant acquaintance. "I have some important business to attend to. Why don't you escort this good merchant chum of yours to my home, and take along the golden chain necklace that you've yet to deliver along, too. I'll get my promiscuous rich wife to cough-up the money that I owe you for the chain. Until and when I can borrow the same sum from you to pay her, then my sexually-inactive spouse will extend me credit from her inheritance to purchase Adriana another overpriced gift from your store."

"Then, you'll finally bring the chain to her, and I'll receive my money, to avoid being apprehended and consigned to this man's trading ship?" the now-paranoid Angelo nervously asked. "I can't afford to tarnish my good reputation among the GLBTQRDKFU Community if I can't afford to pay this man my debt."

"No, you Dolt!" Antipholus (of Ephesus) verbally returned. "Didn't you hear me? You must first deliver the golden necklace, and then, I'll meet you at the Phoenix for dinner to witness some terrific advanced adult entertainment in my master bedroom."

"What the fuck do you mean?" Angelo incredulously asked. "Then give me the goddamned golden chain back, so that I can sell it to another interested customer I know, and cancel-out my debt to this very civil gentleman, who as you can tell, is big and brawny and can brutalize my ass without the help of this burly proud police officer. Now, get your damned oversized ass into donkey-cart gear!"

"You sound like my fucked-up wife speaking!" Antipholus (of Ephesus) charged his very nervous voyeur and furniture friend. "Stop acting and sounding like a neurotic, horny, dry-holed shrew! A friggin' untrained parakeet makes more goddamned verbal sense than you do!"

"Look Asshole, my boat's leaving port in less than two hours!" the austere and aggravated voyeur furniture merchant reminded Angelo.

"Now, shape up or ship out! If you don't make the sale and get my money, then you'll most definitely make the sail!"

"Listen, Antipholus," Angelo pleaded with tears forming in his eyes. "If you don't have the chain in your possession, either give me the money owed for it, or give me something of equal value that you own, preferably another piece of jewelry from your wife's extensive-expensive collection that she's already paid for. Stop fuckin' joking around when it's quite obvious that my fate is in peril!"

"Look Angelo, either settle this matter with this idiotic, petty debt competitor of mine you call Antipholus, or this police officer will arrest you and make you give comprehensive blow-jobs to all the homo' prisoners in the city jail, and to all the gay guards, too," the livid out-of-patience furniture guru spoke his ultimatum.

The burly police officer had something relevant to contribute to the conversation. "My friend the goldsmith, claims that he has not received the money for the gold chain, and I believe Angelo's testimony that *you,* Anti-Folly, Antifa, or whatever the hell your screwed-up name is, will be consigned to work on Angelo's ship all the way to Persia and back if you don't fuckin' pay the fuckin' money owed to him for the gold chain."

"I gave you that chain just a couple of hours ago!" Angelo scolded Antipholus (of Ephesus). "Don't deny it, you dirty son-of-a-bitch!"

"You've wronged my name in public! You bear false witness!" Antipholus vehemently protested to Angelo. "You haven't given me anything but a hard time, and a lot of nonsensical bullshit!"

"You've ruined my credit rating and simultaneously maligned my good reputation in the city!" Angelo volleyed-back. "You treat me like a lowly blacksmith, when indeed I'm an honorable goldsmith!"

"Enough of this adolescent bickering and preposterous invective-laden conversation!" the pissed-off furniture merchant shouted at the two inferior rank debaters. The furniture tycoon next yelled, "I demand Officer that you arrest and interrogate this obnoxious swindler Angelo for general stupidity, if not for forfeiting on his substantial debt obligation to me!"

The appalled goldsmith felt compelled to defend his integrity. "Officer, this devious man Antipholus owes me for an elaborate, golden chain, and I demand that you arrest the bastard for not satisfying his debt to me," the very upset jewelry merchant declared.

"In the name of the Death Duke, which I can't remember at the moment," the not-too-bright Officer said, "I hereby arrest you Angelo for juvenile delinquency, er I mean delinquency of payment."

"Here is the fee for your service," Angelo yelled as the livid goldsmith gladly handed the Government Police Officer a gold coin, and a few seconds later, a three-coin additional generous bribe, too. "I've been needlessly scorned by this frivolous Retard, enough today. If

Antipholus were my brother, I would still legally persist and have the jerk-off arrested and incarcerated. Gentlemen; I hereby no longer consider this debt-owing villain my friend!"

"The allegations presented by Angelo the Goldsmith I deem legitimate. I judiciously arrest you in the name of the anonymous Death Duke!" the Officer announced to the suddenly-shocked Antipholus. "Give me your hand, you're going to become a sailing homo' on the ship leaving for Persia!"

"You've maligned my good name, and I shall hold *you* accountable!" the indignant Antipholus (of Ephesus) bellowed to Angelo the Goldsmith. "I've never before been so egregiously betrayed in all my goddamned life!"

"Go kiss a she lion's ass, and then try stealing her cub!" Angelo countered. "Better yet, Antipholus; go munch on your wife's putrid pussy during the middle of her bloody period!"

"I'll obey you, Officer, and soon I shall obtain the necessary release bail from my sympathetic wife," Antipholus promised. "And as for you Angelo, you can lick my dick after I screw my wife while she's having her disgusting, goddamned period, that usually lasts for the entire month!"

"Shame on your name, you bloody Fool!" Angelo yelled-back to his new-found adversary as the solidly-built Officer/Constable escorted Antipholus (of Ephesus) in the direction of the jailhouse. "I hope you choke to death on your goddamned vomit!"

Dromio of Syracuse was in the vicinity looking for a convenient back-alley rat hole to empty his hyperactive bowels. Then, the zany servant spotted Antipholus of Ephesus, whom he naturally perceived as Antipholus of Syracuse.

"Master, there's a bark ready to disembark from the harbor, soon-to-be heading for either Epidamium, Epidamnum, or Epididymis, I can't remember which destination," Dromio (of Syracuse) said to his supposed Master, not realizing that Antipholus (of Ephesus) was in the process of being arrested. "I've already taken aboard all of our traveling possessions including our luggage. And I hope you have money, because all of the crew is gay and might exploit us for undesirable homosexual sex, if we can't pay ransom for our hostage passages out of this fucked-up city."

"What the hell are you talking about Dromio?" the seething Antipholus (of Ephesus) screamed. "Forget about Epidamnum! I'm not heading for either Epidaurus or Epididymis either, you square-headed Ignoramus! What fuckin' bark are you' referring to?" the angry fellow barked. "Can't you see that I'm being arrested?"

"I'm referring to the ship that you had sent me to book passage on out of this fucked-up ass-backwards city!" Dromio (of Syracuse) steadfastly stated. "Don't tell me that you've forgotten your explicit instruction already!"

"You fucked-up slave Asshole!" Antipholus (of Ephesus) went ballistic on Dromio (of Syracuse). "I had dispatched you to buy or obtain a rope, and now you return and foolishly tell me that all of my possessions are aboard a sailing vessel! I'm living in a veritable, ongoing insane asylum, and fuckin' jail now seems like a suitable paradise of escape!"

"Here Dromio, you inimitable Idiot, take this key to Adriana," Antipholus (of Ephesus) instructed. "Tell my unpredictable and forgetful wife to open a desk under the Turkish taffy tapestry. Inside the drawer is a purse full of ducats. Bring the pouch to the jail so that I can be released on bail. Do as I say, Dromio, or I'll delightfully crush your balls with my own personal razor-sharp nut cracker!"

The impish Dromio (of Syracuse) rushed to the Phoenix to fulfill Antipholus's "implausible command". All the while, the naughty servant was fondly thinking about Nell (Luce), his corpulent fantasy kitchen maid "dreamboat".

* * * * * * * * * * * *

"Luciana, I strongly suspect that my delusional husband has tried wooing you to deliberately betray me, and for some obscure reason, undermine *our* already-rocky marriage," Adriana intimated to her sister in *her* house's kitchen. "What the hell kind of horse manure was he feeding you in the small parlor room?"

"Your insecure husband was saying very peculiar things that made no damned sense at all," Luciana answered. "First, he claimed to be a stranger to this house and to this city. Then, Antipholus told me he wasn't married to anyone, including you, dear Sister. After that, the psycho' said that he wanted to court and marry me, claiming that he had never slept or had sex with you. The flake next praised my beauty and my speech, and then flattered me by saying I should become a damned politician or high priestess. What a lying jerk-off your insane husband is, twisting the truth while in total denial!"

"Luciana, you don't know how badly I really want to publicly slander and humiliate the no-good son-of-a-bitch!" Adriana confided. "Either Antipholus has a deformed and crooked mind, or he's extremely mentally-ill, and needs an accomplished exorcist. My charlatan husband is an ungentle, blunt, conniving, covetous, parasitic, drone-like, vicious and prevaricating bastard, and I've had just about enough of his deceitful bullshit! Not even a beautiful gold chain from him at his own expense would change my set mind!"

413

"How could I ever be jealous of you being married to such a conniving moron?" Luciana asked in empathy with her sister's sentiments. "Antipholus is not even qualified to be second-hand gravel under your feet!"

"My heart prays for his recovery from his mental breakdown, while my tongue curses him, and my mind abhors his atrocious antics; be they deliberate, or be they involuntary," Adriana replied. "Antipholus is like shit. He starts out good as delectable food, but comes out bad as stinking feces! That fair objective evaluation of mine just about sums him up completely!"

Dromio (of Syracuse) entered the house with the key for the desk drawer that was situated under the hanging Turkish taffy tapestry. The inane dwarf encountered the two women, inadvertently interrupting their confidential conversation.

"Hello, gorgeous Woman!" Dromio (of Syracuse) facetiously said to Adriana. "Go to the desk and open the locked drawer. My Master desperately requires something inside. Here's the rusty-crusty key that he had entrusted me with to access the drawer!"

"Why are you all out of breath Dromio?" Adriana sarcastically asked. "Have you just had sex with all of the neighborhood dogs, both male and female?"

"I'll have you know I've been running like a maniac to perform an important key errand for my fucked-up Master," Dromio related as the Syracusan servant again tried capturing and controlling his breath. "I ran so hard I almost wound-up in mythical Iran. I think that my goddamned balls are still a full city block behind me."

"Where *is* your Master?" Adriana curiously asked. "Is that gigolo Antipholus somewhat-well in his head?"

"No; he's captured in a terrible limbo far worse than any hell," Dromio (of Syracuse) panted. "He's being framed to go to jail by an old friend who has malignantly betrayed him. If I don't get the revenue from the drawer to bail him out, my Master is fucked, because he'll be sodomized by all of the queer-bait convicts and jailers in the fucked-up local prison. Your husband will have to miraculously cut a second asshole in order to shit!"

"Exactly, why has Antipholus been arrested Dromio?" Adriana queried. "Was he taken into custody for mental illness that has been mistaken for illicit lying? Has another woman pressed charges against him, finding out that he's already married? Give me some solid answers, you drooling Fool!"

"All I know Mistress is that my Master desperately needs money; the money that's stashed in the desk, and he needs it fast, before his asshole is penetrated by a variety of diseased jail and ship erections!" Dromio (of Syracuse) pleaded. "Please hear my entreaty, and send him the

414

redemption money immediately, or else he'll need ten times as much dough to purchase a new asshole, if there's a fucked-up asshole donor stupid enough to surrender his!"

"Go Luciana. Take this key and fetch the purse of ducats from the desk," Adriana directed. "Now Dromio, be honest with me, you' loose-tongued, servile Shit-head. Is my surreptitious husband in serious deep debt again without my knowledge? I'm tired of bailing the chronic violator out, and to tell you the unvarnished truth, I'm ready to bail-out of our marriage and maybe marry the gay bailiff over at the jail," Adriana belligerently stated to Dromio (of Syracuse). "My husband is a thief who exploits my love, only to then act like a scheming scoundrel. You must agree with my assessment of him!"

"No Madam; I'm quite sure that my Master loves you and only gets into trouble because he doesn't know what else to do, or how to behave in an orthodox manner," Dromio (of Syracuse) defended his presumed boss's character. "I'm sure there're bigger assholes than him in this world, although I've never encountered any of them."

"Okay, you miniature, droll cretin; here's the purse of ducats to satisfy the exorbitant bail!" Adriana offered as the upset wife snatched the ducats' bag from Luciana. "Bring the money straight to the jail, and then escort Antipholus home to me. I'm beginning to feel sorry for that mentally-ill, retarded, no good cheating son-of-a-bitch. His philandering is probably an inexplicable mental sickness unknown to modern medical science, as primitive as it is and sounds. Who needs this kind of extraneous bullshit; especially in my emotionally depressing middle age?"

* * * * * * * * * * * *

Antipholus of Syracuse was slowly ambling down an Ephesus side street, admiring the magnificent gold necklace that the goldsmith had given to him for free (with Angelo all the while thinking that *he* was Antipholus of Ephesus). 'Even though I feel quite effeminate wearing this beautiful piece of ladies' jewelry, everyone on the street is greeting me as if they've known me for a long time, even though I've only been in this weird city for less than a day. Some resident assholes wave as if they recognize me, and several have buttonholed me and asked to lend me money at low loan shark interest rates,' the visitor to Ephesus curiously mused. 'A tailor just called me into his shop to buy silk garments, but then when he said, 'I want to measure your crotch!' I got the hell out of there. I just can't trust anyone in this fucked-up city more than I can trust a desperate criminal robbing me, back in Syracuse!'

Exploited Dromio of Syracuse soon encountered the discouraged Antipholus of Syracuse rapidly exiting the gay tailor's shop. The servant

415

instinctively scurried-over to that side of the narrow street to speak with his Master.

"Sir, I'm glad I recognized you," Dromio prefaced his remarks. "Here's the bag of gold ducats you had sent me to obtain. I'll bet you've bought a brand-new suit from that seemingly content gay tailor standing over there with that broad smile on his queer-looking face!"

"Dromio, what the hell are you talking about?" Antipholus (of Syracuse) yelled. "I didn't send you anywhere to get a purse of gold. Who did you sack this sack from? I understand absolutely nothing that you're describing, even though I understand all of the incredible words your square mouth is uttering! What demon is inhabiting your screwed-up mind?"

"Look Boss; stop acting fucked-up again, just like all of the fucked-up people in this entirely fucked-up enchanted city," Dromio (of Syracuse) responded. "Is there a club, battle-axe or other heavy weapon that has, without my knowledge, fallen from an overhead balcony and smashed against your head? Let me inspect your skull for injury or damage!"

"Dromio, I have a splendid idea," the Master imagined and declared. "Let's make new arrangements to get the hell out of this uncanny city before someone in this enigmatic and peculiar place is making funeral arrangements for us to be buried. Once we're dead, we won't be able to talk about this crazy shit, so my good advice at the moment is for us to evacuate this nutty town as soon as possible. If I can't get the resident Devil out of your fucked-up mind, then I definitely gotta' get the hell outa' here right away!"

"But Sir, I overheard the Officer of the Jail say that this money ought to be delivered to the bailiff as soon as possible, or else you would most positively be lustfully sodomized this evening a multitude of times by a bevy of prisoners and jail keepers," Dromio (of Syracuse) informed his authentic Master. "That is, before you're sodomized by all of the gay sailors on the ship to Persia!"

"Now that's the last straw that breaks the dromedary's back!" Antipholus loudly answered. "Everything out of your deformed mouth is ridiculous drivel sounding like comical fiction, if it weren't so absurdly frightening. If we were back in Syracuse, I'd take you to the temple priest so that your ass could be properly sacrificed to the apathetic gods."

"Well Master, if you insist," the pesky servant qualified. "The vessel *Expedition* sets sail tonight going to somewhere, so here are the ducats in this purse to set you free from prison."

"But I'm not in fuckin' prison or going to fuckin' prison!" Antipholus (of Syracuse) ranted. "Can't you see, my ludicrous knuckle-headed Companion, that I'm out here on the street, have purchased some new silk rags with my own money, and that I'm presently speaking quite emphatically to you. Say Dromio, feast your eyes and check-out this gorgeous woman advancing in our direction. God, I hope she's a horny whore slut!"

"Hello Antipholus," the amiable Tiger Inn courtesan greeted. "I must say that you look rather hot and desirable in your fancy new silk apparel. I see you've finally made contact with the goldsmith, so you can now give me that glorious lustrous chain draped around your alluring neck."

"What the hell's going on here?" Antipholus of Syracuse exclaimed. "Who the hell are you, lovely Lady? I don't know you from Aphrodite or Hera!"

"Master, this must be the Mistress Satana herself that I saw on posters outside the Centaur House of Whores!" the awed Dromio (of Syracuse) commented. "I'll bet you'll get lots of red-hot tail from this sultry bitch! She might even be worth a dozen golden necklaces!"

"She must be the devil in disguise," Antipholus (of Syracuse) agreed with Dromio's first statement, "and she probably has a sharp pitchfork concealed under her ruffled dress to stick into me like I'm a roasted bird. Stay away from the alluring, tantalizing bitch, Dromio. At best, she's a witch, and at worst, a fallen angel of Satan. But wow! What enticing firm tits she possesses!"

"You two bozos are having a merry chat at my expense," the insulted courtesan assessed. "But jolly each other all you want. Just surrender the golden chain you had promised me, Antipholus, and I guarantee that I'll make you a happy and most-gratified man. We'll discuss all the essential details tonight at the Tiger Inn, right Tiger?"

"Don't spoon with this long-spooned, spoiled, demanding bitch!" Dromio (of Syracuse) counseled Antipholus of Syracuse. "She eats with a long spoon because she usually dines with the Devil, and her pernicious plan is to stick a knife into your back after you fork over all your money, in addition to the shiny gold chain, along with the heavy bag of gold ducats specifically intended to bail you out of jail."

"Get away from us, you whoring, Fiend!" Antipholus (of Syracuse) yelled at the conniving courtesan, who naturally believed that he was Antipholus of Ephesus, one of her more generous regular clients. "Thou art a conjuring, mesmerizing sorceress, and I'm telling you to leave us the fuck alone! I'll neither eat supper with you, nor munch on your hairy pink love tunnel, if it's still pink at all!"

"Well then, my favorite debt-ridden Patron, I'll afford you a choice. Either give me the ring you had at dinner last night that you had promised me, or give me the golden chain around your neck that you've also promised me, and I'll leave you alone until you regain your sensibility," the courtesan sternly requested. "My offer is more than fair! If not, I'll summon a constable and have you arrested."

"Master, be wise and sage," Dromio redundantly recommended. "Either she's obeying the Devil's evil commands, or she's a manifestation of Satan himself, this time complemented with rock-solid tits and a nice firm ass. I'll race you to the docks; that's my final feasible statement at the moment."

The Ephesus courtesan then addressed the totally-addled merchant from Syracuse, "Look, Antipholus. I was politely asking you, but now I'm doggedly and imperatively telling you; hand over either the fuckin' expensive ring or the fuckin' gold necklace," the high-society hooker insisted. "If you don't, I'll get my brother, the dedicated muscle-bound Jailer Officer, after your raunchy ass!"

"You're a Witch! You're a sinful slut Sorceress! But most of all, you're an enchantress that's scaring the living shit out of me! Come Dromio!" Antipholus (of Syracuse) ordered. "Let's run away from this fucked-up, promiscuous, whoring woman soliciting extortion and prostitution in this fucked-up city!"

"It's hard to fly like an eagle when I *am* the unfortunate companion of a fat, clumsy turkey like you!" Dromio (of Syracuse) exclaimed as the servant and his Master quickly fled down the street in the direction of the maritime docks.

'That fuckin' asshole is definitely over the edge and in need of psychiatric help,' the distressed courtesan reckoned. 'And the other girls at the Tiger Inn, and also at the Centaur, were absolutely right in their unanimous opinion of him. That ring he owes me is worth at least forty gold ducats, and the gold chain at least forty more. And earlier today, that crazy Antipholus told me about the door being locked and about complete strangers, including himself with his own freakin' voice, being locked inside,' the mixed-up harlot considered. 'I'm heading straight for the Phoenix, and I intend telling his wife all about his mental illness, and learn what the fuck she has to say about his odd dilemma, and also about mental case Antipholus being a schizophrenic-psychopathic lunatic. Eighty beautiful ducats happen to be too big of a fabulous windfall fortune for me to lose!'

* * * * * * * * * * * *

"You don't have to hold me by my garments," Antipholus of Ephesus objected to the very rough Officer/Jailer. "You'll get your blasted damned bail money soon enough, when my very competent servant Dromio returns from my home with the sack of ducats. My thrifty wife Adriana is one of the richest dames in all of Ephesus!"

"If your fucked-up servant is anything like you, he too deserves to be persecuted, man-handled and punished," the grim-faced Jailer harshly replied. "Here comes your buffoon assistant now carrying a dumb-ass

418

rope. The fool probably wants to be the one to dramatically execute your ass instead of the official Executioner to be assigned performing the much-needed service. That act would be quite a wonderful irony! Ha, ha, ha!"

"Here's the thick rope you had instructed me to bring to you!" Dromio of Ephesus indicated to the thoroughly-disappointed and flabbergasted *jailed* Antipholus of Ephesus. "I've exchanged the money you had given me for the lengthy rope. Isn't it a grand piece of hemp? Why are you frowning, Master?"

"Dromio, what the hell are you saying, you daft moron?" Antipholus yelled at his normally obedient and efficient servant. "You've paid five hundred gold ducats for a cheap one-half ducat rope? Are you taking heavy-duty drugs, or imbibing gallons of alcohol? Tell me the goddamned truth!"

"Show some additional patience for this poor lowlife imbecile," the Jailer laughed to Antipholus (of Ephesus). "Obviously, his burlesque is more warped than yours is, and you my Friend, happen to border on comedic insanity."

"I wouldn't dishonor your instructions Master, because you've already beaten the shit out of me once today, and I wish to avoid a second undeserved administration of cruel punishment, if possible," Dromio attested. "I cherish my tender ass, because without it, I can't shit, and if I can't shit, I could easily die or explode from massive accumulated intestinal gas."

"You fucked-up lying whore's son!" Antipholus (of Ephesus) screamed at Dromio (of Ephesus). "Your brains are inside your rectum, and any ordinary ass has more intelligence than either your fucked-up head or your fuckin' ass. I'm surprised that you haven't somewhere in your mediocre life shit your brains out!"

"Even though you believe I have lame ideas," Dromio argued and begged, "that's no reason or excuse for you to make my body lame. Such an unwarranted, wicked beating might even cripple my already-hampered thought processes."

"Get the hell out of the jail cell area, Dromio!" Antipholus bellowed at his totally-confused subordinate. "Wait outside! Here comes my wife Adriana and Luciana, along with two other people I'd rather not identify and discuss."

Dromio (of Ephesus) was frozen from fear, and the petrified fellow did not budge to leave the area of confinement. And soon, Antipholus's (of Ephesus) wife; his sister-in-law; the grieving courtesan; and Dr. Pinch, a quack conjurer and psychiatrist, entered the aforementioned jail cell area. Antipholus (out of sheer anger and frustration) began strangling Dromio through the cell's bars as the servant (already-in-shock of all his master's pent-up anxiety) became resigned to his plight. The four newly arrived entrants all had befuddled looks on their faces.

"I told you all the way over to the jail that your husband was crazy," the complaining courtesan said to Adriana. "He's more fucked-up than the entire fucked-up city of Ephesus is!"

"Good Dr. Pinch; stop goosing me you senile old Pervert!" Adriana boisterously shouted. "Now go about your business and determine what the hell's wrong with my afflicted husband, so that an appropriate cure or remedy can be employed. His abundant defects are greatly affecting both him and me."

"Antipholus's eyes are bulging out of their sockets like his erection used to bulge out of his robe!" Luciana noted and expressed. "He's trembling in his ecstasy, gaining emotional triumph from thoroughly choking and beating the shit out of his weak, defenseless, helpless slave! My brother-in-law's outrageous behavior definitely proves that Ephesus needs a good, reliable mental hospital!"

"Let me feel your pulse," Dr. Pinch stated as the sex-pervert deliberately pinched Antipholus's (of Ephesus) ass through the jail cell bars to gain a cheap thrill. "Sometimes, too much blood is in the genital area for too long, and it has a tendency to constipate the brain! Ah yes, you do have a pulse!" the provocative Dr. confirmed as the deviate eagerly pinched Adriana's ass a second time with his other free hand.

"Get your fuckin' filthy paws off me, you perverted homo'!" Antipholus (of Ephesus) screamed as the prisoner finally released his grip on Dromio's neck, and then deeply raked his fingernails across Dr. Pinch's scarred face. "You're a charlatan, an impostor, and a goddamned disgrace to your quack profession!"

"This belligerent jerk-off is definitely without a doubt possessed by Satan, or by one of *his* scurrilous henchmen like Caliban," Dr. Pinch authoritatively certified without any further examination of the captive patient. "I could pray for his soul until doomsday, with no favorable results ever being achieved," Pinch phlegmatically stated as the masochistic/sadistic predator wiped a quantity of crimson from his forehead and cheeks. "This mentally disturbed fellow standing behind bars is indeed a bloody mess. Yes, indeed, a fuckin' bloody mess."

"Peace to you revered, Wizard!" Antipholus (of Ephesus) exclaimed after the jail cell occupant realized and rationalized the gravity of Dr. Pinch's negative evaluation. "I'm not mad, but only angry, and who is to tell the difference between the two abstractions?"

"You need an able-bodied nurse and a mental guardian until you recuperate from your wicked emotional instability, dear Husband," Adriana sympathetically related. "You're either hallucinating or imagining crazy things and ideas, Antipholus. You need plenty of sleep, lots of bed rest, but now I fear you might smother yourself with the

420

sheets, pillow or mattress. I forgive you, Husband, for all your weird antics, because now the renowned Dr. Pinch has ultimately verified that you're indeed mentally sick."

"I'm not mentally ill!" Antipholus (of Ephesus) verbally stormed. "Why did you earlier this day deny me entrance into my own house? Why did you lock the goddamned front door, Adriana? Were you having an illicit and immoral love affair, and didn't want me to intrude on your carnal pleasure?"

"Oh, suspicious and psychotic, Husband; you did dine at home, and then you had the audacity of making a pass at Luciana, you shameless, sex-starved hypocrite!" Adriana nastily hollered as masochistic/sadistic Dr. Pinch (still profusely bleeding from the face and not giving a shit about it) again goosed her firm ass.

"Dined at home, you say?" Antipholus shrieked in total disbelief. "Dromio, I want you to tell the goddamned truth. Did I dine at home as my wife is fallaciously implying?"

"You did not dine at home, Sir, and your front door was locked-up when you had arrived a bit tardy for supper," Dromio (of Ephesus) swore. "And Madam Adriana's voice reviled and ridiculed you through the closed front door, and her fat kitchen maid Luce mercilessly taunted and scorned you, also. It certainly was not a heavenly experience with all that bellicose berating and mocking going on. And finally, Master. You departed the scene in disgust, thinking that you had caught your wife having sex with another unlucky man. However, you were extremely pissed-off that you had not the opportunity to prove your suspicion."

"Obviously, Dromio is lying and humoring your husband out of fear of having the piss, blood, sweat, tears, and shit beaten out of him again," Dr. Pinch theorized and persuasively articulated. "The whole scenario is a fucked-up conglomeration and collaboration of fantasy lie stacked upon fantasy lie."

"Adriana, didn't you secretly bribe the goldsmith to have me mortified in public with me being arrested in broad daylight near the downtown mart?" Antipholus (of Ephesus) boldly accused his wife.

"Why would I ever do or even consider doing such a terrible thing?" Adriana argued. "I had sent Dromio here to this jail with a purse of gold ducats to bail your ass out, and all I see in his possession is a goddamned length of cheap, shitty rope. Is Dromio contemplating becoming the city hangman starting with you, or what?"

"The frugal Bitch, er, I'm sorry, Master; your Wife gave me no money for bail!" Dromio maintained.

"He's a crazy liar, just like my mentally-ill spouse is!" Adriana indicted what she believed to be two scheming, criminal, mentally-sick corroborators. "Dromio came to me with the secret desk key, and then requested the ducats in the drawer directly under the hanging Turkish taffy tapestry."

"And I saw my honest sister give Dromio the purse of gold ducats!" Luciana testified and verified. "What Adriana should've given the fat, bow-legged bastard was two swift kicks, one to the ass and the other to his balls!"

"As God is my Witness, I was only given one ducat to purchase an ordinary rope from a marketplace vendor," Dromio testified. "I was not dispatched to get any purse; only a cheap rope!"

"Both men have pallid-looking faces and fixed eyes," the bleeding Dr. Pinch stated, as the motivated maniac aggressively goosed both Adriana and Luciana simultaneously. "They're each either under the influence of Satan, or mentally sick, or a rare combination of both. I suggest that these two dangerous Assholes, Antipholus and Dromio, be kept in a dark, damp room with poor ventilation," Dr. Pinch prescribed. "Perhaps the lack of oxygen in their brains will starve the vile spirits that are presently possessing them!"

"Why do you deny receiving the bag of gold when both my wife and my sister-in-law say that it had been given to you?" Antipholus (of Ephesus) inquired of Dromio (of Ephesus) through the cell's vertical bars. "Why do you lie, Dromio?"

"I received no gold from either of these two conspiring bitches!" Dromio (of Ephesus) insisted. "These two viperous douche bags had no bag to give me; not even a lousy bag of shit!"

"I know that both of you absurd connivers are lying!" Adriana attested. "You both piss out of your ears, and shit out of your mouths!"

"You loathsome, nymphomaniac viper!" Antipholus (of Ephesus) bellowed at Adriana. "You want me to think and believe that I'm insane, while you scorn my good name and reputation here in this despicable, filthy jail. I ought to pluck-out your eyes and feed them to the ravens!" Antipholus (of Ephesus) boomed as the jail cell occupant lunged his hands through the vertical bars for his wife's face.

"Bind this out-of-control fiend, Officer!" Adriana yelled to the Jailer. "He needs to be strapped and shackled down upon a flat table."

Four supervisor/wardens fumbling with the appropriate keys entered the jail cell to subdue the man having a fit of rage (for the jail was top-heavy from a bureaucratic perspective).

"Leave the imbecile alone!" the Officer/Jailer ordered the four overzealous wardens. "Return to your office and enjoy your coffee and doughnuts, and other donated delectable pastries."

"I'll reluctantly pay my husband's bond debt to you, if you promise to release him from your custody and into mine," Adriana begged the Jailer. "This cell is a hostile place where gruesome consequences often happen. Even though my spouse is temporarily insane, and possibly possessed by haunting demons. I don't want to see him abused and mistreated in this grimy prison. I've heard many strange tales about excessive and gross sodomizing going on inside here, and as you know, both in and around Ephesus, rumor is often more damned accurate than either fact or reality."

"Thank you for your sweet kindness, oh most unhappy Strumpet!" Antipholus (of Ephesus) strangely remarked. "And I want my only true friend, Dromio here, to be my attendant and nurse in order to make sure that I'm not poisoned at home by either of you two vicious, nefarious Wenches. On second thought, Dromio; get the fuck out of my disjointed life completely!"

Dr. Pinch again goosed the two ladies (Adriana and Luciana) one final time, and exited the jail-cell area, accompanied by Antipholus (of Ephesus) and the often-abused Dromio (of Ephesus). Meanwhile, Adriana, Luciana, the Bondsman Officer of the Jail, along with the very vivacious, curvaceous courtesan Tiger Inn prostitute remained in the open cell where symbolically, and in reality, all three abusive bitches deserved to be caged.

"Do you know an accusative, petulant goldsmith named Angelo?" the Officer asked Adriana.

"I know the Fool! His name *is* Angelo," Adriana acknowledged. "What sum does my husband owe the nuisance Troublemaker?"

"I believe at least forty shiny, new ducats with the coins' dog faces not eroded from wear and tear," The Jailer explained. "The handsome sum is owed because your husband had obtained, but not yet paid for, am expensive gold chain."

"Your addled husband owes me eighty ducats," the courtesan suavely mentioned to Adriana. "Forty for an expensive ring, and forty for a gold necklace he had promised, but never gave to me."

"I'm not negotiating anything right now with you, you whoring Slut!" Adriana bluntly told the greedy and disappointed courtesan. "Jailer, take me to where the goldsmith is. I need to evaluate more facts before I ever pay my husband's capricious debts, or kill him, and then just pay for his funeral and burial expenses. And that naughty Dr. Pinch claims *he* loves to be spanked! Maybe Jailer, you should hostilely whip his skinny ass, good too!"

Antipholus (of Ephesus) and his assistant (Dromio of Ephesus) entered the jail building's central office sector, after finally being released from the cell area by the prison's irresponsible, bureaucratic, pastry-loving supervisory staff.

"Let's run for cover, but obviously there's no place to hide!" Luciana shrieked in feigned horror. "The two dangerous hoodlums are on the loose again!"

Almost everyone (in a frenzy of pandemonium) bolted out of the dark, dingy, grimy prison, and only Antipholus (of Ephesus) and Dromio (of Ephesus) were left behind to put all the pieces together.

"I see that those oddball witches are afraid of our masculinity," Antipholus (of Ephesus) bragged to his irascible assistant. "Now that we're free men once again, Dromio, let's venture into town where we should momentarily be safe and sound from the banes of petticoat tyranny and female exploitation."

"If I may curse, Sir, those loud-mouthed bitches are indeed fucked-up as you have asserted!" the perplexed servant opined. "And the fact that your wife wants to pay for debts you had never amassed makes her even a full, yet-unidentified, level above and beyond simply being ordinarily fucked-up! And how come every asshole in this fucked-up play has no last name?"

Meanwhile Antipholus (of Syracuse) and Dromio (of Syracuse) were planning to have dinner at the raucous Centaur Inn in the center of metropolitan downtown Ephesus, and then catch the next ship out of port to escape "the wildest, most fucked-up, demon-possessed city on the whole goddamned planet."

Act V

The distraught furniture merchant, to whom Angelo owed a substantial debt, again hastily accosted the goldsmith near the city's mooring docks. The aggravated trader was not-too-happy with Angelo's litany of inane excuses.

"I'm sorry that I've hindered you from disembarking out to sea," Angelo apologized, "but I honestly did give the gold chain to Antipholus, yet the dumb-shit liar denies that the transfer ever happened. Whatever you do, don't throw me into the harbor and use my ass as a disposable raft."

"This man Antipholus is esteemed all over Ephesus, yet now for some peculiar reason, the fellow refuses to honor and pay his debts," the peeved merchant griped. "His wealthy prostitute wife is reputed to satisfy his debt credit, I have heard, delivering coins for debts owed in various stalls around the mart."

"She's not a prostitute, Sir. She's an out-and-out whore!" Angelo clarified. "But anyway, Adriana dutifully satisfies both her husband's debts and other men's sexual needs as well, at least that's the gossip around Ephesus. Now speak softly, for I believe that your unreliable debt-owed competitor and his pinhead slave are right this minute walking toward us," Angelo observed and reported.

Antipholus (of Syracuse) and Dromio (of Syracuse) had just rounded the corner, and were rapidly walking in the direction of the departure docks. Angelo noticed that Antipholus (of Syracuse) was wearing the golden chain that Antipholus (of Ephesus) had ordered for the flirtatious courtesan. The on-the-lam escaping visitors from Syracuse were intercepted and immediately interrogated.

"You have no fuckin' shame, you dirty, unreliable Fuck," Angelo the Goldsmith accused Antipholus (of Syracuse). "You pilfer my gold chain; you lie to me about its use; you don't pay me for my craftsmanship, and now you're trying to abscond from port with your lunatic slave," Angelo berated and railed his new-found adversary. "And to add to the indictment, you've irresponsibly wronged my honest friend here, to whom I owe money. He can't set out to sea until I recompense him for a personal loan."

"I never denied I have your chain," Antipholus (of Syracuse) admitted. "But no one in this fucked-up city ever asked me if it was mine or not."

"I heard you talking about acquiring that chain at the mart just this afternoon," the aggrieved curio and desk importer/exporter hollered at the disillusioned Syracuse visitor. "You're an insult to civilization, and also to all humanity. You disgraceful arrogant Fuck have no acceptable code of conduct, except perhaps the unethical laws of the jungle and the desert."

"Thou art a cutthroat Villain to attempt impeaching me, even though I'm not President of your corrupt City Council," Antipholus (of Syracuse) furiously replied. "I'll prove my honor and my honesty by challenging you to a duel. Here's my dull-bladed sword that I shall now wield above my head."

Adriana, Luciana, the courtesan/whore and other curious spectators assembled around the scene of dispute and of potential violence. Adriana cautioned restraint.

"Don't slice him up, Husband," the wench begged Antipholus of Syracuse. "You're mad and need mental rehabilitation and emotional reconstruction administered by that renowned sado-masochistic practitioner, Dr. Pinch."

"Please Master, this is an extremely, highly dangerous situation developing," Dromio (of Syracuse) pleaded. "Let's run into this nearby nunnery and find sanctuary among the holy women."

The apprehensive Syracuse men hastily climbed-up and then awkwardly fell over the top of the locked priory gate, and were quickly met by the Lady Abbess, who had plenty of blubbery porterhouse upon her frame. The Chief Nun immediately lifted-up, and then simultaneously flipped the two interlopers onto the ground.

"What are you two uncouth jesters doing trespassing on my property?" the Lady Abbess quizzed the still-dazed encroachers. "Be quiet, for my novices are busy praying, or else I'll have no alternative but to mercilessly trounce and squash both of you into human juice!" stated the enormous four-hundred-pound woman, threatening the pair of dazed foreigners, lying on the lawn.

The in-control Lady Abbess then opened the gate to allow Adriana, Luciana, Angelo, the courtesan/whore, and the pissed-off furniture merchant admission, in order to civilly resolve the ongoing crisis. Everyone stood at attention out of fear of the formidable woman behemoth's wrath.

"Why are you here?" the enormous Abbess asked Adriana. "This is a legitimate, respectable convent, and not a grimy unlicensed city whorehouse, you know!"

"I specifically came here to fetch my mentally-ill husband off the street before he accidentally injures someone, or accidentally kills himself," Adriana explained. "And I must tell you that my spouse obstinately refuses the suggestions and advice of anyone and everyone, including the renowned Dr. Pinch."

"Do you agree with this woman's statement about her fucked-up husband?" the peeved Lady Abbess asked the more-peeved Angelo. "I'm a tranquil, serene religious woman, so don't you make me fuckin' curse or swear. The last time I fuckin' cursed was when I strangled a pimp to death with my bare hands when the bastard tried hiring me as a hooker over in the crowded marketplace. The Death Duke didn't prosecute my ass because His Majesty knew I was a devoted woman of God."

"This man Antipholus is certifiably insane, and needs a straightjacket, or some similar restraining device right this instance," Angelo affirmatively disclosed to the agitated Lady Abbess. "His erratic mind is undoubtedly possessed!"

"I think my crook of a husband might need a crooked-jacket, because he has a bad case of scoliosis!" Adriana contributed to the chaotic discussion. "His diminutive dick might require a similar, much smaller restraining device!"

"I should've slain the insane bastard and retrieved the golden necklace as satisfaction of Angelo's personal debt to me," the disgruntled international furniture merchant opined. "This goldsmith Angelo here owes me a sum of money," the dealer explained to the Abbess. "In fact, the same sum of money that this careless trespasser onto your property owes him! This careless interloper can care less about his careless obligations!"

"Does this pretentious cavalier idiot always behave in this sort of unruly manner?" the appalled Lady Abbess (who was suffering from an infected abscess in a front tooth, and who was planning to undergo an intricate sex operation to become an abbot) asked Adriana.

"This week my fuckin' husband, er, pardon my poor street language Lady Abbess," Adriana corrected her slang vernacular. "This week my husband was acting strange and weird, more so than usual. But it hasn't been until today that Antipholus has gone completely bonkers; throwing outrageous fits of rage, and intimidating other citizens all throughout our peaceful and pleasant metropolis."

"There must be some plausible explanation to account for his aberrant, unorthodox change in deportment," the Lady Abbess with the major gum abscess speculated and conveyed to her concerned alien audience. "Has he just buried a dear friend? Has he just buried a dear girlfriend? Is he daily living in the mortal sin of constant adultery? My fellow citizens, I do believe in the existence of cause and effect, you know! What the hell's wrong with this rather crazed, deplorable dolt?"

"I believe that some love, probably of this whore/courtesan standing next to me, has drawn my husband out of the house and compelled him to engage in dangerous errant activities," Adriana conjectured and expressed. "Antipholus, I believe, is addicted to young, fresh pussy!"

"Each and every one of you that has been offended by this inconsiderate man should beat the living shit out of him, all at the same time," the Lady Abbess advised. "And if you've already kicked his scoliosis butt, it certainly wasn't hard enough, for this churlish asshole apparently still acts like a churlish asshole. I believe that this reprehensible imbecile you've been chasing onto my property has a conscience saturated with latent guilt, and his insolent and incorrigible conduct reflects *that* very obvious fact," the set in her ways Mother Abbess maintained. "Your collective jealous tirades have forced this man into a protective shell, as if he was a frightened turtle, and now the retard is coming out of his shell of passivity, just like a gay man or adulterous woman comes out of the closet announcing his or her sinful sexual liberation," the Mother Abbess, who was a real Mother, elucidated.

"My sister only scolded the bastard son-of-a-bitch, er, excuse me Lady Abbess; my sister only chided my brother-in-law mildly, even though the reprimand should've been done rambunctiously and wildly with an abundance of physical abuse," Luciana attested. "Let's lynch the bothersome betrayer and disgusting professional thief, and enjoy engaging in some impromptu vigilante justice, without getting the Death Duke involved in our enterprise."

"There'll be no vengeance or violence on my property, unless it's initiated, orchestrated and completed by me," the militant Lady Abbess very loquaciously and quite competently trumped Luciana's punishment recommendation. "I'm hereby allowing this troubled man sanctuary in my convent, until this entire bullshit, er, I mean this entire matter is resolved to my satisfaction. Now Man," the Abbess ordered Antipholus (of Syracuse). "Enter my house, and don't flirt, fuck with, or feel-up any of my virgin novices." Then, the Abbess austerely spoke to the other concerned participants assembled on her lawn. "I'll thoroughly rehabilitate the uncouth son-of-a-bitch, er, I mean your husband or friend, and I'll release my hostage from my safe custody when I'm good and ready."

"Let me have my husband back," Adriana pleaded to the excessively corpulent six-foot-five Abbess. "I'll nurse him back to health, even if it requires breast-feeding him. And I promise that I'll not take legal, punitive, divorce action against him, even if he deserves punishment resulting from marital litigation."

"Drugs, whiskey, holy prayer, elixir syrups, and penis massage is what your husband really needs, and my very capable staff can provide those extra-curricular essential services," the Lady Abbess argued and maintained. "So, you all-too-concerned Fruitcakes, I demand that you depart my sacred premises immediately, before I decide to kick the shit, er, I mean the feces out of all of you!"

"Go on religious Bitch; kick the shit out of me if you dare!" Adriana challenged the wildebeest-sized Abbess. "It's not holy or even kosher for an avowed nun such as yourself to separate a wife from her troubled husband, even if his scoliosis has traveled-down to his Z-shaped pecker. From the tone of your nomenclature, you'll probably capitalize on my spouse's psychological dilemma by selling poor Antipholus into sexual slavery at some foreign brothel."

"You've indiscreetly insulted and offended me more than enough," the Abbess yelled at Adriana while making a clenched fist, "so scoot out of here, or you'll all regret the tragic consequences. Scram, I say!" Then the tall corpulent Abbess swiftly entered the convent with her new ward.

"Let's go and register a complaint with the Death Duke," Luciana suggested to her livid sister. "Maybe His Grace will do us a favor, of course, for promised favors later on. Hopefully, our Ruler will come to this dear abbey, and perhaps his notorious imperial judgment will efficaciously overrule this vociferous, fat Lady Abbess hussy."

"The Death Duke is prepared right now to execute an invader from Syracuse named Aegeon; at least I've learned that the Duke's Headsman is prepared to execute the condemned jackass," the pissed-off chair and sofa merchant chimed-in. "I'll go and fetch His Grace at the always-morose death ditch, and escort him here, either before or after the scheduled beheading of the Syracusan. The delirious Duke is my fucked-up cousin, and the royal dick-head owes me a couple of big political favors."

* * * * * * * * * * * *

The Death Duke of Ephesus, Aegeon (the convicted Merchant of Syracuse), and the formidable Executioner and his very qualified black-robed assistants, were passing the abbey on their way to the town death ditch, where the scheduled decapitation was to occur. The devious Duke was figuring he would "Kill two birds with one boulder", and perhaps execute two condemned men (Aegeon and Antipholus) instead of just one. His Grace was expounding on poor Aegeon's unenviable situation.

"If anyone will pay this piss-head Syracusan's debt of one thousand ducats, then I shall mercilessly spare this man's ribs, er, I mean life," Duke Solinus was overheard saying. "Now, what the hell's this other urgent difficulty that is necessitating my immediate attention, happening right here in peaceful, metropolitan downtown Ephesus? Please tell me some background Madam!"

"I seek justice from a perpetual, ongoing, madness Your Grace," Adriana begged on her right bended knee (for she was aware that if she was on her left bended knee, she too would be instantly executed). "Benevolent Duke. I seek immediate justice against the obese, obstinate Lady Abbess that lives in and manages *that* supposedly holy building."

"But my cousin Lady Abbess is a wonderful, virtuous woman that never wronged anyone, including myself," the now-suspicious Duke answered Adriana. "You must be mistaken in your allegation."

"May it please Your Royal Grace," Adriana proceeded with her complicated exposition. "My personal difficulty involves my husband Antipholus, who had been normal up to this very day, but now he behaves like a bizarre, insane fellow demonstrating outrageous fits of madness. My spouse has displeasured and inconvenienced citizens; has accumulated massive debts without my knowledge or permission; has stolen platinum rings and golden necklaces, and now the shameless prick hides in this abbey where the Abbess gives him sanctuary, after he has violated innumerable laws and people. I plead, kind Duke. to allow my husband to come outside and accept the penalties and the consequences for his inconsiderate, crazy, illegal, unethical, and immoral actions."

"Your husband Antipholus was very loyal to me during several foreign wars, and earned commendations and high praise for his many valorous contributions," Duke Solinus reminded Adriana. "You and your friends go and knock on the abbey's door, and I'll speak with the Abbess and settle this peculiar mounting controversy once and for all. I'll determine if your pathetic *lunatic* Antipholus is insane like a flea on the moon, or not."

Then when everything seemed fairly tranquil and placid, an acquaintance of Adriana rushed onto the scene to convey a critical message. "Madam, your psychotic husband and his neurotic slave have broken loose from jail, have beaten-up several barmaids, and have maliciously bound-up Dr. Pinch at the Tiger Inn; and then the pair committed the vulgar sacrilege of singeing-off the good doctor's beard with fire brands, and next the vandals extinguished the facial blaze with great pails of animal urine. Their fucked-up behavior can only be characterized as an abomination, er, please excuse my unwarranted obscenity, Your Grace."

"Shut your foul mouth, you rambling Fool!" Adriana admonished the over-descriptive female messenger. "Your gossip is totally false, because my husband and Dromio have fled inside this dear abbey, and have sought asylum when they actually needed an asylum."

"Lady Adriana; I swear on my life that my lips have produced the honest-to-Zeus truth," the female courier anxiously insisted. "Your husband was frenetically screaming that if you were inside the Tiger Inn, the barbarian would vindictively torch and scorch your face, and next, deliberately and meticulously disfigure your desirable, curvaceous figure. Holy Shit! He and Dromio are now approaching this location as I speak!"

"Bearers of the spears and battleaxes come forward for my protection," the fearful Death Duke instructed his soldiers while neglecting to mention everyone else's safety and welfare. "And if she exits the priory, I can also use the Abbess for my defense, because ny obese cousin looks like a battle-axe, too!"

When Antipholus (of Ephesus) and Dromio (of Ephesus) arrived at the abbey, the newcomers immediately stopped and bowed-down in deference to the craven Death Duke's presence. Then, Adriana had some pertinent words to say to her strange-acting husband.

"What kind of sorcery is in play here? My husband is behaving so crazily that he's already escaped his sanctuary inside the nunnery, and has run around the block with his blockhead servant Dromio, while we spectators to insanity gathered here this odd day, all have believed that Antipholus is being given safe sanctuary and much-needed rest inside the abbey!" Adriana exclaimed in astonishment.

"I seek true justice!" Antipholus (of Ephesus) insisted in an all-too-familiar refrain. "I had served you nobly, esteemed Duke, in the military during those fucked-up, er, excuse me Your Grace, during those atrocious sea wars, and I suffered deep physical and emotional scars, so you already know that my unwavering loyalty to you is genuine. I've sacrificed and bled for your fair city, so please grant me justice, which from experience I do not take for granted."

Then, the condemned and doomed prisoner Aegeon courageously spoke-up, much to everyone's consternation and amazement. "My ancient eyes are not deceived. They see my son Antipholus and his servant Dromio!"

"Ignore this loony condemned Asshole!" Antipholus (of Ephesus) entreated everyone assembled, so that the gathered witnesses would focus their attention exclusively on *his* situation. "I've always espoused justice, my Duke, but my loose, promiscuous wife has constantly irritated me, abused me, and dishonored me to the point where in one day, I've become an absolute psychological disaster! She has shamelessly and discriminately heaped disgrace and humiliation upon me to the point where I don't give a shit about anything, anymore. Condemn me to Hades to suffer with Sisyphus and Tantalus, for all the fuck I care!"

"What do you mean Antipholus?" Duke Solinus marveled and questioned his faithful subject. "Speak your fucked-up, er, I mean express the essence of your confused mind, and I promise that I shall administer swift justice on the spot."

"This very day, Omnipotent Duke, my wife Adriana shut and locked the front door to my residence at the Phoenix, and kept me outside while she feasted inside with other perverted harlots and male sex-addicts, making me excessively jealous of their orgy of infidelity, and consequently putting me in a state of delirium."

"This all sounds like heavy shit to me!" the Death Duke decided and shared. "Adriana. Is this testimony true or is it fraudulent? I like saying the word 'fraudulent' because it sounds more-fancy than the common word 'false'!"

"It is somewhat-undeniably true, Your Grace, that myself, my sister, and my husband did dine together, but this man whom is accusing me was inside with us and not locked outside the house," Adriana adamantly maintained. "Now my husband's fabricating this canard right before our very eyes and ears, just as Antipholus has mischievously and maliciously been doing all damned day long."

"I confirm all that my sister is saying," Luciana chimed-in. "And her freaked-out husband, I believe, is suffering from a severe mental breakdown, or perhaps even Angry Cow's Disease."

"Yes, oh Omniscient Imperial Duke," Angelo the Goldsmith fearfully and almost-tearfully vociferated. "Luciana is uttering the absolute truth, and her husband is a no-good bastard liar, and the principal prevaricator in this web of turmoil that's now unraveling."

"My Liege," Antipholus (of Ephesus) replied. "I'm not under the influence of drugs, wine or Satan, as has been alleged; nor do I have a fever, even though I'm still hot for my wife's crotchola. It is indeed reality that this afternoon, my spouse Adriana locked me outside my house, and she was enjoying dinner with her licentious, baneful, sinful companions, and I believe that a sidebar love affair was going on between her and the goldsmith Angelo, although he was outside with me being denied entrance, also," Antipholus (of Ephesus) claimed. "Then, I appointed this numbskull Angelo to go and manufacture the golden chain that I planned to give to my unfaithful wife to make amends with her. Alas, when the merchant Balthasar and I dined for supper, there was no evidence or sign of Angelo anywhere, for he had reneged on having dinner with us. Later, I walked down the street and ran into Angelo conferring with a second city merchant, who sold wholesale and retail furniture."

"Well, what happened next?" the befuddled Death Duke pressed Antipholus (of Ephesus). "Did you obtain the gold necklace from reputable Angelo?"

"That's precisely the damned problem, or an aspect of the general problem," Antipholus intelligently insisted. "Angelo swore before the pissed-off second merchant that I had already received the goddamned gold chain, and the vengeful goldsmith had me arrested on the spot when I denied that I had ever received the necklace. Then, I sent my servant Dromio home to get money to bail me out of jail," the perplexed husband elucidated, "but my servant never returned with the leather purse of gold dog-faced ducats. Next, my unpredictable wife showed-up at the jail with a rabble of confederates, along with that detestable and sadistic psychopath Dr. Pinch, who specializes in cheap tit, ass, and pussy feels, and who professes to be a quack sex therapist/psychiatrist," Antipholus of Ephesus gasped, almost out of breath from all of his excitement and mental duress.

"I agree that Dr. Pinch is a hollow-eyed, greedy, fortune-telling wannabe' successful jerk-off, er, I mean idiot," Duke Solinus confirmed and stated. "Pinch has publicly declared on many occasions that everyone in Ephesus is fucked-up, er, I mean 'demented and possessed', so in the near future, I intend to settle matters with that vile pernicious traitor Dr. Pinch, who incidentally never served me reputably in a pinch. Now then; does anyone here have any additional details to relate pertinent to this rather bewildering investigation?"

"My Lord," Angelo the Goldsmith spoke-up again. "It is true that this crazy fellow Antipholus did not dine at home, even though his effeminate voice was coming from inside while he was still outside. This is a very bizarre mystery that plagues my sanity right up to this very moment, for I had indeed experienced the phenomenon with my own wax-filled ears. The last thing I knew, Antipholus and his clown servant fled into yonder abbey, and now the two itinerant sots are out here in broad daylight pretending as if nothing is peculiar or highly irregular!" Angelo testified and stammered. "This all seems like an immense conundrum. I do believe that the entire fiasco is the work of a diabolical sorcerer, making the Devil's evil appear to be a goddamned convoluted miracle."

"This is the most extraordinary pile of bullshit I've ever heard, or seen, or smelled!" the Death Duke marveled and commented. "I hypothesize that you've all been drinking from the enchantress Circe's goblet, who incidentally also sported D cups!"

Then Dromio (of Ephesus) added more crazy information to the fantastic mayhem. "Sir," the sleazy slave said to Duke Solinus. "My Master often dines with this lusty-busty prostitute, er, I mean courtesan, standing right over there, and he promised her the golden chain, which as you can plainly distinguish, he is not wearing."

"But he was wearing it when he had dashed into the abbey!" Adriana testified, as she had so perceptively witnessed. "I saw the sparkling chain with my own two eyes!"

"It's true that the self-appointed lover boy has dined with me on many occasions including today," the classy hooker publicly claimed. "And the bastard, er, I mean gentleman, owes me eighty ducats for the platinum ring and for the gold necklace chain he had promised, that in truth, I've never received or enjoyed."

"And you claim that Antipholus entered the abbey with the gold chain around his neck, and now he stands out here with it missing?" Duke Solinus objectively rehashed those pieces of the major puzzle. "This whole matter is quite incomprehensible and disconcerting! I need respite and independence from it in order to regain my sanity."

"Yes, My Liege!" Adriana, Luciana, Angelo the Goldsmith and the courtesan/whore all yelled in unison. "Yes, My Liege!" they repeated in perfect harmonic unison.

"This entire scenario is awfully irregular. just like my bowels are today, and virtually every other day!" Duke Solinus summarized and articulated. "I think that all of you have become mentally unstable funny farmers! So, you all go with dispatch and summon the obese Abbess. I want to speak with that chubby Mother right now!"

* * * * * * * * * * * *

While Adriana, Luciana, Angelo and the courtesan/whore were fetching the Abbess for the Duke, Aegeon, the condemned Syracuse merchant, addressed the city Monarch and attempted to implore his Grace's clemency.

"Most Eminent Duke. I vouchsafe that you permit me to speak a few sentences about *my* sentence," Aegeon requested.

"I pride myself on being stoic and judicious, so make it short and sweet, you piece of useless rubbish; you chunk of talking garbage," the unimpressed Death Duke very pompously and condescendingly answered. "Soon, bankrupt Merchant of Syracuse, you'll lose your head in a worse way than poor attention-deficit Antipholus has lost his. Commence with your brief narrative."

"Sir, is not your name Antipholus, and your goofy mentally challenged servant Dromio?" Aegeon asked the totally befuddled Antipholus (of Ephesus). "I'm sure that both of you psycho' fools vaguely remember me."

"You aren't another one of Dr. Pinch's forgetful mental patients having amnesia, are you?" Dromio of Ephesus seriously asked Aegeon. "You appear to have all of the attributes of one of those myriad giddy victims!"

"You know my identity well, dip-shit, and should automatically recognize me," Aegeon grieved, while soliciting much-needed royal sympathy for his plight.

"I never saw your visage before in my fucked-up life, and never want to see it again you, demented loser!" Dromio (of Ephesus) insulted the aged condemned man. "You're just what we don't need here in Ephesus; another crazy, deranged, delusional, accused liar from Syracuse!"

"Well granted, you might have inferior vision," Aegeon said to Dromio. "But let's test your auditory perception. Don't you recognize my goddamned voice?"

"Old Man, I recognize nothing, and I have twenty-twenty vision and twenty-twenty hearing, too!" Antipholus of Ephesus replied to the question Aegeon had specifically asked to Dromio of Ephesus. "I trust my eyes and my ears more than I trust anyone here, er, that is everyone except you, Most Eminent Supreme Duke!"

"I don't know who the fuck you are, Old Man, and nor do I particularly care!" Dromio dittoed his Master's negative sentiments. "Stop talking gibberish!"

"You two ungrateful freaks don't remember my very distinct and incomparable voice!" the chained-up Aegeon angrily screamed. "Must my truths fall upon the deaf ears of blind men? Antipholus my cherished son, I am your long-lost father."

"I never saw my father in my life, and I doubt strenuously that you are he," Antipholus (of Ephesus) solemnly expressed. "I suppose you're married to a partridge and a pear tree, that looks like a wild huckleberry bush too, you whimsical Loon!"

"But you had spent many years in Syracuse, too, until you ran away and went to sea in search of your mother and twin brother," Aegeon pleaded. "Surely you must recollect our intimate association in Syracuse."

"Not only have you succeeded in obtaining your sentence to be beheaded, but now you're trying to have me decapitated too!" Antipholus of Ephesus yelled at his yet-to-be-acknowledged father. "I've never been to Syracuse in my life, and never wish to visit that fucked-up city!"

"Look you Syracusan spy," Duke Solinus interrupted the debate with a prodigious frown evident upon his face. "I've known Antipholus here for twenty memorable years, and I can vouch that he's never been near Sicily, let alone Syracuse. Why condemned Aegeon do you subject my loyal subject to such a sensitive detrimental subject? Was your goal in life to become a geography instructor at some foreign Syracuse university?"

* * * * * * * * * * * *

Adriana, Luciana, Angelo the pissed-off Goldsmith, and the sexy blonde courtesan/whore together returned to the front abbey yard accompanied by Antipholus and Dromio (of Syracuse), along with the chunky, fat-assed Lady Abbess.

"Greetings Lady Abscess, er, I mean Lady Abbess," Duke Solinus said. "Perhaps you can clarify this great mystery that has wickedly befallen our fair city."

"Most mighty and benevolent Duke, behold a man that I believe has been unjustly maligned and terribly wronged," the corpulent Lady Abbess answered, much to everyone's befuddlement.

"What the hell's going on here?" Adriana hollered. "I must visit the optometrist, because I have double vision and see two husbands standing out here. This must either be vile sorcery, or mystical chicanery, I know not which!"

"I'm the real Dromio, so Distinguished Duke, I implore you to command this other Dromio impersonator to be taken away to be flogged," Dromio of Syracuse all-too-theatrically insisted to spare his vulnerable body from physical harm. "I can't fuckin' stand phony impostors and great pretenders."

"I, my Esteemed Duke, am the real Dromio, and *this* punk smart-mouthed, artificial conniver to my left is certainly a masquerader," Dromio of Ephesus argued while pointing at Dromio of Syracuse.

"Are you not Aegeon, my father, who thank goodness art not yet in Heaven?" Antipholus of Syracuse uttered in complete amazement. The twin son with the excellent memory stood still with his mouth agape, waiting for a favorable response from the old man sentenced for brutal execution.

"Speak old Aegeon," the Lady Abbess sternly demanded. "For I have gained a husband from this evolving farce. You don't recognize me, ever since I've put on a flabby three hundred pounds, but I'm your very patient, ever-vigilant wife, Aemilia. I bore you twin sons, but then the infant boys and we had been separated in a terrible shipwreck, much worse than any edifice wrecks!"

"Two Antipholus jerk-offs, and two fucked-up Dromio nutcases," the Delirious Duke laughed. "There better not be two Dukes present here, or I'll surely become mighty pissed-off!"

"Tell me Aemilia, what had transpired after we were parted, following the catastrophic shipwreck?" Aegeon pleaded to learn. "Did you immediately enter the convent? I mean, Antipholus and Dromio entered the convent too, and thank goodness those incompetent jerks weren't in there long enough to become mean-spirited nuns."

"I was clinging with Antipholus and Dromio to the partially sunken mast, and shiver me timbers, it was fuckin' cold in the water," Aemelia (the abscessed Abbess) recollected and shared. "Fishermen on a crude clam boat out of Corinth picked us up. From Corinth I saved sufficient money to travel back to Epidamium, and not finding you there, Husband, I gave you up as drowned. So, I journeyed here to Ephesus and worked as a lowly scrub-woman until I was eventually promoted up the ranks to Lady Abbess."

"I can verify that this woman and her son Antipholus had arrived from Corinth via Epidamium," Duke Solinus vouched, "because I was at the time vacationing in Epididymis and voyaged to Ephesus on the same bark with the mother, the child, and the goofy male servant now known as Dromio."

Then Adriana had an inspiration on how to further clarify matters. "Which of you two husbands dined at my house this afternoon?" she curiously asked.

"I, gentle Mistress," Antipholus of Syracuse truthfully stated. "And I'm not your fucked-up husband, as everyone here had originally thought. But needless to say, I wouldn't mind hopping in the sack with your saucy sister, Luciana. She's certainly hot enough to be my personal spice girl."

"You, Sir are wearing the gold chain around your neck that I had specifically manufactured for your usually dependable twin brother," Angelo the Goldsmith realized and articulated as the jewel merchant impolitely pointed to the elaborate necklace. "I must humbly admit that I do very intricate and admirable work."

"I don't deny that it is yours!" Antipholus of Syracuse contritely confessed. "But if the chain had been meant for my bizarre twin brother, I can now comprehend why you wanted me arrested for possessing it!"

"I now fully fathom why I was arrested for not possessing it!" Antipholus of Ephesus comprehended and communicated. "Let's face it; we're all fucked-up; that is, everyone but you, Most Eminent Supreme Duke!"

"This leather purse filled with dog-faced golden ducats that Dromio had brought to me," Antipholus of Syracuse informed and showed everyone, "and all of this zany comedy of errors, had happened because my twin brother and I had been mistaken for each other from time to time by all of you dumb-shit assholes, er, that is, by all of you' noble people, except the Most Eminent Supreme Duke."

"I submit that the gold ducats in the pouch should be used as ransom to free my father Aegeon from being beheaded," Antipholus of Ephesus suggested and announced. "I'm quite sure that my accommodating wife, Adriana, won't mind if I use her blood money so that she can gain a grouchy, grumpy old, rich father-in-law!"

"Keep your shiny ducats!" the wise Duke Solinus commanded. "It's my distinct privilege to proclaim that the Syracusan Aegeon has been released from his execution at no cost to anyone! And Angelo," Solinus added, "I'll gladly pay for the golden necklace from my royal treasury at taxpayers' expense, of course!"

Then, the aggrieved courtesan/whore roughly pulled Antipholus of Ephesus aside to have a confidential conference with him. "You still owe me either the promised platinum ring or the gold necklace chain," the sophisticated well-endowed, prostitute declared.

"I must give both of these fabulous presents to my wife, but I double-promise on my heart," Antipholus of Ephesus insincerely whispered and pledged, "as soon as my bitchy, dry-welled wife again gives me an adequate allowance from her colossal inheritance, I'll go directly to Angelo and have duplicate pieces of jewelry fabricated."

Then, the obscenely obese Lady Abbess (Aegeon's long-lost formerly skinny wife Aemilia) constructively suggested that everyone enter the abbey (which was really a whorehouse under re-construction) to review their particular roles in "this un*convent*ional story". The Abbess then reported to her strange entourage that she had suffered twenty-three years of travail along with chastity and abstinence, and that if she were lucky, she could stimulate and arouse old Aegeon and enjoy her "first marital intercourse in over three decades". "When I finally arrived in Ephesus from the coast of Greece," the Lady Abbess explained, "Duke Solinus felt sorry for me, and adopted my ass as his ward and honorary cousin-in-law."

"Master," Dromio of Syracuse addressed Antipholus of Syracuse. "Your personal possessions from the notorious Centaur Inn that I had placed in the captain's custody aboard a ship in the harbor, well, the boat has just embarked out to sea. I'm afraid you'll never again see your thousand ducats, along with your other valuable gems, nude drawings of well-endowed women, and assorted rare jewels."

"That's perfectly all-right and acceptable, short-fat Dromio," Antipholus of Syracuse softly spoke into his servant's ear. "After I marry Luciana, Adriana's rich sister, who will also be my generous sister-in-law, I'm certain that the charitable dolls will recompense me the thousand dog-faced ducats, and then some extra spending money, too. I'll start a brand-new importing and exporting business, and within several years, I'll become rich again. Life is good when it's not rotten!"

"A slave's life is always fuckin' rotten!" Dromio (of Syracuse) philosophically clarified to Dromio of Ephesus. "Now, twin brother; let's follow our mother, who apparently has become a real Mother, into the abbey to mutually bullshit and figure-out all of the remaining dumb-ass pieces to this quite-sensational, fucked-up enigma."

"Macbeth"
William Shakespeare

Act I

During the eleventh century in Scotland (before there was Scotch tape or potent Scotch whiskey), there was Macbeth, a man of dignity and honor, and Lady Macbeth, who through excessive greed, ambition, and pride, drove her husband to commit wicked acts of murder and villainy. And as Macbeth attempted to cover-up his initial crimes, the thane became deeper mired inside a quagmire of self-incriminating lies and deception. Shakespeare's craftiness and craft in this famous play begins with the sorcery of three ugly, wart-faced witch bitches, who amazingly, all unanimously proclaimed in unison: "Fair is foul, and foul is fair!" without ever-knowing a damned thing about American baseball.

On a desolate and isolated Scotland heath, Macbeth, the heralded intrepid Thane (nobleman/ruler/Duke) of Glamis, had just vanquished a rebellion of an alliance of feudal Vikings and warlike Scots. Hearing of his General's valor, appreciative King Duncan desired to reward his cousin Macbeth's victories by conferring upon the audacious champion dominion over the lands that had been formerly governed by the defeated and traitorous Thane of Cawdor.

Three scabby-skinned, lice-infected witches sang their weird runes among the ruins of an ancient castle, situated along the Scottish heath. Their enigmatic riddles would riddle Macbeth throughout the story, and at the end, the main character wished that he had never encountered the prognosticating, grotesque-looking, very hideous sorcerers. The "bitch witches" gathered around their steaming cauldron and predicted that soon their presence would confront the great hero, Macbeth, who would be passing by their vicinity after waging a successful war against the Norway Vikings and their Scot collaborators; including the usurped thanes of Cawdor and Chowder.

On another foggy and hazy peninsula of the rocky Scottish coast, King Duncan was reassessing the fate of numerous former followers that had participated in the bloody insurrection against his benign authority. Duncan was commiserating with his sons Malcolm and Donalbain, along with the feudal lord Lennox, and several other high-ranking nobles, along with their attendants.

A wounded sergeant was brought forward before the kind King to report the final incidents of the recently-fought battle. The soldier was told to describe exactly what had transpired while the battered warrior still had enough energy to do so, before collapsing onto the ground (and possibly dying).

"King Duncan," the bleeding-to-death sergeant gasped. "During the height of the savage battle, neither side was enjoying an advantage or was winning, for it appeared that the forces were equally-matched, and of equal size and strength. But then several thousand enemy Irish mercenary foot soldiers were led by the fearless MacDonwald, whose absolutely wild and berserk soldiers soon made hamburger meat out of *our* combatants and their helpers," the dying sergeant explained.

"Well, what the fuck happened next?" Malcolm insisted on learning. "Does old MacDonwald still have his farm? Did any thanes clam-up at Chowder? Tell us everything sergeant; before you fuckin' die! If you die before you tell us, then you'll really be sorry!"

"But then, King Duncan, my revered doughnut-eating ruler," the bleeding from the mouth sergeant proceeded with his admirable elaboration. "The armies of Macbeth and Banquo battled the enemy ferociously, and everyone in their path was slaughtered. And when some of those enemy soldiers weren't slaughtered, those others soon became victims and were actually massacred, too. Macbeth and MacDonwald met on the battlefield, and wildly fought with swords. And Macbeth finally emerged the victor, chopping-off MacDonwald's head with one fierce swipe of his mighty blade."

"Well now," majestic King Duncan said to his sons Malcolm and Donalbain. "Since MacDonwald has been slain, we can elevate Macbeth to be the new area burgher king, after we alert all the burghers, even those burghers that are the (charcoal) pits. When awesome Macbeth eliminated MacDonwald," Duncan emphasized, "obviously, that courageous act with his new-*fang*led sword was analogous to cutting-off a poisonous snake's head."

"That's quite totally correct, father," Malcolm readily agreed. "Macbeth literally severed relations with MacDonwald. The rebels had no viable alternative except to retreat in shame after their fearless leader had been abruptly dispensed with."

"I maintain that Macbeth deserves to be rewarded for his unflinching valor, and also for his contribution to the defense of Scotland," King Duncan mandated to his sons. "I shall confer upon the victor a new title!"

"And finally, the brave Macbeth attached MacDonwald's head to a nearby castle rampart to instill intense fear into the enemies' hearts," the virtually dead sergeant verbally shared just before taking his last breath, and then expiring and gratefully leaving this complicated world. Everyone conspicuously standing around ignored the sergeant's demise, and the aspirants focused their attention on King Duncan, on Malcolm, and on Donalbain.

"I concur with everything you had earlier reported, my son," Duncan finally agreed with Malcolm's assessment spoken ten-minutes before. "I'll have to pay Macbeth a visit and announce his new royal appointment. I'll send several of my yahoo messengers out to tell Macbeth of the thane's newly-earned title, and to extend to the celebrated Thane of Glamis my rightful praise. And I can't wait to see the enchanting Lady Macbeth again, and avariciously gaze upon her superb, outstanding breasts, which stick-out so firmly that it appears they're extending outside the castle when she's standing erect near a window! I hope those huge suckers aren't booby trapped!"

In the meantime, Norway's King Sweno the Swedo had his fresh reinforcements attack those commanded by Macbeth and Banquo on a hilly battlefield, but the new assault was repelled and driven back. King Duncan then declared that the captured Scot traitors (the Thane of Cawdor and the Thane of Chowder) had to be swiftly executed in order to quell future rebellions, and that an honorable peace treaty would have to be signed with King Sweno the Swedo of Norway. Two noblemen named Ross and Angus were assigned the task of informing the triumphant Macbeth of *his* new Scottish land and prestige, which the valiant nobleman had earnestly earned in *his* dedicated efforts to protect his King, his kinsmen, and his homeland.

"Which one is Angus?" Malcolm asked King Duncan.

"The one that looks like a cow!" the knowledgeable king replied.

* * * * * * * * * * * *

On the dirt trail that meandered through the misty heath, Macbeth and Banquo (on horseback) encountered the three scabby, warty-faced witches standing in their path like a trio of medieval psychopaths. The trio of witch-bitches seemed to be huddled-together and hovering a foot or so above the marshy ground, but their legs and feet had been obscured by a heavy swirling mist that seemed to mystify and baffle both Macbeth and Banquo. Suddenly, thunder and lightning lit-up the overcast sky (above the actors in this overcast play).

"It's the height of day, and not the witching hour! Which witch is which?" the superstitious Macbeth asked the three women with a tone of uneasiness in his normally strong voice.

"I don't have the foggiest notion of what the hell my General is talking about! Do any of you three witches standing there above the sand have any sand-wiches?" Banquo asked. "I'm quite hungry and promise not to waste a crummy crumb."

"Yes!" Macbeth confirmed. "My partner Banquo here could use some sandwiches in an impromptu banquet, so that my friend could have some more gas in his intestines during his merry smor-gas-bord, ha, ha, ha! That's why Banquo and I always like to fart-around together after we've enjoyed consuming a scrumptious, sumptuous buffet!" Macbeth jested to alleviate the great anxiety his heart was feeling at the sight of the reprehensible-looking wretches, all' of whom had their hands bloody from recently butchering swine, and from drinking the pigs' blood as if it were delicious grape juice.

"Hail. Macbeth, Thane of Glamis!" the first witch yelled.

"You got *that* accomplishment right, you' ugly dragon!" the proud military commander replied. "Macbeth *is* indeed Thane of Glamis. Any asshole living around this part of Scotland knows *that* truth to be an elementary fact."

"Hail, Macbeth; Thane of Cawdor and Thane of Chowder!" the second grotesque-looking, contemptible oracle declared. "May you muster-up enough happiness to catch-up on and relish your new title, you totally arrogant son-of-a-bitch!"

"Now, I'm becoming nervous with clammy hands and I feel like clamming-up altogether!" Macbeth neurotically answered in a worrisome voice directed at Banquo.

"Hail Macbeth, the next King of Scotland!" the third witch bitch oddly predicted. "Your excellent glory will be short-lived, but whatever you do, beware of a terrible golfer that's a *duff*er!"

"It might yet hail, Macbeth!" Banquo spoke softly to his General. "It's already thundered off in the distance, and we've seen wicked lightning bolts suddenly coming from out of nowhere and flashing overhead! You and I Macbeth don't need any more moors and their strange gas emissions that smell like gross farts around this sector of Scotland!" Banquo nervously described and related. "And besides that-less-than-pertinent observation, General Macbeth, I don't like all of this surprise, ominous, and environmental shit we're presently witnessing and experiencing one bit! These three witches are raunchy bitches, all speaking from their separate ditches without any hitches!"

'Shit! I'm already Thane of Glamis, which in retrospect wasn't too glamorous!' Macbeth pensively thought. 'But what's with this Thane of Cawdor and this Thane of Chowder bull-shit, not to mention that I'm slated to be 'King of Scotland' illogical nonsense! King Duncan is still alive, and the monarch has two eligible sons to take his place; Malcolm and Donalbain! Perhaps it's time for a lengthy vacation searching for sea monsters over at Loch Ness, along with pursuing a little well-earned rest and relaxation.'

"Don't let the witches' statements affect your thinking, Lord Macbeth!" Banquo wisely counseled his already power-hungry General. "These three retarded old fucks couldn't predict which witch will take the next shit! Tell me, ugly Women that profess having the gift of prophecy," Banquo insisted. "What' is my destiny? Will I be king of the world or emperor of the universe? If Zeus dies, will I ascend to the throne." Banquo joked.

"You won't ever become a fuckin' king, but your fate is that you'll someday become the father of many fuckin', fucked-up kings!" the third and most raunchy-looking old, haggard-looking bitch forecasted. "You, brave warrior with the diarrhea mouth, seem to have had the right sperm in your worm!"

"You three Bitches need some serious vanishing cream on your faces to hide all of those ugly wrinkles, warts and wens!" Banquo sarcastically yelled from atop his horse. "Each of you hags-from-hell is uglier than mortal sin, and the sight of all three of you together is uglier than all Hell! Speak to us, you pathetic-looking hick Dregs!"

And without the aide or assistance of any vanishing cream, the three horrible-looking witches incredibly disappeared into the hazy mist. Macbeth yelled for the hoary prognosticators to reappear and explain their predictions more in detail, but his desperate solicitations were to no avail. But several minutes later, Angus (whose face looked a little like a bull's), accompanied by Ross, arrived on horseback to tell Macbeth some amazing news.

"Macbeth," Ross excitedly announced. "King Duncan has appointed you the Thane of Cawdor. You should now be one happy dude! You're a Duke, almost doubled the size of his Dukedom!"

"And Macbeth," Angus informed without giving the General a bum steer, or some much-needed hair tonic for his severe cowlick. "You're also the new Thane of Chowder."

"But I believe that the Thane of Cawdor and the Thane of Chowder are still both alive!" Macbeth questioned the King's assigned emissaries. "Are you two warped fellows fibbing and ribbing me? What the fuck's this irrational bull-shit all about? Did you two jerk-offs just have sex with three ugly-looking witches, and have had your sperm-worms and your brains contaminated?" Macbeth conjectured and stated. "Am I to buy similar clothes to *theirs,* and masquerade-around the marshes and heaths of Scotland as the illustrious Thane of Cawdor, and as the effeminate Thane of Chowder? How the hell can I be two additional thanes at the same time, when I have enough trouble just being the goddamned Thane of Glamis?"

"King Duncan has sentenced the Thane of Cawdor and the Thane of Chowder to death for being traitors to Scotland, and also traders with the Vikings!" Ross revealed. "You've been conferred *their* titles and properties, which incidentally, have already been confiscated and transferred. Congratulations, mighty Macbeth. You happen to be the new fucked-up Thane of Cawdor/Chowder! And all of this astonishing shit happened when *our* invincible armies were vanquishing the Norwegian legions. It's certainly a glorious day in your dramatic life!"

'Holy Loch Ness Monster!' Macbeth realized. 'The fuckin' witches knew what the hell the three diseased cunts were saying, especially the second one. Now, Banquo. I'm on the road to becoming the next King of Scotland! I'm glad I still have my good eyesight. because blind ambition could get me into hot water; maybe even into hotter water than that which is inside the three witches' steaming cauldron! I must be careful, or else my entire future might go to pot!'

And then, Macbeth snapped-out of his brief reverie of acquiring more power and asked his loyal subordinate, "Banquo; what the hell do you make of all this unbelievable bull-shit that Ross and Angus have just disclosed? Is this for real, or what?"

"I don't fuckin' trust the evil witches any further than my dick can stretch across the English Channel all the way to France!" Banquo indicated with a two-inch gap showing between his right thumb and forefinger. "Now then, Macbeth. I believe that some jealous have-nots desire sabotaging your success, and might be attempting to get you to do what is both wrong and hazardous. And those three untrustworthy witch bitches might fall into *that* negative category! But let me say that confidentially Macbeth..."

"Yes, yes, go on!" the General urged while contemplating being three thanes at once. "Tell me; what's on your mind besides your scalp and bald head."

"Well General, I do implicitly trust Ross and Angus's veracity. On the other side of the coin, with me being a human member of the Natural World, I've always been leery and skeptical of superstitions concerning the supernatural!" Banquo objectively qualified and declared. "Don't allow those three nefarious-minded witches to cleverly trick you into attempting to fulfill *their* three reckless prophecies! Those disciples of Satan might just be baiting you for future disastrous consequences!"

"But friend Banquo; the second witch's prediction about me being the Thane of Cawdor and the Thane of Chowder has already come to fruition!" Macbeth maintained. "I'll have to send you to a furniture store to purchase me at least three new thrones."

"Only a mere coincidence and nothing more!" Banquo insisted. "She just happened to guess right what might be ten-years from now behind invisible Door # 2, that's all!"

"Well then, I suppose we ought to think about the third witch's bizarre prediction, Banquo, as we ride-off into the sunset to meet with King Duncan and his mentally-challenged sons," Macbeth commented to his faithful aide. "If I become King of Scotland, I'll most certainly appoint you Duke of Edinburgh, and then my friend, Banquo, we'll both become royal pain-in-the-asses to every already overtaxed person living in Scotland!"

"I hope *that* improbable bull-shit really happens, Lord Macbeth; no ifs, ands, or pain-in-the-butts about it!" Banquo answered. And then both men hardily laughed until the two equestrians fell off their horses and tumbled into a nearby, misty swamp.

* * * * * * * * * * * *

King Duncan was the ideal ruler who governed Scotland with a majestic kindness and with aristocratic suavity. But Macbeth now perceived Duncan's older son Malcolm as the prospective successor to the throne, and the ambitious thane envisioned the heir-apparent as *his* principal adversary representing an obstacle for the new Thane of Cawdor/Chowder, who now really desired accomplishing the Thane of Glamis's great desire to attain imperial power. The mental impression of Malcolm existing as an impediment to absolute power became a fixation in Macbeth's avaricious mind; a haunting that the Thane could neither shake nor forget.

Malcolm had told King Duncan that the former Thane of Cawdor and the deposed Thane of Chowder had both been promptly executed for their demonstrated brazen treason against Scotland, which could be interpreted as their rebellious treason directed against King Duncan. The King and his sons were impatiently waiting to congratulate "the invincible Macbeth" upon the hero's triumphant arrival at Duncan's Forres Palace, that had a prosperous coffee and doughnut shop in the dungeon.

The following morning, Macbeth, Banquo, Ross, and Angus all entered King Duncan's throne room where the moderate monarch communicated that he was deeply indebted to *their* cooperative service, and that Macbeth would be greatly rewarded for his indispensable contribution to squelching the rebellion and making the Vikings retreat back to Scandinavia, where the assholes could stare at their women's exotic and erotic bellybuttons all day long.

After officially making Macbeth the Thane of Cawdor/Chowder with a thirty-second sword-dubbing, King Duncan had another special announcement to deliver. "I hereby appoint my favorite son, Malcolm, as the official Prince of Encumberland, er sorry, I meant Cucumberland; er forgive me, my distinguished noble lords. I had really meant to say 'Prince of Cumberland'!" Duncan finally correctly enunciated. "And in case any of you geniuses are wondering what the hell that title Prince of Cumberland means, it expressly indicates that Malcolm is to be the next King of Scotland, sometime in the future! And Macbeth," the King continued his exposition. "Soon my entourage will be traveling to visit you at your splendid castle in Inverness. I'm so glad that you've sold your white castle down south in New Castle to several wealthy burghers!"

When Macbeth finally left King Duncan's fortress at Forres, all that his convoluted mind could think about was the third witch's prediction, and how he should eliminate Malcolm (and Donalbain, too) to fulfill the prophecy that *he* would ascend to become the next King of Scotland. 'I wonder if the heir-apparent to the throne has a last name?' Macbeth speculated and considered. 'Oh well, in my mind, I'll just think of the targeted gutless asshole as Malcolm X!'

* * * * * * * * * * * *

Lady Macbeth was busy reading a letter from her now-famous husband that described how the three witch bitches had predicted that her spouse would become the new Thane of Cawdor/Chowder, and then soon thereafter, achieve the honor of gloriously becoming King of Scotland. Lady Macbeth exactly pondered exactly how the latter prediction could come true with Malcolm and Donalbain being in the line of succession in front of her greedy husband (who was Duncan's first and worst cousin). But the prospect of being the Queen of Scotland seemed rather most enticing, and Lady Macbeth was very fascinated with that soul-consuming possibility.

Then, an exhausted messenger from Forres arrived at Inverness, and the courier informed Lady Macbeth that King Duncan was traveling to the castle, and that he and his sons would be getting there soon, possibly before Macbeth would be arriving home. The essence of the dispatch inspired Lady Macbeth to stealthily contrive a plan that would allow her and her husband to ascend to becoming the new Queen and King of Scotland. The conniving woman evaluated all of the particular circumstances.

But then Macbeth rode upon the open drawbridge, and over the moat, into Inverness, and was warmly and affectionately greeted by his scheming wife, who was evilly thinking during their extended embrace, 'Screw Glamis; pork Cawdor, and fuck Chowder. I want to regally screw everyone in Scotland after I become its Queen.'

"Duncan and his naïve attendants will arrive at Inverness tomorrow morning," Macbeth conveyed to his covetous wife. "Time to make the doughnuts! But more seriously, how can *we* exploit this wonderful opportunity to the hilt?"

But Lady Macbeth was worried that her husband was not ruthless enough to have the sage King and his ill-prepared two sons assassinated. "Don't worry, my dear Spouse!" Lady Macbeth arcanely answered. "You'll be the next King after I satisfactorily take care of your royal guests. Just leave everything up to me. Duncan will wish all-too-late that he had abdicated his throne, rather than foolishly risk coming here to Inverness to be entertained by us," Lady Macbeth spoke to her husband, sounding much like a crazed maniac. "That asshole and his butt-hole sons won't have assholes to shit out of after I get done with them! And what I'm going to have done to them isn't taught in proctology school classrooms, either! Now Husband; the spirits of our cheated ancestors will give us the power and the courage to eradicate all those weak imbeciles that stand in our way! I'll invoke *their* supernatural assistance to ensure the implementation of my devious plan!" the obsessed wife furtively articulated to her already-confused husband, the truly-thrilled-to-death, and now newly-commissioned, proud-as-a-peacock regal Thane of Cawdor/Chowder.

'Before I take care of Duncan, Malcolm, and Donaldbain, I think I'm have the three numbskulls manacled to a dungeon wall, and then I'll have my husband cauterize their assholes with sconce torches so that the three assholes won't be able to shit!' Lady Macbeth fantasized.

The fiendish Lady Macbeth warmly met Duncan and his entourage when their traveling party finally arrived at Inverness. Macbeth's wife welcomed the royal company inside her castle, which in her evil mind, was analogous to setting a treacherous spider's web with *her* being the dangerous trap's arachnid architect, and with Duncan, Malcolm, and Donalbain being the unsuspecting visiting insect victims.

"The air around Inverness Castle smells fresh and clean," King Duncan (who valued civil environmental green small talk) mentioned to Lady Macbeth. "Your beautiful residence certainly does not portray any gloomy atmosphere."

"At present. the atmosphere *here* does not suggest the utmost fear!" Lady Macbeth strangely rhymed to her royal guest. "Come on inside, King Duncan, and I'll see that you and your sons get properly situated in your respective rooms. Lord Macbeth and I are happy to accommodate you! In fact, I'm thrilled-to-death to be your hostess."

* * * * * * * * * * * *

That evening, Macbeth and his diabolical wife had served a fabulous feast to their unassuming guests. While the prolonged merriment was continuing in the banquet hall, Macbeth's plotting wife surreptitiously stepped outside to discuss future strategy with him.

"Husband, why did you suddenly leave the dinner table and leave your guests wondering where the hell you were?" Lady Macbeth asked. "I know you have a lot of get-up-and-go, but that discourtesy was so obviously ridiculous! Duncan, Malcolm, Donalbain and the rest might suspect something rotten in Scotland'!"

"I'm having second thoughts about doing anything nefarious!" Macbeth confided. "Duncan's my first cousin, and his sons are my second cousins. They're welcomed guests in my castle. I don't think that a King should be rooked on a chessboard, or inside *my* fortress."

"But you can't tell me that you weren't the one who first contemplated killing Duncan to attain the crown of Scotland! Why let absurd idiots like wimpy Malcolm and that profane Donalbain hinder your progress!" Lady Macbeth argued. "You're a lot stronger than those two wimps!"

"Well, then Wife. What do you have in your mini-mind besides this grandiose obsession of murder?" the indecisive husband asked. "Your ambition seems to be virtually equal to mine!"

"Tonight, I'll make sure that Duncan's guards, ends and tackles are completely drunk, and then my loyal husband, you can stab the clueless King to death while he sleeps in his room," Lady Macbeth divulged her demonic scheme. "Then, Duncan won't be able to give you any bunk when he's dead in his bunk! Ha, ha, ha! That's why, my conniving Husband, there are two 'asses' existing in the word 'assassination'! Your all-too-trustworthy cousin Duncan will be the first unfortunate ass. and meek and humble Malcolm the second unlucky ass to perish! Ha, ha, ha!" Diabolical Lady Macbeth jubilantly laughed, covering her mouth. "This royal homicide scheme is too rich and too tempting to resist! Ha, ha, ha!"

Act II

Banquo and his dog-loving son Fleance had accompanied King Duncan as part of the royal entourage that had traveled from Forres to Inverness Castle. Superstitious Banquo couldn't sleep soundly because of nightmares Macbeth's friend had been having regarding the uncanny predictions of the three fucked-up witches.

That night Fleance finally chased after and caught-up with his father, who was restlessly pacing around the castle gardens and bruising-up and lacerating his exposed legs, clumsily tripping over bushes, shrubs and tree stumps during his restless nocturnal episode. Banquo then heard rustling from a bracken, and pulled-out his sword in case some sinister individual would be conducting a sneak attack. 'Perhaps it's a band of robbers or some area punk juvenile delinquents,' Banquo thought without any awareness that Fleance was walking right behind him.

"Who the hell is rustling there in the bushes?" Banquo yelled into the dark nightscape. "It better not be cows, because I fuckin' hate cattle rustling!"

"It's just me," a familiar voice declared as a figure stepped out of the shadows and into the light of the full moon. "I haven't been able to sleep too well tonight either, after being appointed as the new Thane of Cawdor/Chowder," Macbeth intimated to his military colleague. "And besides that, Banquo. Lady Macbeth has been such a witch lately by denying me sex that I'm inclined to trade her beautiful ass and the rest of her hourglass body too for one of the three fucked-up witches *we* had encountered on the heath."

"Well now; Fleance and I will go back inside to catch some much-needed shuteye," Banquo promised Macbeth. "I suppose that the inability to fall asleep is not quite as bad as hallucinating, or having recurrent annoying illusions. I now bid you 'good night', omnipotent Thane of Cawdor/Chowder."

"Father, aren't you forgetting something?" Fleance asked Banquo. "You know; your expensive gift to Lord Macbeth for earning his new appointment from King Duncan."

"Oh yes!" the army commander realized and expressed, removing a precious jewel from his pocket. "Macbeth, please accept this token, this three-carat diamond in commemoration of your military triumphs and of your becoming the new imperial governor with the esteemed title of Thane of Cawdor/Chowder," Banquo congratulated his superior commander. "I stole this precious gem from a dead Viking officer's pocket. Now then Macbeth; you can cut your ass, er, I mean you can cut your glass easily with this new exquisite glimmering gem of a gem. I know you were expecting a plate-sized golden doughnut from Duncan and me, but this diamond will have to do."

"Why thank you, my dear Banquo!" the great Thane exclaimed, admiring the dazzling-sparkling object in the moonlight. "I'll have a jeweler make it into part of a ring, and then present the exquisite gift to Lady Macbeth on our diamond wedding anniversary, whenever the hell that event ever rolls around!"

After Banquo and Fleance re-entered Inverness Castle, Macbeth roamed around the dark gardens, trying to harness the rampant emotions frenetically fleeting about within his sinister mind. 'Lady Macbeth is now getting Duncan's guards drunk!' Macbeth considered. 'They're drinking moonshine, while I'm watching the moon shine out here! Ha, ha, ha! What a stupid fucked-up coincidence! And I'm sure that my scheming wife will give me good sex once this daring murder caper is enacted, just after midnight,' Macbeth imagined. 'But I can't rationally explain it; I feel influenced by a terrible force that has evilly drawn me out to these shadowy gardens, as if my body has been magnetized and attracted to it!'

But then, consistent with Banquo's casual comment about "hallucinating," suddenly a ghostly dagger appeared in the pale moonlight, and the object floated and then drifted all about, finally hovering only several-yards above shocked Macbeth's head. 'What the hell's this incredible shit my eyes are seeing? The dagger's jeweled handle points directly at my ass, but this unearthly knife has no material existence; for I'm now passing my hand right through the ominous object, and I'm not touching it, let alone accidentally receiving a goddamned cut from the supposedly sharp blade. This is the eeriest sensation I've ever experienced, and I'm no great fan of supernatural occurrences!' the worried Thane thought. 'I do believe that this goddamned' 'other world weapon' is some kind of fucked-up omen! In truth, I'm less afraid of a thousand attacking Viking barbarians, than I am of this spectral phenomenon that's making my knees knock; my teeth clatter; my hands tremble, and my pecker hurtfully pissing my *mail* underwear!'

* * * * * * * * * * * *

Macbeth heard a certain bell tolling that was (according to design) Lady Macbeth signaling that the guards had been intoxicated (drugged) with good wine, and symbolically, the ringing meant that a death knell was sounding for King Duncan and his two targeted sons. 'It's now time for me to assassinate the King,' Macbeth realized. 'Long live Duncan in either Heaven or Hell! Ha, ha, ha!'

Stepping inside Inverness Castle, Macbeth quickly encountered his duplicitous wife. "The guards are sound asleep and never heard the sound of the bell. Husband," Lady Macbeth specified in a whisper. "Borrow their daggers and proceed to slay Duncan as we had previously discussed. Then, we can blame the King's drunken and drugged sentinels for committing the cold and calculating unthinkable, heinous act!"

Five-minutes later, Macbeth returned to the stone hallway from Duncan's room carrying two daggers that were dripping with blood. "I regret what you had compelled me to do!" the Thane of Cawdor/Chowder said to his roguish wife. "I had always thought that my cousin Duncan was a cut above the rest, and now I'm convinced of that truth! You've persuaded me, Wife, to commit a detestable assassination! You've persuaded me to take a stab at obtaining power. Actually, several stabs!"

And then, as if in a trance, Macbeth entered Donalbain and Malcolm's assigned bedchamber and lacked the motivation to stab Duncan's sons to death, too. But upon exiting the second bedchamber, the General did not possess the wherewithal to re-enter Duncan's room and place the bloodstained knives into the sleeping guards' hands, so Lady Macbeth completed the felonious deed and had the audacity to smear (from the assassination daggers) the sleeping drunken guards' faces with what the unscrupulous wife presumed was Duncan, Malcolm and Donalbain's blood. Then, thinking about murdering Malcolm and Donalbain, Macbeth savagely killed the two drunken sleeping guards.

Macbeth looked-down at his bloodstained hands and thought, 'It would take both the goddamned *Atlantic Ocean* and the friggin'

Mediterranean Sea to wash away these terrible stains. It's like I have a filthy, skin-infected, medieval plague of some sort rotting-away my vulnerable flesh from the inside-out!'

And then, Macbeth perceptively noticed that his wife's hands were just as scarlet as his own. Now, the guilt-laden husband indeed regretted doing the wicked deeds that the brave thane had just maniacally performed. 'My wife has made me execute something ugly and evil!' Macbeth thought. 'I've committed cowardly mortal sins! Upon my death, I'll be denied Purgatory, and my soul will hastily speed directly to Hell!'

The following morning, two nobles, Lennox and MacDuff, visited Inverness Castle to congratulate Macbeth on his newly-acquired titles, and also to discuss certain domestic political matters with King Duncan. "Let us in Servant? Do you have any coal Porter?" Lennox laughed through the door from outside.

An elderly, drunken servant, wearing a loose-fitting sleeping gown, along with a pointed nightcap, and holding a three-foot-high lit candle in his left hand, and a nightcap of scotch whiskey in his right palm, admitted the two warriors inside. "Tell your Master that Lennox and MacDuff are here!" Lennox sternly ordered the senile servant.

"Greetings, Thane Macbeth!" Lennox strongly saluted. "Nice going on also becoming Thane of Cawdor/Chowder. Now then cousin, enough preliminary praise and pomp have been expressed from my loose lips. MacDuff and I must pursue some pithy business with our esteemed Monarch. Succinctly speaking, MacDuff and I would like to converse with King Duncan and establish some priorities and precedents that specifically need to be addressed; that is, if it's perfectly alright with you Macbeth! The King was dead-tired yesterday, and we didn't want to disturb his slumber with boring routine matters, and with touchy Scottish politics. Duncan was dead tired yesterday; but I hope not stone-cold dead today!"

The castle host volunteered to escort Lennox and MacDuff to Duncan's room, but the robust soldiers refused Macbeth's polite offer. And then the visiting pair strolled-down the drafty stone corridor. MacDuff knocked three-times upon the guest's door, and soon casually entered the chamber. Seconds later, the mighty thane loudly screamed accusatory exclamations, "Murder! Treason! Assassination! Murder! Disgrace! Scandal!"

Soon, the terrible murder news resounded throughout Inverness Castle, and Lady Macbeth creatively feigned fainting as she intentionally collapsed to the stone-slated floor in a very theatrical diva dive. Confusion and chaos abounded throughout the fortress. Everything seemed like a total frenzy, a veritable, accelerating, frenzied whirlwind in action.

"Who killed the King?" MacDuff cried-out. "Who was the villainous assassin? Ring the alarm bell! The castle must be searched for evidence! The culprit or culprits must be in here somewhere! Emergency! Someone ring the goddamned alarm bell, I say!"

"It looks like his own guards committed the wicked deed, or should I say committed the wicked misdeed," Lennox stated to his furious companion. "Look MacDuff! The guards have bloodstained daggers in their greedy hands, and apparently the knaves were lying there drunk on the floor where their bodies were just discovered."

Then Macbeth arrived at the bloody murder scene. During a moment of weakness, he confessed to having the guards killed.

"But Macbeth, why did you immediately kill the guards with your sword?" MacDuff interrogated his close friend and distant relative. "The rogues could've confessed their crimes, and then be hung on the basis of factual evidence!"

"I had such love for my cousin Duncan that I acted impulsively; almost reflexively!" Macbeth fraudulently lied with a contrived straight face. "I was strongly motivated by hate and not by reason, and now I grievously regret how stupidly I had reacted. Please forgive my impetuosity, MacDuff. You would've done the same damned thing if the defenseless King had been killed in his sleep inside *your* castle!"

"But why hadn't you told Lennox and me about King Duncan's assassination when we had arrived here at Inverness?" MacDuff skeptically asked. "Your lack of judgment seems to be irrational."

"Because I wanted you and Lennox to see for yourselves exactly what had transpired," Macbeth incredibly lied. "That way, you'd know exactly what motivated me to kill *his* drunken guards. I believe that the soldiers were hired killers; mercenary hit-men involved in a power-play conspiracy."

But after the killing of virtuous King Duncan, much to Lady Macbeth's frustration and anger (upon finding-out the full truth), the evil-hearted woman became extremely distraught when she learned certain additional information. Macbeth, petrified with horror, hadn't garnered the compulsion to murder Malcolm and Donalbain in their quarters, and so, the two young men were still alive and discussing the mutiny-in-progress in their bedchamber.

"I say, Donaldbain. Let's get the hell out of here," Malcolm suggested to his brother with emphatic gesticulations. "Someone's conspiring to take Scotland's throne. I mean, figuratively, and not literally stealing it. And whoever had Father assassinated is now going to try and exterminate us as if we're infected vermin. I think we ought to split-up, Donalbain. By that, I mean we ought to split-up literally and not physically," the totally nervous and suddenly paranoid Malcolm expressed to his younger sibling. "I'll secretly depart to England and then you could...."

"Escape to Ireland," Donalbain finished Malcolm's declarative sentence. "We'll be safer if we're hiding-out in two separate locations; that is two different locations in two distant countries. That way, hopefully, we could avoid a twin killing, even though we're not really twins! Oh well Malcolm; I'm speaking under duress, but you know what the fuck I mean!"

* * * * * * * * * * * *

Ross and MacDuff still had their reservations (although they weren't traveling far to anywhere) about King Duncan's unexpected death. The suspicious pair of renowned military officers conferred in a remote sector of Inverness Castle.

"Who the hell could've ordered the guards to murder Duncan?" Ross incredulously asked. "I mean, the sentinels were Duncan's personal bodyguards to begin with, weren't they? Maybe," Ross seriously speculated and paused. "Just maybe we'd know more, MacDuff, if the guards were still alive to make confessions. Now with no reliable witnesses, a decent investigation can't be conducted."

"Indeed Ross!" MacDuff readily agreed. "The guards might've been caught off-guard. Perhaps it could've been either Malcolm, or Donalbain, or maybe even both of those hundred-pound wimps had collaborated in a daring power-grab maneuver! If both those morons were put together, those two gutless assholes' weight still wouldn't comprise that of a fully-grown man! It sure makes Duncan's sons look bad that they've both run-away after the king's assassination. It sort of makes the scared assholes fuckin' look guilty, doesn't it Ross?"

"Under these bizarre circumstances, Thane Macbeth will undoubtedly be the next King of Scotland," Ross predicted to MacDuff. "I hope that his stiff dick won't get his kilt all out-of-kilter during his coronation ceremony. Will you be heading to Scone to see Macbeth crowned?"

"No, thank you!" MacDuff tersely answered. "I have bad vibrations about the whole fuckin' lousy, stinking scenario! I'll be thinking about and discussing all this crazy bull-shit with my flute-playing wife in my warm comfortable Castle Fife. And now that my wife is learning how to beat a drum, she and I will be able to practice giving our first fife and drum concert!"

"Farewell and Godspeed MacDuff!" Ross formally replied. "One final thing, though: How's your golfing game coming along? Are you still a Mac-duffer?"

"Divots everywhere, but for me, Ross; that's par for the course!" MacDuff smartly responded. "But let me say in a more serious note that

King Duncan's abominable murder has really teed me off! There's the unethical way to replace somebody, and then there's the fair-way! I have to comprehensively think this whole matter through to come-up with a believable solution! Farewell Ross! If there was more than a single assassin, I'd definitely like to put a hole in one of them! Farewell again Ross!"

Act III

Contrary to the type of nonsense that happens in standard fairy tales, power-hungry Macbeth became King of Scotland and fulfilled the third swamp witch's prophecy. Many eminent nobles and foreign country dignitaries were invited to the famous castle at Forres to celebrate the momentous occasion. While eating a hamburger inside the white castle, Banquo was contemplating how Macbeth had achieved everything that the second and third foggy swamp witches had predicted.

'Now, it's my turn to have some good luck kick-in to advance my own fame and fortune,' Banquo selfishly thought. 'The witches; well one of them anyway, predicted that my heirs would become future kings, and I'm sure the old warty-faced hag wasn't referring to either prom or cotillion kings. But I have this gut feeling, and it's not acid indigestion or appendicitis either, and I'll bet anyone dollars to doughnuts that Macbeth was the one responsible for Duncan's bloody death,' Banquo theorized. 'Maybe I can get a little eminent domain action started around here and confiscate Forres and Inverness castles for demolition, and then commission the construction of some highly-profitable, low-income, new village housing projects.'

Soon, trumpets sounded, and strumpets, still is various bedrooms, shrieked-out, "Yes! Yes! Yes!" just when King Macbeth' and his royal court entered the fortress. Banquo consented to Macbeth's explicit request that the war hero join the new King's grand entrance in order to project the illusion of unity to all those jabbering, gossiping attendees assembled in the mammoth banquet and dining hall.

"Yes, My Lord!" Banquo affirmed, the military leader pretending that he was speaking to Jesus Christ. "Fleance and I must leave early this afternoon because I had promised my mentally-challenged son that we would go horseback riding to see if we could capture some rabid wild mountain dogs. My son Fleance, as you know, King Macbeth," Banquo awkwardly rambled-on; "well, the lad collects tics, fleas, and ants as an ordinary hobby, and the mental case possesses the largest such collection in all of Scotland. Fleance sells the parasites at major flea markets all over the country. and the young entrepreneur is the second leading tic distributor in the entire land."

"Okay Banquo, my Friend. But I insist that you and Fleance must return for the second even more regal gala feast scheduled for eight o' clock this evening," Macbeth maintained, remembering what the witch had predicted for Banquo's heirs, and simultaneously perceiving Fleance as a prospective claimant to the crown. "I don't want to be ticked-off later this evening. Be there, Banquo. with your eccentric faggot son, or else you'll be both square and queer!"

"Now, I know why you refuse to stand outside in the brilliant sunshine, King Macbeth," Banquo hesitantly complimented his new Monarch. "Because obviously, you have it made in the shade! No one in Scotland will ever eclipse the great Macbeth!"

"Okay; but don't forget our banquet Banquo, later tonight!" Macbeth reminded his fellow commander. "It's going to be a super supper on which to feast your eyes, and expand the circumference of your gargantuan stomach, too! But more importantly, I wish to discuss with you some crazy shit that's going on in England, and also in Ireland, that might pertain to us. God be with you, friend Banquo, and with your dispirited spirit."

Before the second and more grandiose feast of the day was to begin that evening, Macbeth gazed at a small tranquil lake situated outside his new-residence, Forres Castle bedroom window, and pondered how Fleance constituted an imminent threat to *his* imperial power. 'I have no sons, so this bastard asshole, craven, gay son-of-a-bitch Fleance presents a distinct danger to my current reign. Now that I have absolute power, and am totally corrupted and spoiled by it, I'll delegate two of my professional hit-men that specialize in assassinations to do my dastardly dirty work for me,' the all-too-sinister new Scottish King plotted. 'That little thug Fleance must be eliminated! Yes, exterminated like an insect! Forget feckless Malcolm and Donaldbain. Banquo's obnoxious kid now represents my only major remaining obstacle!'

After the newly-crowned King gave the assigned murderers their evening duties, Lady Macbeth entered the bedroom suite a half-hour later finding her pallid-faced husband sitting in a wooden chair.

"I despise pomp and ceremony, Husband. I can't stand all of that goddamned entertaining and socializing downstairs, so I felt like sitting-down and escaping all of the absurd nonsense for fifteen-minutes," Lady Macbeth complained to her emotionally-distraught husband. "This bull-shit business of being Queen is rather demanding, and I'm friggin' disgusted by all the stress of it already. I can't wait until our so-called guests are the hell out of here. Then, after we control all of Scotland, we can focus on conquering vulnerable England and Ireland!"

"But I have another impending project of paramount importance to initiate!" Macbeth disclosed to his Queen (who incidentally was never a prom queen or a dairy queen, either). "My scepter shall be my interceptor. And when this necessary enterprise to which I allude has been satisfactorily completed, I'll fill you in on all the gory details, and then I'll complete the evening by filling your hungry love tunnel in, too," the King promised his horny spouse.

And next, the now-paranoid Macbeth meditated on his imagined crisis some more. 'After tonight's superlative buffet is served, Banquo and Fleance will both be buffeted; yes, they most certainly will!'

"I thought that our killing mission had been completed once you had disposed of Duncan and ascended like clockwork to the throne of Scotland," Queen Lady Macbeth declared (after mysteriously mentally-intercepting her husband's contemplation).

"The snake's head has been scorched, but the serpent has not been killed!" Macbeth spoke in a nebulous riddle/metaphor. "The remainder of the serpent's body is still wriggling-around. Now the entire viper will perish!"

"In the final analysis, husband, deceased Duncan is really the lucky one!" the Queen maintained. "He no longer has to worry about enemies, and the cadaver just has to account to the Almighty for what sins he had enacted on this Earth as an indecent human being."

"Your fucked-up mind is half full of scorpions, and half full of shit!" pernicious Macbeth descriptively accused, chastising his odious wife. "Your psyche is definitely an anomaly of sorts!"

* * * * * * * * * * * *

A third assassin was hired by Macbeth to make the killings of Banquo and Fleance more proficient and foolproof. When the father and the son returned to Forres Castle from their bizarre riding/bug-hunting expedition, the three assigned hit-men were waiting in the garden shrubs, because in reality, *they* were really only amateur bush league murderers. As Banquo and Fleance ambled near the designated area of attack at dusk, the trio leaped-out with their daggers and began flailing-away. The son broke away and took-off like a falcon with scorched wings out of Hades. Seriously wounded, Banquo intrepidly drew-out his sword from its scabbard, and tried retaliating, but being wounded, his futile effort was much too late.

"Run Fleance!" Banquo weakly screamed. "Flee with your fleas you had collected, Fleance!" In the furious scuffle that ensued, the father stumbled and tripped over a misplaced jardiniere. That's when Banquo was pounced upon by his assailants, and mercilessly and violently knifed and pummeled to death.

The three assassins assessed their incomplete mission, and drew straws to see which one would have to report the half-success to "No-bull-shit Macbeth", who was already-seated with his invited guests at the fabulous coronation feast going-on inside resplendent Forres Castle. Seeing the rogue (that had drawn the shortest straw) peeking from behind a black curtain, Macbeth excused himself from the head table and exited the huge banquet room to discuss the individual fates of Banquo and Fleance.

"What the fuck happened?" Macbeth asked the 'loser assassin'. "You've gotten blood on your face! You look like a big disgrace, smearing my husband's name all over the place! Are you bleeding from the inside-out?"

"This is Banquo's blood you see splattered all over me!" the befuddled killer reluctantly reported. "He's dead with at least twenty puncture wounds, just in his face! We tossed his body into a ditch, in a last-ditch effort to make it a little harder to find!"

"And what about your chief target, Fleance?" Macbeth inquired. "Is that punk hoodlum dead, too?"

"I'm sorry to divulge that the little jerk-off escaped our clutches," the hired assassin with the killer instinct disclosed. "The uncooperative asshole ran away screaming 'Bloody murder', and so *that* aspect of our clandestine plot had not been completed!"

"Well, you managed to erase the threat of Banquo, anyway!" Macbeth half-praised. "Now get the fuck out of here looking like a mess, before I give you a bloody nose to match the rest of your crimson-stained face! Wash-up, because you're too easy to spot! You've got blood on your face, you' big disgrace! Now get the fuck out of this place, before I really feel compelled to rock you!"

Macbeth returned to the raucous feast with a disappointed and worried expression upon his frowning countenance. But upon reaching his position at the table's head chair, the King was astounded to observe a ghost (visible only to him) occupying the seat specifically reserved for the new Monarch.

'Oh my God! It's Banquo's ghost sitting like royalty in *my* high-chair! This colossal bullshit is real, and not imagined folly!' Macbeth marveled and then shuddered. 'Everyone else including Ross and Lennox thinks that my seat is fuckin' empty, but *my* eyes and fears know otherwise!' the King worried. 'I think I'd better excuse myself before I empty the contents of my intestines all over the goddamned stone floor! I don't need the stool from my ass on the floor!' Macbeth angrily thought, as the thoroughly-distraught-monarch intentionally and instinctively knocked-over his King's royal chair (momentarily thinking it was a stool), with Banquo's awesome grim-faced ghost no longer occupying it. The King's strange awkwardness immediately gained everyone's attention.

But before scurrying-out of the immense banquet chamber, Macbeth boisterously yelled, much to everyone's consternation and alarm, "You can't accuse me of fuckin' treachery! Stop shaking your bloody head and hands at me, vile Banquo; even though you're my bloody blood relative!"

"The King is not well!" Queen Macbeth stood and apologized for her husband's erratic deportment. "He's having a bizarre fit, and needs to be tied. Confidentially, my husband's had this epileptic condition ever since childhood, and his convulsions are comparable to Julius Caesar's seizures back in ancient history," the Queen attempted to clarify to the assembled noble guests. "Throughout the ages, epilepsy has been a sign of superior leadership ability! But I'll take care of his present needs, and administer worst aid, er, I meant to say, 'first aid'."

Up in the castle's master bedroom (where Mistress Macbeth slept too), the apprehensive Queen asked her emotionally-disturbed husband: "What the fuck happened?" The unnerved King found it difficult to describe his supernatural encounters with the floating dagger in the garden, and with Banquo's apparition at the banquet occupying the Monarch's chair, ostensibly symbolizing that Fleance was to be the next King of Scotland.

"I have blood mysteriously appearing on my hands for no natural reason or cause, and besides *that* terrible phenomenon Wife, strange hallucinations are insidiously decaying my mind!" Macbeth attested to his evil-inclined spouse. "I must revisit the three witch bitches at the swamp and see what the hell's going to happen. I must learn my density, er, I meant to say 'my destiny'. I think that the homeless sorceresses are hanging-out in a rowboat near an eerie lake that the locals call Lake Eerie. I'll be able to identify each of them, or all of them, by their unique witch craft!"

"Witchcraft! It's only witchcraft. People say that it's only taboo!" Lady Macbeth strangely articulated. "Get to sleep, Husband, if you can, while I wander around downstairs and attempt to mingle with and entertain our assembled five-hundred, all-too-curious, gossiping, gluttonous guests!" Macbeth's wife urged her fatigued husband. "Then tomorrow, you can venture-out and again make contact with the three raunchy bitch witches! Maybe as a novelty, we could hire the three grotesque hags as special performers and fortunetellers for a future party!" the wife facetiously jested, trying to shake her husband out of his disconsolate mood. "That booking would certainly be an all-time-first amusement for our noble friends and acquaintances!"

The following morning, Macbeth rode his favorite black horse from Forres Castle, and the ever-suspicious Lennox remained inside the palace section of the fortress, discussing with Ross recent developments, along with Macbeth's strange behavior (at the weird coronation feast), which was also peculiarly exhibited while the new King had been speaking with several inner-circle confederates.

458

"I hear that MacDuff is extremely pissed-off at King Macbeth, and had refused to attend last night's oddball castle banquet!" Lennox told Ross along with *his* very interested associates. "Is MacDuff back in Fife tooting and smoking his bagpipe? Has Lady MacDuff learned how to beat her drum?"

"Haven't you heard the latest, you big Lummox?" Ross rhetorically asked Lennox. "MacDuff has journeyed to England to negotiate important alliances with King Edward, and also with the expatriated Prince Malcolm, who is welcomed and presently staying at the King's court where all of Edward's judges and magistrates sleep and conduct their judicial matters! Now doesn't that nutcase alliance seem highly irregular?"

"What gives besides mothers' breasts?" Lennox asked the bewildered Ross. "You seem to be holding-back some information."

"MacDuff is requesting that King Edward send Siward, the bellicose Earl of Northumberland, to assist Malcolm in promoting and waging a civil war against Macbeth, right here in foggy old Scotland," Ross explained to Lennox and *their* henchmen. "Just about everyone, including you and me, suspects that Macbeth had Duncan murdered in cold blood over at Inverness. Something drastic in good conscience must be done before the suspicious King has all of us commanders systematically rubbed-out!"

"And I know good old Mac-duffer like I know my reflection image in a dirty mirror!" Lennox stated to Ross and his companions with an austere expression upon his visage. "That lousy, obstinate golfer won't quit until he gets what he wants! That stubborn fellow MacDuff was indeed born with a stubbed-head!"

Then, Macbeth, standing in his lonely bedroom, thought about something fascinating. 'Maybe my assassins could catch that little faggot Fleance hanging-out at one of the major foreign flea markets.'

Act IV

Searching all over the desolate heath (where Macbeth had previously encountered the three witches), the tenacious King finally discovered the ugly dames stirring-up their steaming cauldron inside their "Cave Sweet Cave". Immediately, Macbeth demanded that the trio of grotesque-looking bitches divulge to him his future.

The first-witch stirred the cauldron, and conjured-up an armed head (looking somewhat like an octopus crossed with MacDuff's face) and rhymed, "By lizard's leg and scorpion's tail, beware of the Thane of Fife named MacDuff, over hill and dale. Bubble, bubble, he'll cause you plenty of double-trouble!"

The second image that glowed in the fire's flames, being emitted from the huge steaming kettle, was that of a bloodied child, and in an instant, the second-witch augured and rhymed, "Macbeth, by goat's gall and by hemlock's gruel, you' unscrupulous rogue should know, that no one born from a woman can do you harm or defeat."

The third witch beckoned-out and caused a vision of a child holding a tree branch in its right clenched fist (that inexplicably expanded and contracted while wavering in and out of focus). The aberration hovered above the "porridge cauldron" having "boiling poisonous animal entrails" bubbling inside. The third grotesque-looking witch scrutinized the image and verbally interpreted, "Macbeth, by wolf's tooth and by dragon's scale, you'll remain in power and never fail; or your great dominion will be fully vanquished, if Birnam Wood marches to Dunsinane Hill; and then everyone in Scotland will either Malcolm, or Fleance's will, fulfill."

"That's really double-talk information that's a trifle vague and nebulous," Macbeth shouted to the three old hags that were alternately-but-vigorously stirring the secret ingredients boiling inside their back magic crucible. "But could you tell me something relevant about that past prophecy I had heard you make about Banquo being the father of future kings. Now, ugly and preoccupied ladies, that totally queer utterance requires additional interpretation, and seems to wholly defy my understanding."

Banquo's image, along with those of five sons in a row, appeared inside the mysterious and foreboding flickering fire, and the grim-faced ghost was pointing at the quintet, indicating that *they* were his heirs and also, the apparent successors to Macbeth's throne.

"Why does Macbeth look like he's pissed-off?" the first witch yelled-out and then cackled. "You've asked us for the truth, and we've shown it to only you, a complete asshole who lacks couth."

"This is entirely fucked-up nonsense!" Macbeth exclaimed. "You Harpy-faced Hags have somehow projected an image into the fire through some sort of obscure swamp trickery! I'll bet anyone that you three Bitches used smoke and mirrors to produce those oddball illusions! If you three grotesque-looking Whores were really magical, then you could make yourselves young and beautiful, and not live in this dump, the nearby dilapidated cave! Your steaming caldron is full of shit just like you three fucked-up Old Bags are! When I come back here, politically speaking, I'm going to drain the swamp!"

The witches instantaneously disappeared, leaving Macbeth alone with his thoughts and fears, standing next to the shadowy, dank, dismal cave residence. 'According to the weird prophecy, a forest can't move to a hill; that's physically impossible!' Macbeth logically reckoned, trying to allay his rampant worries, and also endeavoring to soothe his guilty conscience. 'That particular prediction will protect my reign, and I'll live a long and prosperous life. And when the fuckin' time finally comes, and there's no more sand descending in my hourglass, I'll then have a natural death!'

Macbeth was instantly startled when Lennox's right hand touched his shoulder. "Lennox, did you see the three witches vanish?" Macbeth asked with a timorous tone evident in his stammering voice. "Did you see where the fuck they disappeared to?"

"No, Your Majesty, but I have urgent news to announce to you, so I've trailed your ass to this unearthly site," Lennox reported. "Lord MacDuff has gone to England, probably to ally with cowardly Prince Malcolm, and also partnering with the belligerent Duke of Encumberland, er I mean Slumberland, er, I meant to say the ruthless cucumber Duke of Northumberland."

"I'll intimidate that bastard MacDuff by sending a hit squad of soldiers to his castle in Fife, and have his wife and children eradicated while the ambitious knave is preoccupied secretly fucking-around over in England!" Macbeth confided to the now-apprehensive and suspicious Lennox. "I've had about enough of MacDuff!"

'Macbeth's mind is all gnarled, twisted, and entirely fucked-up!' Lennox hypothesized and believed. 'Who the hell knows whom the demented fiend will think of killing next? I better get the fuck home in a hurry and protect my wife Annie from this psychopathic, crazed maniac and his belligerent minions! On second thought, who needs that sort of family responsibility? I'll hang-out here in this part of Scotland and enjoy some wine, women and song! This misty swamp is pretty nifty, and it doesn't seem to be that horrible after all!'

* * * * * * * * * * * *

In the meantime, Ross had ridden his dependable steed to Fife to consult with Lady MacDuff, who had no idea why her normally reticent and laconic husband had fled to England. Ross explained what he believed had happened to King Duncan and to Banquo, and that MacDuff was probably the next fellow on Macbeth's hit list.

"My husband's a deadbeat traitor who has left his family defenseless in the face of certain danger," Lady MacDuff cried and maintained. "He's a no-good, unreliable son-of-a-bitch, just like the rest of the men in his fucked-up family, starting with his cousin, Macbeth. It's in his genetics; I tell you, Ross; it's in his goddamned genes. And when Macduff is feeling blue, it's in his blue genes!"

"I believe that your husband hasn't abandoned you in the same sense that you've just surmised," Ross comforted Lady MacDuff as the notorious sex-maniac gently placed his hand on her soft shoulder. "I think your husband is organizing an army in England that'll ultimately vanquish Macbeth, and have Banquo's son, Fleance, or Duncan's son Malcolm rightfully ascend to the Scottish throne!" Ross predicted as he began slowly rubbing Lady MacDuff's breasts. "And MacDuff knows what's best for Scotland!"

Three-days later, Ross left Lady MacDuff and *their* son (who MacDuff had thought was *his* logical biological offspring) and rode *his* stallion (after riding MacDuff's "Old gray mare, she ain't what she used to be!") all the way to England to join-up with MacDuff and Prince Malcolm. The three conspirators were uniting to give Macbeth what Ross had described as "an *MMR*" *(a Macbeth, Macduff, Ross)*.

Lady MacDuff was now very saddened that her paramour Ross had also abandoned her to meet-up with the wench's husband MacDuff, who had recently deserted her to journey to England. "The wife's son tried comforting her, but could not remedy his mother's prolific melancholy. But that afternoon, a fatigued and sweating messenger arrived at the Fife Castle, warning Lady MacDuff that Macbeth's merciless assassins were coming.

"Your endangered life, along with your child's, are in jeopardy!" the dispatched courier hollered in a rapid prattle. "I suggest that you get the hell out of here before the shit hits the tempest."

"You're a man, a brave soldier!" Lady MacDuff sarcastically yelled. "Stay here and protect us!"

"I would stay and screw you, but I don't like sloppy thirds!" the neurotic courier explained. "In ancient times, kings would kill messengers, and I'm not going to fuckin' hang-around to see if Macbeth has continued that disgusting tradition that's been around since Old Testament Biblical times!"

Fifteen minutes later, crazed, ruthless soldiers barged into MacDuff's small castle, raped Lady MacDuff, and then killed both her and her son (Ross's biological child).

* * * * * * * * * * * *

Ross arrived in northern England a week later and met-up with MacDuff and with Prince Malcolm, about a mile from Siward's (the hostile Earl of Northumberland's) military encampment. The conversation immediately turned to current events in Scotland.

"Macbeth is an absolutely insane fuck, and everyone that lives in Scotland now has an endangered life," Ross conveyed to MacDuff and to Malcolm. "Forget the forest animals. It's a fact that the entire human race living in Scotland is now an endangered species."

"Don't worry Ross!" MacDuff austerely answered, exhibiting an enthusiastic spirit. "King Edward has provided us with Siward and ten-

462

thousand ferocious soldiers set to attack Macbeth's army when the time is right. And I predict that Fleance's old man Banquo will soon be vindicated and honored as a brave hero!"

"If I become King of Scotland," Malcolm stated with a degree of swagger, "there'll be free bagpipes for every male in and around Fife, and free drums for every female all over the goddamned land. And a capon in every pot for everyone, too!"

But then Ross felt compelled to tell MacDuff of *his* wife and son, who were rumored being killed by an elite vanguard of Macbeth's bodyguards. Normally quiet MacDuff went into a furious tirade.

"That fuckin' prick Macbeth has performed his last heinous deed!" MacDuff screamed, raising his sword skyward in a wild fit, representing something between a rant and a tantrum. "Decapitation will be too good of a punishment for that fuckin' bastard!"

'Gee, I better not ever tell MacDuff about my sultry affairs with his promiscuous wife and that his dead son was actually *my* son!' Ross considered, cautiously using discretion. 'I want my head to remain attached to my shoulders, so that I could enjoy many years of good head expertly performed by highly-skilled and licensed, disease-free, official prostitutes!' Ross concluded. 'MacDuff's great grief has now converted into tremendous anger that I dare not interrupt!'

Meanwhile, self-exiled Prince Malcolm had his own doubts about MacDuff's unanticipated arrival in England. 'Perhaps MacDuff is just a pawn on Macbeth's chessboard; a double-agent pretending to be my ally to get me back into Scotland to be maliciously abducted and then viciously assassinated. I better be on my guard as far as this madman MacDuff is concerned. Who the fuck knows?' Malcolm theorized. 'I don't trust Macbeth's cousin any more than I trust Lucifer himself! Maybe Ross, too, is in on Macbeth's wicked conspiracy against me? All Scotsmen, including myself, are in essence, treacherous, betraying fiends! I mean, I don't even want to own old Macdonwald's farm, anymore,' Malcolm considered, understanding the associated grave danger. 'The only one I feel I can now trust is Siward, Earl of Northumberland', a pessimistic Englishman that I hardly even know!'

Act V

Back in bonny Scotland, Lady Macbeth was going crazy and perpetually sleepwalking with her eyes open in broad daylight. Her concerned nurse contacted a doctor, who recommended that the Queen needed to leave Forres Castle and be with her husband at Dunsinane.

"Doctor; My Lady keeps talking gibberish about not being able to wash the red stains off of her hands!" the Nurse whispered and related. "I really wish that she would abstain from talking about and continuously rubbing those imaginary crimson stains off her palms! And then, Mistress Macbeth claimed that she was changing into a vicious leopard having peculiar red spots all over her body that too had to be either cleansed or surgically removed!"

"Keep her out of the garden and definitely away from the mountain ridge!" the Doctor suggested. "Also, keep her away from her bedroom window! We wouldn't want to see Queen Lady Macbeth go off the deep end, now, would we? Even her jumping for joy at the wrong place might have Lady Macbeth plummeting to her death upon impacting with the hard frozen ground. But be careful Nurse! She's definitely showing suicidal tendencies, and must be thoroughly watched and confined to safe quarters at all times!"

"I'll do as you say, Doctor," the Nurse promised, crossing her heart. "And I'll make sure that My Lady is safely transported in a cage from here all the way to Dunsinane Castle. But I think I'll have her mouth gagged en route, so that Mistress doesn't incessantly repeat in some sort of queer mantra the particular names: Duncan, Banquo and Lady MacDuff, over and over again! I believe that Lady Macbeth is hallucinating! There's almost nothing worse than a delusional Mistress in Distress!"

A month later, a dozen noblemen were actively rebelling against Macbeth's presumed tyranny, along with the sadistic king's harsh treatment of feudal lords and vassals alike. Several thanes combined their rebellious forces, and the merged army organized at Birnam Wood, not far from one of Macbeth's many rural castles, the one on Dunsinane Hill. The English troops to be led by Siward (Earl of Northumberland), self-exiled Prince Malcolm, and MacDuff were slated to join forces with the revolting nobles and their poorly-trained armies at the forest's edge. The renegade barons believed that Macbeth's soldiers were only following the King's orders out of fear, but not out of loyalty or duty. Civil War in Scotland was considered imminent among the eminent thanes and hated new king.

"When you get to the top of the high mound where Macbeth's Dunsinane Castle is situated, don't go over it," Lennox cautiously told Ross and *his* assistant, Peter Paul.

"Why not?" Ross asked. "Is there a tunnel pit to Hell on the other side? I don't give a hill of beans about that mound."

"No, stupid Jackass!" Lennox yelled. "We're old men that must stop at the summit; otherwise, people will say we're over the hill!"

But inside Dunsinane Castle, Macbeth was quite smug and complaisant, believing that supernatural forces were aligned with him according to the witches' amazing statements upon his second encounter with the three hideous oracles. 'Lady Macbeth thinks I can't see the forest for the trees, but there's no way in Hell that a forest can move, except maybe during a fuckin' earthquake!' the King plausibly reflected. 'Trees don't have goddamned legs, ankles, knees or feet, so I see the idea of trees marching toward this castle as no deep-rooted problem! Birnam Wood is going to stay right the fuck where it is! And that big crybaby MacDuff better not get in my way, or he'll not live to fuckin' talk or brag about it!'

An excited aide entered the throne room and reported to Macbeth that an enemy force of approximately twenty-thousand troops was assembling outside Birnam Wood. The haughty King dismissed the information as "hilarious, nonsensical, fantasy, dumb-shit bull-shit". King Macbeth fancied. 'I'm not afraid of those wimpy jerk-offs! They're not out of the woods, yet! Ha, ha, ha! They're probably lost looking for arrow signposts pointing the way to Dunsinane Castle! I'll wear my heavy battle gear, anyway, just in case I need it for display proposes. I'll be frightening my craven adversaries while standing and pacing around on the castle's ramparts!' Then, the General/King gave his personal attendant a direction. "Seton, don't hang around the hall! Come here and tighten-up this strap around my right shoulder!" Macbeth imperatively commanded his left-handed, right-hand man.

The English troops and the Scottish rebels soon met at Birnam Wood, and swiftly initiated their strategic battle plan. The attacking soldiers cut-down small tree branches, along with several twigs to stick into their helmets, so that when the allied forces moved ahead, it would give the impression to anyone observing from Dunsinane Castle that the entire forest was moving forward. The advancing men all congratulated each other for doing a "tree-mendous job"!

Meanwhile, Macbeth ordered that his banners, insignias, dirty underwear, and flags be hung from the castle walls. 'Those idiotic fuck-heads Malcolm, Siward, and MacDuff are fully helpless against me. There's no fuckin' way that Birnam Wood is going to march forward to Dunsinaine Castle, and the clairvoyant witches told me that no man born of woman can ever harm me. Shit, I'm leading a friggin' charmed life, and it doesn't fuckin' matter how many enemies I have! Shit, world! Life is good!'

Women's screams broke Macbeth's fanciful musing, and Seton (who had been hanging-out in the Seton Hall wing of the majestic castle) rushed into the throne room. The aide relayed the bad news that woebegone Lady Macbeth had insanely committed suicide. 'This is a bad omen among so many positive ones on the opposite side of the ledger,' Macbeth erroneously hypothesized in an effort to boost his flagging confidence. But then, a hyperactive guard having occasional amnesia entered the chamber and conveyed some rather startling news to the suddenly-beleaguered Monarch.

"King Macbeth!" the ashen-faced messenger panted all out of breath. "If you look over the south and east rampart walls, it appears that Birnam Wood is advancing without legs up Dunsinane Hill. What the fuck's that incredible shit all about?"

"You lying Asshole!" Macbeth yelled while throwing a savage punch that knocked the guard out and directly onto Weird Street. "You're trying to break my stones and pulverize them into sperm dust. Your excessive jawboning has gotten you a broken mandible!"

But then, the King reconsidered something that rather intrigued his distrustful mind. 'How did this lowlife guard know about the witch's weird prediction pertaining to the walking forest riddle? Lennox must've told him! That's it! Lennox told the loud-mouthed jerk-off! And even if the forest walks, no mortal man can defeat me in combat, because it stands to reason that all men are born from women! Ha, ha, ha! That's my superior ace in the hole that never came out of the birth hole! Ha, ha, ha! It pays to have tunnel vision! Ha, ha, ha!"

Everyone inside Dunsinane Castle rushed to grab their weapons when trumpeters sounded the call to arms. But then Macbeth made a crucial military mistake when the illicit king foolishly ordered his soldiers outside to "wage battle against the imaginary, weaponless forest", rather than to stay inside and defend the seemingly impregnable fortress upon the high hill.

The English/Scottish army led by Siward, Malcolm, and MacDuff eventually reached the perimeter of the castle, and the soldiers were ordered to toss aside their utilitarian tree branches and accompanying helmet twigs. Soon, Macbeth commanded that his soldiers attack the enemy forces surrounding the almost non-penetrable fortress.

Siward's son encountered Macbeth, but was no match for the fierce warrior, and the inexperienced youth soon was overpowered and smitten, with his form lying motionless upon the wet turf. "You should've been a steward, Siward Junior, because you fight like one!" Macbeth mocked and laughed-down at the incapacitated dying youth. "You'd still be fuckin' alive and kicking if you were a goddamned steward instead of a delusional Siward! Ha, ha, ha!"

Since Dunsinane Castle was unoccupied and offered no resistance (in that overconfident Macbeth had ordered his soldiers to evacuate and fight the enemy on Dunsinane Hill), Prince Malcolm and Siward, Earl of Northumberland, led their troops into the deserted fortress, claiming it to be captured. Showing his triumphant emotions, Malcolm sang to MacDuff, "I found my thrill; on Dunsinane Hill!"

Meanwhile, the battle outside raged-on, and audacious MacDuff, filled with enmity for Macbeth, confronted the King in about-to-happen man-to-man combat. But before swinging-away with his sword, MacDuff scoffed at his new-found adversary.

466

"After I capture you, Cousin Macbeth," MacDuff boasted, "I'll have you put into an animal cage and carted all over Scotland so that ordinary folks will mock, deride, and scorn your pathetic, miserable ass. What do you think of *that* radical development, oh mighty King?"

"Thane MacDuff, the notorious MacDuffer, you lousy golfer, you; you cannot injure or kill me! Don't you know, Villain, that I'm both invincible and indestructible!" Macbeth bragged. "I can only be harmed by a man not born of woman! Now dumb-fuck; you bungling leader of lowlife rabble; your precious wife and child are now deader than moon dirt, and you'll be next on my short-list agenda! Run away while you still have breath in your fuckin' emphysema lungs!"

"First of all, Asshole False King," MacDuff loudly answered. "I wasn't born naturally, but was roughly ripped-out of my mother's womb. And secondly, I'm not a fuckin' man like you fallaciously believe I am! I'm a transvestite woman who thinks and behaves like a fuckin' man! That's why Ross was the father of my only son that you fuckin' had slain, along with my bi-sexual wife, Lady MacDuff!"

Staggered and stunned by MacDuff's startling stark revelations, Macbeth was virtually petrified and simultaneously paralyzed. But then, the gallant warriors frenetically parried and sparred for fifteen long minutes, as the intense battle continued and raged all around them, with clanking and clanging metal clamorously hitting against shields, armor, mail, and swords. But being exceptionally motivated by hate and revenge, the irrepressible MacDuff had the psychological advantage, and was finally able to mortally wound his bitter enemy.

After Macbeth had been killed, his forces realized that his demise had occurred, and soon the army surrendered. Ross carefully surveyed the field of battle, and the commander mentioned to the Earl of Northumberland that "two key men" were missing in action: "MacDuff and your juvenile delinquent son, Siward Junior"!

But then Lennox sadly approached Northumberland and reported that Siward Junior had been slain by Macbeth, and the British Earl was somewhat encouraged to learn that his son "had died valiantly while battling a veteran and ruthless warrior".

MacDuff stepped across the dusty battlefield, ambling past scores of dead bodies, and the hero meandered-around downed and severely wounded men moaning and groaning as if they were all having bad sex with porcupines. And in his right hand raised above his helmet, the chivalrous Thane MacDuff held the bloody head of Macbeth.

All of the surviving thanes, earls, dukes, Dukes of Earls, and commanding officers gathered around MacDuff and wildly cheered his magnificent accomplishment, all boisterously shouting, "The butcher King is dead!", and "Hail the great MacDuff", and finally, "Hail Malcolm! The new King of Scotland!"

"But what about Fleance, Banquo's homo' tri-sexual son?" Lennox asked Ross in a confused tone of voice. "Where does he fit into the power equation?"

"Sorry to hear of your wife Annie's recent death, Lennox."

"Forget that trivial shit," Lennox replied.

"Well then, here's the more-important news," Ross informed. "Who the hell cares about that dumb fuck, Fleance?" Ross emphatically insisted. "That dwarfish gay faggot will never become a respected Prince in a million years, let alone an all-powerful King of Scotland! Duncan's son Malcolm is the new big man in Scotland."

"Hamlet"
William Shakespeare

Act I

The primary setting for "Hamlet, Prince of Denmark" is Elsinore Castle in Denmark around 1200 AD. Hamlet, (whose fraternal twin brother Omelet had died at birth from being conceived in a defective egg), was not-too-skeptical when his mother had married his uncle Claudius shortly after his father's premature death. But soon later, the alert Prince became suspicious of a possible conspiracy (and love affair) after being visited by *his* father's ghost, who compelled *his* only son to seek vengeance on the new King Claudius, and also a milder punishment on Prince Hamlet's treacherous mother that had betrayed her own husband, and had been grossly guilty of infidelity, the deceitful Queen Gertrude.

King Hamlet of Denmark (Hamlet's father) had an avowed enemy, King Fartinbras of Norway (who had the bad habit and fetish of habitually farting inside women's bras). Hamlet Senior had killed his rival Fartinbras in a decisive battle, and Denmark then acquired vast lands from Norway, thus expanding its territories and the country's *Baltic Sea* influence. But soon thereafter, King Hamlet died (presumably from a venomous snakebite), and his nefarious brother Claudius took over the throne as King. A month later, avaricious King Claudius married Queen Gertrude, Prince Hamlet's suspected unfaithful mother.

Soon after those peculiar developments had occurred, a ghost began appearing on the ramparts of Elsinore Castle, and the two-dimensional, pale-faced apparition looked exactly like Prince Hamlet's deceased father. Three guards Marcellus, Francisco, and Bernardo had individually seen the spectral image, and were very apprehensive and nervous about the supernatural phenomenon; and quite ostensibly, the soldiers were fearful of discussing the specter with Horatio, a close friend of Prince Hamlet.

Francisco had just been relieved of guard duty (to relieve himself in the guard crap-house), leaving Marcellus and Bernardo to keep the graveyard watch. But then, the spooky image again appeared above the rampart; its brilliant glowing form contrasting against the dark starlit sky.

"Speak, oh elusive Spirit!" Bernardo nervously implored the shimmering image. "Shit Marcellus!" the guard yelled as Bernardo felt posterior wetness drenching his undergarments. "We must've drunk too much *spirits* last night for this illogical bullshit to be happening! I'm really being freaked-out! I wonder, Marcellus, if this fucked-up haunting ghost has a hollow-weenie?"

"Say something; explain your purpose; you dreadful deaf-mute Ghost!" Marcellus neurotically uttered while trembling and quivering and also pissing himself. "What the fuck do you want with us? Do you need directions? If you're fuckin' lost, my clogged brain is in Limbo. I don't know the damned way to either Heaven or Hell, let alone Purgatory!"

But then, the spectral illumination seemed to pulsate several times, and in seconds, the apparition amazingly crystallized into infinity. Horatio came dashing around the corner and accosted the two other recently flabbergasted guards. The sentinel's demeanor had suddenly lost its military discipline.

"Horatio, did you see the ghost, or ghoul, or whatever the fuck it was?" Bernardo asked his superior officer. "The scary thing looked just like Prince Hamlet's father!"

"Yes Bernardo; I did get a glimpse of it!" Horatio acknowledged. "And I must admit, it looked exactly like our deceased King Hamlet, and the haunting spirit was wearing the same armor the former King had on when our ruler had fought and killed King Fourteen Bras, er, I mean Fartinbras, who must be now, for diversion's sake, also farting incessantly into women's panties and bras in the afterlife!"

"Well, Guys; I see this eerie apparition's visitation as some sort of negative omen," Marcellus pessimistically evaluated. "The whole damned country is on the verge of civil war, and there's widespread talk of a power struggle developing all over Denmark involving Prince Hamlet and others. And also, Fellas'," Marcellus added. "There's big trouble brewing with fucked-up Norway again."

"Yes, Marcellus," Horatio promptly confirmed. "That asshole Young Fartinbras wants to again fart around, just like his crazy father, and cause havoc inside Denmark. And the greedy asshole has organized an immense army to take back the lands that noble King Hamlet had won fair and square from *his* big daddy," Horatio authoritatively elaborated. "Perhaps that's why King Hamlet's ghost is presently restless and on the prowl above Elsinore Castle. Maybe the spirit is trying to warn us from another dimension of some crucial, fucked-up, impending calamity!"

The evasive ghost suddenly reappeared above the rampart, and Horatio was determined to communicate with it. "Speak your peace, or your piece, restless wandering Spirit! Are you attempting to warn us of some treachery or forthcoming tragedy? Have you secretly buried fabulous treasure somewhere? Have you been evicted from Heaven by St. Peter for not paying rent money? Do you want us to fuckin' help you ghostwrite your dumb-ass autobiography?"

Horatio futilely tried hitting the elusive image with his three-dimensional sword, especially since the visiting ghost had remained reticent without verbally responding to his worried inquiries. But then, the weak-hearted guards heard a half-chicken, half-blackbird cockcrow, and suddenly, the mysterious, itinerant spirit again disappeared into oblivion. Then, the loose-boweled Francisco returned to his guard watch.

"This can't be an illusion, because it would have to be classified as a mass hallucination amongst at least three of us, which is highly unlikely!" Bernardo claimed and exclaimed to his still-astounded peers. "I'm just glad that you three Knuckleheads are here to verify and substantiate my eyewitness account. Your presence has allowed me to avoid having a spirited debate with the know-nothing castle psychiatrist about my sanity and my suspect mental stability."

Then, something significant dawned on Prince Hamlet's close friend. "Spirits cannot face daylight," Horatio told his scared and overanxious underlings. "Kindly remember, Bernardo, Francisco and Marcellus, *that* special bullshit information I've just revealed to you in the twilight years of your lives. Now then, men," Horatio aptly summarized while still facing east. "I want you three stooges to keep quiet about this weird manifestation we've just seen. I'll privately confer with Prince Hamlet about the vision, and if the ghost is truly his father's spirit, perhaps it's specifically seeking him out, and not wanting to communicate with us. I mean, let's give this meandering apparition the benefit of the doubt."

"Yes Horatio," Marcellus nervously agreed. "The freaky ghost probably has poor geography and navigation skills, not to mention its apparent speech deficiency. But at least it had the wherewithal to find its way to Elsinore Castle."

"I agree with Marcellus's general assessment," Bernardo stated and dittoed. "When I first saw the glowing son-of-a-bitch, I deliriously yelled out 'Great Caesar's ghost'! But then," Bernardo continued, clearing his throat. "I realized that I might be involved in a classic case of mistaken identity! That fucked-up spirit was really Prince Hamlet's father; no fuckin' doubt about it! I would wager my left testicle on *that* general observation."

"Excuse me Guys, but I think I have to take another shit!" Francisco told his shocked companions. "That ghost was more effective than any damned apothecary's laxative that I know."

* * * * * * * * * * * *

King Claudius called his family, his athletic supporters, and his main subjects and predicates to a brief audience, and thanked the castle employees for coming to his brother King Hamlet's funeral, and also attending *his* rushed wedding to the one-month-widowed Queen Gertrude, whom the avid ice cream freak would always publicly solicit by yelling, "Yo Gert! Yo Gert! Yo Gert!"

After sending two incompetent emissaries (the jokester Cornelius and the electrifying Voltemand) to the new King of Norway requesting that young "Fourteen Bras" (King Claudius meant to say Fartinbras) was to stop assembling an army threatening to invade Denmark. Finally, the pompous Monarch got-down to discussing pertinent family business. The new Ruler of Denmark was quite self-conscious about reviewing certain recent developments that didn't involve public housing.

"I had to swiftly marry Queen Gertrude to project the appearance to prospective foreign and domestic enemies that Denmark was still strongly unified, and fully capable of handling crises; despite the fact that some of you Numbskulls think that our hurried wedding was not-too-swift," Claudius justified and explained to his diplomats. And then, King Claudius noticed pouting Laertes, the son of the royal chief counselor Polonius, and summoned the sulking lad to stand before the throne. "Is there anything I can do for you, Laertes? You've always been out of the loop, so to speak; you LGBTQZYX gay fruit loop!"

"Yes, Your Highness. I've been in Denmark for a whole month for King Hamlet's funeral, for your coronation, and for your quick wedding to Queen Gertrude," Laertes recollected and remarked. "I would now like to return to the university in France to continue my liberal studies (in pornography and panty raids)."

"Now, I understand why you're such an atrocious, unpatriotic Dane, Laertes," the new King punned and laughed. "If your father Polonius consents to your consensual sex behavioral studies in France with your Spanish girlfriend Lucie Morales, without *him* having a French hemorrhage about it here in Denmark," Claudius declared, "then I'll be more than glad to agree to get you out of my hair, er, I mean get you active again into your *other* foreign affairs."

Claudius then recognized the disillusioned Prince Hamlet, who was disgustedly standing on the left side of the regal throne with a broad sneer upon his face, and the new Monarch asked the youth if anything of interest was bothering him besides his "snarling wolf imitation syndrome".

"I'm very troubled by my father's rather sudden, unexpected death!" Prince Hamlet declared all-too-honestly. "I'm suspicious that it wasn't entirely accidental as had been reported!"

"Could you clarify your concerns?" the new King demanded while shrugging his shoulders. "Your words border on treason!"

"I mean, Uncle Claudius. There are about as many poisonous yellow-belly snakes here in this city slithering around Elsinore Castle as there are virgin prostitutes in Paris! I smell something rotten in Denmark!" Hamlet explained. "And it's not old, fish-odor pussy, either!"

"Forget the hyperbole and explain what the hell you actually mean!" Claudius rankled. "Any dud can shoot off his mouth thinking that he's a booming cannon!"

"But what really confuses and upsets me, Uncle Claudius, is that my father is dead; that you're my uncle, and that now you're also my goddamned new father! I think that this overall, crazy, fucked-up situation is drastically affecting my mental health, and also negatively impacting my sexual orientation!"

Sitting on her throne next to Claudius, Queen Gertrude answered her son's inquiry to help conceal her new husband's guilt and embarrassment at having to address such a candid and challenging question. "My arrogant and loquacious, Son. Everyone including the Pope and Jesus Christ must die one way or another someday!" the Queen steadfastly and austerely maintained. "And someday, you'll be King of Denmark, so if you'd like *that* prospect ever realized, I suggest that you return with Laertes to France, and smell something rotten in Paris of a sensitive feminine nature."

"No, Mother! Denmark might need me, and I don't wish to be assassinated or smelling lousy pussy in France that quite *frankly* stinks like rotten fish in Copenhagen!" Hamlet bluntly replied. "I'll prefer staying right here at good old Elsinore Castle, and be perfectly content passing the time calling the Spanish ambassador El Senor, Culo!" Hamlet cleverly answered.

"Look no further to find a father!" Claudius imaginatively remarked to the totally-peeved and now-antagonized Hamlet. "In the immediate future, I see London, I see France, I see Laertes's and young Hamlet's underpants. Ha, ha, ha! That is, his underpants hanging from some Left Bank ghetto clothesline! Ha, ha, ha!"

* * * * * * * * * * * *

Prince Hamlet met his old friend (well, his young old friend) Horatio in the corridor outside the throne room (the room actually looked like a giant throne). The two youths nostalgically reminisced about their shared childhood experiences, but then the conversation switched to King Hamlet's swift death, and to Queen Gertrude's all-too-soon marriage to Claudius.

"I gotta' tell you Hamlet, a strange occurrence has been happening just after midnight on the night watch," Horatio confided in a timorous voice. "A ghost having a grizzled, silver-sable beard, and resembling your father, has been appearing and disappearing without it ever saying anything. I don't think that traveling ghosts get stage fright or laryngitis, and believe me, Young Hamlet, when I say that I'm no fuckin' expert on *that* arcane subject. And Bernardo and Marcellus have seen it, too, and possibly also Francisco. But I'm not so sure about the veracity or the integrity of that unreliable booze hound, who always has the damned runs!"

"The specter might be trying to convey some esoteric message to me, and then realizes that you're someone else!" Hamlet theorized and commented. "Regardless, Horatio. This is truly fascinating bull-shit, and I'll attempt investigating into the matter immediately. I'll be faithfully showing-up to inspect the night watch just before midnight! I'll bring along some anthracite to help you burn the midnight coal! I'm glad we're forming this confidential coalition between us, Horatio!"

* * * * * * * * * * * *

Before leaving for the prestigious university in Gay Paree, France, Laertes stepped into the palace gardens to chat and say "Goodbye!" to his emotionally naïve sister, Ophelia, who was deeply in love with the handsome Prince Hamlet. But Laertes felt that Hamlet was using and manipulating his sister and just flirting and teasing her affections, because the prince was royalty, and Ophelia was not of blue blood, and was heading for eventual disappointment and discouragement in *their* "silly fantasy relationship".

"Hamlet is okay around the guys, but be wary of any amorous overtures or foreplay activity initiated by him," Laertes honestly warned the chaste and immaculate Ophelia. "And that scoundrel Hamlet is basically a libertine, too dangerous of a free spirit for your vulnerable virginity to effectively resist! In the end, according to tradition, Prince Hamlet must marry other royalty for strict political purposes, and will not feel obligated to marry for love, and for love alone. If love comes with politics, then he'll consider it a terrific bonus. Do you fathom my fucked-up words of advice, Ophelia?"

"Well Brother, do you have any other un-propitious opinions to share?" saddened and suicidal Ophelia asked. "I'd rather masturbate every minute for a full month than listen to your perpetual, cynical complaining! Don't you ever think positive?"

"And finally, dear Sister, if Hamlet takes you out to a hamlet and rudely says 'Oh, feel ya' tits,', then slap the phony scoundrel son-of-a-bitch heartbreaker straight in the mouth, and quickly kick him thrice in the testicles with all your' might," Laertes wholeheartedly lectured. "Hamlet definitely deserves to be neutered!"

"Aren't you confusing love with physical sex?" Ophelia asked. "You're treating them as one and the same!"

"Remember, dear Ophelia; to Prince Hamlet's mind, the word 'love' *is* the word 'sex', and nothing more. For your privileged information, Prince Hamlet was getting laid every night when away at the university, and now he's here at Elsinore with all that sperm fluid building-up inside him, ready to explode like Mt. Vesuvius or Mt. Vernon, or some other fucked-up volcano like that! I know all this significant shit, because I was observing Hamlet in action while I was doing a research paper on the topic of 'voyeurism' for my sex education course," Laertes divulged to his appalled sister.

"How can I place any credence in your pessimistic and inflammatory words?" Ophelia asked. "How do I know that you're just not inventing fiction out of your jealousy for Prince Hamlet?"

"And furthermore, Ophelia. Hamlet needs to become a skinhead, having both his scalp and his dick circumcised!" Laertes continued his scathing dissertation. "Remember Sister; the road to Heaven is both steep and thorny, so therefore, chastity and the denial of your natural urges are equally essential conditions for you to gain admission beyond the Pearly Gates! Watch out for all of the bumps along the way! St. Peter keeps an accurate record of both mortal and venial sins."

"I'll remember your sage advice during your absence, kind benevolent brother!" Ophelia sarcastically answered Laertes. "You used to be a wise ass when we were younger, but now you seem to be a wise-minded smart-ass!"

The brother and sister's father Polonius arrived at the castle gardens to bid farewell to Laertes. "Goodbye, my son!" the King's principal counselor told his often-recalcitrant offspring. "And don't do anything 'in-Seine' while studying female anatomy in Paris; ha, ha, ha!" Polonius chauvinistically remarked. "As you well know, my boy, Paris is not only the city of lights, but also the city of delights! Ha, ha, ha! And young, energetic Laertes, don't forget to mount a broad when abroad! Ha, ha, ha! But make sure you choose the best aristocrat honey-wells to stick your stiff dingle into!"

After Polonius made his embarrassing suggestive remarks to Laertes, the sex-starved boy expediently exited Elsinore Castle on his way to the fabulous Paris red light district, which was opposite the bawdy university fraternity houses. Polonius then inadvertently reiterated to his subordinate daughter a similar litany comparable to Laertes' critical evaluation of Prince Hamlet's "ignoble and selfish sexual intentions". The now-confused Ophelia submissively listened to her father's sanctimonious pontification. But then, the disenchanted girl presented her own perspective to her somewhat concerned father.

"Prince Hamlet has mentioned on numerous occasions the word 'love' in our dialogues; indeed many, many times," the obedient Ophelia confessed to her aged father as if having *that* type of personal conversation with a young man, in itself, were a mortal sin. "Now father; Prince Hamlet must do plumbing as a hobby, because he keeps mentioning something about 'laying pipe'."

"Ophelia, you're more like a green vegetable, and not quite yet a red ripe hot tomato. I'm commanding you to never be alone with that perverted sex maniac! Don't allow that brash, licentious fellow to seduce and traduce you!" Polonius warned his pristine, chaste daughter. "Hamlet wants to pork you with his pee and sperm shooter, and that's the long and short of his erection! I assure you, Daughter, that he'll never be able to take the *ham* out of Hamlet."

"I understand completely, Father!" Ophelia meekly sobbed and wept. "Although Prince Hamlet's words sound honorable and sincere, ultimately, the truth of his lustful desires stands erect between his hairy legs!" And then Ophelia seriously thought about all that had been reviewed with Laertes and with her all-too-dominant father. 'What a fuckin' bummer this lousy mixed-up horse-shit is! It's a goddamned fuckin' man's world out there! And it's also that way inside this shitty-ass castle!' the disillusioned girl very rationally-but-regretfully imagined.

* * * * * * * * * * * *

At midnight, on that frigid winter evening, Hamlet met Bernardo, Marcellus and Horatio on the Elsinore castle ramparts while Francisco was again away from his duty-watch taking an extended dump. After the men were curiously waiting for a half-hour, the mystical ghost amazingly appeared above the northern wall.

"See how it wanes and waxes, especially around its ears!" Horatio pointed-out to Hamlet as a million or so scintilla glows were eddying-around above their mundane heads. "I do believe it's earmarking something to say to you!"

"Ghost; why are you acting so aloof, floating up above the roof?" the astonished and jittery Prince Hamlet interrogated the glimmering spirit. "I insist; Identify yourself!"

The stubborn, radiant manifestation would not speak to an audience, so Hamlet ordered the guards to move away from *his* supernatural encounter. The weird spirit then addressed the Danish Prince in a familiar, firm, bass voice. and clued the dumbfounded Hamlet in on what had truly transpired immediately before King Hamlet's death.

"I promise while hovering up here above Elsinore Castle to address you, my beloved Son, in non-ambiguous terms. First of all, I am indeed your Father's restive spirit, and I'll not achieve eternal tranquility until you diligently avenge my death," Hamlet's father's ghost explained. "I had been murdered, very imaginatively, too, if I may add. The false palace line is that I had been killed by a serpent's bite, but that's not entirely true. That afternoon, my son, I had been in my apple orchard taking a lengthy leak inside a rabbit's hole, which confidentially was a favorite pastime of mine. But then, a snake came out and attempted to

476

bite my foot, but I pissed in its open mouth, and soon the serpent plunged-back down into its hollow. When I told the story of the pissed-off, or should I say pissed-on snake, to Queen Gertrude," the Ghost disclosed to his son, "I believe that *that* description about the snake gave your viperous mother an inspiration of how to contrive my death, the whoring harlot!"

"Holy fuck!" Prince Hamlet exclaimed with his hairs standing straight-up and out as if his separate follicles were generating porcupine quills. "This is not a game of trivial pursuit! Exactly father; how the hell were you ever eliminated from life, if not by a serpent's venom?"

"Well, my son; a lethal snake in the form of my covetous Brother, who was conveniently aided by my scheming unfaithful Wife, pilfered my cherished crown," the Ghost matter-of-factly answered. "When I was in my study taking my standard afternoon siesta, that felonious Claudius poured a poisonous substance into my right ear. Be spiteful, young Hamlet, against my diabolical sibling Claudius! But I beg you, my flesh and blood dear son," the Ghost sternly implored. "Please don't take revenge out on your whoring Mother. Allow her conscience and her guilt to gradually destroy her. These are my expressed true wishes! Goodbye, my dear Hamlet, and remember me always!"

'Now that I know exactly what the fuck the real deal is, I'm pretty goddamned angry and perturbed!' Hamlet evaluated. 'Fuckin' Uncle Claudius isn't going to have a ghost of a chance of surviving my fierce wrath. But first, I must obtain some tangible proof of family guilt and conspiracy, assuming that my father's ghost had been accurate and contrite. Oh, here come my good friends Horatio, Marcellus and Bernardo returning to this northern rampart now!'

"Guys, I'm going to need your indispensable help," Hamlet related to his loyal comrades. "There are more fucked-up things in Heaven and on Earth than you can imagine. You mustn't tell anyone else about my father's ghost, under any circumstances. Swear a sacred oath on my sword! Now, maybe later-on, I'll bring you Fellas' up to speed, but first, I need to conduct a preliminary investigation and search for convicting evidence of a committed crime. If and when I ascertain the truth, then all Hell's going to break loose inside Elsinore Castle!"

Hamlet was acting very peculiar during the next several weeks, and many castle eyewitnesses prattled and gossiped that the disturbed youth was on the brink of insanity. Then, Ophelia stupidly reported a bizarre behavior incident to her two-faced father, Polonius, who was always interested in causing trouble and creating mayhem around the castle to advance his own personal agendas.

"Father, I'm so scared that I've had the diarrhea all damned morning! I'm nearly dehydrated, and even my crotch has dried-up!" Ophelia mentioned to Polonius in the otherwise empty castle dining room. "First of all, Prince Hamlet scurried into my room when I was busy sewing, the *darned* Nitwit. His face was pallid and as white as his exposed dingle; his clothes were extremely rumpled, and quite frankly, the prince smelled like he had just shit himself. Young Hamlet then held me tightly in his arms, while I cringed at inhaling his atrocious, reeking malodor," Ophelia divulged to her attentive father. "The stench-laden Prince then stared into my eyes, and sighed incessantly like a complete retard. Next, the petulant royal asshole ejaculated all over my favorite shoes, and soon hastily ran-out of my bedchamber! From now on, father; I'm going to keep my door locked, even if the fuckin' castle's burning to the ground with only me being inside!"

'Could it possibly be? Maybe that callow jerk-off is really in love with my commoner daughter?' Polonius curiously wondered. "Now tell me, Dear. Have you been gruff with Prince Hamlet lately; spit in his face' punched or kicked him in the testicles, or slammed him in the ass with a sharp battle-axe?"

"Well, Father; quite truthfully; I've returned his letters with envelopes unopened, and I've refused to see him anywhere, especially when he's grumpily sitting on the outhouse toilet," Ophelia answered. "What do you suppose that regal creep wants to share with me besides his throbbing erection? I was only following your explicit instructions to avoid the sanctimonious, haughty asshole like he was Satan Incarnate personified!"

"We must go to King Claudius and reveal Prince Hamlet's crazy antics and semantics!" Polonius insisted as the greedy, demented counselor harshly grabbed his daughter's arm. "Crazy bullshit from that churlish, juvenile maniac must not go unabated!"

Act II

Being very concerned about the Prince Hamlet's erratic behavior, King Claudius and Queen Gertrude summoned two of Hamlet's closest friends, Rosencrantz and Guildenstern, all the way across the *Baltic Sea* from Norway to Denmark, just to console Gertrude's biological son. But even though Hamlet had always liked the two visiting young men, the royal asshole instinctively and distrustfully suspected that the pair were castle spies operating for his deceitful mother and for his stealthy uncle/stepfather.

"My Son thinks highly of you two, fine Fellows!" Queen Gertrude commended R and G. "You've taught him just about everything Hamlet knows, and absolutely nothing about what the defiant bastard should know. But thanks, anyway, for returning to Denmark from wherever the hell you came from, to help rehabilitate Hamlet into the importance of obedience to royal adult authority! It's the thought, and not the success, that really matters; do you two geniuses fathom my nomenclature?"

"I hope you two Gentlemen can lift-up Prince Hamlet's spirits!" King Claudius expressed to Rosencrantz and Guildenstern from his ebony throne. "Something's troubling Hamlet, and making him approach the threshold of insanity. Besides counseling my nephew, who's now my stepson, perhaps you two quixotic geniuses can find-out what his major problem is, and tell us, so that we can render the best solutions possible. Maybe Prince Hamlet should leave the city, and move into a rustic hamlet out in the country."

"Yes," Gertrude automatically concurred. "If Hamlet requires the services of a priest, a psychiatrist, an alchemist, a competent prostitute, or a proctologist, or whatever, we'll fully cooperate and do whatever it takes to get him back to his former normalcy. There has to be some plausible explanation for my son's erratic disposition," the Queen articulated. "I mean, no one is intermittently crazy. Either he or she is, or he or she isn't! I mean to say, life's so much easier to interpret and comprehend when everything is either black or white. This gray area shit is what causes major problems!"

"We're here to help solve the evolving dilemma!" Guildenstern concluded and pledged. "Rosencrantz and I want to be part of the solution and not part of the damned problem!"

"We promise to cheer him up!" Rosencrantz imperatively added. "Every time we lift-up our wine cups, my buddy Guildenstern and I will both yell out the word 'cheers'! That way we can lift-up all *our* anemic spirits, and not just fucked-up, depressed Prince Hamlet's!"

Soon after Rosencrantz and Guildenstern left the dimly-lit throne room, to raid the palace's almost empty wine cellar, Polonius entered, carrying several of Hamlet's love letters to Ophelia that *he* had recently confiscated. The two-faced political advisor addressed the King and Queen in an arrogant, indicting tone of voice, like a prosecutor would speak to a wimpy judge.

"King Claudius and Queen Gertrude," Polonius prefaced with a tone of urgency in his vocal delivery. "I believe I've discovered the precise source of Prince Hamlet's uncharacteristic, deviant behavior, and the good news is that your aberrant son is not coming out of the closet and announcing a new-type of disgraceful and scandalous sexual orientation other than homosexuality," Polonius stated. "My Liege, as I've already alluded, I think I've discovered the cause for Hamlet's lunatic behavior when he was defiantly mooning me an hour ago, as I had exited my quarters. Everything makes complete rational sense now."

"Get to the goddamned point, Polonius! What the hell's wrong with him?" King Claudius instantly responded, showing his mounting aggravation. "Is the callow punk growing a second brain that's gone malignant? Is his original cerebrum evaporating or melting-down? I must know the cause of Hamlet's very egregious and defective deportment, or else Polonius, I'm liable to violently strangle the obnoxious voice box right out of your wrinkled throat."

"Here's *my* theory, Lord Polonius, and correct me if I'm wrong," Queen Gertrude interrupted her illogical, facetious and murderous husband's diatribe. "I think that young Hamlet's mind is bent out of shape from his father's unexpected death, and also by my hasty marriage to King Claudius, shortly thereafter. Now, I know that I frequently jump to conclusions, but am I correct in making those particular assumptions, oh wise and cowardly Polonius?"

"Oh no, my Queen! The evidence that I present is something entirely different!" Polonius mildly and politely challenged. "I believe that I have adequate proof to substantiate that Hamlet is deeply in love with my daughter Ophelia. In these love letters in my possession, which I've temporarily purloined, I've learned that he's calling my daughter 'beautiful', 'a heavenly angel', 'gorgeous,' 'lovely' and 'a virgin cock-teaser'!" Polonius cavalierly reported. "Prince Hamlet claims in these flowery, all-too-mushy, disgusting missives that he's an atrocious poet, but despite his glaring grammar deficiencies, the absolute moron still states that he loves Ophelia with all of his heart and with all of his dick. True, Queen Gertrude," Polonius summarized. "Prince Hamlet's definitely fucked-up, but not because of why you had imagined."

"And how did Ophelia answer Hamlet's amorous solicitations?" Claudius asked his chief counselor. "Did she write love letters back, or go to the beach during the height of winter and write love letters in the sand; a sort of April Love? I mean Polonius," the King curtly maintained. "Does that little squirt Hamlet have enough semen in his body to sustain himself through this perilous love crisis?"

"My daughter has always been obedient to my parental demands, and Ophelia refused to break her self-discipline and write back to him, or even open the letters or her legs, as far as that's concerned," Polonius confidently communicated to his two royal employers. "Ophelia's even refused to accept any dildos or other disgusting sexual paraphernalia from the confused and fucked-up juvenile pervert. But I've conceived a terrific plan outlining how *we* can confirm all of this bullshit that I'm asserting!"

"What is your recommendation, you blabbering Bullshitter?" Claudius demanded knowing. "Do you wish for me to hire Prince Fourteen Bras, or whoever the hell that fucked-up Norwegian punk enemy is, to do some additional espionage?"

"No, my Liege," Polonius replied. "You, King Claudius, and I will hide behind a curtain in the palace parlor room, and listen to Hamlet either arguing with Ophelia, or crazily talking to himself. That way we'll learn once and for all whether Hamlet's fucked-up because he loves Ophelia, and is disconsolate by being rejected by her; or if the prince is fucked-up because he's angry at his father's sudden death and at his mother's rush to marriage. In his fucked-up letters," Polonius very specifically editorialized, "the prince refers to my innocent daughter as his 'celestial cherub'. Now if that isn't inferior poetry, then I don't know what the hell is!"

"I endorse your impeccable strategy, Polonius, and will join you for the intriguing spying mission behind the iron, er, I mean, velvet curtain, but if your behind-the-drapes idea fails," Claudius warned his chief advisor, "then Asshole; it'll be certain curtains for you!"

* * * * * * * * * * * *

Rosencrantz and Guildenstern eventually caught-up with Hamlet, and the former comrades enjoyed a few cups of wine together at a corner tavern. Then, the conversation turned from reviewing the past to more serious matters besides getting drunk and getting laid when the three old chums were mere adolescents, fooling-around and carousing in various European cities.

"Did my father and mother send for you two Dimwits, or did you return to Denmark at your own volition, simply to see and socialize with me?" Hamlet candidly interrogated his all-too-jolly visitors. "If you're my Friends as you both claim, you'll tell me the fuckin' truth! Now what the hell's the story here?"

Both men admitted that the duo had returned to Denmark at the King and Queen's insistence, for the purpose of cheering-up Hamlet. Then, the Prince went-off on a verbal tangent and confessed that ordinary sex with ordinary girls no longer gave him pleasure or amusement, and that his heart was troubled far-beyond the skills of any medical cardiologist. "Maybe I am mad and am suffering from an emotional disorder, and erectile dysfunction, too!" Hamlet confided. "The only time I get a hard-on is when I'm around that naïve and immature doll, Ophelia! I need something interesting to distract me from my mind-consuming obsession of her! Maybe when I return to the university in France, I'll take an advanced pornography course on how to get blood to travel from my brain to my dick when I see other more-endowed hussies! But right now, I feel like I need transfusions into both my brain and my flaccid pecker!"

"Well Hamlet," Rosencrantz empathetically contributed to the discussion. "You know how fond of fondling nipples and beaver we all were in our illustrious fraternity pasts! That's why Guildenstern and I must drink all of this wine, for we must replenish all of the fluids that we've squirted into myriad curly blonde pussies; pink love tunnels, and open throats during our recent stay in Norway. Isn't that right, Guildy baby?"

"Don't despair about your current embarrassing impotency, good friend Hamlet!" Guildenstern affectionately commented while enthusiastically slapping Hamlet on the back. "I have some excellent news to exchange for your enthusiastic attention, and I'm convinced that it'll certainly snap you out of your dismal lethargy. A company of jovial traveling actors has arrived here at Elsinore, and they're the same ones we had seen doing that fantastic, nifty porno' play two years ago in Paris."

"That's right!" Rosencrantz interrupted his verbose traveling colleague. "And the accommodating actors have consented to perform any play *you* so desire. Now Prince Hamlet, for discretion's sake, you can't have any porno' plays given here inside the palace before such a dignified audience of noble sluts and pimps, but as far as any other subject, either in the areas of tragedy or comedy, the fuckin' choice is all yours! You get to choose your poison, so to speak! Ha, ha, ha!"

Later that afternoon, Hamlet met with the traveling actors and indicated that the prince wished that the thespians would perform the little-known tragic play "The Murder of Gonzago". The prince also gave the main actor several dozen extra-lines to say that weren't in the original script. This was a very clever maneuver on young Hamlet's part, because the play's story line paralleled what the prince's father's ghost had revealed above the castle rampart while describing *his* unexpected death. "I hear that you actors are the finest touring company this side of the *Tiber!*" Prince Hamlet commended the head thespian. 'Your motto has always been, "Get your act together, but don't make a scene. However, this time I wish for you to indeed make a scene!"

"Thank you for the wonderful compliment!" the seasoned stage veteran gratefully acknowledged. "Drama simply reflects real life situations, and also real-life conflicts! We assiduously try to be most visceral and graphic in all of our dumb-ass melodramatic presentations, regardless of the demographics! Would you like a demo' or a graphic exhibition, Prince Hamlet?"

"No thanks, that's perfectly okay!" Hamlet judiciously answered the exuberant fellow. "I fully believe, without question, the excellent reputation that has preceded your company's coincidental arrival here in Denmark. I've seen several other of your terrific plays in Paris, and also two more performed right here in Elsinore Castle."

"Yes, Prince Hamlet. My fellow actors and I have been very influenced by Sophocles, Aeschylus, Aristophanes and by those wacky and creative ancient Greek tailors, Euripides and Eumenides, ha, ha, ha!" the head thespian ludicrously guffawed. "But sometimes, in my earnest, I must put a throttle on my Aristotle, because I have too much fuckin' food on my goddamned Plato, ha, ha, ha! Prince Hamlet, I think I'm going to fuckin' piss myself! Ha, ha, ha! Give me a full-gallon of beer to chug-down so that I can piss my leotards all fuckin' night, ha, ha, ha!"

Then, the Prince did some deep contemplation while the head actor was thoroughly amusing himself with his cornball humor. 'Gonzago will be killed in the play, by having poison poured into his ear, just like I suspect Uncle Claudius had done to my father. If Claudius had indeed committed the heinous crime, then he'll show signs of guilt or distress when the actors are inadvertently re-enacting what the cruel and greedy fuck-head had done to my dear old Dad,' Hamlet keenly hypothesized. 'And I'll also get to gauge my mother's emotional reaction to the 'Murder of Gonzago', relevant to her alleged involvement in my father's death, too! I'll use the obscure play as a tool to accurately test the King's conscience, and if Uncle Claudius seems culpable, then that conniving, avaricious, despicable maggot bastard's going to get exactly what the fuck the wily prick deserves!'

* * * * * * * * * * * *

While Hamlet was preoccupied conferring in the palace auditorium with the chatty actors on how to best present the hardly-known play saga, "The Murder of Gonzago," Polonius and King Claudius were surreptitiously hiding behind the purple curtains in the palace parlor to hopefully eavesdrop on a private conversation between Hamlet and Ophelia, who incidentally had been instructed by Polonius to be waiting for "the romantic encounter" while pretending to be reading a sex education book for pre-schoolers.

"That's a really terrific book!" Hamlet observed and said to Ophelia. "I read it at the university studying Ben Jonson for my Master's while learning how to use my Johnson! Life is a grotesque bastard, and death is an abominable bitch!" Hamlet philosophized and shared with his imagined sweetheart. "Both conditions are cruel and callous! If death is like eternal sleeping, then I'd rather be deceased. But then again, Ophelia," Hamlet emphatically communicated. "Death can't be like sleeping, because when someone dies, he or she is no longer fuckin' breathing."

"Well Prince Hamlet, I really don't give a flying shit about your asshole problems! Like Ben Jonson, I really don't give an airborne fart about your Johnson," Ophelia abruptly answered as Claudius and Polonius overheard the bizarre exchange from behind the purple curtains. "Here in this commonplace sack, you can ransack all of your screwball tokens and the remainder of your asinine letters you had presumptuously sent to me!" the irate girl yelled at her imagined suitor. "I need them like my vagina needs an asshole! Your hollow, shallow words, Prince

Hamlet, mean nothing when all you fuckin' want from me is all kinds of sex in every which way, except in the standard missionary position taught by traveling nuns!"

"Are you honest, or are you beautiful?" Hamlet cryptically asked and further confused Ophelia.

"What the hell do you mean by that verbal chicanery?" Ophelia retorted. "You have a way of contaminating words by farting strange gas out of your mouth when you enunciate them! Or is that foul odor I detect your horrible breath?"

"I meant that beautiful women often twist the truth into complicated lies!" Hamlet indirectly accused. "I loved you once, Ophelia, but now I believe that you should enter a nunnery, you lesbian wench! Why should you have children who'll mature into psychopathic sinners and adulterers?" the prince rhetorically asked. "If you marry, then marry a devout fool. Wise men throughout the ages have completely understood the evil nature of women, originating all the way back to the Biblical Eve's pink love tunnel, right up to the period of the lovely Greek, Pandora's hairy box."

"What the fuck are you' saying?" Ophelia yelled-back at her tormentor. "You're talking gibberish!"

"Women are veritable monsters with their made-up clownish faces; with their painted red lips; with their treacherous sweet talk; and with their fucked-up phony acting!" Prince Hamlet elaborated. "Now then; if you're a typical bitch, Ophelia, I insist that you acknowledge and admit it right here and now!"

"I need asylum from you, you schizophrenic asylum candidate!" Ophelia screamed as the frightened girl bolted out of the parlor-room chamber. "You're loony mad! You're absolutely mad! You must live on Psycho Path Lane, but in the future, you'll most certainly reside on Divorce Court!"

"I was and am madly in love with you!" Hamlet yelled as the suitor pursued his heart's desire. "Come back to me, sweet Ophelia, and I'll shower you with love and affection!"

"You're mad! You're stark-raving mad!" Ophelia repeated as the girl fled down the hall into her bedroom, and immediately double-locked the door.

After the wild argument between Hamlet and Ophelia had moved to another sector of the palace, Claudius and Polonius came out from behind the purple curtains, which in medieval times (just like today) was much better than them coming out of their gay purple closets.

"Prince Hamlet might be confounded by his love urges and sex drive, but something else is mysteriously troubling him!" Claudius told Polonius. "I fear that my nephew hates me, and wishes my ass malice!

This could fuckin' be dangerous for me! I'm too young to be joining my deceased Brother Hamlet, who was never at all a monk."

"I suggest that Queen Gertrude discuss Reality 101 with Hamlet, your wife might be able to guide the lad through the perilous strait separating Scylla and Charybdis!" Polonius academically advised. "Your even-tempered spouse might be able to get through to Hamlet before the imbecile executes this presumed secret contemplation that you, My Liege, have alluded to."

"Hamlet must be monitored at all times before the defector attempts something drastic, like assassinating me!" Claudius worriedly conveyed to his almost-senile advisor. "I know what the fuck I'll do! After the play is performed in the palace theater, I'll send Hamlet on a mission to England to collect some debts, tribute, and marks that are owed Denmark. Do you have any more-bright ideas Polonius, before I either diss or dismiss you?"

"As you know, My Liege, I like to listen to private conversations and have taken several advanced higher-education eavesdropping courses in spying and in voyeurism," Polonius eloquently reminded the King. "I'll again hide behind the purple parlor-room curtains, and listen to your wife discussing some personal business with her distraught son. Then, I'll be better equipped to assess what the fuck's wrong with the deviant jerk-off!"

"Good idea Polonius!" Claudius praised. "Your fuckin' ears should've been mouths! By that utterance, I mean that they should be fuckin' open, but not fuckin' speaking!"

* * * * * * * * * * * * *

After going over the last-minute details with the traveling actors, and reviewing the new lines that had been added to the little-known tragedy "The Murder of Gonzago," Hamlet again conferred with Horatio about the changes in the script, and about the new lines that had been included.

"Keep both of your eyes on Claudius!" Hamlet told the ever-vigilant Horatio. "If my uncle shows signs of guilt, and begins sweating or squirming-around upon his throne, like he has to take a lengthy royal shit, then the dirty bastard is guilty. But if my uncle acts like nothing irregular is happening, then perhaps we had been visited by a fuckin' false ghost," Hamlet reckoned and declared. "I've always loved this theatrical bull-shit, and I simply relish drama, trauma, and an excess of suspense. Okay now; the palace's theater is beginning to fill-up, Horatio. Get a good seat and enjoy the production, and think of me and my strategy during the altered murder scene!"

Upon entering the castle's small auditorium, Queen Gertrude requested that Hamlet sit next to her, but the youth declined the royal invitation. Much to the Queen's chagrin, Hamlet brazenly stepped over to (the woman of his choice) Ophelia's couch, laid his head on the surprised and embarrassed girl's lap, and then began wildly sniffing-away like a face-down bloodhound.

"You seem very happy and gay this evening?" Ophelia remarked for a lack of something better to say during her uncomfortable moment. "More happy than gay, I would definitely say!" the girl rhymed as her buttocks wiggled and wriggled-around upon the richly-upholstered couch.

"In this marvelous play, I'll have the opportunity to see a cruel murder re-enacted," Hamlet predicted and snidely chuckled as the prince smelled and sniffed away inside Ophelia's ruffled gown. "A great man's accomplishments will be remembered before this ominous night is through! I can just smell it!" the prince obtusely commented. "Yes Ophelia; I can just smell it!"

The actors skillfully performed their drama with precision and with fine elocution. The opening scene portrayed a King and a Queen having a conflictive dialogue about personal matters in regard to their lousy love life. In the dramatic play's following scene, the King (Gonzago) requested to be left alone to take a nap, and get his mind off of having terrible uninspiring sex with his terrible, shrew of a wife. Then, an actor playing Lucianus (Gonzago's greedy brother) entered the room, and slowly poured a vial full of poison into Gonzago's ear while the King was dozing like a contented bull. "His riches and his kingdom will soon be mine!" Lucianus arrogantly bellowed to the appalled audience. "Death is too good a fate for this no-good son-of-a-bitchin' King! Now, I'll continue my sultry love affair with my sister-in-law, and future wife, the Queen! Ha, ha, ha!"

"Look at King Claudius!" Ophelia alerted her pussy-sniffing male companion. "He's on his feet and almost in a trance! Now, King Claudius is yelling some strange, embarrassing prattle!"

"Stop the play! Stop the fuckin' play immediately!" Claudius hollered above the audience's hush. "Get me the fuck out of here, Gertrude! I'm quite upset! Get me the fuck out of here right this goddamned second!"

Hamlet stopped eagerly sniffing Ophelia's crotch (through her heavy-material gown) and ecstatically paced over to his pal Horatio, who had incidentally been conducting serious polls and interviews, calculating and keeping vital statistics of the *whore ratio* to virgins in Paris, which Horatio represented in an imbalanced equation of 10 to .01. The vigilant guard's concentration was suddenly interrupted by Hamlet's incisive declaration.

"Well, good friend, Horatio; my father's ghost was real and authentic, but more importantly, the specter had spoken the truth," Hamlet confided to his most-trusted comrade. "Uncle Claudius ought to tie himself to an anchor and push it off the top of Elsinore Castle. Anchors aweigh! Anchors away! Ha, ha, ha!"

"I saw the expression on his pallid face, when King Gonzago was being poisoned by his brother," Horatio commented. "It was surreal!"

"What did Claudius look like?" Hamlet asked. "And don't say he looked like shit, because that's how the hell the no-good piss head usually looks!"

"His countenance reflected genuine excruciation!" Horatio described his personal impression. "The abundant guilt present on Claudius's sourpuss really showed when Lucianus duplicated the ear poisoning. The King's expression was evil enough to rot Medusa's cunt right off the monster's body! That detestable bastard is guiltier than Judas Iscariot ever was after the infamous *Last Supper!*" Horatio argued. "Why don't you let your ferocious pet panther loose on the treacherous bastard, Hamlet? Your Uncle Claude deserves clawed testicles more than any other male we know!"

By that time, nearly everyone except a few gossipy stragglers had evacuated the small palace auditorium. As Hamlet and Horatio were discussing the results of the play, soon Rosencrantz and Guildenstern paced-over and conveyed some well-received news to the gloating Prince Hamlet, who believed that his bold social experiment had been a resounding success.

"King Claudius is having an onslaught of convulsions in his bedroom!" Rosencrantz nervously informed Hamlet and Horatio. "He's vomiting and barfing his freakin' guts out, all over the fuckin' place. The disgusting bastard must've eaten a horse, a hippopotamus, and a bull elephant before he became so fuckin' nauseous!"

"Too fuckin' bad for the bastard!" Hamlet un-sympathetically answered, showing his utter disdain and contempt for his devious uncle. "Call a doctor! Better yet, call a veterinarian! Better yet, call a fuckin' mortician! The Grim Reaper is about to harvest his next afterlife candidate!"

"Your Mother wishes to speak with you!" Guildenstern informed Hamlet. "You're still being nursed, are you? I figured by now you'd finally be fed-up with being breast fed!"

'I now hate my mother, and can easily identify with the troubled ancient Greek tragic figure Oedipus!' Hamlet lamented and pondered. 'I'll be sarcastic to her because of her wanton infidelity, and because of her harsh betrayal of my pure-hearted father! But I'll speak daggers and not throw them, not fuckin' yet!'

Act III

Finally recovering from his near-mental breakdown, Claudius had his head steward summon Rosencrantz and Guildenstern to the throne room to provide the ignoramuses with some last-minute vital instructions. The pair of amateur spies soon showed-up, and then stoically received the news of their next espionage assignment.

"Hamlet is a dangerous person wandering around and causing chaos inside and all around this palace," the King began his biased remarks. "I'm going to send the jealous moron on an important expedition with you two adventurers at once, so that some unforeseen-but-feared calamity can be averted here in Denmark. You'll have sealed orders, and the confidential documents are not to be opened until you can clearly view the British coastline, but if it's a foggy day when you arrive, be careful, or else your ship might collide with a hidden shoal or a shallow-water reef."

After Rosencrantz and Guildenstern had received their special assignment from beleaguered King Claudius, in another palace chamber, Polonius was hiding behind the parlor-room's purple drapes and ducking-down, to listen-in on the conversation between Gertrude (who knew of the advisor's clandestine presence) and the duped Prince Hamlet.

On the way to a secluded private suite to speak with Queen Gertrude, Hamlet caught a glimpse of Claudius praying on his knees inside the castle chapel. The King was silently begging forgiveness from the Almighty for killing his brother and selfishly wishing that he could retain the imperial crown, and thus continue governing Denmark and its conquered territories.

'I ought to slay the villainous bastard right here and now!' Hamlet thought as the vindictive-minded prince reached for his sword to rudely interrupt the King's deep introspection and mumbling. 'But then the dirty rotten son-of-a-bitch's soul might ascend up to Heaven, because he's now in the fuckin' act of praying. I'll have to catch the insane mother-fucker when he's not in the act of being penitent, and then I'll bludgeon and kill his dumpy ass!'

A moment later, Hamlet stepped into a hallway and (out of despair) suddenly had intentions of committing suicide, so the mentally-unstable youth held his dagger up to his heart and nervously said, "2 B or not 2 B! That is the algebraic question!" But fortunately, the young royal snapped-out of his odd stupor, changed his mind about self-annihilation, and then focused his instincts on standard self-survival. The prince stridently entered his mother's private parlor located right next to the aforementioned chapel. "Mother, you seek to speak with me? Well, I'll not hide! Here I am, ready or not!"

"Hamlet, you've made your stepfather very angry with that embarrassing play you had deliberately tampered with," Gertrude began in a superior mode of voice while role-playing being the disappointed parent. "Your Uncle Claudius and I both know all about your creative theatrical changes in the play, because the actors told us about your weird and malicious modifications when we threatened to kill them. Even I was extremely humiliated by your stupid juvenile trick, and I'm your damned mother!"

"Just like the main character in 'The Murder of Gonzago', I too am going through changes in my heart and in my soul," Hamlet answered in an impressive, mature manner. "I feel like a caterpillar exiting from its chrysalis, ready to fly away as a butterfly, and curiously explore the world and all its mysteries. The growth process into adulthood is now in progress! I'm ready to assert myself!"

"Stop talking foolishly and impractically, my naïve, idealistic only son!" Gertrude severely admonished. "You're a prospective future King, and you're thinking like a goddamned traveling minstrel, or a pathetic wandering bard. Show me a rich poet, and I'll show you the ass side of the moon!"

"Better to speak foolishly than wickedly, like you do, you bitching whore!" Hamlet boldly alleged and railed. "I ought to wrench your neck from your goddamned head while strangling you!" Hamlet threatened as the young prince went berserk, grabbed Gertrude around the throat, and began violently squeezing her windpipe. "You're a goddamned sleazy whore, who cheated on my kind father, and then fuckin' betrayed his authority! You depraved nympho'. Harlot! Haven't you ever heard of virtue; of chastity; of fidelity; of abstinence?" Hamlet emphatically screamed as the son applied more pressure to his mother's throat while Gertrude continued gagging. "And you too, mother, conspired with your future husband to wickedly poison my dear father! There was never any such thing as a fuckin' poisonous snakebite, now was there?" Hamlet furiously yelled. "If so, explain to me how the hell you and Uncle Claudius got that venomous snake inside that tiny lethal vial?"

At that moment, Hamlet's attention was distracted with a loud fart originating from behind the room's purple curtains. A slight movement was discernible, and Hamlet quickly removed his sword from its scabbard, thinking that Claudius had been eavesdropping on the bizarre conversation. As Gertrude coughed and choked, trying to regain her normal breath, Hamlet vigorously thrust his sword through the drapes, and a loud cry followed by soft moaning was heard. Then, through the crack between the curtains, the mortally wounded Polonius plunged to the stone floor.

"Goodbye you conniving fool, forever damned!" Hamlet bid adieu to the King's manipulative advisor. "You repugnant worm! You, who had turned Ophelia's precious heart against me! I hope you've already said your prayers, because where the fuck you're going, you'll need all the damned divine help you can get!"

"Hamlet! What rash, bloody mortal sin have you done? You've turned into a destructive monster! A beast! A fiendish felon!" Gertrude screamed, finally regaining her voice. "Your blemished soul is stewing in both corruption and sin! What have I done to engender such hateful deportment?"

"Just look at those portraits of my noble Father and of your former devoted husband hanging on yonder walls!" Hamlet dared his mother. "You had the unmitigated audacity to marry his lying thieving Brother, after you evilly conspired with my scumbag uncle to poison Father in his ear. Your new husband is a weak and cowardly criminal, a fucked-up, feckless, gutless villain of the most vile and satanic magnitude!"

"Can't we speak of something else upon which we could mutually agree?" Gertrude suggested from her self-preservation instincts, while still fearing for her life. "I understand that you've been delegated a very important assignment; an essential mission to England I believe."

"Rosencrantz, Guildenstern, and I are being sent to Britain with sealed orders!" Hamlet grimly stated. "But now that I'm especially wary of all the jealous, dangerous, and greedy individuals around me, I'll be on my guard and be ready to turn the tables on any adversary if defensive measures are necessary. I'm learning how to fuckin' play this deceit game of yours, Mother," the fast read declared. "And I want you to know that I'm getting pretty fuckin' good at it."

"Now that you've murdered Polonius, our beloved Denmark will never again have peace with Poland!" Gertrude criticized her son's impulsive reaction. "You'd better get going with dispatch to England quickly, because now, whether you know it or not, you're a renegade; a marked fugitive escaping from justice! Let's hope that King Claudius has mercy on you, and gives you safe passage!"

Hamlet and Gertrude stepped out of the chamber and approached Claudius, who was moving from the chapel on his way to the throne room. Regaining his composure, Claudius was back into his imperial, assertive mood.

"Where the hell is Polonius?" the King lividly demanded. "I need to talk with that pragmatic Polack right away about our endangered treaty with Poland!"

"Polonius is not here because he's now in either Heaven or Hell!" Hamlet firmly answered. "It's too late for him to be penitent in a penitentiary. Quite possibly, your key political advisor may be already purging his besmirched soul away in Purgatory!"

"Hamlet stabbed Polonius through the purple curtains in my private parlor," Gertrude explained to Claudius, while also accusing her son of committing a grave felony. "We really have to switch the color of the drapes in this mediocre-looking castle, because they're all purple in every damned room!" the Queen incoherently added. "Tomorrow I'm contacting the palace's interior decorator. Yes; I'll do that first thing in the morning."

"You realize Hamlet that by killing Polonius, whether on purpose or by accident, you're now a wanted murderer?" Claudius accused and reminded the prince. "A desperate criminal on the lam; a vile curse to this castle's enviable reputation and proud heritage! Do you understand the magnitude of what the fuck you've done?"

"What should I do, uncle?" the prince insolently asked. "Kill both you and my mother too, before running-away to England?"

Claudius ignored Hamlet's defiant bravado and instructed, "A ship is waiting at the harbor mooring dock. Rosencrantz and Guildenstern have been issued sealed orders, and while sailing on the way to England, you three bird-brain assholes can behave like university fraternity brothers, just like old times in Paris!" the King enunciated and then snickered. "Once there in Britain, you'd better sober-up in a hurry because you'll be officially representing Elsinore Castle and the King of Denmark on highly-important government business! And one final thing, Prince Hamlet!" Claudius snidely stressed. "Rosencrantz and Guildenstern are the only ones allowed to open the secret orders in the sealed scrolled documents."

When Gertrude and Hamlet departed the chamber in dual somber moods, King Claudius reflected on the contents of the secret orders. 'Wet behind the ears Hamlet is to be put to death before he ever has the chance of setting foot in Britain! Ha, ha, ha!'

Act IV

Thanks to the now-dead Polonius's effective diplomatic skills, peace between Denmark and Norway had already been negotiated, and finally achieved. King Claudius permitted Young Fartinbras the privilege of marching his army through Denmark to attack Poland, and the Norwegian invader solemnly agreed not to plunder and sack Denmark while reclaiming eastern lands that his father had lost to the Warsaw Duke.

When Prince Hamlet arrived at the dock to board his ship bound for England, the youth encountered sailors and soldiers from Young Fartinbras' regiments heading toward Poland. Naturally, Hamlet was curious about Norwegian troops arriving in a Danish port.

"Why are you going to fight for land that isn't worth too much?" Hamlet asked an officer disembarking from a ship. "I don't think there are any natural resources in what you Norwegians are attempting to get back! Conquering Poland is like fighting for drab wasteland! I mean, what you originally lost to the Duke of Warsaw wasn't worth much to begin with, so why fuckin' bother going into combat over useless territory?"

The high-ranked soldier answered in a rank disciplined fashion, and what the officer revealed really affected Hamlet's mode of thinking. "Fartinbras is going to win the Polish land back because it's not only a matter of principle, it's a matter of honor, which really matters to our Norwegian prestige! Get the picture, Chicken Shit?"

'This is what an honorable son should do for his father,' Hamlet considered. 'I should be like brave Young Fartinbras and audaciously fulfill my true father's goals and ambitions. I'm a fuckin' Prince, too, and ought to begin acting like one by showing courage and resolve, instead of exhibiting petty revenge and animosity like my Uncle Claudius does!' Hamlet imagined and regretted. 'As I weigh my options without taking prompt action, and as I worry about possible consequences, my father's murderer is getting away Scot free, even though he's a not-so-great Dane. From now on, I'm not interested in obtaining *petty* revenge! I'm dedicated to having *major* revenge, and my prime target is that fuckin' black-hearted scoundrel, Uncle Claudius!' the young Prince decided, gritting his teeth and making a clenched fist. 'But first I must survive my English expedition; then to come back to Denmark, and avenge my father's death! I'm beginning to actually like this vigilante justice shit! I'll get onto this ship bound for England, and I hereby vow to return to complete my objective!'

Back at majestic Elsinore Castle, Ophelia was beginning to act crazily because of her father Polonius's murder. And in fact, the young woman started behaving just like Prince Hamlet had done before departing for England. The following day Ophelia requested a private consultation with Queen Gertrude.

The loony girl entered the dimly-lit throne room singing a song using ordinary pronouns "he" and "his", without any specific noun antecedents. "He is dead and gone, rude Lady Gertrude; he is dead and gone. At his head a green and verdant turf, crude Lady Gertrude; and at his heels a cold stone!"

Queen Gertrude immediately yelled for her Husband to come into the chamber to keenly evaluate Ophelia's unorthodox deportment. "Claudius, what the hell's wrong with Ophelia?" Gertrude asked for an objective opinion. "She's now more fucked-up than Hamlet is, or ever was! And it's broad daylight outside, with nary a sign of any full moon! There's only one thing worse than a talking head, and that's a singing air-head!"

"How long has she been conducting herself in this fucked-up manner?" the King asked. "Isn't what she's exhibiting inordinate behavior for even her? I hope that naïve Ophelia is not seeking some malevolent form of poetic justice!"

"She's been acting strangely ever since her father's murder, er, to be more politically-correct, my sweet husband, ever since his untimely death!" Gertrude nervously indicated. "Polonius was such a decent man! Anyway, I don't know how she'll act at his burial! She's already-drowning herself in a flood of tears!"

"I must tell my brother, Laertes, of this heinous act! Yes, benevolent and gallant Laertes will know what the hell to do!" Ophelia wildly ranted. "My Father's soon to be planted in the cold ground, soon to be chewed-up by disgusting worms and insects, no matter how thick and dense his coffin will be! Something must be done about it, Lady! Something must fuckin' be done, do you hear?" Ophelia yelled while vigorously shaking Gertrude's shoulders. "Thank you for listening to my painful woes, Lady. Now it's time for me to enter my coach. Good night, Lady; good night, Gentleman. Good night, Lady; I'm going to leave you now!" the nutcase girl chanted before exiting the regally-decorated castle chamber.

Claudius assigned a Danish-eating guard to follow Ophelia, to make sure the sorrowed girl didn't injure herself, or accidentally kill an innocent God-fearing taxpayer. The King and the Queen were very disturbed about Hamlet and Ophelia's unpredictable behaviors; about Hamlet killing Polonius, and about the population of Denmark gossiping and whispering about crazy young people randomly roaming around Elsinore Castle and causing excessive chaos, grief, and turmoil. Of course, the two evil, self-righteous, sanctimonious royal adult plotters were unconcerned and guiltless about their efficient elimination of good King Hamlet.

"Laertes has furtively returned from Paris to Denmark from his fraternity parties and perverted porno' classes at the French university," Claudius informed Gertrude. "The ignoramus is being exposed to all of this extremely damaging gossip about his father's assassination, er, I mean about *his* untimely death, and about *that* tragedy causing Ophelia's present insanity. And worst of all, I fear that the angry young asshole is going to lead a bloody insurrection against my rule. I should've read Homer's *Odyssey* more astutely," Claudius shared with Gertrude. "In that story, if I remember correctly, Laertes was a lousy dog."

Just then, a guard dashed into the throne room to make a startling announcement. "Anarchy is flourishing! Brash Laertes is leading a raucous mob, and the out-of-control rabble has successfully broken into the palace and is looting and rioting. The hostile vandals want to make that mental case Laertes king. If that happens," the guard paused and took a deep breath, "I'm heading to China or India and fuckin' becoming a Buddhist monk!"

Laertes and his demonstrative supporters wildly and loudly rushed into the throne room, and then when silence finally prevailed, Polonius's son defiantly addressed the frightened Claudius, still sitting and shitting on his luxurious ebony throne, and too petrified to move or pull the deep splinters out of his ass. "Where is my father, evil King? What has happened to him? Tell me the truth or die!"

"Remain tranquil!" Gertrude illogically shrieked to the incensed intruder and his rabble of insurrectionists. "The King did not kill your father, or have him killed! But *your* father, Polonius, who by no means was ever a priest, is dead as a wall sconce, and I must confess with an honest heart, Laertes, that Prince Hamlet had violently stabbed your father with *his* sword!"

But then, Ophelia pranced and danced into the throne room, singing nonsensical poetic verses and distracting Laertes from his primary focus. "Oh, sweet Sister! What has ever happened to you?" the brother incredulously asked. "Why are you eating rosemary? I meant to say, I know you have lesbian tendencies, and I'm aware that Rosemary is one of your girlfriends, but more exactly; why are you eating the fragrant mint herb known as rosemary?"

"To make me remember all that has happened!" Ophelia strangely answered. "Yes; Rosemary will make me recall everything, that gossiping, two-timing, bisexual bitch!"

Queen Gertrude took advantage of the situation by yelling to Laertes's castle-crashing followers, "Here's some copper coins so that all of you loyal citizens can go-out and treat yourselves to some coffee and Danish!" Soon, true to her statement, the Queen tossed several hundred bronze coins onto the floor, and a wild scramble ensued as the mob members (no notorious gangsters present) got their meager reward, and then bolted-out of the castle to patronize nearby coffee and Danish pastry shops.

Meanwhile, Ophelia was industriously passing-out daisies, daffodils, violets, and pansies to Claudius, Gertrude, Laertes, and to palace guards before the loony girl passed-out herself. Then, Claudius attempted to assuage and console Laertes and form a strategic alliance with the disenfranchised young rebel.

"I too am sorrowed at your father's unexpected death!" Claudius apathetically consoled the emotionally-disturbed Laertes while awkwardly placing his right arm around the grieving lad's left shoulder. "Listen to Queen Gertrude and me, as we tell you the whole unedited story, so that you aren't influenced downtown by either coffee, or Danish house cheap damaging gossip!"

After learning that Hamlet had methodically stabbed his father (the counselor Polonius) through the purple curtains, thinking that the intended victim had been Claudius, Laertes privately asked the King why he hadn't had Hamlet punished or executed.

"Because his mother the Queen loves him dearly, and I happen to love her more than oxygen, or even lobster tail, or penne with tomato sauce," the deceitful Claudius lied. "And Hamlet, like yourself' Laertes, has plenty of disciples among the Danish-loving Danish people." Next, the King abruptly dismissed Gertrude from the discussion so that *he* could iron-out particular details with the still-irate Laertes, who now loathed Prince Hamlet.

"Then, I'll accuse Hamlet of killing my father and courageously challenge him to a duel!" Laertes vowed to the unscrupulous and cunning Claudius. "I've become one of the finest fencers in all of Europe, you know, and I don't mean constructing animal enclosures around smelly pastures, either!"

"I have an excellent plan to execute, as usual!" Claudius confidentially shared with Laertes. "Not even Queen Gertrude will be able to play the blame game after it's executed, er, I meant to say, 'after Hamlet is swiftly executed by you'!"

"What's your demented scheme?" Laertes defensively asked. "I don't mind the notion that Hamlet's going to get killed, but I don't want to perish during the fiasco, too! Fill me in on your strategy! I gotta' know all of the sordid details!"

"Hamlet has heard that you're now one of the best fencers in Europe, as you've already mentioned," Claudius reminded the proud and rambunctious Laertes. "And I must warn you that Hamlet's been diligently practicing his skill at the art, too, and I've heard that after he returns from England, he'd like to go up against you in a practice match! But the idea of the contest being a simple practice match will only be from *his* point of view, but it will be a real fuckin' grudge-battle from your end! Do you get the fuckin' picture, now, my stouthearted Young Fellow?"

"We'll be using practice sabers, but how can I kill Hamlet when the points won't be sharp?" Laertes questioned the devious royal plotter. 'I don't want to be fooled, er, I meant foiled again!"

"Ha, ha, ha!" Claudius indulgently laughed. "Your blunt end will have poison on it, so all you'll have to do is simply scratch Hamlet's skin, and then soon, the fucked-up moron will die! Ha, ha, ha! A tiny little scratch will scratch Hamlet right out of the human race, and off the fuckin' planet forever! Ha, ha, ha!" Claudius laughed like an obsessed madman. "This is really rich, marvelous bull-shit! Ha, ha, ha! You get your revenge on Hamlet, and I get rid of the irritating asshole once and for all! Ha, ha, ha!"

"But what if my designated practice opponent accidentally survives, or what if I fail to puncture him enough for the poison to effectively work?" Laertes asked the evil Monarch.

"If the bout goes on for longer than fifteen-minutes, as you know, Laertes, it's customary to take a brief intermission, a break in the action," Claudius coyly told his *foil*. "There'll be cups to drink out of to refresh yourselves before continuing the match!" the King informed and snickered. "Hamlet's cup will coincidentally have poison mixed in the wine, so that when the unsuspecting dumb-ass proceeds with continuing the match....."

"He'll slowly falter and collapse to the floor, wriggle around like a worm, and then painfully die after having swallowed-down the toxic poison!" Laertes realized and endorsed. "That raunchy cock-sucker's going to have an affinity for infinity! Ha, ha, ha! He'll be known as 'Socrates Junior' throughout Europe! We'll bury him beneath a cemetery hemlock tree!"

"And I'll even announce and bet on Hamlet to win the match, so that my wife and others don't catch-on that you and I are partners! Ha, ha, ha!" the King humored himself. "Who would ever suspect Laertes, you and me being amenable partners, ha, ha, ha!"

The confidential conversation was quickly interrupted when a hysterical Queen Gertrude darted into the throne room with more distressful news.

"Ophelia has just drowned in the nearby river. A guard you had assigned to follow her reported that she took some flowers to a spot where a weeping willow tree grew beside the water to weep for her father's death, her demise occurring just alongside the appropriate weeping willow," Gertrude sadly related and sobbed. "Then the crazed girl climbed-up the weeping willow to attach some artificial flowers to the uppermost branch, soon lost her balance, and plummeted into the cold river. She drifted along in the rapid-moving current for a brief time, sang some bizarre surface and underwater lyrics for a while, and then drowned doing the dead man's, er, please excuse my improper nomenclature, doing the dead woman's float!"

"Please forgive me during my moment of emotional weakness," Laertes pleaded, "but I must seek a private place to mourn my sister's accidental suicide! I say that diabolical Hamlet is now responsible for the deaths of both my sister and my father! Poison is too good for that no-good son-of-a-bitch! Er, please excuse me, Queen Gertrude! I meant to say that poison is too good for that no-good bastard!"

* * * * * * * * * * * *

In another sector of expansive Elsinore Castle, sailors had arrived with news concerning Prince Hamlet. Upon interviewing the arrived mariners, Horatio learned that barbarous pirates had attacked Hamlet's ship, and that the prince had been captured and taken prisoner. The rest of the armada had escaped, and was presently sailing toward the British Coast. But Hamlet had shrewdly used his ingenuity and negotiated his own release for a promised ransom, and the wily Prince had miraculously made it safely back to Denmark, and was currently eating pastries and Danish while waiting for his friend Horatio to join him at the docks.

Act V

Horatio met-up with Hamlet at the docks, and the two comrades trekked back towards Elsinore Castle, taking a shortcut through the city cemetery after Hamlet had specifically directed Horatio to walk past the local *seminary,* but the idiot's specific instruction was misunderstood during their intensive discourse. Hamlet spotted men laboring on the evening graveyard shift, digging a new hollow, and then the Prince of Denmark innocently inquired about the identity of the recently-deceased, who was soon to be interred.

"It's a woman residing at Elsinore Castle, but I don't know her exact name," one of the diggers named Doug phlegmatically answered. "Some sort of crazy poet or bard I've heard. All we know is that the King wishes this person buried in a damned hurry, and that's why we're working overtime despite our union regulations."

"It must be Polonius! That senile nutcase always wanted to be an actor or a poet!" Hamlet conjectured and told Horatio. "The idiot often bragged that he was part of the Polish underground, and now he's a full-fledged member of the Danish underground. Pretty ironic, isn't it?"

"It can't be Polonius because the digger told us that the deceased person is, or was, a female! Let's hang around and observe who it is!" Horatio suggested to Hamlet. "Maybe now Polonius can be an adviser to Jesus Christ and to His apathetic apostles, too! Death must be okay Hamlet, because everyone's dying to get into the cemetery, and nobody's dying to get the hell out. Say wait a minute!" Horatio exhorted. "There's King Claudius and Queen Gertrude approaching. It looks like they're going to pay their last respects!"

"Farewell, Young Lady. I was planning on throwing rice and flowers on your wedding day," Gertrude uttered and sobbed. "Perhaps your marriage to my son was never intended by Heaven's grace! As they say, all things happen for the best, and are, in the end, designs of God's will!"

"Holy shit Horatio!" Hamlet exclaimed. "Ophelia is the one being buried. That's her coffin being lowered into the ground. This is the absolute pits this side of mythical Pittsburgh! And to think that I was almost killed last week on the high seas by pirates!"

Before Hamlet and Horatio could completely fathom the significance of the shocking spectacle, Laertes suddenly dashed-up to the gravesite and recklessly leaped into the pit, landing on top of his sister's wooden coffin. After crying with his face pressed against the lid, the brother turned his head and shouted to the stunned gravediggers, "Toss the dirt upon me so that I may be buried alive with my dear sister, Ophelia!"

Being quite distressed himself, Hamlet rushed to the gravesite and also jumped into the cavity, his body colliding with Laertes. The two young men began grappling and wrestling inside the recently dug cemetery grave, as the bewildered diggers watched in awe at the all-time-first spectacle.

"Stop them! Stop the crazy Fools!" Claudius ordered the six guards that had acted as Ophelia's pallbearers. "Hamlet's having another one of his characteristic fits! Subdue the desperate asshole! Separate the two antagonists right this minute! This crazy incident is most embarrassing! I hope there aren't any news reporters around to document this bad publicity!"

Five-minutes later (after the grave scuffle had been stopped), Horatio tried calming-down Hamlet as the pair headed in the direction of the local seminary (to watch gay sex being performed for donations), located a block away from the castle's cemetery. Meanwhile, Claudius spoke to Laertes about the recent graveyard incident being most-advantageous to *their* alliance, because it made the planned fencing match against Hamlet more probable to transpire. Laertes was now Claudius's obedient marionette with all strings attached.

On the way to Elsinore Castle, Hamlet explained to Horatio exactly what had occurred on his eventful voyage from Denmark to England, and how the clever prince had intelligently escaped the jaws of treachery.

"I was smart enough to read the secret orders that my fucked-up immoral Uncle Claudius had entrusted to his incompetent agents, who were pretending to be my friends, namely Rosencrantz and Guildenstern. The parchment document authored and signed by Claudius prescribed that I was to be beheaded," Hamlet angrily related. "I had no time to procrastinate. I quickly rewrote the mendacious charlatan King's mandates that had been addressed to the British authorities, and my instructions specified that Rosencrantz and Guildenstern should be executed, and then I adroitly resealed the papers. Oh well, my friend Horatio. I suppose I have two less so-called acquaintances listed in my black address book."

A messenger met Hamlet inside the palace, and reported that King Claudius was willing to wager on the prince in a practice-fencing duel between the Monarch's nephew and aggrieved stepson, against aggrieved

Laertes. "The King believes that you and Laertes are comparable in skill, but that your notorious coolness of mind will definitely give you the edge and make you prevail," the court courier told Hamlet. "King Claudius has such confidence in your ability, Prince Hamlet, that he's bet six of his finest thoroughbred horses against a wager of a half-dozen French daggers, which roughly translates into a hundred-to-one odds that you'll emerge victorious over Laertes in the scheduled practice match."

"Tell the King and Laertes that I accept my adversary's challenge, as long as we use practice sabers and nobody gets seriously injured in the gentlemen's exhibition," Hamlet declared to the gambling-addicted messenger. "Ophelia's death has indeed pierced both of *our* hearts already, and perhaps after this friendly contest, Laertes and I can make amends and be drinking buddies with Horatio once again!" the Prince of Denmark fully-explained to the better bettor.

Later that afternoon, the dueling match was about to commence. As the two opponents met in the center of the small basement arena, Hamlet candidly conveyed to Laertes that he had not deliberately killed Polonius, and that he didn't wish to offend his old friend in any way. "That unfortunate killing of your father Polonius would've never occurred if King Claudius had installed an iron curtail," Hamlet informed Laertes.

Then, without further delay, the two rivals selected their "practice sabers" (with Laertes choosing first), and next the participants immediately took opposite positions in the fighting chamber, with both men awaiting King Claudius's command to start the contest.

The first furious exchange of swings and swipes went on for over ten-minutes, and then Hamlet's agility and dexterity enabled the prince to score a hit to Laertes' chest. King Claudius called a five-minute refreshment intermission for the combatants to swallow- down some "delicious and well-deserved wine". But amazingly, Hamlet refused the cup offered to him, explaining that he would partake in drink after the second crucial round had been completed.

Not knowing that the goblet offered Hamlet was full of poisoned wine, Queen Gertrude grabbed the cup, and much to King Claudius's astonishment, his wife gave a salute to her "valiant Son", and then gulped-down a quantity of the tainted substance. Several minutes into the second dueling round, Queen Gertrude slumped-over in her chair, just as Hamlet robustly scored a second hit on the now-shocked and overmatched Laertes. But not obeying the rules of engagement, Laertes savagely lunged at Hamlet when the prince's guard was down, and his blunted blade scratched the dueler's chest with *his* artificial weapon's flat-but-poisonous end.

Being pissed-off at Laertes' flagrant cheating (and not aware that *he* had just received a lethal wound), Hamlet wildly swung his sword, and the impact was so great that both men's weapons clanked onto the dungeon's stone floor. Instinctively, the combatants quickly stooped-down to retrieve their dual dueling weapons.

Laertes was soon tagged again in his ribs, and then realized too late that he also was destined to die, because the frustrated dueler lucidly remembered that he and Hamlet had inadvertently switched identical sabers when the objects had fallen from their grasps. Laertes couldn't quickly rise from his horizontal position lying upon the stone floor, and while desperately gasping for air, informed his worthy opponent that *he* was dying.

"Lock the doors!" Hamlet yelled to the guards on duty. "I must find-out what the fuck's going on here!"

"The saber you're holding in your hand, Hamlet, is poisoned, and both you and I have been scratched by it!" Laertes coughed and stammered from his position lying face-up on the hard cold floor. "Yes, my Friend; you'll be dead in about ten-minutes, and I in around five. And your mother just drank from the poisoned chalice upon her table, and I must confess that the cunning King is both the cause and the blame of all of *this* incredible horrendous scenario!"

"This debacle is entirely fucked-up!" Hamlet angrily screamed. "If this fuckin' saber is poisoned, then it should be intended for the one that was the genesis of all of this unwarranted tragedy! God save my immortal soul!"

And with those pathetic prophetic words, the exhausted-but-incensed Prince rushed forward, and with all his might, violently thrust his blunt weapon into the chest of the appalled and helpless, craven King Claudius. And as the King's face slumped forward, Hamlet quickly grabbed the poisoned goblet with his right hand, pulled Claudius's head back with his left appendage, and then generously poured most of the remaining lethal wine down the doomed Monarch's throat, just to make sure that Claudius's fate had been permanently doomed.

The noble Horatio leaped-forward and latched-onto the tilted goblet, wrenching it from Hamlet's weakened grasp. "I'll gladly drink the last ounce of this vile substance, My Liege, and we'll all go to Kingdom-Come together!"

"No, Horatio!" Hamlet pleaded as the afflicted Prince began panting for breath. "I'm dying, and someone reliable such as yourself must live to retell this crazy, fucked-up story from beginning to end! Please don't drink the poison for my sake, and more importantly, for posterity's sake!" Then, the weakened Prince of Denmark gasped and asked, "What's that noise I hear outside the castle? It sounds like war-drums!"

"I believe it is Young Fartinbras and his army returning from his victorious military campaign in Poland," Horatio sadly stated. "Yes, My Liege. I'm sure it's Young Fartinbras! I understand that he greatly admires you!"

"I swear to you in my dying moment, Horatio," Hamlet wheezed and coughed. "Fartinbras has my endorsement to become the next King of Denmark. I've always aspired to be as daring as he!" And with those amazing and noteworthy historic words, Hamlet, Prince of Denmark, inhaled his last breath.

"My Master's noble heart has stopped beating!" Horatio recognized and wept. "Now it's up to me to sort-out all that has happened!"

Young Fartinbras and his passing-gas bodyguards entered the small fighting arena inside Elsinore Castle's dungeon. His face reflected both consternation and astonishment. "What the fuck's happened here? Is it a mass cult suicide?"

"No, Sir!" Horatio answered in a disconsolate-but-respectful tone of voice. "I'll explain everything in detail as well as my memory will serve me! Reality and truth are often stranger than weird fiction, as these unbelievable circumstances aptly prove. Quite frankly, I'm overwhelmed by the tremendous responsibility of it all. But I'll endeavor to do my best to figure-out and fit all of the incredible puzzle pieces together into some logical sequence!"

"I'm curious to learn exactly what has occurred here. But for now, I command my four captains to hoist-up young Hamlet's body, and carry his revered corpse to a place of honor and praise!" Young Fartinbras directed his personal bodyguards. "Had he lived, noble Hamlet would've made a hell of a King; perhaps the best monarch that Demark has ever had, or will have ever known!"

501

About the Author

Jay Dubya is author John Wiessner's initials (J.W.) and also his pen name. John is a retired New Jersey public school English teacher, having taught the subject for thirty-four years. John lives in southern New Jersey with wife Joanne and the couple has three grown sons.

Jay Dubya has written other adult literature besides *Thirteen Sick Tasteless Classics, Part III*. *So Ya' Wanna' Be A Teacher*, *The Wholly Book of Genesis'*, *Black Leather and Blue Denim, A '50s Novel* and its sequel, *The Great Teen Fruit War, A 1960' Novel* are humorous literary endeavors. *Frat Brats, A '60s Novel* completes Jay Dubya's coming-of-age action/adventure trilogy. *Pieces of Eight*, *Pieces of Eight, Part II*, *Pieces of Eight Part III and Pieces of Eight, Part IV* are short story/novella collections featuring science fiction, paranormal and humorous plots and themes. *Nine New Novellas, NNN, Part II, NNN, Part III* and *NNN, Part IV* are other sci-fi/paranormal story collections. *Two Baker's Dozen* is another collection of short fiction works.

Ron Coyote, Man of La Mangia is adult humor and a satire/parody on Miguel Cervantes' *Don Quixote*, published in 1605. *The Wholly Book of Exodus* is adult satirical humor. *Thirteen Sick Tasteless Classics*, *Thirteen Sick Tasteless Classics, Part II* and *TSTC, Part IV* are adult satirical rewrites of famous literary short fiction. Other satirical works are *Mauled Maimed Mangled Mutilated Mythology, Fractured Frazzled Folk Fables and Fairy Farces* and *FFFF & FF, Part II*.

John has also authored a trilogy of young adult fantasy novels, *Enchanta*, *Pot of Gold* and *Space Bugs, Earth Invasion*. *The Eighteen' Story Gingerbread House* is a new collection of eighteen diverse children's stories.

Jay Dubya likes '50s rock and roll music, and he also enjoys pop' songs by the Beach Boys', Fleetwood Mac, the Eagles, the Rolling Stones, *ELO*, John Mellencamp and by John Fogerty. When not writing or listening to music, Jay Dubya likes watching *76ers* basketball and *Phillies* and *Yankees* television baseball games.

Author Biography

Born in Hammonton, NJ in 1942, John Wiessner had attended St. Joseph School up to and including Grade 5. After his family moved from Hammonton to Levittown, Pa in 1954, John attended St. Mark School in Bristol, Pa. for Grade 6, St. Michael the Archangel School in Levittown for Grades 7 and 8 and then Immaculate Conception School, Levittown, Pa. for Grade 9. Bishop Egan High School, Levittown PA. was John's educational base for Grades 10 and 11, and later in 1960, the aspiring author graduated from Edgewood Regional High, Tansboro, NJ. John then next attended Glassboro State College, where he was an announcer for the school's baseball games and also read the nightly news and sports over WGLS, GSC's radio station.

John Wiessner had been primarily an English teacher in the Hammonton Public School System for 34 years, specializing in the instruction of middle school language arts. Mr. Wiessner was quite active in the Hammonton Education Association, serving in the capacities of Vice-President, building representative and finally, teachers' head negotiator for 7 years. During his lengthy teaching career, John had been nominated into "Who's Who among American Teachers" three times. He also was quite active giving professional workshops at schools around South Jersey on the subjects of creative writing and the use of movie videos to motivate students to organize their classroom theme compositions.

John Wiessner was very active in community service, being a past President of the Hammonton Lions Club, where he also functioned for many years as the club's Tail-Twister, Vice-President and Liontamer. John had been named Hammonton Lion of the Year in 1979 and in 2009 received the prestigious Melvin Jones Fellow Award, the highest honor a Lion can receive.

John also was a successful businessman, starting with being a Philadelphia Bulletin newspaper delivery boy for two-years in the late 1950s in Levittown, Pennsylvania. After his family moved back to New Jersey in 1959, John worked at his grandparents and his parents' farm markets, Square Deal Farm (now Ron's Gardens in Hammonton) and Pete's Farm Market in Elm, respectively. He later managed his wife's parents' farm market, White Horse Farms in Elm for three summers.

Also in a business capacity, for 16 summers starting in 1967 John Wiessner had co-owned Dealers Choice Amusement Arcade on the Ocean City, Maryland boardwalk and also co-owned the New Horizon Tee-Shirt Store for eight summers (1973-'81) on the Rehoboth Beach, Delaware boardwalk. In addition, "Jay Dubya" was a co-owner of Wheel and Deal Amusement Arcade, Missouri Avenue and Boardwalk, Atlantic

City. And then, for 18 summers beginning in 1986, John had been the Field Manager in charge of crew-leaders for Atlantic Blueberry Company (the world's largest cultivated blueberry farm), both the Weymouth and Mays Landing Divisions.

After retiring from teaching in 1999, writing under the pen name Jay Dubya (his initials), John Wiessner became the author of 64 books in the genre Action/Adventure Novels, Sci-Fi/Paranormal Story Collections, Adult Satire, Young Adult Fantasy Novels and also Non-Fiction Books. His books exist in hardcover, in paperback and in popular Kindle and Nook e-book formats.

In January of 2022, John Wiessner (Jay Dubya) was nominated into Marquis Who's Who in America, and in April of that same year, was one of nine distinguished Who's Who in America members honored with Lifetime Achievement Awards, all nine sharing an article of recognition appearing in the Wall Street Journal.

Google: Jay Dubya books